SECOND EDITION

America in the Twentieth Century

A History

SECOND EDITION

America in the Twentieth Century

A History

★ JAMES T. PATTERSON ★

Brown University

Under the General Editorship of
John Morton Blum
Yale University

HARCOURT BRACE JOVANOVICH, PUBLISHERS

San Diego · New York · Chicago · Washington, D.C. · Atlanta
London · Sydney · Toronto

To Steve and Marnie; and in memory of Nancy

ISBN: 0-15-502224-5
Library of Congress Catalog Card Number: 82-82590
Printed in the United States of America

COPYRIGHTS AND ACKNOWLEDGMENTS

For permission to use the selections reprinted in this book, the author is grateful to the following publishers and copyright holders:

IRVING BERLIN MUSIC CORPORATION for excerpts from lyrics of "This Time" by Irving Berlin on page 316. © Copyright 1942 Irving Berlin. © Copyright renewed 1969. Reprinted by permission of Irving Berlin Music Corporation, Chappell & Co., Ltd., Reuter & Reuter Förlags, A.B., Allans Music Australia, Ltd., and Victor Music Publishing Co., Inc., of Japan for their respective territories.

DOUBLEDAY & COMPANY, INC. for "The Reckoning," copyright 1941 by Theodore Roethke, from the book *The Collected Poems of Theodore Roethke.* Reprinted by permission of Doubleday & Company, Inc.

FARRAR, STRAUS & GIROUX, INC. for "When I get to the other side" from *Anyplace But Here* by Arna Bontemps and Jack Conroy. Reprinted with the permission of Farrar, Straus & Giroux, Inc., from *Anyplace But Here* by Arna Bontemps and Jack Conroy, Copyright © 1945, 1966 by Arna Bontemps and Jack Conroy.

MARCUS GARVEY, JR. for "Black queen of beauty, thou hast given color to the world" by Marcus Garvey, Sr. Reprinted by permission of Marcus Garvey, Jr., literary executor of the estate of Amy Jacques Garvey.

HARPER & ROW for "Superman" from *The Carpentered Hen and Other Tame Creatures* by John Updike. Copyright © 1955 by John Updike. Reprinted by permission of Harper & Row, Publishers, Inc.

HOUGHTON MIFFLIN COMPANY for "When the organizers needed dough" from *Coming of the New Deal* by Arthur M. Schlesinger, Jr. Reprinted by permission of the publisher.

EILEEN LAMB for "Where are You, God?" from *So Far, So Good! An Autobiography* by Elsie Janis. Reprinted by permission of Eileen Lamb.

MACMILLAN PUBLISHING CO., INC. for "The Leaden-Eyed" by Vachel Lindsay. Copyright © 1914 by Macmillan Publishing Co., Inc., renewed 1942 by Elizabeth C. Lindsay.

SANGA MUSIC for "I don't want your millions mister" by Jim Garland. © Copyright 1947 by Stormking Music Inc. All rights reserved. Used by permission.

CHARLES SCRIBNER'S SONS for "Richard Cory" by Edwin Arlington Robinson. Reprinted by permission of Charles Scribner's Sons from *The Children of the Night* by Edwin Arlington Robinson.

TWAYNE PUBLISHERS, INC. for "If We Must Die" from *Selected Poems of Claude McKay;* copyright 1953 by Twayne Publishers, Inc., and reprinted by permission of Twayne Publishers, a Division of G. K. Hall & Co., Boston.

PREFACE

This second edition of *America in the Twentieth Century* revises my thoughts concerning United States history from about 1900 to the present, a subject I have taught for nearly twenty years. Like the first edition, this one pays due attention to political and diplomatic events. It also devotes more space to areas of special interest to many students today: black history, women's history, urbanization, the role of ethnic groups, the rise of presidential power and of the federal bureaucracy, the power of corporations and the conflict of economic groups, changing sexual mores, and trends in regional and national values.

I have tried to give pace to the narrative by including anecdotes and quotations, by describing key personalities, and by setting aside selections from primary sources that illuminate passages in the text. However, I hope readers will not conclude that my purpose is to entertain or to avoid serious issues. On the contrary, I have tried to offer up-to-date interpretations and to state my conclusions on major questions. Without sacrificing my own viewpoint, I have also tried to present various sides of controversial issues. My aim is to stimulate the thinking of college-level students in survey courses and in courses dealing with twentieth-century American history.

Many people helped me during the writing and production of this second edition. I am grateful especially to Professor Nancy Weiss of Princeton University, Professor John Dittmer of Massachusetts Institute of Technology, and Professor Joseph R. Conlin of California State University, Chico, for thorough criticism of the first edition; and to my friend and editor at Harcourt Brace Jovanovich, William J. Wisneski. He has been unfailingly supportive and intelligent in all his dealings with me.

James T. Patterson

CONTENTS

Preface   v

1 A frayed society: America at the turn of the century   3

Movement and Tension   4
The Pains of Growth   24

2 The ambiguities of progressive solutions   33

Nineteenth-century solutions   33
Progressivism   43
The successes and failures of progressivism   67

3 National politics, 1900–1917   71

Congress and the Court   72
Enter Theodore Roosevelt   75
William Howard Taft   80
Woodrow Wilson   84

4 From expansion to war, 1900–1917   93

Pressures of imperialism   95
War in Europe   105

5 The divisiveness of war   119

The burdens of war   121

The Red scare 127
The fight for the League of Nations 129
Disillusionment with the war and withdrawal 137

6 The 1920s: the modern decade 141

Avenues to the future 141
The new era 148
Affirmations of the past 154
The rise of ethnic consciousness 170

7 Crash and depression, 1929–1939 179

The crash of 1929 179
The depression 188

8 Political modernization in the 1930s 205

The Hoover years 205
Franklin D. Roosevelt and New Deal solutions 210
The second term: programs and frustrations 231
The New Deal: an evaluation 236

9 From nonintervention to war, 1929–1941 241

Hoover and foreign affairs 241
The rise of noninterventionism, 1933–36 243
The hope for appeasement, 1936–38 245
America and Hitler, 1939–41 247
Roosevelt and Hitler: an evaluation 254
Toward war with Japan 255

10 World War II: the great divide 267

The military effort 267
Wartime diplomacy 273
The expansion of government 278
The war and American society 284

11 Acrimony at home and abroad, 1945–1952   **295**

Domestic controversies   298
Cold War, 1946–48   307
Truman's second term   314
Reversal in 1952   330

12 The middle-class world of the 1950s   **337**

The case against the 50s   337
President Eisenhower   353
The civil rights movement   357
The Cold War continues, 1953–61   360
The end of the Eisenhower order   367

13 The 1960s: from altruism to disenchantment   **373**

The New Frontier   373
The revolution in civil rights   378
New Frontiers abroad   382
The Johnson years, 1963–68   387
Affluence—bane of social change?   402

14 Turmoil, 1965–1968   **407**

From interracialism to black power   407
Vietnam, 1964–68   414
The youth rebellion   420
The counterculture   422
Black power, red power, women's power   427
The incredible campaign of 1968   430

15 Unsettling times: from Nixon to Reagan   **439**

Limited advances, 1969–73   439
The persistence of discord   443
Vietnam, Cambodia, and Laos   447
The great turnabout, 1971–72   450

Acrimony again, 1973–75   453
In the aftermath of Watergate   461
Bicentennial and after: social problems   464
Reagan and the 1980s   474

The Constitution of the United States of America   **481**

Presidential Elections, 1900–1980   **494**

Index   **497**

Tables

The growth of cities, 1860–1900   6
Industrial growth, 1860–1920   21
American enterprise abroad, 1900–20   96
Economic growth, 1919–29   142
Economic collapse, 1929–39   181
Rise of labor unions, 1900–50   226
America's mood, 1949–52   301
American enterprise abroad, 1925–55   311
Economic growth, 1950–60   348
America's mood, 1953–60   360
America's mood, 1961–63   378
Economic growth, 1961–70   403
White and nonwhite family income, 1950–70   412
America's mood, 1964–68   419
Median annual earnings by sex, 1962–72   429
America's mood, 1969–74   456

Maps and Graphs

Relation of immigration to total population, 1870–1930   14
Election, 1912   85
Election, 1916   89
U.S. involvement in the Caribbean in the early twentieth century   101
The changed face of Europe after the Treaty of Versailles, 1919   133
Election, 1928   160
Election, 1932   211
Growth of federal services, 1905–45   224
Aggression of Axis powers in Europe, 1936–42   249
Election, 1940   253
Japanese aggression in Asia and the Pacific, 1931–42   256
Division of Europe, 1945–55   309
Election, 1948   315
Changes in Gallup Poll rating of Truman   316
Korean War, 1950–53   325
Election, 1952   332

Changes in Gallup Poll rating of Eisenhower   353
Election, 1960   369
Changes in Gallup Poll rating of Kennedy   375
Federal services and distribution of funds   396
Changes in Gallup Poll rating of Johnson   408
Vietnam war and the fall of Indochina, 1954–75   415
Election, 1968   434
Election, 1972   453
Middle East, 1947–75   456
Changes in Gallup Poll rating of Nixon   457

Photo Credits

SECOND EDITION

America in the Twentieth Century

A History

A frayed society: America at the turn of the century

The historian Frederick Jackson Turner had every reason to rejoice as the nineteenth century ended. In 1893, when he was only thirty-one years old, he had delivered his widely acclaimed paper describing the influence of the frontier on American history, and by 1899 he was a well-established professor at the University of Wisconsin. Although his salary was only $3,000 per year and he usually had to teach summer school six days a week to pay his bills, Turner still lived comfortably. Food, fuel, and light for him, his wife, and three small children cost less than $1,000 a year, taxes and interest on his house around $500, clothes $200, and medical bills $100. Like other Americans, he paid no income tax, and he did without such later "necessities" as a car, freezer, or refrigerator. He owned his lake-front home, employed two servants, and had ample time for the bicycling, fishing, and walking that kept him close to the beauty of his native state.

Turner seemed secure and content, like many contemporaries born and raised on farms and in small towns at the turn of the century. Burton Wheeler, later a senator from Montana, grew up in Hudson, Massachusetts, an industrial town twenty-five miles from Boston. His father was a cobbler, and the family owned an eight-room frame house on the outskirts of town. They kept a horse and a cow and raised pigs and chickens. Wheeler recalled easy-going days when he picked blueberries for pocket money and wandered through Hudson, a "classic Victorian setting." Hugo Black, who was later to achieve fame as a Supreme Court justice, also remembered happy hours of horseshoe pitching, baseball, croquet, and fishing in east-central Alabama. Paul Douglas, later a senator from Illinois, cherished the Maine woods in which he lived as a small boy and where his mother and uncle cleared land for cabins and a summer hotel. Bruce Catton, the Civil War historian, recalled fondly the measured pace and opportunity of the lumber country in upstate Michigan during the 1890s. Born in 1901, the famed anthropologist Margaret Mead was perhaps most rhapsodic of all in remembering her early years in Hammonton, New Jersey, not far from Philadelphia. Like the others, she was struck by the simplicity of life and the immediacy of the outdoors, where she could roam at will. Among her joys were playing with her mother's possessions and, living in an extended family, listening to her grandmother's imaginative stories.

These young people enjoyed life styles enormously more comfortable than those endured by the large number of people who crowded the cities or scratched at the land. Class distinctions existed, but opportunity also beckoned, and right conduct (or "character," as it was popularly called) was believed to count for almost as much as social standing. As the historian William Leuchtenburg described it, the life of middle-class youth featured "the clang of the trolley, the cry of the carnival pitchman, the oompah of the military band on a summer evening, the clatter of Victorian sulkies, the shouts of children playing blindman's bluff and run-sheep-run." For nostalgic Americans in later decades this description offered an image of a world that seemed to have been overwhelmed by the complexity, breathlessness, and divisiveness of twentieth-century life.

Movement and tension

Only an elite, however, could hope to live so well. America had 76 million people in 1900, of whom 35 million were generally underprivileged Negroes, Indians, or immigrants. Of the remaining 41 million, few enjoyed the advantages of people like the Turners. For every socially secure girl like Margaret Mead there were scores, like Theodore Dreiser's Sister Carrie, who fled farm or small town, only to be buffeted about in the cities. Many thousands, in fact, resorted to prostitution in order to make a living. For every upwardly mobile young man like Wheeler or Douglas there were many more who migrated constantly without advancing up the social ladder. Continuous geographical mobility and social insecurity characterized the lives of all but the favored few at the time.

Moreover, memories suffused with nostalgia have a way of distorting historical reality. Even for people like Turner and his well-placed contemporaries, that reality could be frightening indeed. For Turner the blows were personal, and they came with the suddenness that made life so uncertain for people of that generation. In 1899 he lost both a daughter and a son, his wife had an emotional breakdown and was confined to a sanitarium, and he, stricken by the events, went briefly into seclusion. Personal tragedies also disrupted the early lives of Mead and Douglas. When Mead was a young girl, her father grew withdrawn from the family following the death of her baby sister. When Douglas was four, his mother died; his father took to drink, making life intolerable for a second wife and two sons, who fled to the Maine woods. Black and Catton were spared similar family crises but lived amid social and economic dislocations: Black in a farm region suffering from depression and Catton in a once-thriving lumber region cut barren by the loggers. By 1900 conservationists began to lament such reckless commercial exploitation of natural resources.

Sensitive Americans worried deeply about this social instability. Some young people reacted by seeking opportunity in the city, and some by moving West—young Burt Wheeler did both. Others, like Douglas, who watched lumberjacks killed or maimed every year, came to demand action from the government, which in the 1890s remained more a symbol of unity than an active force affecting lives directly. Many others, however, turned to saloons or, perhaps most frightening to contemporaries, to socialism, radicalism, or newly forming special-interest groups. This apprehension about potential class warfare, intensified by the belief that the frontier was a thing of the past, obsessed many respectable Americans in the depression-ridden 1890s. They were alarmed especially by the pace of social change, which appeared to be destroying the Republic. As the historian Henry Adams complained, "the individual crawled as best he could, through the wreck, and found many values of life upset."

Ethnic and racial tensions, already acute in the large American cities, disturbed even the lives of small-town Americans. Black's area of Alabama had comparatively few Negroes, but like all who lived in the South, they were systematically oppressed and terrorized. When a local white boy shot and killed a Negro, he was acquitted because his father was respectable. Wheeler had no experience with Negroes, but when he tried to date local Catholic girls, he was driven from their neighborhood by people throwing rocks. Douglas recalled that the Irish in Maine were stoned as they tried to walk to parochial schools. These racial and ethnocultural tensions, sharp and open in late-nineteenth-century America, profoundly shaped the residential, educational, and political contours of the era.

Epidemics, high mortality rates, drunkenness, immorality, agricultural disaster, unemployment, radicalism, ethnic and racial divisions—all these frightened well-placed Americans in the 1890s. A supposed harmony of interests seemed in danger of demolition. In retrospect it is clear that the wellborn were to maintain their social and economic hegemony under a capitalistic economy and a republican form of government—in short, that in twentieth-century America much from the nineteenth century was to be preserved. Yet many values and life styles did change rapidly after 1900. Moreover, the strength of existing institutions was by no means so clear at the time, for three overwhelming forces seemed destined to transform the nation. These were urbanization, massive immigration, and industrialization.

FEAR OF THE CITY

The scope of urbanization in America by 1900 is sometimes exaggerated. Only 21.5 million of the country's population of 76 million dwelled in places with 25,000 or more people. Many cities that later became metropolises were still moderate in size: the population of Dallas in 1900 was 42,000, of Houston, 44,000. In all but a few large cities it was still possible to climb aboard a trolley and ride quickly into the country. The slums, tenements, and ghettos described by Jacob

Riis and other urban reformers proliferated in only a few older, predominantly eastern urban areas. Only one city, Boston, had a subway, and very few had sky-scrapers. New York, whose tallest building in 1900 had only twenty-nine stories, was not the vertical wonder it was to become in the next thirty years but a sprawling conglomeration of low, gray tenements, brownstone houses, and commercial build-ings with cast-iron grillwork.

Yet contemporaries were correct in pointing to the pace of urban growth, for it had been astonishing. In 1860 Pittsburgh had a population of 67,000 people; by 1900 it had 450,000. During the same period the population of Minneapolis grew from 2,500 to 200,000, that of Los Angeles from 5,000 to 100,000. Chicago, with 30,000 inhabitants in 1850, had 1.7 million by 1900, and Kansas City, only a small town in 1850, had 200,000. By 1900 not only Chicago but also Philadelphia, with 1.3 million, and New York–Brooklyn, with 3 million, housed more than a million residents. And the urban expansion continued: by 1930 nearly 50 million Americans (of 122 million in all) lived in places with 25,000 or more people. Almost 30 million of these dwelled in large metropolitan areas of 250,000 or more.

At the root of this growth were sweeping developments in technology. Electrifi-cation made possible trolleys, which transformed the "walking city" of antebellum days and promoted the rapid expansion of suburbs; these housed millions of people as early as 1900. Electrification led also to the installation of elevators, without which the vertical metropolis could not have developed. Steam and electricity also accelerated the urban concentration of industry, which had previously relied heavily on scattered sources of water power. The mechanization of farming, the growth of railroads, and the increasing use of the refrigerator car facilitated the rapid shipment of foodstuffs and other raw materials in the quantities necessary to support huge agglomerations of people. The rise of cities and of suburbs, like much else in modern American history, stemmed in large part from the technological imperative.

The growth of cities: the ten largest cities from 1860 to 1900 and in 1970
(in thousands)

1860		1880		1900		1970	
New York[a]	1,072	New York[a]	1,773	New York[a]	3,437	New York	11,571
Philadelphia	585	Philadelphia	847	Chicago	1,699	Los Angeles[b]	7,032
Baltimore	212	Chicago	503	Philadelphia	1,294	Chicago	6,978
Boston	178	Boston	363	St. Louis	575	Philadelphia	4,817
New Orleans	169	St. Louis	351	Boston	561	Detroit	4,199
Cincinnati	161	Baltimore	332	Baltimore	509	San Francisco[c]	3,109
St. Louis	161	Cincinnati	255	Pittsburgh	452	Washington	2,861
Chicago	109	Pittsburgh	235	Cleveland	382	Boston	2,753
Buffalo	81	San Francisco	234	Buffalo	352	Pittsburgh	2,401
Newark	72	New Orleans	216	San Francisco	343	St. Louis	2,363

SOURCE: Donald B. Cole, *Handbook of American History* (New York, 1968), p. 166; and George E. Delury, *World Almanac and Book of Facts 1975* (New York, 1974) p.148
[a]Manhattan and Brooklyn   [b]Includes Long Beach   [c]Includes Oakland

Technological change also disrupted rural and small-town life. The mechanization of agriculture contributed to regular overproduction of cash crops and to plummeting prices (especially before 1897) on domestic and world markets. Small farmers, tenants, and rural laborers found themselves squeezed off the land or burdened with ever-greater debts. Faced with ruin, thousands of people, especially in the Plains and the South, joined the Populists in the early 1890s and cursed their enemies. "The great common people of this country are slaves," said Mary Ellen Lease, a prominent Populist orator, "and monopoly is the master. The West and South are prostrate before the manufacturing East." The folk singer Woody Guthrie, son of poor rural folk from the Plains, remembered his mother rocking him to sleep:

> Rock-a-bye baby, on the tree top;
> When you grow up, you'll work in a shop.
> When you are married, your wife will work, too
> So that the rich will have nothing to do.
>
> Hush-a-bye baby, on the tree top;
> When you grow old, your wages will stop.
> When you have spent the little you've made
> First to the poorhouse, then to the grave.

Some of the reforms sought by the agrarian rebels—the eight-hour day, progressive taxation of incomes, popular election of senators, governmental control of railroads and utilities, public support for farm prices—later became part of American life. In the 1890s, however, the Populists succeeded chiefly in frightening "respectable" people, who perceived them as harbingers of class warfare. More important, the embattled farmers were fighting a losing battle against inexorable technological forces, and thousands gave up the struggle every year by fleeing to the cities. Though America's rural population continued to rise, the urban population jumped much more rapidly. Millions of these urbanites were immigrants from abroad. Millions more, however, came from the American countryside. This vast rural-urban migration testified vividly to the unsettled economic and social conditions of the age.

A variety of motives impelled the throngs who left the farms and small towns. For some, the city was a magnet—a place where bright lights, noise, and color might bring excitement to life. For others, urban life was the new frontier—a place that promised to enhance social status or economic opportunity, a "safety valve" for economic discontent, cultural isolation, and social stagnation. To such migrants rural life had been monotonous, lonely, and exhausting. "I'm sick of farm life," one of Hamlin Garland's characters complained bitterly. "It's nothing but fret, fret, fret, and work the whole time, never seeing anybody but a lot of neighbors just as big fools as you are. I spend my time fighting flies and washing dishes and churning. I'm sick of it all."

Many Americans responded to the massive shift from country to city and suburb by reaffirming the presumed virtues of rural life. Contradicting Garland's realistic portrayals of rural hardship, rhapsodies about life in small towns survived as staples of fiction until writers like Sherwood Anderson and Sinclair Lewis delivered pow-

Poor rural families often helped support themselves by setting up "home factories" in their backyards.

erful (though still not fatal) blows to them in the 1910s and 1920s. Booth Tarkington's *Gentleman from Indiana,* published in 1900, was a characteristic hymn of praise to small-town values. The inhabitants of fictional Plattville, a Tarkington character observed, were "one big happy family." Plattville was "the one place for a man to live who likes to live where people are kind to each other, and where they have the old-fashioned way of saying 'Home.'" Even Theodore Dreiser, product of a harsh, lower-class background in small-town Indiana, was moved by a trip through his native state in 1916. "Every one of those simple towns through which we had been passing," he conceded, "has its red light district." But "the center of Indiana is a region of calm and simplicity, untroubled to a large extent . . . by the stormy emotions and distresses which so often affect other parts of America and the world."

The celebration of the small town was but one manifestation of the desire to affirm a usable past, which Americans needed in order to find an anchor amid the storms of social change. Other indications were the nostalgia implicit in Turner's thesis that democracy and individualism were products of the frontier, the joyful release many Americans felt at the "safe" William McKinley's triumph over the "radical" William Jennings Bryan in 1896, and the passion with which people

When Aunt Em came there to live she was a young pretty wife. The sun and wind had changed her, too. They had taken the sparkle from her eyes and left them a sober gray; they had taken the red from her cheeks and lips, and they were gray also. She was thin and gaunt, and never smiled now. When Dorothy, who was an orphan, first came to her, Aunt Em had been so startled by the child's laughter that she would scream and press her hand upon her heart whenever Dorothy's merry voice reached her ears; and she still looked at the little girl with wonder that she could find anything to laugh at.

Henry never laughed. He worked hard from morning till night and did not know what joy was. He was gray also, from his long beard to his rough boots, and he looked stern and solemn, and rarely spoke.

The reality of life on the Plains, as described by Lyman Frank Baum in his *The Wonderful Wizard of Oz* (1900). Aunt Em and Uncle Henry were the guardians of Dorothy, the heroine, who is swept away from her humdrum life.

embraced the "splendid little war" against Spain in 1898, a conflict that William James thought might "hammer us into decency." Disoriented by social change, many Americans persistently emphasized the virtues of their agrarian heritage. Accordingly, their portrayal of cities was hardly flattering, and even historians have echoed their emphasis on the dingy, the violent, and the pathological side of urbanization. Such a portrayal, sometimes distorted and overgeneralized, deserves a careful look.

THE QUALITY OF URBAN LIFE

James Bryce, the sophisticated English observer whose *American Commonwealth* (1888) remains one of the most discerning descriptions of late-nineteenth-century American life, emphasized one theme that underlay the verbal assault on American cities. This was esthetic revulsion. American cities, he observed, "differ from one another only herein, that some are built more with brick than with wood, and others more with wood than with brick." A year later, his countryman Matthew Arnold agreed. "American cities," he wrote, "have hardly anything to please a trained or a natural sense for beauty . . . a great void exists in the civilization over there [in America]; a want of what is elevating and beautiful, of what is interesting."

Bryce and Arnold reflected a widespread view that American cities, among the fastest growing in human history, were unplanned and therefore ugly. The architect Louis Sullivan described Chicago as "this flat smear, this endless drawl of streets and shanties, large and small, this ocean of smoke. . . . New York may be revolting to you, but this Chicago thing is infinitely repulsive to me. . . . Seventy years ago it was a mudhole—today it is a human swamp." Rudyard Kipling concluded simply of Chicago, "I urgently desire never to see it again," while the novelist Henry James, who moved to London to escape the crassness of his native land, called the American city a "huge continuous 50-floored conspiracy against the very idea of the ancient graces."

To contemporary observers ugliness was merely the most obvious manifestation of urban ills. Another was city government, which by 1900 was too often in the hands of immigrant political "machines" to suit old-stock residents and "goo-goos," or "good government" reformers. In fact, these urban machines served important functions, sometimes offering to city government the same organization and regimentation that graded urban schools were bringing to education. At their most humane they furnished welfare services to people in need. As Martin Lomasney, the boss of Boston, put it, "there's got to be in every ward somebody that any bloke can come to—no matter what he's done—and get help. *Help, you understand; none of your law and justice, but help."* Men like Lomasney or New York's Charles Murphy, boss of Tammany Hall, provided on the local level the beginnings of welfare functions that state and federal government were later to assume.

Some of these bosses proved wasteful or corrupt. More often, they treated politics as an occupation, not as a forum for disinterested public service. "There's an honest graft," Tammany's George Washington Plunkitt observed, "and I'm an example of how it works. I might sum up the whole thing by sayin': I seen my opportunities and I took 'em." By this comment Plunkitt meant that the political machine—for him and for many other aspiring immigrants—was a business like any other. Those who worked for the machines provided services to people in need and were paid for their efforts. In these ways the immigrant political organizations were sources of social mobility for ethnic groups (especially the Irish then), as well as institutions that offered what nothing else did at the time—a more centralized way of managing increasingly large and unwieldy urban centers. It was not surprising that such organizations tended to overturn the older Yankee elites.

Many people recoiled from such machines, especially because immigrants ran them. Bryce contemptuously referred to the "ignorant multitude, largely composed of recent immigrants, untrained in self-government." Novelists of the period commonly agreed. The progressive David Graham Phillips in his political novel *The Plum Tree* (1905) described a city boss, Dominick, as a "huge tall man, enormously muscular, with a high head like a block, straight in front, behind and on either side; keen, shifty eyes, pompous cheeks, a raw, wide mouth; slovenly dress, with a big diamond on his puffy little finger." Tarkington in "The Aliens," a short story, portrayed a precinct chairman as a "pockmarked, damp-looking, soiled little fungus of a man." Even the social worker Jane Addams believed that immigrants were "densely ignorant of civic duties."

Observers of the city around 1900 were especially distressed by crowding. Actually, urban densities were generally manageable in American cities, most of which sprawled outward rather than upward. But in a few older areas such as New York City, the situation seemed ominous. The urban reformer Jacob Riis estimated in 1890 that 330,000 people lived in one square mile of the Lower East Side, and that the death rate for children under five in some of these blocks was almost 140 per thousand, compared to 88 per thousand for the city at large. The density of population in Manhattan in 1894 was 143.2 people per acre. One section had 986.4 people per acre, a density surpassing even that of Bombay.

The cause of such crowding, then and later, was the increasingly high value attached to scarce urban land, which led builders and landlords to make optimal use of space. The result in New York was the "dumbbell" tenement, the dominant form of residential construction in that city between 1879 and 1900. These tenements were five- or six-story buildings, each floor of which had two hallway water closets and fourteen rooms divided into four apartments. The buildings occupied small lots of 25 × 100 feet, and the largest rooms were 10½ × 11 feet. The tenements left no space for landscaping and were attached to each other in front and back. The name "dumbbell" was applied because of narrow (28-inch) air shafts that separated the buildings in the middle and provided the only lighting for the interior rooms. One New York block in 1900 contained thirty-nine such tenements with a total of almost 2,800 inhabitants. In that block only forty apartments had running water, and thirty-two cases of tuberculosis had been recorded in the previous five years.

Writers of the time were almost unanimous in deploring the results of this crowding. Frequently the water closets jammed, leaving overpowering odors that mingled with those of horse manure on the streets and garbage tossed down the air

Tenement dwellers: fire escapes were the chief place to get relief from summer heat in the slums.

shafts. These odors, a report on sanitation in Philadelphia concluded, created "such a pernicious influence upon the atmosphere that one feels an indescribable sense of relief in going to the park or moving out of town, where the air is not laden and polluted with the fetid vapors and foul odors everywhere prevailing." The air pollution of the 1970s and 1980s, however noxious, has been considerably less pungent than in the days of privies and the horse.

Middle-class reformers were understandably appalled. Though they worried about disease, they tended in that Victorian age to dwell on the presumed connection between slum life and sexual immorality. Charles Loring Brace, organizer of the Children's Aid Society, stressed that theme as early as 1880 in his book *The Dangerous Classes of New York*. "If a female child be born and brought up in a room of one of those tenement houses," he exaggerated, "she loses very early the modesty which is the great shield of purity. Personal delicacy becomes almost unknown to her. . . . it is well nigh impossible for her to retain any feminine reserve, and she passes almost unconsciously the line of purity at a very early age."

Complaints such as these ignored the fact that privacy—new to the Victorian era—had hardly characterized rural life in America. Still , others followed Brace's lead. Crowding, said the Tenement House Commission of New York in 1894, led to a "condition of nervous tension; interfering with the separateness and sacredness of home life; leading to the promiscuous mixing of all ages and sexes in a single room—thus breaking down the barriers of modesty and conducing to the corruption of the young, and occasionally to revolting crimes." Josiah Strong, a widely read Protestant minister and reformer, called slum life a "commingled mass of venomous filth and seething sin, of lust, of drunkenness, of pauperism and crime of every sort." A popular song concluded:

> She wanted to roam so she left the old home
> The old people's hearts were sore,
> She longed for the sights and the bright city lights
> Where hundreds had gone before.
> She went to the heart of the city
> And mingled with strangers there,
> But nobody said, "You are being misled,"
> For what did the stranger care?
>
> In the heart of the city that has no heart
> That's where they meet, and that's where they part,
> The current of vice had proved too strong
> So the poor little girlie just drifted along,
> Nobody cared if she lived or died,
> Nobody cared if she laughed or cried,
> She's just a lost sister and nobody's missed her,
> She's there in the city
> Where there's no pity,
> In the city that has no heart.

Although songs such as these tended toward sentimentality, there was no doubting the economic privation and medical catastrophe that threatened millions of people in the cities. One contemporary who witnessed such conditions first-hand was Margaret Sanger. One of eleven children whose mother died young of tuberculosis, Sanger became a nurse on the Lower East Side of New York at the turn of the century. What she saw made her a pioneer for birth control. The way women live, she wrote later, "is almost beyond belief. They hate and fear any prying into their homes or into their lives. They resent being talked to. The women slink in and out of their homes on their way to market like rats from their holes. The men beat their wives sometimes black and blue, but no one interferes. . . . Women whose weary bodies refuse to accommodate themselves to their husbands' desires find husbands looking with lustful eyes upon other women, sometimes upon their own little daughters, six and seven years of age."

Not all areas were as disorganized and miserable as those that Sanger saw in New York. Workers in Paterson, New Jersey, for instance, maintained such unity in the late nineteenth century that they were able to enlist the backing of police and municipal leaders against factory owners. Similarly, many Italian-American families retained the tradition of the old country that males earned the family's daily bread while the wives worked, if at all, in the home; many of these families adapted well to urban life. Many other urban families, while poor and ill-educated, managed to accumulate property and to take part in a range of community activities; few were part of an intergenerational "culture of poverty." Most important, the cities, for all their problems, still offered displaced rural people a standard of living they could not have found anywhere else, and millions of Americans flocked to them through most of the twentieth century.

Nevertheless, the vision of the city as ugly, corrupt, crowded, disease-ridden, and above all immoral caught hold with many Americans who were small-town born and bred and who were adults by the turn of the century. The slum, and by extension the city, appeared a frightening symbol of the decline of civilization and the disruption of the natural order of things.

THE FOREIGNERS

In 1908 Israel Zangwill scored a hit on Broadway with his play *The Melting Pot.* "The real American," one of his characters explained, "has not yet arrived. He is only in the Crucible, I tell you—he will be the fusion of all the races, the coming superman." Four years later a young Russian-Jewish immigrant, Mary Antin, wrote a book, *The Promised Land,* that sold more than 85,000 copies in the next four decades. Like Zangwill, she advanced the idea that America could melt all newcomers into a superior common nationality. "I have been made over," she exulted. "I am absolutely other than the person whose story I have to tell."

It is doubtful, however, that the many Americans who saw the play or read the book really believed in the optimistic message of the melting pot. On the contrary, hostility to free immigration mounted steadily after the 1870s. As early as 1882 Congress excluded Chinese immigration, and in 1897 it approved a law that required incoming migrants to pass a literacy test. President Cleveland vetoed it. In 1917, only five years after Antin's cry of affirmation, Congress overruled Wilson's veto, and in the 1920s it went further by applying quotas that discriminated against southern and eastern Europeans. The nativism revealed by these laws was not new to the late nineteenth century, for Americans had periodically erupted in waves of ethnocentrism, religious intolerance, and persecution of aliens. But the depth of turn-of-the-century nativism—which ultimately overrode the pressure of otherwise powerful industrialists seeking cheap labor—exposed a lack of confidence in the nation's ability to absorb the ''wretched refuse'' (as even the Statue of Liberty labeled immigrants) of foreign lands. The ''immigrant problem,'' along with the rise of cities, profoundly unsettled many turn-of-the-century Americans.

The anti-immigrationists worried first about the sheer size of the ''invasions,'' which dwarfed all previous mass movements in Western history. Besides newcomers from Asia and from Mexico, approximately 25 million Europeans entered the United States in the five decades before 1900. The census of that year showed that 26 million of America's 76 million people were foreign-born or children of immigrants. In the next fourteen years, the peak of immigration, another 14.5 million arrived—a rate of more than a million per year. Alarmed, the head of the Daughters of the American Revolution concluded in 1910 that ''we must not so eagerly invite all the sons of Shem, Ham, and Japhet, wherever they may have first seen the light, and under whatever traditions and influences and ideals foreign and antagonistic to ours they may have been reared, to trample the mud of millions of alien feet into our spring.''

The restrictionists worried especially about the nature of this latest wave of immigration. Prior to the 1890s close to 90 percent of immigrants had come from northern or western Europe. Many, like the Irish, spoke English; others, like the Germans or Scandinavians, physically resembled Americans of Anglo-Saxon

Relation of total immigration to total population, 1870–1930

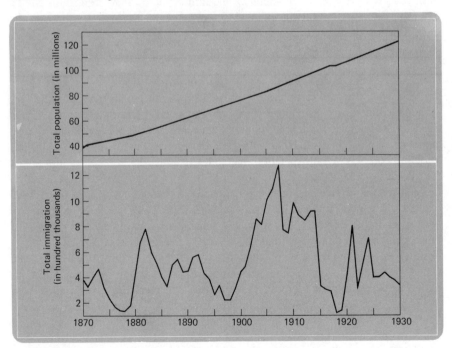

SOURCE: Adapted from *Historical Statistics of the United States*, pp. 7, 56, 57.

stock. Many of these migrants had eventually brought their families and had settled on farm land rather than congregating in cities. Increasingly, however, the new migrants fled from southern or eastern Europe, which provided 70 percent of the wave that entered between 1900 and 1914. To Anglo-Saxons they seemed poorly educated and politically ignorant (or subversive). They were much more likely than the earlier immigrants to be Catholic or Jewish. Arriving in a country with little good land left for farming, they concentrated in eastern and middle western cities. By 1910 one-third of the population of America's eight largest cities was foreign-born.

Preoccupation with such a picture led contemporaries into several oversimplifications. One was that the new migrants, as Woodrow Wilson said in 1902, were "men out of the ranks where there was neither skill nor energy nor any initiative of quick intelligence." In fact, the bottom elements of European society lacked the money to migrate. More commonly, the newcomers were restless sons and daughters of peasant families that could subdivide their meager acreage no further. Or they were people who had already been uprooted to European cities and had moved again to America. Or, if Jewish, they had fled from persecution in Russia and eastern Europe. Far from being lazy or unenterprising, these new migrants were willing to work long hours at heavy physical labor—perhaps to give their children the advantages they had lacked, perhaps to save the money necessary to buy a house in the city or land in the old country.

Contemporaries also assumed wrongly that the percentage of foreign-born Americans in the population was growing rapidly. That was not the case. Many of the new migrants left their families behind, and those who brought them did not reproduce faster than native Americans. Millions of these immigrants were single men who came to America in search of jobs. If they were lucky, they found them, worked hard, and amassed savings far beyond what they could have accomplished in their native lands. If they were unlucky—and millions were after the panics of 1893 and 1907—they suffered. Either way, many availed themselves of the cheap (as low as $10) steamship voyage home to the old country—for good. Between 1870 and 1900 it is estimated that 24 percent of the immigrants—"birds of passage," they were called—left America; between 1900 and 1914 the percentage approached 40. For these reasons the foreign-born in America in 1914 comprised only 14.5 percent of the population, barely higher than the 13.2 percent discovered by the census of 1860.

The extent of this outward migration suggests that images of heavy ethnic concentration need revision. Even between 1900 and 1914 in America the ethnic ghetto did not exist in the eastern European sense of the term, which usually implied a rigidly bounded area to which Jews were confined. Large concentrations of ethnic groups developed mainly in those few older cities or mill and factory towns where abundant aged (and therefore cheap) housing existed. Moreover, these enclaves were not "spider webs" trapping all who blundered in or "spawning grounds" for crime and immorality, to use the words of one contemporary observer. On the contrary, they were usually highly fluid neighborhoods that featured huge inward and outward migrations. And statistics on crime and immorality in these enclaves or among foreign groups are so notoriously imprecise as to be useless. Even the Mafia, sometimes explained as a characteristically criminal out-growth of "ghetto" life, was in fact part of the cultural baggage of some of those who emigrated from Sicily.

Historians have qualified the notion that there was one representative immigrant experience. While the bulk of southern and eastern Europeans fled peasant or village backgrounds, throngs, especially from Italy, came from cities. Also, the foreign arrivals from any given country possessed such a bewildering variety of mores and dialects that it is hazardous at best to speak of a common experience by nationality. Southern and northern Italians, for instance, might as well have come from different countries. Sometimes whole villages resettled in American enclaves; some of these colonies refused to mix with nearby residents who happened to derive from different villages. Such differences, often exploited by employers, helped to prevent the unified class consciousness that radicals attempted to develop.

The immigrants also brought with them widely different values and aspirations. Thousands of Italians and Chinese, for instance, were single men or were husbands who had left their families behind. Many of these migrants sought above all to earn as much money as possible in order to return and live like kings in the old country. Many Slavic workers who labored long hours in heavy American industry also had left families behind; their goal, however, was frequently to save enough to call their families to the United States. Most of these workers—whether Italian, Chinese, or Slavic—were restless and geographically mobile. Poor and exploited, they were often slow to put down deep roots in their new communities. In this way they differed from some other immigrant groups, notably the eastern European Jews, who tended to arrive in family groups, to settle in one place (most often New York City), and to encourage their children to work hard in American schools and to acculturate themselves quickly to New World ways. Partly for these reasons, second- and third-generation Jews moved relatively quickly up the social and occupational ladder.

Marked differences distinguished even those immigrants who settled as family groups. The Jews, for instance, tended to come from towns and cities (in many places they had been forbidden to work as farmers). Unlike many peasant migrants from southern Europe, they were accustomed to city life and to urban occupations. Millions of Jews established themselves in New York City as peddlers, or as garment workers operating out of their own tenements. Setting high value on education, they saved what they could and urged their children to stay in school. Few therefore managed to acquire real estate, or even much personal property outside of the essentials needed for subsistence. Italian-American families, by contrast, often plowed their meager savings into property. To achieve this goal, they had to pull their children out of school and set them to work adding to the family income. The wives turned extra rooms, if any, over to boarders. This "property mobility," as it has been called, was slow—very few immigrants rose from "rags to riches"—but it was substantial by the early twentieth century. It fostered hopes of upward mobility, thereby lessening the attraction of radical doctrines. It facilitated the development of ethnic enclaves with varied community organizations that lasted many generations. For such people, proud of their heritage, rapid acculturation was not necessarily a preeminent goal.

Clothing workers demonstrate for better working conditions and the right to organize a union. The signs are in Italian, Yiddish, Russian, and English.

Other groups tried still different means of getting ahead. For the Irish (who of course had the advantage of speaking English), a preferred route was less through education or property (though many valued these goals, too) than through political power. By World War I the Irish were either dominant or strongly represented in the police forces, fire departments, and political machines of many eastern cities. A generation later, other groups—Italians, Slavs—also managed to secure some power in urban politics. The possession by these ethnics of political resources provided employment and modest welfare to fellow countrymen. Such power was of considerable symbolic value; it helped to soften the resentment of ethnics against the superior class position of the Americans of older stock. In this way ethnic pride helped to defuse class tensions.

If the experiences of immigrant men differed, so did that of the women. Irish immigrants, for instance, included many single women. Necessarily, these quickly moved into the labor force, often as domestic servants. Joining them were thousands of other young immigrant women—daughters and granddaughters of families who had migrated to America—and of American blacks. The labor of such people was repaid with little more than room and board; it facilitated an inexpensively comfortable style of life for the urban and suburban middle classes. Women in some other ethnic groups rejected domestic service and worked—like many Jewish women—as seamstresses, taking work home on consignment. Still other women, following Old World customs, were expected to remain at home and tend to domestic duties. Some took in washing and sewing from wealthy neighbors but otherwise did not work for pay.

Over time, however, millions of young, unmarried women found it economically essential to work outside their homes. Some became nurses or teachers. Most moved into low-paying jobs as garment workers in factories or as clerks and salesgirls in the growing retail trades of the cities. Many had to leave home and to accustom themselves to the new world outside their ethnic communities. In this way, as in many others, the need to make a living clashed with the desire of ethnic Americans to cling to familiar ways.

As the children of immigrants moved into the American schools and workplaces, they developed habits and ideas that bewildered their parents. The younger generations insisted on speaking English and on wearing American-style clothes. More fundamentally, many broke with the religious practices of the old country. This is not to say that the younger generations rejected their heritages—ethnic ties (as exemplified especially in marital choices) remained vital. Ethnic communities also persisted. But the experiences of the second- and third-generation ethnics nonetheless required a degree of acculturation that broke with the habits of their parents. The tensions between generations, like the differences between ethnic groups, testify to the very great variety that characterized the immigrant experience in America.

Just as rural Americans exaggerated the seamy side of the city, so old-stock residents failed to appreciate this great variety among foreign migrants. The result was a nativism as varied as the immigrants themselves. As early as the 1870s nativists included some people like the New Jersey professor who was esthetically disgusted by the "beer-drinking" and "brute-like" people who "eat, drink, breed, work, and die" and who require the "rich and more intelligent classes" to "guard them with police and standing armies, and to cover the land with prisons, cages, and all kinds of receptacles for the perpetrators of crime." Others joined the antialien American Protective Association and campaigned for such abiding institutions as Flag Day and the pledge of allegiance to the flag. Anglo-Saxons established increasingly exclusive orders to separate themselves from the immigrant masses (and from native whites scrambling up the social ladder). Between 1883 and 1897 these people founded such organizations as the Sons of Revolution, Groton School, the Social Register, the Colonial Dames, the DAR, the Society of Mayflower Descendants, the Aryan Order of St. George, and the Baronial Order of Runnymede. By 1897 the DAR, founded in 1890, had 397 chapters in thirty-eight states.

Not all those who worried about the rising tide of immigration were nativists or political and social conservatives. In 1885 a group of progressive economists founded the American Economic Association to promote social reform. At the same time they offered a prize of $150 for the best essay on the "Evil Effects of Unrestricted Immigration." Free immigration, they recognized, was welcomed by employers seeking cheap labor. It resulted in poverty and exploitation. The sheer size of the migrations—of people who had had no experience with democratic institutions—threatened to overwhelm America's political system.

The depression of the mid-1890s temporarily decreased the rate of immigration, but it also sharpened the social tensions under which nativism spread. The use of nasty stereotypes increased. *The New York Times* referred to "hatchet-faced, pimply, sallow-cheeked, rat-eyed young men of the Russian-Jew colony," while Francis Walker, an eminent economist and restrictionist, talked of "beaten men from beaten races, representing the worst failures in the struggle for existence." The appearance of heightened nativism at the very moment that immigration was decreasing suggests that restrictionism stemmed from a significant loss of confidence among Americans in the 1890s as well as from alarm about the numbers of foreign-born people who were arriving.

Walker's phrase "struggle for existence" revealed a growing use of Darwinian language in the battle against free immigration. This kind of argument received its most scholarly support in the writings of William Z. Ripley, who published his *Races of Man* in 1899. Ripley used cephalic indexes to describe three "races," the Teutonic, the Alpine, and the Mediterranean. Though Ripley avoided ranking these "races," restrictionists were not so careful, and his book became a Bible for proponents of a Darwinian view that justified Anglo-Saxon imperialism as well as discrimination against certain ethnic groups. The restrictionist case henceforth stressed that some groups were by nature better "fit" to assimilate. Because assimilation to the dominant culture—the white Anglo-Saxon Protestant descendants of the earlier immigrants—was the perceived ideal, those immigrants who failed to conform were not only less "fit" but by definition inferior.

As scientific ethnocentrism became common during the first decade of the twentieth century, articles advocating eugenics proliferated in the magazines and newspapers. Between 1907 and 1917, sixteen states passed laws permitting sterilization of various types of presumably hereditary defectives (none of the laws was regularly enforced). The Dillingham Commission of congressmen and other experts, which set out to discover "whether there may not be certain races which are inferior to other races," not surprisingly concluded (in a forty-two-volume study published in 1911) that restriction of the newer groups was justified by "economic, moral, and social considerations." Madison Grant, an anthropologist with the American Museum of Natural History, summarized the racist argument in 1916 with publication of his *Passing of the Great Race*. Grant's book exalted the "specialized traits of Nordic man; his stature, his light colored eyes, his fair skin and light colored hair, his straight nose and his splendid fighting and moral qualities.'' Grant lamented the emancipation of the slaves and ridiculed the notion of human brotherhood. *Science* magazine, impressed, called it a "work of solid merit.''

Restrictionism attracted some reformers as well. In California, progressives talked of the "Yellow Peril" and forced anti-Japanese laws through the legislature. At the time California had approximately 50,000 Japanese residents in a total population of 2,250,000. Members of the Immigration Restriction League included Robert A. Woods, Boston's leading social worker, John R. Commons and Edward A. Ross, eminent reformers and economists at the University of Wisconsin, and President David Starr Jordan of Stanford University. Florence Kelley, a socialist and a militant social reformer, worried after the Lawrence textile strike of 1912 that anarchy had "become hereditary from generation to generation among immigrants and their children.''

In 1916 the progressive *New Republic* revealed how far America had departed from the model proposed by Zangwill and Antin. "Only recently,'' it observed, "we had absolute confidence in our power of assimilation. Serb, Armenian, Lithuanian, we assured ourselves, would put off their national characters and become good Americans . . . as Irish, Germans, and Scandinavians had become merged with the original English stock. . . . This optimism is hard to remember.'' The older ways of small-town, Anglo-Saxon America appeared to be vanishing as rapidly as the frontier, and with them went some of the characteristic American confidence in the future.

INDUSTRIALIZATION

"Every American who lived into the year 2000,'' Henry Adams wrote in 1904, "would know how to control unlimited power. He would think in complexities unimaginable to an earlier mind. . . . To him the nineteenth century would stand on the same plane with the fourth—equally childlike—and he would only wonder how both of them, knowing so little, and so weak in force, should have done so much.''

Adams was merely expressing the awe that many people felt about industrialization. As early as the 1880s the value of manufactured goods exceeded for the first time that of farm products, and the number of nonagricultural laborers rose above the number working on the farms. In 1860 American industries had ranked fourth in the world with products totaling $1.9 billion. By 1890 they were worth $10 billion, and by 1900 the United States stood first in the world with goods valued at $13 billion.

Other statistics suggest the magnitude of this growth, which even in the depression-ridden 1890s averaged 4.6 percent per year. Between the mid-1860s and 1900 railroad trackage increased from 35,000 to 193,000 miles, steel from 20,000 long tons produced per year to 10 million, and bituminous coal from 13 million short tons extracted per annum to 212 million. Oil production rose from zero in 1860 to 1 billion gallons of kerosene, 300 million gallons of fuel oils, and 170 million gallons of lubricating oils in 1900, while horsepower from all sources (steam,

The explosion of industrial growth, 1860–1920

	1860	1880	1900	1910	1920
Population (millions)	32	50	76	92	106
Exports of merchandise (millions of current dollars)	316	824	1,371	1,710	8,030
Nonagricultural exports (millions of current dollars, followed by percent of total)	49(16)	122(15)	485(35)	767(45)	4,163(52)
Iron ore production (thousands of tons)	2,873	7,120	27,300	57,015	67,604
Crude petroleum production (thousands of barrels)	500	26,286	63,621	209,557	442,929
Workers in nonfarm occupations (thousands, followed by percent of all workers)	4,325(41)	8,807(51)	18,161(63)	25,779(69)	30,985(73)
General imports (millions of current dollars)	354	668	850	1,557	5,278
GNP (billions of dollars 1929 prices)	9.1[a]	16.1[a]	37.1[a]	55.0[a]	71.9[a]

SOURCE: Adapted from *Historical Statistics of the United States*, pp. 7, 14, 72, 139, 356, 357, 360, 361, 365, 366, 416, 417, 427, 429, 544, 545, 552, 553

[a]Annual averages, 1869–73, 1877–81, 1897–1901, 1907–11, and 1917–21

electricity, wind, water, and work animals) increased from 2,535,000 in 1860 to 46,215,000 forty years later. It was no wonder that Adams added, "power leaped from every atom. . . . Man could no longer hold it off. Forces grasped his wrists and flung him about as though he had hold of a live wire."

Inventions accompanying this growth seemed equally astonishing to contemporary observers. Before 1860 Americans had taken out 30,000 patents; during the next thirty years they took out 440,000. These led to such developments as the transatlantic cable, the telephone, refrigerator cars, typewriters, the linotype, and the Pullman car. After 1900 the parade of technological advances and innovations continued: the first transmittal of speech by wireless (1900), the Wright brothers' airplane (1903), the first connected film story, *The Great Train Robbery* (1903), the Diesel engine (1904), the nickelodeon (1905), and Ford's Model T (1908).

Despite these innovations, America remained an awkward giant in many ways. Roads were so poor as late as 1901 that Roy Chapin, publicizing the new "Merry Oldsmobile" by driving it from Detroit to New York, followed the Erie Canal towpath for 150 miles rather than trusting the highways. The trip took seven and a half days. Cars were so frightening that President Theodore Roosevelt was commended for his "characteristic courage" in riding in one. Urban housewives used canned vegetables and some processed foods, but they lacked such modern conveniences as refrigerators. Most people relied on gas jets or candlepower for lighting and did without indoor plumbing or central heating. Even the telephone, developed in the 1870s, was a rarity in private houses—only 1.3 million existed for 16 million American households in 1900. It was not until the 1920s that technological advances were concentrated in consumer goods, or that the middle classes began to enjoy the domestic conveniences that the elite possessed at the turn of the century.

Yet technological changes were leading to a host of less-publicized but profoundly influential industrial innovations. In the glass industry, machines were developed after 1880 that made bulbs, bottles, tumblers, glass tubing, and continuous sheets of window glass. Innovations also transformed the media. In 1840 editions of large urban newspapers consisted of between four and six pages; they had circulations of up to 4,000, and their cost was between five and ten cents. By 1890 there were machines that not only set type but also printed both sides of a continuous sheet of paper, then automatically folded and cut the pages. By the turn of the century the *New York World,* a giant among papers, was reaching perhaps a million readers daily with editions of sixteen or more pages, which sold for two cents. Sunday editions, including colored supplements, were sometimes as large as sixty-four pages.

Perhaps the most astonishing improvements occurred in the production and handling of grains, lumber, and metals. Corn production increased from 800 million bushels in 1860 to 3 billion in 1915, while wheat output in bushels rose during the same period from 173 million to 1 billion. Developments in mining iron ore after 1880 included not only exploitation of the rich Mesabi Range in Minnesota but also new loading procedures. In 1890 it took a week to discharge 2,000 tons of ore from a lake ship onto railroad gondolas, but by 1910 it was possible to load a 10,000-ton cargo in less than two hours. Trains filled with ore clattered down the Duluth, Missabe, and Iron Range Railroad every forty-five minutes.

Many nontechnological developments assisted these improvements. Among them were the techniques of "scientific management" popularized by Frederick Winslow Taylor. His aim was primarily to increase output by organizing work more efficiently. Higher productivity, he argued, would allow for better wages, more harmonious labor-management relations, and, ideally, lower prices on manufactured goods. These lower prices, in turn, would decrease the cost of living for consumers, including factory workers. These ideas anticipated Henry Ford's dramatic announcement in 1914 of a $5-a-day minimum wage and helped some employers grasp the relationship between decent wages and the profits to be made through mass consumption. But Taylor's methods usually meant that workers toiled at the ever-faster, machine-ruled pace memorably caught in Charlie Chaplin's film *Modern Times*. "If a man won't do what is right," Taylor said, "*make* him." "Remember," he told students, "that the kind of engineering that is most wanted is that which saves money; that our employer is first of all in business to make money and not to do great and brilliant things."

Increasing capital derived from profits also contributed to industrial growth, especially among large concerns. Between 1860 and 1890 the average rate of savings by American business was 5 percent yearly, and so funds were available for reinvestment and expansion. Successful manufacturers were able to set up their own warehouses, eliminate jobbers, develop their own advertising, patent brand names, and sell directly to wholesalers. Retailers, assisted by Rural Free Delivery, starting in 1896, and parcel post, starting in 1913, were able to branch into a mass national market. The circulation of the Sears general catalogue increased from 318,000 in 1897 to 3 million for the fall of 1907. Well before the mid-1920s, when some 75 million Sears catalogues circulated annually, they were known as the "Farmer's Bible." With other developments, such as the interurban railway and the mass-circulation newspapers, the Sears catalogues did much to bridge the gap between urban and rural life styles and to chip away at the insularity of the countryside.

A final important source of industrial development was urban growth. In many consumer-goods industries the enticement of this vast urban market led entrepreneurs to develop new business strategies and structures that were as innovative as technological changes. In meat packing and tobacco men like Gustavus Swift and James B. Duke created vertical combinations permitting them to control operations from production through sales to consumers. Other entrepreneurs worked out horizontal mergers by absorbing competitors, especially during the depression of the 1890s, which ruined weaker competitors. Either way, these giant combinations boomed as cities grew. And by the 1890s the urban market also brought huge growth to producer-goods industries. In 1887, for instance, the Carnegie Steel Company shifted its production at the Homestead Works from rails to building materials for the booming urban construction industry. The continued urban and suburban growth of the three decades after 1900 remained a prime source of the dramatic increases in American industrial power.

The pains of growth

As Americans quickly discovered, such unprecedented expansion did not come without serious pressures and pains. Among these was the concentration of financial power in the hands of a few well-situated bankers and life insurance executives, particularly in New York City. Their command of vast pools of capital for investment, especially in the 1890s, when many businessmen were scrambling for cash, gave them considerably more leverage over the economy than that possessed by the national government, which in the 1890s had to turn to J. P. Morgan's syndicate for a high-interest loan. Because the money market was in the hands of unregulated private entrepreneurs, the economy was subject to periodic overspeculation, mismanagement of stockholders' fund, and occasional panics. One of these panics, in 1901, left half the brokerage firms in New York bankrupt.

Another panic, in 1907, was more serious, forcing banks to close their doors to frightened depositors who wanted to withdraw their money. Further damage was averted only when Morgan himself gathered the top financiers in his imposing library, locked the door, and took the key to make certain that none of them resumed the selling that had been slashing market values. The congressional investigating committee formed in the aftermath of this panic later published findings showing that Morgan and Rockefeller interests controlled 341 directorships in 112 corporations with aggregate resources of $22,245,000,000. This sum was more than the assessed property in all states west of the Mississippi.

The power of the investment bankers (which later declined slightly as rich corporations developed their own funds for expansion) was but one sign of the increasing concentration of resources in the hands of a few industrial giants. The main wave of mergers occurred after the depression of the 1890s, which suggested that size could be a hedge against hard times. At that time, 95 percent of railroad trackage fell into the hands of six large combines dominated by Morgan and the Kuhn-Loeb bank. By 1900 there were 73 industrial combinations with capitalizations exceeding $10 million, 53 of which had been chartered in 1898 or 1899. By 1904 the 305 largest firms in America, with an aggregate capital of some $7 billion, controlled almost two-fifths of manufacturing capital in the country.

The most spectacular merger of all developed in 1901, when Charles Schwab, Carnegie Steel's chief executive, concluded a deal with Morgan. The result was the United States Steel Company, America's first billion-dollar corporation. In many ways the deal made economic sense, for it prevented the excess in capacity that was already hurting the railroads. The new corporation was able to pay higher wages than other steel companies and to maintain satisfactory dividends. For Morgan, who argued that concentration maximized profits and rationalized growth, the deal was amply justified.

But the new corporation terrified many of Morgan's contemporaries. U. S. Steel swallowed 213 manufacturing plants and transportation companies; 41 mines; 1,000 miles of railroad; 112 ore boats; 78 blast furnaces; and vast coal, coke, and ore holdings, including those in the Mesabi. It controlled more than 60 percent of America's steel capacity and exercised enormous leverage over the production of finished goods. It directly employed some 170,000 workers. Its capitalization, at $1.4 billion, was three times the amount spent annually by the federal government. It was falsely capitalized at twice the value of the stocks and bonds of the companies it had absorbed, enabling the House of Morgan to make an initial profit of $12.5 million on the new watered stock. The huge, unprecedented size of the combination caused President Hadley of Yale, a conservative, to warn that if the trusts were not "regulated by public sentiment," there could be an "emperor in Washington within twenty-five years."

The profits amassed by people like Morgan also gave Americans concern. In 1900 Carnegie himself earned $23 million and paid no income taxes (which were then unconstitutional). The Vanderbilt family had seven houses worth a total of $12 million within seven blocks on New York's Fifth Avenue. In 1900, 1 percent of the population owned more national wealth than did the remaining 99 percent, and by 1910 it was estimated that seventy Americans owned $35 million or more each, or one-sixteenth of the nation's total wealth. Far from hiding these fabulous riches, many of the new millionaires flaunted them in displays of conspicuous consumption.

At the other end of the income ladder millions of Americans lived in conditions best described by Robert Hunter, who published his widely read book *Poverty* in 1904. Hunter discovered that during the prosperous years between 1897 and 1903 approximately half of America's families owned no property, and that 10 million Americans, one-eighth of the population, were "underfed, underclothed, and poorly housed." Such people, Hunter warned, "live miserably, they know not why. They work sore, yet gain nothing. They know the meaning of hunger and the dread of want. They love their wives and children. They try to retain their self-respect. They have some ambition. They give to neighbors in need, yet they are themselves the actual children of poverty." The poet Vachel Lindsay simply called them the "Leaden-Eyed."

> Not that they starve, but that they starve so dreamlessly,
> Not that they sow, but that they seldom reap,
> Not that they serve, but have no gods to serve,
> Not that they die, but that they die like sheep.

These 10 million people were but a fraction of the total who were needy; approximately half the population lacked the wealth to make ends meet. Such widespread deprivation helps explain some staggering statistics about turn-of-the-century America. In 1900 only 95,000 Americans graduated from high school. This was only 7 percent of young people aged seventeen. The average educational level was between grades five and six. More staggering still are health statistics. The infant mortality rate in 1900 was 1 per 100 live births; sixty years later it was 1 per 400. Life expectancy at birth for whites was forty-eight years, for nonwhites only thirty-three. While comparative statistics leave something to be desired, it is probable that these health figures ranked America in 1900 at the bottom of the industrialized Western world.

Books like Hunter's, or John Spargo's *The Bitter Cry of the Children* (1906) and John A. Ryan's *A Living Wage* (1906), also offered insights into the impact of industrialization on American labor. By 1900, 18 million of America's work force of 29 million people were engaged in nonagricultural jobs. Those in essentially blue-collar positions (perhaps 11 to 13 million people) earned an average annual wage of around $500, often too low to match the cost of living for an urban family of four. The work force included 1.75 million children under fifteen and more than five million women, many of whom worked in southern mills at wages as low as ten cents for a ten-hour day. Most industrial workers labored sixty or more hours per week, and many, including those at U. S. Steel, toiled more than seventy hours, which included one twenty-four-hour shift per week. Close to a million industrial workers were hurt per year in uncompensated work-related accidents. A total of 146 women died in a fire in 1911 at the Triangle Shirt Waist Company in New York City. These women had been working a seventy-four-hour week for between $14 and $15, or approximately twenty cents an hour.

Well before 1900 such conditions had prompted militant reactions from labor spokesmen. The Haymarket affair (1886), the Homestead strike (1892), and the Pullman strike (1894) had already terrorized the upper classes. After the turn of the century the agitation continued, including a general strike in San Francisco in 1900, a national hatters' strike in 1901, a walkout of anthracite miners (1902), which forced presidential involvement, and a bitter strike in the Colorado coal fields (1904), which led to the imposition of martial law. Between January 1902 and June 1904 such outbreaks caused the death of 180 men, injuries to 1,651, and arrests of

---

O masters, lords and rulers in all lands,
Is this the handiwork you give to God,
This monstrous thing distorted and soul-quencht?
How will you ever straighten up this shape;
Touch it again with immortality;
Give back the upward looking and the light;
Rebuild in it the music and the dream;
Make right the immemorial infamies,
Perfidious wrongs, immedicable woes?

O masters, lords and rulers in all lands,
How will the future reckon with this Man?
How answer his brute question in that hour
When whirlwinds of rebellion shake all shores?
How will it be with kingdoms and with kings—
With those who shaped him to the thing he is—
When this dumb Terror shall rise to judge the world,
After the silence of the centuries?

Edwin Markham's "The Man With the Hoe," first printed in the *San Francisco Examiner* in 1899, "flew eastward across the continent like a contagion." The frightened reaction to it suggested the concern Americans felt about potential class conflict.

Why workers struck: company-owned houses in a coal mining town.

5,000 more. Total union membership, only 440,000 in 1897, increased to more than 2 million by 1904.

But the American labor movement, which even in 1904 attracted only 12 percent of the nonagricultural work force, stalled during the next decade, and by 1915, unions represented only 8 percent of the nonfarm labor. Many formidable obstacles caused this poor showing by unions, which were considerably less successful than in industrial areas of western Europe at the time.

One of these was the enormous political and economic power enjoyed by American employers. This power stemmed in part from a simple fact: thanks to heavy immigration, the supply of labor in many areas exceeded the demand for it, thus permitting employers to exploit the situation. To ensure such a large supply, American industrial leaders spearheaded lobbying against all efforts to restrict the flow of immigration. Employers also acted purposefully to keep workers in their place. Steel executives, for example, shrewdly placed workers of different ethnic groups together in work teams. This strategy of "divide and conquer" assumed—often correctly—that ethnic misunderstandings would override class solidarity. Other employers did not hesitate to call in armed police to suppress unrest; many bloody conflicts erupted between labor and management in America at the time. Business leaders finally could count on the support of antiunion judges, who were quick to issue restraining orders against strikes, and on political leaders in most of the towns and states. With such formidable resources arrayed against them, union leaders were frequently powerless.

Another handicap facing unions was the ethic of work that equated success with individual effort. "You cannot wetnurse people from the time they are born until the time they die,'' proclaimed Henry Havemeyer, the sugar baron. ''They have got to wade in and get stuck.'' The popular preacher Henry Ward Beecher added, ''no man in this land suffers from poverty unless it be more than his fault—unless it be his *sin*.'' Underlying such statements was the sweeping power of social Darwinism, which applied evolutionary theory to the marketplace. Champions of this view such as William Graham Sumner, an influential Yale professor, asserted that successful human beings were those most fit to survive. Failures—the poor—were by definition unfit. Labor unions, the social Darwinists thought, artificially assisted people who were destined not to survive; they interfered with evolution by natural selection. ''Leave things as they now are,'' Carnegie counseled in promoting his ''Gospel of Wealth.'' ''If asked what important law I should change, I must perforce say none; the laws are perfect.''

Another obstacle to unionization was the fear among moderates, especially in the turbulent 1890s, that labor agitation might erupt in class warfare. During the Pullman strike William Howard Taft, later a mild progressive, complained that the police ''have only killed six . . . as yet. This is hardly enough to make an impression . . . it will be necessary for the military to kill more.'' Theodore Roosevelt added, ''the sentiment now animating a large proportion of our people can only be suppressed as the Commune in Paris was suppressed, by taking ten or a dozen of their leaders out, standing . . . them against a wall, and shooting them dead. I believe it will come to that. These leaders are plotting a social revolution and the subversion of the American Republic.''

Though reactionary groups such as the National Association of Manufacturers continued to resort to such language in the 1900s, some leaders of big business like J. P. Morgan used more sophisticated arguments aimed at co-opting labor agitators. By promising company pension plans, employee representation, and profit sharing, they promoted ''welfare capitalism.'' To advance this cause, Morgan and others collaborated with labor leaders like Samuel Gompers, head of the American Federation of Labor, to form the National Civic Federation. Business and labor, federationists believed, had an identity of interests that could prevent conflict. As if to practice what he preached, Morgan induced recalcitrant coal mine executives (over whom he had financial control) to accede, during a nationwide strike in 1902, to arbitration.

This welfare capitalism was hardly popular with smaller businessmen, most of whom could ill afford to be generous amid the fierce competition and insecurity of the age. Businessmen, indeed, were never a united interest group. Moreover, the welfare capitalists were scarcely prolabor. Those few corporations that inaugurated pension plans ordinarily required workers to stay on the payroll for fifteen (or even thirty) years before qualifying for benefits. Meanwhile employees who agitated for unions ran the risk of being fired. Employee representation plans were euphemisms for company-run unions. Profit sharing, really wages withheld for distribution later, reached only a handful of workers. Still, welfare capitalism sounded more enlightened than the crass social Darwinism of the Robber Barons. The flexibility of magnates like Morgan, then and later, did much to maintain the peculiarly unchallenged power of corporations in modern America.

The ethnic composition of the work force also posed difficulties for labor unions. Most recent migrants knew little of labor organizations, and they did not like to pay union dues. Contrary to a prevailing stereotype, they tended to be politically apathetic: few were radicals. They were too anxious about job security and their savings to risk becoming blacklisted. Many immigrant steel workers, for instance, endured twelve-hour shifts, stumbled home to boarding house dormitories, and fell into the beds just vacated by laborers taking the next shift; long hours meant more pay. If they could survive the backbreaking toil and avoid accidents, they could acquire enough money to return home, find a wife (or rejoin one), buy land, and achieve a standard of living undreamed-of before their voyage to the New World.

This dream of affluence surely conspired against unions. Working conditions were not much better, if at all, in America than in the industrialized parts of Europe. But real wages, however inadequate, were higher than they were in England or France, and incomparably better than those in eastern Europe. For thirty years after the Civil War native as well as immigrant workers also benefited from a long deflationary spiral that had the effect of increasing real earnings even when dollar wages stayed the same.

These facts suggest that the processes of industrialization and technological change were not the strictly destructive forces that some modern writers have described. Witness the occupational structure in 1900. Though still heavily weighted toward industrial labor (11 to 13 million workers) and farming (11 million), it also included 1.2 million professional and technical workers, 1.7 million managers and officials (not counting farm owners), 900,000 clerical workers, 1.3 million sales workers, and 1 million service workers, or more than 6 million in all. These white-collar workers, who had numbered less than 1 million in 1870, were engaged in the fastest-growing areas of the economy. Moreover, of the 11 to 13 million industrial workers in 1900, 3 million were defined by the census as "craftsmen, foremen and kindred workers." Despite the pace of change, these people had managed to retain their skills or to develop new ones. Many achieved positions of status in their neighborhoods or moved to better locations. Many others were able to acquire property, or money that enabled their children to stay in school or go to college. This upward social and geographical mobility was far less common than the novels of Horatio Alger suggested. Moreover, business leaders were recruited from among the children of the educated middle classes. People did move gradually up the social ladder, however, and many more thought they could, which was more important than the reality. Union organizers constantly confronted this refusal of industrial workers to consider themselves part of a permanent laboring class.

For all these reasons the dominant union, the American Federation of Labor, tended to recruit primarily among skilled workers and to eschew the task of organizing industry-wide unions. Gompers, the longtime head of the AFL, typified this mentality. The son of a Dutch-Jewish cigar maker, Gompers was apprenticed at the age of ten to a shoemaker and then to his father. At age thirteen, in 1863, he migrated to America and assumed his trade in New York. Young Gompers became a union member at fourteen and knew well the writings of Marx and Engels, but he never joined the Socialist party. He branded theoreticians as "so-called intellectuals or butters-in." Socialism, he added, "is a proposition to place the working people of this country in a physical material strait-jacket." Gompers insisted instead on skilled craftsmen working within capitalism for better conditions. "Unions, pure and simple," he said, "are the natural organization of wage workers to secure their present material and practical improvement and to achieve their final emancipation. . . . The way out of the wage system is through higher wages." Gompers distrusted the state, which he argued (with considerable truth at the time) was as likely to oppress as to assist working people, and he was open in his contempt for blacks and Orientals, who were competing with other workers for jobs. "Caucasians," he announced, "are not going to let their standard of living be destroyed by Negroes, Japs, or any others."

Not surprisingly, Gompers' brand of craft unionism offended socialists and militants. Eugene Debs, head of the Socialist party, said that to work with Gompers was as "wasteful of time as to spray a cesspool with attar of roses." But the socialists, like other militants, found that generating class consciousness among geographically mobile, ethnically divided workers, especially amid an extremely hostile judicial and governmental climate, was a very difficult struggle. For all his limitations, for all his racism, Gompers and men like him came close to anticipating one model of the future: a nation of increasingly self-conscious interest groups, each with an existing stake in the system, and with a set of practical economic goals.

But a nation of interest groups was of course precisely what many influential Americans were fearful of at the turn of the century. "Welfare capitalists," for instance, denounced such a development precisely because they, as a dominant group, had the most to gain by arguing that society was harmonious as it was. Even Richard T. Ely, a progressive economist, felt obliged to defend himself against charges of having uttered heretical ideas by denying that he had ever counseled workers to strike or that he favored the principle of the closed shop. To hold such beliefs, Ely said, would "unquestionably unfit me to occupy a responsible position as an instructor of youth in a great University." In making such a statement Ely, product of a small-town, middle-class background, joined his colleague Frederick Jackson Turner—and many others at the time—in asserting the hope that the turbulent social forces of turn-of-the-century America could be directed into peaceful channels. This effort to maintain order amid the forces of urbanization, immigration, and industrialization—in short, to halt the dangerous fraying of society—was to be a central theme of the "progressive era" that followed.

Suggestions for reading

Among the many books offering interpretations of American life at the turn of the century are Robert Wiebe, *The Search for Order, 1877–1920** (1968); Samuel Hays, *The Response to Industrialism** (1957); and Rowland Berthoff, *An Unsettled People* (1971), and Robert Wiebe, *Segmented Society* (1975), both of which offer a broader view of American history. Small-town existence is covered in Lewis Atherton, *Main Street on the Middle Border* (1954); Robert Walker, *Life in the Age of Enterprise* (1967); and Mark Sullivan's six-volume *Our Times* (1926–34). For descriptions of life on the farms, and for accounts of Populism, see Ray Allen Billington, *Westward Expansion: A History of the American Frontier** (1967); Lawrence Goodwyn, *The Populist Moment* (1978); John Hicks, *The Populist Revolt** (1931); Norman Pollack, *The Populist Response to Industrial America** (1962); Walter T. K. Nugent, *The Tolerant Populists: Kansas Populism and Nativism* (1962); Theodore Saloutos, *Farmer Movements in the South, 1865–1933* (1960); C. Vann Woodward, *Tom Watson* (1938), and *Origins of the New South, 1877–1913** (1951).

For urban history consult Howard Chudacoff, *Evolution of American Urban Society** (1975); Constance M. Green, *The Rise of Urban America** (1965); Charles Glaab and A. T. Brown, *A History of Urban America** (1967); and Zane Miller, *Urbanization of America** (1973). All are useful surveys. Studies of mobility include Stephan Thernstrom, *Poverty and Progress** (1964), which deals with Newburyport, Massachusetts, and *The Other Bostonians**, which covers 1880–1970; and Howard Chudacoff, *Mobile Americans: Residential and Social Mobility in Omaha, 1880–1920* (1972). Sam Bass Warner's *Streetcar Suburbs: The Process of Growth in Boston 1870–1900* (1971) is excellent. Morton and Lucia White, *The Intellectual Vs. the City** (1962) surveys antiurban attitudes of selected American thinkers. Books on immigration and nativism include Oscar Handlin, *The Uprooted** (1951); Maldwyn Jones, *American Immigration** (1960); John Higham, *Strangers in the Land: Patterns of American Nativism** (1955); Moses Rischin, *The Promised City: New York's Jews, 1870–1914* (1970); Humbert Nelli, *The Italians in Chicago, 1880–1930** (1973); Barbara Solomon, *Ancestors and Immigrants* (1956); Milton Gordon, *Assimilation in American Life** (1964); Thomas Kessner, *The Golden Door: Italian and Jewish Immigrant Mobility in New York City, 1860–1915* (1977); John Bodnar, *Immigration and Industrialization: Ethnicity in an American Mill Town, 1870–1940* (1976); and Irving Howe, *The World of Our Fathers* (1976), on Jews.

For developments in business and technology students might start with Daniel Boorstin, *The Americans,** vol. 3 (1870–1960) (1974). See also Adolf Berle, Jr., *The Twentieth-Century Capitalist Revolution** (1954); Frederick Lewis Allen, *The Big Change** (1969); Edward Kirkland, *Industry Comes of Age, 1860–1897* (1961); and Thomas Cochran and William Miller, *The Age of Enterprise** (1942). William Miller, ed., *Men in Business* (1952), contains stimulating essays, as does Thomas Cochran's *Inner Revolution** (1964). Books on business leaders include Joseph Wall, *Andrew Carnegie** (1970); and Matthew Josephson, *Edison* (1959). Useful works on turn-of-the-century social and economic thought are Sidney Fine, *Laissez Faire and the General Welfare State** (1956); Samuel Haber, *Efficiency and Uplift: Scientific Management in the Progressive Era, 1890–1920** (1964); Richard Hofstadter, *Social Darwinism in American Thought** (rev. ed. 1959); Robert McCloskey, *Conservatism in the Age of Enterprise, 1865–1910** (1951); James Weinstein, *The Corporate Ideal in the Liberal State, 1900–1918** (1969); and Daniel T. Rodgers, *The Work Ethic in Industrial America, 1850–1920* (1978).

Accounts of the poor and of labor include Robert Bremner's excellent *From the Depths: The Discovery of Poverty in America* (1956); David Brody, *Steelworkers in America: The Nonunion Era** (1970); Henry Pelling, *American Labor** (1960), a survey; and Bernard Mandel, *Samuel Gompers, a Biography* (1963).

Important primary sources are Jacob Riis, *How the Other Half Lives** (1890); Jane Addams, *Twenty Years at Hull House** (1910); Lincoln Steffens, *Shame of the Cities** (1904); Robert Hunter, *Poverty* (1904); John Spargo, *The Bitter Cry of the Children* (1906); and Mary Antin, *The Promised Land* (1969 ed.), a glowing account by an immigrant.

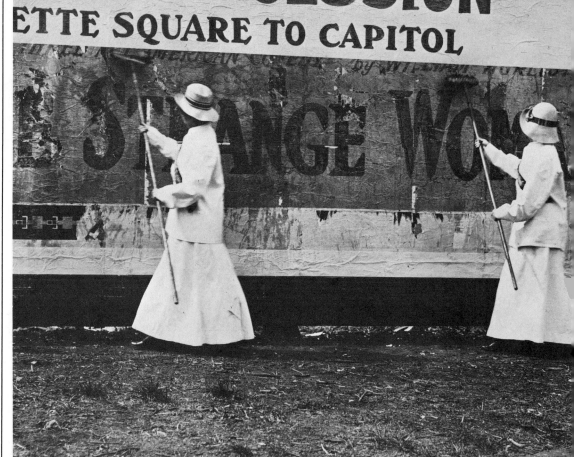

The ambiguities
of progressive solutions

Nineteenth-century solutions

In 1906 William James complained of the "moral flabbiness born of the exclusive worship of the bitch-goddess SUCCESS. That—with the squalid cash interpretation put on the word success—is our national disease."

It was no great feat for men like James to identify the pervasive materialism and commercialism of the age. It was much harder, however, for social critics and reformers to develop solutions to the problem. The quest by reformers to improve society intensified in the late nineteenth century. Many who joined the search attempted—unsuccessfully, as it turned out—to change society through restoration of the past. They were counterrevolutionaries struggling against often intractable economic forces of the modern age.

Among those who sought to preserve older, rural values of the past were some of the reformers who worried about the extremes of wealth and poverty. Until 1900 many called themselves "charity workers," and they considered poverty—revealingly referred to as "pauperism"—the result of individual failings, not of environmental conditions. Leaders in the field, while well-intentioned, believed that generous assistance bred dependency, and they usually doled out as little aid as possible. One critic of this cost-conscious approach wondered later if the Charity Organization Society was really just a "business enterprise, designed to keep poverty out of sight and make life more comfortable for the rich." A poet concluded:

> The organized charity scrimped and iced
> In the name of a cautious, statistical Christ.

Even Jacob Riis, the reporter whose *How the Other Half Lives* (1890) did so much to alert people to poverty, could not blot out happy memories of village life in Denmark, whence he had emigrated at the age of twenty-one. Though he supported reforms ranging from model tenement legislation to settlement houses, he hated the city, and he relied heavily on such palliative solutions as playgrounds, home economics teaching, kindergartens, and boys' clubs. Like other nineteenth-century reformers, Riis opposed public housing legislation, and he despised "bums," tramps, and people who relied on charity. "Nothing is more certain," he said, ". . . than this, that what a man wills himself, that he will be." He added, "Luck is lassoed by the masterful man, by the man who knows and who can."

Reformist ministers promoting the so-called social gospel revealed some of the same nostalgia. Typical of late-nineteenth-century social gospelers was Washington Gladden, a Congregational minister of small-town background who refused to welcome an urbanized, bureaucratized society. Gladden supported compulsory education, abolition of the saloon, and child labor legislation, but he also quoted social Darwinists on the evils of "over-legislation." Frightened by growing class divisions, he yearned for the harmony he had experienced as a boy.

The social gospelers were especially ambivalent about the major forces of the age: urbanization, immigration, and industrialization. Caught in an increasingly secularized world, their response as churchmen and women was to demand the Christianization of society. This was an appeal that aimed more at awakening the conscience of individuals than at developing collectivist approaches to social problems. It did not give serious attention to whether Christianity, under assault from secular values, retained the power to move individuals toward reform. Such a

---

Our scientific political economy has long been an oracle of the false god. It has taught us to approach economic questions from the point of view of goods and not of man. It tells us how wealth is produced and divided and consumed by man, and not how man's life and development can best be fostered by material wealth. It is significant that the discussion of "Consumption" of wealth has been most neglected in political economy; yet that is humanly the most important of all. Theology must become christocentric; political economy must become anthropocentric. Man is Christianized when he puts God before self; political economy will be Christianized when it puts man before wealth. Socialistic political economy does that. It is materialistic in its theory of human life and history, but it is humane in its aims, and to that extent is closer to Christianity than the orthodox science has been.

Walter Rauschenbusch's *Christianity and the Social Crisis* (1907) expresses a militant critique of materialism and of capitalism. Others, such as Washington Gladden, expressed a more characteristically moderate view.

---

probing assessment of religion itself had to await the writings of Reinhold Niebuhr and others in the 1930s.

Nothing reveals better the ambivalence inherent in late-nineteenth-century reformism than the ideas of the two towering social thinkers of the age, Henry George and Edward Bellamy. George, Philadelphia-born, sailed as a young man to California, where he published his immensely influential book *Progress and Poverty* in 1879. The book offered contemporary readers a sharp indictment of the wastefulness and rapaciousness of American capitalism. It influenced a galaxy of later activists and intellectuals, including the municipal reformers Tom Johnson and Newton Baker of Cleveland, Samuel ("Golden Rule") Jones and Brand Whitlock of Toledo, the writer and muckraker Lincoln Steffens, and the "people's lawyer," Clarence Darrow. Bellamy, a newspaper reporter and novelist, published his influential utopian novel *Looking Backward* in 1888. By 1890 American readers of Bellamy's book had already founded 127 so-called Nationalist clubs to promote his doctrines.

George's solution for the problem of capitalistic excesses was the so-called single tax on unused or unimproved land. The threat of such a tax, he argued, would force landowners to develop their property for the good of society. Revenue from the tax would enable government to abolish other levies. George did not want to create a centralized, positive government or a welfare state. Instead he proposed the single tax as the panacea for the ills of society. Populists in the 1890s rejected George's antistatist perspective, and a later reformer dubbed his ideas "a single draft of Socialism with unstinted individualism thereafter." These critics were harsh, for George's writings did much to challenge the rusty "iron laws" of economics. But the critics were correct in noting that George tended to look backward to a Jacksonian society of freeholders and entrepreneurs, not forward to an urban, bureaucratic nation.

Bellamy's vision was more modern. Few social thinkers, in fact, were keener about the potential of rational planning and centralization. His utopia accepted urbanization, and it glorified technological progress. It was run by a highly bureaucratic state in the hands of benevolently inclined former workers. But this utopia, aptly named the "Republic of the Golden Rule," was above all free of class division and unrest, the specter of which in the 1880s had prompted his creative outburst. Bellamy's world of the future was harmonious, free of factious interest groups—an urbanized version of small-town values. Bellamy, and many other Americans in the late nineteenth century, yearned for community, for stability, for virtues supposedly associated with the small towns in which they had grown up.

THE GENTEEL TRADITION

Another manifestation of turn-of-the-century thought was what the philosopher George Santayana in 1911 called the Genteel Tradition. Narrowly defined, the Genteel Tradition meant discreet and decorous optimism in the arts. Painters and sculptors were supposed to depict what one critic called "beautiful things seen beautifully." The business of art, another proclaimed, "is to afford joyance . . .

what a shame it is the great gifts of expression should be wasted on heinous and joyless subjects.'' When Thomas Eakins, one of America's most gifted artists, painted a picture of doctors operating on a human body, an outraged critic denounced it as a ''degradation of art . . . the scene is so real that [people with nerves] might as well go to a dressing room and have done with it.'' In 1886 Eakins was dismissed from his teaching post at the Philadelphia Academy because he posed nude males with females.

Similar conventions governed literature at the turn of the century. Critics praised the optimistic mysticism of Emerson while fearing (or ignoring) the more tragic visions of Poe or Melville. Theodore Roosevelt seriously dismissed *Anna Karenina* as ''altogether needlessly filthy.'' Among the best sellers in 1901 were historical romances and novels celebrating traditional values. Included were such titles as *Quo Vadis, When Knighthood Was in Flower,* and *Alice of Old Vincennes.* Even a ''realist'' like the novelist William Dean Howells, who honestly portrayed the tensions of middle-class life, appeared to Sinclair Lewis in 1930 to be a ''pious old maid whose greatest delight is to have tea at the vicarage.'' Lewis was unfair, but his remark revealed the contempt that some later writers held for the literary traditions of 1900.

The Genteel Tradition in culture reflected a broad affirmation of pious beliefs, which the historian Henry May called the ''reality, certainty, and eternity of moral values.'' These included truth, justice, patriotism, and decency, all of which the educated classes had a duty to inculcate in other people. Thus Roosevelt insisted that ''the greatest historian should also be a great moralist. It is no proof of impartiality to treat wickedness and goodness as on the same level.'' A manual for high school teachers in 1914 asserted: ''My teacher of history should increase my capacity for real happiness, and sharpen my appreciation for all things beautiful and for all persons noble and honorable. He should help me to see that righteousness exalts a nation, and that sin not only is a reproach to my people, but has also been the downfall of great empires.''

Decorous relations between the sexes was a major goal of supporters of the Genteel Tradition. Proper women were supposed to imprison themselves in corsets, to wear layers of skirts covering their ankles, and to keep their feelings hidden from young men. Well-bred suitors had to pursue young ladies with punctilious respect. ''Even when I was thirty years old,'' a New York gentleman recalled, ''if I had asked a girl to dine with me alone, I would have been kicked down the front steps. If I had offered her a cocktail, I would have been tossed out of society for my boorish effrontery.'' Such propriety was not typical of informal courtship in the country or the casual encounters of lower-class urban life. But it represented an ideal that well-bred young people followed. And talk of sexual matters was taboo in polite society. G. Stanley Hall, a prominent psychologist and expert on adolescent behavior, felt obliged to be positively saccharine about the subject. ''In the most unitary of all acts,'' he wrote of sexual intercourse, ''which is the epitome and pleroma of life, we have the most intense of all affirmations of the will to live and realize that the only true God is love, and the center of life is worship. Every part of mind and body participates in a true pangenesis. This sacrament is the annunciation hour, with hosannas which the whole world reflects. Communion is fusion and beatitude. It is the supreme hedonic narcosis, a holy intoxication.''

Social dancing, c. 1914. Dances that featured close body contact were frowned upon by guardians of traditional values.

By 1910 the "conspiracy of silence" against the mere discussion of sexual questions was under assault. But many of the warriors against it were not incipient Freudians demanding sexual expression, but doctors and other guardians of traditional values who led the social hygiene and "purity" movements. Alarmed at statistics indicating the spread of gonorrhea and syphilis, some of these reformers went so far as to call for frank sex education in the schools. The main thrust of these movements, however, was preservation of marriage and the family. Indeed, "purity" reformers also campaigned against prizefighting, ballet, and intercollegiate football. Meanwhile, traditionalists stood firm against perceived breeches of the code. In 1910, 30,000 readers of the *Ladies Home Journal* canceled their subscriptions in protest against an article that suggested that ignorance about sex could cause illegitimate conceptions.

As the career of Theodore Roosevelt was to reveal, there was no necessary contradiction between adhering to traditional moral values and adopting a "progressive" position on political issues. Progressivism for such people was frequently counterrevolutionary in its intent—a way of rejecting trusts, class conflict, and commercialization, and returning to the older ways. So long as the Genteel Tradition remained intact, it was difficult for more "modern" thinkers to receive a hearing.

THE ASSAULT ON GENTEEL VALUES

One of the guardians of traditional values, *Nation* magazine, complained in 1913 of "the tango, eugenics, the slit skirt, sex hygiene, . . . the double standard of morality . . . a conglomerate of things important and unimportant, of age-old problems and momentary fads, which nevertheless have this one thing in common, that they do involve an abandonment of the old proprieties and the old reticences.'' In the same year, another magazine, *Current Opinion,* phrased it more simply by saying that in America it had now struck ''Sex O'Clock.''

Many manifestations of this cultural change were indeed merely ''momentary'' or faddish. These included such dances as the turkey trot, the chicken scratch, the kangaroo dip, the bunny hug, and the grizzly bear. Traditionalists also worried about less transient developments such as the rise of the ''flapper,'' the popularity of jazz and abstract art, and the spread of cigarette smoking, which by 1914 led ten predominantly rural states to pass laws banning the sale of cigarettes. Americans especially feared more alarming manifestations of cultural change like divorce, which ended approximately one marriage in twelve by the eve of World War I. It seemed that the formerly solid props maintaining the genteel way of life had been cut away.

An increasingly self-aware group of literary leaders, many of whom were congregating in places like Greenwich Village, led the push for these changes in behavior. As early as 1900 some of them founded *Smart Set,* a magazine aimed at promoting new cultural forms, and by 1908, when bright young critics like George Jean Nathan and H. L. Mencken worked for it, *Smart Set* enjoyed a circulation approaching 200,000. Four years later, in 1912, radical young intellectuals like Max Eastman, John Reed, and Floyd Dell founded the *Masses.* Known for its left-wing political views, the *Masses* also ridiculed genteel values. Its masthead proclaimed it a ''Revolutionary and not a Reform Magazine: A Magazine with a Sense of Humor and No Respect for the Respectable: Frank, Arrogant, Impertinent, Searching for the True Causes . . . A Magazine Whose Final Policy Is To Do As It Pleases and Conciliate Nobody, Not Even Its Readers.''

By 1917 these cultural radicals—aptly named the ''lyrical left'' by one historian—had found two especially articulate spokesmen for their cause. One of them, the sharp-tongued Randolph Bourne, celebrated a youth movement. ''How well we know the type of man of the older generation who has been doing good all his life,''

It was understood that no girl was interested in a man or showed any liking for him until he had made all the advances. You knew a man very well before you wrote or received a letter from him, and those letters make me smile when I see some of the correspondence today. There were few men who would have dared to use my first name, and to have signed oneself in any other way than "very sincerely yours" would have been not only a breach of good manners but an admission of feeling which was entirely inadmissible.

You never allowed a man to give you a present except flowers or candy or possibly a book. To receive a piece of jewelry from a man to whom you were not engaged was a sign of being a fast woman, and the idea that you would permit any man to kiss you before you were engaged to him never even crossed my mind.

Eleanor Roosevelt's recollections of girlhood at the turn of the century.

Bourne wrote bitterly. "How his personality has thriven on it! How he has ceaselessly been storing any moral fat in every cranny of his soul! How goodness has been meat to him." The other, Van Wyck Brooks, broke decisively with genteel ("highbrow") writers, who "produced a glassy inflexible priggishness on the upper levels that paralyses life," and with "lowbrow" writers, who appealed to "self-interested practicality." He concluded by demanding a "middle plane. . . . On the economic plane this implies socialism; on every other plane it implies something which a majority of Americans in our day certainly do not possess—an object in living."

Many of these cultural critics were visionaries: socialism, sexual liberation, and youthful values were to sweep away bourgeois conventions. Other young writers, however, were affected by a deep pessimism about contemporary conditions. Three such pessimistic books were Stephen Crane's *Maggie—A Girl of the Streets* (1896), Frank Norris's *McTeague* (1899), and Theodore Dreiser's *Sister Carrie* (1900). All embraced a literary naturalism that asserted the inexorable power of the environment over humankind. As Crane's title suggested, Maggie fell victim to urban living and became a prostitute. The book, Crane told a friend, showed that "environment is a tremendous thing in this world, and often shapes lives regardlessly." *McTeague,* which one genteel critic termed "about the most unpleasant American story that anybody has ever ventured to write," sketched the moral and social decline of a San Francisco dentist. Dreiser's novels were relentless in describing the adverse effects of urban life. "The rich were rich and the poor poor," he said, "but all were in the grip of imperial forces whose ruthless purposes or lack of them made all men ridiculous, pathetic, or magnificent as you choose."

Whenever Richard Cory went down town,
We people on the pavement looked at him:
He was a gentleman from sole to crown,
Clean favored, and imperially slim.

And he was always quietly arrayed,
And he was always human when he talked;
But still he fluttered pulses when he said,
"Good morning," and he glittered when he walked.

And he was rich—yes, richer than a king—
And admirably schooled in every grace:
In fine, we thought that he was everything
To make us wish that we were in his place

So on we worked, and waited for the light,
And went without the meat, and cursed the bread;
And Richard Cory, one calm summer night,
Went home and put a bullet through his head.

The vogue of naturalistic pessimism. A poem by Edwin Arlington Robinson.

This pessimistic naturalism encouraged cynicism about reform (Dreiser said he "didn't care a damn for the masses"), unflattering stereotyping of small-town life as in Edgar Lee Masters' grim *Spoon River Anthology* (1915), and the sophomoric despair of men like Mencken or Sherwood Anderson. As Anderson put it in 1916, "the idea is very simple; so simple that if you are not careful you will forget it. It is this—that everyone in the world is Christ and they are all crucified." Yet for all their oversimplification the naturalists ripped away the façade of propriety that the genteel writers had erected.

SOCIAL DARWINISM UNDER SIEGE

Paralleling the assault on the Genteel Tradition was a gradual, ultimately successful war against social Darwinism. By 1917 this war was still being fought, but the major battles had been won. Among the many writers engaged in these battles were young journalists who wrote scathing indictments of American conditions for the new mass-circulation magazines. These included Upton Sinclair, a phenomenally productive socialist whose book *The Jungle* (1906) exposed conditions in the meat-packing industry; David Graham Phillips, whose *Treason of the Senate* (1906) attacked congressional irresponsibility and corruption; and Lincoln Steffens, a reporter whose *Shame of the Cities* (1904) exposed the links between urban malfeasance and corporate power.

These men were reporters, not philosophers engaged in intellectual combat with formal social Darwinian thought. They were stronger on providing facts than on offering theoretical solutions. They tended to exaggerate, so much so that Roosevelt denounced them as "muckrakers." However labeled, they were reformers who rejected the older faith in the unimpeded blessings of evolution. They also enjoyed an unprecedented readership. If they did not cause a reorientation in popular thinking, they surely reflected and reinforced it.

Other critics of social Darwinism used universities or scholarly organizations to voice their views. These included such figures as John R. Commons, a Wisconsin economist; Lester Ward, a sociologist and paleontologist who became the first president of the American Sociological Society in 1905; and Franz Boas, a cultural anthropologist at Columbia who attacked the theories underlying racial and ethnic discrimination. Though these academicians differed widely in their views, they

There is filth on the floor, and it must be scraped up with the muck-rake; and there are times and places where this service is the most needed of all the services that can be performed. But the man who never does anything else, who never thinks or speaks or writes, save of his feats with the muck-rake, speedily becomes, not a help to society, not an incitement to good, but one of the most potent forces of evil.

Theodore Roosevelt's view of muckrakers, 1906.

shared the basic belief that men and women could redirect evolutionary forces toward more progressive ends. Academicians such as these exercised growing influence within their disciplines and on the early generations of American graduate students in the social sciences.

Perhaps the most original of these turn-of-the-century social theorists was the iconoclastic Thorstein Veblen. Conventional in some ways—he defended the profit motive—he was very unconventional in others. Veblen had little use for entrepreneurs like Carnegie or financiers like Morgan. Such men, he argued, were motivated not by an ''instinct for workmanship'' but by ''pecuniary emulation.'' His heroes were engineers, who, if given power, could deliberately reshape the economy along more efficient, rational lines. This emphasis on planning was the clearest sign of Veblen's break with established economic thinking and an inspiration to younger, reform-oriented economists of the 1920s and 1930s.

New developments in legal thought assisted this revolt against social Darwinism. As early as the 1880s Oliver Wendell Holmes, Jr., began questioning the prevailing nineteenth-century view that abstract judicial principles, or precedent, must form the essence of decisions. ''The life of the law has not been logic; it has been experience,'' Holmes argued in *The Common Law* (1881). ''The felt necessities of the time, the prevalent moral and political theories . . . even the prejudices which judges share with their fellow men, have had a good deal more to do than the syllogism in determining the rules by which men should be governed.'' Named to the Supreme Court by Theodore Roosevelt, Holmes quickly disappointed the President by refusing to vote in 1904 for the dissolution of the Northern Securities Company, a railroad combine. But Holmes's view that experience must be the basis for the law also led him to insist that judicial decisions reflect changing social conditions. Thus Holmes dissented when a majority of the court in *Lochner* v. *New York* (1905) overturned a state law setting a ten-hour day for bakers. The court justified its decision by arguing that laws regulating work violated the freedom of contract guaranteed by the Constitution. Holmes, however, insisted that the Constitution was ''not intended to embody a particular economic theory.'' He argued also for judicial restraint: courts should avoid striking down democratically enacted legislation. This practical view, dubbed ''sociological jurisprudence'' by Harvard law professor Roscoe Pound, rarely convinced a majority of the Supreme Court before 1937. But well before World War I it had attracted such able lawyers as Louis D. Brandeis, who used social statistics to defend labor legislation. In law, as in economics, new ways of thinking were challenging the abstractions of the past.

Educational theorists joined this revolt against nineteenth-century dogmas. One such theorist was G. Stanley Hall, a psychologist, philosopher, and educator who led the so-called child study movement at the turn of the century. To Hall, as to other ''progressive'' educators, the graded, formalistic schools of late-nineteenth-century America placed so much emphasis on rote learning that the needs of individual children were ignored. The title of his best-known book, *Adolescence: Its Psychology and Its Relation to Physiology, Anthropology, Sociology, Sex, Crime, Religion, and Education* (1904), suggested the range of his interests and the depth of his belief that educators should consider the particular needs of individual children.

Among the younger men influenced by Hall was John Dewey, whose almost unending stream of books and articles (including his brief, readable *School and Society* [1899]) lambasted contemporary educational methods. Schools, Dewey argued, should be "embryonic communities" that could "shape the experiences of the young so that instead of reproducing current habits, better habits shall be formed, and thus the future adult society be an improvement on their own." Dewey hoped schools could sponsor a cooperative community spirit such as he had known as a boy in rural Vermont. But Dewey was not nostalgic, for he wished such cooperativeness to promote collective social action. Education, he said, was the "fundamental method of social progress and reform."

Like many educational theorists, Dewey placed too much faith in the potential of schools to alter society—schools remained highly structured and bureaucratic reflections of society at large. Dewey's ideas also left an ambiguous legacy on progressive educational theory. Some of his followers used him to promote industrial education (which he often favored), and others, to defend unstructured "play schools" (which he opposed). Many progressive educators forgot that Dewey, far from opposing intellectual training, wanted to develop in students what he called a "creative intelligence," which could be put to "pragmatic" or "instrumental" use in improving society. Like Veblen, Dewey hoped that institutions, if led by purposeful, intelligent people, could become flexible, adaptable agents of change.

But if it was not always clear what Dewey's "instrumentalism" stood for, it was easy to tell what he was against: dogma, rigidity, formalism. Like the philosopher William James, who advocated what he termed "pragmatism," Dewey insisted that human intelligence (what James called "will") could alter the course of history. "The knower is the actor," James said. "There belongs to mind from its birth upward, a spontaneity, a vote." In this sense Dewey and James ranged well beyond their chosen disciplines of philosophy, psychology, and educational theory and offered the opponents of social Darwinism a powerful set of arguments.

Men like Dewey, Veblen, and Holmes also provided reformers with a rationale for replacing older abstract "principles" with empirical study. "The man of the future," Holmes said, "is the man of statistics and the master of economics." W. E. B. DuBois, the militant black leader, added, "there is only one sure basis of social reform, and that is Truth—a careful, detailed knowledge of the essential facts of each social problem." A host of contemporary developments—muckraking, the collection of labor statistics, "scientific" studies of social conditions, the Brandeis brief—reveal that many reformers questioned one older method of effecting change: creating moral outrage leading to conversion. Instead, experts must collect the facts, and planners use them in rational ways.

This faith in expertise, in administration, in planning properly struck some critics as undemocratic. How "progressive" was it to rely on an intellectual elite? Others predicted that "experts" could never be wholly impartial and that it was naive to suppose that administrators could free themselves from moral or political pressures. The assertion that truth was relative, that it depended in part on the facts one could amass, also alarmed observers who argued that pragmatism ultimately disavowed moral principles. "The younger cosmopolitan America," Santayana complained later, "has favored the impartial confrontation of all sorts of ideas. . . . Never was the human mind master of so many facts and sure of so few principles." As Santayana and others correctly perceived, the faith in facts could cause political and economic leaders to stress the practical over the honorable.

Still, pragmatism developed a growing appeal after the turn of the century. To younger, forward-looking members of the professional classes it substituted empiricism for metaphysics. The stress on planning promised to give direction to modernization as well as to take control of society away from corrupt bosses and plutocrats and place it in the hands of "experts." Finally, pragmatism gave little offense even to conservatives. For all their ridicule of social Darwinism, instrumentalists like Dewey, who celebrated community cooperativeness, planners like Veblen, who glorified the ethic of meaningful work, and philosophers like James, who insisted that human beings could impose their wills on the course of events, still believed deeply in the potential of individuals to survive the collectivization of life. The pragmatic revolt, in short, promised to preserve as well as to plan. Like the "progressivism" that embraced it in the name of reform, it was counterrevolutionary as well as reformist.

Progressivism

Broadly speaking, the attacks on the Genteel Tradition and social Darwinism were part of intellectual currents throughout the industrialized Western world. In the United States they accompanied the so-called progressive era between roughly

1900 and 1918. But intellectual ferment is ordinarily as much a reflection as a cause of broader forces. Such was the case during these years, when the major social forces—industrialization, bureaucratization, urbanization—grew so threatening that people felt they had to adopt new methods to control them. In a society as diverse and complex as the United States, these methods necessarily varied widely. Some people organized to battle high tariffs, others to eliminate the slum or restrict immigration. Still others promoted conservation, urban reform, trust busting, or improvement in the status of blacks, labor, or women. Most of these people called themselves "reformers" or "progressives."

These progressives also worried, naturally enough, about their own well-being. Confronted with collectivization, they concluded that they had to develop pressure groups of their own. From this perspective the progressive era was not simply a morality play starring "reformers" against "special interests." It also featured a cast of specialized and increasingly bureaucratized groups, some of which overlapped in ways that facilitated effective (if temporary) reform coalitions. So it was that "progressives"—the broad-based and diverse collection of reformers who proliferated in these years—were frequently moralistic in their rhetoric while being simultaneously practical, self-interested, and professional in their means.

The proliferation of pressure groups at the time supports this functionalist description of progressive reform movements. The pressure groups included reform-conscious organizations like the Anti-Saloon League, the General Federation of Women's Clubs, the Farmers' Union, the Immigration Restriction League, and the National Association for the Advancement of Colored People. More specialized business groups included the National Civic Federation, the National Business League, and the National Rivers and Harbors Congress, all of which sought to change, or "reform," the existing order. The growing number of professional organizations included the American Medical Association, the American Sociological Society, and the American Association of University Professors. These groups, and many more like them, were either first organized or expanded rapidly during this period. All became increasingly self-interested (and, with some exceptions, more powerful) as professionalization and specialization advanced later in the century. The universalist reform impulse of Edward Bellamy no longer seemed as applicable in the modern age.

Why these organized groups gathered strength when they did is difficult to explain. Simple economic interpretations of the progressive spirit confront the fact that America enjoyed unprecedented prosperity in the twenty years following the depression of 1893–97: large-scale commercial farmers, the vanguard of protest in the 1890s, benefited as never before from rising prices for their produce. The view that "the people revolted" against exploitation fails to identify the "people" or to answer why they did not do so earlier. The explanation of "social lag"—that people only belatedly articulate their problems and turn to reform—tells more about what happened than why.

An equally unsatisfactory explanation of progressivism argues that the reformers were middle-class Americans concerned primarily about enhancing their social status. Such a view correctly identifies the rapid growth of the middle classes in the late nineteenth century. It correctly asserts that many professional people—lawyers, doctors, teachers, ministers—felt threatened by immigrants beneath them and plutocrats above them. But this theory of "status revolt" is based on the questionable psychology that threatened people become reformers, when in fact they might have become revolutionaries or drones. The theory also tends to forget that most political movements in modern societies are led by people in the middle or upper middle classes. It fails to explain why such people, who had been threatened long before 1900, waited until then to lash out. And it is empirically wrong, for studies of reform on the state level have shown no significant difference in the social origins of progressives and standpatters. The theory of status revolt, while helpful in directing attention to the social tensions of the age, cannot explain why some middle-class Americans became reformers after 1900 and others did not.

Still, economic and social forces did contribute to pressures for change. The years after 1897, while free of serious depression, featured periodic panics and much financial uncertainty. They were also the first years of sustained inflation since the 1860s. The cost of living increased some 30 percent between 1897 and 1917, while wages and salaries rose only slowly. It is not certain that middle-class people caught in this economic squeeze comprised the backbone of support for progressive causes, or that blue-collar workers provided a mass following. Indeed, later inflationary periods such as the mid-1940s or the 1970s and early 1980s caused people to demand budgetary retrenchment, not reform. But it is clear that Americans at the time complained often against the cost of living, and that for them retrenchment—and honest government—was the essence of reform.

The depression of the mid-1890s, which angered not only farmers but also thousands of urban dwellers, also moved various groups of people to call for change. These disaffected groups began by demanding an end to waste and then went on to insist that politicians eradicate special privilege, support progressive taxation, and finally be held accountable themselves (through initiative, referenda, recall, and direct election of senators) to the people. As economic conditions improved, these groups insisted that their politicians offer not only efficient but also positive government. In this way the depression of the 1890s, like the hard times of the 1930s, helped develop new ideas of what government could and should do.

Any satisfactory explanation of the sources of progressivism must finally keep in mind the regional differences of turn-of-the-century America. Massachusetts seemed quite "conservative" simply because it had already accomplished many of the social reforms being demanded after 1900 in less industrially advanced regions of the nation. In Virginia, "progressivism" was promoted by anti-industrial reactionaries anxious to restore the state's Jeffersonian heritage. In many areas of the South and the Plains, progressives complained most bitterly about absentee corporate ownership of their economic resources: such people were not embattled former Populists but merchants, entrepreneurs, and professional people angry at high freight rates or processing costs. In California, progressivism began as a movement of antirailroad ranchers and landowners and developed later into a coalition of urbanites, labor unions, and ethnic groups. And in highly urbanized states like New York, workers and city machines provided steady support for a host of social and political reforms. In this general way shifting local coalitions tended naturally to call for changes befitting their peculiar situations.

Viewing progressivism in this way, as a mixed and shifting collection of self-interested pressure groups, helps explain why it was difficult to identify its base. For though it enjoyed diverse support (an advantage the Populists had lacked), it depended always on cooperation among potentially conflicting groups. Thus, many small businessmen gladly supported efforts to regulate railroad rates, but opposed the NAACP, the AFL, or women's suffrage. Social reformers included those who promoted immigration restriction, those who favored protective labor legislation, and those who worked for both. Feminists divided, often fiercely, into those who proclaimed the virtues of suffrage, those who demanded sexual liberation, and those who sought to protect women workers from economic exploitation. These divisions among progressives ensured that the reform spirit of the age, while real and significant, never acquired the power of a unified social movement.

The divisions also helped to ensure another central aspect of progressive reforms: their essential moderation. Few progressives were seeking to develop a large welfare state, much less socialism. Many, indeed, supported reform in order to ward off the threat of radical solutions. Others—especially those who promoted prohibition and immigration restriction—were "progressives" who feared the masses. These reformers sought to organize and to excise the blemishes that scarred American life. They did not wish to institute racial, social, or sexual equality or to transform such basic and hallowed values as individualism, the work ethic, and the nuclear family.

BROAD VISIONS

Social justice The most satisfactory way to understand progressivism is not to talk generally about motives and ideas but to see what the reform groups did. Among such groups were the advocates of better working conditions. These reformers fell far short of achieving their objectives, but many of them offered a vision of social justice that transcended the interest group model of progressivism.

Many of these social justice reformers were young, well-educated, middle-class women. The role of such women, indeed, was vitally important in a range of contemporary quests for social reform. Florence Kelley, daughter of a Pennsylvania congressman, graduated from Cornell University in 1882. Because she was a woman, the University of Pennsylvania refused to admit her to law school. Kelley traveled to Europe, attended the University of Zurich, and translated into English Friedrich Engels' *The Condition of the Working Class in England*. In 1886 she returned to America, lived briefly at Jane Addams' Hull House in Chicago, and became chief factory inspector in Illinois. In 1899 she became general secretary of the National Consumers' League, which battled for laws protecting women and children workers. She also joined the Socialist party, helped organize the NAACP, and in 1919 became a founding member of the Women's International League for Peace and Freedom.

The most revered social worker of the time was Jane Addams. Like Kelley, she came from a solid middle-class background. But after dropping out of medical school she became restless, traveled twice to Europe, and returned home deter-

Fostering a different life in the city: the Henry St. Settlement, New York.

mined to found a settlement house for the poor. Hull House, started in 1889, offered services including a day nursery, a dispensary, a boarding house, a music school, and an art gallery. Addams branched out to crusade for child labor laws, juvenile courts, women's suffrage, and international peace. In 1912 she seconded the nomination of Theodore Roosevelt for the presidency on the Progressive party ticket.

Addams frankly noted that settlement house activity gave middle-class women something useful to do; it was a "subjective necessity." She rejected socialism, supporting Roosevelt in 1912 in part because she distrusted the power of labor unions within the Democratic party. Though sensitive to the cultural patterns of immigrant life, she said that newcomers could learn much from America, which "represented a distinctly superior standard of life and thought." Part of Addams' great appeal to contemporaries (many of whom idolized her as "Saint Jane") lay in her ability to call for humanitarian reform while at the same time upholding traditional values.

The settlement house movement, vigorous before 1917, declined rapidly after the 1930s. One reason was the virtual end after 1914 of mass immigration; another was competition from governmental services, especially under the New Deal, which revealed that settlement workers seldom reached poor people beyond their neighborhoods. Indeed, they seldom tried, for most social workers during the progressive era were cool to the idea of a welfare state. Unlike more radical reformers, they wished to humanize the social community, not to restructure it.

Still, the social justice movement left an impact on its times. It was in many ways the vanguard of progressive reform activity. By 1914 there were some 400 settlement houses in America. By 1916, thirty-two states had passed laws providing workmen's compensation, thirty-nine were regulating working hours for women and children, and all had approved some controls over child labor. Eleven states were experimenting with minimum wage legislation—for women only. Though these state laws affected relatively few people, and though the Supreme Court struck down the minimum wage laws, many social workers emerged as forceful advocates of New Deal measures in the 1930s. In the progressive era they did much to expose social conditions, to develop model legislation, to popularize the fact-oriented investigative method of understanding social problems, and to extend the idea that environmental, not personal, problems lead to social disorder.

More militant members of the social justice movement began looking beyond the neighborhood to class action. Among these were young labor organizers who sought industry-wide unions as alternatives to the conservative craft unionism of

Troops and workers during a textile strike, Lawrence, Mass., 1912.

the AFL. In 1909 the New York Women's Trade Union League and a local of the International Ladies Garment Workers Union succeeded in gaining support for a massive strike—the Uprising of the Twenty Thousand—against sweatshops in New York City. For three months thousands of women workers, mostly young Jewish immigrants, endured winter cold and abuse from police and thugs trying to break their picket lines. The strike resulted in the unionization of only a few shops, but even this limited success encouraged organizers. In Chicago a strike in 1910 of 40,000 men clothing workers, though again only partially successful, led to the growth of Sidney Hillman's Amalgamated Clothing Workers Union of America. By World War I these industrial unions remained weak. But they were established as industrial unions and later became bulwarks of the CIO.

Most social justice progressives managed to support such working-class activity. But they feared class warfare and were cool to more radical efforts to promote social change. One of these efforts was the Western Federation of Miners, an industrial union whose greatest strength lay in the metal-mining areas of the Far West. Led by flamboyant figures such as William ("Big Bill") Haywood, a powerful activist who had lost one eye in an accident at the age of nine, these miners engaged employers in a series of bloody strikes at places like Coeur d'Alene, Idaho (1899), and Cripple Creek, Colorado (1903). In 1905 Haywood helped to gather these miners and other migratory workers such as lumberjacks into the Industrial Workers of the World. By 1910 the IWW, or Wobblies, as they were called, comprised the radical, direct action wing of American socialism, and in the next two years they branched into organizing textile workers in the East. In 1912 the IWW won a protracted struggle for unionization in the mills at Lawrence, Massachusetts. An unsuccessful strike of textile workers in Paterson, New Jersey, then weakened the IWW in the East. But it remained a vital force in the West, where it claimed 60,000 to 100,000 workers in 1915.

The revolutionary militancy of the IWW terrified conservatives, and even the Socialist party felt obliged to recall Haywood from its executive board in 1913 because he advocated violence and sabotage. The man of the future, said the IWW, was not the theorist but "the obscure Bill Jones on the firing line, with stink in his clothes, rebellion in his brain, hope in his heart, determination in his eye, and direct action in his gnarled fist." Haywood said, "The working class and the employing class have nothing in common. . . . Between these two classes a struggle must go on until the workers of the world unite as a class, take possession of the earth and the machinery of production, and abolish the wage system."

In fact, the IWW talked more militantly than it behaved, and its leaders avoided violence and sabotage. Most of the members were nonideological miners and migratory workers who supported the IWW not because it called for a class struggle but because it promised them—unrealistically—a personal freedom such as they had enjoyed prior to the advent of large-scale corporate mining and lumbering. Their heroes were Lincoln, Jefferson, and John Brown, as well as Karl Marx. Haywood himself wanted workers, not the state, to own private property.

Still, Haywood's radical demands alarmed many Americans, who avidly supported repressive measures against the IWW once the nation entered World War I in 1917. After the Wobblies led a few strikes, the government retaliated by staging

Young girls working in a textile factory, about 1909–1913.

unconstitutional raids on IWW offices. Vigilante groups physically attacked IWW leaders, killing some. By 1918 almost all the IWW leaders were in jail on charges brought under the wartime Espionage Act and Sedition Act, which gave broad latitude to superpatriotic public officials who wanted to stamp out antiwar ideas or left-wing activities. Haywood, prosecuted, jumped bail in 1921 to flee to Russia, where he died ignored and embittered in 1928. The IWW proved an exciting, romantic model of industrial unionism that continued to attract syndicalists, cultural radicals, and even anarchists long after its demise. From the beginning, however, it attempted the difficult task of organizing migratory workers against corporate power, and it played a negligible role after its suppression during the war.

The other left-wing thrust for social justice at the time was the Socialist party, which grew dramatically during the years between 1900 and 1912. Its leader, Eugene Debs, had turned to socialism in 1897 after being jailed for his part in the Pullman strike. No intellectual or organizer, Debs was charismatic, openhearted, and eloquent. Under his leadership, the party managed by 1912 to elect 160 councilmen, 145 aldermen, 1 congressman, and 56 mayors, including leaders in cities like Milwaukee, Berkeley, and Schenectady. During this same period socialists published more than 300 newspapers, one of which, the Kansas-based *Appeal to Reason,* had 700,000 weekly subscribers. In 1912 the party boasted a membership of 125,000, and Debs as presidential candidate received 900,000 votes, or 6 percent of the total presidential vote. Of third-party candidates in the twentieth

Eugene V. Debs speaking to a crowd in Canton, Ohio.

century, only Theodore Roosevelt the same year, Robert La Follette in 1924, George Wallace in 1968, and John Anderson in 1980 received higher percentages of the vote.

Debs spoke for a broad following ranging from immigrants in the cities to former Populists on the Plains to writers like Jack London and Upton Sinclair. He probably appealed above all to blue-collar workers ignored by the AFL. Although he insisted he was a Marxist, he talked more eloquently about poverty and injustice than about the class struggle or the dictatorship of the proletariat. After the election of 1912 his following began to diminish. Some members placed their hopes in Woodrow Wilson. Others, including the IWW, were expelled. By 1917 party membership had slipped to 80,000. In 1920, Debs received almost 920,000 votes in his campaign for the presidency, the most ever earned by a Socialist candidate. But observers agreed that the vote, which was only 2 percent of the total, represented disillusion with the war and admiration for Debs, who ran his campaign from a prison cell. By the mid-1920s the party was a deeply divided, insignificant political force that failed to revive substantially even in the depression-plagued 1930s.

The decline of the American Socialist party was not the fault of Debs, an inspiring leader. It stemmed rather from many sources, including savage repression by the public and government in World War I, and from internal factionalism intensified after 1920 by Communists. The party also faced the problem of trying to appeal to mobile workers who yearned for membership in the middle class, not in a revolutionary proletariat, and who were divided along racial and ethnic lines. The socialists also found lukewarm support, at best, from most progressives, and deep hostility from conservatives. With so many obstacles it is not surprising that Debs tended to stress social justice as much as socialism, or that his party, like the IWW, failed in the long run to expand.

Women's rights To activists like Addams and Kelley women's rights were part of the broader crusade for social justice. For other women reformers of the era, they became the central issue. Though these feminists differed sharply among themselves, some of them raised arguments later revived by advocates of women's liberation.

Far on the fringe in that decorous era were a few militant champions of sexual liberation. One of the most visible was Emma Goldman, a Russian-Jewish immigrant who fled to America in 1885. After a brief marriage she moved to New York City and embraced anarchism, birth control, and free love. Women, she said, "must no longer keep their mouths shut and their wombs open." Frequently jailed for her radical activities, she was ultimately deported to Russia in 1919. Goldman appealed more to a small group of intellectuals and anarchists than she did to most feminists or to the masses, whom she once termed "inert and indolent, crude, lame, pernicious in their demands and influence." Even before her deportation she had little influence on her times, except to serve as a symbol for all that was "dangerous" in the radical tradition.

A slightly less radical phase of feminism was the birth control movement led by Margaret Sanger. The middle-class women behind this cause rarely proposed anything so extreme as free love or the restructuring of the nuclear family. Some of them were conservatives motivated by fears that Anglo-Saxon Protestants were committing "race suicide": birth control, they believed, could reduce the population growth of immigrant masses. Still, the birth control advocates encountered impassioned hostility from traditionalists. In 1914 the government indicted Sanger on nine counts of obscenity that if upheld could have imprisoned her for forty-five years. But Sanger persevered, the charges were later dropped, and in 1918 the courts permitted doctors to distribute birth control information. Though state laws continued to prohibit the sale of contraceptives, the advocates of birth control had begun to show some women a way out of the tyranny of unwanted pregnancies.

A more economically oriented feminism appeared in the writings of Charlotte Perkins Gilman, whose *Women and Economics* (1898) put forth much of what the National Organization for Women was to say seventy years later. Gilman grew so unhappy with the burdens of housework and motherhood (she had one daughter) that she had a nervous breakdown and obtained a divorce in 1894. *Women and Economics* reflected her own unhappy experience by challenging the widespread belief in the joys of domesticity. "Only as we live, think, feel, and work outside the home," she wrote, "do we become humanly developed, civilized, and socialized." Gilman disagreed that sexual freedom was the way to transform or liberate women. Rather, she argued, women were like men in finding freedom and satisfaction through meaningful work and creative effort. Gilman did not oppose marriage but crusaded for a form of communalism featuring large housing units, day nurseries, central kitchens, and maid service to relieve women of domestic chores. Because the number of working women was rapidly increasing—from 5 million in 1900 to more than 7 million in 1910—she was clearly addressing a central social trend of the modern era.

Most of these women, however, were not working because of some quest for personal fulfillment or social standing, or because they felt trapped in domestic tasks. Rather, they were predominantly from the working classes—blacks, immigrants, poor girls from the farms and small towns looking for subsistence in the cities. They worked at menial jobs and for very low pay. Those with a little education found places as clerks or salesgirls—jobs thought fitting for the "weaker" sex. Of course, they had little or no economic or political power, and little time for feminist reforms. Gilman's ideas, while provocative, stood no chance whatever of being adopted at the time.

The limited appeal of sexual freedom and of economic justice for women left the field clear for women's suffrage reformers. These leaders, mostly middle-class women of progressive bent, spearheaded the movement for women's rights by 1910. Membership in the National American Women's Suffrage Association, the central agency of the reform, increased from 17,000 in 1905 to 75,000 in 1910. In that year Washington became the first state since 1896 and only the fifth (all western) to approve women's suffrage. Four other states, including California, followed in the next two years. In 1912 Roosevelt's Progressive party endorsed the measure, and when his party started to dissolve in 1913, politicians began promoting the cause in hopes of gathering former Progressives to their side for the elections of 1914. After 1915, when the highly organized Carrie Chapman Catt assumed control of NAWSA, the movement rapidly gathered momentum. Though unenthusiastic about America's entrance into World War I, Catt shrewdly reminded politicians that women were selling war bonds, working in factories, and enlisting in the Red Cross. At the same time she maintained a prudent distance from more radical suffragists whose headline-grabbing tactics of picketing and other means of direct action probably alienated potential supporters. By the end of 1917 NAWSA claimed two million members, and in 1919 the Senate sent the proposed Nineteenth Amendment to the states. In mid-1920 the amendment was finally ratified by the necessary three-fourths of the states. The moderate, pragmatic tactics of NAWSA provided a classic illustration of a well-organized pressure group operating within the political process for well-defined ends.

Passage of the amendment led some reformers to perceive a golden age ahead. "There is little doubt," a woman wrote in 1922, "that within twenty years the corrupt city machine as we now know it, with its party bosses, its inner cliques and

. . . More than two-thirds of the negroes of the town where I live are menial servants of one kind or another, and besides that more than two-thirds of the negro women here, whether married or single, are compelled to work for a living,—as nurses, cooks, washerwomen, chambermaids, seamstresses, hucksters, janitresses, and the like. . . . The condition of this vast host of poor colored people is just as bad as, if not worse than, it was during the days of slavery. Though today we are enjoying nominal freedom, we are literally slaves. . . . I frequently work from fourteen to sixteen hours a day. I am compelled by my contract, which is oral only, to sleep in the house. I am allowed to go home to my own children, the oldest of whom is a girl of 18 years, only once in two weeks, every other Sunday afternoon—even then I'm not permitted to stay all night. . . . It's "Mammy do this," or "Mammy do that," or "Mammy do the other," from my mistress all the time. So it is not strange to see "Mammy" watering the lawn in front with the garden hose, helping the cook, or darning stockings. . . . I don't know what it is to go to a lecture or entertainment or anything of the kind; I live a treadmill life; and I see my children only when they happen to see me on the streets when I am out with the children, or when my children come to the "yard" to see me, which isn't often, because my white folks don't like to see their servants' children hanging around their premises. You might as well say that I'm on duty all the time—from sunrise to sunrise, every day in the week. I am the slave, body and soul, of this family. And what do I get for this work—this lifetime bondage? The pitiful sum of ten dollars a month.

An anonymous Negro nurse describes her life in the South, 1912. From her earnings she was expected to pay rent of four dollars a month and to feed and clothe herself and her three children.

grafting gangs, will be a thing of the past, as extinct as the dodo.'' It soon became clear, however, that these were wildly euphoric expectations. Women, it developed, did not vote as a bloc; they therefore were unable to command political influence for the causes they favored or to gain admission to positions of political or economic influence. The Nineteenth Amendment, the social worker Grace Abbott admitted realistically in 1925, ''provided a ticket of admission to the political fairgrounds. It does not admit us to the races nor to the side shows, nor does it insure us a place on the committees which award the prizes.''

The expectation that women could abolish the ''corrupt city machines'' veiled a less attractive side of suffragism as it developed after 1900. In the nineteenth century crusaders like Elizabeth Cady Stanton and Susan Anthony had appealed directly from the Declaration of Independence. Women, they argued simply, deserved full equality with men. But suffragists after 1900 tended to be middle-class Protestants who, like many people in the North, feared the immigrant and laboring masses. Suffragists from the South opposed voting by blacks. Many of these women favored the imposition of a literacy test to ''abolish the ignorant vote.'' Such a test would obviously discriminate against blacks, ethnics, and lower-class working men and women. ''Those [suffragists] who thought 'Patrick' was bad enough,'' one historian has explained, ''did not want to add 'Bridget' to their

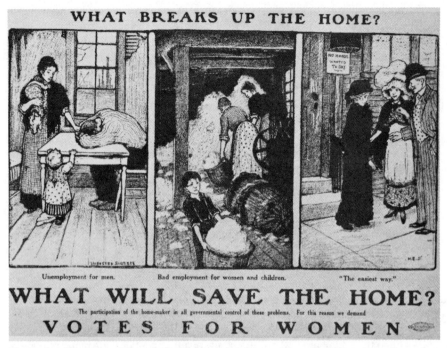

WHAT BREAKS UP THE HOME?

Unemployment for men.   Bad employment for women and children.   "The easiest way."

WHAT WILL SAVE THE HOME?

The participation of the home-maker in all governmental control of these problems. For this reason we demand

VOTES FOR WOMEN

The National American Women's Suffrage Association seeks working-class support.

problems.'' Other advocates of women's suffrage hoped that middle-class Protestant women, who outnumbered their ethnic sisters, might gain the most with the approval of suffrage. And still others promoted women's suffrage as a way of achieving moralistic reforms aimed in part at immigrants: all seven states that adopted prohibition between 1914 and 1917 were states in which women had recently been granted the vote. The crusade for women's suffrage, like many progressive reforms, included racism and nativism, which stained its vision.

Still, pragmatists like Catt—the mainstream of the suffrage movement—did not stress racist or nativist reasons for their cause. Rather, they emphasized that women were being denied basic rights. In so doing, they confronted widely held contemporary views that women were not intelligent enough to vote and belonged

---

No other country has subjected its women to the humiliating position to which the women of this nation have been subjected by men. . . . In Germany, German women are governed by German men; in France, French women are governed by Frenchmen; and in Great Britain, British women are governed by British men; but in this country, American women are governed by every kind of a man under the light of the sun. There is no race, there is no color, there is no nationality of men who are not the sovereign rulers of American women. . . .

Nativism and feminism: The argument of Dr. Anna Howard Shaw, President of NAWSA, in 1914.

---

in the home as wives and mothers. "The man or woman who deliberately avoids marriage," Theodore Roosevelt (who finally supported women's suffrage in 1912), had intoned in 1903, "and has a heart so cold as to dislike having children, is in effect a criminal against the race. . . .if the women do not recognize that the greatest thing for any woman is to be a good wife and mother, why, that nation has cause to be alarmed about its future." L. Frank Baum, widely read creator of the Wizard of Oz, reflected the contemptuous attitude toward feminists by creating a female character in 1904 called General Jinjur, leader of an "army of revolt." General Jinjur ran a female-dominated society in which "men were sweeping and dusting and washing dishes, while the women sat around in groups, gossiping and laughing." Her army, equipped with knitting needles, jabbed at guards protecting the Scarecrow (a straw man) and plotted to use the jewels of Emerald City for rings, bracelets, and necklaces, and the city's wealth to "buy every girl in the Army a dozen new gowns." Countless other manifestations of popular attitudes explain why people like Charlotte Perkins Gilman received such a perfunctory hearing. Under the circumstances the suffragists accomplished a good deal. The right to vote, indeed, represented one of the most significant democratic advances of the century.

Racial justice Unlike women, America's blacks remained a relatively concentrated group in the years prior to World War I. In 1910 four-fifths of American blacks (who then numbered 10 million in all, or 11 percent of the American population) still lived in the South, where most worked at menial tasks. Harlem was described in 1893 as a white district "distinctly devoted to the mansions of the wealthy, the homes of the well-to-do, and the places of business of the tradespeople who minister to their wants." The ghettoization of blacks in northern cities had barely begun as the nineteenth century came to a close.

These were years of mounting racial discrimination. In the 1890s southern whites, fearful of a developing interracial alliance under Populism, began the systematic disfranchisement of blacks (and often of poor whites). They also perfected an unsurpassed demagoguery based on Darwinian concepts of black "retrogression" or "reversion to savagery" after emancipation. Benjamin Tillman, a senator from South Carolina, announced that the Negro was "a fiend, a wild beast, seeking whom he may devour." A character in Thomas Dixon's novel *The Clansman* (1905) added that the Negro was "half child, half animal, the sport of impulse, whim, and conceit . . . a being who, left to his will, roams at night and sleeps in the day, whose speech knows no word of love, whose passions, once aroused, are as the fury of a tiger."

Disfranchisement was but the newest form of racial discrimination suffered by blacks. Segregated in schools that in 1910 spent approximately $2.20 per pupil (the amount spent for southern whites was $4.90, for the nation at large, $21.15), they were lucky if they learned to write; the illiteracy of blacks in some states approached 50 percent, four to five times that of southern whites. Three-fourths of blacks were tenants or share croppers, with an annual wage of approximately $100, and thousands were held to the land by contract labor systems that amounted liter-

That was the end of that! Mob justice administered! And there the Negro hung until daylight the next morning—an unspeakably grisly, dangling horror, advertising the shame of the town. His head was shockingly crooked to one side, his ragged clothing, cut for souvenirs, exposed in places his bare body: he dripped blood. And, with the crowds of men both here and at the morgue where the body was publicly exhibited, came young boys in knickerbockers, and little girls and women by scores, horrified but curious. They came even with baby carriages! Men made jokes: "A dead nigger is a good nigger." And the purblind, dollars-and-cents man, most despicable of all, was congratulating the public:

"It'll save the country a lot of money!"
Significant lessons, these, for the young!

But the mob wasn't through with its work. Easy people imagine that, having hanged a Negro, the mob goes quietly about its business; but that is never the way of the mob. Once released, the spirit of anarchy spreads and spreads, not subsiding until it has accomplished its full measure of evil.

From Ray Stannard Baker, *Following the Color Line* (1908). This particular lynching occurred in Springfield, Ohio.

ally to peonage. If blacks complained, there was always the ultimate sanction of lynching. During the 1890s lynchings averaged 188 per year in the South, and blacks (who previously had shared the distinction with some whites) became the almost exclusive target.

The first decade of the twentieth century saw the beginnings of a long-term decline in lynchings: 93 occurred per year between 1900 and 1910, and 62 per year in the next decade. But peonage remained so common that one Florida citizen concluded in 1907, "slavery is just as much an 'institution' now as it was before the war." And tensions occasionally erupted into race riots, one of which took place in 1908 in Abraham Lincoln's home town of Springfield, Illinois, and prompted the founding of the National Association for the Advancement of Colored People a year later. By then northerners as well as southerners regularly endorsed racial discrimination, viewing blacks as "children" in need of protection or as biologically inferior brutes. The novelist Jack London spoke of "the dark-pigmented things, the half-castes, the mongrel bloods, the dregs of long-conquered races," and the progressive editor William Allen White conceded that "we [whites] are separated by two oceans from the inferior races." Henry L. Mencken added in 1910:

The educated Negro of today is a failure, not because he meets insuperable difficulties in life, but because he is a Negro. His brain is not fitted for the higher forms of mental effort; his ideals, no matter how laboriously he is trained and sheltered, remain those of a clown. He is, in brief, a low caste man, to the manner born, and he will remain inert and inefficient until fifty generations of him have lived in civilization. And even then, the superior white man will be fifty generations ahead of him.

In the face of such attitudes it is not surprising that the advice of Booker T. Washington, head of Tuskegee Institute, remained popular among American blacks until early in the twentieth century. "The agitation of questions of social equality," he insisted, "is the extremest folly, and progress in the enjoyment of all the privileges that will come to us must be the result of severe constant struggle rather than of artificial forcing." Yet even in Washington's time blacks were far from passive. In 1890 the black editor T. Thomas Fortune helped found the National Afro-American League as an alternative to the two major parties. In that same year an estimated one million blacks belonged to the Colored Farmers Alliance, which eventually joined white Populists in the fight for agrarian reform. Throughout the period Washington himself—in public so accommodating—privately funded the legal struggle against peonage.

After 1900 men like William E. B. Du Bois began rebelling against Washington's leadership. A product of the middle class, Du Bois was raised in Massachusetts and educated at Fisk and Harvard, where he received his PhD degree in 1895 and where he grew highly sensitive to racial slurs. In his *Souls of Black Folk* (1903) he declared that "the problem of the twentieth century is the problem of the color line." Two years later he joined other militants to demand equality. Blacks, he said in criticizing Washington, could not sit in "courteous and dumb self-forgetting silence" until time rescued them. Four years later, in 1909, he co-founded the NAACP. This interracial organization did not demand social mixing of the races, or total integration—which few blacks or whites wanted. However, it did seek to overturn the legal and economic barriers to equal opportunity. In so doing it went well beyond the accommodationism of Washington. By the time of Washington's death in 1915 Du Bois was already recognized as the leader of militant blacks. "We must lay at the soul of this man," Du Bois wrote of his departed rival, "a heavy responsibility for the consummation of Negro disfranchisement, the decline of the Negro college and public school, and the firmer establishment of color caste in this land."

If somewhere in this whirl and chaos of things, there dwells Eternal Good, pitiful yet masterful, then anon in His good time America shall rend the Veil and the prisoned shall go free. Free, free as the sunshine trickling down the morning into these high windows of mine, free as yonder fresh young voices welling up to me from the caverns of brick and mortar below—swelling with song, instinct with life, tremulous treble and darkening bass. My children, my little children, are singing to the sunshine, and thus they sing:

> *"Let us cheer the weary traveler,*
> *Cheer the weary traveler,*
> *Let us cheer the weary traveler*
> *Along the heavenly way."*

And the traveler girds himself, and sets his face toward the Morning, and goes his way.

W. E. B. Du Bois, *Souls of Black Folk* (1903).

In seeking racial justice, Du Bois and his white allies in the NAACP found some supporters. Among them were leaders of the newly formed National Urban League, a black organization that focused on improving the lot of workers. Other supporters included some social workers in the northern cities. These cities, indeed, seemed to many such reformers the most propitious places for reform, for it was at that time that large-scale migrations of blacks from South to North began to change the historic concentration of blacks below the Mason-Dixon line. Responding to employment opportunities in the North (especially during World War I), nearly a million blacks moved north between 1910 and 1920. The black population in northern cities increased by 35 percent in these years, and by 1920 it exceeded 100,000 in Chicago, Philadelphia, and New York. During that decade, the number of blacks in Detroit rose by 600 percent, in Cleveland by 300 percent.

In all these cities blacks encountered harsh opposition from whites, who succeeded in segregating the new migrants in the dingiest parts of the city. It was then that the northern black ghettos took shape. Still, the migrations north, into blue-collar manufacturing jobs, offered thousands of semienslaved persons a better life by far than they had previously known. Their growing concentration in the cities also made possible the development of black-run businesses, and the slow rise of a black middle class. These developments appeared to assist organizations such as the NAACP and the National Urban League in their quests for racial justice.

W. E. B. Du Bois

But these organizations did not enjoy much success. The NUL, poorly financed, could not do much to counter the exploitation of black workers. And Du Bois, for all his intellectual brilliance, was at times a divisive force. Surely he was uncharitable toward Washington, whose accommodationism flowed from awareness of harsh southern racial patterns and whose stress on blacks helping themselves inspired later black nationalists. Du Bois was also an elitist who relied heavily on what he called the "talented tenth" for black leadership and on primarily legal answers to discrimination. This faith in a black elite failed to recognize that there were few blacks as militant and well educated as he, few white liberals who could be counted upon, and few judges who were willing to challenge white attitudes. As the "civil rights revolution" of the 1960s demonstrated, the black masses—the very group to whom Washington had pitched his more accommodationist appeal— would have to be involved and organized before meaningful racial progress could occur.

Yet Du Bois' growing bitterness, which led him to pan-Africanism, socialism, and (as a very old man) communism, was easy to understand, for many progressives had little time for people of color. Southern states, led by progressive governors like James K. Vardaman of Mississippi and Jeff Davis of Arkansas, proceeded with the efficient disfranchisement of blacks, while systematic discrimination began to spread in northern cities such as Chicago and New York. As early as 1905 white school children in Chicago rioted when officials attempted to transfer them to a predominantly black school, and in the next decade blacks in Chicago were banned from amusement parks, dance halls, and even the YMCA. And stereotypes hardened. New York plays about blacks carried such titles as "Gentlemen Coons' Parade," "The Coon at the Door," "Dat Watermillyon," and "The Coon and the Chink." Negro songs at the time, the black writer James Weldon Johnson recalled, were known as " 'coon songs,' and were concerned with jamborees of various sorts and the play of razors, with the gastronomical delights of chicken, pork chops and watermelon, and with the experiences of red-hot 'mammas' and their never too faithful people." In 1915 D. W. Griffith drew all the worst stereotypes together by making Dixon's *The Clansman* into a cinematographically brilliant movie, *Birth of a Nation*. It portrayed the Ku Klux Klan preserving southern womanhood from bestial black men roaming the post-bellum South.

Confronted with such universal prejudice, militants like Du Bois understandably failed to accomplish much in the progressive era or the 1920s. It was not until the 1960s—a very different world for black Americans—that racial patterns advanced significantly in the United States.

NARROW VISIONS

Prohibition The campaigns for social justice, women's rights, and racial equality, for all their compromises and imperfections, possessed a vitality that sustained them in later years. Other reforms sponsored by progressives exposed a more nativist, self-interested side of progressivism.

Among these was prohibition, which critics like H. L. Mencken ridiculed as the creation of fundamentalist preachers and rural Puritans. This image is correct to a point, for the "dry" crusade was strongest in the predominantly rural, Protestant sections of the South and West and was championed by their most revered spokesman, William Jennings Bryan. But as Bryan's involvement revealed, prohibition was also a plank in the platform of many progressive leaders. Frances Willard, the head of the Women's Christian Temperance Union, fought for social justice as well as for prohibition, and the muckraking novelist Upton Sinclair wrote an antiliquor book, *The Wet Parade,* as late as 1932. These progressives favored prohibition because they believed that nothing less drastic could curb the plague of alcoholism and the disorderly behavior of "drunks" on the streets and around saloons. This middle-class Christian impulse, rooted in the social gospel, gave the crusade against alcohol an appeal far broader than men like Mencken were prepared to acknowledge.

Yet later "wets" were correct in pointing to other aspects of the crusade. The most effective workers for the cause were the highly organized lobbyists of the Anti-Saloon League, which converted from support of local option laws to prohibition after 1907. The League was a one-issue pressure group whose lobbyists admitted that they did not care whether people drank or not, so long as they voted dry. The League reminded legislators (as if they needed much reminding) that the liquor interests corrupted politics and that saloons assisted immigrant political machines. It also appealed to employers who wanted a more reliable, efficient labor force. In Sinclair Lewis's novel *Babbitt,* Vergil Gunch, the coal dealer, sips a cocktail and says to his companion, " . . . don't . . . forget prohibition is a mighty good thing for the working classes. Keeps 'em from wasting their money and losing their productiveness."

For all these reasons the Anti-Saloon League scored success in twenty-six states representing half the population by April 1917; prohibition was not the product of wartime emotions but an ongoing part of prewar progressivism and nativism. When America entered the war, the League's pressure became irresistible. The grain used for making liquor, it was argued, was so necessary to feed soldiers that Congress in 1917 approved legislation banning the use of grain for distilling or brewing. Germans, it seemed, controlled most of the breweries. And it did seem unpatriotic to talk about the freedom to drink when the nation was fighting to save the world. In December 1917 the proposed Eighteenth Amendment passed Congress, and in January 1919 it received the necessary ratification of three-fourths of the states. The Volstead Act, approved nine months later, banned the manufacture or sale (but not the private consumption) of liquor (defined as one-half of one percent alcohol by volume) after the amendment took effect in January 1920. The crusade against alcohol was thus transformed into the coercive and divisive "Great Experiment" of the 1920s.

Reform of city government Like the drive for prohibition, the demand for urban reform involved a wide variety of people. Two of these were Tom Johnson, who served as mayor of Cleveland from 1901 to 1909, and Hazen Pingree, mayor of

Detroit from 1890 to 1897. Johnson, product of a poor southern family, rose in classic fashion from newsboy to hard-driving owner and operator of street railways in Cleveland. An advocate of free trade, he became a disciple of Henry George. By the time he became mayor, he had moved beyond the single tax to support municipal ownership of public utilities, women's suffrage, urban home rule, and progressive taxation. At his death in 1911 he was perhaps America's best-known urban reformer. Pingree, like Johnson, was a self-made man (in shoe manufacturing) who brought a solid business background to public life. He too began as a moderate reformer concerned with providing honest, efficient service but was moved by the depression of the 1890s to call for progressive taxation, municipal ownership of utilities, the direct election of senators, and the abolition of child labor. To relieve unemployment, he provided workers with "potato patches," an early version of direct governmental relief.

A still more controversial social reformer was Samuel "Golden Rule" Jones, mayor of Toledo from 1897 to 1904. He too was a capitalist who began as an oil roustabout and ultimately made a fortune manufacturing oil-well machinery. As an enlightened employer he established an eight-hour day, paid vacations, profit sharing, and a minimum wage. As mayor he called for a "Cooperative Commonwealth, the Kingdom of Heaven on Earth," and he practiced what he preached. He recognized labor unions, inaugurated a minimum wage for city employees, financed kindergartens, constructed a municipal golf course, took clubs away from police, planned playgrounds, and maintained a free lodging-house for tramps. Essentially a pragmatic Christian socialist, he argued that "private ownership is a high crime against democracy." Jones's heretical views earned him the emotional support of workers and ethnic groups. Elected four times, he died in office and was succeeded by Brand Whitlock, a disciple who carried on his work.

The careers of such capitalists-turned-reformers reveal the impact of the depression in shaping the impulse for social justice in America. They suggest also that some progressives embraced reform not because they feared for their social status but because their experiences in the ruthless world of business shattered their faith in nineteenth-century solutions.

But such social reformers were relatively rare in city halls during the early years of the century. More common were men and women aptly described by the historian Melvin Holli as "structural reformers." Some of these propagandized for the so-called Galveston Plan of 1901, which attempted to take government "out of politics" and entrust it to a commission of businessmen. Others favored hiring an expert city manager, as Staunton, Virginia, did in 1908. These reformers demanded a nonpartisan ballot, the overthrow of corrupt political machines, and the application of scientific management to government. "Ignorance should be excluded from control," wrote Abram Hewitt, the reform mayor of New York in 1901. "The city business should be carried on by trained experts selected upon some other principle than popular suffrage."

Hewitt's distrust of popular suffrage made it quite clear that these structural reformers yearned especially to destroy the power of immigrants in city politics. Good government, they said, meant rule by the wellborn. "A man's occupation," the reformist Voters League of Pittsburgh argued in 1911, "ought to give a strong indication of his qualifications for membership on a school board . . . small shop-keepers, clerks, workmen at many trades . . . could not, no matter how honest, be expected to administer properly the affairs of an educational system.'' These re-formers began calling for literacy tests as qualifications for voting, for stringent voter registration laws (which tended to exclude the geographically mobile working classes), and for citywide districting, which broke down the ward-based structure of the immigrant machine.

Such structural reformers campaigned against real abuses; much urban corrup-tion did exist. They were also self-interested. Former businessmen like Johnson and Jones—and writers like Steffens—knew better that the ultimate source of corrup-tion was not the immigrant bosses but entrepreneurs seeking favors and franchises. The structural reformers also assumed wrongly that it was possible to take politics (by which they often meant immigrant machines) out of government. This view was not only nativist but also naive, because politics in the broad sense meant the balancing of interest groups, and there was little reason to believe that efficiency-conscious commissioners or appointed city managers could do that any better than could elected, and therefore responsive, politicians. It was not surprising that men like Hewitt seldom lasted in power for long, that commission-style government rarely proved popular in the larger, ethnically diverse cities, or that the political power of ethnic groups persisted long after the crusade for structural reform at the turn of the century.

Reform in the states By 1900 many political figures had concluded that the city offered too small a field for change, and they turned to reform on the state level. ''The state, and the state alone,'' Richard Ely explained in 1898, ''stands for all of us.'' The most prominent among these politicians were Robert La Follette of Wis-consin and Hiram Johnson of California. Both were fiery, outspoken opponents of trusts and special interests who developed formidable vote-getting appeal in their states. La Follette served as governor from 1900 to 1906 and then as senator until his death in 1925. Johnson was chosen for three terms as governor between 1910 and 1916, and then for five terms in the Senate. To many of their generation they were the very symbols of enlightened, progressive government.

Their exalted reputations rested on undeniable accomplishments. La Follette pressed for more stringent control of railroads and public utilities. He got the legislature to approve the nation's first meaningful direct primary, and he estab-lished stiffer tax rates on corporations. By using the resources of the University of Wisconsin he established a model for informed, precise preparation of legislation. Johnson, who rode to power on the slogan, ''Kick the Southern Pacific [Railroad] out of politics,'' achieved laws regulating utilities and child labor, an eight-hour day for working women, workmen's compensation, and political reforms such as the initiative and referendum.

Both men were considerably more complex than they appeared to their more ardent admirers. Like many progressive politicians, La Follette had been a regular Republican in the 1880s and 1890s, whereupon he gradually emerged as a leader of an ''out'' faction within the party. His ideas were no more progressive at that time than those of many others in Wisconsin, and he did much less for social justice than

Senator Robert La Follette
with Senator Smith Brookheart
in Des Moines, Iowa.

did his less-publicized gubernatorial successors. Once elected, he used state employees to construct a potent political machine that helped his family to dominate the state for forty years. "Give us this law," he reputedly said in demanding the direct primary, "and we can hold this state forever." Johnson, a narrow, abusive man who seldom forgave an enemy, was as vain and personally ambitious as La Follette. He was the champion, especially in his early years, of moderates who proclaimed themselves as leading a "movement in behalf of the businessman, the tax-payer, and decent government." As late as his campaign for governor in 1910 he did not know what such reforms as the initiative and referendum were. In 1913 he encouraged racists to pass a bill prohibiting aliens from owning property, and he led sharp crackdowns on strikers. Such was the reality behind the façade of progressive achievement.

Men like La Follette prided themselves especially on their laws setting up commissions to regulate railroads and public utilities. But though these commissions helped curb intrastate discrimination in rate making, they varied so considerably that interstate carriers came to demand uniform federal regulation. Most commissioners also realized quickly that economic nationalism made state regulation rather meaningless. And few commissioners possessed even the authority to examine company records in order to compute "fair" rates. Accordingly they accomplished much less than progressive rhetoric claimed.

A case in point was the model Wisconsin railroad commission law of 1905. Like most state laws that followed, it permitted railroads to set initial rates and granted broad review powers to the conservative courts. As the price for passage, moderates let it be known that they would refuse to confirm nominations of La Follette men to the commission, and the body as finally established became dominated by a member who conceded in 1907 that "no railway commission has ever lived which can prescribe carefully adjusted rates for a state with considerable railway mileage." By 1910 the commission had dropped all pretense of battling the railroad interests and was seeking instead ways of establishing fair, "scientific" rates. A final irony was that La Follette insisted on making the commission appointive, while his enemies, resenting this "undemocratic" plan, called (unsuccessfully) for the popular election of commissioners. The controversy showed that it is dangerous to swallow progressive rhetoric about the virtues of popular rule.

The demand for these state regulatory commissions rarely came from the "common" people, most of whom were too poor even to ride as passengers. Rather, it stemmed chiefly from large commercial farmers and businessmen seeking reduced shipping rates. To the extent that railroads discriminated against certain regions, these businessmen-progressives had a case. But their argument rarely acknowledged that the overall level of railroad rates had remained stable since the 1890s, despite increased railway labor and material costs. They also refused to concede that many American railroads, already struggling to stay alive economically, could not afford rate reductions. It is too much to argue—as some have—that regulation (which was seldom punitive) killed the railroads. Conversely, it is cynical to say that men like La Follette were pawns of shipping interests. Nevertheless, the drive for regulatory commissions was led by well-organized shipper groups with economic motives. This contest between shippers and carriers indicated that business interests often opposed one another—there was no united "industrial complex." It suggested also that it is more accurate to see the politics of regulation as a conflict among interest groups than as a dualistic contest between railroadmen and reformers.

Perceiving the regulatory issue as a battle among interests helps to explain why the commissions frequently left progressives unhappy. Even those few commissions with access to company records found that there was no such thing as "scientific" rate making. They discovered that it was impossible to define the "public interest" or to take the rate question "out of politics." Setting rates meant assigning economic priorities, and someone—shipper, carrier, consumer—inevitably got hurt. Efficiency-conscious progressives nonetheless refused to abandon this ideal of regulation by "experts," and when state commissions proved unable to oversee interstate commerce, they clamored for federal agencies. These, it turned out, were useful in providing a forum for reconciling diverse interests—which legislatures could not have done so well. But to the extent that experts assumed the authority to assign priorities, they took control of basic economic policy from democratically elected officials. In this way the commission idea was more "political" and more elitist than progressives like La Follette ever cared to admit.

ELECTORAL REFORM

If regulation of the "interests" was plank number one for many state progressives, "direct democracy" was second. "The voice of the people," said the progressive Kansas editor William Allen White, "is indeed the will of God." "The people," La Follette also observed, "have never failed in any great crisis in history." To prove they meant what they said, many progressives demanded the direct election of senators, the direct primary, and the initiative, referendum, and recall. All were supposed to take government away from politicians and special interests and return it to the "people."

The rhetoric behind such reforms—that the cure for the ills of democracy is more democracy—had a powerful appeal. It sustained arguments for broadening the suffrage, and it was later to lead Americans into thinking that democratic institutions could be exported to authoritarian countries abroad. But the reformers tended to set up a false dualism between the "interests" and the "people" and to ignore the pluralism of American life. They also forgot that these innovations, if adopted, did not necessarily mean enactment of significant social legislation. There was ever a gulf between political democracy and economic equality or social justice.

For these reasons "direct democracy" fell short of expectations. The popular election of senators, established by constitutional amendment in 1913, caused no discernible improvement in the operations of the Senate. The procedures of initiative, referendum, and recall ordinarily required large numbers of signatures, a cumbersome process that served well-financed interest groups better than it did poor people. Partly for this reason such measures had little impact on state legislation. Many states ignored or repealed them in the years to follow.

Direct primaries also had mixed effects. In a few states they assisted reformist politicians who appealed to the voters and overturned entrenched "state-house rings." In these cases the primaries helped "return government to the people," or at least to different people. Commonly, however, the primary tended to have one of four unsatisfying consequences: to make intraparty competition so expensive that politicians demanded repeal; to assist machines, which possessed the resources to bring out their regulars on primary day; to be used cynically by well-organized "out" groups with no program save that of gaining power themselves; or to play into the hands of demagogic orators previously screened out at conventions. By 1920 it was already clear that the direct primary was working no magical transformation of politics.

The attention given such innovations as the direct primary obscured three other political phenomena that reveal the limitations of using "progressivism" as the model for describing state politics at that time. One of these was the continued prominence of ethnic and religious issues like prohibition, Sunday baseball, blue laws, and aid to parochial schools. These ethnic and cultural divisions had more to do with forming political allegiances than did remoter issues like the tariff, trust busting, or political democratization. The progressive-conservative dichotomy, while a force in states such as Wisconsin, simplistically describes political reality in other states, and even in Wisconsin a Scandinavian newspaper suggested the depth of cultural feelings by proclaiming in 1914 that "the history and record of the Catholic power is black, blood-stained, and rotten, and cannot bear the light of day." Such ethno-cultural cleavages prevented social reformers from getting dependable mass support for economic programs.

The second phenomenon was a drop after 1890 in the percentage of eligible voters who went to the polls. Why this decline, which persisted until the 1930s, occurred is not wholly clear. One cause was the tighter registration laws and voter "purges" directed at immigrants. Another was the secret ballot, aimed at discouraging the practice of buying the votes of indigent people. A third cause was closer supervision of the polls, a reform that prevented people from voting several times.

But while these changes discouraged voting in ethnic areas, they do not account for declines in turnout almost everywhere in the country. Another explanation for the decline was the realignment of political parties following the depression of the 1890s, the demise of Populism, and Bryan's presidential candidacy in 1896. These events shattered the Democratic party in many eastern and midwestern urban states. Voters, left with little choice, may have become apathetic, perhaps even alienated, except concerning sensitive cultural and religious issues. But whatever the cause of this decline in turnout, it is clear that the progressive era, far from attracting Americans into an increasingly broad-based democratic system, witnessed the growing nonparticipation of millions. No other aspect of state politics revealed more clearly that progressive reforms failed to engage the masses.

The third sign that progressive reform had only a limited impact on state politics was what the political scientist Walter Dean Burnham has called the "withering away of the parties." Measures such as the secret ballot and registration laws discouraged massive efforts at recruitment, while the direct primary occasionally promoted the politics of personality or of "friends and neighbors" at the expense of organizational unity. To many progressives, who praised the "people" and denounced the machines, these were steps for the good. In fact, however, the innovations contributed to the factionalization of American parties, to short-lived coalitions of interest groups, to the deliberate blurring of economic and social programs, and perhaps to the decline in partisan loyalty and participation. In so doing they helped sustain the decentralization of parties at a time of rampant economic centralization and interest-group consciousness, and to leave public power at a disadvantage against private power. Because America was a huge, sectionally divided, and ethnically diverse country, it is questionable whether the parties, which had to appeal to broad constituencies, could have developed otherwise. It is also far from clear whether the nation would have benefited from a splintering of parties along class, ethnic, or ideological lines. But it is clear that American parties were unable to implement the kind of coherent social programs occasionally being promoted at that time in western Europe.

The successes and failures of progressivism

Progressive reformism was remarkable because it lasted as long as it did and because it broadened as time passed. Progressive ideas captured sizable segments of both parties by 1912 and culminated in "success" in many ways: settlement houses, social legislation, women's suffrage, the NAACP, prohibition, municipal reform, the popular election of senators, the direct primary, and regulatory commissions. Without these reforms, progressives thought, the imbalances of American capitalism could have led to serious class conflict, to socialism, to authoritarian government, or to other fundamental changes in American institutions.

In the process of fighting for these reforms many progressives recognized that modern developments like the metropolis and the corporation had come to stay. They realized that evangelical crusades or appeals to conscience could not reverse the imperatives of technology, industrialization, and urbanization. So these people counterorganized. They established professional associations and legislative lobbies, and they struggled for their own increasingly well-defined objectives. Their resort to counterorganization and pressure groups represented practical ways of contending with forces that would otherwise have been beyond their control. Their emphasis on ideals of efficiency and rational administration, however elitist, presaged the future.

Their very successes reveal that these progressives worked within existing institutions. Few of them strove for fundamental social change—which usually involves social conflict—but rather for more modest alterations in the status quo. Many reformers preferred moralizing or tinkering to planning for a more egalitarian social system. Others displayed a fear, sometimes bordering on paranoia, of immigrants, blacks, and workers. It took the depression of the 1930s to expose what they could hardly have been expected to recognize: that their modest reforms were considerably less significant in preventing social upheaval in their own time than was the steady, solid growth of the American economy until 1929.

Suggestions for reading

General interpretations of the progressive era include Arthur Ekrich, *Progressivism in America** (1974); William O'Neill, *The Progressive Years** (1975); John D. Buenker, *Urban Liberalism and Progressive Reform* (1973); John W. Chambers, *The Tyranny of Change: America in the Progressive Era, 1900–1917* (1980); and the books by Wiebe and Hays cited in the bibliography for chapter one. Gabriel Kolko, *The Triumph of Conservatism** (1963), focuses on the regulation of business during the period, while Albro Martin, *Enterprise Denied: Origins of the Decline of American Railroads, 1897–1917* (1971), offers a contrasting point of view. Richard Hofstadter's *Age of Reform** (1955) contains original comments on reform thought during the progressive era and afterwards. State studies that offer wide-ranging interpretations include David Thelen, *The New Citizenship, 1885–1900* (1972), which deals with Wisconsin; Richard Abrams, *Conservatism in a Progressive Era: Massachusetts Politics, 1900–1912* (1964); and Sheldon Hackney, *Populism to Progressivism in Alabama* (1969).

Among the books that cover trends in thought are Morton White's valuable *Social Thought in America: The Revolt Against Formalism** (1957); Daniel Levine's brief *Varieties of Reform Thought** (1964); David Chalmers, *Social Ideas of the Muckrakers** (1964); Nathan G. Hale's *Freud and the Americans: The Beginnings of Psychoanalysis in America, 1876–1917* (1971); and Lawrence Cremin's pioneering *Transformation of the School: Progressivism in American Education, 1876–1956** (1961). On education see too Laurence Veysey, *The Emergence of the American University* (1970). Also important are Henry May, *The End of American Innocence, 1912–1917** (1959), which details the attack on the genteel tradition; William O'Neill, *Divorce in the Progressive Era* (1967); Donald K. Pickens, *Eugenics and the Progressives* (1968); Jack Holl, *Juvenile Reform in the Progressive Era* (1971); Charles Forcey, *Crossroads of Liberalism** (1961), on Walter Lippmann, Herbert Croly, and Walter Weyl; R. Jackson Wilson, *In Quest of Community: Social Philosophy in the United States, 1860–1920** (1970); David Rothman, *Conscience and Convenience: The Asylum and Its Alternatives in Progressive America* (1980); James T. Patterson, *America's Struggle Against Poverty, 1900–1980* (1981); and George Frederickson, *The Black Image in the White Mind, 1817–1914** (1971). Gilman Ostrander's *American Civilization in the First Machine Age, 1890–1940* (1970) interprets social and cultural developments.

Other important books dealing with aspects of the period are Roy Lubove, *The Progressives and the Slums: Tenement House Reform in New York City, 1890–1917* (1962), and *The Professional Altruist: The Emergence of Social Work as a Career, 1880–1930* (1965); Allen Davis, *Spearheads of Reform: The Social Settlements and the Progressive Movement, 1890–1914** (1967), and *American Heroine: Life and Legacy of Jane Addams** (1973). See also David F. Musto, *The American Disease* (1973), a study of efforts to control the use of narcotics, 1905–40; C. Roland Marchand, *The American Peace Movement and Social Reform, 1898–1918* (1973); Samuel Hays, *Conservation and the Gospel of Efficiency, 1890–1920** (1959); and James Timberlake, *Prohibition and the Progressive Movement, 1900–1920** (1963). Books dealing with urban reform and bossism include Melvin Holli, *Reform in Detroit** (1973); and Zane L. Miller, *Boss Cox's Cincinnati** (1968).

Trends in religious thought are covered in Henry May, *Protestant Churches and Industrial America (1963); C. H. Hopkins, The Rise of the Social Gospel in American Protestantism, 1865–1915* (1940); John T. Ellis, *American Catholicism** (2nd ed., 1969), a survey; and Nathan Glazer, *American Judaism** (rev. ed., 1972), also a survey. See especially William McLoughlin, *Modern Revivalism** (1959). Books dealing with militant labor include Howard Quint, *The Forging of American Socialism* (1964); Ray Ginger, *The Bending Cross** (1949), a biography of Eugene Debs; Melvyn Dubofsky, *We Shall Be All: A History of the Industrial Workers of the World** (1969); John Laslett, *Labor and the Left* (1970); Graham Adams, Jr., *Age of Industrial Violence, 1910–1915* (1971); David Shannon, *Socialist Party in America** (1967 ed.); Daniel Bell, *Marxian Socialism in the United States** (1952); and James Weinstein, *The Decline of Socialism in America, 1912–1925** (1967). John P. Diggins, *The American Left in the Twentieth Century** (1973), is excellent.

Books concerning the status of women and of feminism include William O'Neill, *Everyone Was Brave: The Rise and Fall of Feminism in America** (1969); Aileen Kraditor, *The Ideas of the Women's Suffrage Movement, 1890–1920* (1965); David Kennedy, *Birth Control in America: The Career of Margaret Sanger** (1970); Carl Degler, *At Odds: Women and the Family from the Revolution to the Present* (1980); Leslie Woodcock Tentler, *Wage-Earning Women: Industrial Work and Family Life in the U.S., 1900–1930* (1978); and Lois Banner, *Women in Modern America** (1974), a readable survey of twentieth-century developments. See also John Sirjamki, *The American Family in the Twentieth Century* (1953). On black life and protest see Elliott Rudwick, *W. E. B. DuBois** (1969); B. Joyce Ross, *J. E. Spingarn and the Rise of the NAACP* (1972); Nancy Weiss, *The National Urban League, 1910–1940* (1974); Louis Harlan, *Booker T. Washington*, vol. 1 (1972); and August Meier, *Negro Thought in America, 1880–1915** (1963). Thorough studies of black life in the city are Gilbert Osofsky, *Harlem: Making of a Ghetto, 1890–1930** (1966); and Allen Spear, *Black Chicago: The Making of a Negro Ghetto, 1890–1920** (1967). The spread of discrimination by law in the South is described in C. Vann Woodward, *The Strange Career of Jim Crow** (rev. ed., 1974). See also John Dittmer's excellent *Black Georgia in the Progressive Era, 1900–1920* (1977).

Important primary sources for the period are Upton Sinclair, *The Jungle** (1906); W. E. B. Du Bois, *Souls of Black Folk** (1903); Edgar Lee Masters, *Spoon River Anthology** (1915); John Dewey, *Child and the Curriculum* and *School and Society** (1899); Charlotte P. Gilman, *Women and Economics** (1898); William James, *Pragmatism and Other Essays** (1905); Edward Bellamy, *Looking Backward** (1888); and Henry George, *Progress and Poverty** (1879).

National politics

1900–1917

"It's easy enough to be President," naval hero George Dewey said in 1900. "All you have to do, I see, is take orders from Congress, and I have been taking orders all my life."

Dewey's image of a passive presidency mirrored Grover Cleveland's a few years earlier. "I shall keep right on doing executive work," Cleveland had said. "I did not come here to legislate." In 1900 President William McKinley handled official business by relying on only ten staff members, four of whom were doorkeepers or messengers. Cabinet departments such as Commerce, Labor, Transportation, Health and Human Services, and HUD did not exist; nor did such agencies as the Federal Trade Commission, the Federal Communications Commission, the Federal Reserve, the Securities and Exchange Commission, and the Social Security Administration.

The small scale of the executive branch did not mean that the federal government was wholly powerless or that it consistently pursued a philosophy of laissez faire. On the contrary, congressional land grants and high tariffs had assisted entrepreneurs throughout the nineteenth century. Federal spending at the turn of the century—for internal improvements, defense, the post office, and other purposes—approximated $500 million annually. This was 3 percent of the Gross National Product, roughly the same percentage as the mid-1920s.

These statistics do not alter the central fact that both the federal government and the presidency remained weak at the turn of the century. To the extent that Americans looked at all for public services, they turned to states and municipalities, which spent twice as much as Congress. During the Spanish-American War, soldiers identified themselves with their local units, not with the Regular Army, and newspapers concentrated on the actions of these local units to the virtual exclusion of political events in Washington. Few newspapers, indeed, bothered sending a correspondent to Washington before 1900, for they recognized that federal activity rarely affected ordinary citizens. As Cleveland had put it, "while the people should patriotically and cheerfully support their government, its functions do not include the support of the people."

Prior to the 1890s, few people complained about this state of affairs. By 1900, however, many writers and politicians were arguing that the growth of private power threatened to overwhelm public authority. As the political scientist M. I. Ostrogorski said in 1902, "from one end of the scale to the other, the constitutional authorities are unequal to their duty; they prove incapable of ensuring the protection of the general interest. . . . The spring of government is weakened or warped everywhere."

Congress and the Court

Those seeking to strengthen this "weakened spring" after 1900 could draw upon some significant contemporary developments. One was the growth of federal employment. In 1861 there were 36,000 civilian federal employees, in 1900 almost 240,000, and in 1910, 389,000. Though most of these 389,000 were post office workers (210,000) or employees of navy yards and arsenals (59,000), the growth showed that government, like other large institutions, was slowly developing a bureaucracy that could consider national approaches to problems. A second advantage was the gradual spread of the merit system, which covered 222,000 of these employees by 1910. This merit system was a mixed blessing, for it protected bureaucrats who were impervious to popular pressures. It also tended to discriminate against lower-class applicants, who, less adequately educated, were at a competitive disadvantage in taking the civil service examinations. But elitist reformers welcomed these developments, for government could now rely on "experts" or at least on "nonpolitical" men and women presumed to be literate and honest. In the absence of the merit system, it is doubtful that many Americans would have supported subsequent efforts of national reformers to expand federal activity.

Formidable obstacles to governmental effectiveness outweighed these developments. These obstacles included the same barriers that impeded progressive action on the state level: factionalized political parties, conflicting interest groups, and ethno-cultural divisions precluding the development of a mass base for social reform. National reformers had to confront two additional institutions, Congress and the courts, which consistently resisted efforts for change.

One problem with Congress was its leadership, which in 1900 meant "Uncle Joe" Cannon of Illinois in the House and Nelson Aldrich of Rhode Island in the

Senate. Cannon had first entered Congress in 1873. By 1901, when he became speaker, he was a disagreeable sixty-five-year-old whose villainous black cigars smeared his lips with tobacco shreds. Known as "foul-mouthed Joe," he made no pretense of sharing his power over committee assignments with proponents of change. "I am god-damned tired," he said, "of listening to all this babble for reform." Aldrich, more cultivated and sophisticated, owed his dominance in the Senate to considerable intellect and personal force. But to reformers, he was a plutocrat whose ties to big business were symbolized by his daughter's marriage in 1901 to John D. Rockefeller, Jr. Aldrich was a Hamiltonian who championed firm ties between big business and government and an elitist who justified his dominance over the Senate by commenting, "Most people don't know what they want."

As the tide of progressivism advanced, new legislators appeared to challenge the almost absolute power that men like Cannon and Aldrich enjoyed in the early 1900s. In the Senate these included La Follette of Wisconsin and Albert Beveridge of Indiana. In the House they were led by George Norris of Nebraska, who staged a revolt in 1910, stripping Cannon of his power over committee assignments. By 1913 these "insurgents" were strong enough to give President Woodrow Wilson important backing. Many of them (like Norris, who served as a senator from 1913 to 1943) remained forceful and widely admired progressives for decades thereafter.

The growing strength of these congressional progressives attracted considerable attention from reporters, who reflected the American tendency to personalize politics. Get heroic reformers in office, they implied, and change will occur. But voters and state legislatures never sent more than a small minority of insurgents to Congress. Moreover, the insurgents rarely formed a cohesive bloc. This failure to coalesce stemmed in part from the cantankerousness of men like La Follette, and in part from local pressures: Congressmen who hope to stay in office must listen to constituents. Given America's diversity of interests and regions, it is not surprising that progressives broke apart on key sectional issues like the tariff. From this perspective Congress was not the reactionary villain that reformist writers described, but simply the political institution most answerable to voters and pressure groups.

> *From the time in earliest records, when Eve took loving possession of even the forbidden apple, the idea of property and the sacredness of the right of its possession has never departed from the race. Whatever dreams may exist of an ideal human nature . . . actual human experience, from the dawn of history to the present hour, declares that the love of acquirement, mingled with the joy of possession, is the real stimulus to human activity. When, among the affirmatives of the Declaration of Independence, it is asserted that the pursuit of happiness is one of the unalienable rights, it is meant that the acquisition, possession and enjoyment of property are matters which human government cannot forbid. . . .*

Justice Brewer, address entitled "Protection to Private Property from Public Attack," 1891.

In this way Congress could claim to be responsive—at least to those who were well organized. The judges of the Supreme Court, however, could not, for they were lifetime appointees free to decide as they wished. To the despair of reformers they chose to echo conservative theorists like Thomas M. Cooley and Supreme Court justices like Stephen Field and David Brewer. Cooley, the dominant legal scholar of the late nineteenth century, argued that the Constitution was intended to protect private property, that it must be interpreted literally, and that reform had to come from amendments, not from legislatures or courts. "What a court is to do," he wrote, "is to declare the law as written, leaving it to the people themselves to make such changes as circumstances may require." Field, the high priest of business enterprise, opposed almost all governmental efforts to improve the social welfare. "Protection to property and to persons cannot be separated," he said in 1890. ". . . Protection to the one goes with the other; and there can be neither prosperity nor progress where either is uncertain."

Apologists such as these usually invoked hallowed documents like the Declaration of Independence or dogmas like laissez faire. In fact, individuals like Field were working consciously for business interests. Between 1890 and 1896 the high court struck down much state regulatory legislation (*Chicago Milwaukee and St. Paul Railway Co.* v. *Minnesota,* 1890), it temporarily undermined the Sherman Antitrust Act (*E. C. Knight* case, 1895), it sanctioned the separate but equal doctrine of race relations (*Plessy* v. *Ferguson,* 1896), and it overturned a progressive federal income tax (*Pollack* v. *Farmers' Loan and Trust Co.,* 1895). Field cast the deciding vote against the income tax by intoning that "the present assault upon capital is but the beginning. It will be but the stepping stone to others, larger and more sweeping, until our political contests will become a war of the poor against the rich; a war constantly growing in intensity and bitterness."

After 1900 the Court generally avoided such blatant statements of political preference. In 1904 (*Northern Securities* case) it began to resurrect the antitrust law and in 1908 (*Muller* v. *Oregon*) sustained a state law setting maximum working hours for women. But it still overturned state minimum wage laws and national child labor acts, and it persisted in regarding labor unions as illegal combinations in restraint of trade. In this way the Court, like Congress, obstructed reformers. It also led them to turn to the presidency as the only hope for change—and to lavish affection on the one man who personified the future. That man was Theodore Roosevelt, who assumed the presidency on the assassination of William McKinley in September 1901.

Enter Theodore Roosevelt

From some vantage points it is difficult to understand why so many progressive Americans made Theodore Roosevelt their hero. Born to a patrician family from New York in 1858, he had been educated at Harvard, served as a regular Republican assemblyman in the 1880s, and advanced in the 1890s to become a civil service commissioner, the police commissioner of New York City, assistant secretary of the navy, hero of the Rough Riders in Cuba, governor of New York, and finally, vice-president. His career to that point, while distinguished, hardly revealed him as a forceful social reformer, and during the turbulent 1890s he had echoed the ferocity of members of his class. He said, "I like to see a mob handled by the regulars, or by good State-Guards, not over-scrupulous about bloodshed."

This lust for combat could be frightening. "Every man who has in him any real power of joy in battle," he said, "knows that he feels it when the wolf begins to rise in his heart; he does not then shrink from blood or sweat, or deem that they mar the fight; he revels in them, in the toil, the pain, and the danger, as but setting off the triumph." During the Spanish-American War, when he galloped through a hail of bullets to capture San Juan Hill, he proudly wrote his friend Henry Cabot Lodge, "I killed a Spaniard with my own hand." Four years later he explained that he was "not in the least bit sensitive about killing any number of men if there is an adequate reason." For him as well as for many Americans the war was a test of character, and killing a patriotic necessity.

Roosevelt was an equally fierce moralist. What mattered in life, he said in urging the wellborn to have large families, were the "strong and tender virtues of a family life based on the love of one man for one woman and on their joyous and fearless acceptance of their common obligation toward their children." While president he overrode existing law to deny readmittance to the United States of a citizen who had traveled to Canada with a woman not his wife. He told the Boy Scouts, "Don't flinch, don't foul, hit the line hard." And he preached repeatedly the necessity of fair play, especially in college football, then a savage sport (it killed eighteen young men in 1905). "Brutality and foul play," he thundered, "should receive the same summary treatment given to a man who cheats at cards." The presidency, he believed, was a "bully pulpit," and he made the most of it.

This impulsive activism in the cause of righteousness alarmed many contemporaries. Mark Hanna, the Republican party's dominant political boss, referred to him as "that damned cowboy." When the GOP nominated TR vice-president in 1900, Hanna wrote his friend McKinley that "your *duty* to the Country is to live for four years from next March." Even Roosevelt's admirers had to laugh at their hero's

President Theodore Roosevelt addressing a street crowd. Some said he spoke as much with his hands as with his voice.

activities. "You must remember that the President is about six," one of them wrote. Elihu Root, soon to be Roosevelt's secretary of state, told him on his forty-sixth birthday in 1904, "you have made a very good start in life, and your friends have great hopes for you when you grow up."

Yet no one denied that Roosevelt cut a colorful figure. While police commissioner he occasionally sallied late at night—dressed in pink shirt and silk sash—into the worst sections of the city to check on his subordinates. At San Juan Hill he wore a sombrero with a blue polka-dot kerchief fluttering in the breeze. As a crusader against vice in New York and as an authentic war hero he was a man whom party chieftains like Hanna could hardly ignore.

His crusades for family, home, and country were as reassuring as they were entertaining. These were traditional, conservative virtues, not assaults on the established order. If part of Roosevelt's appeal lay in his color, much of it stemmed from his ability to appear as crusader and moral conservator at the same time. To the progressive William Allen White, Roosevelt was "reform in a derby, the gayest, cockiest, most fashionable derby you ever saw,'' and for young Walter Lippmann, he was ''the image of the great leader and the prototype of Presidents.'' White and Lippmann spoke for thousands of contemporaries for whom TR ever remained a figure of heroic proportions.

ROOSEVELT AS PROGRESSIVE

One image of Roosevelt's seven and a half years in the White House can never be blotted out. It shows a toothy, swashbuckling TR, America's youngest president, slashing away at the corporations, conserving natural resources, and prodding Congress toward reform.

Like many stereotypes, that one was accurate in part. Though he moved slowly at first, he alarmed big businessmen in 1902 by instituting antitrust proceedings against the Northern Securities Company, J. P. Morgan's railroad combine. Three months later he infuriated reactionaries during a bitter anthracite coal strike by threatening to dispatch troops and dispossess the owners if they refused to agree to arbitration. His threat worked, and the union eventually won a modest victory. That year he also helped secure passage of the Newlands Act, an important conservation measure that set aside federal funds from the sale of public lands for reclamation purposes in the West. In 1903 he worked with Congress to establish a Bureau of Corporations to gather information about business, and to approve the Elkins law prohibiting railroad rebates.

Reelected easily in 1904, over Democratic candidate Alton B. Parker, Roosevelt felt politically secure, and he strayed further from the path of his predecessor. In his second term he instituted antitrust suits against Standard Oil and the American Tobacco Company; he secured passage of the Hepburn Act providing for limited regulation of railroads; and he signed into law the Pure Food and Drug Act and the Meat Inspection Act. By executive order he appointed an Inland Waterways Commission, which drew up plans for multipurpose river development, and he named the conservationist Gifford Pinchot head of a new Forest Service. He also increased the total acreage of timber and forest reserves from 45 to 195 million acres. At the end of his second term he publicly favored stiff inheritance and income taxes on the wealthy, the regulation of railroad securities, strict limits on antilabor injunctions, and extension of the eight-hour day and workmen's compensation.

Roosevelt's economic philosophy reflected this movement from moderation toward progressive causes. In 1902, when he called in the coal operators, he had no idea of promoting unionism; rather he felt he had to stop the strike before it paralyzed the country. And in 1904, when he proclaimed a Square Deal for all people, he spoke as a conservative animated by fears of potential class war. ''It would be a dreadful thing,'' he wrote, ''if we saw this country divided into two parties, one containing the bulk of the property owners and conservative people, the other the bulk of the wageworkers and the less prosperous people generally. . . . The friends of property, of order, of law. . . must realize that the surest way to provoke an explosion of wrong and injustice is to be shortsighted, narrow-minded, greedy, and arrogant.''

By 1908 Roosevelt had moved to the left. He spoke of "certain malefactors of great wealth," referred to himself as a "radical," and lambasted the "speculative folly and flagrant dishonesty of a few men of great wealth." In 1910 he added, "I stand for the square deal, but when I say that I am for the square deal, I mean not merely that I stand for fair play under the present rules of the game, but that I stand for having those rules change so as to work for a more substantial equality of opportunity and of reward for equally good service." The means to this end he called the New Nationalism, which would "put the national need before sectional or personal advantage" and would make the "executive power the steward of the public welfare." In pursuing this course Roosevelt supported social welfare programs, including minimum wages for women, that he had ignored a few years earlier. His move to the left, which paralleled that of the voters, did not make him an advocate of a welfare state, but it left him a proponent of an activist federal government, of a modern presidency, and of social reform.

He also developed a thoughtful position on the dominant issue of the day: control of the trusts. Unlike some other progressive politicians, who attacked all monopolies, Roosevelt regarded centralization as a fact of modern economic life. "This is an age of combination," he said in 1905, "and any effort to prevent all combination will not only be useless, but in the end vicious, because of the contempt for law which the failure to enforce law inevitably produces." Although Roosevelt used the Sherman Act forty-four times against corporations, he placed more faith in regulatory measures such as the Hepburn Act; he tried to "bust" only those few monopolies that struck him as immoral and unreasonable in their restraint of trade. This distinction between "good" and "bad" trusts (adopted by the Supreme Court in 1911) was characteristic of his moralistic approach to problems. It tended also to leave corporations (and their critics) at the mercy of the "dead hand" of judges and officials, who later changed standards of right and wrong. Still, Roosevelt's awareness that the federal government had to become a countervailing power marked him as a more flexible thinker than many nostalgic opponents of bigness in any form.

THE LEGACY OF TR

If Roosevelt was such a spirited and realistic progressive, why did many reformers find him unsatisfactory? La Follette, for instance, complained that TR's "cannonading . . . filled the air with noise and smoke, which confused and obscured the line of action, but, when the battle cloud drifted by and the quiet was restored, it was always a matter of surprise that so little had really been accomplished." Ray Stannard Baker, a perceptive journalist, concluded later that Roosevelt had "wholesome enthusiasms," but that he "ran full-speed on all the tracks at once. Too often he rode down opposition without understanding what it meant, or talked it down with a torrent of phrases."

La Follette and Baker spoke as political enemies of Theodore Roosevelt. Yet they were correct in saying that TR was less of a reformer than he sounded, especially during his first term, when he felt he needed conservative support to be elected in 1904. Aware of congressional hostility, he did not move to lower the tariff and did nothing, despite the financial panic of 1907, to regulate banking. He urged Colorado authorities to crush the Western Federation of Miners in 1904. In 1905, angered by unsubstantiated reports that Negro soldiers had killed a man in Brownsville, Texas, he ordered the blanket discharge from the service of 160 blacks, 6 of whom had won the medal of honor.

TR's detractors also pointed to the questionable "progressivism" of his legislative accomplishments. The Elkins Act regulating rebates was intended to cut costs of railroads, not to assist the public. In practice the law was easily evaded. The Pure Food and Drug Act failed to regulate patent medicines, the sale of adulterated food, or false advertising. It, too, was ignored or abused. The Meat Inspection Act stemmed in part from the demands of the major packers, who recognized that such a law could restrain their smaller competitors. "It is a wise law," Swift and Company said in large ads. "Its enforcement must be universal and uniform." The Hepburn Act, Roosevelt's most impressive legislative achievement, permitted the ICC to set rates on complaint of shippers—an important step—but it failed to authorize the physical evaluation of railroads, and it left ICC rates subject to review by the courts. The act reflected the pressure on Congress of shippers, who benefited from ICC decisions.

Roosevelt's expansion of presidential power also left an uncertain legacy. His activism encouraged Americans to depend on charismatic presidential leadership. Would reform have been served better by efforts to diminish the obstructive potential of the states, or by amendments to curb the jurisdiction of the courts? These are largely unanswerable questions. Moreover, such changes did not have much chance of adoption at the time. But it is true that Roosevelt did more than any other person to institutionalize the modern presidency, and that reformers ever since have tended to place exaggerated reliance on the magic of 1600 Pennsylvania Avenue.

But these criticisms of Roosevelt tend to exaggerate his freedom to act. He never enjoyed a progressive majority in Congress, and he had to deal with a largely conservative Republican party. Had he tried to promote tariff revision or banking reform, he would have succeeded only in alienating potential allies for other legislation. If he had insisted on a stronger Hepburn or Pure Food and Drug act, he would have emerged with no bills at all. Roosevelt, neither radical nor idealist, worked within the system rather than tilting against it.

No man, facing Roosevelt in the heat of controversy, ever actually got a square deal. He took extravagant advantages; he played to the worst idiocies of the mob; he hit below the belt almost habitually. . . . One always thinks of him as a glorified longshoreman engaged eternally in cleaning out barrooms—and not too proud to gouge when the inspiration came to him, or to bite in the clinches, or to oppose the relatively fragile brass knuckles of the code with chair-legs, bung-starters, cuspidors, demijohns, and icepicks.

H. L. Mencken's view of TR, 1920.

Moreover, Roosevelt stood for more than preserving the status quo. He sought not only to maintain capitalism but also to humanize it. He worked to increase executive power in part because he wished to harness it to change. He offered reformers flexible yet purposeful leadership, and he showed that the federal government would try to deal with industrialization. In so doing he helped to preserve the faith of influential Americans in democratic government and in capitalism.

William Howard Taft

Roosevelt's successor, William Howard Taft, was one of the best-trained presidents in American political history. Number two in his class at Yale, he had received a law degree in his native Cincinnati and then progressed rapidly: solicitor general under President Benjamin Harrison, federal judge, high commissioner in the Philippines, and Roosevelt's secretary of war. Though immensely fat (sometimes more than 300 pounds), he was neither lazy nor slow. He had a quick, well-honed, and deeply conventional mind. La Follette, not given to excessive praise of his contemporaries, agreed in 1909 that Taft was "able, balanced, tactful, forceful . . . an honest and honorable man who regards a promise as sacred and a pledge as a bond."

Roosevelt, who handpicked Taft as his successor, emphatically concurred. "Things will be all right," he assured people when he took vacations from Pennsylvania Avenue. "I have left Taft sitting on the lid." He told Taft, "I do not believe that you will ever quite understand what strength and comfort and help you are to me." Taft reciprocated these warm feelings. He told reporters in 1907 that TR's views "were mine before I ever knew Mr. Roosevelt at all." A few weeks after being inaugurated in 1909 Taft wrote his predecessor as "Mr. President." "When I am addressed as Mr. President," he explained, "I turn to see whether you are not at my elbow. . . . I do nothing in the Executive Office without considering what you would do under the circumstances."

Less than two years later these two best of friends had broken apart. Roosevelt complained in 1910 that Taft was a "well-meaning, good-natured man, an excellent judge . . . but not a leader." During the acrimonious campaign of 1912 when he ran against his old friend for the presidency, he was more blunt, calling Taft a "puzzle-wit," a "fat-head," a man guilty of "naked fraud, of naked theft from the people." Taft, though less combative, accepted the challenge. "I do not want to fight," he said, "but when I do fight, I want to hit hard. Even a rat in a corner will fight." The struggle between the two men racked the Republican party and helped to elect Woodrow Wilson president.

In part the breech was caused by differing ideas about how to govern. Where Roosevelt was an activist, Taft was reflective and judicious, a strict constructionist concerning the separation of powers. "I have no disposition to exert any other influence than that which it is my function under the Constitution to exercise," he assured Aldrich. Taft added that he did not care for politics. "I don't like the limelight," he complained. He also assumed that he could function purely as an

Jovial William Howard Taft.

administrator. "My sin," he confessed, "is . . . a disposition to procrastinate." By late 1910 this restrictive concept of the presidency was antagonizing progressives.

Roosevelt, still only fifty years old early in 1909, grew restive on the sidelines. He was ambitious for himself, for his loyal supporters, and for his ideas. As he turned to the left after 1909, he applauded some of Taft's moderately progressive policies, which included legislation regulating safety in mines and railroads, support of the amendment (ratified in 1913) legalizing income taxes, establishment of a Children's Bureau, passage of a law providing for employer liability in work done under government contracts, and the Mann-Elkins Act of 1910, which increased the ICC's power over railroads. But Roosevelt also recognized that Taft was unwilling to go further. "The chief function of the next administration," Taft said in 1909, "is to complete and perfect the machinery." It was Taft's misfortune to be president during a time when many reformers, accustomed to dynamic leadership, pressed for more substantial legislation, and when a youthful hero yearned to return to the helm.

The first of many controversies that widened the break was the tariff. Roosevelt had realized that pressure from constituent interests always forced congressmen to raise rather than lower duties, and he wisely avoided the issue. But Taft, plunging earnestly ahead, called a special session in 1909 to lower the existing high rates. The result was predictable: the so-called Payne-Aldrich Tariff, which increased duties to new highs. This tariff fight of 1909 hardly exposed a clear-cut split between progressives and conservatives, for men like La Follette voted for higher duties on foreign goods competing with home-state products. Still, the insurgents complained accurately that the new tariff would increase the already ascending cost of living and that Taft had not exerted much influence on moderates in order to secure a better bill. When Taft defensively praised the act as the "best tariff bill that the Republican party has ever passed," they were incensed.

The tariff fight convinced progressives that Taft was joining forces with the standpat wing of the party. They were right. Though he initially distrusted Aldrich, he grew close to him during the long special session, and by 1910 called him a "good friend." Though he encouraged insurgents to think he would struggle against Cannon, whom he found "dirty and vulgar," he backed off when he felt he needed the votes of Cannon and his friends for tariff revision. After 1910, when Norris' insurgents stripped Cannon of his power to make committee assignments, they were bitter at the President, whom they owed nothing. Taft, meanwhile, grumbled that the insurgents were "yelping and snarling," "rather forward," and "pretty stupid."

Taft's views on control of trusts added to his growing estrangement from Roosevelt. "We must get back to competition," Taft said. The Sherman Act was a "good law that ought to be enforced, and I propose to enforce it." This faith led him to institute more antitrust suits in four years than Roosevelt had in seven and a half. But his approach repudiated Roosevelt's faith in regulatory action and brought him directly into conflict with TR's New Nationalism, which Taft termed full of "wild ideas." His suit in 1911 against U. S. Steel particularly infuriated TR, who perceived the action as a politically motivated effort to publicize U. S. Steel's acquisition in 1907 of the Tennessee Coal and Iron Company. "To attempt to meet the whole problem by a succession of lawsuits," Roosevelt insisted, "is hopeless. . . . It is practically impossible to break up all combinations merely because they are large and successful and to put the business of the country back into the middle of the nineteenth century."

THE BALLINGER-PINCHOT CONTROVERSY

The most rancorous cause of Taft's break with progressives was the Ballinger-Pinchot controversy, which plagued his administration throughout late 1909 and 1910. This struggle stemmed from charges by chief forester Gifford Pinchot, America's leading conservationist, that Richard Ballinger, Taft's secretary of the interior, had conspired to turn over Alaskan coal fields to a syndicate including Morgan interests. On reviewing these charges Taft sided with Ballinger. But Pinchot (whom Taft regarded as a "radical and a crank") continued his attack by publicly accusing the administration of opposing conservation. Taft then had no choice but to fire

Pinchot for insubordination. In the protracted hearings that followed, Taft loyalists in Congress exonerated Ballinger of fraud. But insurgents sided with Pinchot, Roosevelt's good friend and the symbol of conservation.

The issue was not nearly so clear-cut as the insurgents believed. No enemy of conservation, Taft appointed a friend of Pinchot to replace Ballinger, and he used his executive power to remove more public land from private use than Roosevelt had done in a comparable period of time. Moreover, the line between Ballinger and Pinchot was thinner than many people realized. Ballinger, like many westerners, sided with settlers and entrepreneurs who wished to develop, not preserve, the land. But Pinchot, too, opposed simple preservation. Like Ballinger, he wanted valuable acreage developed, and as chief forester he permitted grazing and lumbering on government property (which he appropriately named "national forests" instead of "forest reserves"). Indeed, ardent preservationists like John Muir, founder of the Sierra Club, vainly fought the attempt of Pinchot and others to transform the beautiful Hetch Hetchy Valley in California into a reservoir for San Francisco. Muir and his friends, Pinchot snapped, were "nature lovers."

Yet Pinchot was correct in arguing that men like Ballinger favored a more exploitative approach. For Pinchot wanted the federal government to manage national resources, while Ballinger preferred free-wheeling private development or state supervision. In this way Pinchot appealed to the anticorporate emotions of many progressives and to the growing passion among the urban middle classes for outdoor recreation and the "strenuous life." His thinking also reflected the desire of many eastern progressives for efficient, "scientific" direction of national policy. The thrust of this argument showed that national progressives were moving toward the modern administrative state.

The Ballinger-Pinchot controversy revealed clearly a key aspect of many "progressive" political issues: they were struggles between different interests for preference. The controversy also exposed the formidable pressures besetting Taft's presidency. Judicious and legalistic, he had supported a subordinate whom Pinchot had determined to destroy. But in doing so he assisted opponents who used the appeal

---

We have become great because of the lavish use of our resources and we have just reason to be proud of our growth. But the time has come to inquire seriously what will happen when our forests are gone, when the coal, the iron, the oil, and the gas are exhausted, when the soils shall have been still further impoverished and washed into the streams, polluting the rivers, denuding the fields, and obstructing navigation. These questions do not relate only to the next century or to the next generation. It is time for us now as a nation to exercise the same reasonable foresight in dealing with our great natural resources that would be shown by any prudent man in conserving and wisely using the property which contains the assurance of well-being for himself and his children.

Conservation as a means to promote national growth and greatness. Roosevelt, 1908.

of conservation to brand him as a reactionary. More broadly, he encountered progressives as they were becoming more aggressive and spirited in their demands. A man of deliberate, judicial temperament, Taft was ill-suited to cope with the political exigencies that these changes demanded.

Woodrow Wilson

By mid-1912 Taft admitted mournfully that he could be overwhelmed in his bid for reelection. "I think I might as well give up so far as being a candidate is concerned," he wrote his wife in July. "There are so many people in the country who don't like me." Though he stayed in the race, he anticipated that either Roosevelt, who stormed out of the GOP convention to head the new Progressive party, or the Democratic candidate, Woodrow Wilson, would win.

Roosevelt's campaign stirred his supporters to evangelical enthusiasm. One newspaper described a convention of Progressives as an "assemblage of religious enthusiasts. It was such a convention as Peter the Hermit had. It was a Methodist camp meeting done over into political terms." Wherever Roosevelt appeared, his backers sang hymns of praise.

> Follow, follow, we will follow Roosevelt
> Anywhere, everywhere, we will follow him.

Or:

> Thou will not cower in the dust,
> Roosevelt, O Roosevelt!
> Thy gleaming sword shall never rust
> Roosevelt, O Roosevelt!

TR, proclaiming himself fit as a "bull moose," did not disappoint his admirers. When shot in the chest during a speech in October, he brushed aside attempts to provide medical help and proclaimed, "I will make this speech or die. It is one thing or the other." The wound proved superficial, and he later resumed campaigning. His speeches offered progressives the most advanced ideas of the day. Roosevelt supported women's suffrage, the initiative, referendum, and recall, a corrupt practices act, minimum wages for women, the prohibition of child labor, the eight-hour day, the abolition of the convict labor system, and the "national regulation of interstate corporations" by a "strong Federal administrative commission." He also favored the recall of judicial decisions in cases where state courts declared laws unconstitutional. His platform attracted most progressive social workers, including Jane Addams, to his side, and it terrified conservatives. *The New York Times* (which backed Wilson) said that TR preached "Socialism and Revolution, contempt for law, and doctrines that lead to destruction." The Louisville *Courier-Journal* commented, "more than ever [we] are sure of his insanity. If he be not of disordered mind, the record would show him a monster of depravity and turpitude."

In contrast to Roosevelt's "radicalism," Wilson's credentials as a reformer seemed fairly good by 1912. The son of a southern Presbyterian minister, he had graduated from Princeton and attended law school before turning to academic life. He then moved rapidly ahead, as a scholar in the field of political science, as a dynamic president of Princeton, and as a reform governor of New Jersey in 1911 and 1912. He owed his presidential nomination to the support of most progressive Democrats, including Bryan.

Actually, however, Wilson's progressivism had been mild until 1909. In the 1890s he had supported the conservative Grover Cleveland, and in 1907 he had denounced "radicals" like Bryan, whom he wished to knock "into a cocked hat." In 1908 he explained that change is slow, that "living political constitutions must be Darwinian in structure and in practice." His voluminous writings on American history heaped scorn on recent immigrants (whom he called "the more sordid and hapless elements of the population") and opposed the growth of federal activity. "We must be careful," he said in 1906, "not to depend too much upon the federal government or turn too often from the remedy which is at hand in the power of the states."

By 1912 he appeared to have moved appreciably beyond such Jeffersonian beliefs about government. "The service rendered the people by the national government," he said, "must be of a more extended sort and of a kind not only to protect it against monopoly, but also to facilitate its life." But he remained less of a social reformer than Roosevelt, and his speeches on control of trusts, a central issue of the campaign, resembled Taft's. The way to prevent monopoly, he said, was to improve

Election, 1912

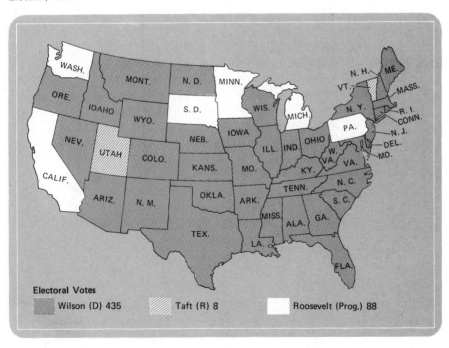

Electoral Votes

Wilson (D) 435   Taft (R) 8   Roosevelt (Prog.) 88

the antitrust laws, not to depend on regulatory commissions. Wilson did not oppose bigness per se, but like Taft he believed that fair competition preserved the entrepreneurial spirit that made America great. "What this country needs above everything else," he said, "is a body of laws which will look after the men who are on the make rather than the men who are already made."

Wilson's view, TR explained, was "outworn academic doctrine which was kept in the schoolroom and the professorial study for a generation after it had been abandoned by all who had experience of actual life." But Roosevelt's criticisms availed him nothing. Wilson proved an energetic campaigner and powerful orator. He capitalized especially on the division within the Republican party. In November he won easily, getting 6,296,547 votes to Roosevelt's 4,118,571, carrying the electoral college by a margin of 435 to 88, and creating Democratic margins over Republicans in Congress of 291 to 127, and 51 to 44. Taft, forgotten man of the campaign, received but 3,486,720 votes and 8 electoral votes, while Eugene Debs got 900,672 votes. The election ultimately destroyed the Progressives, who moved either to the Democrats or back to the GOP by 1916. It also showed that support for progressive candidates was overwhelming. More than TR or Taft, Woodrow Wilson came to office with a mandate for action.

WILSON'S DOMESTIC PROGRAM

Eight years later, when a sick and discredited Wilson left the presidency, it became almost fashionable to deride him as a priggish, self-righteous rhetorician. Abraham Flexner, an educational and medical reformer, complained that Wilson fell in love with phrase-making: "The man cannot pass an ink bottle without sitting down to pen a note." John Maynard Keynes, the English economist, called him a "blind and deaf Don Quixote." And H. L. Mencken, master of hyperbole, dismissed Wilson as a "self-bamboozled Presbyterian, the right-thinker, the great moral statesman, the perfect model of the Christian cad."

These criticisms captured one side of the new president, who had already proved so stubborn during his last years at Princeton that the university's trustees were happy to see him leave. So were New Jersey's Democratic leaders. But such criticisms overlooked his flexible direction of domestic policy between 1913 and 1916. Like Roosevelt, he had an expansive conception of the presidency. He distributed patronage effectively, compromised when he had to, and appealed eloquently to the people in support of his programs. During these four years Congress turned out more significant legislation than it had in the almost twelve years of Roosevelt and Taft.

Three major laws headed this list of legislative achievements. The first, the Underwood-Simmons Tariff of 1913, significantly decreased duties and placed on or near the free list such products as agricultural machinery, wool, sugar, shoes, iron, steel, and steel products. Taking advantage of the Sixteenth Amendment (1913), which made lawful an income tax, it also imposed a surtax of up to 6 percent on incomes. The second, a banking bill signed in December 1913, established twelve Federal Reserve banks regulated by a central board in Washington. This reform, Wilson's most durable achievement, was aimed at bringing some

Woodrow Wilson conferring with his aides.

central direction to monetary policy, hitherto reserved to private bankers. The third major reform, the Federal Trade Commission, approved in 1914, attempted to give the government the same regulatory control over corporations that the ICC had over railroads.

In achieving these laws Wilson showed that he had an open, highly flexible mind. On the banking question he at first endorsed a decentralized plan that gave the government little control over currency. When progressives complained, he reversed himself to call for a tougher bill, though one that still left bankers in control of important decisions about monetary policy. He also acceded to demands by agrarian spokesmen for an amendment authorizing the discounting by reserve banks of short-term agricultural paper—a measure that provided farmers with much-needed credit. Though eastern banking interests rebelled, Wilson stood firm, gathered support from businessmen, and secured a much stronger measure than he had dreamed of at the start of the battle. The final act needed substantial strengthening in the 1930s, but it made a start toward lessening the control over banking then enjoyed by Morgan and others.

His turnabout on the trust issue was more startling. At first he supported the so-called Clayton bill, a measure prohibiting interlocking directorates and specifying unfair trade practices. Its central purpose, to toughen the Sherman law, closely followed his New Freedom philosophy. But he was persuaded by Brandeis in 1914 to make regulatory commissions the major line of offense against the trusts. To the dismay of the antimonopolistic progressives he dropped interest in the Clayton bill (which ultimately passed in weakened form) and supported a measure providing for a Federal Trade Commission. When Wilson signed the commission bill in late 1914, he formalized his acceptance of the New Nationalist philosophy he had denounced less than two years earlier.

Wilson's ability to shift ground manifested itself again in 1916, when, with a difficult campaign ahead against GOP candidate Charles Evans Hughes, previously a reform governor of New York, he moved to attract progressives to the Democratic party. First, he named Louis Brandeis to the Supreme Court. He then advocated several measures he had resisted during the first two years in the White House. These included a bill banning the shipment in interstate commerce of goods made or mined by child labor; a rural credits act providing government capital to federal farm loan banks; and a workmen's compensation bill for federal employees. Faced with a railroad strike, he signed the Adamson Act establishing an eight-hour day for railway workers. Congress also passed a Federal Highway Act authorizing matching money to states for road building, and a Revenue Act (aimed primarily at raising money for defense), which raised maximum surtaxes on incomes to 15 percent. This burst of progressive legislation in 1916 showed that Wilson had moved appreciably toward accepting federal control of American economic life. By 1916 he stood as the leader of an ethnic-worker-farmer coalition that was developing within the Democratic party. This coalition helped bring him a narrow victory over Hughes in November.

AN EVALUATION OF WILSON

Wilson's legislative accomplishments, while impressive, did not satisfy many progressives. The banking act left the reserve banks in private hands and failed to give the central board power to set discount rates. Distressed, La Follette and many other congressmen opposed it. The FTC was potent enough on paper, but it became the virtual captive of large corporate interests, in part because the Supreme Court clipped its effectiveness, in part because Wilson himself named conservative appointees to the commission.

Insurgents also perceived accurately that Wilson's flexibility stemmed in part from lack of profound conviction and from political calculation. Unlike many progressive congressmen, Wilson in 1914 considered his program completed. But sharp setbacks in the off-year elections and the prospect of defeat in 1916 gradually persuaded him that he had to move to the left or face defections from the labor and

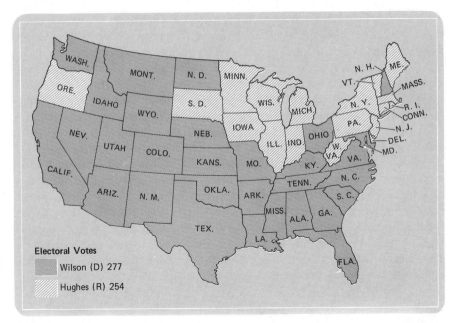

Election, 1916

Electoral Votes
Wilson (D) 277
Hughes (R) 254

social justice wings of his party. His experience indicates that the pressures of party and of Congress were as important to the success of legislation as was dynamic presidential leadership—that the executive branch had no monopoly on "reform." Wilson, unlike Taft or Roosevelt, had responsive Congresses that were ordinarily to his left.

The nature of the legislation passed in these years shows also that Wilson was as much a sectional as a national leader. The income tax pleased agrarians who hoped it would lighten the burden of taxes on land. The Underwood-Simmons Tariff assisted the South and the West by placing agricultural machinery and various finished goods on the free list. The enactment of rural credits, the highway law, and the Smith-Lever Act of 1914 (which authorized federal grants to states for agricultural extension work) were aimed at gratifying the southern and western wings of the Democratic party. All these measures were "progressive" in the sense that they expanded the role of the federal government. They also illustrated clearly the growing power of organized pressure groups in Congress.

Wilson showed many blind spots. Having assured the activists in 1912 that he favored women's suffrage, he refused to support it during his first term. The party as a whole, he argued, opposed it. Though he vetoed nativist bills establishing literacy tests for immigrants, he did so to keep ethnics in the Democratic camp, not because he had overcome his distaste for southern and eastern Europeans. And he openly sanctioned the spread of discrimination against blacks in the government bureaucracy. "I would say," he explained in 1913, "that I do approve of the segregation that is being attempted in several of the departments."

For all these reasons Wilson need not be placed on a pedestal as an economic thinker, social reformer, or legislative magician. But he also has to be evaluated in the context of his times. Coming to office at the high tide of progressive sentiment, and blessed with receptive Congresses, he proved pragmatic and politically shrewd. He was an eloquent speaker and a dynamic congressional leader. If he had blind spots, so did many progressives at the time. His able leadership revived the Democratic party and temporarily anchored its base among urbanites and ethnics. It helped southern and western interests to feel that they too could participate in the federal management of the economy.

Above all, Wilson's first term extended years of growing federal responsiveness to pressures for change. This responsiveness was often more rhetorical than substantive, and the legislation more symbolic than effective: blacks, most of organized labor, and the urban poor continued to be excluded from federal assistance. But the appearance of responsiveness was symbolically important, for it encouraged many Americans to believe that the presidency could contain corporate power. This faith, however exaggerated, sustained the national progressives and preserved a measure of political stability in a time of dramatic economic change.

Suggestions for reading

Five important books on political patterns are William N. Chambers and Walter Dean Burnham, eds., *American Party Systems** (1967), a series of essays on party development; Burnham, *Critical Elections and the Mainsprings of American Politics* (1972), which focuses on the twentieth century; Paul Kleppner, *Cross of Culture: A Social Analysis of Midwestern Politics, 1850–1900* (1970); Richard Jensen, *The Winning of the Midwest: Social and Political Conflict, 1888—1896* (1971); and Arthur Schlesinger, Jr., *The Imperial Presidency* (1973).

For the period prior to 1900 see L. D. White, *The Republican Era, 1869–1901* (1958), an administrative history; H. Wayne Morgan, *From Hayes to McKinley: National Party Politics, 1877–1896* (1969); David J. Rothman, *Politics and Power: The United States Senate, 1869–1901** (1966); and H. Wayne Morgan, *William McKinley and His America* (1963). The key books for national politics, 1900–17, are George Mowry, *The Era of Theodore Roosevelt** (1958); and Arthur Link, *Woodrow Wilson and the Progressive Era** (1954). Important studies are John M. Blum, *The Republican Roosevelt** (1954); and *Woodrow Wilson and the Politics of Morality** (1956). Both are brilliantly written. Major biographies include P. C. Jessup, *Elihu Root* (2 vols., 1938); Henry Pringle, *Theodore Roosevelt** (1931), which is critical; William Harbaugh, *Power and Responsibility** (1961), a balanced biography of TR; Pringle, *Life and Times of William Howard Taft* (2 vols., 1939); Donald E. Anderson, *William Howard Taft* (1973); John J. Broesamle, *William Gibbs McAdoo: A Passion for Change, 1863–1917* (1974); and John Braeman, *Albert J. Beveridge* (1971). See also Walter Johnson, *William Allen White's America* (1947); Richard Leopold, *Elihu Root and the Conservative Tradition** (1954); Alpheus T. Mason, *Brandeis** (1946); Ray S. Baker, *Woodrow Wilson* (6 vols., 1927–37); Alexander and Juliette George, *Woodrow Wilson and Colonel House** (1956), a provocative study using insights drawn from psychology; and David Thelen, *Robert La Follette and the Insurgent Spirit* (1976).

Regulatory policies are covered in Gabriel Kolko, *Triumph of Conservatism** (1963), and *Railroads and Regulation, 1877–1916* (1964); and Hans Thorelli, *Federal Anti-Trust*

Policy (1955). See also Morton Keller, *The Life Insurance Enterprise, 1885–1910* (1963); Robert Wiebe, *Businessmen and Reform** (1962); K. Austin Kerr, *American Railroad Politics, 1914–1920* (1968); and Melvin Urofsky, *Big Steel and the Wilson Administration* (1969).

For the Supreme Court, see Robert McCloskey, *The Modern Supreme Court** (1972), a brief survey; Loren P. Beth, *The Development of the American Constitution, 1877–1917** (1971); James W. Hurst, *Law and the Conditions of Freedom in the Nineteenth-Century United States* (1956); and Samuel L. Konefsky, *The Legacy of Holmes and Brandeis: A Study in the Influence of Ideas* (1974 ed.).

Relevant primary sources include Herbert Croly, *The Promise of American Life** (1909), an influential call for nationalism by a leading American intellectual; Walter Lippmann, *Drift and Mastery** (1914); and Walter Weyl, *The New Democracy** (1912).

From expansion to war
1900–1917

4

In opposing the war against Spain in 1898, former Secretary of State Richard Olney labeled America a "nation of sympathizers and sermonizers and swaggerers." The country, he said, was too immature to pursue a policy of self-interest based on power. Instead, it oscillated between moralizing and a romantic adventurousness that was more dangerous than calculating.

Had he wished to follow this perceptive argument, Olney could have pointed to all kinds of foolish American rhetoric about foreign relations in the 1890s. Some of it came from populist opponents of expertise. Democratic Congressman Champ Clark of Missouri, Woodrow Wilson's chief opponent for the 1912 presidential nomination, urged in 1897 the abolition of America's diplomatic corps. The New York *Sun* concurred. "The diplomatic service," it editorialized in 1899, "is a nurse of snobs. . . . Instead of making ambassadors, Congress should wipe out the whole service." Equally extreme statements came from racists and jingoists who asserted that America could do no wrong. The expansionist Senator William E. Chandler of New Hampshire contended that victory over Spain would require between fifteen minutes and ninety days.

Chandler's confidence reflected the very "swaggering" that Olney described, for America's military establishment was pathetically inadequate for sustained foreign adventures. Ships commissioned in the 1880s, revealingly called "seagoing coastline battleships," represented President Chester Arthur's view that "it is no part of our policy to create and maintain a navy able to cope with that of the other great powers of the world." In the early 1890s Congress authorized eight new battleships, four of which proved useful in the war against Spain in 1898. But the Regular Army remained weak. On the eve of the war, fought ostensibly to liberate Cuba from Spanish oppression, the army consisted of 28,183 officers and men (compared to 180,000 Spanish regulars in Cuba). Promotions had been so slow that Roosevelt claimed to observe white-bearded first lieutenants leading troops into battle. National guardsmen, who soon composed the bulk of American forces, were still equipped with Civil War vintage rifles. America won that "splendid little war" primarily because Spanish admirals foolishly exposed their ships in the harbors of Cavite and Santiago, not because "heroes" like TR killed thousands of Spaniards. American soldiers, ill equipped, poorly trained, and seriously weakened by tropical diseases (perhaps 2,000 died of illness, four times the number killed in battle), were spared what could have been the disaster of fighting sustained battles on land in Cuba or the Philippines.

American understanding of the consequences of a war against Spain was even more primitive than its military readiness. For a while President McKinley had to use schoolbook maps to follow naval movements in the Pacific. "It is evident," he confessed, "that I must learn a great deal of geography in this war." When Admiral Dewey took Manila, McKinley did not know what to do. After much agonizing he decided that America must take over the Philippines (and Guam), for returning them to Spain would be "cowardly and dishonorable," and giving them to a European power would be "bad business and discreditable." The Philippines, he concluded, were "unfit for self-government," and "there was nothing left for us to do but to take them all, and to educate the Filipinos, and uplift and civilize and Christianize them."

McKinley's reasoning, neither impetuous nor hypocritical, rested in part on his unwillingness to let the Philippines fall under the control of Germany or some other colonial power. Similar strategic impulses explain the acquisition of Puerto Rico, which guarded sea lanes to Central America, where American expansionists wished to construct a canal. McKinley's program meant the acquisition of far-flung properties and, in 1903, the establishment of an exploitative American protectorate over Cuba that lasted until 1933. Though America's administration in Cuba proved relatively enlightened for the time, military occupation of the Philippines provoked a bloody revolt—which in turn prompted brutal American countermeasures. Perhaps 200,000 Filipinos died between 1900 and 1903. (Some estimates place the number in the millions.) One American commander ordered his men to "kill and burn and make a howling wilderness of Samar."

In the long run the Spanish-American war had ominous consequences for American policy, for the virtually indefensible Philippines, 5,000 miles away, formed what Roosevelt called "our heel of Achilles." Recognizing their vulnerability— and the economic interests that had to be protected throughout East Asia—Secretary of State John Hay sent the major powers two notes in 1899 and 1900. The first called on them to maintain equal commercial opportunities for all. The second requested that the great powers preserve the territorial integrity of China. The "Open Door" notes did not signify a change in American policy, which had regularly sought secure Asian markets. They received little backing from the other powers, which correctly regarded them as efforts to protect American influence.

But in acting as if he had established the United States as the altruistic guarantor of China, Hay encouraged Americans to cherish exaggerated notions of American influence in East Asia. This gap between perception and reality had dangerous implications for policy.

Pressures of imperialism

America's sudden acquisition of a colonial empire did not go unchallenged by domestic critics. The independent Carl Schurz cried that taking the Philippines marked a "brutal appeal to sordid greed . . . utterly hostile to the vital principles of our free institutions." William Graham Sumner prophetically remarked that "the most important thing which we shall inherit from the Spaniards will be the task of suppressing rebellions." The pacifist Ernest Howard Crosby assailed the Christian sermonizing of men like McKinley:

> Onward Christian Soldiers
> 'Gainst the heathen crew!
> In the name of Jesus
> Let us run them through.

These anti-imperialists were so eloquent that later critics of American expansion could add little to their case. But the opponents of colonialism could not reverse what had been done between 1898 and 1900. The popularity of the war against Spain, the initial complacency with which Americans acquired such distant territory, and the subsequent appeal of Roosevelt's expansionist foreign policy suggested that imperialist impulses flowed from powerful currents of opinion and from interest groups that knew where they were going.

One of these impulses was economic—pressures from commercial farmers and industrialists to establish and expand markets abroad. Great strides in productivity gradually enabled American manufacturers to undersell foreign competitors and to develop favorable trade balances, which ranged between $200 and $700 million every year between 1896 and 1914. The value of American exports rose from approximately $1 billion annually in the early 1890s to $2.5 billion in 1914. More important, American overseas investment increased from $700 million in 1897 to $3.5 billion in 1914.

It is easy to exaggerate the impact of this growth on the Gross National Product, 93 percent of which still depended on domestic markets. It is also easy to overstress the political influence and commercial success of people engaged in this overseas commerce: the United States never managed to develop substantial trade with China. Still, growing numbers of American bankers and businessmen articulated an expansionist point of view by 1900, and important politicians listened. "We now hold three of the winning cards in the game for commercial greatness," the head of the American Bankers Association declared in 1898, "to wit—iron, steel, and coal. We have long been the granary of the world, we now aspire to be its workshop, then we want to be its clearing house." McKinley stated that "it should be

American enterprise abroad, 1900–1920

| | FOREIGN TRADE (In millions of current dollars) | | | | | INTERNATIONAL INVESTMENTS (In billions of current dollars) | | |
| | EXPORT | | IMPORT | | BALANCE (+ OR −) | U.S. INVESTMENTS ABROAD | FOREIGN INVESTMENTS IN U.S. | NET INVESTMENT POSITION (+ OR −) |
	AMOUNT	% OF GNP	AMOUNT	% OF GNP				
1900	1,499	7.4[a]	930	4.3[a]	+ 570	0.7[c]	3.4[c]	−2.7
1905	1,660	5.3[b]	1,199	4.4[b]	+ 461	n.d.	n.d.	. . .
1910	1,919	4.9	1,646	4.2	+ 273	2.5[d]	6.4[d]	−3.9
1915	2,966	6.6	1,875	4.0	+1,091	3.5[e]	7.2[e]	−3.7
1920	8,664	9.3	5,784	5.9	+2,880	7.0[f]	3.3[f]	+3.7

SOURCE: Adapted from *Historical Statistics of the United States*, pp. 537, 542, 564
[a]Average of GNP percentages for 1897–1901   [b]Average of GNP percentages for 1902–06   [c]Data for 1897   [d]Data for 1908
[e]Data for 1914 (to June 30)   [f]Data for 1919

our settled purpose to open trade wherever we can." Secretary Hay's open-door policy merely reflected this conscious demand for commercial expansion.

This drive for markets was part of a broader feeling that grew with the supposed disappearance of the domestic frontier and with the devastating depression of the mid-1890s. These events created widespread alarm. Was the depression the result, as it seemed to be, of the end of the frontier? Could the economy be reinvigorated by expansion beyond the continent? With production escalating, would the domestic market suffice? Admiral Alfred Thayer Mahan spoke for many: "Whether they will or no, Americans must begin to look outward. The growing productivity of the country demands it."

Other expansionists argued that it was America's destiny to expand, not only to promote prosperity at home but also to bring blessings to the rest of the world. Senator Beveridge of Indiana explained in 1900 that the question of absorbing the Philippines was "elemental. It is racial. God has not been preparing the English-speaking and Teutonic peoples for a thousand years for nothing but vain and idle self-contemplation and admiration. No! He has made us the master organizers of the world to establish system where chaos reigns. . . . He has marked the American people as his chosen nation to lead in the regeneration of the world." Like many other imperialists, Beveridge was an evangelical reformer who equated progress with American expansion and was not at all self-conscious about proclaiming the racial supremacy of the Anglo-Saxon peoples.

These economic and racial impulses toward expansion buttressed the strategic arguments of Mahan. A prolific writer who headed the Naval War College, Mahan insisted in books like *The Influence of Sea Power upon History* (1890) that control over international communications was the key to success in modern war. America, he argued, should build a mighty navy that could strike at an enemy's fleet and vital points. It should construct a canal across the central American isthmus, guard access to it, and acquire bases and coaling stations for its fleet throughout the world. Mahan's arguments assisted congressional navalists like Senator Henry Cabot Lodge of Massachusetts. They impressed Theodore Roosevelt, who tried to implement them a few years later.

Mahan urged Americans to awake and grow strong. "The best hopes of the world," he wrote, did not rest in "universal harmony nor in fond hopes of universal peace." Rather, they depended on "that reviving sense of nationality . . . in the jealous determination of each people to provide first for its own. . . . In these jarring sounds . . . are to be heard the assurance that decay has not touched yet the majestic fabric erected by so many centuries of courageous battling." This argument gave Americans a rationale for engaging in the competitive struggle with other colonial powers. It offered a new frontier, a sense of purpose, a way out of the drift and divisiveness of the 1890s. Through national power and expansion, perhaps, the United States could allay the tensions of the frayed society.

ROOSEVELT'S ROMANTIC *REALPOLITIK*

"I utterly disbelieve in the policy of bluff," Roosevelt told Taft in 1910, ". . . or in violation of the old frontier maxim, 'Never draw unless you mean to shoot.' I do not believe in our taking any position anywhere unless you mean to shoot."

Like many of TR's statements, this one was colorful and blunt. But it was not impetuous, for Roosevelt—perhaps more than any other president in this century—had pondered the role of America in foreign affairs. His basic conclusions, while clouded by moralisms, were consistent. America, he thought, had to play the large strategic and economic role that Mahan had envisioned. This policy satisfied Roosevelt's activist temperament. It rested on his characteristically American faith in the blessings of Anglo-Saxon civilization. But it was more than ethnocentrist moralism; it was also *Realpolitik*. Nations, he recognized, ordinarily act in their own selfish interests. They do not readily respond to "bluff" or to sermonizing. American policy, he argued, must recognize this fact by striving to preserve a stable balance of power.

Roosevelt's Asian policy attempted to put these ideas into practice. The Open Door policy, he explained later, was "an excellent thing"—on paper. But it "completely disappears as soon as a powerful nation determines to disregard it, and is willing to run the risk of war." Rather than rely on such a "bluff," TR sought ways to restrain the Russians, who appeared to be acquiring a dominant position in Manchuria. When Japan attacked Russia in 1904, Roosevelt wrote happily that Japan was "playing our game." The war would enhance American interests by destroying the potential for "either a yellow peril or a Slav peril."

At this point, however, Japan scored a series of resounding military successes that threatened to drive Russia out of the region. American magazines, easily alerted to the "yellow peril," began printing stories with headings like "Japan's Closing the Open Door," and "The Menace of Japan's Success." Roosevelt agreed that Japanese victory might signify a "real shifting of equilibrium as far as the white races are concerned." He then inaugurated a series of secret maneuvers that culminated in both Japan and Russia agreeing to attend a peace conference in Portsmouth, New Hampshire, in the summer of 1905. By that time both nations were exhausted by the conflict, and Roosevelt's diplomacy encouraged them to settle. The agreement gave Japan Port Arthur and railroads in Manchuria and recognized Japan's "predominant" interests in Korea. But by preserving Manchuria as a part of China, the treaty kept the rich province officially open to the trade of all nations. Roosevelt's skillful diplomatic intervention sustained America's modest economic presence in East Asia.

Roosevelt then proceeded to seek an accommodation with Japan, now the preeminent power in Asia. This seemed difficult, for migrations of Japanese laborers to the West Coast brought about ugly confrontations by 1906. In that year the California legislature debated a bill to exclude Orientals, and in 1907 anti-Oriental riots exploded all along the West Coast. Roosevelt, though furious at the "idiots of the California legislature," recognized the power of the Hearst press to inflame tensions to the point of war. Accordingly, he negotiated the so-called Gentlemen's Agreement of 1907. By this informal understanding both sides agreed to put an end to all unwanted immigration. The agreement could not erase the affront to Japanese pride, but it did permit tensions to subside. In 1908 Roosevelt further courted the Japanese by approving the so-called Root-Takahira Agreement. This affirmed the status quo, including Japanese hegemony in Korea. Each side pledged to respect the other's interests, to observe the Open Door in China, and to protect Chinese territorial integrity.

When Roosevelt left office a few months later, he had in no sense assured stability in Asia. American businessmen continued to complain about efforts by Japan, aided by Russia and England, to exclude outside interests. However, the instability in Asia did not stem from flaws in TR's policies, but from the inviting weakness of China, which America lacked the power to change. Recognizing these limits on American influence, Roosevelt had done what little he could to develop a balance of power in the area.

Considerations of power also dominated Roosevelt's more bellicose actions in the Caribbean, which he viewed as an American lake. Following Mahan, he was dedicated to building an isthmian canal—in part so that the navy could move freely to defend the new possessions in the Pacific. Because the Caribbean, unlike the Orient, was well within the range of American naval forces, he was quick to act when threatened with opposition.

His role in developing the Panama Canal revealed his willingness to resort to force. In December 1901 the Senate ratified a treaty with England that cleared the way for American construction of a canal. Secretary Hay then negotiated a draft treaty with Colombia, which controlled Panama. It granted the United States the right to build and fortify a canal, in return for which Colombia was to get $10 million, plus $250,000 annual rental. However, the Colombian government then demanded $20 million and specific guarantees of sovereignty in the canal zone. Roosevelt could have accepted the increased price, which was a fraction of the eventual cost, or he could have negotiated (as Hay suggested) with Nicaragua, where an alternative canal route beckoned. Instead, he referred to "those contemptible little creatures in Bogatá" as "foolish and homicidal corruptionists," and he determined to take control of the isthmus "without any further parley with Colombia."

At this point he was assisted by a successful Panamanian revolution against Colombia. Roosevelt immediately recognized the new state of Panama, which signed an agreement granting the United States canal rights for the original price of $10 million. Eleven years later the canal opened under American control.

Roosevelt at first insisted he had behaved properly. In fact, however, he had not only encouraged talk of revolution but had led Philippe Bunau-Varilla, a Frenchman who headed the Panamanian junta, to expect American assistance. (Bunau-Varilla, Roosevelt said later, would have been "a very dull man" to have expected

Roosevelt running a steam shovel at the Panama Canal.

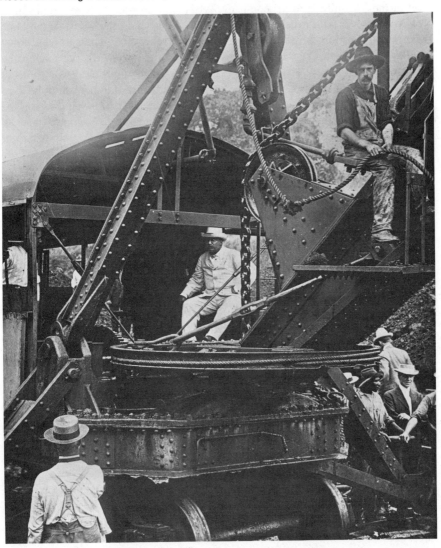

otherwise.) When Colombian troops attempted to bring in reinforcements, an American warship, which had conveniently arrived at the isthmus the night before the revolution, barred their entry. Later TR admitted, indeed bragged about, his covert role in these maneuvers: "I took the isthmus, and started the canal, and I let Congress debate me instead of the canal." He added, "so far from acting unconstitutionally about the Panama Canal, I acted the way every President worth his salt ought to act."

The revolution provides a neat case study of the role of economic interests in American imperialism. Bunau-Varilla was not only leader of the junta but agent for the French canal company that had demanded $40 million for surrender of its prior right to build a canal in Panama. After the revolution he became Panama's representative in Washington, where he negotiated the treaty making possible the payment of the $40 million to his company. Assisting him was William Cromwell, a New York lawyer with excellent political connections and easy access to the State Department. As attorney for the French company Cromwell used this influence first to lobby against the route through Nicaragua, then to develop American sympathy for the revolutionaries. The grateful French later paid him $600,000, some of which, it was later rumored, found its way into the hands of American politicians who had been stockholders in the company. Though Panama may have been the better route and though Roosevelt was not personally implicated in these financial dealings, his actions contemptuously ignored the rights of the sovereign state of Colombia. The Springfield *Republican* accurately labeled the affair "one of the most discreditable performances in our history."

Securing the canal was but part of Roosevelt's broader desire to exclude other powers from the Caribbean. As early as December 1902, when Germany (with help from England and Italy) bombarded Venezuelan ports to secure payment of debts, he had worried about possible European intervention in the area. When a revolution in Santo Domingo in late 1903 threatened to bring on similar actions, Roosevelt's suspicions mounted. Because 1904 was an election year, he acted at first with restraint, telling a friend that he had as little desire to annex the West Indian island as a "boa constrictor might have to swallow a porcupine wrong-end-to." At the same time, however, he said (privately) that "these Dagos . . . will have to behave decently," and in December, after the election, he proclaimed a new policy to Congress. The Roosevelt Corollary, as it became known, asserted that "chronic wrong-doing" or "impotence" by a nation of the Western Hemisphere could "force the United States, however reluctantly, in flagrant cases of such wrong-doing or impotence, to the exercise of an international police power." The corollary broadened the Monroe Doctrine to assert the right of the United States to intervene unilaterally whenever it deemed it necessary.

Like the Open Door policy, the corollary was an assertion of intent by the executive branch, not a law approved by Congress or an international agreement binding on any other power. But unlike the Open Door, the Roosevelt Corollary was well within American power to implement, and TR acted quickly to do so by placing the finances of Santo Domingo under American control. Meanwhile he let American bondholders know he would protect their interests throughout the Caribbean. When the Senate refused to ratify his agreement concerning Santo Domingo, he simply maintained it without consent, until the Senate gave way in 1907.

U.S. involvement in Caribbean in early twentieth century

TR's Caribbean policies were "realistic" in using power in a region where it was effective. They were therefore successful in the narrow sense. America acquired a canal of strategic importance, excluded foreign rivals from the Caribbean, and intervened with impunity to protect economic and political interests. His policies—for all their bluster on occasion—avoided dragging the country into war. But his actions were constitutionally high-handed. They brought him no friends in Latin America. They encouraged Americans to believe that might makes right, that the end justifies the means. Though perceptive concerning the role of power in international affairs, Roosevelt remained one of Olney's "swaggerers," something of a militarist who thrilled to the excitement of victory.

AMERICA, ASIA, AND LATIN AMERICA, 1909–16

Both Taft and Wilson appeared to reverse the romantic *Realpolitik* of Roosevelt. Taft was legalistic, a leading supporter of the international peace movement, and a devoted though frustrated advocate of reciprocity with Canada and of arbitration treaties with other nations. Wishing to avoid shows of force, he acted with restraint when unrest in Mexico threatened American interests. Wilson supported Secretary of State William Jennings Bryan's successful efforts to negotiate conciliation treaties, and tried (in vain) to get Congress to offer an apology and indemnity to Colombia. When revolution erupted in Mexico, he refused to let himself be swayed by American investors. "I am President of the United States," he said, "and not of a small group of American investors with vested interests in Mexico."

Both presidents, however, extended and broadened the interventionist pattern that had developed after 1898. In 1910 Taft explained that he would engage in "active intervention to secure for our merchandise and our capitalists opportunity for profitable investment." His policy of "substituting dollars for bullets," he added in 1912, was "an effort frankly directed to the increase of American trade. . . ." Taft sent marines to Nicaragua to assist a conservative regime with close ties to American interests. He also prodded American bankers into investing in railroad consortiums in Manchuria. However, the bankers struggled vainly against strong coalitions of foreign powers, which the Taft administration lacked the political and military strength to oppose. In pushing for "dollar diplomacy" in Asia, Taft hoped that American money would lessen tensions. But he succeeded only in advertising America's inability to control events in Asia. He had misunderstood TR's essential teaching: "never draw unless you mean to shoot."

Wilson's Asian diplomacy indicated that he, too, had difficulty in preserving the Open Door for American interests there. He seemed motivated by a desire to act honorably. Thus he withdrew support for the American bankers in Manchuria. He was quick to recognize a nationalist regime in China that toppled the corrupt Manchu dynasty. He protested strongly when Japan issued the so-called twenty-one demands on China in 1915. Apparently backing down before Wilson's determined stand, the Japanese dropped their demands. But they did so only because Britain and China also resisted, and their retreat was only temporary. In 1917 Wilson himself accepted the so-called Lansing-Ishii agreement, which recognized Japan's "special" interests in China. Like his predecessors in the White House, Wilson lacked a position of strength in Asia; his policies, therefore, did not have much success.

His efforts to affect politics in Central America were considerably more influential, but hardly popular with the common people there. To prevent anarchy in Nicaragua, Wilson extended Taft's policy of direct intervention by imposing military rule, which assisted American financial interests. He ordered marines into politically unstable Santo Domingo, and by 1916 America ruled the country. He also initiated a military occupation of Haiti, which lasted until 1934. The Haitians, proudly independent, resisted Yankee beneficence. Before marines completed the task of pacification, some 2,000 Haitians had been killed.

The irony of these interventions, which dwarfed those of his predecessors, was that Wilson thought he was acting altruistically. Unlike Roosevelt, he did not fear European pressure, for no such threats existed in Haiti or Santo Domingo. Unlike Taft, he did not cater to American investors (though they did influence the State Department). Rather, as his attempt to indemnify Colombia revealed, he hoped to promote inter-American understanding. His miscalculation, like that of many Americans before and since, was to assume that Anglo-Saxon values—stability, democracy, liberal capitalism—could be exported to countries with different cultural traditions and nationalistic aspirations.

Wilson's intervention in Mexico Nothing exposed this ethnocentrism better than his policies in Mexico, site of one of the twentieth century's major social revolutions. Three weeks before Wilson took office in 1913, the forces of General Victoriano Huerta betrayed and murdered Francisco Madero, the idealistic reformer who had overthrown the old autocracy in 1911. The European countries extended de facto recognition to the new regime, and American interests, seeing in Huerta the only stabilizing force in Mexico, urged Wilson to follow suit. To deny recognition to an established regime, in fact, involved a break with ordinary diplomatic practice. But Wilson took a moralistic view. "I will not recognize a government of butchers," he said. In so doing he created precedent for a doctrine of nonrecognition later used against Japan's conquest of Manchuria in 1932, and against the People's Republic of China in 1949.

When a new Mexican leader, Venustiano Carranza, pledged a revolution against Huerta, Wilson saw a chance to achieve his aims. He supported the Constitutionalists, as Carranza's forces called themselves. Carranza, however, rejected Wilson's efforts to guide the revolution. In need of an excuse to intervene, Wilson found it when Huerta's forces arrested American sailors who had strayed behind Mexican lines. The local Huertista commander apologized, but the American admiral on the scene, acting without clearance from Washington, demanded a twenty-one-gun salute to the United States flag, and Wilson supported him. Insulted, Huerta declined to salute unless the Americans responded volley for volley. Because such a response meant recognition of Huerta's government, Wilson refused. Two days later he used the incident as a pretext to ask for congressional authority to use armed force if necessary.

Wilson then received word that a German steamer was about to land in Vera Cruz with a shipment of arms for Huerta. Without waiting for congressional action, Wilson ordered the navy to take the city. The next day, April 22, 1914, it did so, at the cost of 126 Mexican and 19 American lives. The incident provoked anti-American demonstrations throughout Latin America, and it disturbed informed writers throughout the world. "If war is to be made on points of punctilio raised by admirals and generals," the *Economist* of London observed, "and if the government of the United States is to set the example for this return to medieval conditions, it will be a bad day for civilization."

At this stage war was averted when Wilson accepted an offer from Argentina, Brazil, and Chile to mediate the dispute. And during the summer of 1914 the Constitutionalists finally drove Huerta from power. But Wilson still resented Carranza's refusal to take American advice; so when Francisco ("Pancho") Villa, a dashing but ignorant general, broke with Carranza, Wilson threw him his support. This was a serious miscalculation, for Carranza's forces were too strong for Villa. With no option remaining, Wilson was persuaded in late 1915 to offer Carranza de facto recognition. Villa then turned on his former supporter, first by hauling sixteen Americans off a train in Mexico and shooting them on the spot, and then, in March 1916, by crossing the border to burn Columbus, New Mexico, and to kill nineteen more. Wilson had helped to sponsor a volatile and erratic man.

Villa's defiance prompted Wilson to dispatch a punitive expedition into Mexico under the command of General John J. Pershing. Vainly trying to capture the elusive Villa, Pershing expanded his army to 11,600 men and moved them more than 300 miles into central Mexico. Carranza, who had never envisioned such a formidable force, grew agitated, especially after two incidents, one at Parral in April, which resulted in the deaths of two Americans and forty Mexicans, and the second in June near Carrizal, which killed thirty Mexicans and twelve Americans and left twenty-four Americans captives of Carranza's forces.

The killings at Carrizal appeared to make war with Mexico inevitable. At this point, however, American soldiers admitted they had started the incident. Pacifists deluged Wilson with appeals for restraint. Carranza released the prisoners. Negoti-

Pancho Villa

ations between the two countries then deadlocked over the sensitive issue of Pershing's troops, which Carranza demanded be withdrawn, and which Wilson, facing reelection, did not dare to remove. But with the election safely behind him, and the prospect of having to fight in Europe, Wilson knew he had to retreat. In January 1917 he ordered the withdrawal to begin, and in March, almost three years after Carranza had taken power, Wilson finally offered him de jure recognition.

From one perspective Wilson's handling of Mexican affairs was restrained. Despite clashes such as the one at Carrizal, he had resisted the temptation to engage in full-fledged war. Despite the pressure of economic interests, he—alone among western leaders—had refused to recognize the autocratic Huerta. In so doing he had indirectly assisted the revolutionaries in their battle against autocracy and economic oppression.

From another perspective, however, his Mexican policies represented the "sympathizing and sermonizing" that Secretary of State Olney had deplored. They directly caused several armed clashes, otherwise avoidable, which led to loss of life. They aroused strong anti-American sentiment throughout Latin America. And they revealed two illusions that plagued American policy makers in the years to come. The first assumed that foreign nationalists welcomed attempts to spread the American way of life. The second, stemming from the first, was that America, the most powerful nation on earth, could use its technology and its military force to guide revolutionary movements into channels that would safeguard American interests. These illusions continued as hallmarks of American diplomacy. As subsequent events—in Russia, China, Cuba, and Vietnam—were to demonstrate, Wilson's Mexican policy did not serve as an object lesson in the limitations of missionary foreign policy.

War in Europe

The movement for international peace peaked in the years before the outbreak of World War I in 1914. Andrew Carnegie established a Peace Fund in 1910 with an initial gift of $10 million. Taft worked diligently for arbitration treaties. Norman Angell's popular *The Great Illusion* (1910) argued persuasively that war was useless and obsolete. By 1912 a prominent peace leader concluded, "It looks as though this were going to be the age of treaties rather than the age of wars, the century of reason rather than the century of force."

The Great War shattered these hopes. But it did not lead Americans to plunge immediately into the action. As Wilson put it, the United States "must be neutral in fact as well as in name during these days that are to try men's souls. We must be impartial in thought as well as in action." A year later he heard rumors that the army was preparing contingency plans for battle against Germany. Furious, he summoned the acting secretary of war. If the rumors were true, he commanded, the

Robert Minor, an antiwar cartoonist, expresses opposition to war in 1915. The caption, uttered by an army medical examiner, reads, "At last, a perfect soldier."

secretary should "relieve every officer in the general staff and order him out of Washington." In hindsight his order appears both touching and quaint, but it testified to his sincere desire to stay out of war.

In adhering to this course for almost three years Wilson found he could draw on substantial popular support. Some, including many Irish-Americans, opposed engaging in a war to assist England. Some, including thousands of German-Americans, did not want to fight former countrymen. Others, like Theodore Dreiser, were Anglophobes. "It would be an excellent thing for Europe and the world," he wrote, "if the despicable British aristocracy . . . were smashed and a German viceroy sat in London." Untold thousands of Americans simply felt that Europe's quarrels were its own business, that America must be spared the curse of militarism. "Don't Take My Darling Boy Away" was the title of one popular song of 1915. Another went:

> There'd be no war today
> If mothers all would say,
> I didn't raise my boy to be a soldier.

But from the start of the war Wilson had to contend with many Americans who yearned to discipline the Germans. When Germany marched through neutral Belgium, Harvard President Charles Eliot urged Wilson to conclude offensive and defensive treaties with the Allies. *Life* added (a few days after the war began) that "the unanimity of sentiment in this country against Germany is surprising . . . the English, French, and Russians are fighting in behalf of the liberties of the world." Popular magazines published exaggerated accounts, spread via British propaganda, of German atrocities. *Harpers* (December 1914) titled a story "The Attack on New York." Another popular article, by Richard Harding Davis in *Metropolitan Magazine,* imagined spike-helmeted, bayonet-wielding Germans entrenched in headquarters at a Long Island country club.

Wilson also had to bow to economic pressures. At first he offered token support to Secretary of State Bryan, a near-pacifist who refused to permit American bankers to float loans to the Allies. "Money," Bryan said forcefully, "is the worst of contrabands—it commands all other things." But influential bankers openly favored England. "Our firm had never for one moment been neutral," a Morgan partner recalled, "From the very start we did everything we could to contribute to the cause of the Allies." Wilson understood that the denial of loans to belligerent nations broke with the usual practice, that it was therefore unneutral, and that it would hurt England and France, which needed the help, much more than it would harm the Central Powers. He also realized that loans could facilitate trade and perhaps end the recession that had descended on the American economy in 1913. So in October 1914 he permitted the extension of commercial credits, in March 1915 he approved a $50 million loan from the Morgan interests to France, and in September 1915—after Bryan's resignation from the State Department—he authorized a loan of $500 million more to the Allies. By 1917 America had loaned $2.25 billion to the Allies, and but $27 million to Germany. Trade with the Allies increased from $824 million in 1914 to $3.2 billion in 1916. (With blockaded Germany and Austria-Hungary it declined during the same period from $169 million to

$1.15 million.) Long before American intervention in April 1917, the United States pursued an economic policy that was "neutral" in that it followed the ordinary practice of nonbelligerent nations in time of war but that assisted both the American economy and the Allies.

By far the largest obstacle to a neutrality "impartial in thought as well as in action" was the struggle for command of the seas. England, whose ships controlled the surface, gradually imposed a far-reaching definition of contraband to be confiscated from ships bound for the Central Powers. By early 1915 its list of contraband included not only armaments but such vital raw materials as copper, iron, aluminum, rubber, gasoline, oil, and even foodstuffs. This lengthy list infuriated the Central Powers, and it angered neutrals like the United States, whose shipments were frequently confiscated. But the English, desperate to prevent supplies from reaching their enemies, tightened their economic warfare in 1916 by "blacklisting" some eighty-seven American firms from trading with British subjects in any way.

This blacklist, combined with the British suppression of the Irish, infuriated Wilson. Privately he called the English "poor boobs." He wrote Colonel Edward House, his closest adviser, that he was "seriously considering asking Congress to authorize me to prohibit loans and restrict importations to the Allies. . . . Can we any longer endure their intolerable course?" As late as November 1916 he told House to warn the English Foreign Secretary, Sir Edward Grey, that American feeling was "as hot against Great Britain as it was at first against Germany and likely to grow hotter still against an indefinite continuation of the war."

Various forces kept these tensions from escalating to the point of open conflict. Among these were the ties of language and of economic interest that bound Americans to the English. Individuals also promoted understanding. One of these was America's ambassador to England, Walter Hines Page. An avid Anglophile, he behaved in a flagrantly unprofessional way by making clear to British officials that he did not share Wilson's irritation. On receiving one American protest, he took it to Grey and said, "I do not agree with it. Now let us sit down and see how we can answer it." Another was Colonel House, who served as Wilson's personal emissary on frequent missions to Europe. Still another was Robert Lansing, who succeeded Bryan as Secretary of State in 1915. Lansing believed that American security demanded the defeat of Germany. "If our people only realized the insatiable greed of those German autocrats at Berlin," he wrote early in 1917, ". . . we would be at war today. . . . The Allies must *not* be beaten. . . . War cannot come too soon to suit me."

British sensitivity to American opinion also prevented a rupture. When southern congressmen agitated in 1915 against a British plan to place cotton on the list of absolute contraband, Lord Grey and others negotiated a secret agreement by which the British bought enough cotton to stabilize the price. Grey also instructed his ambassador in Washington to avoid unnecessary misunderstandings. "Do nothing," he advised, "which will be a cause of complaint or dispute as regards the United States government; such a dispute would indeed be a crowning calamity."

The major force driving England and America together was the German submarine, a frightening new weapon that ultimately destroyed Wilson's hopes for peaceful resolution of neutral rights at sea. From the beginning the Germans determined to use their advantage to prevent valuable materials from reaching their enemies. They made it clear that their submarines might have to sink targets on sight—subs that surfaced to warn and then to search armed ships for contraband risked destruction. Early in 1915 they imposed a "war zone" around the British Isles in which they threatened to sink all enemy vessels. Neutral ships, they warned, would be in danger because of British misuse of neutral flags.

Germany's action was a bluff, for it lacked the subs to carry out such a sweeping blockade, and it had no intention at that time of sinking neutral ships. Moreover, Wilson's response, while holding Germany to "strict accountability" for illegal destruction of American ships or lives, did not mention the difficult issue of the rights of American citizens to travel on belligerent ships. By May 1915 German-American relations, though troubled, were far from critical.

At this point a German submarine sank, without warning, the *Lusitania,* a British passenger liner. Among the 1,198 people who died were 128 Americans. The sinking shocked people not yet inured to the ravages of total war. "All the world," Ambassador Page commented privately, "should fall to and hunt this wild beast down." The sinking narrowed Wilson's options, for many Americans demanded that he uphold the nation's honor. Distressed, he sent stiff notes demanding that Germany desist from attacking unarmed merchant ships. His sternness cost him the resignation of Bryan, who argued that Wilson should warn Americans against traveling on belligerent vessels, that he should protest the British definition of contraband, and that ships like the *Lusitania* were secretly carrying arms. Bryan observed that "a person would have to be very much biased in favor of the Allies to insist that ammunition intended for one of the belligerents should be safe-guarded in transit by the lives of American citizens."

Though rejecting Bryan's advice, Wilson too was not ready to go to war, and he was cheered when he declared that "there is such a thing as being too proud to fight." Instead, he resolved to affirm "strict accountability," including the right of Americans to travel on belligerent ships. Germany refused to accede to his demands

---

Where are You, God? . . .
I can't believe that you have seen
The Things that they have done . . .
And yet upon this earth of Yours
There still exists the Hun. . . .

Where are You, God?
  In whom I put my trust?
    You must be there,
  And You are great and just.
Your mighty sea they've turned into a grave,
A little baby slumbers on each wave. . . .

A poem by Elsie Janis, musical actress, 1915, expressing American feelings about the sinking of the *Lusitania.*

---

and in August 1915 sank the *Arabic,* a British liner, causing the loss of two more American lives. But Wilson persevered, and Germany backed off far enough to promise it would no longer attack unarmed passenger liners without warning, unless they tried to escape. Though the *Arabic* pledge left unresolved the status of merchant ships and of armed passenger vessels, it suggested that Germany was bending. Wilson's patience appeared to be paying off.

Wilson then labored hard to mediate an end to the war, and in February 1916 Colonel House reached with Lord Grey an agreement that appeared to be a significant step in that direction. The House-Grey memorandum stated that the President "on hearing from France and England that the moment was opportune," would call a conference to end the war. "Should the Allies accept this proposal, and should Germany refuse it, the United States would probably enter the war against Germany." The memorandum marked the high point of Wilson's wartime effort to mediate for peace.

In fact, however, no such conference was held. The Germans had never shown much interest in one, and the British, who were supposed to initiate the demand for mediation, never did so. Instead, they fought grimly on. Even if a conference had been called, Wilson might have been embarrassed, for he had no authority to commit the United States to war.

Meanwhile, Secretary Lansing, operating with Wilson's approval, suggested that the Allies disarm their merchant ships, in return for which German submarines would agree to give warnings. The delighted Germans announced they would begin attacking armed merchant ships on February 29. But Grey complained that Lansing's suggestion made the "sinking of merchant vessels the rule and not the exception." Wilson then disavowed the plan. The lack of communication between House and Lansing revealed the uncertainty of American diplomacy. And the failure of both their approaches in 1916 suggested that nothing short of total victory would satisfy the exhausted belligerents.

Wilson's rejection of Lansing's idea infuriated antiwar congressmen. What would happen, they demanded to know, if the Germans made good their threat to sink armed merchant ships, on which Americans might well be traveling? Wilson replied that he would hold the Germans accountable. Alarmed, many leading Democrats supported the Gore-McLemore resolutions warning Americans against traveling on armed belligerent ships. Wilson fought back with an open letter to Senator William J. Stone, chairman of the foreign relations committee. "Once accept a single abatement of right," he declared, "and many other humiliations would certainly follow, and the whole fine fabric of international law might crumble piece by piece." Wilson's insistence on preserving national honor (and economic interests) carried the day, and early in March the resolutions failed in the House, 276 to 142.

Having reaffirmed his policy of strict accountability, Wilson now awaited the German response. It came quickly, for on March 24, 1916, a submarine torpedoed the *Sussex,* an unarmed French channel steamer. There were eighty casualties, including several badly wounded Americans. Pressed hard by both Lansing and House, Wilson sent a stiff note to Berlin. It demanded that Germany stop attacking without warning merchant and passenger vessels, armed or unarmed, belligerent or

EDITOR   CAPITALIST   POLITICIAN   MINISTER

Having Their Fling.

The cartoonist Art Young was indicted during the war for cartoons like this one.

neutral. The Germans at first reacted angrily, but on May 4 they promised that submarines would visit and search before sinking merchant vessels, both in and out of the war zone. Though the note was truculent in tone, it met Wilson's demands. The policy of strict accountability, it appeared, had prevailed.

By then, however, American advocates of preparedness were strident. The Germans, one critic said, were "standing by their torpedoes, the British by their guns, and Wilson by strict accountability." Tin Pan Alley turned out songs with such titles as: "I Did Not Raise My Boy to Be a Coward," and "I'd Be Proud to Be the Mother of a Soldier." Theodore Roosevelt, more militaristic than ever, charged that the president, a "peace prattler," had "done more to emasculate American manhood and weaken its fiber than anyone else I can think of." The preparedness advocates forced through a bill more than doubling the Regular Army to 11,327 officers and 208,388 men, increasing the National Guard to an authorized strength in five years of 17,000 officers and 400,000 men, and integrating the Guard into the federal defense structure. They also secured passage of a bill authorizing huge expansion of the navy within three years. House Majority Leader Claude Kitchin, a leader of the antipreparedness forces, complained that "the United States today becomes the most militaristic naval nation on earth."

Wilson dismayed men like Kitchin by signing the army bill and by applying pressure for the naval act. But as the election of 1916 approached, it was clear that the president, not Charles Evans Hughes, the Republican nominee, remained the bright hope for American peace workers. Indeed, he let it be said that he had "kept America out of war." "You Are Working—Not Fighting!" read one widely circulated Democratic handbill. "Alive and Happy—Not Cannon Fodder! Wilson and Peace with Honor? or Hughes with Roosevelt and War?" The misleading refrain

Bayonet drill at Camp Dix.

"he kept us out of war" was the central one of the campaign, and except for a few Socialists (who fared poorly at the polls), Wilson attracted all the advocates of restraint. He won the election by a very narrow margin.

But even during the campaign Wilson recognized a potential danger to his policy of strict accountability: it depended on German restraint. "I can't keep the country out of war," he observed privately. "Any little German lieutenant can put us into war at any time by some calculated outrage." Early in 1917 what he feared (but hadn't explained to the voters) finally happened: Germany announced a new, drastic policy of submarine warfare. After February 1, it announced, submarines would sink without warning all ships, belligerent or neutral, discovered in a zone around Great Britain, France, and Italy, and in the eastern Mediterranean. The German threat against neutral ships was clearly aimed at nations such as the United States. On February 2 the President broke off diplomatic relations with Germany.

Wilson still hoped for peace. "We do not desire any hostile conflict with the Imperial German Government," he told Congress on February 3. Though American ships clung to port, causing cargo to pile up on the docks, he resisted congressional demands that he authorize the arming of merchant vessels. But on February 25 he was shown an intercepted message sent by the German Foreign Secretary, Arthur Zimmermann, to the German minister in Mexico. If America and Germany went to war, the message said, the minister should suggest that Mexico fight against the United States and receive in return the "lost territory in Texas, New Mexico, and Arizona." Wilson temporarily kept the note to himself, but it stiffened his resolve to adhere to strict accountability. The next day he went to Congress and asked for authority not only to arm merchantmen but also to "employ any other instrumentalities or methods that may be necessary and adequate to protect our ships and our people in their legitimate and peaceful pursuits on the seas."

Most congressmen were prepared to arm merchant ships, even though the result would certainly be shooting on the high seas, the loss of American life, and the outbreak of war. But a minority refused to grant Wilson blanket authority to "employ any other instrumentalities or methods that may be necessary." Such power, they contended, belonged to Congress. When Wilson publicized the Zimmermann note on March 1, the stunned House of Representatives gave him the authority to arm ships, but still denied him the broader powers he wished. And in the Senate eleven or twelve noninterventionists, including Norris and La Follette, threatened to talk the bill to death. The American presidency, while much expanded since the days of Roosevelt, could not silence congressional dissent.

Most of the antiwar senators were from the Plains or Middle West, areas with weaker commercial and sentimental ties to the Allies and (in some cases) with relatively large proportions of German-Americans. They also represented the anti-monopolistic wing of the progressive movement. Remembering a simpler era, they refused to accept either bigness in business or arbitrary use of presidential power. As humanitarian progressives they were horrified by the thought of sending Americans to die in far-off Europe. And as opponents of large corporations they suspected economic motives for war. "Who are the patriots of the country?" La Follette asked rhetorically. "They are the Morgans, the Rockefellers, the Schwabs, the Garys, the DuPonts and those who are back of the thirty-eight corporations most benefitted by war orders. Shades of Lincoln! What a band of patriots!'' Norris added later, ''we are going to war upon the command of gold. We are about to put the dollar sign on the American flag.''

In working for nonintervention the filibusterers probably enjoyed considerable popular support until April. But they encountered fierce abuse from superpatriots. Newspapers called them ''descendants of Benedict Arnold,'' while Wilson coldly branded them ''a little group of willful men, representing no opinion but their own.'' When they prevented passage of the bill, Wilson proceeded on his own to order the ships armed and to instruct them to shoot at subs that came within striking range. This action of dubious constitutionality made a naval war inevitable, and on March 18, submarines sank three American ships, with heavy loss of life. Wilson still hesitated, but by March 20, when he called Congress into special session for April 2, he had decided that America must fight.

His call for war on April 2 was magnificently idealistic. The United States, he said, ''had no quarrel with the German people.'' On the contrary, it would fight for ''the ultimate peace of the world and for the liberation of its peoples, and the German peoples included.'' Wilson added that ''the world must be made safe for democracy. Its peace must be planted on the tested foundations of political liberty. We have no selfish ends to serve. . . . We are but one of the champions of the rights of mankind.'' His eloquent speech impressed even such partisan critics as Roosevelt and Henry Cabot Lodge. And though men like Norris, Kitchin, and La Follette fought him to the end, the die was cast. The Senate adopted the resolution for war by a vote of 82 to 6, and at three in the morning of April 6 the House concurred, 373 to 50. Wilson signed the country into war the next afternoon.

There is no necessity for war with Germany—there is no necessity for war with any of the belligerent powers. Three thousand miles of water make it impossible for us to be drawn into that vortex of blood and passion and woe if we are true to the American people. If this administration shall put a higher estimate upon human life than commercial conquest; if we shall put the immortal soul above the dollar, and regard justice of more importance than financial success, there will be no war. It is not for the vindication of the principles of human justice that imperil our peace, but rather the avaricious reaching out for pelf that threatens to involve this Nation in this world war. I submit it would be more profitable to the people of the United States—better for the peoples of the world, rather than involve the United States in that war, to suspend commerce between Europe and America so far as American shipping interests are concerned. Not that I believe that Germany or England, or any other power, has a right to prevent our ships from going where they have a right to go on the high seas. I might have a right to go in the streets where a duel was being fought by participants in a drunken mob, but it would be better for me if I exercised the prudence of a brave, sane man, and remained away from the danger zone until order should be restored.

Sen. James Vardaman of Mississippi, one of the group of "willful men," speaks out against war, March 1917.

AMERICAN POLICY RECONSIDERED

Two major questions arise concerning American policy toward Europe in the years between 1914 and 1917. Why did the United States go to war? Could war have been avoided?

The first question has called forth various answers. Some people, like House and Lansing at the time, thought war necessary to protect American security. Others, following Wilson's war message, assumed that American motives were primarily idealistic: to make the world safe for democracy. Critics like La Follette blamed the corporations and the bankers. Still others have qualified this economic interpretation by pointing to a broader national demand for a world in which American capitalism must be permitted to expand.

None of these answers is wholly satisfactory. The view that America fought to preserve its security simply ignores the fact that neither Wilson nor most Americans thought in such Rooseveltian terms. The argument that Wilson sought to make the world safe for democracy confuses his rhetoric of April 1917 with more prosaic—and more urgent—causes relating to Germany's submarine warfare. The focus on narrow economic interests ignores the fact that bankers and corporations, though profiting immensely from war, had little impact on Wilson or Congress. The stress on broader economic considerations—on preserving an "open door" for democratic capitalism—captures part of the truth, for Wilson, like many Americans, assumed that America's future depended on its ability to protect and to expand its overseas interests. But such a view is one-sided if it underplays Wilson's peculiar rectitude. His primary aim was to uphold his country's neutral rights—for their own sake as well as for the commercial advantages such rights might maintain. By intervening he also hoped to be in a position to promote his ideals at the peace conference. To Wilson as to many other Americans "national honor" was very much worth fighting for.

This policy worked tolerably well until 1917. It forced the Germans to back down after the sinking of the *Lusitania* in 1915 and the *Sussex* in 1916. It was politically successful, for it satisfied most noninterventionists and pacifists, as well as those who insisted that he protect neutral rights, and it left extremists like Roosevelt isolated on the fringe. Wilson's neutrality policy until early 1917 achieved its basic goal: to preserve American nonbelligerency with honor.

The problem with this policy was that it depended for its success on the restraint of Germany. More generally, it revealed how difficult it was for a nation as powerful as the United States to remain either "isolated" or "neutral" amidst total war in Europe. Having insisted on the right of American ships to sail the seas, Wilson inevitably had to protect them from attack. It was the German decision to wage unrestricted submarine warfare—a decision based on domestic perceptions of military needs—that destroyed these goals and provoked America's declaration of war.

Could American participation in the conflict have been avoided? Two schools of thought answer yes. One argues that Wilson should have worked harder for preparedness, that Germany would never have dared to embark on unrestricted submarine warfare if the United States had shown it was ready to fight. The other insists that Wilson was a "sermonizer," that he should have accepted limits on

American neutral rights, that such "rights" made no sense in the age of the submarine.

The proponents of better preparedness tend to underestimate the difficulties as well as the limitations of such a policy. No such course stood much of a chance in Congress before 1916, and even after America's entrance into the war, conscription encountered stubborn congressional opposition. If Wilson had desired to arm America to the teeth, he could have done so, if at all, only by manufacturing the very crises that he wished to avoid. Most important, it is doubtful that the specter of a well-prepared America would have altered the German decision for unrestricted warfare. On the contrary, that ultimately fatal decision stemmed from the desperation of a government brutalized by the bloodiest war in world history, and it would probably have come regardless of the state of American preparedness.

The argument that Wilson was too righteous at first appears convincing. Seen from the perspective of the 1980s, when experience with total wars makes talk about "national honor" seem dangerous, Wilson's policy appears ill-advised. In defending the privilege—for that is what it was—of Americans to travel on belligerent ships, Wilson also affirmed a provocative definition of neutral rights. Suppose he had backed off on that point: Americans might have thought twice before traveling on such ships; many of the 175 citizens who were killed on such vessels before February 1917 might have been saved; and a major source of tension would have been dispelled. German-American relations would unquestionably have been more amicable between 1914 and early 1917 if Wilson from the start had warned Americans to stay off belligerent ships.

But his stubborn stand on that issue was not the major cause of war. Indeed, the United States remained at peace with Germany for almost two years after the sinking of the *Lusitania*. The basic cause—again—was Germany's decision to sink neutral as well as belligerent vessels. This decision left Wilson with three equally unpalatable courses of action in 1917. The first, to keep American ships out of the war zones, meant the politically perilous surrender of traditional neutral rights and of "national honor." Given America's economic and cultural ties with England, no president could pursue such a policy without playing into the hands of militarists like TR. The second course, to affirm the right of ships to enter the zones but to leave them unarmed, in practice meant the same surrender of neutral rights, for such ships refused to sail. The remaining course was to arm the ships, to let them sail, and to hope the Germans would leave them alone. When Germany did not, Wilson was cornered. If he had still refused to ask for war, the pressure of Congress and public opinion might soon have given him no other choice.

Wilson's defenders thus contend that the Germans left him no choice but to ask for war. If he had shown any signs of backing away from his determined defense of neutral rights, they add, the German decision might well have been made in 1916. However much Americans may like to think that they can always direct world events, other nations sometimes pursue policies that they know will lead to war. Such a policy was adopted by Germany in 1917, by which time the passions of warfare drove all the belligerents to acts of desperation. Given America's crucial economic and strategic role in the world by that time, Wilson's defenders conclude, it is hard to see how he could have kept the United States isolated from such passions or how he or any other democratic leader could have preserved a monopoly of initiative in the cause of peace.

In retrospect, most American observers probably agree that it was in the long-range interest of the United States to see to it that Germany did not win the war—and that Wilson therefore did right to involve the country in the fighting. Many experts nonetheless remain highly critical of his policies. For Wilson did not talk much about such interests. Instead, he pursued an inflexible policy stressing traditional neutral rights. In so doing he refused to admit that the submarine had changed some of the basic rules. He deprived himself of the initiative. When Germany embarked on unrestricted warfare in 1917, America was therefore trapped; it had no clear recourse save to fight. In doing so, it relied on reasons that seemed scarcely worthy of such great sacrifice, and that later prompted disillusion and shrill debate.

Suggestions for reading

General interpretations of American foreign policy—all of which cover a much broader period than the years dealt with in this chapter—are William A. Williams, *The Tragedy of American Foreign Policy** (1962), a revisionist account emphasizing economic forces; George Kennan, *American Diplomacy, 1900–1950** (1950), a ''realist's'' account; and Robert Osgood, *Ideals and Self-Interest in American Foreign Policy* (1953), a well-written ''realist'' interpretation. Other general books are Norman Graebner, ed., *An Uncertain Tradition: American Secretaries of State in the Twentieth Century** (1961); John A. S. Grenville and George Berkeley Young, *Politics, Strategy, and American Diplomacy: Studies in Foreign Policy, 1873–1917* (1966); and Richard D. Challener, *Admirals, Generals, and American Foreign Policy, 1898–1914* (1973).

Important books on late-nineteenth-century foreign policies include Robert L. Beisner, *From the Old Diplomacy to the New* (1974); Charles C. Campbell, *The Transformation of American Foreign Relations* (1976); Ernest May, *Imperial Years: The Emergence of America as a Great Power* (1961); Walter LaFeber, *The New Empire: An Interpretation of American Expansion, 1860–1898* (1963); LaFeber, *The Panama Canal* (1979); and Julius Pratt, *The Expansionists of 1898* (1936). Other relevant books are May, *American Imperialism, A Speculative Essay** (1968); Beisner, *Twelve Against Empire: The Anti-Imperialists, 1898–1900** (1968); and E. Berkeley Tompkins, *Anti-Imperialism in the United States: The Great Debate, 1890–1920* (1970).

The Roosevelt years receive thorough treatment in Howard Beale, *Theodore Roosevelt and the Rise of America to World Power* (1956). See also Raymond Esthus, *Theodore Roosevelt and the International Rivalries* (1970), and the books on TR by Pringle and Harbaugh mentioned in the bibliography for chapter 3. For the Taft years Pringle's *Life and Times of William Howard Taft*, 2 vols. (1939), also mentioned in chapter 3, is thorough. More recent is Walter and Marie Scholes, *The Foreign Policies of the Taft Administration* (1970). Easily the most careful account of Wilson is the multivolume biography by Arthur Link listed in the bibliography for chapter 3. *Wilson: The Diplomatist** (1957), by Link, is a collection of lectures that provide important insights.

Coverage of Caribbean affairs can be found in Dexter Perkins, *The Monroe Doctrine, 1867–1907** (1937); Robert Freeman Smith, *The U. S. and Revolutionary Nationalism in Mexico, 1916–1932* (1972); Dana G. Munro, *Intervention and Dollar Diplomacy in the Caribbean, 1900–1921* (1964); Robert E. Quirk, *An Affair of Honor: Woodrow Wilson and* *the Occupation of Vera Cruz** (1962); and P. Edward Haley, *Revolution and Intervention: The Diplomacy of Taft and Wilson with Mexico, 1910–1917* (1970). For Asian affairs, see Charles E. Neu, *An Uncertain Friendship: Theodore Roosevelt and Japan, 1906–1909* (1967); Akira Iriye, *Across the Pacific: An Inner History of American–East Asian Relations* (1969); Paul A. Varg, *The Making of a Myth: The United States and China, 1879–1912* (1968); and Roy W. Curry, *Woodrow Wilson and Far Eastern Policy, 1913–1921* (1968).

For American involvement in World War I see vols. 3–5 by Link on Wilson. Also Ernest May, *The World War and American Isolation, 1914–1917* (1959); Ross Gregory, *The Origins of American Intervention in the First World War** (1971); Daniel M. Smith. *The Great Departure: The United States in World War I, 1914–1920** (1965); and John M. Cooper, Jr., *The Vanity of Power: American Isolationism and the First World War, 1914–1917* (1969), an account of domestic opinion.

5

The divisiveness of war

"If this war had not come," wrote Ray Stannard Baker, "we should all have been rotten."

Baker, an ardent Wilsonian, meant that American intervention would end the war to end all wars. Like many contemporaries, he also hoped that it would heal divisions at home. The war was to bring justice to the world and unity and progress to the United States.

Much that happened in 1917 and 1918 appeared to confirm Baker's expectations. American military strength, for instance, was indispensable to a fairly early and decisive end to the war. Early in 1917, German U-boats were sinking nearly 900,000 tons of shipping per month. By November 1917 American warships helped cut losses to less than 300,000 tons per month, and after April 1918 the Allies never lost more than 200,000 tons per month. Had the pre-1917 rate been maintained, Britain would have run out of grain within two months. On land the United States supplied 1 million troops by July 1918 and 2 million by November. The Americans cracked the southern front at St. Mihiel between the Argonne Forest and the Vosges Mountains and helped the Allies break the long stalemate in the trenches. The war cost 116,000 American lives (53,000 in battle) and 204,000 wounded—stiff losses for so short a time. But the deaths numbered only a third of those killed in the Civil War, and they were trifling compared to those sustained by England (900,000), France (1.35 million), and Russia (1.7 million). The apparent ease of victory encouraged Americans to take a somewhat lighthearted view of war.

A woman welder in a munitions factory. Because of the shortage of men during the war, many women were able to work at jobs from which they had previously been excluded.

To progressives like Baker, the war appeared especially salutary at home. Reformers cheered the institution of prohibition, women's suffrage, and progressive taxation, all of which were promoted by the exigencies of war. They applauded the liberal policies of the War Labor Board, which helped union membership grow from approximately 2.5 million in 1915 to more than 5 million in 1920. War orders also brought prosperity. Wages for all workers increased from an average of $628 per year in 1915 to $672 (real 1914 dollars) in 1920, while stock prices, which had wallowed in 1913, broke upward in 1915 and remained high until 1920. And war caused the GNP to leap from an average of $39 billion between 1912 and 1915 to more than $80 billion between 1917 and 1921. This was a per capita increase from $408 to $835, a rate of progress never approached thereafter. In all these ways, World War I marked not the end, but rather the fulfillment of many causes central to American progressives.

An unprecedented federal partnership with business interests promoted this economic boom. To the applause of those progressives who welcomed the rise of public authority, the government took over the railroads, and it established new agencies such as the Food Administration, the Fuel Administration, the Shipping Board, and the Emergency Fleet Administration, to supervise and assist the private sector. However, antitrust progressives deplored some of these wartime developments. In particular, they opposed the activities of Bernard Baruch, a canny financier whom Wilson named as head of a new War Industries Board. The WIB established an entente between government and big business that featured informal price fixing and collusive bidding. "The great difficulty about the distribution of work among smaller manufacturers," Baruch said frankly, "is the difficulty of getting the work done. . . . We have been trying to meet this situation by endeavoring to get a number of firms to consolidate." Baruch's partiality toward mergers assisted the long-range movement toward economic concentration. In this way the war helped kill one of the major goals of many progressives—breaking up (or at least firmly policing) the trusts. For these reformers, the domestic legacy of war was ambiguous indeed.

Wilson's favoritism toward big business showed that he had moved far from the New Freedom of 1912 and that the election of Warren G. Harding in 1920, instead of signifying a return to "normalcy," meant a continuation of federal policy already well entrenched. But the fact of business profits did not mean that large corporations overwhelmed their smaller competitors. On the contrary, big business sometimes lost ground—as was the case in steel and automobiles—to newer, more efficient companies that profited from access to the vast wartime markets. The partnership between government and business also stopped short of developing into highly centralized or compulsory public planning. Both Bernard Baruch and Herbert Hoover, the efficient engineer who headed the Food Administration during the war, prided themselves on employing voluntaristic methods to secure cooperation. Still, the potential of agencies like the Food Administration and the War Industries Board seemed to confirm the faith of some progressives in governmental planning. As early as 1917 this faith led Americans to accept such "advancements" as psychological placement and standardized testing of soldiers. In 1933 it led New Dealers to believe that the experience of government-business cooperation in World War I offered an answer to ending the depression.

The burdens of war

Almost from the beginning, however, it was clear that the war could not eradicate the prewar divisions of American society. Prosperity and economic growth, though enlarging the size of the pie, stimulated the expectations of pressure groups, who scrambled for their shares. Reflecting these pressures, Congress resisted price control and allocation of food until August 1917, four months after the American declaration of war. Arguments erupted constantly over such sensitive questions as profiteering, the location of army bases, the staffing of wartime agencies, outbreaks of pneumonia and meningitis in training camps, and shortages of coal that caused misery among the urban poor in the winter of 1917–18. Contrary to a common impression, Wilson's problems with Congress did not begin during the struggle for the League of Nations in 1919: they were commonplace during the war.

Easily the most important domestic issue was inflation. Food prices more than doubled between 1915 and 1920, as did the cost of living in general. Though wages overall kept pace, many individual workers quickly felt the strain. So did some pressure groups, for government policies favored some groups over others. The southern bloc in Congress successfully resisted attempts to impose price controls on cotton, and clothing tripled in cost during those years. Spokesmen for the wheat farmers, whose prices were partially controlled, resented this favoritism and turned on the Democratic party in the election of 1918. Other citizens complained bitterly about the increased income taxes imposed to support the war: "progressivism" in this guise lost its appeal when people had to pay for it. For all these reasons Wilson faced a Republican Congress when he looked for help with the Versailles Treaty in 1919.

The war years also intensified racial tensions. The economic boom combined with the ravages of the boll weevil in the South to spur mass migrations of blacks to northern cities. Thousands more were lured north as strikebreakers. Southern whites were so troubled by this exodus of cheap labor that they resorted to intimidation and violence. One mob in Mississippi even derailed a train to keep the blacks at home. (In the 1950s and 1960s, when agriculture was more mechanized, southern whites were happy to see the blacks go.) Northerners, alarmed by the "invasion" of 1915–19, retaliated by imposing discriminatory residential requirements very different from housing patterns in southern towns and cities, where whites and blacks tended to live in close proximity to each other. Northerners also resorted to intimidation. Mobs beat blacks who strayed out of their neighborhoods and stoned families who dared to move into white areas of the cities. Racial tensions erupted in riots in twenty-six cities during 1917, including frightening confrontations in East St. Louis, Omaha, and Houston. The riot in East St. Louis left thirty-nine blacks dead, victims of shooting, lynching, and burning by white mobs.

Headlines in the *Chicago Tribune,* July 1919.

These racial confrontations intensified after the war. Black soldiers deeply resented the segregation and discrimination they had encountered in the service. Those who had been abroad returned with memories of more benevolent racial patterns. The result was rising black militancy, especially in northern cities. Alarmed, whites put blacks in their place, sometimes by resorting to violence. The result was another spate of racial disturbances in 1919. These were not "commodity riots," such as those in the 1960s, in which blacks destroyed property. Rather, the riots of 1919 were "communal." Touched off by acts of white violence or persecution, they featured retaliatory violence by blacks followed by white counterattacks. Fighting, accordingly, disrupted white as well as black neighborhoods. The worst of these riots, in Chicago, exploded in four days of fighting that killed twenty-three blacks and fifteen whites before troops stepped in. These race riots shattered hopes for racial harmony and proved that the war had failed utterly to promote racial justice at home.

THE WAR AND CIVIL LIBERTIES

An especially frightening domestic result of the war was the encouragement it gave to superpatriotic conformity. Deluded before 1917 into thinking they could stay neutral, Americans suddenly found themselves engaged in total war. To keep the doubters quiet, Wilson explained that the war would end all wars, that it was a cause of righteousness against evil. Those who dissented, by definition, enlisted on the side of hell.

Such idealistic rhetoric was intended to appeal to people's nobler instincts. But other Americans used the passions of war to unleash campaigns of hatred against the enemy and against "slackers" at home. Others saw in the passions of war the chance to exclude aliens and to preserve older ways of life. The *Saturday Evening Post* demanded the removal of "the scum of the melting pot" from American life, and a popular wartime song warned:

> If you don't like your Uncle Sammy,
> Then go back to your home o'er the sea,
> To the land from where you came,
> Whatever be its name;
> But don't be ungrateful to me!
> If you don't like the stars in Old Glory,
> If you don't like the Red, White, and Blue,
> Then don't act like the cur in the story,
> Don't bite the hand that's feeding you.

Wilson and his aides encouraged this intolerance. "This is a People's war, " he proclaimed. "Woe be to the man or group of men that seeks to stand in our way in this high day of resolution when every principle we hold dearest is to be vindicated and made secure for the salvation of nations." Wilson established the first full-blown propaganda agency in the history of the United States, the Committee on Public Information. Headed by the dynamic progressive journalist George Creel, the agency employed able writers, reformers, and intellectuals to sell bonds, popularize war aims, and encourage voluntary censorship by newspapermen. CPI volunteers distributed some five million "Red White and Blue" pamphlets, and gave one million patriotic "Four Minute Speeches" during the war. They also encouraged thought control and witch hunts. Free speech in wartime was simply out of the question, Creel quoted Wilson as saying. "There could be no such thing . . . it was insanity."

The CPI was an ominous sign of what a purposeful central government could do. But its function was to exhort, not to punish, so in June 1917 Congress approved the Espionage Act, which permitted the government to ban newspapers and magazines from the mails and which subjected people convicted of obstructing the draft to fines of $10,000 and twenty years in prison. Postmaster Albert S. Burleson immediately interpreted the law to mean that he could censor any printed matter that "interfered with the success of any Federal loan . . . or caused insubordination, disloyalty, mutiny, or refusal of duty in the military or naval service, or obstructed the recruiting, draft, or enlistment services . . . or otherwise embarrassed or hampered the government." Within a month he denied mailing privileges to fifteen major publications, including the *Masses,* a socialist publication. In 1918 Burleson received even greater authority through the Sedition Act, which authorized the prosecution of people who attempted to obstruct the draft or who used "disloyal, profane, scurrilous, or abusive language" concerning the government, the Constitution, the armed forces, or the flag. More than 2,100 people were prosecuted under these statutes.

Conscientious objectors were one target of this campaign for "right thinking." Secretary of War Newton Baker tried to be fair by offering them the possibility of alternative noncombatant service. In fact, America's treatment of c.o.'s—some 65,000 of 24 million registrants for selective service—was more enlightened than that in other belligerent nations during the war. But only members of pacifistic religious groups, perhaps 5,000 of the 21,000 conscientious objectors inducted, qualified for alternative service; others faced prison sentences ranging up to twenty-five years. An estimated 400 c.o.'s went to jail, including Roger Baldwin, head of the National Civil Liberties Bureau, which was the precursor of the American Civil Liberties Union. According to Attorney General Thomas Gregory, Baldwin was "one of a very dangerous class of persons . . . an active pacifist . . . not leading a moral life."

C.o.'s, however, were hardly numerous or threatening. Radicals and antiwar socialists, who struck many Americans as subversive, were a much more inviting target. Among socialist leaders prosecuted under the Espionage Act were Victor

Berger of Milwaukee, who was twice denied his seat in Congress as a result of his conviction; Debs, who urged people to "resist militarism, wherever found" (and who spent thirty-two months in prison); and Rose Pastor Stokes, whose mistake was to assert that "no government which is *for* the profiteers can also be *for* the people, and I am for the people." The government also pounced on the IWW, confiscating its office materials (including typewriters and petty cash) and arresting 165 of its most militant members. When Baldwin interceded, Secretary of War Baker urged Wilson to drop the cases. But the President replied that the IWW was "certainly . . . worthy of being suppressed." Most of the leaders were sentenced to terms ranging up to twenty-five years.

In applying such laws men like Gregory occasionally had to confront organizations such as the American Union Against Militarism, a group of pacifists who included Norman Thomas and Jane Addams. (Its symbol for militarism was a dinosaur named "Jingo" and labeled "All Armor Plate—No Brains.") But Gregory safely challenged them, for he could rely on the greatest of all pressures for conformity: an aroused public. Superpatriots organized groups with names like the American Defense Society, the Sedition Slammers, the Terrible Threateners, the American Vigilante Patrol, and the Boy Spies of America. Vigilantes in Bisbee, Arizona, rounded up 1,200 striking copper miners in July 1917 and dumped them in the New Mexico desert. An Indiana jury took two minutes to acquit a man who shot and killed a man who had yelled, "To hell with the United States." A motion picture producer was sentenced to ten years in jail for his movie *The Spirit of '76,* because it allegedly aroused hostility to Britain, America's wartime ally. And almost all things German, from sauerkraut (renamed Liberty Cabbage) to Beethoven to hamburger (renamed Salisbury Steak), were banned or criticized during the war.

In 1919 the Supreme Court catered to such illiberal feelings by sustaining the wartime statutes. The Espionage Act, Justice Holmes held in *Schenck* v. *U. S.* (1919), was justified. "The question in every case," he said, "is whether the words are used in such circumstances and are of such a nature as to create a clear and present danger that they will bring about the substantial evils that Congress has a right to prevent. It is a question of proximity and degree. When a nation is at war many things that might be said in time of peace are such a hindrance to its effort that their utterance will not be endured so long as men fight." The First Amendment, he added, was not absolute, for "the most stringent protection of free speech would not protect a man falsely shouting fire in a theater and causing a panic." In the case of *Abrams* v. *U. S.* (1919) Holmes took a slightly more libertarian view by defending a "free trade in ideas." The "best test of truth," he said, "is the power of the thought to get itself accepted in the competition of the market. . . . we should be eternally vigilant against attempts to check the aggression of opinions that we loathe." But Holmes was outvoted, and the Abrams decision sustained the Sedition Act, seven to two. In reaching such decisions the Court placed its view of the national interest ahead of the Bill of Rights. In doing so it was reflecting the majority view of the time.

An intriguing question remains: Why, with little organized opposition to war, did this crusade against dissent occur? One reason is that the centralized state now possessed the resources to abet such a crusade. Another is that the mass nature of the war—the first total conflict in modern history—caused all peoples involved in it (in Europe as well as in America) to become harsh and even hysterical about "slackers" and "seditionists." From this perspective America was no more repressive than other belligerents. And a third is that the war served as the occasion for "purifying" American life, for restoring to it some of the social harmony that was presumed to have existed in the "good old days" of 1914, or 1890. When these broad forces came together in 1917, they threw the nation into one of the periodic panics of intolerance that have stained American history.

The Red scare

If peace in November 1918 had brought stability to America, these excesses might have faded from sight. But wartime inflation left many American workers dissatisfied, and they determined to strike for recognition and for better pay. In January 1919, 35,000 shipyard workers in Seattle went on strike. When laborers in other trades joined them, it appeared for a few days that a general strike of 100,000 people might paralyze the region. A series of labor disturbances followed in the spring and summer, culminating that September in a strike of Boston police officers, which Wilson called a "crime against civilization." Some 350,000 steel workers went on strike a few days later, shortly to be emulated by coal miners.

This rash of strikes terrified people of property, who were quick to blame aliens, radicals, and communists. In March 1919 the Bolsheviks, who had secured power in Russia in 1917, proclaimed their dedication to worldwide revolution, and communist revolts erupted in eastern Europe. A few weeks later, homemade bombs, timed to go off on May Day, began appearing in the mail of people like John D. Rockefeller, Postmaster General Burleson, and Mayor Ole Hanson, the Red-baiting mayor of Seattle. On June 2, bombs exploded in eight American cities at the same hour, and one damaged the home of Attorney General A. Mitchell Palmer. And in September 1919 radicals appeared to complete preparations for revolution by forming the American Communist and Communist Labor parties. Though divided along ethnic lines (most of the foreign-language speakers joined the CP), both groups were endorsed by the Third International. Their estimated combined membership totaled between 25,000 and 40,000 people.

These events created a Red scare of unprecedented proportions. Chief of Staff General Leonard Wood demanded the deportation of Bolsheviks in "ships of stone with sails of lead, with the wrath of God for a breeze and with hell for their first port." Billy Sunday added, "If I had my way with these ornery, wild-eyed Socialists and IWW's, I would stand them up before a firing squad and save some space on our ships." The Harvard *Crimson* damned the British Socialist Harold Laski, who had defended the striking policemen, as "Laski de Lenin" and "Ivan Itchykoff," Bolshevik seducer of Radcliffe girls.

Elbert Gary, head of U.S. Steel, meanwhile refused even to recognize the steel union. "The contemplated progress of trade unions if successful," he declared, "would be to secure the control of the shops, then of the general management of business, then of capital, and finally of government." Throughout the lengthy and bitter steel strike of late 1919, he determined not only to reject labor's demands (one of which asked for the end of the twelve-hour day then standard for steel workers), but also to break the militant union and to establish the unlimited power of management in labor disputes. With vast financial resources (including huge reserves from wartime profits) and with the support of police in many steel towns, he could afford to hold out, and by early 1920 he had won. The crushing of the steel strike, one of the most dramatic in American history, marked a decisive point in the annals of labor-management relations and left unions weak and demoralized during the 1920s.

Attorney General Palmer, an ardent Wilsonian progressive, was at the same time bringing the full force of the federal government into play against presumed radicals. In August he called on J. Edgar Hoover to run a new antiradical division of the Department of Justice. In November Palmer staged raids on radicals in twelve cities, arresting 250 people and recommending 39 for deportation. In December he deported 249 aliens, including Emma Goldman, to Russia. Few of the 249 were Bolsheviks, many were philosophical anarchists opposed to violence, and most had no criminal records. And on one night in January 1920 Palmer's men arrested more than 4,000 alleged Communists throughout the nation. Many of the suspects were kept for days in jail without charges, kicked about or denied food by police, or held incommunicado. The raids were justified, Palmer said, because the country was infested with the "moral perverts and hysterical neurasthenic women who abound in communism."

The Red scare then subsided almost as quickly as it had started. Cooler heads prevailed in the Department of Labor, which intervened to stem the deportations at 600. Most of the arrested Communists, having committed no crimes, were released. By midsummer of 1920 labor agitation had been quashed and American radicals had become badly split into warring factions of Socialists, Communists, and Communist Laborites. Most important, Americans relaxed as the threat of Bolshevism in Europe subsided. By September Americans refused to respond to Palmer's proclamation of impending revolution even after a wagonload of bombs exploded on Wall Street, killing 33 and injuring 200 more. Warren Harding, no radical, pronounced the epitaph: "too much has been said about Bolshevism in America."

The cruel treatment of dissenters during 1919 and 1920 marked the most widespread attack on civil liberties in American history. It showed that supposedly progressive public officials, like the people at large, lacked an elementary understanding of the Bill of Rights or of the distinctions between socialism, anarchism, and communism. It resulted in 1920 in the arrest for murder of Nicola Sacco and Bartolomeo Vanzetti, Italian aliens and anarchists whose ultimately unsuccessful battles to escape execution were depressing reminders of the excesses of intolerance. And it profoundly discouraged people who might otherwise have worked for reform. Frederic Howe, the immigration commissioner who fought against deportations, confessed that his faith in public power as an agent of reform had been misplaced. "My attitude toward the state," he wrote later, "was changed as a result of these experiences. I have never been able to bring it back. I became distrustful of the state. It seemed to want to hurt people; it showed no concern for innocence; it aggrandized itself and protected its power by unscrupulous means. It was not my America, it was something else."

The fight for the League of Nations

During much of the time that Gary, Palmer, and Hoover were stamping out dissenters at home, Wilson was either at Paris negotiating the peace treaty, on speaking tours defending it, or—after suffering a severe stroke in October 1919—trying vainly to restore his health. But the Senate ultimately refused to approve the treaty. The struggle over ratification showed that neither Wilson nor the Senate as yet had a realistic sense of America's role in world affairs.

Prospects for the "peace without victory" that Wilson desired appeared excellent in late 1918. "We expected," Lewis Mumford recalled, "that at the end of that fierce and rancorous conflict, in which other men had been engaged for four searing years, the beat of angels' wings would at once be heard in the sky, and concord and brotherly love would immediately settle over the earth." When Wilson went to France after the armistice, he was acclaimed by the European people. One woman wrote, "Wilson, you have given back the father to his home, the ploughman to his field. . . . You have saved our children. Through you evil is punished. Wilson. Wilson. Glory to you, who, like Jesus, have said: Peace on Earth and Good Will to Men."

From the start, however, Wilson made tactical errors that did his cause no good in the Senate. The first of these occurred before the midterm elections of 1918 when he asked voters to return loyal Democratic majorities. This ill-advised appeal, which Colonel House regarded as a "needless venture," backfired when the voters sent a Republican majority, angry at Wilson's slurs on their patriotism, to Washington. Wilson then compounded his error by naming himself to head the five-man peace delegation and by including no senators or prominent Republicans on it. California Senator Hiram Johnson observed, "In selecting himself as the head of the American delegates to the conference, President Wilson has named himself five times."

THE PEACE CONFERENCE AT VERSAILLES

Wilson also faced an almost herculean task at Versailles, for Prime Minister David Lloyd George of Britain and Premier Georges Clemenceau of France were determined to secure economic and territorial aims that they had secretly mapped out early in the war. The Italian delegate, Vittorio Orlando, was concerned primarily with gaining disputed territory for his country. The Japanese exerted pressure for further concessions in East Asia. None of these nations welcomed Wilson's Fourteen Points, which called for "open covenants of peace, openly arrived at," freedom of the seas, free trade, the self-determination of peoples, just territorial settlements, fair treatment of Germany, and a "general association of nations." "God gave us the Ten Commandments," Clemenceau said, "and we broke them. Wilson gave us the Fourteen Points. We shall see."

The specter of the Soviet Union further haunted the conference. Wilson loathed Bolshevism and refused to recognize the Soviet Union—or to admit it to deliberations at Paris. The Allies, furious at Soviet withdrawal from the war against Germany in February 1918, had sent in troops to reopen the eastern front. When the conference opened, these troops were helping Russian counterrevolutionaries try to overthrow the Bolshevik regime.

Wilson refused to engage American troops in the Russian civil war. But he did decide in the summer of 1918 to dispatch 5,000 men to northern Russia and 10,000 more to Vladivostok near Manchuria. His motives for sending the expeditions were honorable: to stop supplies from reaching the Germans, to help stranded Czech soldiers get out of Siberia, and to warn the Japanese against overrunning Manchu-

Lloyd George, Clemenceau, and Wilson at the Palace of Versailles.

ria. But Wilson did not remove the American troops from northern Russia until June 1919 and from the Manchurian area until April 1920. During this time they did nothing to keep supplies from Germany, to evacuate the Czechs, who regrouped and fought the Bolsheviks, or to deter the Japanese, who stayed in Manchuria until 1922. Understandably, the Soviets distrusted Wilson's motives, the more so because he refused to deal with them in Paris. The gulf that developed between Russia and the West cast a measure of unreality over the whole proceedings at the conference.

In the face of so many obstacles Wilson did well to salvage parts of his Fourteen Points. With the help of Lloyd George he successfully resisted the French demand for the cession of the Saar basin. Instead, the Saarland was to be turned over to the League of Nations for fifteen years, after which a plebiscite was to determine its fate. The President also resisted Japanese demands to annex the Shantung peninsula, and Italian claims on the port of Fiume. He secured his primary goal: incorporation of the League of Nations as part of the treaty itself.

These were considerable accomplishments—more than any other statesman could have achieved. But they inevitably fell short of the goals he had outlined during and after the war. The treaty said nothing about freedom of the seas or the lowering of international economic barriers. It violated the principle of self-determination by turning over land in South Tyrol to Italy, by granting Japan economic rights in the Shantung peninsula, by placing Germans under Polish rule in Silesia, and by handing over German colonies to the British, French, and Japanese. (Wil-

Wilson's Fourteen Points.

1. *"Open covenants of peace, openly arrived at" and an end to secret diplomacy.*
2. *"Absolute freedom of navigation upon the seas . . . alike in peace and in war."*
3. *"The removal, so far as possible, of all economic barriers" to free trade.*
4. *Reduction of armaments "to the lowest point consistent with domestic safety."*
5. *An "absolutely impartial adjustment of all colonial claims" giving equal weight to the interests of the colonial populations and "the equitable claims" of the imperial governments.*
6. *"The evacuation of all Russian territory" and cooperation to allow Russia "the independent determination of her own political development and national policy and assure her of a sincere welcome into the society of free nations under institutions of her own choosing."*
7. *German evacuation of Belgium and restoration of full sovereignty.*
8. *"All French territory should be freed" and Alsace-Lorraine, taken by Prussia in 1871, should be returned to France.*
9. *"A readjustment of the frontiers of Italy . . . along clearly recognizable lines of nationality."*
10. *Autonomy for the peoples of Austria-Hungary.*
11. *Evacuation of Rumania, Montenegro, and Serbia; international guarantee of the political and economic independence of the Balkan states; and Serbian access to the sea.*
12. *Autonomy for the subject nationalities within the Turkish Empire and free passage through the Dardanelles for ships of all nations.*
13. *An independent Poland with "free and secure access to the sea."*
14. *"A general association of nations."*

son, Clemenceau remarked cynically, "talked like Jesus Christ, but acted like Lloyd George.") The treaty also saddled Germany with the "war guilt" clause and with reparations that ultimately amounted to $33 billion. These, with many domestic problems, made the embittered Germans receptive to Hitler in 1933.

THE VERSAILLES TREATY AND THE SENATE

Well before the conference completed its work in late June, it was obvious that Wilson would have to fight hard for Senate approval. On March 5, thirty-nine senators or senators-elect—six more than the one-third necessary to defeat the treaty—signed a so-called Round Robin that declared that "the constitution of the League of Nations in the form now proposed to the peace conference should not be accepted by the United States." The League, these senators agreed, should not be discussed until the terms of peace were agreed upon. Wilson tried to meet such objections by getting the delegates at Versailles to recognize the Monroe Doctrine and by inserting an "escape" clause permitting member nations to withdraw from

The changing face of Europe after the Treaty of Versailles, 1919.

the League in two years, but he refused to separate the League from the terms of peace. "When that treaty comes back," he declared in New York, "gentlemen on this side will find the covenant not only in it, but so many threads of the treaty tied to the covenant that you cannot dissect the covenant from the treaty without destroying the whole vital structure."

By the summer of 1919, when the struggle for ratification began, the nature of his opposition in the Senate was ominous. His most extreme foes in the Senate were approximately eighteen "irreconcilables" who opposed the treaty in any form. Some of these, like La Follette, were consistent isolationists who objected to American participation in the League with the same passion they had shown against American involvement in 1917. Some, like Johnson, were vehement partisans as well as isolationists. Other irreconcilables, like Medill McCormick of Illinois and James Reed of Missouri, were racist xenophobes. The League, McCormick said, would create a superstate with "economical Japanese operating our street railways . . . Hindoo janitors in our offices and apartments . . . Chinese craftsmen driving rivets, joining timbers, laying bricks in the construction of our buildings." Reed added, "Think of submitting questions involving the very life of the United States to a tribunal on which a nigger from Liberia, a nigger from Honduras, a nigger from India, and an unlettered gentleman from Siam, each have votes equal to the great United States of America."

The strongest tie binding the irreconcilables was a nationalistic insistence that America retain a free hand. Most of them opposed joining the League because they feared even a moral obligation to engage in collective security. In particular they opposed Article X, which said that members would "undertake to respect and to preserve as against external aggression the territorial integrity and existing political independence of all Members of the League." This clause did not require member states to send troops, but only to "advise upon the means by which this obligation shall be fulfilled." As Wilson explained, Article X was a "moral not a legal obligation." But the irreconcilables, like many other senators, were unconvinced. Their leader, William Borah of Idaho, explained that he could support American intervention abroad, but only on his own terms. "I may be willing to help my neighbor, though he be improvident or unfortunate," Borah declared,

> but I do not necessarily want him as a business partner. I may be willing to give liberally of my means, of my council and advice, even of my strength or blood, to protect his family from attack or injustice, but I do not want him placed in a position where he may decide for me when and how I shall act or to what extent I shall make sacrifice.

A larger and more dangerous group of senatorial opponents were the "strong reservationists" led by Henry Cabot Lodge, a Harvard-educated patrician who chaired the Foreign Relations Committee. Standing between La Follette and Wilson, Lodge opposed both isolationism and utopian internationalism. Instead, like Roosevelt, he believed that American influence must be exerted to maintain a stable balance of power, and he favored guaranteeing French security against the Germans. Lodge's nationalistic stance perhaps came closer than Wilson's expansive internationalism to expressing the views, however vague, of Americans in 1919.

But Lodge was a partisan politician who despised the President. "I never expected to hate anyone with the hatred I feel toward Wilson," he had written Roosevelt in 1915. The phraseology of the League Covenant, he sneered, "might get by at Princeton, but certainly not at Harvard." Holding such views, Lodge misused his key position. Instead of educating Americans to their world responsibilities, he engaged in vituperative partisan debate, packed the Foreign Relations Committee with Wilson's enemies, delayed while foes of the League coalesced, and suggested so many "reservations" that Wilson concluded that Lodge could never be placated. The most controversial of these reservations stated that America was not obliged to act under Article X unless Congress approved in each case.

Lodge's delaying tactics permitted a wide variety of opponents of the treaty to express their positions. Among these were supernationalists. "There's no nation in

Europe worth a tinker's damn," one complained. "The whole continent is rotten, or tyrannical." More worrisome to Wilson was the stand of people who might otherwise have supported him. These included pacifists like Jane Addams, who feared that the League sanctioned the possibility of war, and progressive purists who could not stomach the compromises he had made at Paris. "THIS IS NOT PEACE," the *New Republic* proclaimed. "The peace cannot last. America should withdraw from all commitments which would impair her freedom of action." Wilson also faced growing hostility from ethnic groups. German-Americans resented the war-guilt and reparations clauses, Italian-Americans the failure of Italy to gain Fiume, and Irish-Americans the inability of the delegates to do anything for Ireland.

The defection of so many people who had formed his electoral coalition in 1916—peace workers, progressive reformers, ethnic leaders—greatly weakened his chances of persuading fence-sitting senators that he had the masses with him. The treaty gave these people another powerful reason—as if inflation, high taxes, and the Red scare had not been enough—to distrust their government and the Democratic party in particular. In this sense the League issue was a final blow to the chances for a stable reform coalition in the 1920s and to the unity of the Democratic party.

The pragmatic Wilson of 1913 might have tried to meet such opponents halfway. But the Wilson of 1919 was too sure of his vision to listen to reason. These opponents, he said in February, were "blind and little provincial people" who reminded him of a "man with a head that is not a head but is just a knot providentially put there to keep him from ravelling out." When Colonel House urged him in June to be conciliatory, Wilson replied, "House, I have found that one can never get anything in this life that is worthwhile without fighting for it." When his Senate floor leader later warned him to compromise, he shot back, "anyone who opposes me in that I'll crush."

When his foes persisted, Wilson set out in September on a cross-country speaking tour. At first his speeches met with mixed reactions, but by the time he reached California he attracted cheering crowds. His schedule, however, was grueling, and the sixty-three-year-old president grew exhausted as he turned east. After giving a moving speech in Pueblo, he collapsed in pain and had to cancel the rest of the tour. Four days later his wife found him unconscious on the floor. He had suffered a stroke, which paralyzed the left side of his body. Though his mind still functioned, the stroke left him too weak to carry out his duties properly. During that time— October 1919 to March 1921—the business of the country was in the hands of his wife and a few close aides.

Shortly after Wilson suffered his stroke, Lodge reported out the treaty with fourteen reservations. Most Democratic supporters of the League seemed willing to accept Lodge's version. Most of the reservations made little difference, they pointed out, and even the modification of Article X was acceptable to the European powers. Had Wilson followed their advice, it is possible that the treaty would have passed. But Wilson did not compromise. Lodge's reservations, he insisted, re-

Breakers Ahead

moved America's all-important moral obligation. Obstinately, he instructed his Democratic followers to hold firm, and on November 19 they joined the irreconcilables in voting against the treaty with reservations, fifty-five to thirty-nine. A vote on the treaty without reservations then fell before a coalition of Republicans and irreconcilables, fifty-three to thirty-eight. These votes showed that 85 percent of the senators accepted the League in some form, and moderates worked toward compromise. When the Senate voted again on March 19, 1920, twenty-one Democrats broke ranks to accept Lodge's reservations, and the treaty in that form secured a majority of forty-nine to thirty-five. But that was seven short of the two-thirds necessary for ratification. Of the thirty-five, twenty-three were Democrats who followed their stricken leader to the end.

Many forces killed the treaty, including xenophobia, ethnic loyalties, isolationism, and party politics. But Wilson deserves much, perhaps most, of the responsibility. As early as the spring of 1917 he had known of the Allied secret treaties, yet he sent American soldiers to fight in Europe without demanding that the treaties be repudiated. He then persisted in proclaiming that the war was being fought for noble ends. When the Versailles treaty proved otherwise, many Americans were shocked. Others, worried about social problems at home, were simply apathetic about the treaty. Even so, Wilson could probably have secured most of the basic terms had he been willing to compromise. That he did not was his personal tragedy.

Was it a tragedy for the world? Probably not. The resistance to Article X, to say nothing of subsequent isolationism in the 1920s and 1930s, suggested that Americans—League or no League—were not yet ready to assume the burdens of collective security. Neither, as later events were to demonstrate, were the English or the French: nationalism was not unique to America, but dominant throughout the Atlantic world before 1939. In this sense the Senate's rejection of the League was neither tragic nor surprising. Rather, it reflected the national selfishness that the war of 1914–18 had intensified throughout the West.

It was a fact, nonetheless, that the partisan debate accompanying the Senate's rejection of the treaty was unenlightening. Isolationists and irreconcilables oscillated between xenophobia and the unrealistic belief that America could ignore European developments. Wilsonians proclaimed unrealistically sweeping visions, preached a *Pax Americana* to the rest of the world, and went out of their way to offend the Soviet Union. Men like Lodge, who appreciated the nation's expanded role in world affairs, spent more of their time conjuring up frightening consequences of collective security than they did in defining the country's international responsibilities. For all these reasons the nature of America's basic strategic interests received little thoughtful discussion. The Great War, it appeared, had taught Americans only that they should stay out of the next one.

Disillusionment with the war and withdrawal

The experience of war meant to a few intellectuals that idealism was just so much cant, that "progressivism" had been a ghastly mistake. Young people, F. Scott Fitzgerald wrote, had "grown up to find all the Gods dead, all wars fought, all faiths in man shaken." John Dos Passos best described this disillusion with idealism—and with the State—that some intellectuals felt in the aftermath of war.

"Where his chest ought to have been," he wrote of the Unknown Soldier,

> they pinned the Congressional Medal, the D.S.C., the Medaille Militaire, the Belgian
> Croix de Guerre, the Italian gold medal, the Vitutea Militara sent by Queen Marie of
> Rumania, the Czechoslovak war cross, the Virtuti Militari of the Poles, a wreath sent
> by Hamilton Fish, Jr., of New York, and a little wampum presented by a deputation of
> Arizona redskins in warpaint and feathers. All the Washingtonians brought flowers.
> Woodrow Wilson brought a bouquet of poppies.

Few Americans were as bitter as these intellectuals. Indeed, men like Dos
Passos were alienated in part because they sensed that thousands of fellow citizens,
who had much innocence yet to lose, were not listening to them. By mid-1920 most
people simply seemed glad that the heroics were over, that the "Reds" had been
suppressed, that the nation was free of foreign entanglements. They were angry
about inflation, weary of big government, ready for what Wilson's popular successor, Warren G. Harding, called "normalcy." It was time to live again as in the supposedly harmonious days before the divisive and dissatisfying experience of war.

Suggestions for reading

A starting point for military history and the effect of war at home is Russell Weigley, *The
American Way of War** (1973). A helpful survey is Harold and Margaret Sprout, *The Rise of
American Naval Power, 1776–1910* (1939). See also Elting Morison, *Admiral Sims and the
Modern American Navy* (1942); and John G. Clifford, *The Citizen Soldiers* (1972), on pre-
paredness. Useful books on attitudes are Charles Chatfield, *For Peace and Justice** (1971),
which discusses pacifism 1914–41; and Warren Kuehl, *Seeking World Order: The United
States and World Organization to 1920* (1969).

Domestic life is well covered in David Kennedy, *Over Here: The First World War and
American Society* (1980). See also Robert D. Cuff, *The War Industries Board: Business-
Government Relations During World War I* (1973); S. W. Livermore, *Politics Is Adjourned*
(1968), on politics, 1916–18; and Daniel R. Beaver, *Newton D. Baker and the American
War Effort, 1917–1919* (1966). George T. Blakey's *Historians on the Home Front* (1970)
shows how wartime passions influenced scholars. The books by Kerr and Urofsky mentioned
in the bibliography for chapter 3 cover regulatory policies.

The effect of the war on civil liberties is the subject of several good studies. Among them
are William Preston, *Aliens and Dissenters: Federal Suppression of Radicals, 1903–1933**
(1963); H. C. Peterson and Gilbert Fite, *Opponents of War, 1917–1918* (1957); Zechariah
Chafee, *Free Speech in the United States* (1941); and Paul L. Murphy, *World War I and the
Origins of Civil Liberties in the United States* (1979). See also Donald Johnson, *Challenge to
American Freedoms** (1963), the story of the birth and growth of the American Civil Liberties Union; and Joan M. Jensen, *The Price of Vigilance* (1968), which deals with super-
patriotism during the war.

For developments in the period 1918–21 the most important studies are William Tuttle,
Jr., *Race Riot: Chicago in the Red Summer of 1919** (1970); David Brody, *Labor in Crisis:
The Steel Strike of 1919** (1965); Stanley Coben, *A. Mitchell Palmer* (1963); Robert K.
Murray, *The Red Scare** (1955); and Burl Noggle, *Into the Twenties: The United States from*

Armistice to Normalcy (1974). See also Kenneth Jackson, *The Ku Klux Klan in the City, 1915–1930** (1967); G. L. Joughin and E. M. Morgan, *The Legacy of Sacco-Vanzetti* (1948); and Arthur Waskow, *From Race Riot to Sit-in, 1919 and the 1960's** (1966).

Foreign policy and peacemaking, 1917–21, are covered in Thomas Bailey, *Woodrow Wilson and the Lost Peace** (1944), and *Woodrow Wilson and the Great Betrayal** (1945); N. Gordon Levin, Jr., *Woodrow Wilson and World Politics** (1968); John Garraty, *Henry Cabot Lodge* (1953); Arno J. Mayer, *Politics and Diplomacy of Peacemaking: Containment and Counterrevolution at Versailles, 1918–1919* (1967); John M. Thompson, *Russia, Bolshevism, and the Versailles Peace* (1966); and Ralph A. Stone, *The Irreconcilables: The Fight Against the League of Nations** (1970). See also H. R. Rudin, *Armistice* (1944); George F. Kennan, *The Decision to Intervene: Prelude to Allied Intervention in the Bolshevik Revolution* (1956); and Paul Birdsall, *Versailles Twenty Years After* (1941).

6

The 1920s:
the modern decade

"The aspirin age," the "Roaring Twenties," the "era of excess," a time of "Fords, flappers, and fanatics"—these are but a few of the labels pasted on the decade of the 1920s in America. All of them portray a hedonistic populace staggering out of World War I and plunging toward the crash of 1929. The 1920s, it appeared later, were a frenzied interlude between war and depression.

A more accurate way of describing the period is to stress its modernity. While many people hoped to preserve "normalcy," to reaffirm values of the past, millions of others welcomed the first recognizably "modern" decade in American history. The major forces of twentieth-century life—technological change, bureaucratization, the growth of the middle class, suburbanization—accelerated so rapidly that people thought they were living in a capitalist utopia, or—as it was then called—a "new era."

Avenues to the future

ECONOMIC PROGRESS

The most striking manifestation of the "new era" was economic growth. The per capita GNP in current prices jumped from an average of $719 in the prosperous years of 1917–21 to $857 in 1929. Between 1922 and 1929 the national income

Economic growth, 1919–29,
compared to select years before and after this period

	NATIONAL PRODUCT AND INCOME (In billions of current dollars)			PER CAPITA INCOME (In current dollars)
	GNP	NATIONAL INCOME	PERSONAL INCOME	
1900[a]	17.3	14.6	14.3	231
1914[a]	40.3	34.8	33.7	408
1919	78.9	70.2	65.0	755
1920	88.9	79.1	73.4	835
1921	74.0	64.0	62.1	682
1922	74.0	63.1	62.0	672
1923	86.1	74.3	71.5	769
1924	87.6	75.2	73.2	768
1925	91.3	78.2	75.0	788
1926	97.7	83.7	79.5	832
1927	96.3	81.7	79.6	809
1928	98.2	82.8	79.8	815
1929	104.4	87.8	85.8	857
1933	56.0	40.2	47.2	446
1945	213.6	181.2	171.2	1,526
1978	2,107.6	1,703.8	1,452	7,810

SOURCE: Adapted from *Historical Statistics of the United States*, p. 139
[a]Annual averages, 1897–1901, 1912–16

rose from $63.1 billion to $87.8 billion. This was an annual increase in real dollars of 5.6 percent, a rate unmatched for any comparable length of time in modern American history.

At the root of this growth were steady technological advances, many of which had been developed or perfected in the war period. The years between 1917 and 1929 witnessed major industrial breakthroughs, such as the manufacture of continuous strip-sheets in steel and tin, and of machines to make glass tubing, which completely replaced glass blowers by 1925. New machines revolutionizing the construction industry included power shovels, belt and bucket conveyors, pneumatic tools, concrete mixers, and dump trucks. The communications industries developed automatic switchboards, dial phones, and teletype machines. Innovations in chemicals and synthetics included rayon, bakelite, and cellophane. George Washington Carver, a pioneer in developing farm products for industrial use, found ways of turning peanuts into axle grease and shaving lotion, and sweet potatoes into shoe blacking, library paste, and synthetic tapioca.

Ordinary people profited from these technological and economic changes. Real wages for regularly employed factory workers increased by about 11 percent during the decade. Hours for manufacturing workers decreased from 47.4 per week in

1920 to 42.1 in 1930. The long-range trend toward enlarging the middle class accelerated. During the 1920s the number of farm workers decreased (from 11.4 to 10.3 million), and the number of manual and service workers increased only gradually—from 20.3 to 24 million. White-collar workers, meanwhile, jumped in numbers from 10.5 to 14.3 million, or from 22 percent to almost 30 percent of the labor force of 50 million. For the first time in American history a significant percentage of the population was getting the money, and the time, to buy and to enjoy consumer goods.

Reflecting this potential, consumer goods industries boomed as never before. Moderately priced products included radios, wristwatches, cigarette lighters, hand cameras, linoleum, vacuum cleaners, and washing machines. Nine of the top twenty industries in 1930 specialized in consumer goods, compared to one in 1920. The availability of such creature comforts to common people astounded contemporaries. America, the French observer André Siegfried wrote in 1927, "has again become a new world. . . . The American people are now creating on a vast scale an entirely new social structure which bears only a superficial resemblance to the European. It may even be a new age."

Siegfried and others were especially impressed by the revolution in communications—film, radio, and the telephone—in the 1920s. As early as 1915, when *Birth of a Nation* grossed $18 million, the film industry revealed its amazing potential, and in the 1920s movies all but displaced camp meetings and political rallies as essential mass entertainment for Americans. By 1926 every large American city had deluxe theatres seating 2,500 to 4,000 people. By 1930 the average weekly attendance was 90 million. In 1929, the first year of "talkies," revenues reached $720 million, almost three times the amount spent on books and ten times the sum expended on spectator sports.

The growth of radio was equally spectacular. As late as August 1921, KDKA, which had pioneered in news coverage by broadcasting the 1920 election returns, was the only licensed radio station in America. By the end of 1922, there were 508 stations, and 3 million Americans owned sets. In 1926 the National Broadcasting Company began consolidating the stations into a network, and in 1927 the Federal Radio Commission was established to police the industry. By then radio was big business. In 1929 Americans spent $850 million for sets and parts, advertisers paid $10,000 an hour for a national hookup, and NBC's gross income was $150 million.

Easily the most dramatic development was the automobile. Like the movies, cars were prewar innovations: almost 2.5 million were registered in 1915. Yet they did not spread to the masses until after the war, when installment plans and technological advances in production (Ford turned out a Model T every ten seconds by 1925) cut prices to new lows. (Model Ts cost $290 in 1925, roughly the equivalent of three months' wages for factory workers, who were offered all sorts of inducements to buy on time.) In 1920 Americans registered 9.2 million motor vehicles, in 1925 they registered 20 million, and in 1930 they registered 26.7 million, or more than two for every three American families.

The impact of the automobile on the American economy was enormous. The car industry in the 1920s absorbed 20 percent of America's steel, 80 percent of its rubber, and 75 percent of its glass. It built oil into a major industry and ultimately

During the decade, the number of roadside stands climbed into the thousands.

created the fateful dependence of the economy on petroleum. Automobiles made possible real estate booms in heretofore distant Florida and California, facilitated the development of consolidated schools, worked wonders for highways (and road builders), prompted the sprawl of roadside restaurants, motels, and service stations, and assured the decline of railroads. Automobiles were to the 1920s what the railroads had been to the nineteenth century—a major force affecting the entire economy.

Automobiles also abetted the rapid growth of metropolitan and suburban development. As early as 1920 the census reported that the number of Americans who lived in places with 100,000 or more people exceeded the number who resided in all smaller cities. Assisted by the automobile, this metropolitan sprawl accelerated in the 1920s: by 1930, 8 million more Americans lived in places with populations exceeding 250,000 than had ten years earlier. The migration to the cities revealed the restlessness of millions of small-town and rural Americans. It also exposed one especially clear manifestation of the decade: heightened tension between metropolitan and rural styles of life.

These striking economic and demographic changes inevitably provoked sharp controversy and social conflict. Critics of these changes, while conceding some benefits from technological development, argued that machines threw hundreds of thousands of people out of work every year in the 1920s. Plays like Eugene O'Neill's *Dynamo* and Elmer Rice's *Adding Machine,* as well as the Czech term "robot," expressed widespread doubts about scientific management and the effects of the assembly line.

Other critics complained that the "modernization" of economic life accelerated corporate concentration. Before 1910, 200 firms had made cars, but by 1930 the Big Three, Ford, General Motors, and Chrysler, with 83 percent of sales, had already established their oligopolistic control. In the same year CBS and NBC, with control over more than 150 transmitters, dominated the field of broadcasting. Chain stores grew spectacularly, with A&P expanding from 400 outlets in 1912 to 15,500 in 1932, and Drug, Incorporated, a holding company, controlling Vick Chemical, Bayer Aspirin, and Bristol-Myers as well as 10,000 Rexall and 706 Liggetts stores. Adolf Berle, Jr., and Gardiner Means, whose *Modern Corporation and Private Property* (1932) treated the subject authoritatively, estimated that of the 300,000 nonfinancial corporations in America approximately 200 had half of the nation's corporate wealth. These top corporations made such unprecedented profits between 1915 and 1929 that they were able to do much of their own financing, without recourse to investment bankers like Morgan. If the turn of the century had been the golden age of the financier, the 1920s saw the triumph of the oligopolistic, self-sustaining corporation.

The 1920s were also an age of managers. In order to expand, the corporations issued thousands of shares of new stock to many more people. The Pennsylvania Railroad, for instance, had 65,000 stockholders in 1910 and 207,000 in 1930. This growth meant that ownership in many corporations was a little more widely dispersed: the twenty largest stockholders of U. S. Steel, AT&T, and the Pennsylvania Railroad owned but 5.1 percent, 4 percent, and 2.7 percent, respectively, of the outstanding shares. The dispersal of ownership did not take place in all companies: Ford, for instance, still kept control of his operations within the family. Nor did it mean that small shareholders ran big companies. It did mean, however, that day-to-day operation of the larger corporations fell into the hands of managers and highly skilled professionals. The "managerial revolution" directed by the "organization man" was occurring in the 1920s.

Characteristic of the "new" executive was Alfred P. Sloan, the efficient chief of General Motors after 1923. Unlike William C. ("Billy") Durant, his colorful predecessor, Sloan recognized that "General Motors had become too big to be a one-man show." It had to be decentralized, with expert managers placed in control of functionally organized divisions. Modern methods of marketing helped Sloan understand also that car buyers yearned for new and distinctive models every year—the unchanging black Model T was too commonplace. So GM relied shrewdly, profitably on planned obsolescence. By the end of the decade GM had surpassed Ford as the nation's leading automobile manufacturer. Such is progress.

Another corporate manifestation of the 1920s was a booming advertising business, whose earnings jumped from $1.3 billion in 1915 to $3.4 billion in 1929. Such advertising encouraged a sixfold increase in installment buying—to $7 billion—during the same period. Advertising, Calvin Coolidge proclaimed in 1926, "is the most potent influence in adopting and changing the habits and modes of life, affecting what we eat, what we wear, and the work and play of the whole nation."

Many advertisers drew on the cheerless behaviorist theories of John B. Watson, a psychologist and successful advertising consultant. Like Freud, Watson rejected the nineteenth-century notion that physiological processes governed man. He also shared Freud's assumption that psychology, properly applied, could ameliorate the human condition. But unlike Freud, who emphasized instinctual drives within the individual, Watson stressed the power of the environment. Control the environment, he said, and human beings could be shaped at will. "Give me a dozen healthy infants," he proclaimed, ". . . and my own specified world to bring them up in, and I'll guarantee to take any one at random and train him to become any specialist I might select, doctor, lawyer, artist, merchant, chief, and yes, even beggarman and thief, regardless of his talents, tendencies, abilities, vocations and race of his ancestor."

Advertising leaders, like proponents of scientific management, readily applied this view of manipulable humanity. Kenneth Goode and Harford Powel, Jr., wrote in *What About Advertising?* (1927) that the advertiser "must recognize the extreme mental stupidity of the vast majority of his audience, and their pathetic lack of adult mental nourishment. The average normal American, broadly speaking, celebrates his twenty-fifth birthday by shutting up shop mentally and refusing to accept any new ideas. He has then the literate capacity of a twelve- or fourteen-year-old." It followed, Goode and Powel concluded, that people would believe almost anything that kept them up with the Joneses.

This was also the message of Edward Bernays, a nephew of Freud who worked for the Creel Committee in 1918 and who became America's leading public relations man in the 1920s. "The counsel in public relations," he said, "not only knows what news value is, but knowing it, he is in a position to *make news happen*. He is a creator of events." Opinions, he insisted, were developed by groups, not by individuals. The job of the advertiser, the PR man, indeed the political leader, was to appeal to group leaders. Sell new fashions by getting society women to model them. Promote cigarettes by showing debutantes smoking. Sell baseball equipment by telling the people Babe Ruth uses it. And forget progressive nonsense about educating the common people. The American system, he said, "must be a leadership democratically administered by the intelligent minority who know how to regiment and guide the masses."

Traditionalists viewing these innovations lamented the passing of prewar social patterns. Cars, they complained, were hurting church attendance, taking entertainment from the home to the roadhouse, and inducing young people—roaming far in search of opportunity—to neglect the old folks at home. They grumbled especially that cars, movies, and advertising were intensifying materialism and conspicuous consumption and sharpening marital tensions. Wives, they complained, were now suing for divorce because their husbands would not let them go alone to the movies. More commonly, wives broke up marriages on the ground that their husbands were not earning enough to support a comfortable "life style."

"The blue dusk of the deluxe house," one critic wrote, "has dissolved the Puritan strictures that . . . [people] had absorbed as children." Ford, Lincoln Steffens explained in 1931, "was a prophet without words, a reformer without politics, a legislator, a statesman, a radical. I understand why the Bolshevik leaders of Russia admired, coveted, and studied him."

This centralizing tendency of the automobile may be only a passing phase; sets in the other direction are almost equally prominent. "Our daughters [eighteen and fifteen] don't use our car much because they are always with somebody else in their car when we go out motoring," lamented one business class mother. And another said, "The two older children [eighteen and sixteen] never go out when the family motors. They always have something else on." "In the nineties we were all much more together," said another wife. "People brought chairs and cushions out of the house and sat on the lawn evenings. We rolled out a strip of carpet and put cushions on the porch step to take care of the unlimited overflow of neighbors that dropped by. We'd sit out so all evening. The younger couples perhaps would wander off for half an hour to get a soda but come back to join in the informal singing or listen while somebody strummed a mandolin or guitar." "What on earth do you want me to do? Just sit around home all evening!" retorted a popular high school girl of today when her father discouraged her going out motoring for the evening with a young blade in a rakish car waiting at the curb. The fact that 348 boys and 382 girls in the three upper years of the high school placed "use of the automobile" fifth and fourth respectively in a list of twelve possible sources of disagreement between them and their parents suggests that this may be an increasing decentralizing agent.

The baneful effect of the car, as seen by Robert and Helen Lynd in *Middletown* (1929).

Steffens' point was well taken, for the economic and technological changes of the 1920s probably did affect attitudes and behavior. People who went to the movies, who read the ads (or heard them on the radio), and who rode about in cars were bombarded by the variety of the American scene. They discovered what others possessed: bathtubs, up-to-date fashions, household gadgets, matching furniture, and, of course, the latest styles in cars. In the process they were groomed for the most "subversive" change of all: the growth of consumerism and leisure orientation. As one writer observed sadly, Americans were beginning to prefer indulgence to adventure; their travels were marked "not by the whitening bones of pioneers" but "by discarded inner tubes and heaps of salmon cans."

Most important, middle-class Americans were readier than ever to believe in the positive virtues of economic progress. Growth, prosperity, and material possessions, they hoped, could blur ethnic and class distinctions and give everyone a stake in the system. Herbert Hoover, in accepting the GOP presidential nomination of 1928, remarked that "we in America are nearer to the financial triumph over poverty than ever before in the history of our land. The poorhouse is vanishing from among us." Like *Time* magazine, which named Walter Chrysler its "man of the year" in 1929, Hoover was dazzled by technological change and by modern, functional methods of business administration. Millions of Americans welcomed the "new era" that was dawning in the land.

The new era

CHANGING SEXUAL MORES

Another manifestation of modernity in the 1920s was the spread of permissive attitudes toward sex. It was the decade of the "flapper," of flesh-colored stockings, of "petting," of more frequent divorce (100,000 in 1914, 205,000 in 1929), of daring modern dancers like Isadora Duncan, and of Cecil B. De Mille movies with titles like *Old Wives for New, Women and Lovers,* and *Golden Bed.* Where the reigning goddesses of the screen before World War I had been chaste Pollyannas, those of the 1920s, like Clara Bow (the "it" girl), were sex symbols.

Other products of popular culture reinforced this emphasis on sexuality. Songs carried titles like "Hot Lips," "I Need Lovin'," and "Burning Kisses." The "Little Blue Books," five- to ten-cent precursors of paperbacks, featured titles like *Love Letters of a Portuguese Nun, Sex Life in Greece and Rome,* and *One of Cleopatra's Nights.* Popular magazines for men, or "pulps," included *Breezy Stories, Jim Jam Jems,* and *French Stories.* The sociologists Robert and Helen Lynd discovered that the high-school girls of Muncie, Indiana, wore cosmetics (called "paint"), that they checked their corsets in ladies rooms at dances, and that they seemed to spend more time riding around (and parking) with boys than sitting at home.

Sigmund Freud, though a respectable Victorian, became a culture hero to the advocates of the new permissiveness. Distorting his theories, these Americans believed that he advocated the casting off of all sexual restraints. The vogue for Freud led some writers to produce facile psychoanalytic explications of history and literature, and it served to provide justifications for many rebels, including proponents of free schools, surrealist painting, and modern dance. Used as a kind of secular evangelism, Freudianism expressed the progressive faith that human beings have an inalienable right to happiness and the potential to ameliorate their lives.

A daring debutante, ready for a swim, tries a cigarette on the beach at Southampton, Long Island.

You can read essays by American intellectuals to prove . . . that a man can live with three wives; that it is sorrowful to be a Lesbian; that mental telepathy really works . . . that sex should be free . . . that when a bridge breaks, God is Love; that Poe was sexually impotent; that Henry Clay was oversexed; that Carrie Nation Bryan . . . and Buffalo Bill . . . suffered from an Oedipus complex; that Martha Washington suffered from one also; . . . that Henry VIII made British history because he was oversexed; that Abe Lincoln made the Civil War because he was undersexed; that history is sex; that America is sex, that sex is soul; that soul is all; Oom, oom, pfui!

Mike Gold, a Marxist literary critic, ridicules the emphasis on sex.

Taking a different tack, a few feminists campaigned for women's liberation. Thus Dorothy Dix, counsel to the young, advised girls to "learn a trade," for "economic independence is the only independence in the world. As long as you must look to another for your food and clothes you are a slave to that person." Dorothy Canfield Fisher's *The Home-Maker* (1924) made the same point by portraying a woman who was successful in business while her husband did the housework and raised the children. Fisher, like Charlotte Gilman a generation earlier, kept alive the vision of women finding themselves through work.

Sexual permissiveness amused a few urbane observers. "If all the girls at the Yale prom were laid end to end," Dorothy Parker wrote, "I wouldn't be surprised." Others, however, reacted rigidly, exposing yet another division in American society in the 1920s. Self-proclaimed arbiters of public taste imposed censorship on magazines and books and tried—with limited success—to set standards of decency in films. An Ohio legislator introduced a bill outlawing any "garment which unduly displays or accentuates the lines of the female figure" and prescribing that "no female over fourteen years of age shall wear a skirt which does not reach to that part of the foot known as the instep." The town of Norphelt, Arkansas, actually passed a statute that read:

Sect. 1. Hereafter it shall be unlawful for any man or woman, male or female, to be guilty of committing sexual intercourse between themselves at any place within the corporate limits of said town. . . .

Sect. 3. Section one of this ordinance shall not apply to married persons as between themselves and their husband and wife, unless of a grossly improper and lascivious nature.

Sexual behavior was indeed changing, at least among the urban middle classes. Though few women embraced sexual license, they did chafe under Victorian prudishness and the double standard. They also popularized the idea that sex was "fun." These attitudes reflected changes in behavior later documented by Dr. Alfred C. Kinsey and other researchers. Their findings, based on retrospective interviews of middle-class people, revealed that premarital sex was more common in the 1910s and 1920s than previously. To this degree the guardians of conventional morality were correct in complaining that sexual mores were becoming more permissive.

> *One fact is evident, that whether or not they [college students] pet, they hesitate to have anyone believe that they do not. It is distinctly the mores of the time to be as ardently sought after, and as not too priggish to respond. As one girl said—'I don't care particularly to be kissed by some of the fellows I know, but I'd let them do it any time rather than think I wouldn't dare. As a matter of fact, there are lots of fellows I don't kiss. It's the very young kids that never miss a chance.'*

The role of peer group pressure in the youth "rebellion" of the 1920s. From a student, 1926.

As usual, however, the alarmists exaggerated: the movements for sexual freedom and economic equality were contained in reach and scope. In Muncie, for instance, talk of sex was taboo in the schoolroom. Movies featured the wife returning to her husband and the "jazz baby" marrying the small-town boy next door. The wide appeal of *Gentlemen Prefer Blondes,* a popular novel and play of mid-decade, suggested that men—and many women—still expected women to be "feminine" (beautiful, zany, and not too bright), not career women or threats to male domination in the public sphere of things.

Moreover, talk of sexual liberation was essentially a sideshow; it did not much affect the daily lives of most American women in the 1920s. Though a few young, upper-middle-class women in the cities talked about throwing off the older conventions—they were the "flappers"—most women adhered to more traditional attitudes concerning their "place." Few middle-class women, in fact, sought steady employment outside the home. Though contraception and new, time-saving household appliances gave them potentially more freedom to enter the job market, most women concentrated on managing the home and on using spare time at women's clubs or in charitable service. Their daughters, far from taking to the streets against sexual discrimination, were more likely to prepare for careers as mothers and housewives.

Millions of immigrant women and their daughters also clung to cultural traditions that placed men firmly in control of the family and relegated women to the domestic scene. The vast majority of working-class women—immigrants, blacks, and old-stock whites—were busy raising families or clinging to low-skill jobs that continued to command lower pay than those of similarly qualified men.

Poorer women such as these had little time for advanced theories about sex, or for feminist programs calling for equal treatment. The Women's Trade Union League, the National Consumers League, and the League of Women Voters, which tried to make women a force in the economy and in politics, languished in the 1920s. The Women's Party, the home of feminists who sought full social and economic equality for women, attracted only a handful of supporters. A key reason for this weakness of feminism in the 1920s was the continuing power of traditional male attitudes asserting the superiority of men in the public sphere. Confronted with such attitudes, most American women concentrated on making ends meet or on setting aside money to purchase the alluring conveniences that offered some release from household drudgery. This consumerism also weakened the appeal of

After the war, most working women were forced to return to traditional jobs, as typists, secretaries, and the like.

feminism. For women as well as men, it offered some release from the burdens faced by working-class families in the "new era." It was a way of muting class and ethnic tensions in an age of rapid social change.

EDUCATION AND SOCIAL SCIENCE

The 1920s also witnessed important long-range developments in education. First among these was an acceleration in attendance at all levels. Thanks to compulsory attendance laws, to urbanization, and to such basic developments as the school bus, enrollments in high schools rose from 1.3 million in 1915 to 4.4 million in 1930. The number of high school graduates increased from 240,000 (12 percent of seventeen-year-olds) to 667,000 (29 percent). College enrollments during the same period rose from 404,000 (5.5 percent of eighteen- to twenty-year-olds) to 1.1 million (12.5 percent).

This growth was necessarily gradual; 71 percent of American young people, mainly from the lower classes, failed to graduate from high school as late as 1930. Still, the rise in attendance and in per pupil spending for public schools (up from $33.55 in 1915 to $86.70 in 1930) was unprecedented. Schools, like much in American life during the 1920s, were becoming efficient, consolidated, businesslike institutions that abetted and reflected the middle-class development of society.

The same practical considerations led to the growth of college enrollments during the decade. Continued support for federal aid to agricultural extension work and vocational training showed that many people conceived of colleges as places for the inculcation of occupational skills that earlier generations had received, if at all, through apprenticeship.

Nevertheless, alert students, especially the growing numbers of graduate students who were to do much of the university teaching for the next three decades, could not avoid being exposed to new approaches to learning. Many social scientists stressed the need for quantitative and empirical work. The Lynds, whose *Middletown* (1929) remains a classic of empirical sociology, pioneered in team observation of everyday life. The ''Chicago School'' of sociology, led by Robert Park, insisted that environment was a key to human behavior and undertook ecological investigations of the city. ''Legal realists'' like Jerome Frank extended sociological jurisprudence to the point where they argued that judges, utilizing their own observations, could establish new law. One of these legal realists, William O. Douglas, later became a leading liberal judge of the Supreme Court.

Economists and anthropologists also insisted on the necessity for careful empirical study. Rexford Tugwell, Wesley Mitchell, and others made detailed analyses of institutions. Cultural anthropologists ranged still farther afield. Melville Herskovits embarked on his influential studies of African survivals in the New World. And Ruth Benedict and Margaret Mead carried the emphasis on empirical study to its logical conclusion by observing American Indians and South Sea Islanders in their native settings. Their findings challenged monistic explanations of behavior or immutable laws of human conduct.

These empirical approaches hardly swept the older views from the American scene. Moreover, the new social scientists sometimes made questionable claims. Still, they left an important legacy, for many of these social scientists believed in the practical utility of research. Tugwell, a follower of Veblen, believed that empirical studies could assist planners and social reformers. Frank and Douglas conceived of legal realism as an antidote to conservative jurisprudence. Political scientists pioneered in setting up such organizations as the National Institute of Public Administration (1921) and the Social Science Research Council (1924). With many other enthusiastic social scientists they assisted the Committee on Social Trends (1929), President Hoover's attempt to gather data for policy makers. These people, far from succumbing to postwar disillusionment, believed that they could improve and rationalize American life, that a ''new era'' was at hand, and that they could bring the progressive movement to full flower. Their students carried this faith in experimentalism and empiricism into the New Deal.

Under the machine and science, the love of beauty, the sense of mystery, and the motive of compassion—sources of aesthetics, religion, and humanism— are not destroyed. They remain essential parts of our nature. But the conditions under which they must operate, the channels they must take, the potentialities of their action are all changed. These ancient forces will become powerful in the modern age just in the proportion that men and women accept the inevitability of science and the machine, understand the nature of the civilization in which they must work, and turn their faces resolutely to the future.

Charles Beard, 1928, offers a characteristically optimistic view of the "new era."

Affirmations of the past

FOREIGN POLICY

These manifestations of the "new era"—economic progress, technological innovation, changes in sexual behavior, educational change—were powerful and ultimately triumphant. But they were not pervasive enough to destroy older patterns of life and thought. In many areas of activity—foreign policy, politics, small-town life, religion, ethnic and race relations—many Americans affirmed the past. The persistence of these affirmations accounted for considerable cultural conflict throughout the decade.

Statistics on American economic interests abroad in the 1920s suggest the nation's irreversible involvement in world affairs. Exports increased from $2.4 billion in 1914 to $7.03 billion fifteen years later, while private investment overseas jumped during the same period from $3.5 billion to $17.2 billion. The 1920s witnessed the steady Americanization of the Western economy. In Latin America, where American investments literally skyrocketed from $800 million in 1914 to $5.4 billion in 1929, military and political intervention continued to follow the dollar. By 1924 the United States was directing the finances of ten nations in the Caribbean area.

This growing economic influence did not lead Americans to commit themselves politically outside the Western Hemisphere. On the contrary, rejection of the League of Nations was but one manifestation of the broader nationalism and xenophobia intensified by the frustrations of World War I. Other manifestations were America's insistence that the hard-pressed Allies pay their "war debts"; the refusal to guarantee French security; and the passage of the high-tariff Fordney-McCumber Act in 1922.

America's military unreadiness was another sign of the country's aversion to foreign entanglements. Demobilization began as soon as the war ended, and the armed services received little funding for the next twenty years. General Billy Mitchell, a flamboyant advocate of aircraft development, proved in 1923 that planes could sink battleships, but the naval brass learned little from this lesson. Throughout the period the army and navy devoted little attention to air power, to amphibious warfare, or to aircraft carriers. Distressed, Mitchell blamed plane crashes in 1925 on the "incompetency, the criminal negligence, and the almost treasonable administration of our national defense by the Navy and War Departments." Court-martialed, he was convicted and resigned from the service. The aftermath of World War I, unlike the years following World War II, was no time for forceful generals or for military expansion.

The Washington Conference, called in 1921–22 by Secretary of State Charles Evans Hughes, clearly revealed American reluctance to get involved beyond the Western Hemisphere. The conferees successfully negotiated three agreements. One, the nine-power treaty, was a pious reaffirmation of the unenforceable Open Door policy regarding China. The second, the five-power treaty, marked one of the few times in world history that large nations agreed to scrap existing naval vessels. They accepted ratios for tonnage of battleships (smaller vessels were not covered) of approximately 5:5:3 for the United States, Great Britain, and Japan, and 1.75 for France and Italy. The four-power treaty (United States, Britain, France, and Japan) declared that the four signatories were to consult whenever peace in East Asia was threatened.

When Japan attacked Pearl Harbor in 1941, some writers blamed the five-power treaty for weakening American defenses in the Pacific. To a limited extent they were right, for the agreement forbade the United States to fortify Guam or the Philippines. But in 1922 the five-power agreement seemed satisfactory to the United States, which now matched Great Britain, long the world's primary naval power. It was received poorly by many Japanese, who dubbed the ratio Rolls Royce, Rolls Royce, Ford. Moreover, the parsimony of subsequent Congresses concerning defense budgets revealed that America would have limited its naval building even in the absence of a treaty. The United States was relatively weak in the western Pacific by 1941 because Japan increased its naval construction in the 1930s and because Congress, reflecting public opinion, consistently refused to authorize a fleet even to treaty strength. America did not back up the Open Door with arms.

The different congressional responses to the treaties also exposed American fears of overcommitment. The five-power and nine-power treaties—affirmations of honorable intent—swept through easily. But the four-power agreement encountered stiff congressional opposition from men like Borah and Johnson, who tacked on a reservation stating that the treaty involved no "commitment to armed force, no alliance, and no obligation to join in any defense." Reassured, the treaty's foes withdrew their opposition, but their strong stand against even the hint of sustained international cooperation reflected widespread feeling at the time. For most Americans in the 1920s foreign affairs were peripheral concerns. It was all right for policy makers to assist in the search for overseas markets and to intervene in the Caribbean, but they should otherwise stay clear of commitments abroad. The contrast between the dramatic growth in American economic involvement overseas and the return to prewar visions of international policy provided one of the many instances of the decade's uncertain, transitional character.

POLITICS

American politics in the 1920s revealed a similar contrast between modernizing forces and older attitudes. On the one hand, the exigencies of the war, along with the steady bureaucratization of life, had greatly increased the size and scope of government at all levels. Federal employees numbered 395,000 in 1915 and 600,000 in 1930 (in 1918 they had peaked at 850,000). Federal spending, only $760,000 in 1915 ($7.60 per capita), leaped to $18.5 billion in 1919 ($170 per capita) and then leveled off at around $3 billion ($24.00 per capita) annually in the 1920s—more than three times what it had been before the war. State and local spending, only $2.2 billion in 1913, increased just as rapidly, to approximately $8 billion on the eve of the crash of 1929. These statistics suggest the obvious: that government was steadily more capable of influencing the lives of citizens.

Government was also increasingly able to respond to the group orientation of American life. Like large corporations, which were restructuring themselves along functional lines, governments at all levels were slowly developing the specialized skills necessary to preside over a complex society. The federal government, for instance, adopted an executive budget in 1921 in place of the previous "system" that had left spending to the discretion of congressional appropriations committees. (The budget act, however, limited executive freedom by denying presidents the power of item vetoes and by setting up the Comptroller General's office independent of the White House.) Executive agencies like Herbert Hoover's Commerce Department branched far afield to provide businessmen with data and advice. The Agriculture Department developed close ties with powerful pressure groups representing agribusiness. The Federal Trade Commission (FTC), dominated by conservatives, worked purposefully to assist business groups. The idea of resource management also spread within the government, which created a network of migratory bird sanctuaries and gave aid for flood control projects in the Mississippi River valley. Though conservatives overrode efforts to provide public funds for the development of the Tennessee Valley region, they approved plans for Boulder Dam, the first federally sponsored large-scale, multipurpose river basin development. The influence of such agencies reveals that the 1920s—far from being a time of governmental retrenchment or of total break with a "progressive" past—broadened the public sector.

As many reformers realized, however, these structural developments in government did much more to assist well-organized groups than they did to advance the cause of social reform. Settlement house workers, labor leaders, advocates of civil rights, spokesmen for ethnic groups, and feminists all complained bitterly about the response of government during the years between 1919 and 1933. Progressives, while active and energetic in the 1920s, rarely succeeded in forming the political coalitions necessary for success in state legislatures or in Congress. In this sense, it is broadly accurate to say that the decade witnessed a low point—compared to 1900–18 or 1933–38—in the history of progressive reform in twentieth-century America.

One obstacle to reform was clear to all: conservative Republican control of Congress and of the White House under presidents Warren Harding and Calvin Coolidge from 1921 to 1929. Harding was flexible and agreeable. Unlike Wilson, he was popular with Congress, and, contrary to myth, he had ideas of his own. He approved the new budget system, appointed able subordinates like Hughes and Hoover, advocated a federal antilynching law, called for a Department of Public Welfare, intervened to end the twelve-hour day in steel mills, and approved legislation assisting farm cooperatives and liberalizing farm credit. His record in the field of civil liberties contrasted sharply with the repressiveness of Wilson—Harding not only let Eugene Debs out of jail but received him in the White House. His tolerant approach brought Americans a necessary respite from postwar acrimony. When he died, people wept as if they had lost another President Lincoln.

As early as the 1920 campaign, however, Harding was the target for all sorts of gibes about his cliché-ridden oratory. "Keep Warren at home," one cynical Republican boss advised. "Don't let him make any speeches. If he goes out on tour somebody's sure to ask him questions and Warren's just the sort of damned fool who will try to answer them." A Democratic critic sniped that Harding's speeches "left the impression of an army of pompous phrases moving over the landscape in search of an idea." H. L. Mencken concluded that Harding "writes the worst English that I have ever encountered. It reminds me of a string of wet sponges; it reminds me of tattered washing on the line; it reminds me of stale bean soup, of college yells, of dogs barking idiotically through endless nights. It is so bad that a sort of grandeur creeps through it."

Harding's record as president caused few of these critics to change their minds. Though he appointed Hughes and Hoover, he also frequented the company of party hacks, hustlers, and low life. Other appointments appalled reformers. He named Harry Daugherty, a crass party functionary, as Attorney General; former President Taft as chief justice of the Court; James J. Davis, Supreme Dictator and Reorganizer of the Loyal Order of Moose, to Labor; and Albert Fall, a reactionary senator from New Mexico, to Interior. Daugherty was a vigorous foe of labor who secured a crushing injunction against the striking United Mine Workers in 1922. Taft presided over a conservative Supreme Court that struck down a national child labor law, held minimum wages for women unconstitutional (Taft dissenting), and increased restrictions on boycotts and picketing. The role of the Court, he said, was "to prevent the Bolsheviki from getting control." Davis was an uninformed, complacent official who complained of reformers, "I never knew a theorist who wasn't a sick man." And Fall accepted bribes for turning over valuable mineral reserves to private interests. The resulting Teapot Dome scandal failed to implicate the President directly; compared to the Watergate affair of the 1970s, it was a limited misuse of power. But with other lesser scandals it revealed the corruption of many of Harding's friends.

Harding's choice as treasury secretary was the multimillionaire industrialist Andrew Mellon. As head of the Treasury until 1932, he was the high priest of business-oriented welfare capitalism—the J. P. Morgan of the "new era." Like Morgan, he was certain that big business could curb "wasteful" competition and promote the capitalist utopia. It followed, Mellon believed, that government must intervene to assist people who had capital. Throughout the 1920s he recommended cuts in taxes on the rich and on corporations. These policies widened the gulf between rich and poor, concentrated capital in relatively few hands, and did nothing to broaden consuming power, so necessary to sustain prosperity.

Harding's successor, Calvin Coolidge, was a sour and nasty man who took pleasure in playing practical jokes on aides and secret service men. At the same time, however, he was fastidious, plain, and upright—so reassuring a figure that Americans easily forgave his party the scandals under Harding. "Silent Cal," as he was called, had been awarded the vice-presidential nomination in part because people thought that as governor of Massachusetts he had helped settle the Boston police strike of 1919 (actually he had procrastinated and made matters worse), and in part because he seemed a champion of business values. "Governor Coolidge," the Chicago *Tribune* had said approvingly, "is a red, white, and blue American by birth."

Left, Warren Harding's 1920 campaign button. Above, the Coolidge thimble, which was designed to attract women voters in the 1924 election.

The *Tribune* saw Coolidge correctly. He was a safe, do-little president. In part because of metabolic need, he had to have a nap every afternoon as well as ten hours of sleep a night; he averaged four hours of work per day. He believed firmly in the Jeffersonian dictum: that government is best which governs least. "I am for economy and after that for more economy," he said. "Public administrators," he added, "would get along better if they would restrain the impulse to butt in or be dragged into trouble. They should remain silent until an issue is reduced to its lowest terms, until it boils down to something like a moral issue." No twentieth-century American president was a more consistent advocate of small government.

This faith was part of a philosophy that enshrined business values. Where Harding was an amiable moderate who wished to please everyone, Coolidge was a dedicated champion of corporations. "The business of America is business," he said. "The man who builds a factory builds a temple. The man who works there, worships there." Mellon had been an ornament in Harding's cabinet; he was Coolidge's major adviser. Coolidge opposed labor unions, tried (unsuccessfully) to turn over government-owned facilities in the Tennessee Valley to private interests, appointed business spokesmen to regulatory agencies like the FTC, and twice vetoed bills aimed at providing government assistance to agriculture. "Farmers," he said characteristically, "have never made much money. I don't believe we can do much about that."

Coolidge's dour expression, his hatchet face, his taciturn nature, and his legendary laziness made him easy to ridicule. Alice Roosevelt Longworth, Theodore Roosevelt's daughter, sniped that he had been weaned on a pickle. Dorothy Parker, informed that Coolidge had died, responded, "How could they tell?" Mencken complained that "Nero fiddled but Coolidge only snored. . . . He had no ideas and was only a nuisance."

Wise observers realized, however, that the business orientation of men like Coolidge commanded considerable public support. Indeed, the dominant feature of national politics in the 1920s was the majority status of the conservative wing of the Republican party. Representing the most powerful interest groups in American life—large commercial farmers, bankers, businessmen, even some top leaders of the AFL—the GOP successfully claimed to voters that it was the party of prosperity. Largely for these reasons Republicans won easily in presidential elections at the time.

In 1920 Harding beat Governor James M. Cox of Ohio, his Democratic opponent, 16,143,407 to 9,130,328; in 1924 Coolidge trounced John W. Davis, 15,718,211 to 8,385,283; and in 1928 Hoover beat Alfred E. Smith, the progressive governor of New York, 21,391,993 to 15,016,169. These were by far the largest margins in modern American history to that date. Moreover, left-wing third parties trailed badly. Debs received only 919,799 votes in 1920 and Norman Thomas, the Socialist candidate in 1928, only 267,835. La Follette, running as a Progressive with socialist and (lukewarm) union backing, received 4,831,289 votes (17 percent) in 1924, an impressive showing when contrasted to that of other third-party candidates in American history. But he carried only one state (Wisconsin). These statistics are a little deceptive, for voters did maintain a core of determined, if beleaguered, progressives in Congress. These activists, including new urban liberals like Robert Wagner of New York, showed that progressive ideas were not dead in the 1920s. But the activists remained frustrated by the essential weakness of the Left in that decade. People were content to "keep cool with Coolidge."

The presidential elections suggest other aspects of the political universe of the 1920s. One aspect was the division within the Democratic party. Disillusion with Wilson had shattered the urban-ethnic and agrarian coalition the party had been developing before 1918. Amid the wreckage two broad groups struggled for supremacy. One, strong in rural regions of the West and South, rallied behind men like William G. McAdoo, Wilson's secretary of the treasury and son-in-law. The other, which represented the urban ethnic groups, followed Alfred E. Smith, governor of New York, for much of the decade. In the 1924 convention the two men battled for 103 ballots before giving way to the compromise choice of Davis, a Wall Street lawyer whom no one much wanted. Until this urban-rural and sectional gap was bridged—by Franklin D. Roosevelt in the 1930s—the Democrats remained too divided to agree on national policy.

Another characteristic of the political scene in the 1920s was the continuing low turnout of eligible voters, especially before 1928. Many forces contributed to this poor showing, including stringent voter-registration laws and the absence of a meaningful two-party system in many states. Another reason, which feminists and idealists deplored, was light voting by women, again before 1928. Whatever the causes, the low turnouts carried on patterns that had developed in the progressive era. In this regard, as in many other areas of life, the 1920s witnessed considerable continuity with the past.

The politics of the 1920s revealed also that voters appeared to care little for debate about "big" national issues—trust busting, tariffs, conservation—that had animated many progressives. They concerned themselves instead about ethno-cultural questions like immigration restriction, the Ku Klux Klan, fundamentalism, and prohibition. These ethno-cultural divisions had intensified during the war and the Red scare, leaving many ethnic voters unhappy with both parties by 1920. Because of apathy or alienation, millions of them did not vote for the next seven years.

In 1928 they finally found their champion in Smith, an Irish Catholic, an out-spoken foe of prohibition, and a product of New York City's Lower East Side. Though Smith lost badly, he carried America's top twelve cities by 38,000 votes, and he brought millions of ethnics and many women to the polls for the first time. His total vote almost doubled that of Davis, and it was only slightly less than that received by Harding in 1920 or Coolidge in 1924. In strengthening the affiliation of urban dwellers and ethnics with his party he began the historic realignment toward Democratic dominance that the depression and the New Deal completed. This movement of ethnic voters (though not of blacks, who remained Republican, dis-franchised, or apathetic) was perhaps the most significant long-range political de-velopment of the decade. It exposed again, however, the continuing cleavage be-tween the country and the city, between old- and new-stock Americans, and

Election, 1928

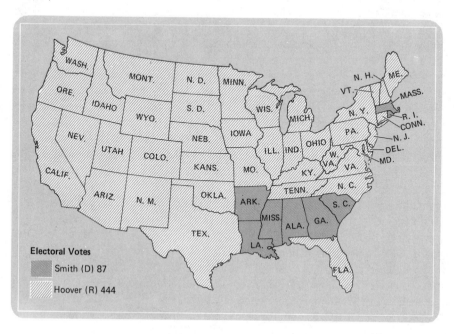

Electoral Votes

Smith (D) 87

Hoover (R) 444

especially between Protestants and Catholics. Millions, in fact, swelled Hoover's vote in order to register their profound unease with what Smith symbolized. No event of the era more clearly revealed the cultural conflict that had been developing for decades.

BABBITTRY SUPREME

Bohemians, expatriates, alienated intellectuals; F. Scott Fitzgerald, Sinclair Lewis, H. L. Mencken: these were among the critics of America in the 1920s. Their writings appeared to suggest that the decade witnessed a fierce and ultimately successful assault on traditional values.

Their critique, hardly subtle, aimed first at small-town mindlessness and materialism. Mencken dismissed the South as the "Sahara of the Bozart," a "gargantuan paradise of the fourth-rate." Lewis complained that "Main Street is the climax of civilization. That this Ford car might stand in front of the Bon Ton Store, Hannibal invaded Rome and Erasmus wrote in Oxford cloisters."

These critics complained especially of the conformity of American civilization. Following Nietzsche, Mencken yearned for philosopher kings, supermen who could rise above the commonplace. The gulf between the cultivated and the masses, he believed, was unbridgeable. Van Wyck Brooks, influenced by Freud, concluded that geniuses like Mark Twain had been repressed by American culture. "A vast unconscious conspiracy," he said, "actuates all Americans against the creative spirit." Babbitt, Lewis' unforgettable conformist, seemed so typically American that the word *Babbittry* passed into the language as a synonym for what people in the 1950s called the Organization Man. Americans, it seemed, were crude, conformist, consumption-crazed Philistines whose gods, as Babbitt conceded, were "Modern Appliances."

Pale druggists in remote towns of the Epworth League and flannel nightgown belts, endlessly wrapping up bottles of Peruna. . . . Women hidden away in the damp kitchens of unpainted houses along the railroad tracks, frying tough beefsteaks. . . . Lime and cement dealers being initiated into the Knights of Pythias, the men at lonely railroad crossings in Iowa, hoping that they'll be able to get off to hear the United Brethren evangelist preach. . . . Ticket-choppers in the subway, breathing sweat in its gaseous form. . . . Family doctors in poor neighborhoods, faithfully relying upon the therapeutics taught in their Eclectic Medical College in 1884. . . . Farmers plowing sterile fields behind sad meditative horses, both suffering from the bites of insects. . . . Greeks tending all-night coffee-joints in the suburban wildernesses where the trolley-cars stop. . . . Grocery-clerks stealing prunes and ginger-snaps, and trying to make assignations with soapy servant-girls. . . . Women confined for the ninth or tenth time, wondering helplessly what it is all about. . . . Methodist preachers retired after forty years of service in the trenches of God, upon pensions of $600 a year. . . .

Mencken's view of Middle American "Virtue," 1922. From *Prejudices,* 3rd series, 1922.

Disgust with American culture led some writers to glorify youth. Like Randolph Bourne before the war, they hoped the coming generation could sweep away the past. "The older generation had certainly pretty well ruined this world before passing it on to us," a critic commented in 1920. "They gave us this Thing, knocked to pieces, leaky, red-hot, threatening to blow-up; and then they are surprised that we don't accept it with the same attitude of pretty, decorous enthusiasm with which they received it."

The gloom of such writers was reflected in growing skepticism about the possibility of promoting progressive change. Lincoln Steffens, rejecting reform, observed, "I can't see why everybody is so anxious to save this rotten civilization of ours." In his autobiography (1931) he praised such diverse autocrats as Mussolini, Lenin, and Henry Ford. Walter Lippmann, no longer an ardent progressive, argued the need for an elite governing class. The protagonists of Dreiser's *American Tragedy* (1925) had to surrender to inexorable natural forces, while Ernest Hemingway's characters achieved manhood only through self-assertion and physical courage. In 1929 Joseph Wood Krutch wondered if people could ever reconcile traditional beliefs with modern experience. "The possibility of an actual human maturity," he wrote, "is problematic. There impends for the human spirit either extinction or a readjustment more stupendous than any made before."

Some of these writers were nostalgic, suspicious of technology and of urban growth. Lewis, while ridiculing small towns, cherished their warmth and friendliness, and he made no effort to praise the city. Other writers, like Hemingway, exalted solitude. Floyd Dell and other bohemians celebrated the virtues of small communities like Greenwich Village. At the root of much cultural criticism in the 1920s was a highly ambivalent attitude toward modernization, and especially toward machine technology.

Now my generation is disillusioned, and I think, to a certain extent, brutalized, by the cataclysm which their complacent folly engendered. The acceleration of life for us has been so great that into the last few years have been crowded the experiences and the ideas of a normal lifetime. We have in our unregenerate youth learned the practicality and the cynicism that is safe only in unregenerate old age. We have been forced to become realists overnight, instead of idealists, as was our birthright. We have seen man at his lowest, woman at her lightest, in the terrible moral chaos of Europe. We have been forced to question, and in many cases to discard, the religion of our fathers. We have seen hideous peculation, greed, anger, hatred, malice, and all uncharitableness, unmasked and rampant and unashamed. We have been forced to live in an atmosphere of "to-morrow we die," and so, naturally, we drank and were merry. We have seen the rottenness and shortcomings of all governments, even the best and most stable. We have seen entire social systems overthrown, and our own called in question. In short, we have seen the inherent beastliness of the human race revealed in an infernal apocalypse.

"Youth culture," 1920s: the response of John F. Carter, a young journalist, 1920.

Ben Shahn. *The Passion of Sacco and Vanzetti.* (1931–32.) Collection of the Whitney Museum of Modern Art.

The painter Ben Shahn bitterly depicts the "justice" given Sacco and Vanzetti.

For these reasons many of these critics stopped short of posing radical challenges to American culture in the 1920s. Relatively few remained bohemians or expatriates for long, and fewer still advocated revolutionary changes in sexual behavior or in familial patterns. Not many writers—Dos Passos and Steffens were among them—went beyond a critique of materialism to engage in a serious reexamination of capitalism itself. The transition from assaults on the "Booboisie" to such economic radicalism began slowly in the late 1920s, especially after the executions of Sacco and Vanzetti. These were carried out in 1927, after seven years of legal maneuvering that prolonged the case and made Sacco and Vanzetti—eloquent advocates of philosophical anarchism—into martyred symbols of the oppression of radicals in America. Still, even their deaths could not make radicalism a potent political force. It took the depression of the 1930s to revive the Left in America.

Above all, writers like Mencken and Lewis failed utterly to undermine the self-confidence of the dominant business elites. Observe a few statements from businessmen of the time.

On the glories of capitalism:

History shows that the prime motive of capitalism—namely, *selfishness*—merely reflects the conviction, *inborn in every living creature,* that *it is his natural right to keep, own, and control whatever he himself has made, saved, thought out, bought, or fought for;* a conviction which works out broadly not only for *justice* to the individual, but to the common good of all.

(Charles N. Fay, *Business in Politics,* 1926.)

On Jesus as the archetypal businessman:

So we have the main points of [Jesus'] business philosophy:

1. Whoever will be great must render great service.
2. Whoever will find himself at the top must be willing to lose himself at the bottom.
3. The big rewards come to those who travel the second, undemanded mile.

(Bruce Barton, *The Man Nobody Knows,* 1925.)

And on the nature of labor:

It is the aim of Scientific Management to induce men to act as nearly like machines as possible, so far as doing the work in the one best way that has been discovered is concerned.
(Frank Gilbreth, successor to Frederick Winslow Taylor as crusader for scientific management.)

Not all business spokesmen were so crude. The larger, wealthier corporations moved further in the direction of welfare capitalism by developing pension plans and providing paid vacations. But most capitalists tended to use workers as automated machines, and to embrace the bureaucratization and corporate concentration that undermined the individualism they professed to cherish. They also continued to crush the American labor movement. Thanks primarily to a concerted strike-breaking campaign in 1919–20, union membership declined from 5 million in 1920 to less than 3 million by 1932. The decline of organized labor in the 1920s was the most impressive display of the power of the business ideology of the time.

Workers, of course, did not accept this state of affairs calmly. The decade featured many walkouts, demonstrations, and wildcat strikes. Militant workers, including women, protested bitterly against their treatment in the mill villages and textile plants of the South. Their employers, like Gary during the steel strike, responded coldly, resorting to violence that killed and injured women workers. Blue-collar people yearned especially for some control over their work—a control that mechanization and scientific management had taken away from them. And while many workers received more in real wages than they had before, they resented the gulf that seemed to be growing between them and the middle classes. Workers had to labor hard indeed to buy the consumer goods, including cars, that now seemed to be the essential manifestations of economic well-being and social status. In all these ways, the lives of many blue-collar workers during the 1920s, though materially a little more comfortable than in the past, exhibited considerable tension.

However, workers who openly asserted themselves confronted not only the substantial power of corporate executives but also a more general ideology of rugged individualism that still exercised considerable appeal in the relatively prosperous 1920s. Many middle-class Americans worshipped Henry Ford, not only because he made inexpensive cars but also because he constructed a colonial village and proclaimed loudly that he was a self-made man. They revered Thomas Edison, an originator of team science, because they pictured him as a solitary genius working with his hands. They adored Charles Lindbergh in part because he was the "lone eagle," a lineal descendant of other frontier-breaking pioneers in American history. They heaped praise on sports figures like Babe Ruth, Bobby Jones, and Gene Tunney. They deeply admired Herbert Hoover, the Great Engineer who defended rugged individualism. All these heroes appeared to personify the characteristics that had made America great: solid achievement and self-reliance.

In so believing, Americans conveniently forgot that many of their heroes—Ford, Lindbergh, Edison, and even Hoover—were helpmates of scientism, technological displacement, and collectivization. But these contradictions did not bother them, for they saw what they wanted to see. Like their fathers and mothers, they cherished a world where traditional values of self-reliance would count, where the masses did as they were told, where government minded its own business, and where the capitalistic system could spread its blessings to all who worked to get them. In this sense the business values of the 1920s easily survived the barbs of Mencken and Lewis, the rejections of the expatriates, and the sneers of the bohemians.

THE PERSISTENCE OF PIETISM

Even the casual newspaper reader in the early 1920s had to be struck by the visibility and power of two related groups: prohibitionists and fundamentalists. By 1932, however, the prohibitionists were fighting an obviously futile battle and the fundamentalists seemed all but forgotten. The diminishing visibility of these groups, allied in their pietistic insistence on right conduct, symbolized the apparent decline of village values and the triumph of more "modern" urban and secular beliefs. In the cultural conflict over modernity, a pronounced feature of the decade, the modernists seemed to emerge the winners.

On the surface this picture of the decade had much to recommend it. Prohibition, for instance, was an obvious failure well before it was repealed in 1933. Though it eradicated the saloon and decreased the alcohol consumption of the lower classes (who could least afford speakeasies or bootlegged stock), it stimulated the illicit sale of awful concoctions. These included Jackass Brandy, which caused internal bleeding, Soda Pop Moon, which contained poisonous alcohol, and Panther Whiskey, which was based on esters and fusel oil. (The joke went around that one customer, suspicious of his bootlegger's stock, sent a sample to a chemist, who replied, "Dear Sir, your horse has diabetes.") The total income of bootleggers, based on annual sales of 150 million quarts of liquor, was $2 billion per year, roughly 2 percent of the Gross National Product.

In gang-ridden Chicago, the failure of prohibition was especially clear. As early as 1920, when vice king "Big Jim" Colosimo was murdered, he was mourned by an estimated 5,000 people. His honorary pallbearers included three judges, eight aldermen, an assistant state attorney, and two congressmen. The cavalcade to his burial, the Chicago *Tribune* noted, was "such as moved behind the funeral car of Caesar." Colosimo's death permitted ruthless men like Al Capone to take over, and violence mounted: one article estimated that 1,291 people were murdered in gang warfare between 1926 and mid-1929.

Prohibition alone did not cause the organization of crime in America during the 1920s. Vice rings, like most American institutions, had grown steadily more centralized in previous decades. Moreover, the economic opportunities offered by

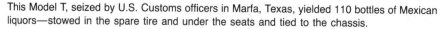

This Model T, seized by U.S. Customs officers in Marfa, Texas, yielded 110 bottles of Mexican liquors—stowed in the spare tire and under the seats and tied to the chassis.

syndicated crime provided a ladder to wealth for ethnic groups denied access to more legitimate businesses. "Prohibition is a business," Capone proclaimed. "All I do is supply a public demand. I do it in the best and least harmful way I can." But the very prominence of men like Capone showed that prohibition remained a dreadful mistake. It discriminated against poor people and ethnics. It diverted attention from people who hoped to promote noncoercive remedies for the curse of alcoholism. It disillusioned progressives who had relied on statutes to bring about right behavior. It encouraged stereotypes about knife-wielding Sicilians and crime-ridden cities. It led otherwise respectable people to act in contempt of the law. No wonder it was eventually repealed.

Fundamentalists (many of whom were prohibitionists) also seemed laughable to sophisticates during the decade. Billy Sunday, the baseball player turned evangelist, confessed that he didn't "know any more about theology than a jack-rabbit knows about ping-pong," but that "that old bastard theory of evolution" was "jackass nonsense." Aimée Semple McPherson, popularizer of the "Four-Square Gospel," used her good looks, modern showmanship, and claims of faith healing to found the Angelus Temple, capacity 5,300, in Los Angeles. "To visit Angelus Temple," one cynic wrote, "is to go on a sensuous debauch served up in the name of religion." The Reverend J. Frank Norris, head of the First Baptist Church of Fort Worth, Texas, built a 6,000-seat church and bathed it in searchlights making it visible for thirty-two miles. A crude, violent man who once shot and killed someone in his office, Norris hotly opposed "that hell-born, Bible-destroying, deity-of-Christ-denying, German rationalism [known as] . . . evolution."

Assertions such as these led to the wide publicity given the trial of John Scopes, a biology teacher in Dayton, Tennessee, for the illegal teaching of Darwinian theories. At the trial William Jennings Bryan defended the state's antievolution law by insisting that "it is better to trust in the Rock of Ages than to know the age of rocks; it is better for one to know that he is close to the Heavenly Father than to know how far the stars in the heavens are apart." He conceded, however, that the "day" of creation might mean a million years. Clarence Darrow, who cross-examined Bryan at the trial, expostulated, "I am examining you on your fool ideas that no intelligent Christian on earth believes."

Because Scopes made no pretense of denying his "guilt," no one was surprised when the court ruled against him. The antievolution law remained on the books for forty-two more years. Yet the case enabled journalists like Mencken to ridicule Bryan (who died immediately after the trial) and pietists generally. A handful of extreme fundamentalists, like Gerald B. Winrod, counterattacked by embracing anti-Semitism, anticommunism, and authoritarianism—beliefs that made them precursors of fascism in the 1930s. However, most fundamentalists nursed their resentments more quietly. Fundamentalism, modernists thought prematurely, was as doomed as prohibition.

In fact, these expressions of pietism remained considerably more vigorous than many people realized. The dry forces, far from renouncing their cause, might have held out longer if the depression had not led people to believe that the legalization of liquor would produce tax revenue. At that point in 1933, the "great experiment" was repealed, but the pietists did not embrace the values of their opponents. Instead, they withdrew into themselves, more conscious as a group than ever before and more certain that the dominant elites—eastern, urban, corporate—were their enemies.

Modernists could not even take solace from assaults on fundamentalists like Bryan. Convinced of their rectitude, many fundamentalists advanced the once-radical idea that ordinary people could build their own pipelines to God. In so doing they promised individuals faith amid secularization, and group solidarity amid the pressures of migration and rapid social change. As millions of rural and small-town Americans moved to unfamiliar urban surroundings—like McPherson's Los Angeles or Norris' Fort Worth—the fundamentalists increased their strength. From this perspective the fundamentalists offered much to people in need of certitude amid rapid change. Like many other out-groups of the decade, these people counter-organized in order to maintain their bearings.

THE KU KLUX KLAN

Another manifestation of pietism in the early 1920s was the Ku Klux Klan, which was resurrected in 1915 by William J. Simmons, an evangelist and insurance sales-man from Atlanta. Inspired by the racist film *Birth of a Nation,* Simmons pro-

A KKK meeting in the 1920's.

claimed himself Imperial Wizard, burned crosses, and spread the gospel of native white supremacy. When he enlisted the services of public relations specialists in 1920, his organization blossomed into both a profitable racket and a national movement. Despite the then costly membership fee of $10 (to pay, among other things, for sheets), 4 to 5 million Americans joined the Klan in the next five years.

The new movement was anti-Catholic, anti-Semitic, anti-immigrant, and anti-radical as well as antiblack. It represented, with prohibition and fundamentalism, an assertively Christian indictment of urban, ethnic, modern America. Championing decorous personal behavior, it asserted the old moral code; in some places Klansmen concentrated on beating up young couples in lovers lanes. The KKK stood for "Americanism," a euphemism for white Protestantism and for God-fearing, law-abiding behavior. It openly sanctioned night-riding, tar-and-feathering, and other acts of physical intimidation. "The Klan is intolerant," bragged Hiram Wesley Evans, a Texas dentist who headed the organization in the mid-1920s, ". . . of the people who are trying to destroy our traditional Americanism . . . aliens who are constantly trying to change our civilization into something that will suit themselves better."

By 1924 the Klan had become a potent political force, not only in the South but also in California, Ohio, Indiana, and Oregon. It showed considerable strength in northern cities, especially those to which blacks and immigrants had streamed during the war and postwar years. Though influential in both parties, it was especially powerful in the Democratic party, which refused (by one vote) to condemn it in the divided convention of 1924. The nineteenth-century Klan had never amassed such national support.

The KKK, more than the prohibitionists and the fundamentalists, fell from grace after 1925. One blow was publicity given the sordid leadership of David Stephenson, Grand Dragon of the Indiana Klan, who kidnapped and assaulted his secretary on a train to Chicago. When she died from taking poison, Stephenson was sentenced in 1925 to life in prison. When the governor, a Klansman himself, refused to pardon him, Stephenson produced evidence that sent a congressman, the mayor of Indianapolis, and other officials to jail. Elsewhere voters belatedly voted Klansmen out of office. The decline of the KKK after 1925 suggested that Americans were coming to their senses, that the repressiveness that had blighted the country since the early days of the war was declining.

There are three great racial instincts, vital elements in both the historic and the present attempts to build an America which shall fulfill the aspirations and justify the heroism of the men who made the nation. These are the instincts of loyalty to the white race, to the traditions of America, and to the spirit of Protestantism, which has been an essential part of Americanism ever since the days of Roanoke and Plymouth Rock. They are condensed into the Klan slogan: "Native, white, Protestant supremacy!"

The gospel of the KKK by Imperial Wizard Hiram Wesley Evans, 1926.

The rise of ethnic consciousness

THE BLACK EXPERIENCE

In fact, the decline of the Klan was at best a surface victory for the champions of racial, ethnic, and religious toleration. The 1920s witnessed the continued subjection of blacks. Peonage on southern farms was so widespread that Secretary of Commerce Hoover had to appoint a "Colored Advisory Committee" in 1927. The committee tried to investigate the situation, but plantation owners intimidated witnesses, and the Red Cross interfered with efforts to publicize conditions. In the North the continuing migrations of blacks made the modern racial ghetto a reality. Chicago's black population increased from 109,458 to 233,903 during the decade, while New York's rose from 152,467 to 327,706. Penned in slum housing, blacks also faced rigid discrimination in employment. Most black men who found jobs worked as porters, waiters, or janitors; black women served as cooks, domestics, and washerwomen. Blacks often had to resort to strike breaking to find jobs at all. There were two kinds of businesses in New York, the sociologist E. Franklin Frazier commented, "those that employ Negroes in menial positions, and those that employ no Negroes at all."

Of course, there were a few encouraging signs. During the 1920s, as in previous decades, the movement of blacks into the middle classes continued. The ghettos featured much-heralded success stories—of entrepreneurs in real estate, undertaking, hairdressing and other small business ventures. The ghettos also developed a range of community activities that brought some cohesion to the otherwise harsh existence of the slum. Moreover, places like Harlem, for all their horrors, offered blacks more hope than did the rural South. "I can never put on paper the thrill of the underground ride to Harlem," the black poet Langston Hughes wrote. "I went up the steps and out into the bright September sunlight. Harlem! I stood there, dropped my bags, took a deep breath, and felt happy again."

Black intellectuals like Hughes, Alain Locke, Claude McKay, and James Weldon Johnson thought places like Harlem would create what Locke called the "New Negro." Harlem, Locke said, "has the same role to play for the New Negro as Dublin has for the New Ireland or Prague for the New Czechoslovakia." Hughes explained that it was the "duty of the young Negro artist . . . to change through the force of his art that old whispering 'I want to be white,' hidden in the aspirations of his people, to 'why should I want to be white? I am a Negro—and beautiful.' " Artists such as these led the Harlem Renaissance, a flowering of jazz, poetry, and fiction.

Other black spokesmen offered a more militant form of black pride. For years, W. E. B. Du Bois had worked to develop interracial cooperation. By the 1920s, however, he had begun to despair. He not only drifted away from white liberals, but freely confessed his racial prejudice. Hearing of the lynching of a white man in 1923, he wrote, "We're sorry we're glad. We wish we were big enough to be dissolved in tears. . . . But we're not; we're just plain tickled at this blood-soaked land." He also propagandized for Pan-Africanism. By this he did not mean that

James Weldon Johnson, poet, was a member of the Harlem Renaissance.

American blacks should migrate to Africa but that they should establish their kinship with oppressed people throughout the world. "The spell of Africa is upon me," he wrote in 1924. "The ancient witchery of her medicine is burning in my drowsy, dreamy blood. This is not a country, it is a world—a universe of itself and for itself, a thing Different, Immense, Menacing, Alluring. Africa is the Spiritual Frontier of human kind."

The most colorful black leader of the decade was Marcus Garvey of Harlem. Like many prominent blacks (others in the twentieth century included McKay, Stokely Carmichael, Shirley Chisholm, and Bayard Rustin), Garvey was a West Indian migrant. One of his early inspirations was Booker T. Washington, apostle of black self-help. Unlike Washington, however, Garvey urged blacks to reject everything white. He took as his colors red (for slave blood), black (for skin color), and green (for African fertility), and he refused to let his newspaper, *Negro World*, accept ads for hair straighteners or skin bleachers. Founding the Universal Negro Improvement Association, he crusaded above all for the economic self-sufficiency of his race.

If we must die let it not be like hogs
Hunted and penned in an inglorious spot,
While round us bark the mad and hungry dogs,
Making their mock at our accursed lot.
If we must die, o let us nobly die,
So that our precious blood may not be shed
In vain; then even the monsters we defy
Shall be constrained to honor us though dead!
O kinsmen! We must meet the common foe!
Though far outnumbered let us show us brave,
And for their thousand blows deal one deathblow!
What though before us lies the open grave?
Like men we'll face the murderous cowardly pack,
Pressed to the wall, dying but fighting back!

Black militance in the 1920s. A poem by Claude McKay.

He also called for a back-to-Africa movement, to be assisted by the Black Star shipping line. A master showman, Garvey relied heavily on fancy uniforms, and he rewarded lieutenants with such grandiose titles as the African Virgin Mary, Duke of Uganda, and Knight Commander of the Nile. His flamboyance, together with the pride in color that he evoked, gave his movement an unprecedented mass appeal in Harlem in the early 1920s.

A more thoughtful, though less sensational, program of black militancy came from the creative mind of A. Philip Randolph, a socialist who had cofounded the *Messenger* (subtitled the ''Only Radical Negro Magazine in America'') in 1917 and who had been arrested in 1918 for opposing the war. In 1925 he started the Brotherhood of Sleeping Car Porters, a pioneering effort to forge a black labor union and to develop working-class consciousness among American blacks. Though it was twelve years before the Pullman Company agreed to sign a contract with the union, Randolph's persistence proved that blacks could sustain an efficient, effective, nationwide organization. Meanwhile, Randolph continued to speak out for interracial organization of workers and to call for militant demonstrations aimed at break-

Black queen of beauty, thou hast given color to the world!
Among other women thou art royal and the fairest!
Like the brightest jewels in the regal diadem,
Shin'st thou, Goddess of Africa, nature's purest emblem!

Black men worship at thy virginal shrine of purest love,
Because in thine eyes are virtue's steady and holy mark,
As we see no other, clothed in silk or fine linen,
From ancient Venus, the Goddess, to mythical Helen.

A poem by Marcus Garvey.

ing the power of corporate elites. Randolph tried to reach the vast majority of American blacks, blue-collar workers, and to forge an interracial coalition of low-income people. His example proved inspiring to later militants.

These expressions of racial pride and of militancy showed that blacks were struggling to organize against their foes. But they fell far short of success. The Harlem Renaissance was heavily dependent on white patronage, and venturesome whites who flocked to the night clubs and jazz halls of Harlem transformed black art forms into variations more suitable for mass white consumption. Other whites saw in jazz confirmation of the stereotype that blacks were rhythmic, spiritual, attuned to the beat of the jungle. Robert Park, the nation's leading sociologist, explained that the Anglo-Saxon was essentially "a pioneer and sociologist," while the black was "primarily an artist, loving life for its own sake. His métier is expression rather than action. He is, so to speak, the lady among the races." Most discouraging of all, the Harlem Renaissance failed to assist the black masses. "Some Harlemites," Hughes lamented, "thought the race problem had been solved through Art. They were sure the Negro would lead a new life from then on in green pastures of tolerance. . . . I don't know what made Negroes think that— except that they were mostly intellectuals doing the thinking. The ordinary Negroes hadn't heard of the Negro Renaissance. And if they had, it hadn't raised their wages any."

The spokesmen for black protest also failed to accomplish much in the 1920s. Du Bois, proud and outspoken, still argued for a "talented tenth" and did not reach the masses. Randolph's days of influence lay far ahead. Garvey, who denounced Du Bois as "purely and simply a white man's nigger," antagonized blacks as well as whites. Du Bois dismissed him as an ignorant demagogue, and Randolph called him the "Supreme Negro Jamaican Jackass." Garvey's Black Star line foundered, the victim of poor management and of unscrupulous dealers who sold him aged ships. The federal government then jailed him in 1925 for mail fraud and deported him in 1927. His decline did not mean that his followers disappeared—on the contrary, some of them founded the Black Muslims in 1931. But it did encourage whites to ridicule his cause.

Garvey's fall revealed another obstacle in the way of black progress: blacks themselves were divided into groups. Some middle-class blacks, restless in the ghettos, tended to blame the lower-class migrants for intensifying white racism. And in Harlem, the presence of some 50,000 West Indian blacks was a constant source of intraracial tension. These migrants were often better educated, more militant, and prouder of their color than the newly arrived southern blacks. Some of them spoke French or Spanish, and even the English speakers had accents different from the southerners. Most West Indians were Episcopalians or Catholics, whereas the southerners tended to be Baptists or Methodists. These differences led native blacks to refer to the West Indians as "monkey-chasers," "ring-tails," and "cockneys." Ditties ridiculed the back-to-Africa movement:

> When I get to the other side
> I'll buy myself a mango,
> Grab myself a monkey gal
> And do the monkey tango. . . .

Garvey, Garvey, is a big man
To take his folks to monkey land.
If he does, I'm sure I can
Stay right here with Uncle Sam. . . .

When a monkey chaser dies,
Don't need no undertaker.
Just throw him in the Harlem River
He'll float back to Jamaica.

The largest barrier to racial justice remained intolerance by whites. Contemporary editors of the *Encyclopedia Brittanica* explained that the "Negro" had a "less voluminous brain as compared with the white races," was "on a lower evolutionary plane than the white man," and was "more closely related to the highest anthropoids." "After puberty," the encyclopedia concluded, "sexual matters take the first place in the negro's life and thoughts." Even well-meaning whites sounded patronizing. "The Negro," one explained in 1923, "has good points that many other races do not. He is a patriot. He loves the South. He loves his white folks. He understands the southern white. He has a genius for religion. . . . Let us be faithful to God and help the southern Negro to work out to wholesome and worthy ends the strange destiny which has placed him here among us." Attitudes such as these showed that in racial matters, as in much else in the 1920s, Americans held to established notions. So long as this racism persisted, and until blacks were able to manage effective organization against discrimination, the status of blacks remained low.

There is nothing in the make-up of a Negro, physically or mentally, which should induce anyone to welcome him as a neighbor. The best of them are unsanitary, . . . ruin alone follows in their path. They are as proud as peacocks, but have nothing of the peacock's beauty. . . . Niggers are undesirable neighbors and entirely irresponsible and vicious.

A passage from the *Property Owners' Journal,* 1920, Chicago, cited in Allan Spear, *Black Chicago: The Making of a Negro Ghetto, 1890–1920.*

ETHNIC CONFLICT IN THE MELTING POT

This discrimination against blacks was but part of a broader bigotry that manifested itself in many ways during the 1920s, and that—together with pietism—exposed the deep cultural conflicts of the decade. One manifestation was anti-Semitism, reflected in the steady popularity of Madison Grant's *Passing of the Great Race,* first published in 1916. "The man of the old stock," Grant explained, "is today being literally driven off the streets of New York City by the swarms of Polish Jews." Kenneth Roberts, a widely read historical novelist, referred to eastern European Jews as "human parasites." Henry Ford had his car dealers circulate the "Protocol of the Elders of Zion," the spurious creation of a Czarist secret policeman that supposedly "proved" that Jews were engaged in a conspiracy to take over the world. Anti-Semitic feelings affected universities and businesses, which imposed religious quotas or simply closed their doors to Jews.

Stereotypes surfaced in countless other forms, especially in a resurgence of prejudice against the newer ethnic groups from Asia and southeastern Europe. Such feeling was an undercurrent in the writings of Mencken, who stereotyped immigrants with sensuality in order to indict the Puritanism of native whites. It sustained psychological tests "proving" that the foreign-born had low IQs. It powerfully reinforced the Americanization movement, at full flower in the 1920s. Three years after the decline of the Klan, ethnic and religious prejudice flared openly in slurs on Al Smith, a Catholic many Americans believed was a stooge for the Pope.

The most enduring legislative result of this nativist feeling was the Immigrant Restriction Act of 1924, which only six senators opposed. This law set up a "quota" system of immigration that discriminated deliberately and unashamedly against southern and eastern European immigrants. It also excluded Japanese—a blatant slap that badly damaged Japanese-American relations. The act reflected the racist science of the day; it also exposed the political power of old-stock Americans, who worried deeply about a renewed "invasion" of ethnics after the war. Even industrialists, hitherto opposed to cutting off the flow of cheap labor, nervously acquiesced in the nativism of the day. (Most employers could well afford to, for with unions badly demoralized, wages could be kept low in any event.)

All these displays of intolerance and of nativism intensified ongoing patterns of counterorganization and fragmentation in the United States. At the turn of the century many immigrant groups had been too new to the American scene to organize effectively. Blacks had been oppressed and isolated in the rural South. By 1930, however, some of these people were joining the host of interest groups in

America. Many Jews, including Justice Brandeis, sought to preserve common bonds by embracing Zionism. Militant blacks looked to Garvey or Randolph. Millions of ethnics buoyed the strength of urban political machines. These efforts at counterorganization, in turn, led disaffected fundamentalists, prohibitionists, and Klansmen to tighten their own group loyalties. This fragmentation—of city versus country, of pietists versus modernists, of ethnics against Anglo-Saxons, of blacks versus whites, and of subgroups within these categories—tended to blur class divisions between workers and capitalists—divisions that had seemed so threatening at the turn of the century. But they exposed with special clarity the cultural divisions that characterized American life even in the relatively prosperous 1920s. The "new era," it seems, sharpened many of the tensions of older ones.

Suggestions for reading

Four starting points for interpretive accounts of the 1920s are William Leuchtenburg, *The Perils of Prosperity, 1914–1932** (1958), a skillful, well-written treatment; John Braeman et al., eds., *Change and Continuity in Twentieth-Century America: The 1920s* (1968); Robert Elias, *Entangling Alliances with None: An Essay on the Individual in the American Twenties* (1973); and Ellis Hawley, *The Great War and the Search for a Modern Order: A History of the American People and their Institutions, 1917–1933* (1979).

Books focusing on currents in thought are Roderick Nash, *The Nervous Generation: American Thought, 1917–1930** (1969); Alfred Kazin, *On Native Grounds** (1942), on literary trends; and Robert Crunden, *From Self to Society: Transitions in American Thought, 1919–1941** (1972).

For politics, a useful survey is John D. Hicks, *Republican Ascendancy** (1960). Harding is treated in Andrew Sinclair, *The Available Man** (1965); and Robert K. Murray, *The Harding Era* (1969). Donald McCoy, *Calvin Coolidge* (1967), is an excellent study. Important biographies are Richard Lowitt, *George W. Norris: The Persistence of a Progressive* (1971); William Harbaugh, *Lawyer's Lawyer: The Life of John W. Davis* (1973); Matthew and Hanna Josephson, *Al Smith* (1970); and Arthur Mann, *LaGuardia . . . 1882–1933** (1959). George Tindall, *The Emergence of the New South, 1913–1945* (1967), is almost encyclopedic. Donald Swain, *Federal Conservation Policy, 1921–1933* (1963) is an admirable monograph. Important studies of electoral trends are David Burner, *The Politics of Provincialism* (1968), on the Democratic party; Samuel Lubell, *The Future of American Politics** (1952); and Allan J. Lichtman, *Prejudice and the Old Politics: The Presidential Election of 1928* (1979). J. Joseph Huthmacher, *Massachusetts People and Politics, 1919–1933** (1959) is a first-rate state study. Clarke Chambers, *Seedtime of Reform, 1918–1933* (1963) concerns itself with the ideas and activities of social reformers.

Many books deal with social and cultural trends in the 1920s. They include Robert and Helen Lynd, *Middletown** (1929); John Rae, *The Road and Car in American Life* (1971); William Chafe, *The American Woman: Her Changing Social, Economic, and Political Roles, 1920–1960** (1972); and J. Stanley Lemons, *The Woman Citizen: Social Feminism in the 1920s* (1973). Also Don Kirschner, *City and Country: Rural Responses to Urbanization in the 1920s* (1970); Norman H. Clark, *Deliver Us From Evil: An Interpretation of American Prohibition* (1976); Lawrence Levine, *Defender of the Faith: William Jennings Bryan, the Last Decade, 1915–1925* (1965); Norman Furniss, *The Fundamentalist Controversy, 1918–1931* (1954); David M. Chalmers, *Hooded Americanism: The First Century of the Ku Klux Klan** (1965); Paul Carter, *The Decline and Revival of the Social Gospel** (1954); and Ray

Ginger, *Six Days or Forever?** (1958), which deals amusingly with the Scopes trial. Otis Pease, *The Responsibilities of American Advertising, 1920–1940* (1958) covers an otherwise neglected subject.

A solid economic history of the decade is George Soule, *Prosperity Decade** (1947). Equally valuable is the briefer account by Jim Potter, *The American Economy Between the Wars** (1974). Milton Friedman and Anna Schwartz, *The Great Contraction** (1965), focuses on monetary problems; see also Elmus Wicker, *Federal Reserve Monetary Policy, 1917–1933* (1966). James Prothro, *The Dollar Decade** (1954), describes business thought. A durable interpretation of corporate trends is Adolf Berle, Jr., and Gardiner Means, *The Modern Corporation and Private Property** (1932). Alfred Chandler's *Strategy and Structure** (1962) is an indispensable guide to changes in corporate structure. The basic book on labor is Irving Bernstein, *The Lean Years** (1960), to be supplemented with Robert Zieger, *Republicans and Labor, 1919–1929* (1969). See also some of the essays by David Montgomery, *Workers' Control in America* (1979).

Black History receives coverage in E. David Cronon, *Black Moses** (1955), which deals with Marcus Garvey. See also Theodore Vincent, *Black Power and the Garvey Movement* (1971). Other useful studies are Nathan Huggins, *Harlem Renaissance** (1971); Eugene Levy, *James Weldon Johnson* (1973); and the books on Harlem and Chicago by Osofsky and Spear cited in the bibliography for chapter 2.

For judicial trends consult Alpheus Mason, *The Supreme Court from Taft to Warren* (1958); and Paul Murphy's detailed *Constitution in Crisis Times, 1918–1969** (1970). Foreign policy is surveyed in L. Ethan Ellis, *Republican Foreign Policy, 1921–1933* (1968). See also Joan Hoff Wilson, *American Business and Foreign Policy, 1920–1933* (1971); Thomas Buckley, *The United States and the Washington Conference* (1970); Akira Iriye, *After Imperialism: The Search for a New Order in the Far East, 1921–1931** (1969); and Joseph Tulchin, *The Aftermath of War: World War I and United States Policy Toward Latin America* (1971).

Primary sources include H. L. Mencken, *Prejudices* (6 vols., 1924–27); James Weldon Johnson, *Autobiography of An ex-Colored Man** (1927); Lincoln Steffens, *Autobiography** (1931); John Chamberlain, *Farewell to Reform** (1933); and Joseph Wood Krutch, *The Modern Temper** (1929).

Crash and depression
1929–1939

For millions of Americans who suffered through it, the Great Depression was the most numbing experience of their lives. It threw millions out of work, disrupted families, fomented class conflict, and inspired sharp criticism of capitalism itself. It threatened the faith in economic growth and business values that had been at the core of twentieth-century American life. It helped cause lasting changes, especially in politics and in attitudes toward the government. "The experience" of depression, the sociologists Robert and Helen Lynd observed in returning to Muncie in the 1930s, "has been more nearly universal than any prolonged recent emotional experience. . .it had approached in its elemental shock the primary experiences of birth and death."

In retrospect, however, it is striking how little was altered in the long run. Most of the major trends of previous decades continued, some at accelerated rates. Bureaucracy spread, the economy centralized, and technology advanced. Interest groups, more self-conscious and insistent than ever, added to the fragmentation of American society. Cultural conflicts, while obscured by the economic crisis, persisted. Hard times or no, older values were cherished.

The crash of 1929

Among the many specialized groups that proliferated in the 1920s was the National Association of Credit Men. In 1925 it issued a warning about the rising level of private debt in America. "There has been built up in our country," its resolution said, "a large peak of installment credit, and it is wise for our business people to exercise caution, for undoubtedly in a credit pinch this condition would prove a very disturbing factor."

A year later their fears were borne out in Florida, where a land boom finally collapsed. The immediate reason for the bust was a hurricane, which caused millions of dollars of damage. But the underlying cause was the speculative fever that had led to the blindest sorts of investment and had enabled avid promoters to stake out more house lots in Florida than there were families in the entire country.

But few Americans appeared to pay much attention to the credit men or to the lesson of boom and bust in Florida. On the contrary, net private debt increased from $139 billion in 1926 to $161 billion in 1929. During the same period brokers' loans—a measure of borrowing for investment—also increased, from $3.5 billion to more than $8.5 billion. Much of this expansion occurred during the summer of 1928, when the Great Bull Market lifted industrial stocks more than 100 points. Thereafter it became more difficult to make a killing. But stock prices continued to rise. Calvin Coolidge, symbol of Yankee frugality, advised that stocks were "cheap at current prices."

Because these increases in stock prices far outran real economic growth, it was but a matter of time before the nation experienced the bust that had afflicted Florida in 1926. That was precisely what happened when the market crashed in September and October of 1929. By November 13, when prices hit their low for the year, industrial stocks had fallen 228 points, or 50 percent. The magnitude and suddenness of the crash dwarfed previous panics in American history.

Most of the early losers were speculators, not ordinary workers or citizens. If the market had stabilized, as it appeared to by mid-1931, the economy itself need not have been seriously harmed. But stock prices then plummeted again until July 1932. So it was that from October 1929 to June 1932 GM fell from 73 points to 8, U.S. Steel from 262 to 21, Montgomery Ward from 138 to 4, and RCA from 101 to 2.5. The market then stabilized, but despite record-low interest rates for borrowers, investment was sluggish during the 1930s, and stock prices stayed well below 1929 levels.

It was primarily during this second decline, from mid-1931 to March 1933, that the stock market troubles were accompanied by an ever-deepening economic depression. Thousands of brokers and investors simply went under, and 31,822 businesses folded in 1932 alone. Schools released teachers, cut the length of terms, or closed down entirely: Georgia shut 1,318 schools with a total enrollment of 170,790. Some 5,000 banks, with aggregate deposits of $3.2 billion, folded between October 1929 and August 1932. Demand slackened, and the prices for farm and industrial products fell off sharply. The resulting deflation staggered debtors, who now had to pay off predepression obligations in more valuable dollars. Surviving corporations cut production and slashed wages: regularly employed manufacturing workers were paid an average weekly wage of $25 in 1929, and $16.73 in 1933. Employers also laid off workers, until 13 million Americans—one-fourth of the work force—were idle in 1933. All these events caused an unprecedented decline in the national income, from $88 billion in 1929 to $40 billion four years later. They culminated in frantic runs on banks, which President Franklin D. Roo-

Economic collapse, 1929–39			
	1929	**1933**	**1939**
Population (millions)	122	126	131
GNP (billions of dollars, 1929 prices)	104	74	111
Per capita GNP (dollars, 1929 prices)	857	590	847
Exports of merchandise (billions of current dollars)	5.2	1.6	3.1
General imports (billions of current dollars)	4.4	1.5	2.3
Wholesale commodity prices (1926 = 100)	95	66	77
Farm products price index (1926 = 100)	105	51	65
Wheat price (current dollars per bushel, received by farmers)	1.04	0.38[a]	0.69
Realized gross farm income (billions of current dollars)	13.9	7.1	10.6
Average weekly earnings for production workers in manufacturing (current dollars)	25.03	16.73	23.86
Unemployed (millions, followed by percent of labor force) (estimates only)	1.6(3)	12.8(25)	9.5(17)
Common stocks price index (1941–43 = 100)	260	90	121
Volume of sales on the New York Stock Exchange (millions of shares)	1,125	655	262
Bank suspensions	659	4,004	72

SOURCE: Adapted from Cole, *Handbook of American History*, p. 211
[a]1932

sevelt was forced to close in March 1933. The world's strongest, most modern economy had virtually ground to a halt.

The human dimension of these statistics is very hard to describe. Testimony before a Senate committee in early 1932 revealed that Philadelphia had 280,000 unemployed, four-fifths of whom received no relief. The other one-fifth got grants of $4.23 per family per week, two-thirds of what they needed for food alone. The diets of these people consisted of bread and coffee for breakfast, and bread and carrots or canned soup for supper. In Chicago, an estimated 11,000 children had to be fed by their teachers (who did not receive all their back pay until World War II). Thousands of families, evicted from their homes, slept outdoors in parks or huddled in shacks and tents on unused land in "Hoovervilles" on the outskirts of cities. The situation in Washington, D.C., was terrifying. "I come home from the Hill every night filled with gloom," a newsman wrote. "I see on the streets filthy, ragged, desperate-looking men such as I have never seen before.'' Another observer added,''these [unemployed] are dead men. They are ghosts that walk the streets by day. They are ghosts sleeping with yesterday's newspapers thrown around them for covers at night.''

The search for jobs led countless Americans to leave home. *Business Week* reported in 1931 that 100,000 Americans applied for 6,000 openings for skilled workers in the Soviet Union. A Missouri Pacific official told the Senate two years later that the number of transients illegally riding trains had risen from 13,700 in 1928 to 186,000 in 1931. Hundreds of thousands rode on other railways, hitchhiked, or gathered their families into an old truck or car and took off. Some communities gave these transients a meal of beans and stale bread in return for a day's work, then herded them to the city limits. Others simply rounded them up, threw them back on the trains or into their trucks, and sent them on their way.

Many of these transients were migrant agricultural laborers. The Farm Security Administration later estimated that 500,000 such workers, with families of 1.5

American migrants on the road west. This picture was taken by Dorothea Lange.

A Hooverville: shacks on a vacant lot, housing the unemployed.

million, roamed the country during the decade, and that they found employment an average of twenty-one to twenty-four weeks a year for total annual wages of between $110 and $124 per worker. In California, mecca for thousands of "Okies" displaced from the Dust Bowl areas of the Plains and from the South, migrants were shunted from town to town, or crowded into unsanitary camps. Many thousands despaired and turned back. Mexican-American workers, who had moved across the border in better times, now encountered violence from fearful local officials. An estimated 500,000, including some American citizens, were deported during the decade. "The Mexicans are trash," one California official declared. "They have no standard of living. We herd them like pigs." Still, the migration northward continued, and by 1940 there were 2.5 million "Chicanos" in America—500,000 more than ten years earlier.

Optimists argued that the situation was not hopeless. Many young people, they pointed out, were finishing school rather than dropping out to look for jobs they knew they couldn't find. The proportion of seventeen-year-olds who finished high school jumped from 29 percent in 1930 to 50 percent in 1940, the greatest advance in American history. Hard times, optimists added, forced many marginal employers of child labor out of business. Optimists also pointed to the enormous efforts made by relief officials at all levels of government, especially by New Dealers after 1932. In December 1934, one of the worst months of the depression, an estimated 19 million Americans received some form of public assistance. Despite impaired diets, they appeared to be coping: life expectancy at birth rose from 59.7 years in 1930 to 62.9 in 1940. Such statistics reveal that the depression did not reverse long-range demographic trends.

Other observers were aware that opportunity beckoned in the midst of poverty. J. Paul Getty, who had already grown rich in the 1920s, amassed millions more in

---

In one of the two rooms a six-year-old boy licked the paper bag the meat had been brought in. His legs were scarcely any larger than a medium sized dog's leg, and his belly was as large as that of a 130-pound woman's. Suffering from rickets and anemia, his legs were unable to carry him for more than a dozen steps at a time; suffering from malnutrition, his belly was swollen several times its normal size. His face was bony and white. He was starving to death.

In the other room of the house, without chairs, beds, or tables, a woman lay rolled up in some quilts trying to sleep. On the floor before an open fire lay two babies, neither a year old, sucking the dry teats of a mongrel bitch. A young girl, somewhere between fifteen and twenty, squatted on the corner of the hearth trying to keep warm.

The dog got up and crawled to the hearth. She sat on her haunches before the blazing pine-knots, shivering and whining. After a while the girl spoke to the dog and the animal slunk away from the warmth of the fire and lay again beside the two babies. The infants cuddled against the warmth of the dog's flanks, searching tearfully for the dry teats.

Erskine Caldwell describes the shack of a southern tenant farmer, 1935.

---

the 1930s by buying oil companies cheaply. Norton Simon bought a bankrupt cannery for $7,000 in 1931 and scrambled to the top of Hunt Foods, a multimillion-dollar business, by 1942. The actress Constance Bennett earned $30,000 in one week endorsing products, and Maurice Chevalier signed on at a Chicago night club for $12,000 a week. Despite hard times, some small business people in the tourist trade—motel owners, used car dealers, gas station operators—made profits during the decade. So did other people well placed in "luxury" occupations—cosmetics manufacturers, movie theater and race track owners, cocktail bar managers, major league baseball players. Corporate lawyers and tenured professors were among the professional people who lived fairly well in the 1930s; so did skilled white-collar workers and managers of technologically advanced companies like IBM and AT&T.

The 1930s also witnessed ongoing advances in the products of technology. These included nylon, aluminum, pneumatic tires for tractors, hybrid corn, television, coaxial cables for simultaneous long distance calls, and FM radios. Travelers welcomed completion in the early 1930s of the first coast-to-coast paved road (the Lincoln Highway) and the first uninterrupted air service across the country. (Previously, passengers had had to spend nights in Pullman cars on the ground and fly again by day—a tiring three-day process.) In 1939 alone newspapers reported the introduction of regular air service across the North Atlantic (Long Island to Lisbon in 26½ hours), of the hydraulic clutch, nylon stockings, fluorescent lights, and—ominously—the successful accomplishment of nuclear fission. Some of these advances were promoted by industries that were desperate for marketable new products or for labor-saving devices. Others stemmed from long-range researches begun before the crash. Either way, it was clear that the technological imperative remained at the essence of modern American life.

However, these success stories concealed precipitous declines in the opportunities available to most workers, especially small farmers and farm laborers, unskilled industrial workers, and employees engaged in all forms of construction, which was paralyzed during the decade. The success stories failed to blot out daily reminders of the misery, malnutrition, and hopelessness of millions of Americans. As late as January 1937, with prosperity apparently returning, President Franklin D. Roosevelt admitted that one-third of the nation was still "ill-housed, ill-clad,

---

Going into the mill was a little like entering a deserted city. There was no movement, no sound. Men worked joylessly at little tasks that had no meaning. The open hearth and rail mills were vast echoing caverns with a single light here and there and a man, sometimes two, puttering around the still machines, the dead furnaces. They looked up eagerly at the sound of a footstep: when they spoke they kept their voices low. But not even the silence and the emptiness were as profoundly disturbing as the all pervading cold, the strange unnatural chill of these places of iron and flame. Leaving there was like worming out of a tomb.

The steel industry in the 1930s, as described by Thomas Bell, *Out of this Furnace,* 1941.

---

ill-nourished." If anything, he underestimated the extent of need, for the Great Depression hit America harder and longer than it did other Western countries. And the pockets of wealth amidst poverty made the depression all the more infuriating. The humorist Will Rogers observed: "We've got . . . more of everything in the world than any nation that ever lived ever had, yet we are starving to death. We are the first nation in the history of the world to go to the poorhouse in an automobile."

WHY DID IT HAPPEN?

Economists have tried to analyze the forces behind the crash and to explain why the depression lasted as long as it did. They do not agree. Nevertheless, it is possible to offer a few tentative explanations.

One cause of the crash was the jerry-built nature of America's corporate structure by 1929. The most flagrant example was Samuel Insull's utilities empire, a vast complex of holding companies and interlocking directorates that rested on the gullibility of investors. Among other highly vulnerable institutions were investment trusts, which were corporations that used the capital of investors to speculate in the securities of other companies. Some of these trusts, and Insull's holding companies, engaged in stock manipulation and fraud; others were capitalized at levels far above their real value. Either way, they were unable to meet their obligations once stock prices declined. Their fall carried with them brokerage houses, banks, corporations, and thousands of private investors.

The proliferation of investment trusts and holding companies in the 1920s exposed another cause of the crash: the vastness of unregulated speculation. Investors were allowed to borrow heavily in order to purchase stock, and to run up still higher debts through installment buying of consumer goods. This runaway speculation also enticed corporations and banks. So long as speculating firms could get high returns from stocks, they had no problems. But when the market slipped, the lenders (which included corporations and banks) called for their money. If they were lucky, they got it—from borrowers who liquidated their investments and thereby further depressed the market. If they did not get their money, both borrowers and lenders defaulted on their obligations. This unprecedented involvement of large institutions in speculation created a vicious circle once prices started to fall.

The instability of banks added to the downward spiral after 1929. Despite efforts by reformers, no federal deposit insurance existed before 1933. Many state banks operated apart from the Federal Reserve system, quite as local capitalists engaged in entrepreneurial ventures. Because banks were not required to separate their banking and investment arms, they used depositors' money for speculative purposes. As the economy declined, people pulled out their deposits to make ends meet. Others, worried that their deposits were not insured, put their money under their mattresses. Caught with huge outstanding liabilities and dwindling deposits, banks foreclosed mortgages, demanded repayment of loans, or went under. To millions of small property owners and depositors nothing was more devastating.

Government policies in the 1920s aggravated these weaknesses. In theory, the Federal Reserve system had the power to curb violent swings in the business cycle. It could make speculation more expensive, either by increasing the interest rate at

Run on banks. Americans, afraid that banks would fail, flocked to withdraw their deposits in the early 1930's.

which member banks had to borrow or by increasing the ratio of reserves they had to withhold from investors. In practice, however, important decisions were not made in Washington, but by private bankers with the Federal Reserve bank in New York. These men were slow to act or even to warn against the speculative mania. When they did, by raising rates to 5 percent in 1928 and 6 percent in 1929, they were too late to stop speculators, who proved willing to borrow elsewhere at exorbitant rates. If higher interest rates had any effect at all in 1929, they turned the screws on solid investment in plant and equipment and accelerated the uncertainty that often precedes a crash.

Federal Reserve officials also showed an undue concern for the welfare of the English pound, which had been unstable since World War I. Keeping American interest rates low, they realized, might encourage excessive speculation. But raising them might induce English capitalists to invest their money in America, thus draining capital from England and increasing pressure on the pound. Accordingly, the New York bankers kept American interest rates low between 1926 and 1928. This concern for the stability of the pound revealed the extent to which international investments affected the domestic economy.

All these destabilizing forces—investment trusts, holding companies, rampant speculation, shaky banks, counterproductive government policies—were important causes of the crash. But they do not explain the depression. Many of these weaknesses, in fact, were hardly new in 1929. Speculative manias and unstable corporations had always plagued the economy, and American banks had long been decentralized. And monetary policy, while uninformed, was not necessarily the panacea that some later economists claimed. In 1929, for instance, higher interest rates failed to prevent speculation, in part because so many corporate investors could employ profits for idle purposes, in part because the psychology of boom made the cost of borrowing almost irrelevant. The reverse psychology in the 1930s meant that record-low rates failed to bring money out of hiding. Investors cannot be moved by interest rates alone.

The depression

What, then, did turn the crash into such a devastating depression?

One cause lay in international economic instability of a peculiarly severe nature. The war had left England and France heavily in debt to America, which insisted on repayment of its loans. But the Allies, even after squeezing Germany dry, were hard pressed to pay. Until 1928 American investors sustained a circular state of affairs by literally pouring loans into Germany. By 1929, however, they found the fantastic domestic possibilities on the stock market more alluring than European investments. So they began to invest and to speculate more heavily at home. As Europe's financial institutions began to weaken, investors throughout the world sought safer places for their money. By September 1931 these forces led to the devaluation of the English pound and the collapse of the Kreditanstalt, Austria's central bank. Frightening withdrawals from banks—what economists call a rush for liquidity—then followed throughout the Western world. In America alone 3,800 banks failed in 1931 and 1932.

Fundamental domestic weaknesses also made the crash of 1929 more lasting than those in the past. Among these weaknesses were "depressed areas," as they were later called, in mining, textiles, and agriculture. The distress of America's farmers, who had overexpanded during the years of wartime demand, was especially significant, for farmers and farm workers comprised about 10 or 11 million people, or more than one-fifth of the work force. Their plight was contagious, especially in the many towns and small cities sustained by agriculture. (In the "prosperous" years between 1923 and 1929, for instance, banks folded at the appalling rate of two per day. Most of these were in rural areas.) For all these people the crash on Wall Street made a difficult situation worse. Their hard times—and loss of purchasing power—were important reasons why the depression lasted as long as it did.

Cyclical downswings in the economy coincided with and intensified these structural weaknesses. The "new era" of the 1920s had been heavily sustained by the automobile and construction industries. As early as 1925, however, residential construction began to level off, and in 1927 auto sales declined. Though the car industry recovered in 1928, construction continued to lag. By the summer of 1929 this "temporary stagnation" began to worry businessmen with large inventories.

Their uneasiness, in turn, helped provoke the crash. Thereafter, the sluggishness in these important consumer durables—and the absence of great innovations in the 1930s—compounded the economic problems of the era.

At the root of this stagnation was the maldistribution of income in America. While the real wages of regularly employed production workers in manufacturing were increasing by 12 percent between 1921 and 1929, corporate profits jumped 62 percent and dividends 65 percent. In 1929 the richest 5 percent of the population received 33.5 percent of disposable income; the richest 1 percent got 19 percent. The 36,000 wealthiest families (less than 1 percent of the total) earned more than the combined income of the 12 million families who got less than $1,500 a year, a minimum standard of living.

This distribution of income was no worse than it had been in earlier decades. The middle classes, in fact, formed a higher percentage of the population. But therein lay another problem: "new era" prosperity depended as never before on mass purchasing power. Until 1925 or so this consumer power, fueled by gains during the war years, was sufficient to promote growth. People were able to buy cars and houses, and businesses to expand. By 1927, however, most people who could afford by buy such goods had already done so. As this "saturation point" was approached, demand slackened, production leveled off, and payrolls stabilized. If corporations (which had profited immensely since 1915) had dramatically lowered prices or raised wages, they could have pumped life into purchasing power. But few producers in the 1920s felt much pressure to do so, for labor unions were struggling and price competition (especially in oligopolistic industries like automobiles) was often weak. Fewer still perceived the vital connection between consumption and prosperity. These impediments to increased purchasing power helped make the depression of the 1930s deeper and more severe than any in the American past.

A lack of economic expertise also helped prolong the depression. There was in 1930 no Council of Economic Advisers to assist public officials, and no coherent body of economic theory stressing the need for sustaining purchasing power. Keynesian ideas concerning the uses of compensatory fiscal policy were not fully set out until 1936 or well known among American economists until the end of the decade. Thus it was that government, like private corporations, did little to assist mass purchasing power in either the 1920s or the 1930s.

Instead, many Americans persisted in thinking that the "utopia" of the 1920s had rested on rugged individualism and welfare capitalism. The answer to hard times, Andrew Mellon said cavalierly, was to wait for the cycle to hit bottom. "Liquidate labor, liquidate stocks, liquidate the farmers, liquidate real estate . . . enterprising people will pick up the wrecks from less competitive people." Myron Taylor, head of U.S. Steel, added in 1932 that government attempts to stabilize industry would "take out of life its chief elixir, the element of competition, and would eliminate profit, which is the reward for the energetic and patient and farsighted." Ideas such as these prevented Americans from adopting the programs of social insurance that softened the blow of depression in European countries. As late as 1932 these same ideas stopped politicians of both parties from recognizing that positive state intervention can ameliorate hard times.

The deepest cause of prolonged hard times was psychological. Having experienced a "new era" in economics during the 1920s, Americans expected the crash to be short-lived. The market, they told themselves, inevitably falls off from time to time; when it hits bottom, investment will pick up, and growth will resume. But as the downward spiral persisted, surprise turned to shock, panic, and desperation. People who had money refused to risk it, even at the lowest interest rates in history. The shattering sequence of events of 1929–33, following so abruptly on the high expectations of the 1920s, created a depression psychology of unprecedented proportions that affected all levels of society.

REPERCUSSIONS

Sexual mores and family life To listen to the moralists in the 1930s, one could easily conclude that hard times were undermining the home and family, leading to widespread sexual immorality and promoting a fatal dependency on relief that undermined individualism and the work ethic.

These alarmists buttressed their case with seemingly formidable evidence. The depression induced thousands of husbands to move far from home and countless thousands more—no one knows how many—to abandon their families. Prolonged idleness forced others to feel ashamed, emasculated; many left home early in the day for no purpose other than to get out from under the eyes of reproachful wives or children. And millions of the jobless, after trying fruitlessly to get work, went to the relief office. Some of these, especially the older and unskilled workers, never got another steady job. Young people leaving home for better opportunities deprived themselves of the security of roots and their parents of companionship and assistance in their old age. Hard times also delayed marriages and sharply depressed the birth rate: the book *Live Alone and Like It* (1936), by Marjorie Hillis, was a best seller. John Steinbeck's epic *Grapes of Wrath* (1939), which portrayed the desperate efforts of the Joad family to stay together under the pressure of poverty and migration, was a fair (if somewhat romanticized) picture of family tensions in the 1930s.

The great need for millions of the unemployed was to find ways to cope with idleness. Many people turned in on themselves to pursue solitary pleasures. Americans read more, took up stamp collecting, and avidly joined boxtop contests. Other popular pastimes included dance marathons and six-day bicycle races—escape hatches for bored, jobless spectators who lost themselves in the crowd. Above all, people tried to forget their troubles by going to the movies or listening to the radio. Some 85 million Americans (65 percent of the total population) saw movies at least once a week. The number of Americans who owned radios increased from 10 million in 1929 to 27.5 million a decade later. Each radio, one survey found in 1937, was used for an average of 4½ hours a day.

It also seemed that the moralists had a case in arguing that sexual license was spreading in the 1930s. Observing the delay in marriages, the American Association of School Administrators complained of "increases in masturbation, clandestine relations, prostitution, and homosexuality.'' The Lynds concluded soberly that the inability of young people to afford marriage, combined with advances in contraception, encouraged premarital sexual relations. They also reported that family tensions caused ''a great deal of married women's running around with single men.''

As usual, the moralists were unduly alarmed. While many husbands headed off for better opportunity, others, recognizing the futility of migration, clung more firmly than ever to the familiar ties of home and family. Many Americans, remembering their lives in the 1930s, recall fondly that their families grew closer under the pressures of hard times. They remember that neighbors and friends gathered around to help in especially trying periods. Nor did all the young people race off to ride the rails: it is probable (statistics are sketchy) that the amount of geographical migration declined—as it ordinarily does when economic opportunities are limited. The cost of going out also forced many families to stay at home, and to enjoy simple domestic pleasures like bridge, cookouts, and Monopoly instead of rushing off in their cars. Divorce rates actually decreased in the early 1930s (though the main reason was probably the cost of going through the courts).

The moralists also failed to prove their point about changes in sexual behavior. Organized prostitution probably declined—most businesses did. Alleged increases in masturbation, homosexuality, or adultery simply were—and are—impossible to document. The apparent rise in premarital sexual activity was neither new nor alarming. Rather, it extended a trend which had already surfaced in the 1920s. And mainstream attitudes toward discussion of sex were no more liberated than in the 1920s. The 1930s witnessed the peak in strength of such organizations as the Legion of Decency, the Episcopal Committee on Motion Pictures, and Hollywood censorship under ''Movie Czar'' Will Hays (who cut the offensive line of Mae West, ''I wouldn't let him touch me with a ten-foot pole'').

Those who worried about sexual immorality also underestimated the desire of young women for security in those troubled times. Those feminists who called for sexual liberation—or for economic equality—did not receive much of a hearing. Middle-class women, a few of whom had tried to enter the professions in the 1910s and 1920s, seemed readier to accept marriage and domesticity as primary goals. As if to underline this attitude, they paid less attention to such visible symbols of emancipation as bobbed hair or clothing that flattened the figure. They tended to wear their hair naturally, used practical shoes, and dressed in simple, sensible clothes. Facing widespread opposition to the hiring of women in a time of massive male unemployment, they had to live with regulations against hiring women as civil servants and laws that denied jobs to married women teachers if qualified men could be hired in their place. A Gallup poll revealed that 82 percent of Americans, including 75 percent of women, agreed that wives should not work if their husbands were employed. A women's magazine concluded: ''no matter how successful, the office woman . . . is a transplanted posey. . . . Just as a rose comes to its fullest beauty in its own appropriate soil, so does a home woman come to her fullest blooming when her roots are struck deep in the daily and hourly affairs of her own most dearly beloved.'' The depression years, far from promoting sexual liberation or economic feminism, sustained traditional beliefs in marriage and in the father as head of the household.

Americans felt above all that the family must be preserved. They eagerly read Gasoline Alley, the comic strip about ordinary family problems. They applauded the Hardy family movies, which received a special Oscar in 1942 for "furthering the American way of life." They made big sellers of Clarence Day's *Life with Father* (1935) and *Life with Mother* (1936), and of *Good Housekeeping's Marriage Book: Twelve Ways to a Happy Marriage* (1938). They responded warmly to Steinbeck's heroic Ma Joad, guarantor and preserver of familial unity. While the connection between popular culture and mass values cannot be firmly established, it seems fairly clear that the 1930s made domesticity a primary virtue. It was three decades before "women's liberation" and the "counterculture" of the 1960s popularized an alternative.

The alarmists who worried about the disintegration of the work ethic also oversimplified a complex matter. For many chronically poor people—the aged, the disabled, members of broken families, blacks, Mexican-Americans—the hard times of the 1930s made relatively little difference. "The reason why the Depression didn't have the impact on the Negro that it had on the whites," one contemporary black writer explained, "was that the Negroes had been in the Depression all the time." Chronic poverty had also afflicted millions of textile workers (many of them women and children), miners, small farmers, and migrant workers. All these people were used to hard treatment, and they did not expect to go far in life. As one poor farmer observed, "always going to be more poor folks than them that ain't poor, and I guess always will be. I ain't saying that's the government's fault. It's just down right truth, that's all."

The largest group of these very poor were small farmers, especially blacks, in the South. One such area was Macon County, Alabama, a cotton-growing region that included Tuskegee Institute, the black college founded by Booker T. Washington. It was 82 percent black. Charles Johnson, a sociologist who studied the culture of these blacks in the early 1930s, concluded that it featured a "static economics not unlike that of the Mexican *hacienda,* or the condition of the Polish peasant—a situation in which the members of a group are 'muffled with a vast apathy.'" Of the 612 households he visited, 144 had illegitimate children, 443 rented as tenant farmers or croppers, and 108 lived in plantation cabins. Most of the dwellings were more than thirty years old, unpainted, without windows. They had open privies or no sewage disposal at all on the premises. They were very crowded. "The crowding together of families in these small rooms," Johnson said, "destroys all privacy, dulls the desire for neatness and cleanliness, and renders virtually impossible the development of any sense of beauty. It is a cheerless condition of life for those who keep alive a flickering desire for something better."

Macon County was an extreme case; few regions were as depressed. Nor were the poor people there depraved and disorganized—an impression that other writers about black family life sometimes conveyed. On the contrary, these and other blacks tried hard under oppressive conditions to maintain stable family lives and their cultural heritage. Still, the central point remained true: for millions of chronically poor Americans, the depression merely prolonged their plight. It did not

A common sight during the depression. Many Americans held fiercely to the work ethic at a time when unemployment was very high.

wreak much new havoc in their lives or cause fundamental changes in their values or family patterns.

For the newly poor and unemployed, of course, the depression mattered greatly; it was often a shattering and totally demoralizing experience. Social workers worried that hard times were indeed destroying people. "There is a terrible problem," one said, "of salvaging human material, or letting it permanently rot . . . this ailment [of poverty] is chronic." Another cried, "the young are as disheartening as any group, more so, really. They are apathetic, sinking into a resigned bitterness. . . . They don't believe in man or God, let alone private industry. The only thing that keeps them from suicide is this amazing loss of vitality." A third reported a "decline in morale of our relief clients as each month goes by . . . we are beginning to notice what I would call a complacency on relief."

Some of these social workers perceived a vast apathy among the unemployed. "There are no protest groups," one wrote. "There are no 'dangerous reds.' If anything, these people are a sad gray; waiting, hoping, trusting." Another added, "the more articulate go into relief offices and kick. Mostly, however, their attitude is one of patience—a rather terrible sort of patience, I think." Reporters who watched the so-called Bonus Army come into Washington in 1932—this was a group of veterans who marched to Congress in order to seek help—were struck by the veterans' "curious melancholy." The group, one observer noted, was not a dangerous bunch of radicals but an "army of bewilderment."

But it is inaccurate to stress the loss of morale or the apathy of the unemployed in the 1930s. Rather, most of the jobless showed remarkable resiliency, and they adhered stubbornly to older values, including the work ethic. The vast majority procrastinated as long as possible before heading for the relief station. "I'd rather be dead and buried," one commented. An accountant on a work project said, "I'd rather stay out there in that ditch the rest of my life than take one cent of direct relief." A third, reflecting the pervasive racism of the day, added, "I'd do anything if only I could get a job—even to cleaning cuspidors, or doing any other Nigger work." The depression, far from promoting a "relief ethic" or destroying morale, tended to intensify the importance of hard work and individual effort. The old values persisted.

It is equally simplistic to stress the political apathy of the down-and-outers. Many raged at the rich and powerful. "Why don't the big corporations dig down and donate a little?" one complained in 1930. "It is always the poor devil that has to fork over. . . . Now is the time for all *rich men* to come to the aid of their country." Poor people also blamed government "big shots." One wrote Harry Hopkins, head of the federal relief effort, "when the half-starved unemployed get a job cutting grass these days, they sing, every tuft of grass, a big shot's head. That gives them strength; when I come to your head, I get roots and all." Some of these people joined protest movements, such as the national drive for publicly paid old-age pensions, or the "Share Our Wealth" crusade of Senator Huey Long of Louisiana. Others lobbied for stiffer taxes on the wealthy. Many joined demonstrations, rent strikes, and—in the mid-1930s—labor unions by the millions. A general strike briefly gripped Seattle in 1932, terrifying conservatives. Miners and textile workers struck on a massive scale in 1934–35. Ordinarily peace-loving farmers angrily dumped milk on the highway rather than sell it at low prices. Blacks in Harlem rioted in 1935. Strikes, even by workers on public relief projects, disrupted industrial peace throughout the decade.

Given the depth and duration of the depression, it is arguable that Americans were remarkably patient and submissive. This view is true insofar as it underlines the inability of America's needy to mobilize and get adequate relief, much less to promote and institute radical economic programs. Disparities in wealth and power, great in 1929, were perhaps greater in 1939. But the problem facing the poor was not so much apathy as lack of resources and of organization. Desperate for work, they lacked the time and the money to become a vital political force. They therefore had to rely on sporadic, uncoordinated protests. These were easily quashed, but in quashing them, more fortunate Americans grew unsure and uneasy. Amid such turbulence—few decades witnessed more unrest—it was wrongheaded indeed to see only apathy among the underclasses.

Thinkers on the Left Nothing could be sillier than the notion, spread later by demagogues like Senator Joe McCarthy, that the 1930s were a "Red decade" in America. It is almost as simplistic to generalize and apply the term "left-wing" to

American social thought in the depression years. Still, hard times naturally prompted a variety of leftist prescriptions for social action. The writers and thinkers on the Left had never been more articulate or more relevant.

Unrest in the universities revealed that left-wing ideas generated more interest among the young than they had in the 1920s. College youth joined such leftist organizations as the National Student League and the Student League for Industrial Democracy. Others joined the Young Communist League and led demonstrations against tuition costs or local power elites. In 1934 an estimated 25,000 students went on strike in support of Anti-War Week, and in 1935, 175,000 turned out for a repeat performance. Compared to the demonstrations of the 1960s, those of the 1930s were peaceful and unthreatening. Campus life, including fraternities and football, went on as before. But the radical youth of both eras agreed in distrusting the older generation. "A man might be of some use to the community until he was thirty years old," James Wechsler, a young radical, wrote in 1935, "but after that he was automatically aligned with the legions of darkness."

Some leaders of the progressive education movement welcomed this turn to the left. Like George S. Counts, a professor at Teachers College, Columbia, they rejected one monument of progressive educators in the 1920s: the child-centered school. Teachers who concentrated on developing the expressiveness of individual children, Counts argued, were neglecting their social duties. Schools, he said, must "face squarely and courageously every social issue, come to grips with life in all of its stark reality, establish an organic relation with the community, [and] develop a realistic and comprehensive theory of welfare. . . ." The title of his best-known book, *Dare the School Build a New Social Order?* (1932), expressed his programmatic orientation. The depression was no occasion for "play schools" or for experiments aimed at enhancing individual creativity; it was the time to indoctrinate people for social change.

The master progressive educator, John Dewey, agreed. In 1934 he helped found, with Counts and others, the magazine *Social Frontier,* which became a forum for leftist intellectuals for the rest of the decade. Though he had long advocated experimentalism, he now emphasized that it must not become an end in itself. "Organized social planning," he said, " . . . is now the sole method of social action by which liberalism can realize its professed aims. . . . Liberalism must now become radical." In stressing the social mission of America's political and educational leaders Dewey revealed a leftist orientation characteristic of many intellectuals of the time.

A growing number of law school teachers shared this reformist bias. Among them were Jerome Frank and William O. Douglas, who had already spread the gospel of legal realism in the 1920s. Another was Thurman Arnold, a Yale law school professor whose *Symbols of Government* (1935) and *Folklore of Capitalism* (1937) included broad-ranging assaults on absolutist dogmas of all kinds. "So long as preconceived principles are considered more important than practical results," he wrote, "the practical alleviation of human distress and the distribution of available comforts will be paralyzed." America, he added, needed "new public attitudes toward the ideals of law and economics" so that a "competent, practical, opportunistic governing class may rise to power." On one level Arnold's plea for "practical results" embraced value-free experimentalism. But his relativism also stemmed from impatience with the existing order. Like Dewey, Arnold hoped to "alleviate human distress" through social engineering.

The planners and relativists did not go unchallenged. Robert Hutchins, the influential president of the University of Chicago, insisted that educators had a duty to provide young people with enduring truths; students at Chicago were required to read the "great books." Walter Lippmann complained of the "aimless and turbulent moral relativity of twentieth-century social thought." Planners, he added, were potential tyrants: "there can be no plan to find the planners: the selection of the despots who are to make society so rational and so secure has to be left to the security of irrational chance." Though these writers differed widely in their politics, they were searching for absolutes more transcendent than social engineering or experimentalism. As the threat of fascism grew in the late 1930s, their call for a return to first principles seemed increasingly relevant.

None of these thinkers was radical in his economic thought. However, others turned to the Communist party, which attracted some 50,000 Americans by mid-decade. For such people, socialism was too slow and evolutionary; only proletarian revolution could abolish capitalism. When Hitler came to power in 1933, they concluded that the Soviet Union was the only bulwark against the spread of fascism. In the late 1930s, when word of Josef Stalin's ruthless purges reached the West, and especially in 1939, when Russia signed a nonaggression pact with Germany, thousands of these American communists broke with the party. Until then, however, revolutionary rhetoric and communist sympathy were common among left-wing intellectuals of the 1930s.

Among these communist sympathizers were established writers like Theodore Dreiser and Lincoln Steffens, younger men like John Dos Passos, Erskine Caldwell, and Lewis Mumford, and rising literary critics like Edmund Wilson, Malcolm Cowley, and Granville Hicks. These sympathizers also included radical playwrights who banded together in collectives like the Group Theatre, or in The Theatre Union, whose motto was "theatre is a weapon in the class struggle." Other young writers, including Richard Wright, joined the John Reed clubs, named after the romantic American radical who had embraced the Bolshevik revolution. Promoting the *New Masses,* the leading communist organ in America, the John Reed clubs called upon "all honest writers and artists to abandon decisively the treacherous illusion that art can exist for art's sake, or that the artist can remain remote from the historic conflicts in which all men must take sides." Writers, the manifesto added, must "break with bourgeois ideas which seek to conceal the violence and fraud, the corruption and decay of capitalistic society."

Chief guru of these radical artists was Michael Gold, an editor for the *New Masses* and author of *Jews Without Money* (1930), an unrelievedly grim novel about poverty in New York. Gold angrily rejected the older bohemian left, which he felt spent too much time propagandizing for cultural liberation and sexual freedom. (He called Floyd Dell, a former bohemian, "the historian of the phallic-hunting girls of Greenwich Village."). Gold insisted that writers and artists employ proletarian themes and advance the inevitable class struggle. This literary theory left nonproletarian writers like Thornton Wilder beyond the pale. Wilder,

The *New Masses,* a Communist magazine, predicts a proletarian revolution. Cover by William Gropper.

Gold charged, was the "prophet of the genteel Christ," the "poet of a small sophisticated class that has recently arisen in America—our genteel bourgeoisie. . . . This Emily Post of culture will never reproach them; or remind them of Pittsburgh and the breadlines."

Gold's crudely Marxist approach to literature offended many writers, including leftists like Wilson and Cowley. It also failed to inspire an outpouring of proletarian writing. But many intellectuals agreed with Gold that writers and artists must be men and women of action and that social criticism was a necessary aspect of true art. These beliefs led social realist painters like Ben Shahn to show the same contempt for expressionist painting that Counts had heaped on free schools. "Is there nothing," Shahn asked, "to weep about in this world any more? Is all our pity and anger to be reduced to a few tastefully arranged straight lines or petulant squirts from a tube held over a canvas? All the wheels of business and advertising are turning night and day to prove the colossal falsehood that America is smiling. And they want me to add my two percent. Hell, no."

Other writers and artists echoed Shahn's faith in the social value of art. Pare Lorentz, a gifted documentary film maker, produced *The Plow that Broke the Plains* (1936) and *The River* (1937), lyrical efforts to propagandize for conservation of natural resources. Warner Brothers films such as *I Am a Fugitive from a Chain*

Gang (1932) and *20,000 Years in Sing Sing* (1933) reminded audiences of poverty and injustice. Gangster movies featuring tough-guy heroes like James Cagney attempted to show that the lower classes possessed tenderness and human dignity. Folksingers, especially Woody Guthrie, sang the virtues of ordinary working people and Dust Bowl migrants. Playwrights like Clifford Odets composed inspirational dramas such as *Let Freedom Ring, Awake and Sing,* and *Waiting for Lefty* (which stirred audiences to shout "strike, strike, strike" at the end of performances).

Novels of social criticism enjoyed an unprecedented vogue in the 1930s. Dos Passos' *Big Money* (1936), the concluding volume of his massive trilogy *U. S. A.,* described the pernicious effect of materialism on the ordinary characters who crowded his panorama of twentieth-century American society. Caldwell's illiterate, almost subhuman tenant farmers in novels such as *Tobacco Road* (1934) exposed readers to the poverty of the rural South. James T. Farrell's *Studs Lonigan* (1932–38) chronicled the pathology of Irish-American slum life in the city. Richard Wright's *Native Son* (1940), set in Chicago's black belt, dealt with the evils of racism and capitalism; one of its most sympathetically drawn characters was a communist lawyer. Steinbeck's *In Dubious Battle* (1939) also included a communist protagonist, while his socially conscious *Grapes of Wrath* (1939) became a best-selling movie.

Even Ernest Hemingway, champion of individual courage, seemed affected by the depression. *To Have and Have Not* (1937) was the story of a smuggler ruined by society. At the end of the novel, he gasps, "A man ain't got no bloody fucking chance." And in *For Whom the Bell Tolls* (1940), a novel featuring antifascist heroes in the Spanish Civil War, Hemingway took an openly political stance. His title was taken from a John Donne poem in which also appeared the words, "No man is an island, entire of itself." The depression, it appeared, was provoking a revolutionary change in literature as well as in social theories.

Search for a usable past Appearances, however, were deceptive. Though social consciousness grew in the early 1930s, it was neither pervasive nor lasting. "If you want to hear discussions of the future revolution in the United States," George Soule observed accurately in 1932, "do not go to the breadlines and the mill towns, but to . . . gatherings of young literary men. . . . Searching for actual flesh-and-blood revolutionary proletarians is a thankless task. Most of those who really suffer from the depression are . . . simply stricken dumb by it." These people were shocked by hard times and ashamed to be trapped in them. Though angry, they often blamed themselves, not capitalism, for their troubles. They looked backward for usable values, not forward to revolution. Despite ten years of unparalleled economic hardship, they succeeded in reaffirming much that they had cherished in the years before the crash.

One manifestation of this search for a usable past was renewed appreciation of small-town, rural ways of life. Because of hard times, some Americans promoted a back-to-the-land movement that romanticized the virtues of self-sufficient living close to the soil. New Dealers, including Eleanor Roosevelt, championed a Subsistence Homestead program. Twelve southern agrarians wrote a manifesto of essays,

Walker Evans photographed the kitchen of an Alabama tenant farmer, 1936.

I'll Take My Stand (1930), which combined a critique of industrial capitalism with nostalgia for the antebellum South. Thousands of others applauded films like Frank Capra's *Mr. Deeds Goes to Town* (1934) and *Mr. Smith Goes to Washington* (1939), which celebrated the virtues of simple, small-town Americans. The works of artists such as Lorentz, Guthrie, and Steinbeck, while exposing the excesses of free enterprise, also were hymns of praise to the countryside and the agrarian way of life. And many radical intellectuals, including Theodore Dreiser, Edmund Wilson, and Sherwood Anderson, as well as gifted photographers like Walker Evans and Dorothea Lange, traveled the land to record affectionately the everyday scenes they had ignored in the 1920s.

A self-conscious rejection of things foreign accompanied this affection for the American heartlands. Frederick Jackson Turner's frontier thesis, which apotheosized the rural pioneer, explicitly rejected the "germ" theory tracing American traits to European beginnings. His ideas were generally accepted by textbooks in the early 1930s. Painters like Thomas Hart Benton and Grant Wood ignored European fashions in art and promoted a Regionalist movement that focused on scenes of the American Plains and Midwest. "No good painting has come out of France since 1890," Benton pronounced with characteristic (and calculated) truculence. Like the isolationists, who also developed imposing influence in the 1930s, the Regionalists sought recompense for hard times by reaffirming their faith in the heartland of America.

Other Americans sought roots far in their past. Van Wyck Brooks, once the harsh critic of American writers, published essays praising a host of second-rate nineteenth-century literary figures. Carl Sandburg wrote an appealing multivolume biography of Abraham Lincoln, who came across as a lovable folk hero. High prices for paintings by primitives like "Grandma" Moses, as well as for antique furniture, suggested that Americans cherished visible reminders of their past. The popularity of tough guys in the movies, of westerns, and of the hard-boiled heroes of detective fiction revealed that Americans enjoyed being reminded of the good old days when rugged individualists still had a chance against social forces.

Popular and elite culture   Other purveyors of popular culture outdid themselves in appealing to similarly escapist impulses. Popular radio programs included "The Green Hornet," "The Lone Ranger," and the ever-present "Amos 'n Andy." The enormously popular soap operas ("Portia Faces Life," "Life Can Be Beautiful," "Ma Perkins," "Just Plain Bill") almost always featured white, middle-class, small-town Protestants—just plain folks—enduring all manner of minor tragedies before surmounting the forces against them. Housewives, it was assumed, were relieved to know that ordinary people faced tribulations more trying than theirs, just as they were reassured by larger-than-life heroines like Ma Perkins, stabilizers of all that was good and holy. Escapist novels included such best sellers as Margaret Mitchell's *Gone with the Wind* (1936) and Walter Pitkin's *Life Begins at Forty* (1932). The comics, more popular than ever, featured new strips like *Tarzan* (1929), *Dick Tracy* (1931), and *Terry and the Pirates* (1934). Many of these reinforced stereotypes about apelike blacks and wily orientals. That may have been part of their appeal. In any event, they offered readers rugged, he-man heroes. Milton Caniff, creator of *Terry and the Pirates,* knew that he was providing a kind of narcotic. "The strip started out," he said later, "in October, 1934, and the country was already on its way out of the muddle, but the people were so exhausted by the emotional drain that I used the simple picaresque device of attempting to take them out of their post-depression milieu and at least pretend for a Scheherazade moment that they are somewhere else dreaming Walter Mitty dreams of their position (in the manner of Don Quixote). In the very nature of this a certain order was implied."

Even the leftists—except for self-styled proletarians like Gold—could be understood on different levels. Though members of the Group Theatre submerged their individual personalities in a collective effort, they often did so to experiment with new dramatic forms, not necessarily to promote social art. Caldwell's tenant farmers, like Steinbeck's migrants, cared little for socialism; they wanted only land and meaningful work. Many apparently leftist books—Farrell's *Studs Lonigan,* Wright's *Native Son*—were autobiographical and existential as much as they were programmatic calls for social change.

The work of Dos Passos, who had criticized capitalism even in the 1920s, revealed similar ambiguities. Though money corrupted many of his characters, he offered no political solution. His heroes were hard-working, rugged young men like "Vag," the hitchhiker who is kicked about as he wanders—alone—toward some unknown opportunity in the future. A writer, Dos Passos concluded, should resist oppression and injustice. But he "must never, no matter how much he is carried away by even the noblest political partisanship in the fight for social justice, allow himself to forget that his real political aim . . . is [artistic] liberty.''

This refusal to surrender artistic sensibility to communist ideology motivated most of the well-known writers of the decade. Intellectuals, Edmund Wilson observed, were free to work for collectivist programs but should insist on remaining independent custodians of ultimate values. Archibald MacLeish believed that the true artist should never follow the ''social and intellectual fashions of the day.'' James Agee, coauthor with Walker Evans of *Let Us Now Praise Famous Men* (1941), a photo-poetic attempt to recapture the daily lives of southern tenant farmers, characterized the feeling of many critical intellectuals in the 1930s. ''A good artist,'' he said, ''is a deadly enemy of society, and the most dangerous thing that can happen to an enemy . . . is to become a beneficiary.'' Agee meant that sensitive intellectuals could not help being alienated by the crassness and injustice of American life—he did not defend the status quo. He also meant that artists must remain free to express their alienation as they saw fit.

The quest for self-respect The Lynds, describing Muncie at mid-decade, were persuaded that the depression did not much affect the attitudes of the residents. ''In the main,'' they argued, ''a Rip Van Winkle, fallen asleep in 1925 while addressing Rotary or the Central Labor Union, could have awakened in 1935 and gone right on with his interrupted address to the same people with much the same ideas.''

The Lynds recognized that it was risky to make such sweeping statements about the attitudes of an entire city. Muncie, in any event, was not necessarily ''typical.'' Yet many clues existed to support their argument that the desire for material goods, so sweeping in the 1920s, survived the hard times of the 1930s. Among these clues were the fantastic sums bet on football pools, the proliferation of slot machines, the passion for the game of Monopoly, and the popularity of Dr. Napolean Hill's *Think and Grow Rich*, which sold 5 million copies. The anthropologist Margaret Mead concluded that parents persisted in inculcating such values in their children throughout the decade.

All profits disappear; the gain
Of ease, the hoarded, secret sum;
And now grim digits of old pain
Return to litter up our home.

We hunt the cause of ruin, add,
Subtract, and put ourselves in pawn;
For all our scratching on the pad,
We cannot trace the error down.

What we are seeking is a fare
One way, a chance to be secure:
The lack that keeps us what we are,
The penny that usurps the poor.

"The Reckoning," a poem by Theodore Roethke, 1941, reveals the desire for security.

In 1936 *Fortune* magazine offered a slightly different interpretation. Surveying the "present-day college generation," it concluded that it was "fatalistic . . . it will not stick its neck out. It keeps its pants buttoned, its chin up, and its mouth shut. If we take the mean average to be the truth, it is a cautious, subdued, unadventurous generation. . . . Security is the *summum bonum* of the present college generation."

The very success of a magazine named *Fortune* might suggest that the Lynds were closer to the mark, that Americans were as hungry as ever for material wealth. But *Fortune* (which pioneered in the new "science" of polling) was also correct to stress that this hunger had security as the ultimate goal. As Dale Carnegie explained in his best-selling manual, *How to Win Friends and Influence People* (1936), one should not shake the social ladder too hard in climbing to success. One should learn to adjust, to become socialized. If the popularity of Carnegie's book was any indication, the 1930s were the decade when Americans, in William F. Whyte's terms, began to substitute the Social Ethic for the Protestant Ethic of years past.

Such an argument is impossible to document or to apply to millions of people. Yet it is plausible. For a time the depression turned many Americans to the left. But as early as 1936, when the worst appeared to be over, many Americans began to long for the old ways. Though some of these people hoped to rise like Horatio Alger characters, from rags to riches, most of them yearned primarily to exorcise the guilt and shame they had felt on losing their jobs, their homes, or their social position. They wanted self-respect, dignity, the security of work, home, and family. They continued to be cautious, scared, and "unventuresome" long after prosperity returned. No one put it better than Woody Guthrie:

> I don't want your millions mister
> I don't want your damned ring
> All I want's just live and let live
> Give me back my job again
>
> Think me dumb if you wish, mister,
> Call me a green or blue or red.
> There's just one thing that I know, mister
> Our hungry babies must be fed. . . .

Suggestions for reading

Among the clearest accounts of economic trends in the late 1920s and 1930s are J. K. Galbraith, *The Great Crash** (1955); Robert Sobel, *The Great Bull Market** (1968); Broadus Mitchell, *Depression Decade** (1947); and Charles Kindleburger, *The World in Depression, 1929–1939* (1973). See also works by Friedman and Schwartz and by Potter cited in the bibliography for chapter 6. Other useful books are Murray Rothbard, *America's Great Depression* (1963); Herbert Stein, *The Fiscal Revolution, 1931–1963** (1969); Robert Lekachman, *The Age of Keynes** (1966); Lester Chandler, *American Monetary Policy, 1929–1941** (1971); and Susan Kennedy, *The Banking Crisis of 1933** (1973).

Social trends are covered in Dixon Wecter, *The Age of the Great Depression, 1929–1941** (1948); Robert and Helen Lynd, *Middletown in Transition** (1937); David Brody, *Workers in Industrial America* (1980); and Irving Bernstein, *The Turbulent Years** (1970), on labor; David Conrad, *Forgotten Farmers* (1966); John Shover, *Cornbelt Rebellion*

(1965); Donald Worster, *Dust Bowl: The Southern Plains in the 1930s* (1979); and Walter Stein, *California and the Dust Bowl Migration* (1970). Other subjects are treated in Robert Angell, *The Family Encounters the Depression* (1936); Mirra Komarovsky, *The Unemployed Man and His Family** (1940); and Abraham Hoffman, *Unwanted Mexican-Americans in the Great Depression** (1974). John Dollard, *Caste and Class in a Southern Town** (1937), is a sociological study. Caroline Bird, *The Invisible Scar** (1965), is a general account of social trends. Sidney Fine, *Sit-Down: The General Motors Strike of 1936–37* (1969), is a thorough account of its subject.

Books dealing with American thought in the 1930s are Richard Pells, *Radical Visions and American Dreams: Culture and Social Thought in the Depression Years** (1973); Charles Alexander, *Nationalism in American Thought, 1930–1945** (1969); Edward Purcell, Jr., *The Crisis of Democratic Theory* (1972); Donald Meyer, *The Protestant Search for Social Realism, 1919–1941* (1960); and David O'Brien, *American Catholics and Social Reform: The New Deal Years* (1965). Barry Karl, *Charles E. Merriam and the Study of Politics** (1974), is an important book dealing with political science at the time; on left-wing and radical thought see Frank A. Warren, *Liberals and Communism: the "Red" Decade Revisited* (1966); Irving Howe and Lewis Coser, *The American Communist Party* (1957); Daniel Aaron, *Writers on the Left** (1961); and Bernard Johnpoll, *Pacifist's Progress* (1970), on Norman Thomas.

For black history consult Raymond Wolters, *Negroes and the Great Depression** (1970); and Dan T. Carter, *Scottsboro: A Tragedy of the Modern South** (1969). A moving account of race relations (and medicine) is James M. Jones, *Bad Blood: The Tuskegee Syphilis Experiment* (1981). Primary sources include twelve southerners, *I'll Take My Stand** (1930), which is a collection of essays by southern agrarians; Thurman Arnold, *Folklore of Capitalism** (1937); Edmund Wilson, *American Earthquake** (1958); Richard Crossman, ed., *The God That Failed** (1949), essays by disillusioned former communists; Walter F. White, *A Man Called White** (1948), a memoir by the leader of the NAACP; James Agee and Walker Evans, *Let Us Now Praise Famous Men** (1941), a moving account of life among poor farmers in the South; and James Burnham, *Managerial Revolution** (1941). William Stott, *Documentary Expression and the 30s America* (1973) is a very relevant study.

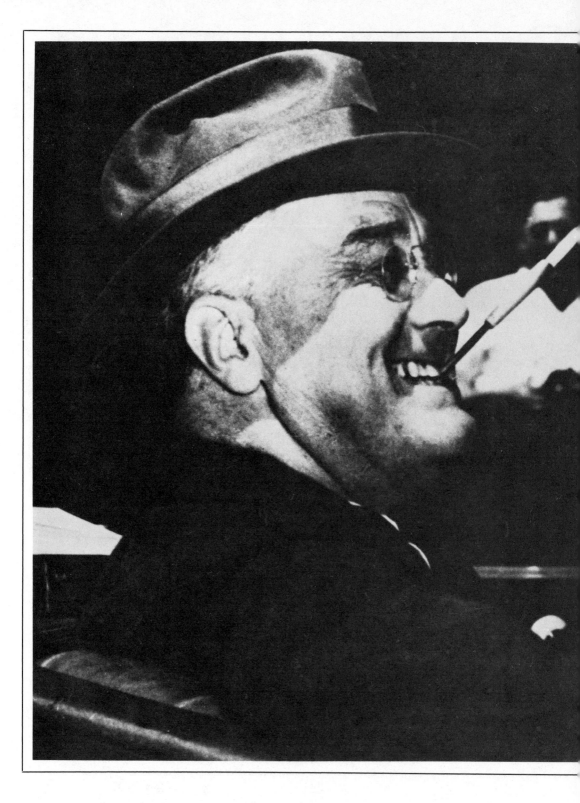

Political modernization in the 1930s

8

"Under Franklin D. Roosevelt's New Deal," a conservative complained in the late 1930s, "America took a decisive step toward Caesarism. The remarkable feature of this subtle evolution was that it could take place constitutionally, without any illegal move, simply by stretching the extremely pliable fabric of America's political institutions."

Such talk about "Caesarism" was characteristic of the exaggerated rhetoric of the Right in the 1930s. But FDR did indeed stretch the pliable fabric of governmental institutions. The expansion of public authority—at the local, state, and national levels—began to modernize American governments. That development proved central to the fight against the depression—which was national in scope—and to the management of World War II. It assisted interest groups in their ongoing efforts to influence the government. It accelerated the "subtle evolution" toward the concentration of power in the presidency, and the rise of a large and complex bureaucracy. Political centralization was therefore a mixed blessing. No developments of the decade were more significant.

The Hoover years

Few Americans seemed better qualified to deal with hard times than Herbert Hoover, who succeeded Coolidge in 1929. Orphaned at eleven, Hoover left his native Iowa to live with relatives in Oregon, then to work his way through Stanford

University. On graduating he became a mining engineer, in which capacity he traveled the world. Intelligent and efficient, he moved speedily ahead. By the age of forty he was a millionaire and a recognized expert in streamlining complex operations. Woodrow Wilson made him director of relief efforts in Belgium in 1914, of the Food Administration during the war, and finally of postwar American relief operations throughout Europe. Impressed by his expertise in these capacities, Franklin D. Roosevelt exclaimed in 1920, "Hoover certainly is a wonder, and I wish we could make him President of the United States. There could not be a better one."

At that time Republican regulars were cool to Hoover, who had worked for a Democratic administration and who had never run for office. But the regulars also recognized that he was too prominent to be ignored. Harding made him secretary of commerce, and Coolidge, while grumbling about Hoover's activist expansion of the Commerce Department, kept him on. By 1928 Hoover was the obvious choice for the GOP presidential nomination, and he beat Al Smith with ease.

Like most Americans in 1929 and 1930, Hoover assumed that the crash was a temporary dip in the business cycle. But from the beginning he was not prepared— as Coolidge would have been—to sit back and do nothing. On taking office he called a special session to deal with depressed farm prices, and after much wrangling Congress passed a law that provided federal loans to farm cooperatives. In 1930 he asked for and received a tax cut of $160 million. He also engaged in what later presidents called "jawboning"—using his prestige to urge businessmen and labor leaders to cooperate.

When conditions deteriorated in 1931, Hoover moved further in the direction of governmental intervention. In June he called for a moratorium in the payment of war debts to America. He accelerated work on Boulder Dam and developed plans for Grand Coulee Dam, started in 1933. He signed the Norris–La Guardia Act of 1932, which outlawed "yellow dog" (antiunion) labor contracts and restrictive antistrike injunctions. Acting under pressure from congressional progressives, he approved creation of the Reconstruction Finance Corporation in late 1931. The RFC was authorized to lend some $500 million (later much expanded) to financial institutions, which in turn were to direct the "trickling down" of money to the public. In 1932 he agreed, though reluctantly, to let the RFC lend $300 million to states for the relief of unemployment.

These measures proved to be too little too late. The modest tax cut made little difference, primarily because few Americans in that more innocent age paid federal taxes anyway. "Jawboning" helped sustain some wage rates until 1931, but only at the expense of the millions of workers who were laid off. The new Agricultural Marketing Administration did not try to control overproduction—the central cause of depressed prices—and its revolving fund to aid cooperatives was quickly exhausted. The belated loans for relief were far too small to combat hard times as they had developed by 1932.

The RFC, though helpful to a few large financial institutions, involved only loans, not grants. It failed to prevent bank panics or to save hundreds of smaller companies that needed massive aid. By following the "trickle down" theory the RFC also became an easy target for critics who wondered why Hoover was willing

A caricature of Herbert Hoover from *Liberty* magazine. The background suggests his interests—engineering and government.

to earmark federal money for business while denying it to the unemployed. The progressive economist Rexford Tugwell said the RFC's policies were like putting fertilizer in the branches of a tree instead of its roots, and Will Rogers irreverently concluded that the trickle down theory always operated in reverse. "You can drop a bag of gold in Death Valley," he quipped, "which is below sea level, and before Saturday it will be home to Papa J. P. [Morgan]."

Hoover pursued other policies that actually harmed the world economy. One of these was the Hawley-Smoot Tariff, which he signed in 1930 despite the advice of most economists. The record-high rates of this tariff probably had little impact on domestic prices or on foreign exporters (who had already found difficulty in cracking the American market). But the tariff did provoke sharp retaliation from other countries: America's exports were cut in half between 1930 and 1932. It also intensified the pessimism spreading through the Atlantic world. The United States, it was clear, was not going to use its immense economic power to be a banker or creditor "of last resort."

Another counterproductive move was the decision of the Federal Reserve Board in October 1931 to increase the discount rate from 1½ percent to 3½ percent. This action, taken after Britain had abandoned the gold standard, was intended to dissuade foreign investors from pulling their money out of the United States. It probably assisted in preserving the gold standard at home. But it also dampened economic activity by raising the cost of borrowing. In so doing it compounded the already deteriorating conditions of late 1931 and helped provoke the serious problems of 1932–33.

Hoover also resisted congressional efforts toward more substantial farm relief; he vetoed a bill to strengthen the United States Employment Service; and until the summer of 1932 he stopped all congressional appropriations for direct relief of unemployment. His tenacious defense of the gold standard and of balanced budgets (which falling tax revenues nonetheless made impossible) prevented him from devaluing the dollar to promote American exports or from approving inflationary measures to assist debtors.

His stance on all these issues stemmed from a consistent economic philosophy. As a humanitarian he recognized that the government must sometimes intervene: he was not a reactionary social Darwinist. But as a self-made man he believed that America provided equality of opportunity to all who made the effort to advance. And as an old Wilsonian he cherished voluntarism and states' rights. It followed that the federal government should try to keep its hands off the economy. "We must not be misled by the claim that the source of all wisdom is in the government," he said. "The way to a nation's greatness is the path of self-reliance, independence, and steadfastness in times of trial and stress."

Hoover's philosophy rested on his understandable faith that American capitalism was essentially sound. This conviction led him to believe that reassuring White House statements could restore public confidence. It caused him also to argue that the root of economic maladjustment lay abroad. European banks, he maintained, were unstable in the aftermath of World War I. When they began to fail in 1931, they forced nations like England off the gold standard. The failures staggered American investors, whose loans had sustained these banks until 1929. This blow to American capital, together with unscrupulous dealings by Wall Street speculators, led to the panicky runs on banks after 1931.

Hoover's belief in the overseas origin of the depression was comforting, for it sustained his reluctance to engage in large-scale governmental intervention at home. But his analysis was one-sided. The serious domestic problems—maldistribution of income, depressed agriculture, bad banking practices—cried out for attention. The centralization of the economy during Hoover's lifetime meant that these problems had become national in scope and in need of governmental redress.

Hoover also displayed unfortunate personal and political limitations. His background in the world of business and administration had given him little appreciation of the problems faced by congressmen, who found him cold, distant, and unwilling to compromise. The 1930 elections brought scores of Democrats into power, and when they joined with Republican progressives, Hoover was outnumbered. Sure of his course, the President refused to compromise with these adversaries, and by 1932 few on the Hill wanted to defend him. "Politics," the journalist William Allen White explained, "is one of the minor branches of harlotry, and Hoover's frigid desire to live a virtuous life and not follow the Pauline maxim and be all things to all men, is one of the things that has reduced the oil in his machinery and shot a bearing."

Because Congress was not only divided but (like all Americans at the time) bewildered by the persistence of economic difficulties, it is questionable whether any president could have led it in fruitful directions. But Hoover made it easy for congressmen to oppose him by doing little to gather public support. "This is not a showman's job," he insisted. "I will not step out of character." The sickness of the economy made him ever more glum, sensitive to criticism, isolated from other people. His Secretary of State, Henry Stimson, remarked after talking with him that "it was like sitting in a bath of ink in his room." Even outside the political arena Hoover's personality was severely criticized. The sculptor Gutzon Borglum added, "if you put a rose in his hand, it would wilt." The story circulated that Hoover asked an associate for a nickel to phone a friend. "Here's a dime," came the reply. "Call all your friends."

Hoover's most grievous error was to move against the "bonus army" of 1932. This "army" was actually a ragged bunch of some 22,000 unemployed citizens, most of whom claimed to have been veterans of World War I. By the summer of 1932 they had descended on Washington to lobby for immediate payment of bonuses due them (in 1945) for their service. When the Senate rejected the bonus bill, many of the veterans left for home. However, others camped in ramshackle quarters on Anacostia Flats across the river from the Capitol. A politically sensitive president might have visited them or at least shown some sympathy for their plight. But Hoover believed in law, order, and efficiency. So he ordered the reluctant police to clear the veterans from the area near the White House. When bricks started to fly, a policeman panicked, and two veterans were killed by gunfire. Hoover then com-

The Bonus "Army" is burned from Anacostia Flats, 1932.

manded the army to chase the veterans across the river to Anacostia Flats, and the city witnessed the spectacle of four troops of cavalry, four troops of infantry, a machine gun squad, and several tanks proceeding along Pennsylvania Avenue. The troops, under the leadership of General Douglas MacArthur, then charged into the Flats, where they chucked tear gas into tents, plunged, bayonets drawn, into crowds of men, women, and children, burned the shacks, and ran the "army" out of the District. Perhaps 1,000 people were gassed, and 63 were injured. Seldom in American history have troops been used with so little cause.

Franklin D. Roosevelt and New Deal solutions

THE TRIUMPH OF DEMOCRATIC RHETORIC, 1932

The deterioration of Hoover's presidency made it virtually certain that he would be overwhelmed at the polls in 1932. John N. Garner of Texas, Franklin D. Roosevelt's Democratic running mate, half seriously suggested a do-nothing campaign. "All you have to do," he told FDR, "is to stay alive until election day."

However, Garner recognized that Roosevelt was too appealing a candidate to stay at home. Over the years FDR had changed from an arrogant, supercilious young aristocrat (product of private tutors in Hyde Park, New York, of Groton School, and of Harvard) into a charming, gregarious, seductively charismatic man. He had begun his political career as a good-government state senator in 1910, and as a fervent admirer of TR, a distant relative. (FDR's wife, Eleanor, was also TR's niece.) In 1913 he became Wilson's assistant secretary of the navy, and in 1920 he was the party's popular choice for the vice-presidency. Crippled by polio in 1921, he refused to retire to a life as country gentleman. In 1928 Smith and other Demo-

FDR campaigning in West Virginia, October 1932.

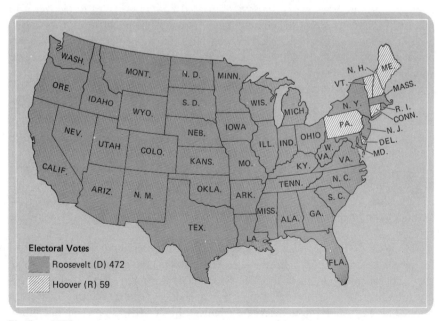

Electoral Votes

Roosevelt (D) 472

Hoover (R) 59

Election, 1932

cratic leaders pressed him back into active service by making him the party's nominee for governor of New York. When Roosevelt withstood the Hoover landslide to win—and then to prove himself a vigorous and popular governor—he emerged as a leading presidential contender for 1932. At the convention he had to overcome bids by Smith and Garner. But he ultimately prevailed. The Roosevelt-Garner ticket, by bridging the fatal urban-rural split in the party, united the Democrats as they had not been united since 1916.

Roosevelt waged an energetic, well-organized campaign. Wealthy backers like Bernard Baruch and Joseph Kennedy supplied him with money, and "brain trusters" like Raymond Moley and Rexford Tugwell, Columbia professors, offered him ideas and well-written speeches. Savvy politicos like Louis Howe, a newsman who had long counseled Roosevelt, and James A. Farley, the campaign director, provided expert counsel on strategy and tactics. Roosevelt's campaign revealed one of his great assets as president: an ability to attract able associates from diverse backgrounds and political persuasions. Unlike Hoover, he was assuredly all things to all men.

Finally, FDR seemed ready to act. He promised to look after the "forgotten men, the unorganized but indispensable units of economic power." He pledged to end prohibition, to "restore purchasing power to the farming half of the country," and to bring "relief to the small banks and homeowners." Washington, he added, "will assume bold leadership. . . . The Federal government has always had and still has a continuing responsibility for the broader public welfare. It will soon fulfill that responsibility." "I pledge myself," he declared, "to a new deal for the American people. . . . This is more than a political campaign; it is a call to arms."

All these assets, combined with Hoover's obvious liabilities, brought Democratic triumph in November. Roosevelt amassed 22 million votes to Hoover's 15 million. Democrats swept to power in many previously Republican states, and in both houses of Congress, 311 to 119, and 60 to 35. Considering the subsequent power of Democrats in urban areas, it was interesting that Hoover carried Pennsylvania and Connecticut. The election marked an astounding reversal in voter preference. After nearly forty years, America was becoming a Democratic country.

But what was the new president to do with his mandate? Speeches suggested he planned to promote conservation, lower tariffs, regulate public utilities, and curb the excesses of Wall Street. They also revealed that he wished to revive capitalism, "avoiding alike the revolution of radicalism and the revolution of conservatism." America, he said, "demands bold, persistent experimentation. It is common sense to take a method and try it: if it fails, admit it frankly and try another. But above all, try something." This speech indicated his experimental method: unlike Hoover, he was not to be bound by a consistent economic philosophy. But it promised nothing specific.

Many observers, however, considered FDR too conservative. Though a few of his speeches suggested he believed in governmental planning, he said nothing about such subsequent programs as the Tennessee Valley Authority, the National Recovery Administration, extensive public works spending, or labor reform. Though he implied he was willing to unbalance the budget, his focus was on economic orthodoxy. "I regard reduction of federal spending," he said, "as one of the most important issues of this campaign." Roosevelt was not making idle promises: like Hoover, he wanted very much to avoid deficit spending.

For these reasons the Left was as discouraged by the campaign as was the Republican Right. Both party platforms, one reformer complained, were "rehashes of old proposals, political croquettes concocted from the leftovers of former years and dressed up with a little fresh verbal parsley." Socialists noted gloomily that Norman Thomas, their presidential candidate, received only 880,000 votes, less than Debs had gotten in 1912 or 1920, and but 2.4 percent of the total turnout. William Z. Foster, the Communist candidate, got but 100,000. The weakness of the American Left in such difficult times revealed the vigor of the two-party system and the reluctance of Americans to abandon traditional beliefs about the government's role in the economy.

THE 100 DAYS

The four months between election day and inauguration in March 1933 were among the most dismal in American history. Consistent to the end, Hoover tried to commit Roosevelt to his deflationary program, but the President-elect refused to be trapped into cooperation. The lame-duck Congress managed to send repeal of prohibition to the states for ratification but otherwise debated fruitlessly. It was then that the final wave of panic swept depositors and forced state governors to declare "holidays" lest the banking system collapse altogether.

In the long run, however, the interregnum worked to Roosevelt's advantage, for it left people ready to do almost anything he might wish. As Will Rogers put it shortly after the inauguration, "I don't know what additional authority Roosevelt may ask, but give it to him, even if it's to drown all the boy babies." Senator Arthur Vandenberg of Michigan, a Republican conservative, added, "I think we need a 'dictator' in this particular situation. But a dictator is of no particular use unless he *dictates*. I think the country is crying to heaven for the announcement of a firm, comprehensive banking plan."

The new president's inaugural address hinted that he planned to seek the sort of power that Rogers and Vandenberg wanted to give him. Though he remained unspecific, he spoke of the need for "national planning" of utilities and transport, for "strict supervision of all banking and credits and investments," and—taking a neo-Populist phrase from Justice Brandeis—"an end to speculation with other people's money." Invoking wartime metaphors, he announced he would call a special session immediately and would "ask the Congress for the one remaining instrument to meet the crisis—broad executive power to wage a war against the emergency, as great as the power that would be given to me if we were in fact invaded by a foreign foe."

In the "100 Days" that followed, Roosevelt kept his promise to act, and an unprecedented volume of important legislation flowed from Congress. After declaring a national bank holiday, he hurried through a bill outlawing hoarding and providing federal assistance to solvent banks. In the next few weeks most of the bigger banks reopened, and when Congress (with Roosevelt's reluctant approval) created the Federal Deposit Insurance Corporation later in the session, it erected a barrier against unreasoning banking panics. Indeed, the FDIC became a major prop sustaining the role of private banking in a capitalist economy. Roosevelt then honored his pledge to cut government spending by securing passage of an Economy Act cutting $400 million from veterans' payments and $100 million from the salaries of federal employees. The President concluded his early program by dispatching a popular message calling for the legalization of 3.2 beer. Congress approved the measure, and on April 7 beer was legally sold in America for the first time since 1919.

As many progressives noted in anguish, these early measures were far from radical. His original banking act discriminated against smaller institutions and left the system, such as it was, in the control of private interests. The economy bill was deflationary and harsh. The beer bill, which imposed taxes on sales, did nothing to improve purchasing power. It was obvious that fiscal conservatives, especially Budget Director Lewis Douglas, were closest to the President's ear. It was also clear that many congressmen stood to the left of the executive branch and that Roosevelt, though distinctly more progressive than Hoover, was definitely not a radical. Rather, he was a flexible and humane politician—neither the Caesar perceived by the Right nor the crass opportunist depicted by many on the Left.

Subsequent actions were more far-reaching. Reversing Hoover's policy, Roosevelt moved cautiously toward relief of exporters and debtors by taking the nation off the gold standard, by devaluing the dollar, and by encouraging Federal Reserve officials to pursue an easy money policy. He secured passage of the Civilian Conservation Corps, which ultimately gave more than 2 million men useful and remunerative work in camps administered by the army. Congress also approved funds for the Home Owners Loan Corporation, which could buy mortgages from banks and offer owners generous, long-range terms for repayment. With the Securities Act he began to honor his promise to oversee Wall Street. And a new Public Works Administration was authorized an initial fund of $3.3 billion for large-scale projects.

A more momentous act set in motion the Federal Emergency Relief Administration. The FERA began with an initial appropriation of $500 million (the amount FDR had "saved" through the Economy Act) and received billions more before expiring in 1935. Under the direction of Harry Hopkins, a fast-acting humanitarian, it gave grants (not loans) to states on a matching basis of $3 of state money to $1 from Washington. Hopkins further had power to spend as he felt necessary, whether states matched the grants or not. When the FERA failed to meet the needs of the unemployed, Roosevelt set up a temporary work relief program (the Civil Works Administration) during the winter of 1933–34. It is frightening to think of the suffering that would have continued without the FERA and CWA. Perhaps no New Deal programs did more to promote the faith of masses in government, in Roosevelt, and in the Democratic party.

Roosevelt also broke with Hoover's policies by working for passage of a bill creating the Tennessee Valley Authority. Progressives, spearheaded by George Norris of Nebraska, had long urged public development of the backward, poverty-stricken region, but Coolidge and Hoover had stood firmly in their way. The legislation that Roosevelt signed empowered the Authority not only to control floods and to provide fertilizer and electric power but also to encourage social reconstruction of the entire valley. An admiring Norris confessed that FDR "plans to go even further than I did." Private utilities in the area protested vigorously that the government would drive them out of business. Still other critics complained that the TVA, the New Deal's most far-reaching intervention into the preserves of private enterprise, was state socialism. But Roosevelt thought not. The TVA, he said with characteristic pragmatism, was "neither fish nor fowl, but . . . it will taste awfully good to the people of the Tennessee Valley."

Subsequent conflicts within the TVA board limited the effectiveness of this great experiment, as did resistance by vested interests, who turned TVA Director David Lilienthal's faith in "grass-roots democracy" to their own advantage. Tugwell observed in 1936 that TVA should be called the "Tennessee Valley Power Production and Flood Control Corporation." Even in this somewhat limited fashion, however, TVA did benefit thousands of farmers by providing them with low-cost electricity for their homes. Decades later, it remained overwhelmingly popular in the many states affected by it.

Though some of these measures contributed to economic recovery, their primary purpose was relief—or, as in the case of the TVA, long-range reform. To break the depression, Roosevelt relied on two other creations of the 100 Days, the National Recovery Administration (NRA), and the Agricultural Adjustment Administration (AAA). These agencies, the core of his recovery program, showed the basic philosophy of the early New Deal.

NATIONAL RECOVERY ADMINISTRATION

The central aims of the NRA were to stabilize industrial prices and provide minimal guarantees to organized labor. Like many New Deal measures, it emanated primarily from the executive branch after conferences among brain trusters like Raymond Moley, big business leaders, and labor unionists. Their compromise bill attempted to satisfy everyone by authorizing management and labor within each industry to formulate "codes" of fair competition. These codes were supposed to outline production and pricing policies. Section 7-a of the bill stipulated that the codes guarantee minimum wages, maximum hours, and the right of collective bargaining for unions. While the government could not coerce industrialists into signing a code—Roosevelt shied away from such federal compulsion—it could shame noncooperators by withholding its insignia of approval—a blue eagle—from recalcitrant employers. The Justice Department was also empowered to prosecute violators of the codes. Roosevelt called the NRA "the most important and far-reaching legislation ever passed by the American Congress."

The NRA showed that Roosevelt wished to work with, rather than against, business interests. Indeed, the NRA favored big business by exempting code signers from antitrust prosecution. As Moley put it, "any attempt to atomize big business must destroy America's greatest contribution to a higher standard of living for the body of its citizenry—the development of mass production." Antimonopolistic progressives bitterly opposed this aspect of the plan in Congress. But Roosevelt applied pressure, and their cause failed. The President, it was clear, placed more faith in the progressive New Nationalism of TR and in the government-business partnership of World War I than in the trust-busting philosophy of Wilson's New Freedom.

Thanks to Hugh Johnson, the NRA's super-energetic chief executive, the recovery program at first seemed assured of success. Working quickly, he herded reluctant employers and labor leaders into his office, and by midsummer more than 500 industries, including such important ones as shipbuilding, wool textiles, and electrical manufacturing, had signed codes. In all, the codes covered some 2½ million firms and 22 million workers. Equally heartening was the index of factory production, which nearly doubled between March and July.

By midautumn, however, the NRA was having serious troubles. Johnson, who had worn himself out negotiating so many codes (even gravediggers and strip-tease artists were included), grew snappish and erratic. Antimonopolists grumbled that big businessmen, best able to survive downturns in the economy, were negotiating codes that put small competitors into bankruptcy. Labor leaders complained that Johnson and FDR were unsympathetic. Critics noted especially that some NRA codes attempted to sustain prices by limiting production. In so doing they penalized consumers. This basically deflationary approach, the reverse of what was needed, was intensified by Secretary of the Interior Harold Ickes, the churlish, fiercely honest administrator of the Public Works Administration. Ickes moved so cautiously in approving projects that purchasing power, necessary if production were ever to be increased, developed only slowly.

For a brief time in 1933 many American businesses advertised their cooperation with the NRA.

POLITICAL MODERNIZATION IN THE 1930s

Oh, I've kidded myself along, trying to believe that the codes were working, at least in the big industries—that the textile people, for instance, were complying probably to the extent of 60%. But I wonder. I'll bet you right now that 99% of American big businessmen are trying to beat them and succeeding. And the little fellows aren't even pretending to live up to them. They can't. The whole damned outfit are simply grabbing everything they can for themselves out of improved business stimulated by the Government priming and public confidence in the President. They're not contributing anything.

Lorena Hickok, a social worker, reports a characteristic progressive view of the NRA to Harry Hopkins, late 1933.

Opposition from business interests also hurt the NRA. Some major industries, like oil, dragged their heels before signing. Others, like coal, underwent strikes before cooperating. "Rugged individualists" like Henry Ford (who pointed out that working conditions in his factories were superior to those prescribed in the automobile code) simply refused to sign. Leading steel executives, fearing that talk with labor spokesmen implied union recognition, had to be dragooned by Secretary of Labor Frances Perkins into discussing a possible steel code.

Small businessmen presented still larger obstacles. Many such operators, often ignored in the code-negotiating process, discovered that they could not comply with pricing and labor provisions. Faced with the alternative of bankruptcy, they resorted to evasion. But Johnson lacked the staff to police so many codes, and violators soon acted with impunity. By mid-1934 the administrative breakdown of the NRA, derisively branded the "National Run Around" by opponents, was apparent to all.

The NRA was not a total failure. However temporarily, it gave people the idea that the New Dealers were trying. Section 7-a, though subject to circumvention by employers, prompted labor leaders to sponsor unionization drives. But the NRA's inability to secure recovery suggested the need for better coordination between spending and industrial policy. Its failure to secure cooperation from private interests showed that centralized planning had to involve stronger government enforcement powers. Recognizing the difficulties inherent in voluntary cooperation between government and business, FDR turned by 1935 to tougher measures against big business.

AGRICULTURAL ADJUSTMENT ADMINISTRATION

Like the NRA, New Deal agricultural policies grew out of prolonged discussion within the executive branch, especially by Milburn Wilson, a Montana professor and farm expert, Secretary of Agriculture Henry A. Wallace, a progressive farm editor from Iowa, and Rexford Tugwell, whom Roosevelt made an assistant secretary of agriculture. Their primary concern was to increase farm income, which had fallen by 60 percent since 1929. Conditions were so desperate in rural areas that conservative, property-owning farmers from the eastern seaboard to the Plains had intimidated lawyers and judges who attempted to foreclose mortgages, and had sponsored "farm holidays" keeping goods from market until prices increased.

To stabilize the farm sector, Wallace and his advisers devised a complex of proposals. These aimed at extending farm credit, assisting cooperatives, and encouraging marketing agreements and export trade. Their key proposal outlined a "domestic allotment" plan to guarantee "parity," prices restoring the favorable ratio with industrial goods that farm products had enjoyed in the prosperous years between 1909 and 1914. This goal was to be achieved through crop controls to battle the chronic problem of overproduction. These proposals, like many other New Deal innovations, stemmed from progressive ideas that had circulated in the 1910s and 1920s. They were neither brand new nor revolutionary. But in some respects—notably the use of government authority to encourage limits on production—they broke sharply from policies then in effect.

The AAA, which administered domestic allotments, stopped short of full-scale national planning. Because he feared excessive centralization, Roosevelt insisted that farmers growing major crops decide policies themselves. These farmers were to hold periodic referenda to determine total output and set acreage quotas for each producer. Farmers who reduced their acreage could benefit in two ways: by receiving higher prices for their goods, and by getting government subsidies for cooperating. In this way the government was intervening with a carrot, not a stick, for farmers who thought they could do better without the subsidy were free to grow all they liked. The AAA was also expected to run in the black, for the cost of the subsidies was to be met by a federal tax on agricultural processors. Like the NRA, the AAA was an effort to promote cooperation between government and major producers. Though more far-reaching than anything attempted before, it preserved the principles of voluntarism and decentralization.

Because extensive droughts in 1933–35 cut output in places, it is difficult to measure precisely the economic impact of the AAA. But it undoubtedly did much to curb overproduction and to raise farm income, which doubled between 1933 and 1936. Other farm programs—the Soil Conservation Service, the Rural Electrification Administration, the Farm Credit Administration, and the Commodity Credit Corporation (which offered loans on storable products)—also assisted commercial farmers. Agricultural radicals, who had capitalized on widespread rural unrest in 1932, found relatively little support four years later. And Democrats made huge inroads in normally Republican rural areas in 1934 and 1936. In all these respects the farm program of the New Deal was successful.

But the AAA exposed many anomalies and contradictions in the New Deal approach. One of the most glaring was the policy of curtailing production—indeed, of destroying crops and livestock already planted or born in early 1933—at a time when millions of Americans were desperate for food and clothing. As one critic observed, Roosevelt seemed to be solving the paradox of want amidst plenty by doing away with plenty.

Roosevelt's preference for decentralization also presented problems. It meant that local committees of farmers enjoyed wide discretion. Some of them inflated the value of land taken from production. "It's a miracle," one farmer noted, "how the prospect of getting a little extra cash out of Uncle Sam has improved South Carolina dirt.'' Worse, decentralization left major policy decisions in the hands of large commercial farmers and of local Agriculture Department officials who echoed their points of view. It was yet another example of Roosevelt's reluctance to upset the power of well-entrenched groups.

George Peek, the AAA administrator, accepted this world as he found it. ''No democratic government can be very different from the country it governs,'' he answered. ''If some groups are dominant in the country, they will be dominant in any plan that government undertakes.'' But subordinates in the Department of Agriculture thought otherwise. Led by General Counsel Jerome Frank, they complained that acreage reductions were displacing thousands of tenant farmers, especially in the South. When Wallace, caught in the middle, appeared to back the rebels, Peek resigned in late 1933. But infighting continued to plague the AAA until 1935, when Wallace bowed to the pressures of large commercial farmers and dismissed the rebels. The struggle exposed the administrative hassling that accompanied the rapid growth of bureaucratic power during the New Deal.

Meanwhile, tenants continued to suffer. Perhaps 3 million people were displaced from the land between 1932 and 1935 alone. In 1935 Tugwell and others attempted to deal with the problem through the Resettlement Administration, which aimed at relocating people in garden cities. In 1937 Congress approved loans for further relocation of tenants on small farms, and FDR set up the Farm Security Administration to tackle such problems. But conservatives prevented these programs from receiving adequate funding. And even with larger appropriations, it is very questionable whether government aid for rural resettlement of small farmers, who had been struggling against economic centralization for decades, was a realistic long-range answer. Opportunity for small farmers depended heavily on rapid industrial expansion, and this the New Deal was unable to promote.

Two final problems hurt the long-range effectiveness of domestic allotment. One was continuing technological change, especially in chemical fertilizers, which created dramatic increases in production per acre. To combat this rise in supply, some farmers opted for compulsory production quotas in 1934. Others relied on the government to store the excess so that it would not glut the market: by 1939, after six years of cotton subsidies, the carryover to be stored was 3 million bales greater than in 1932. Though the demand generated by World War II temporarily alleviated this problem, it became obvious in the postwar years that the cycle of subsidies, crop loans, and government storage was costing the taxpayers billions of dollars and that it was enriching an ever smaller number of commercial farmers.

The other problem was that the American agricultural depression was only a part of the larger decline at home and abroad. Limiting domestic production assisted foreign farmers, who acquired a larger share of the world market. At home, increased prices for farmers meant higher costs to consumers for the necessities of life. Moreover, to the extent that the NRA brought about higher prices for industrial goods, it worked against the interest of farmers, who had to buy them. Some reformers concluded that Roosevelt should have combined the best features of the NRA and the AAA into a comprehensive national plan. Others, perceiving the complexity of the national economy, replied that no such plan could work in time of peace. Perhaps they were right—for interest groups throughout twentieth-century American history have proved too strong for government planners. Still, it remained true that the NRA and AAA sometimes worked at cross purposes and that neither did much for mass purchasing power—the key to recovery.

REMEMBERING THE FORGOTTEN MAN

Any activist administration inevitably confronts hostility before long, and Roosevelt's was no exception. The Securities and Exchange Commission, approved in 1934 to define a federal role in regulating the stock exchange, was particularly controversial. Though it permitted the financial community considerable latitude in managing its own activities, it nonetheless infuriated rightwingers on Wall Street. Some of these joined the Liberty League, which led reactionary opposition to the New Deal in 1934–36. Other conservatives complained loudly about deficit spending. Budget Director Lewis Douglas resigned in August 1934, warning the President that upon a balanced budget "hangs not only your place in history but conceivably the immediate fate of our civilization." Deriding the presidential "royal family," one reactionary wrote,

> The King is in the White House
> Handing out the money.
> The Queen is on the front page
> Looking very funny.
> The knave [their son James] is up in Boston,
> Picking up the plums
> While the country alphabetically
> Is feeding all the bums.

But criticisms such as these made little mark on voters. Though the depression persisted, Roosevelt's measures were obviously popular. Accordingly, Democrats won heartening victories in 1934, the first time since 1902 that the party in power gained seats in an off-year election. Encouraged, Hopkins saw a mandate for further reform. "Boys," he told his aids, "this is our hour. We've got to get everything we want—a works program, social security, wages and hours, everything—now or never!"

Hopkins correctly assessed the activist mood of the new Congress, which in 1935 passed more important laws than in any previous session of modern American history. Heading them were three landmark acts: a relief bill leading to creation of the Works Progress Administration, a social security act, and the National Labor Relations (or Wagner) Act providing unprecedented guarantees to labor. These assisted the so-called forgotten man in ways scarcely dreamed of by many New Dealers themselves during the 100 Days.

WPA The relief program stemmed in part from Roosevelt's unhappiness with the dole. "Continued dependence on relief," he complained, "induces a spiritual and moral disintegration fundamentally destructive of the national fiber." Unlike some conservatives, however, he shrank from throwing the unemployed back on their own. The answer was to require work from the able-bodied unemployed. Congress responded with an initial fund of $4.8 billion—the largest peacetime appropriation in American history. The newly created WPA, focus of the administration's relief efforts for the next five years, received a substantial portion of the money, and Hopkins set to work spending it.

Right-wing spokesmen quickly assailed the plan. Even work relief, they insisted, would create a nation of parasites, and would plunge the country into everlasting debt. "If the government keeps handling relief, manicuring ladies' nails, and giving relief people cars to ride around in," one reactionary state governor lamented, "it will stifle religion in the country." Other right-wingers repeated stale jokes about WPA "workers." "There's a new cure for cancer," one went, "but they can't get any of it—it's sweat from a WPA worker." Southern conservatives grumbled that relief wages assisted "lazy blacks" who would otherwise have increased the supply of inexpensive farm labor. Leaving nothing to chance, they successfully excluded blacks from coverage in many regions. Republicans insisted that the WPA was a Democratic racket devised to employ party hacks and to swell the New Deal vote in 1936.

None of these criticisms was based on fact. Though some people may have preferred easy jobs with the WPA to regular work, the vast majority struggled to avoid the stigma of accepting public employment. "I didn't want to go on relief," one said. "Believe me, when I was forced to go to the office of the relief the tears were running out of my eyes." And while a few state relief officials played politics

WPA projects not only provided assistance to the unemployed, but also provided services to the community, such as building and repairing roads, bridges, and the like.

Mr. Gordon had a good wife, one daughter of 17, another of 15, and three other young children. He was an intelligent, hard-working man and had never before been in straits. . . . Then came the depression, no work, tension. . . . When their resources were exhausted the public welfare department allowed the family $5 a week of relief and the man got one day's public work at $3. . . . Finally one night Evelyn disappeared. She had gone to work in a "closed dance hall." She earned about $4.85 a week and what she could get from the sale of her tired body. . . . Meanwhile her family had lost its place in the community.

A case study of a New York State family hit by unemployment, mid-1930s.

with relief money, most—under strict orders from Hopkins—acted with remarkable nonpartisanship. Nonetheless, criticisms persisted, for some of the projects were makework in character.

Criticism from the Left was more persuasive. Spokespeople for the unemployed complained that the appropriation was too small, that millions of people still had to hope for charity from local agencies. These complaints were justified, for the WPA provided an average monthly wage of $52, which was rarely enough for heads of households, and it never employed more than 40 percent of the unemployed. Far from being a lavish expenditure of tax money, it proved that much remained to be done.

These criticisms could not diminish the great popularity among the needy of the WPA, especially during its first two years of operation. During that time it provided relief to between 1.9 and 3.2 million people per month, and by 1941 it had pumped more than $11 billion into the economy. Though most of this money went to unskilled or semiskilled workers, some of it aided artists and writers who enriched the nation's cultural experience. The Federal Theatre Project, sponsored by the WPA, employed 12,500 actors and stagehands, who performed before 350,000 people a week in 1936. The National Youth Administration offered aid to some 2 million students and 2.6 million nonstudents during the 1930s. The WPA, like the FERA and CWA before it, revealed the New Deal at its most humanitarian.

Social Security Where the WPA tried to offer immediate relief, social security, the other half of Roosevelt's welfare program, promised longer-range protection. The measure featured three forms of aid. The first, pensions for people over sixty-five, was to be financed by a tax on payrolls. The federal "reserve fund" thus built up was to provide pensions to people who had worked long enough in covered occupations to qualify. The second type of aid was unemployment compensation. Such compensation, directed by states, was to come from taxes on employers, who were to receive federal rebates provided that they did not lay off workers. The third form of aid was money given to categories of poor people—blind, dependent children, and disabled—who could not qualify for WPA work or find other forms of employment. This "categorical assistance" involved federal-state coordination. Funds were to come from federal grants, provided that states appropriated matching funds.

Progressives recognized flaws in this "system" from the beginning. The old-age pension plan excluded millions of workers who pursued occupations not covered by the original legislation. Moreover, the government was not to begin to pay pensions until 1940. Meanwhile, money for pensions was to be drawn from employers and employees. It required little imagination to see that the old-age pension plan was limited in scope and that it reduced purchasing power at the time the economy most needed stimulation. Like the Economy Act of 1933, it showed that Roosevelt was at heart a fiscal conservative.

A major weakness in the unemployment compensation plan was its federal-state nature, which meant that states, unwilling to penalize business interests within their borders, tended to enact only the minimum federal requirements. The result was stingy, short-lasting benefits for workers. By penalizing employers who laid off workers the plan also reflected the view that irresponsible firms were responsible for unemployment. Given the magnitude of the economic crisis, this was a false assumption. The plan also discouraged employers from hiring workers whom they might have to lay off if conditions failed to improve. Overall, it was ill-formed in conception and ungenerous in benefits.

The categorical assistance plans were plagued by their federal-state administration. Many states proved unwilling to spend much money for the programs, and the recipients suffered accordingly. Some states made no provision at all for so-called unemployables, a large group of people covered neither by the WPA nor by the categories. Even the more generous states felt obliged to provide relief on a pay-as-you-go basis. Accordingly, they resorted to sales taxes to find the money. These, like the payroll taxes to support old-age pensions, were regressive. The federal-state nature of categorical assistance also caused wide variations in benefits and prevented establishment of a national "floor" under income. Any law that permitted, indeed exacerbated, such regional variations was obviously inequitable. Both unemployment compensation and categorical assistance would have been fairer had they used funds raised by progressive federal taxation and been administered with an even hand from Washington.

Some of these weaknesses stemmed from Roosevelt's fiscal orthodoxy and from his faith in decentralization and states' rights. But FDR was not a social reactionary. On the contrary, his faith in a "cradle to the grave" system of "social

Fear and worry based on unknown danger contribute to social unrest and economic demoralization. If, as our Constitution tells us, our Federal government was established among other things "to promote the general welfare," it is our plain duty to provide for that security upon which welfare depends.

These three great objectives—the security of the home, the security of livelihood, and the security of social insurance—are, it seems to me, a minimum of the promise that we can offer to the American people. They constitute a right which belongs to every individual and every family willing to work. They are the essential fulfillment of measures already taken toward relief.

Roosevelt's welfare philosophy, 1934.

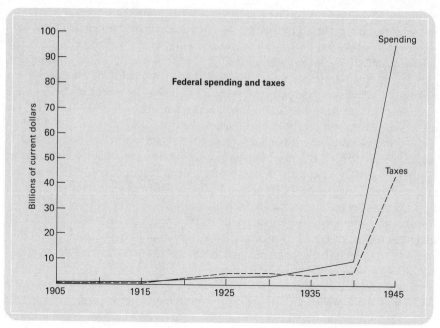

Growth of federal services, 1905–45

insurance'' was enlightened for its time in the United States. Roosevelt also recognized that the Supreme Court as then constituted might overturn a law that failed to give states a role in the operation. And he foresaw the vulnerability of any plan that depended for its success on annual congressional appropriations. Hence he defended the payroll taxes on employees. "Those taxes," he admitted, "were never a problem of economics. They are politics all the way through. We put those payroll contributions there so as to give the contributors a legal, moral, and political right to collect their pensions and their unemployment benefits. With those taxes in there, no damned politician can ever scrap the social security program."

In this prediction the President was accurate, for the mixed system enacted in 1935 remained the basis of American welfare for decades thereafter. Subsequent Congresses felt obliged to provide more generous benefits (and to increase payroll taxes) so that social security became virtually unrepealable. With all its faults, the social security law was a major step forward in the assistance of the "forgotten man." As one social worker wrote, "during the years between 1929 and 1939 more progress was made in public welfare than in the hundred years after this country was founded."

Wagner Act: NLRB   The third major accomplishment of the 1935 Congress, the Wagner Act, was demanded by reformers who had chafed under the ambiguities and limitations of NRA's Section 7-a. Their bill called for a permanent, independent National Labor Relations Board, which was to have the power to conduct elections determining bargaining units. The NLRB was also to prevent such "unfair" management practices as firing workers for union membership or fostering employer-dominated company unions. Henceforth, the bill stipulated, bargaining agents for workers were to be chosen by a majority of employees. These far-reaching provisions—which promised to throw the balance of power toward unions for the first time in American history—were not FDR's doing. Indeed, the squire of Hyde Park was barely informed concerning the intricacies of labor-management relations. Labor Secretary Frances Perkins conceded later that he "never lifted a finger" for the bill. But Wagner and others did not need FDR's expertise, only his benevolent neutrality. And that he gave them. With the White House offering no comfort to spokesmen for management, the National Labor Relations Act passed both houses in May and June of 1935. In early July FDR signed it into law.

From the beginning the NLRB found itself engaged in one of the most tumultuous periods of labor-management controversy in American history. This conflict had begun to escalate in 1933, when Section 7-a of the NRA had encouraged militant labor leaders like John L. Lewis of the United Mine Workers to conduct organization drives. These drives deeply frightened employers, for they aimed at developing nationwide industrial unions composed not only of skilled craftsmen (many of whom were already members of the AFL) but also of masses of unskilled and semiskilled workers. By 1934 these campaigns for new members had led to a wave of strikes involving 1.5 million workers. Some of the strikes erupted in battles between workers and authorities. And in October 1935, only three months after passage of the Wagner Act, the militants forced a break within the labor movement itself. Following a wild AFL convention, Lewis and other industrial unionists split off to form the Committee for Industrial Organization (later renamed the Congress of Industrial Organizations). Free of the inhibiting influence of the AFL, the CIO leaders redoubled their drives for membership.

In this kind of controversy the NLRB could hardly satisfy everyone. AFL unions complained that its decisions favored the CIO. Employers grumbled that the Wagner Act should have enumerated unfair union practices and that the NLRB was riddled with "left-wing bias." William Knudsen, head of General Motors, exclaimed in 1938 that the NLRB was "the largest drawback to good industrial relations." This conservative opposition, frequently savage and unreasoning, revealed the insecurity behind welfare capitalism.

THE RISE OF UNIONS

The NLRB also had to contend with the new tactics of CIO militants in 1937. These militants, acting without Lewis' approval, dramatized their struggle for union recognition by occupying factories, most importantly in the rubber, automobile, and steel industries. Such "sit-down" strikes involved perhaps 400,000 workers. They terrified men of property, and they were later declared illegal by the Supreme Court. But they were hard to combat, for the use of force by management could easily damage valuable plant and equipment. By 1938 such strikes had compelled antiunion strongholds like General Motors and U.S. Steel to bargain collectively with the CIO. By 1940 American unions claimed almost 9 million members, compared to 3.2 million in 1932.

In some ways the benevolent neutrality of the New Deal promoted this growth. In particular, the NLRB proved important in clarifying the rights of labor and in helping to settle disputes. No single New Deal reform had greater long-run significance. And ordinary Americans appreciated this new, more sympathetic attitude in Washington. One person said simply, "Mr. Roosevelt is the only man we ever had in the White House who is not a son of a bitch." "Every house I visited," a social worker reported after a tour in South Carolina, ". . . had a picture of the President. These ranged from newspaper clippings (in destitute houses) to large colored prints, framed in gilt cardboard. The portrait holds the place of honor over the mantel; I can only compare this to the peasant's Madonna."

Union members expressed this gratitude at the polls. As early as 1934 industrial wards began developing large voting margins for the Democratic party. In 1936, when Lewis campaigned for FDR, the alliance between the CIO and the New Deal became open. The frank partisanship of the CIO, and the overwhelming support that prolabor Democrats consistently received from working-class areas, were among the most significant political developments of the 1930s—and thereafter.

In retrospect, however, it is clear that FDR's services to the labor movement were not as crucial as some people thought. During the controversy over the sit-down strikes, he was benevolent enough not to call out troops, as many of his predecessors might have done. But he also determined not to take sides and pronounced a "plague o' both your houses." This statement infuriated Lewis, who later defected to the Republican party. However, workers continued the strikes without the assistance of FDR. In this sense their militancy, and their achievements, owed relatively little to the New Deal. Moreover, the triumph of industrial unionism in the 1930s was far from complete. As late as 1940 American unions embraced only 28 percent of nonagricultural workers. In 1945, a peak year of union power, they had but 36 percent. Most of the unskilled remained unrepresented and relatively powerless.

Corporate attitudes showed little change either. For every industrial leader like Myron Taylor of U.S. Steel, who recognized the futility of combatting unions at every turn, there were many who battled on. Among them was aging Henry Ford, who refused to recognize the CIO until the eve of World War II, when the promise of profits through labor peace proved too alluring to resist. Ford entrusted labor matters to thugs who beat up United Auto Workers organizer Walter Reuther. Another recalcitrant employer was James H. Rand of Remington, whose "Mohawk Valley Formula" appealed strongly to antiunion businessmen. This formula, effec-

Rise of labor unions, 1900–50
(In thousands)

	1900	1910	1920	1930	1940	1950	1979
Total labor force	29,030	37,291	42,206	50,080	56,180	63,858	104,444
Total union membership	791	2,116	5,034	3,632	8,944	15,000	21,000
Percentage	2.7	5.7	11.9	6.8	15.5	22.3	20

SOURCE: Adapted from *Historical Statistics of the United States*, pp. 75, 97; U.S. Department of Labor, *Handbook of Labor Statistics: 1973* (Washington, D.C., 1973), p. 345

Police intervene to quell labor disturbances in Ohio.

tive in one-company towns, prescribed that employers brand union organizers as
Reds and anarchists, that citizens' committees and local police restore "law and
order," and that companies threaten to leave town if strikes were not stopped
quickly. Perhaps the most adamant corporate leader of all was Tom Girdler, president of Republic Steel and, by example, of "little steel" companies that resisted the
sit-down strikes. "I won't have a contract," Girdler proclaimed, "verbal or written, with an irresponsible, racketeering, violent, communistic body like the CIO,
and until they pass a law making me do it, I am not going to do it." Girdler was
prepared to fight, and he purchased quantities of billy clubs, shells, rifles, and
grenades. Like many such employers, Girdler succeeded: "little steel" was not
unionized until the 1940s.

The labor militancy of the mid-1930s did not last beyond 1950. As time passed,
the CIO learned that corporations would never surrender control over pricing policies. Once established, the CIO also evolved from a militant defender of the industrial working class to an increasingly self-interested pressure group, which worried
little about minority groups, consumers, or workers in nonunionized areas. By 1950
it was securely established as one of the many influential interest groups within the
fragmented society, and by the 1950s it differed little from the AFL.

Union organizers also came to realize that most blue-collar workers had little
interest in the "working class" as a concept. As in the past, American laborers

were captivated by the dream of monetary success. They longed for the consumer goods, especially cars, that technological advances had brought within their reach during the 1920s. They wanted security and self-respect, not conflict. When prosperity returned, most of them continued to pay their union dues and to vote Democratic. They formed a "countervailing power" against employers, who were not to regain the awesome and arbitrary power they had had before the 1930s. But workers tended to stop there. They had as little use as ever for proletarian revolution or for racial equality. The class consciousness of 1937, half-formed even then, barely outlasted the hard times that created it.

THE OPPOSITION AND NEW DEAL RESPONSES

The passage of landmark social legislation in 1935 earned Roosevelt the support of many members of the Left. But recovery remained as elusive as ever, and disaffected groups grew steadily more impatient. By mid-1935 they had grown so insistent that Roosevelt's political advisers grew alarmed about the prospects for reelection in 1936.

The spokesmen for these groups were a mixed lot. Minnesota Governor Floyd Olson demanded increased federal spending to assist farmers and workers. Mayor Fiorello La Guardia of New York insisted on more generous relief and housing measures to assist the urban, ethnic masses. Congressional progressives Robert La Follette, Jr., and Burton Wheeler of Montana demanded tougher measures against monopolies. Easily the most outspoken critics, however, were three leaders who appealed to disaffected Americans on the Left and Right alike. They were Father Charles Coughlin, Dr. Francis Townsend, and Senator Huey Long of Louisiana.

Father Coughlin of Royal Oak, Michigan, was already a well-known "radio priest" during the Hoover administration, which he flayed with abandon. At first he warmly supported Roosevelt's policies, even asserting that the New Deal was "Christ's deal." But from the beginning Coughlin called for monetary inflation and for the nationalization of banking. Ambitious and vitriolic, Coughlin became steadily more anti-Semitic. Millions of Americans listened to his broadcasts, and many appeared ready to follow his apparently egalitarian Union for Social Justice. By early 1935 he seemed a threat Roosevelt could not afford to ignore.

Townsend, an elderly California doctor, was a gentler, more decent man than Father Coughlin. But he was no less determined, and his cause of government aid for old people cried out for attention. With the aid of shrewd promoters, Townsend set up Old Age Revolving Pensions, Ltd., and gained hundreds of thousands of converts by 1935. His plan called for the government to provide people over sixty with $200 per month, providing the recipients spent the money within that time and retired if employed. Money for the pensions was to come from a "transactions tax" (essentially a sales tax). Critics were quick to show that the plan would have cost some $20 billion a year for a minority of old people. They also exposed corruption within Townsend's organization (though he himself was honest). But to Townsend's impassioned followers these matters made little difference. Even after passage of social security, agitation for the plan continued.

Long, the self-styled "Kingfish" who was virtual dictator of Louisiana, posed the greatest danger of all to Roosevelt. Like Father Coughlin, he had supported much of the New Deal in 1933. But even then he had balked at the exemption of the NRA codes from antitrust suits, and by 1934 he had broken with the administration. Roosevelt, he said, differed hardly at all from Hoover. "Maybe you see a little change in the men working in the dining room," he sneered, "but back in the kitchen the same old cooks are back there fixing up the vittles and the grub for us that cooked up that mess under Hoover. There has never even been a change in the seasoning." By 1935 Long was promoting his "Share Our Wealth" plan, which promised to soak the rich and make "every man a king." Shrewd, quick-witted, and fiercely ambitious, Long claimed some 5 million followers. It was obvious that he longed to take FDR's place in the White House.

The moderate Roosevelt of 1933, seeking to promote business–government cooperation, might well have ignored these challenges. But at this very time in late 1934 and early 1935 the Right also began to recover from its shock and despair of 1933. Most alarming, the conservative Supreme Court began to counterattack. Its most momentous decision, *Schechter* v. *US,* unanimously struck down the NRA in May 1935. In doing so it proclaimed what Roosevelt aptly denounced as a narrow "horse and buggy definition of interstate commerce." It also ruled against the delegation of legislative authority to code makers. These were essentially *obiter dicta* stemming from the conservative economic philosophies of the judges. If the TVA, AAA, and other agencies ran into the same biases, the New Deal could be destroyed.

Until the Court's decision Roosevelt had continued to hope for cooperation from conservative business interests. He had accordingly refrained from rhetoric aimed at stealing the thunder of men like Coughlin and Long. But the Court, which appeared to typify the uncompromising obstructionism of conservatives generally, helped persuade FDR of the futility of trying to appease the Right. He therefore swung to the left. Acting quickly, he supported legislation against special privilege. Some of this legislation, such as an act to establish more centralized control of banking, was already moving through Congress. But the most controversial results of Roosevelt's turn to the left were the Public Utilities Holding Company Act and the "wealth tax."

The holding company bill clearly reflected the administration's new hostility toward big business. Its drafters, Benjamin Cohen and Thomas Corcoran, were young Washington lawyers who admired Justice Brandeis. Like him, they believed in trying to restore a measure of decentralization and free competition to the economy. Their bill revealed this philosophy by applying a "death sentence" to large, integrated holding companies in the utilities field. As Wheeler, its Senate sponsor, put it, the bill was a "federal tax on bigness . . . the only program that can eventually restore to us the reality of that economic and political democracy by which we fondly like to think this nation lives."

The "wealth tax" began as a Treasury bill—aimed at increasing revenue from high income brackets and corporations. By the summer of 1935, however, Roosevelt seized on it to placate followers of men like Long. He wrote a friend that he was "fighting Communism, Huey Longism, Coughlinism, Townsendism. . . . To combat . . . crackpot ideas, it may be necessary to throw to the wolves the forty-six men who are reported to have incomes in excess of one million dollars a year. This can be accomplished through taxation." When Long saw Roosevelt's tax message, he crowed that FDR was "copying my share-the-wealth speeches now that I was writing when I was fourteen years old. So he's just now getting as smart as I was when I was in knee breeches."

Both measures aroused excited protests from conservatives. Wendell Willkie, a leading utilities executive, led a well-organized lobbying campaign against the holding company bill, which John W. Davis, Democratic presidential nominee in 1924, termed the "gravest threat to the liberties of the American citizen that has emanated from the halls of Congress in some time." Hearing of the wealth tax, William Randolph Hearst told his editors to refer to it as "Soak the Successful" and to label the New Deal the "Raw Deal." Walter Lippmann called it the "work of tired brains, relying on their wishes and their prejudices and throwing out suggestions which they are too hot and bothered to think about."

Such vocal opposition was partly successful. Congress softened the holding company bill to permit the continued existence of geographically defensible empires. It amended the wealth tax bill into an innocuous measure that failed either to soak the rich or to produce much additional revenue. Congress's response to conservative pressure showed again that organized interest groups were not to be denied. It also revealed that Roosevelt, while still in command, backed away from fighting Congress for long on such issues. A congressional renaissance was underway.

The battles over the holding company and tax bills suggested further that Roosevelt was an inconsistent economic thinker. Having failed in 1933 to establish business–government cooperation, he had switched—in part for political reasons—to a New Freedom animus against bigness. Given the hostility of businessmen and the gross inequities in wealth, this change of course was understandable. But it did not promote economic recovery.

Nevertheless, Roosevelt's sally against big business paid political dividends.

Though it ultimately failed to silence implacable critics like Long, it suggested that he stood for economic and social justice. Roosevelt, the master politician, realized that throwing plutocrats "to the wolves" was almost always popular with the voters.

The second term: programs and frustrations

VICTORY IN 1936

As the 1936 campaign developed momentum, the Right outdid itself in hurling invective at the New Deal. Mark Sullivan, an influential conservative columnist, worried that 1936 might witness the "last presidential election America may ever have. . . . It is tragic that America fails to see that the New Deal is to America what the early phase of Nazism was to Germany." Switchboard operators at the Chicago *Tribune* greeted callers with, "Good morning, Chicago *Tribune*. There are only——days in which to save the American way of life."

Demagogues were equally unhappy. Though Long had been assassinated in late 1935, Gerald L. K. Smith, an anti-Semitic rabble rouser, moved in to direct Long's followers against the President. Coalescing with Coughlin and Townsend, they nominated William Lemke, a progressive North Dakota congressman, for the presidency on the Union party ticket. "Liberty Bell" Lemke, as he was called, stood for the inflationist, anti–Wall St., quasipopulist platform of Coughlin's Union for Social Justice.

Roosevelt also confronted discontent among militant spokesmen for blacks. The NRA, they maintained, had displaced black workers; its initials represented "Negroes Ruined Again." The AAA had dispossessed thousands of black tenants. TVA towns were for whites only. The NAACP complained especially about Roosevelt's refusal to endorse a federal bill against lynching, only to be told, "If I come out for the antilynching bill now, they [influential southern congressmen] will block every bill I ask Congress to pass to keep America from collapsing. I just can't take that risk." This was a politically correct assessment, for few Americans paid much attention in the 1930s to the plight of blacks. But it angered black leaders. *Crisis,* magazine of the NAACP, concluded that blacks "ought to realize by now that the powers-that-be in the Roosevelt administration have nothing for them."

The President welcomed the self-defeating rhetoric of the Right. "Economic royalists," he proclaimed, had never "been so united against one candidate as they stand today. They are unanimous in their hatred of me—and I welcome their hatred. . . . I should like to have it said of my second administration that in it these forces met their master." Raymond Moley, who had broken earlier with the President, recalled that "thoughtful citizens were stunned by the violence, the bombast, the naked demagoguery of these sentences." Perhaps. But assaults on the privileged few won a great many more votes than they lost.

As the election drew near, it became equally obvious that Roosevelt had little to fear from the Union party, which clumsily combined populism, anti-Semitism, and rhetorical excesses. Lemke, though an earnest candidate, suffered from reminders that the Liberty Bell was cracked. Compared to headline seekers like Coughlin and Smith, he was all but forgotten by election day.

The Republican party also offered little challenge. Its candidate, Governor Alfred M. Landon of Kansas, was a decent, moderate man who had little in common with right-wing extremists. But he was too restrained and too plain to develop much popular appeal. The "Kansas Coolidge," as he was unfairly labeled, never posed much of a threat.

Roosevelt knew also that most blacks would have to support him. Neither the GOP nor the Union party seemed likely to help them, and Norman Thomas, who had eloquently supported black tenant farmers, seemed such an unlikely winner as the Socialist presidential candidate that few blacks considered wasting their votes on him. Blacks also recognized that many New Dealers sympathized with them. Mrs. Roosevelt often intervened on their behalf, and Harold Ickes secured places in the federal bureaucracy for black spokesmen. Other department heads challenged the Jim Crow practices that Wilson had developed years earlier. Most important, programs like the Civilian Conservation Corps, Public Works Administration, and Works Progress Administration employed thousands of poor blacks, who at last felt the direct benevolent hand of Uncle Sam. Far from antagonizing the black electorate, FDR's policies swung it into the Democratic column. Some 75 percent supported him in 1936, compared to but 21 percent four years earlier.

In this same positive way Roosevelt attracted ethnic voters to his side. New Deal welfare policies pumped millions of dollars into the cities, where the established ethnic machines became the natural distributors and beneficiaries. Roosevelt also spread patronage generously to ethnic leaders. By 1936 most of these leaders, especially Jews and Irish-Americans, were fervent supporters of Roosevelt and the Democratic party. They, too, retained these loyalties for decades.

With all these advantages Roosevelt scored a spectacular victory on election day. He swept every state but Maine and Vermont, and carried with him into Congress unprecedented Democratic margins of 331 to 89 and 76 to 16. (Progressives and Independents like La Follette and Norris added to his margin of support.) His total vote of 27.8 million swamped Landon's 16.7 million, Lemke's 880,000, and Thomas' 187,000 (700,000 fewer than in 1932). Roosevelt's total, more than 5 million more than he had gotten four years earlier, was swelled by throngs of people who previously had not voted. These people—blacks, ethnics, workers, and poor people—formed an enduring coalition of forgotten men and women for the Democratic party.

STALEMATE

Shortly after the election, Senator Hiram Johnson of California prophesied the future. "I think," he wrote, "that Roosevelt during this next session will give free rein to his imagination. There will be nobody to stop him, and but few to protest. All sorts of experiments we may see, some of which will give us the cold shivers." It is difficult to explain why this did not happen and why the New Deal advanced no further.

One important reason was the "court reform" bill with which Roosevelt polarized the country in February 1937. The reform called for the addition of new judges to the federal courts when the incumbents refused to retire at the age of 70. The

Supreme Court (which then had six judges over 70) could be expanded to a maximum of 15. With new blood, the President argued, the courts could stay abreast of their work.

Roosevelt's desire to curb the "nine old men," as progressives called them, was understandable. After overturning the NRA, the judges had proceeded in 1936 to reject the AAA (six to three) and state minimum wage acts (five to four). Justice Harlan Stone, one of the three consistent liberals on the Court (Brandeis and Benjamin Cardozo were the others) called the 1936 term "one of the most disastrous in history." With other key legislation, such as social security and the Wagner Act, soon to reach the high tribunal, New Dealers feared for the worst.

But the President's message badly misjudged popular reverence for the Court and for the sanctity of separation of powers. The New York *Herald Tribune,* a Republican paper, typified this sort of reaction by proclaiming that "it was a French King, Louis XIV, who said: 'L'Etat c'est moi'—I am the state. The paper shell of American constitutionalism would continue if President Roosevelt secured the passage of the law he now demands. But it would only be a shell." Liberals, too, worried about the President's plan. The Court, they agreed, was not falling behind in its work. Aged justices—their hero, Brandeis, was eighty-one—were not the problem. Roosevelt had said nothing about Court reform during the election, nor had he consulted his congressional backers. "The President's plan," Wheeler complained, "is a fake and a sham proposal. It does not accomplish one single thing that the liberals of this country have been fighting for."

Roosevelt professed to be unperturbed by the outcry. "Conservatives," he chortled to a friend, "are running about tearing their hair and using language about me that surpasses even that of the campaign." But during the prolonged hearings

The "nine old men" of the Supreme Court. From left to right: (front row) Associate Justices George Sutherland and James Clark McReynolds, Chief Justice Charles Evans Hughes, Associate Justices Louis Dembitz Brandeis and Pierce Butler. (back row) Associate Justices Benjamin N. Cardozo, Harlan Fisk Stone, Owen J. Roberts, and Hugo L. Black.

on the plan, opposition mounted steadily. Charles Evans Hughes, the formidable, white-bearded chief justice, showed conclusively that the Court was fully abreast of its duties. The Court itself—in a "switch in time that saved nine"—then undermined Roosevelt's effort by sustaining (by votes of five to four) the social security and Wagner acts and by reversing its decision of 1936 on state minimum wage laws. Thereafter, even Roosevelt's most loyal supporters pleaded for an end to the divisive debate. After holding out stubbornly for five months, the President finally gave up the struggle.

In some respects Roosevelt could argue that the Court had appeared to reverse itself under pressure. Moreover, the retirement of one of the conservative judges in May promised to give the New Deal a safer margin of support in the future. (By 1941 four other judges had retired, and Roosevelt had safely assured himself of support for liberal legislation by naming men like Hugo Black, William Douglas, and Felix Frankfurter to the Court.) But such an argument failed to recognize that the decision sustaining minimum wages, though announced after the release of the President's court-packing announcement, had actually been arrived at beforehand. What motivated the two "swing men," Hughes and Owen Roberts, to change their minds in 1937 was not wholly clear—perhaps the Democratic triumph of 1936— but it was not the plan itself. Instead, Roosevelt's proposal alarmed the country, split the Democratic coalition, and encouraged congressional moderates, who had previously feared to challenge such a popular president, to resist. From that point on, Roosevelt had to fight for what he could get from an increasingly hostile Congress.

Other developments added to Roosevelt's difficulties in his second term. One was the sit-down strikes, which business spokesmen were quick to blame on the administration's friendliness toward the CIO. Another was the state of the economy. Early in 1937 it seemed that prosperity was returning at last. But Roosevelt, anxious as always to reduce federal spending, cut back on relief. At the same time the Federal Reserve tightened money. Businessmen held back on new investment. For all these reasons one of the most serious recessions in American history descended in late 1937. Within ten months some 4 million people lost their jobs, and unemployment rose to 11.5 million.

Conservatives responded to this state of affairs by saying, "I told you so." Moderates wondered if the New Deal had done any good at all. Keynesian economists and progressives demanded that FDR resume heavy public spending. Caught in a crossfire, Roosevelt procrastinated, agonized, and finally (after sensing trouble ahead in the 1938 elections) supported the spenders. By late 1939 the economy moved sluggishly out of the recession. But Roosevelt's policies (and indecision) had contributed to two more years of hard times. Under such conditions it was not surprising that Republicans made strong inroads on his congressional majorities in 1938.

Despite these setbacks, Roosevelt pressed for further reforms: regional resource development, minimum wages, maximum hours, protection of child labor, assistance to tenant farmers, reorganization of the federal government. Persuaded that big business was holding out on him, he encouraged the antitrust division of the Justice Department to move against monopolies. Contrary to the view of some

Business men have a different set of delusions from politicians; and need, therefore, different handling. They are, however, much milder than politicians, at the same time allured and terrified by the glare of publicity, easily persuaded to be 'patriots,' perplexed, bemused, indeed terrified, yet only too anxious to take a cheerful view, vain perhaps but very unsure of themselves, pathetically responsive to a kind word. You could do anything you liked with them, if you would treat them (even the big ones), not as wolves and tigers, but as domestic animals by nature, even though they have been badly brought up and not trained as you would wish. It is a mistake to think that they are more immoral than politicians. If you work them into the surly, obstinate, terrified mood, of which domestic animals, wrongly handled, are so capable, the nation's burdens will not get carried to market; and in the end public opinion will veer their way.

Lord John Maynard Keynes advises Roosevelt on handling businessmen, 1938. Roosevelt paid him little heed.

disenchanted leftist historians, he had neither run out of ideas nor given up the struggle.

But he was unable to translate his personal popularity into legislation. The interest groups that comprised his formidable electoral coalition repeatedly failed to work jointly for legislation unless it directly affected them individually. And the conservative coalition in Congress complained accurately that the Democratic party had been transformed since 1928 from the largely southern and western bloc it had been in the days of William Jennings Bryan to a predominantly urban agglomeration symbolized by people like Robert Wagner of New York. Angered by the demands of the urbanites—money for relief and housing, assistance for blacks, laws protecting labor—the rural forces determined to mount a strong opposition. With their demoralization of 1933–35 overcome, they were no longer willing to help the New Deal.

The result was stalemate. Between 1937 and 1939 Congress approved laws providing small sums for public housing and tenant farmers. It enacted a second

The New Deal has been carried to extremes by the more radical element, and they are the worst enemies of the New Deal. They propose now to destroy the Democratic Party and build upon its ruin a party of their own—a New Deal Party. They seem now to be making desperate efforts to drive all others out of the Democratic Party and the remarkable thing about this is that many of them were never Democrats. They have come into the house which was built by others and intend to take possession and drive the builders out. . . . It would be better for them to be a little more tolerant of the Democrats who have always been faithful to the party. For those are they who carry elections.

Sen. Josiah Bailey, Democrat of North Carolina, offers a characteristic conservative complaint (1939) about the "new" Democratic party.

AAA, without the tax on food processors to which the Court had objected. In a change which foreshadowed many later moves to expand the White House staff, it authorized Roosevelt to create the Executive Office of the President. Most important, it finally approved a law abolishing child labor in interstate commerce and providing for federal minimum wages and maximum hours. But these laws were heavily amended before passage. Congress also dismissed Roosevelt's requests for regional development, it whittled away at the WPA, it cut off funding for the Federal Theatre project, it rejected an expansion in government lending, and it ushered in a new age of congressional investigatory activity by authorizing a probe into the NLRB and providing generously for the new House Un-American Activities Committee. It was clear that Congress had moved from the left of the White House (where it had usually been between 1909 and 1936) to the right, and that it was resuming the assertive behavior it had demonstrated from 1919 to 1933. Presidential success, it appeared, inevitably bred congressional counterreaction.

The New Deal: an evaluation

Because Roosevelt attempted so much, it is easy to criticize him. Conservatives were correct in complaining about the maze of bureaucratic agencies; even Roosevelt conceded in 1936 that "administration" was his greatest weakness. They were also correct in accusing Roosevelt of inconsistency. And they were wise to be wary about the dangers of executive direction. "The old Jeffersonian emphasis on schools for citizenship and on self-government," one critic observed, "has changed to a Rooseveltian emphasis on response to a heroic leadership."

Other critics focused on what they perceived as the synthetic quality of Roosevelt's personality. The President, they agreed, was flexible, buoyant, charismatic, an eloquent speaker who evoked mass loyalty unprecedented in American politics. But, they added, he was primarily a political animal who concealed a calculating nature behind a façade of good humor and patrician assurance. Worse, he was a drifter and an improviser who lacked the intellectual capacity to understand economics and the courage to act when—as during the recession of 1937–38—decisive responses were required. According to this perspective, Roosevelt was sheer personality—a con artist supreme.

Critics on the Left stressed the limitations of the New Deal. Roosevelt, they said, was often cautious and conservative. He refused to nationalize banking, to sponsor laws against lynching, or to work hard for public housing. He was slow to perceive the needs of organized labor and he was virtually blind to those of the city. Before 1942 he barely mentioned such later reforms as federal aid to education, health insurance, or civil rights legislation. Despite his rhetoric against big business, he did little to stem the growth of monopoly, which proceeded apace in the 1930s. After his abortive attempt for a "wealth tax," he left the tax structure as it was. Income distribution in 1940 was much as it had been ten years before.

Other reformers argued that FDR hardly affected the sources of power in America. He remained a firm believer in decentralization and in a responsive approach to interest groups. Large farmers and businessmen expanded their influence, while newer groups, especially labor unions, added to the pressures on government. In theory this state of affairs culminated in a balance of "countervailing powers," bringing rough justice to all groups. In practice, however, it meant that the strongest groups got what they wanted while others—consumers, unskilled workers, women, blacks—got little or nothing.

Finally, critics observed that the New Deal failed to arrest the depression. Even in the "good" times of early 1937 some 7.5 million Americans (out of a work force of 54 million) were unemployed. In the same year gross private domestic investment was only $11.7 billion, compared to $16.2 billion in 1929. Per capita national income did not reach 1929 levels until early 1940.

Why this was so remains in dispute. Some conservative economists maintain that more sophisticated monetary policy was the answer—that the Federal Reserve in 1931, and again in 1937, tightened money at the wrong times, thereby deterring potential investors. However, this view perhaps exaggerates the potential of monetary policies. It also downplays the fact that cheap money between 1933 and 1937 had little impact on investment.

Another argument blames conservative fiscal policy for the persistence of hard times. Federal tax rates, instead of being reduced to stimulate consumption (and investment), were sustained, and new levies (including social security) were added. Though federal spending increased—from approximately $3.3 billion in 1929 to $4.6 billion in 1932–33 to $8.9 billion in 1939—this was perhaps too little too late. Moreover, the modest federal deficits (averaging $3 billion a year between 1933 and 1939) caused by these increased expenditures were counterbalanced by surpluses in state and local budgets throughout the decade. Accordingly, there was no public deficit spending by governments—federal, state, and local—in the 1930s. As public works expenditures in Germany during the 1930s were already suggesting, the best remedy for hard times may have been higher public spending at all levels, and neither Roosevelt nor Hoover ever fully accepted that fact.

These criticisms, however, exaggerated Roosevelt's alleged opportunism. Unlike some of his successors in the White House, he was concerned with more than augmenting his own position (though he cared very much about that). While uninformed about labor organization, he wanted to assist ordinary people, and he expressed their needs in simple language they could understand. In his "fireside chats," his numerous press conferences, his attention to the avalanche of mail that poured into the White House, he projected the image of a man who cared, and in his dealings with Congress he proved supple and forceful. His air of confidence gave people hope and restored faith in democratic institutions. "He showed," one admirer concluded, "that it is possible to be politically effective and yet benevolent and civilized."

Critics also underestimated the obstacles to thoroughgoing reform. The Supreme Court, which caused him to introduce his ill-fated packing plan, was one. Congress, malapportioned to favor conservatives, became another. The federal system was a third, for Roosevelt could not change state fiscal policies, which were regressive, or state political parties, which remained free to dilute the effect of programs. Roosevelt might have worked harder than he did to place progressives in power at the grass roots. But he did not have time to do everything, and when he attempted (rather hastily) to "purge" conservative Democrats from Congress in 1938, he failed.

The largest obstacle to reform remained the economic interest groups. If Roosevelt had chosen to confront them in 1933, when even conservatives yearned for strong leadership, he might have battered them about. Trusts might have been weakened, utilities, banks, and stock exchanges more rigorously regulated. Such policies, if combined with massive spending, might have brought recovery as well as reform. But few political leaders were willing to go that far, even in 1933, and it is highly unlikely that the President could have moved that fast without prompting divisiveness and loss of confidence at the very start of his administration.

Above all, Roosevelt's detractors tend to neglect his accomplishments. In part because of the New Deal, the economy stopped its disastrous slide of 1930–32. Farm prices increased, debtors received relief, banks reopened. The New Deal introduced modest centralization of banking and limited regulation of stock issues. It created landmark achievements such as social security and TVA and pioneered in the federal development of public welfare. The Wagner Act helped to give federal protection to workers. And while Roosevelt rejected deficit spending as a long-range policy, so did most of his contemporaries: his willingness to resort to it at all stamped him as a flexible leader.

These acts were "conservative" in that they maintained the capitalistic system. But they were also reforms, and they were partially successful. They resulted—at last—in a measure of political modernization capable of struggling with the economic centralization of previous decades. Compared with what had come before, the growth in the 1930s of the welfare state was considerable.

Suggestions for reading

Books on the Hoover years include Joan Hoff Wilson, *Herbert Hoover** (1975); Harris Warren, *Herbert Hoover and the Great Depression** (1959); Jordan Schwarz, *Interregnum of Despair* (1970); Albert Romasco, *The Poverty of Abundance: Hoover, the Nation, the Depression** (1965); and David Burner, *A Public Life* (Hoover) (1979). See also Roger Daniels, *Bonus March** (1971).

The most important general works on the New Deal are William Leuchtenburg, *Franklin D. Roosevelt and the New Deal, 1932–1940** (1963); Arthur Schlesinger, Jr., *The Coming of the New Deal** (1959) and *The Politics of Upheaval** (1960); James M. Burns, *Roosevelt: The Lion and the Fox** (1956); Otis Graham, Jr., *An Encore for Reform** (1963); Paul Conkin, *The New Deal** (1967), a brief interpretation; and the four volumes on Franklin D. Roosevelt by Frank Freidel. These volumes take Roosevelt into 1933. See also Joseph Lash, *Eleanor & Franklin** (1971). Books revealing the impact of the New Deal on politics are Theodore Lowi, *The End of Liberalism** (1969); Grant McConnell, *Private Power and American Democracy** (1966); Bruce Stave, *The New Deal & The Last Hurrah* (1970), on urban politics; and the book by Lubell cited in the bibliography for chapter 7.

Studies dealing with New Deal programs include Randolph Paul, *Taxation in the United States* (1954); John M. Blum, *Roosevelt and Morgenthau* (1970); Ellis Hawley, *The New Deal and the Problem of Monopoly** (1966); Richard Kirkendall, *Social Scientists and Farm Politics in the Age of Roosevelt* (1966); and James T. Patterson, *The New Deal and the States: Federalism in Transition* (1969). Also Roy Lubove, *The Struggle for Social Security, 1900–1935** (1968); Paul Conkin, *Tomorrow a New World* (1959), which deals with community programs; Jane D. Mathews, *The Federal Theater, 1935–1939** (1971); Joseph Arnold, *The New Deal in the Suburbs** (1971); Thomas McCraw, *TVA and the Power Fight, 1933–1939** (1970); Michael Parrish, *Securities Regulation and the New Deal* (1970); John Salmond, *The Civilian Conservation Corps* (1967); William Graebner, *A History of Retirement* (1980); Anthony J. Badger, *Prosperity Road: The New Deal, Tobacco, and North Carolina* (1980); and Mark Gelfand, *A Nation of Cities: The Federal Government and Urban America, 1933–1965* (1975). See also Robert J. Zangrando, *The NAACP Crusade Against Lynching, 1909–1950* (1980); and Harvard Sitkoff, *A New Deal for Blacks: The Emergence of Civil Rights as a National Issue* (1979).

For Roosevelt's opponents, see Charles Tull, *Father Coughlin and the New Deal* (1965); David H. Bennett, *Demagogues in the Depression: American Radicals and the Union Party, 1932–1936* (1969); Abraham Holtzman, *The Townsend Movement* (1963); and Donald McCoy, *Angry Voices* (1958). Conservatives are covered in James Patterson, *Congressional Conservatism and the New Deal** (1967); John Hudson and George Wolfskill, *All But the People: FDR and His Critics** (1969); and McCoy, *Landon of Kansas* (1966). See also Richard Polenberg, *Reorganizing Roosevelt's Government . . . 1936–1939* (1966); Barry Karl, *Executive Reorganization and the New Deal* (1963). Important biographies include T. Harry Williams, *Huey Long** (1969); Ellsworth Barnard, *Wendell Willkie* (1966); and J. Joseph Huthmacher, *Senator Robert Wagner and the Rise of American Liberalism* (1968). For the Supreme Court consult Leonard Baker, *Back to Back: The Duel Between Franklin D. Roosevelt and the Supreme Court* (1967); Robert Jackson, *The Struggle for Judicial Supremacy** (1941), an account by a New Deal partisan who later joined the Court; and C. Herman Pritchett, *The Roosevelt Court, 1937–1947* (1963).

9

From nonintervention
to war
1929–1941

"There is the most profound outlook for peace today," President Hoover told
Secretary of State Henry Stimson in 1930, "that we have had at any time in the last
half century." Five years later, *Christian Century* accurately reported that
"ninety-nine Americans out of one hundred would today regard as an imbecile
anyone who would suggest that in the event of a European war the United States
should again participate in it." In 1940 President Roosevelt assured an audience in
Boston, "while I am talking to you, fathers and mothers, I give you one more
assurance. I have said this before but I shall say it again and again: your boys are
not going to be sent into any foreign wars."

Events forced Hoover and *Christian Century* to revise their predictions, and
they made a liar out of FDR. By 1945, when World War II finally ended, 50 million
people, including 405,000 Americans, had been killed. Yet the three quotations tell
much about the movement of American thinking at the time: from optimism for
peace, to assertions about the virtues of isolation, to desperate, deceiving assurances about the prospects for noninvolvement.

Hoover and foreign affairs

Hoover, with a Quaker background, was perhaps the most pacifistic of American
presidents. During his administration he worked earnestly toward renouncing the
Roosevelt Corollary, which had justified American military intervention in Latin

America. He attempted—unsuccessfully—to commit the leading powers to broaden the naval limitations established in 1922. Though he signed the nationalistic tariff act of 1930, he attempted to lessen international economic tensions by declaring the moratorium on war debt payments in 1931.

Hoover was also a staunch nationalist. At Versailles he had concluded that Europeans were irreparably selfish and quarrelsome. Like most Americans, therefore, he showed little interest after 1920 in the League of Nations. When confronted with demands that America take a hard line against overseas aggression, his instinctive reaction was to refuse. Like George Washington, he believed America should mind its own business.

The Manchurian crisis of 1931 revealed the strengths and limitations of Hoover's pacifistic nationalism. The area had long been a source of conflict between Russia, Japan, and China. The Japanese secured leaseholds and railroad rights there after World War I. Their presence antagonized Chinese nationalists under Chiang Kai-shek, who encouraged local warlords to compete with Japan. Chiang, indeed, enjoyed only nominal control over many areas of China, which at that time was far less unified than many Westerners believed. Perceiving China's weakness, the Japanese attacked Manchuria in September 1931. The League called rather vaguely for sanctions. But it lacked an army, and Britain and France, the League's strongest powers, were ill prepared to resist. What, therefore, were Herbert Hoover and the United States prepared to do?

The answer was, very little. Hoover authorized an American to sit in at meetings of the League Council but to speak only if the delegates attempted to utilize the pious Kellogg-Briand Pact of 1928, which ''outlawed'' aggressive war. He also refused to recognize Japanese conquests in Manchuria. Following this American approach, the League embraced this doctrine of nonrecognition. However, the Japanese ignored the League and then, in February 1933, withdrew from it. Japanese armies remained in China and Manchuria until 1945.

This Western weakness later encouraged both Germany and Japan to pursue aggressive policies. But what was Hoover (and later Roosevelt) to do? In the depth of the depression it seemed foolhardy to retaliate by cutting off American trade with Japan, which bought four times as much as China, or to try to resist the well-equipped Japanese armies. It seemed equally unwise to defy the American public, which wanted no part of military involvement in Asia. The historian Charles Beard spoke for many in proclaiming that it was not worth ''killing American boys in a struggle over the bean crop in Manchuria.'' Hoover could have done nothing to stop Japan in 1931.

Hoover also asked the broader question: Was it really in America's national interest to defend the Open Door against Japan? Unlike Stimson—and many later ''experts'' on Oriental behavior—he did not believe the Japanese could be scared into submission. Challenging them, he thought, was like ''sticking pins in tigers.'' America's only vital interests, he added, lay in the Western Hemisphere. This argument stemmed from his rather narrow nationalism, and it led to appeasement. But in 1931–33 it was restrained, and —given the temper of the times—politically realistic. Only later, when the aggressive powers banded together, did its limitations become clearer.

The rise of noninterventionism, 1933–36

Roosevelt's first term witnessed the spread of virtually unchallenged militarism and aggression. In January 1933 Hitler assumed power, and in October he pulled out of the League. He followed this action by intensifying his persecution of Jews and leftists. In 1935 Mussolini invaded Ethiopia, and Germany started conscription. In 1936 Hitler further violated the Versailles treaty by moving into the Rhineland. Meanwhile, Japan tightened control in Manchuria and refused any longer to be bound by the five-power treaty limiting naval armaments.

On the face of it Roosevelt appeared well prepared to deal with such a world. As Wilson's assistant secretary of the navy he had shared Wilson's faith that America must play an active role in world affairs. "Modern civilization," he said in 1920, "has become so complex and the lives of civilized men so interwoven with the lives of other men as to make it impossible to be in this world and not of it." By 1932 such influential forces as the chauvinistic Hearst press had induced him to back away from support of the League. But he never shared Hoover's instinctive suspicion of Europe or his faith that America should go it alone.

During his first years in office he occasionally acted on cautiously internationalist premises, especially where they promised to aid the economy. Following Hoover, he worked toward what he called the "good neighbor" policy in Latin America. In 1934, with a conservative regime in Cuba protecting American interests, he ended the United States protectorate there. By 1940, America's relations with Latin America were warmer than before. FDR also recognized the Soviet Union in 1933, primarily in the misplaced hope of developing trade. And he named as his secretary of state Cordell Hull, an ardent believer in lower tariff barriers as the way to peace and prosperity. Thanks to Hull's efforts, Congress approved the Reciprocal Trade Agreements Act of 1934, which stopped congressional logrolling by empowering the executive branch to negotiate rates. In the same year Roosevelt established the Export-Import Bank, which extended credit to potential customers abroad.

But neither Roosevelt nor Hull was a profound thinker concerning foreign affairs. Hull, indeed, was a rather rigid moralist obsessed with the vision of free trade. Roosevelt kept many important matters out of Hull's hands, and in so doing reduced morale in the State Department. Worse, FDR occasionally acted as if his charm and adaptability could bring to international relations the same soothing results they brought to domestic affairs. The diplomat George Kennan complained later that some of Roosevelt's problems stemmed from his "superficiality, the forced and often unsuccessful humor, the studied avoidance of every serious issue."

Roosevelt's greatest handicap was the depression, which forced him to place domestic policies above all else. Accordingly, he sent a "bombshell" message to the London Economic Conference that met in June 1933. Efforts to stabilize currencies, he proclaimed, were "old fetishes of so-called international bankers" and were "purely artificial and temporary." The United States must act alone to develop "the kind of a dollar which a generation hence will have the same purchasing and debt paying power as the dollar we hope to obtain in the near future." This nationalistic message was defensible economically, for it promised to free Western nations from the inhibitions of the gold standard and to permit expansionary fiscal policies at home. At the same time, the message was blunt and curt. It effectively torpedoed the conference.

This economic nationalism was part of a much broader current of isolationist thinking in the mid-1930s. Abroad isolationism led to the growth of pacifism and "appeasement" in England and France. Both countries felt doubts about the treatment accorded Germany at Versailles, and both shrank from another war. In America isolationism was reflected in books like Charles Beard's *Open Door at Home* (1934), which maintained that overseas adventurism blocked domestic reforms. Among young people it helped promote a rise in pacifism, which led to creation of the mock-serious Veterans of Future Wars (whose members demanded pre-service bonuses) and to a wave of student strikes for peace.

This understandable fear of a World War II also prompted a wave of historical revisionism that blamed Wilson and profiteers for dragging America into World War I. *Merchants of Death* by Helmuth Englebrecht and Frank Hanighen, a tract against munitions makers, became a best seller in 1934. Walter Millis' *Road to War,* which stressed the role of economic motives and of Allied propaganda, was a Book-of-the-Month Club selection in 1935. Robert Sherwood's *Idiot's Delight,* a play featuring an evil arms manufacturer, received a Pulitzer Prize in 1936. To one bitter revisionist, "platitude-mongering Wilson, who was willing to have young men die for old men's dividends," was no longer the magnificent idealist who had stirred people's visions in 1919, but the arch villain of his time.

All these feelings—fear of war, hatred of profiteers, distrust of presidential power—were strong on Capitol Hill. As early as 1933, at the height of Roosevelt's popularity, Congress refused to give him discretionary power to apply arms embargoes against nations he labeled aggressors. In 1934 it passed a law prohibiting American loans to nations defaulting on war debts. At the same time it authorized a special Senate committee to investigate munitions making during World War I. The committee, headed by Gerald P. Nye of North Dakota, discovered only the obvious:

> Munitions men, bowed down with care
> And worries here and everywhere,
> Each nite must breathe this little prayer—
>   Now I lay me down to snore,
> I hope tomorrow there'll be war—
> Before another day shall pass
> I hope we sell some mustard gas;
> Bless the Germans, bless the Japs,
> Bless the Russians, too, perhaps—
> Bless the French! let their suspicions
> Show the need for more munitions!
> Now I lay me down to snooze;
> Let the morrow bring bad news!

Characteristic antiwar doggerel, mid-1930s.

that munitions manufacturers had made money and that they had engaged in collusive bidding. It did not uncover a conspiracy to get the nation into war, nor did it succeed in implicating Wilson, who was no friend of arms manufacturers. But neither Nye nor his wide audience worried much about lack of such evidence. It was enough that rich manufacturers (already scapegoats for the depression) had made huge profits while American boys died on European soil. The economic motive for war must not be allowed to develop again.

In mid-1935 Congress took a still more fateful step by debating a ''neutrality'' bill applying the "lessons" of 1914–17. Among the bill's provisions was an automatic embargo on American arms and ammunition to all parties at war. Alarmed, Hull sought amendments enabling the president to discriminate between aggressor and innocent. Roosevelt recognized that the bill not only tied his hands but repudiated traditional American shipping rights—which Wilson had gone to war to protect. But FDR's top priority remained domestic legislation against the depression. To challenge Congress over the neutrality bill, he realized, was futile and counterproductive. So he told Hull to submit. When Congress approved the measure at the close of the session, Roosevelt signed it and called it "entirely satisfactory."

A few weeks later Mussolini launched a long-expected attack on Ethiopia. Roosevelt immediately applied the arms embargo against both sides. His action probably made little difference, for Italy did not need American arms, and Ethiopia could ill afford to buy them. More significant was the failure of the United States to ban the shipment of oil, the key to the success of mechanized armed forces such as Italy's. When American exporters sent oil to Italy, Roosevelt and Hull urged them to apply a "moral embargo." But the hard-hit companies were anxious to make a profit, and they saw little reason to comply with a president who had turned against big business. The shipments proceeded.

American policy was by no means the only obstacle to Ethiopia's cause. Britain and France also shied away from taking a stand that might involve them in war. Both countries shipped oil to Italy throughout the crisis. Nor could Roosevelt have secured repeal of the neutrality act, which had passed the Senate by a vote of seventy-nine to two, and the House without even a roll call vote. Still, the neutrality law showed how far America was willing to go to keep the nation out of war. The "lessons" of 1917 had been learned too well.

The hope for appeasement, 1936–38

In August 1936 Roosevelt again appealed to isolationist feelings. "I hate war," he proclaimed. "I have passed unnumbered hours, I shall pass unnumbered hours, thinking and planning how war may be kept from this nation."

His hopes for peace were sincere. But in reiterating them he was concealing from the public his own private anger at the aggressors. He was also ignoring the advice of many emissaries abroad, especially William Dodd in Berlin and George Messersmith in Vienna. "The Hitler triumvirate," Dodd warned in 1935, "is . . . far more powerful than the Kaiser was. . . . You may infer . . . that war is their direct and major aim.'' In 1936 Messersmith added, "there is only one way to deal with the German regime of today, and that is to meet its brutal, ruthless action by an equally determined stand. It is the only language which that regime understands. . . .''

Congress, of course, would not have permitted Roosevelt to follow such a course in 1936, or even in 1938. Still, he could have begun the process of educating the public for the ordeal that he recognized might lie ahead. That he did not, that he persisted in appeasing the isolationists, revealed him as less than forthright. It marked him also as one of the many, including Britain's Prime Minister Neville Chamberlain, who clung to illusions about the chances for real neutrality in a world being overrun by men like Hitler.

Roosevelt's hopes for peace proved useless against the even more aggressive behavior of the antidemocratic forces. In November 1936 Germany and Japan signed the Anti-Comintern Pact, forerunner to later agreements that bound the two powers (and Italy) in military defense alliances. Fascists under Franco then revolted against the legitimate republican government of Spain. In 1937 Japan launched a full-scale invasion of China. In 1938 Hitler annexed Austria, and then the Sudetenland of Czechoslovakia.

Confronted with these threats, Congress pursued a still more nationalistic course. In 1936 it prohibited citizens from advancing loans or credits to belligerents. Early in 1937 it hurried through a law extending this ban, as well as an arms embargo, to the civil war in Spain. Progressives, including many who had supported previous neutrality legislation, complained that the act would assist Franco. They were overruled, and America stood by while Hitler aided Franco and used the Spanish war as a testing ground for his weaponry.

In May 1937 Congress, still preoccupied with learning lessons from 1914–17, completed its pursuit of peace by passing a comprehensive neutrality law. It banned American ships from war zones, prohibited Americans from traveling on belligerent ships, and extended the mandatory embargo on arms and ammunition. Making sure that the United States had its cake and ate it too, it placed other vital exports, including oil, steel, and rubber, under the rubric of "cash and carry" for two years. Foreign belligerents could buy such goods only if they paid for them in cash and carried them in their own ships. Cash and carry, Congress recognized, enabled American producers to sell their goods abroad, without exposing American ships to enemy submarines and without giving Wall Street any cause to press for defense of its loans.

As in earlier years, Roosevelt wasted little effort trying to dissuade Congress from enacting these measures, which obviously commanded popular support. But in the fall of 1937 he appeared to move cautiously away from his hands-off policy. Taking advantage of the fact that no "war" was declared in Asia, he refused to apply an embargo, thus permitting American ships and creditors to deal with China in the years ahead. In October he followed by giving a "quarantine" speech in Chicago. "The epidemic of world lawlessness," he said, "is spreading. When an epidemic of physical disease starts to spread, the community approves and joins in a quarantine of the patients in order to protect the health of the community against the spread of disease. . . . There must be positive endeavors to preserve peace." At last, so it seemed, Roosevelt was moving toward a policy of resistance.

Having ventured toward activism, Roosevelt failed to follow it up. In fact, it remains unclear what he had expected to do in the first place, for the quarantine speech was equivocal. It talked of action by the "community" and of "positive endeavors," but it offered no concrete suggestions for collective measures, and it reiterated that "America hates war. . . . America actively engages in the search for peace." When a few isolationist newspapers exploded in protest, Roosevelt ignored contrary reactions, and said nothing more. Amid such an atmosphere of caution it was not surprising that Japanese planes over the Yangtze felt bold enough in December to sink the American gunboat *Panay*, to strafe its crew, and to kill two American sailors in the process. Though Roosevelt privately considered responding with economic sanctions, he did nothing when Japan apologized; he wanted no part of using such incidents to fan the passions of war.

By 1938 many influential Americans were chafing openly at Roosevelt's temporizing. Former Secretary of State Stimson was one, Harold Ickes another, Secretary of the Treasury Henry Morgenthau, a close advisor of the President, a third. But the isolationist House of Representatives grew so alarmed about the *Panay* incident that it nearly approved a constitutional amendment requiring a national referendum before America could go to war, and polls suggested that sizable majorities of the people supported the neutrality laws. Ever sensitive to the popular pulse, Roosevelt contented himself with stopping the amendment and with working successfully for more generous naval appropriations.

It was at this point, in mid-1938, that Hitler demanded the Sudetenland of Czechoslovakia. Pursuing appeasement to its logical conclusion, Prime Minister Neville Chamberlain of England and Premier Eduard Daladier of France went to the Munich Conference in October and surrendered to Hitler's demand. Actually, Chamberlain and Daladier had a difficult choice, for their nations did not want war, and even with the aid of the Czech army they might have been hard pressed to defeat Germany. Chamberlain was nonetheless foolish to proclaim that he had secured "peace in our time." Winston Churchill, a foe of appeasement, was closer to the mark in exclaiming that "Britain and France had to choose between war and dishonor. They chose dishonor. They will have war."

The United States played no direct role in the Munich Conference. ("It is always best and safest," Chamberlain remarked, "to count on nothing from the Americans but words.") Roosevelt also showed little sympathy for Churchill's position. Two days after the conference he told Chamberlain, "I fully share your hope and belief that there exists today the greatest opportunity in years for the establishment of a new order based on justice and law." As Hitler prepared for his greatest conquests, the United States remained as doggedly neutral as ever.

America and Hitler, 1939–41

When Hitler seized the remainder of Czechoslovakia in March 1939, it became difficult to doubt his insatiable ambitions. Further German expansion, the British and French warned, would mean war. Unimpressed, Hitler negotiated a nonaggression pact with Stalin to protect his eastern front, and in September the two nations

Hitler enters Brno, Czechoslovakia in March, 1939.

invaded Poland. "Close your hearts to pity," Hitler told his generals. "Act brutally. Eighty million people must obtain what is their right. Their existence must be made secure. The strongest man is right. . . ."

Before the invasion Roosevelt asked for and received expanded funds for defense. He also made a belated effort to get Congress to repeal the mandatory arms embargo. However, Congress had refused. So when war broke out in September 1939, Roosevelt tried again. After prolonged debate, Congress repealed the mandatory embargo in November, and munitions began to flow across the Atlantic. At the same time Roosevelt quickly provided funds to scientists eager to develop an atomic bomb. But he still insisted that America "will keep out of this war. . . . there will be no blackout of peace in the United States." And Congress persisted in adhering to cash and carry—the Allies must buy all goods, including munitions, in cash and transport them in their own ships.

Hitler then overran Denmark and Norway in April 1940 and France and the low countries in May and June. Only Britain, whose troops fled across the Channel from Dunkirk, remained to fight the fascist menace. For many Americans the fall of

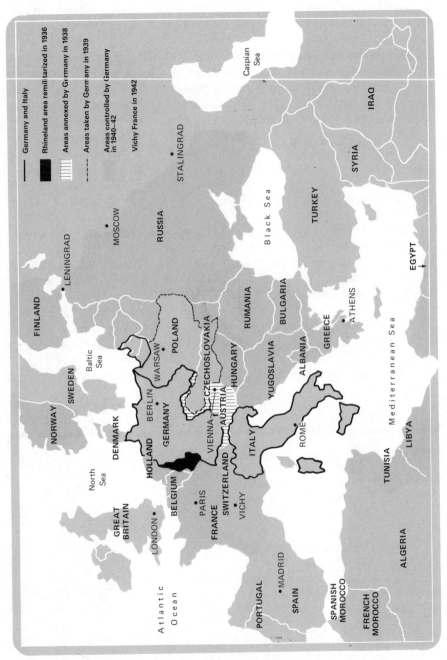

Legend:
— Germany and Italy
▮ Rhineland area remilitarized in 1936
▦ Areas annexed by Germany in 1938
▦ Areas taken by Germany in 1939
- - - Areas controlled by Germany in 1940–42
Vichy France in 1942

Aggression of Axis Powers in Europe, 1936–42

France was especially sobering. They formed the Committee to Aid the Allies under the leadership of the veteran publisher William Allen White. Equally alarmed, Roosevelt proclaimed, "we will extend to the opponents of force the material resources of this nation, and, at the same time, we will harness and speed up the use of these resources."

Other moves in mid-1940 suggested that FDR was ready to pursue a more resolute course against Hitler. In June he named Stimson, an ardent foe of appeasement, as secretary of war. He lent passive support to Stimson's drive, which proved successful, for the nation's first peacetime draft. He received quick congressional backing for additional defense spending. After assuring himself that Wendell Willkie, the Republican presidential nominee, would not attack him, he agreed in September to the unneutral "destroyer deal," whereby America released fifty aged destroyers in return for leases on British bases in the Western Hemisphere. Because some of the ships could barely make it to sea, they were of limited use in Britain's desperate defense against German submarines. But the deal symbolized America's increasing readiness to help.

The drift away from neutrality aroused the anti-interventionists to renewed activity. Many of them joined America First, a broad isolationist front. Others, like Senators Robert Taft of Ohio and Arthur Vandenberg of Michigan, led a Republican onslaught in Congress. Many socialists and pacifists, including Norman Thomas, added their voices. So did former President Hoover, flying hero Charles Lindbergh, progressive Senator Robert La Follette, Jr., Charles Beard, John L. Lewis, Frank Lloyd Wright, Joseph Kennedy, America's ambassador to Great Britain, and some spokesmen for German, Italian, and Irish ethnic groups. Though the isolationists were probably outnumbered after the fall of France, they were strong in the Midwest, in a few German-American enclaves, and among nonseaboard Republicans.

I'll sing you a song, and it's not very long
It's about a young man who never did wrong
Suddenly he died one day
The reason why no one could say
　　. . . Only one clue as to why he died
　　—A bayonet sticking in his side.

Would you like to see the world
Billy boy, Billy boy?
Would you like to see the world
Charming Billy?
　No it wouldn't be much thrill
　　To die for Dupont in Brazil.
　　　He's a young boy and cannot leave his mother.

Two songs by the left-wing, antiwar Almanac Singers, 1940–41.

They attracted enough liberals and progressives to represent a broad political spectrum. It was a formidable coalition of people who believed passionately in their cause.

Some of their arguments were crude and ill informed. Lindbergh, one of the stalwarts of America First, reflected the anti-Semitism that persisted in America in the 1930s and that contributed to a callous policy toward Jewish refugees seeking escape from Hitler. "The three most important groups which have been pressing this country toward war," he said, "are the British, the Jewish, and the Roosevelt administration." His wife, the author Anne Morrow Lindbergh, conceded that fascism was often "evil and horrible," but added with defeatism that it was the "wave of the future. . . . there is no fighting the wave of the future any more than as a child you could fight against the gigantic roller that loomed up ahead of you."

More thoughtful anti-interventionists worried that the European war was concentrating power in the presidency and creating a potential threat to civil liberty. If America decided to enter the war, Vandenberg charged angrily, "we would get such a regimentation of our own lives and livelihoods . . . that the Bill of Rights would need a gas mask, and individual liberty of action would soon become a mocking memory." Professor Edward S. Corwin, a distinguished specialist in constitutional law, observed that the destroyer deal, an executive agreement negotiated without congressional consent, represented "unrestrained presidential power in the conduct of our foreign relations." Charles Beard observed that the war was giving the President extraordinary powers. "With a political machine, a judicial machine, an industrial machine, and a military machine combined under his control, a President of dictatorial propensities could find ready instruments at hand for extending and entrenching his authority." Though these arguments exaggerated Roosevelt's power—and distorted his intent—they were prophetic in warning against the long-range constitutional effects of modern war.

Central to the isolationist case was the argument that the European war, like World War I, was none of America's business. As Joseph Kennedy put it, "England is not fighting our battle. This is not our war." (Kennedy, Roosevelt complained privately, "has been an appeaser and always will be an appeaser. . . . He's just a pain in the neck to me.") American communists also called for noninvolvement—that was then the party line as advanced by Stalin after the Soviet-German nonaggression pact of 1939. The antiwar wing of the Socialist party reached a similar conclusion from a more principled and pacifistic perspective. "The cause for which Hitler has thrown the German masses into war," it concluded in April 1940, "is damnably unholy. But the war of England and France is not thereby rendered holy. . . . The Allied governments have no idealism in the conflict, no war aims worthy of the sacrifice of overthrowing fascism except to replace it by a more desperate and brutal government, if need be. . . ."

Few of the isolationists went so far as did these Socialists. They recognized that Hitler was a barbarian, that only the Allies could claim to be defending democracy. But even after the fall of France they persisted in arguing that Britain could survive and if not, that Hitler posed no direct threat to a well-armed United States. Even with Hitler controlling all of Europe—which they thought impossible in the long

Wake up! Wake Up, Uncle!

run—America had the resources to stand alone as a beacon of freedom and self-sufficiency. Because the enemy powers lacked planes that could attack the Western Hemisphere and return, the isolationist concept of "fortress America" was particularly difficult to contest.

None of these arguments convinced Roosevelt. But he did not dare to confront such an articulate minority—at least until the election was safely behind him. Accordingly, he gave no hint in 1940 that he might request further alterations in the neutrality law. And he uttered his misleading promise that Americans would not "be sent into any foreign wars." With Willkie, an internationalist, proclaiming, "If you elect me I will never send an American boy to fight in a European war," the campaign degenerated into a contest between two charismatic leaders who lacked the courage to admit the probability of war.

After winning the election, Roosevelt moved more directly into the British camp. In December he called for neutrality revision to permit the lending and leasing of American equipment to Britain and her allies. The proposal called in effect for the end of the "cash" aspect of cash and carry. In January he authorized secret staff talks between British and American army officers. In April he negotiated an executive agreement with Denmark permitting the United States to take over bases in Greenland. In July America went still farther into the North Atlantic by occupying Iceland. In the fall Roosevelt belatedly revealed that American destroyers were escorting British convoys across the Atlantic.

These moves infuriated the noninterventionists. Unsuccessfully opposing lend-

There was considerable opposition to a third term for FDR.

lease, Senator Burton Wheeler called it a Triple A foreign policy that would plow under every fourth American boy. Bitterly, isolationists warned, "when your boy is dying on some battlefield in Europe, and he's crying out, 'Mother, Mother,' don't blame Franklin D. Roosevelt because he sent your boy to war. Blame YOUR-

Election, 1940

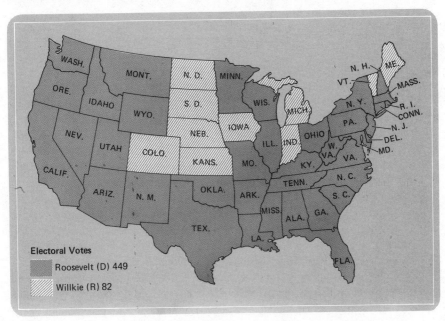

Electoral Votes

Roosevelt (D) 449

Willkie (R) 82

SELF, because YOU sent Franklin D. Roosevelt back to the White House.'' Such rhetoric aside, the isolationists were correct about the President's lack of candor.

As Roosevelt had hoped, lend-lease proved to be of vital assistance not only to Britain but (after Hitler invaded Russia in June 1941) to the Soviet Union; by 1945 it totaled some $50 billion, or four times the amount loaned the Allies between 1917 and 1919. But the isolationists were equally correct in predicting the use of American naval vessels as escorts, which began in late summer. However, Roosevelt at first concealed this fact from the public. He also resorted to deliberate falsehood when the American destroyer *Greer,* which had been tracking German submarines for the British, was harassed early in September. The *Greer,* the President announced angrily, had been carrying passengers and mail to Iceland when it was attacked without provocation. Henceforth, he added, American naval vessels were authorized to shoot at hostile vessels on sight.

Further incidents on the Atlantic followed quickly. Eleven Americans on the destroyer *Kearney* were killed after a submarine attack October 11, and 115 lost their lives on the destroyer *Reuben James* October 31. These assaults led FDR to ask for permission to arm merchant ships, to send them across the Atlantic, and to let them enter European ports in the previously prohibited war zones. When Congress reluctantly agreed, it dismantled the ''carry'' part of cash and carry and tore down the last important prop in the neutrality legislation it had laboriously erected in the 1930s. Full-scale war with Germany was now but a matter of time.

Roosevelt and Hitler: an evaluation

The case against Roosevelt's European policy was never made better than by the isolationists themselves at the time. The President, they insisted, decided sometime in 1940 (perhaps earlier) that Hitler must be defeated, even if it later meant American participation in the war. To that end, he deceived the people. Involvement in the war, critics added, was not necessary to advance United States interests. By March 1941 Britain, without lend-lease assistance, had succeeded in deterring Hitler from invasion, and after June, when Germany invaded the Soviet Union, America could have watched the two dictatorial countries tear each other apart. Even if Hitler defeated the Soviet Union and then overran Britain, he would be too absorbed in managing his far-flung empire to threaten the Western Hemisphere. The administration, isolationists concluded, need not have adopted lend-lease. Or, having done so, it should have been restrained enough to avoid incidents on the Atlantic and patient enough to await European developments.

Some of these arguments were convincing. Though Roosevelt vacillated until mid-1940, it is clear that he thereafter seriously entertained the possibility of entering the war. In the election campaign, in his argument for lend-lease, and in his handling of the convoy question, he did not tell the whole truth. The isolationists may also have been correct in maintaining that Russia and Britain could hold out (though lend-lease was already of some help in 1941), that Germany was overextended, and that Hitler—at least in 1941—had no quarrel to pick with the United States. As late as November, America could have prevented an escalation of hostilities on the Atlantic if it had refrained from arming its ships and sending them into the war zones.

Later critics were persuasive in rejecting the argument that Roosevelt's ends justified his means. Granted that the isolationists had become an increasingly unbending obstacle. Still, he relied much more heavily on deception than on democratic methods of persuasion. Placing the end before the means set precedents for presidential aggrandizement and dishonesty, which later occupants of the White House were to emulate for ignobler ends.

Nevertheless, the President's conduct of European affairs after 1939 has to be understood in the context of the times. Unlike some of his opponents, Roosevelt was correct in suspecting that Hitler's ambitions truly knew no bounds. If Hitler had gained control of all of Europe, he would have been free to exterminate even more of European Jewry and to develop jet planes, rockets, and atomic bombs (on which his scientists were working) to threaten the Western Hemisphere. With Japan and Italy, with whom he had signed the Tripartite Pact in September 1940, he would have controlled most of the industrial world. It so happened, of course, that Britain and Russia still stood in his way in late 1941. But as Germany slashed toward Moscow that summer, the need for all-out aid to Britain and Russia seemed overwhelming. As any head of state must, Roosevelt acted on the basis of his perception of the world at the time.

Roosevelt was also less bellicose than his critics like to think. Until 1939 he appeared resigned to, if not in fact content with, a policy of appeasement. Thereafter he worked to aid the Allies, but until mid-1941 he still hoped to keep America from the fighting. Even on December 7, with blood coloring the waters of the Atlantic, he desisted from asking for war against Germany. That came on December 11, when Hitler acted first. That Hitler did not have to declare war on the United States (the Tripartite Pact required him to aid his allies only if they were attacked) was final testimony to his ambitions and to his weakening grasp on reality. So long as such a madman existed, no great power could feel safe for long.

Toward war with Japan

One of Hitler's excuses for aggression was the need for *Lebensraum*—space to expand. The military leaders who dominated Japan during the 1930s made the same claim. Japan, they insisted, needed guaranteed access to raw materials and foodstuffs to feed a rapidly growing, highly industrialized population. Only through the

Greater East Asia Co-Prosperity Sphere, an empire embracing much of China, Southeast Asia, and the western Pacific, could Japan feel secure in the future.

In contending with this bellicosity, Roosevelt was much freer to act tough than he was in Europe. One reason for this freedom was the mystique of the Open Door policy, which presumably made the United States the protector of China—and of American economic interests in Asia. Many Americans embraced the vision of Pearl Buck's best-selling *The Good Earth* (1937), a sugary glorification of the Chinese peasant. Roosevelt (whose maternal grandfather had made a fortune in the

Japanese aggression in Asia and the Pacific, 1931–42

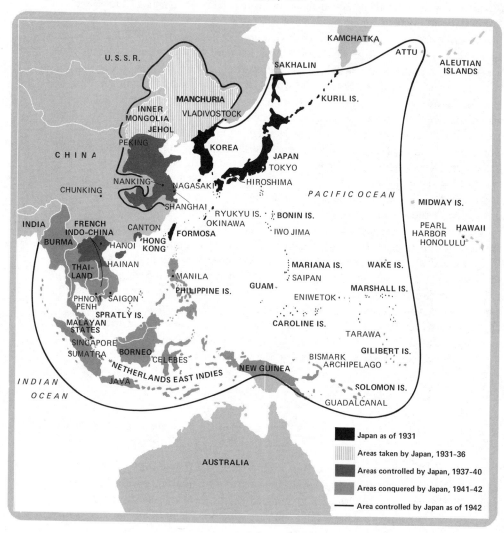

China trade) also sentimentalized the Chinese as a potentially great but exploited people who needed Western beneficence to achieve their destiny. It followed that the United States must protect this helpless giant from the predations of foreign powers like Japan.

American images of Japan reinforced these feelings. Compared to the Chinese, they seemed competitive, expansive, militaristic—the "yellow peril" that racist writers had described for decades. Exploiters of labor, they threatened to engulf the West with "cheap Jap goods." For all their energy, they were little people who built top-heavy ships and whose nearsighted pilots were no match for a determined enemy. As Freda Utley implied in her *Japan: Feet of Clay* (1937), Japan would never dare to fight, much less attack, a Western nation like the United States.

What little sympathy existed for Japan evaporated in the wake of events after 1937. Japanese forces, uncontrolled by civilian leadership, bombed Chinese cities and pillaged the countryside. In Nanking they slaughtered 100,000 Chinese. When France and Holland fell to Germany in 1940, Japan moved quickly to dominate French Indochina and the oil-rich Dutch East Indies. By the end of the year the blueprint for the co-prosperity sphere was clear: Japan was to conquer China, insist on control of valuable resources in Indochina and the Indies, and demand that the West mind its own business.

Roosevelt determined to resist these goals. In July 1939 the United States served notice that in six months it would feel free to impose economic sanctions, and in July 1940, after the Japanese demands on Southeast Asia, America clamped an embargo on shipments of top grades of gasoline and scrap iron to Japan. The embargo left Japan free to buy iron ore and lower grades of oil, which could be refined for military use. But the message to Japan was clear: refrain from expansion or face further reprisals. When Japan nonetheless moved its armies into Indochina on September 24, America responded immediately with an embargo on scrap iron and scrap steel.

America's policy of economic warfare had much to commend it. Restrained, it awaited overt Japanese acts before being applied. Incremental, it gave Japan time to reconsider its course. Roosevelt hoped it might assist Japan's more moderate leaders and deflect the military from its course of conquest. And what else was he to do? With the threat of Hitler to worry about, he could hardly push for war in Asia, nor could he happily provide Japan with the means to overwhelm China and the Indies.

The trouble with economic war was that the Japanese were determined to achieve their co-prosperity sphere. Moderates there were much too weak, and indeed intimidated by assassinations, to stand in the way of the armed forces, who argued that American trade reprisals made command over the resources of Southeast Asia that much more essential. FDR's reliance on economic warfare—as often in world history—proved more provocative than persuasive.

The war of wills then proceeded. Japan's answer to the tightened embargo was to announce the Tripartite Pact with Germany and Italy two days later. In April 1941 it protected its northern flank by negotiating a five-year nonaggression pact with Russia. In July it demanded air bases in southern Indochina, within range of the East Indies. Hull responded to these demands by joining with the Dutch and English to freeze Japanese assets and to impose a total embargo. As American Ambassador to Japan Joseph Grew observed, "the vicious circle of reprisals and counterreprisals is on. . . . Unless radical surprises occur in the world, it is difficult to see how the momentum of the down-grade movement can be arrested, or how far it will go. The obvious conclusion is eventual war."

In the months of peace that remained several issues divided the two powers. One was Japan's relationship with Germany. America demanded that Japan reveal its obligations under the Tripartite Pact, which Tokyo refused to do. Another issue was China. Hull clung to the Open Door: Japan must withdraw. The Japanese countered by insisting on retaining troops and economic rights in China. They demanded also that America stop aiding Chiang Kai-shek and that it recognize Manchukuo, the puppet government in Manchuria. A third bone of contention was the status of southern Indochina, which Roosevelt insisted the Japanese evacuate. Japan said no and went on to demand that America end its embargo on oil. Indochina was already an important pawn in the chess game of international politics.

At times it appeared that compromise might break the deadlock. In August 1941 Prime Minister Fumimoro Konoye, who hoped for peace, proposed a conference with Roosevelt. However, Hull rejected the idea by pointing out that the Japanese promised no concessions and that militarists were insisting on accompanying Konoye to the conference. Two months later Konoye fell and was replaced by War Minister Hideki Tojo, who made a final proposal in November. If America agreed to stop helping Chiang, if it assisted Japan to secure access to raw materials in the East Indies, and if it restored economic relations to their status before the freeze in July, Japan was to promise to pull its troops out of southern Indochina. When the war with China was over, Japan was to withdraw from Indochina entirely. After rejecting suggestions that America make concessions, Hull drafted a so-called modus vivendi of November 25. It called on Japan to renounce further expansion in any direction, to reduce her forces in northern Indochina, and to get out of southern Indochina immediately. In return America was to admit small quantities of Japanese imports and send some cotton and oil (for civilian use only) to Japan. But Hull recognized that America was being asked to make economic concessions right away, *after* which Japan was to respond. Given past Japanese behavior, he had little trust in such assurances. He knew that a Japanese task force was even then steaming toward the Indies. And he was under strong pressure from China and Great Britain to make no concessions whatever. The modus vivendi was never delivered.

In failing to respond Hull knew that war must follow. "I have washed my hands of it," he told Secretary of War Stimson. "It is now in the hands of you and [Secretary of the Navy] Knox—the Army and the Navy." Four days later, on December 1, Japan secretly reaffirmed its decision for carrier-launched attacks on December 7. Its task forces, already under way, ploughed toward Hawaii and the Indies. Roosevelt toyed with the idea of appealing to Emperor Hirohito, but did nothing about it until December 6. That night American experts, who had broken

The USS *Arizona, Tennessee,* and *West Virginia* after the attack on Pearl Harbor, 1941.

many top Japanese codes, began to decipher a truculent fourteen-part message sent from Tokyo to the Japanese ambassador in Washington. Informed of the first thirteen parts that night, Roosevelt remarked simply, "This means war."

The Japanese attack on Hawaii came at dawn the next day, Pearl Harbor time. Fortunately for the United States, American carriers were out at sea. But Japan's torpedo bombers were otherwise devastating. The raid destroyed or severely damaged 8 battleships, 3 light cruisers, and 188 planes, and inflicted 3,435 American casualties. It was the worst loss in American history.

When the Japanese attacked Pearl Harbor, it was about 2:00 P.M. on Sunday in Washington. Cordell Hull, awaiting two Japanese emissaries in his office, already had heard from Roosevelt the news about Hawaii. The Japanese, including the ambassador, then arrived and handed Hull an uninformative note. Kept in the dark by the military in Tokyo, they had negotiated in good faith with Hull for months; they did not even know of the attack. Hull kept them standing while pretending to read their message. Then he burst forth. "In all my fifty years of public service," he said, "I have never seen a document that was more crowded with infamous falsehoods and distortions—on a scale so huge that I never imagined until today that any Government on this planet was capable of uttering them." The Japanese struggled for words, but Hull cut them off with a nod towards the door.

The next day Roosevelt called for a declaration of war. With but one dissenting vote (that of Jeannette Rankin, a Montana pacifist who had also voted against World War I), the House agreed. The Senate vote was unanimous. When Germany then joined Japan, America was involved in World War II.

REVISIONISTS AND PEARL HARBOR

The Japanese success at Pearl Harbor naturally prompted outraged calls for an investigation of "blundering" American officialdom. In later years it led revisionist historians to lambaste the whole course of Roosevelt's diplomacy.

Some of these revisionists were bitter in the extreme. The historian Harry Elmer Barnes charged that "Roosevelt's political ambitions and his mendacious foreign policy" led "some 3,000 American boys [to be] quite needlessly butchered at Pearl Harbor." Charles Tansill, in his appropriately entitled book *Back Door to War,* concluded that Roosevelt, having failed to draw Germany into war, deliberately provoked the Japanese. "In 1941," he wrote, "Roosevelt's orchestra of death was anxiously waiting for the signal to begin the new symphony. He had hoped for a German motif but Hitler had refused to open with a few martial notes. Perhaps some Japanese statesman would prove more accommodating? At any rate . . . he turned his eyes toward the Orient and sought new inspiration from the inscrutable East."

Though Tansill went so far as to imply that Roosevelt invited the attack, most revisionists contented themselves with uncovering American blunders. Some of these errors were military. Why had American naval leaders placed the battleships so invitingly close together in the harbor? Why were planes bunched together on the airstrips? How had a virtual Japanese armada steamed within fighter plane range of Hawaii? Why didn't army chief General George Marshall send his final warning—of the fourteen-part note—by wireless instead of by Western Union? (The message took more than ten hours to reach American commanders in Hawaii and was delivered by a messenger on a bicycle after the attack had caught the United States by surprise.)

Many revisionists focused on the government's role in the Pearl Harbor debacle. Why had Roosevelt, despite contrary advice from some naval experts, sent the Pacific fleet from the West Coast to the more exposed base in Hawaii? Since America had broken some top Japanese codes, why were the military commanders at Pearl not informed that a rupture in relations was imminent? As early as January

1941 Ambassador Grew had told Washington: ''there is a lot of talk around town to the effect that the Japanese, in case of a break with the United States, are planning to go all out in a surprise attack on Pearl Harbor.'' Why wasn't Hawaii alerted to evidence of this nature?

Some of these questions were well founded. Though short of equipment, the military at Pearl could perhaps have done a more thorough job of searching the Pacific west and north of Hawaii. Junior officers and enlisted men could have acted more quickly to report last-minute signals, such as the blips representing Japanese planes found on a radar screen, or the Japanese midget submarine discovered in the harbor itself shortly before the attack. Given the possibility that the Japanese would soon declare war (a Honolulu paper on November 30 had carried the headline, ''Japanese May Strike over Weekend''), the military at Pearl should have been better prepared.

These errors, however, were of the human kind that all nations tend to make. There was no conspiracy to tempt the Japanese into attacking. Roosevelt had moved the fleet to Hawaii to warn Japan, not to expose it. The planes were bunched together so that they could be guarded against sabotage, which is what the Hawaiian commanders had been ordered by Marshall to expect. The final warning had gone by Western Union so that the Japanese could not pick it up on the wireless. Washington failed to keep Hawaii fully informed because it had to refrain from sending messages that might tip off the Japanese that their codes had been cracked.

Cultural and racist presuppositions lay at the root of these human errors. Assuming the Japanese to have ''feet of clay,'' Americans doubted that they could develop torpedo bombers capable of sinking large ships in shallow water, or that their ''nearsighted'' pilots could maneuver so capably. The blips, radar watchers thought, must be American planes circling in for a landing; the submarine must have strayed. Americans dismissed the very idea that Orientals would dare to attack a bastion of Western defense like Pearl Harbor. Instead, the attack—if it came at all—would be on British and Dutch possessions in the East Indies, toward which a Japanese task force was known to be heading. (The attack came there, too.) It was

---

Including the movement of aviation now in progress, Hawaii will be defended by 35 of our most modern flying fortresses, 35 medium range bombers, 13 light bombers, 150 pursuit bombers of which 105 are of our most modern type. In addition Hawaii is capable of reinforcement by heavy bombers from the mainland by air. With this force available a major attack against Oahu is considered impracticable.

In point of sequence, sabotage is first to be expected. . . .

General Marshall explains to FDR, May 1941, that sabotage, not Japanese attack, is the likely problem at Pearl Harbor.

these failings—a lack of imagination, of historical perspective, of cultural understanding—and not gross stupidity or conspiracy that made the attack so successful.

ROOSEVELT'S ASIAN DIPLOMACY

The furor over Pearl Harbor obscured three basic questions about Roosevelt's Asian
diplomacy.

1. Could America have deterred Japan from its aggressive course without getting involved in war?
2. Could the United States have postponed the impasse?
3. Should the United States have engaged in the war against Japan at all?
The answer to the first question is almost certainly no. The Japanese longing for
the Greater East Asia Co-Prosperity Sphere was shared by practically all shades of
influential opinion, including Konoye as well as Tojo. It was repeatedly reaffirmed
in 1940 and 1941. If America hoped to discourage Japanese ambitions, its best
course short of war was probably the one it pursued: economic warfare. As it
happened, this course drove the Japanese to acts of desperation, including the
attack on Pearl Harbor. But the alternative, desisting from economic sanctions,
would obviously have played into Japanese hands. So long as the administration
made it its policy to deter Japan, armed conflict was highly likely.

America could have tried harder to postpone the impasse. In July 1941 Roosevelt could have thought twice before tightening the economic sanctions that had
already proved provocative. If so, Japan might not have felt driven to move so fast.
In August he could have stalled for time by agreeing to meet Konoye or by ex-
changing long notes about the agenda for the conference. Such an exchange might
have sustained the Konoye government for a few more weeks and delayed the more
aggressive plans of Tojo. In November a secretary of state less rigid than Hull
might have delivered the modus vivendi or proposed some other softening of America's economic war. The Japanese might then have paused to consider an answer.

Such possibilities were unlikely, since by August 1941 the Japanese military
had set an almost irreversible timetable. It is therefore unlikely that Roosevelt could
have done much to postpone the war beyond very early 1942. Still, it is sad that
America did not exhaust all hopes for postponement. And to secure time to prepare,
it is unfortunate that Hull did not try harder to coordinate diplomatic responses with
the needs of the army and the navy. If he had, such disasters as Pearl Harbor, and
the defeats at Bataan and Corregidor, might have been less severe.

Should America have fought the war at all? A tempting answer to this question
is no, for America's real interests in Asia, except for Guam and the Philippines
(which were due to be granted independence in 1946), were limited. Despite the
rhetoric about the Open Door, China was of little value economically or militarily
to the United States. Nor were Indochina and the atolls of the western Pacific. Even
the tin and rubber of the East Indies could have been dispensed with or replaced by

synthetics and alloys. To go to war in defense of these areas was to aid British, Dutch, and French imperialism and to tie up American forces needed for the fight ahead against Hitler.

In retrospect it is not clear whether the war did much to advance long-range Western interests in Asia. The turmoil unleashed anti-Western feelings that ultimately destroyed British, Dutch, and French power in the area. It permitted the Soviet Union to move into the vacuum left by Japan. It assisted the growth of communism in China and Indochina. As John MacMurray, the former chief of the Far Eastern division of the State Department, phrased it in 1939, "the defeat of Japan would not mean her elimination from the problems of the Far East. . . . It would merely create a new set of stresses and substitute for Japan the USSR as the successor. . . . Nobody except Russia would gain from our victory in such a war."

But these arguments, like those that criticize American toughness toward Hitler, fail to appreciate the crisis atmosphere of the time. Japan had been molesting China, land of the supposed Open Door, for years, and by 1941 Americans were understandably impatient. Why, they asked, should America keep on sending vital supplies to such an aggressor? Why also should Japan be permitted to take over the rich resources of the Indies? China urgently asked the same questions, as did England, which in 1941 desperately needed American support in Asia. It was politically hazardous for FDR to refrain from retaliatory economic measures—the only ones he could employ—against the accelerating Japanese advance.

This is another way of saying that Roosevelt, far from seeking a "back door to war" in Asia, wanted very much to avoid it. But the Japanese, like Germany in 1917, had determined on a course that narrowed his choice of policy. In so doing, they invited war against a nation they knew they could never conquer. Indeed, their great "success" at Pearl Harbor, which they hoped would neutralize the United

---

I recall talking to the President many times in the past year and it always disturbed him because he really thought that the tactics of the Japanese would be to avoid a conflict with us; that they would not attack either the Philippines or Hawaii but would move on Thailand, French Indo-china, make further inroads on China itself and possibly attack the Malay Straits. He also thought they would attack Russia at an opportune moment. This would have left the President with the very difficult problem of protecting our interests.

He always realized that Japan would jump on us at an opportune moment and they would merely use the 'one by one' technique of Germany. Hence his great relief at the method used. In spite of the disaster of Pearl Harbor and the blitz-warfare with the Japanese during the first few weeks, it completely solidified the American people and made the war upon Japan inevitable.

Harry Hopkins, six weeks after Pearl Harbor, reveals that FDR was "relieved" by the attack.

States long enough to solidify their conquests in Southeast Asia, was their greatest blunder of all, for it united America as nothing else could have. Senator Wheeler, an avid isolationist, commented, "The only thing to do now is to lick hell out of them." The *Chicago Tribune* changed the slogan on its masthead from "Save our Republic" to "Our Country Right or Wrong." Others, "remembering Pearl Harbor," later thought nothing of demanding unconditional surrender, of firebombing Japanese cities, and of obliterating Hiroshima and Nagasaki.

The intractability of Japan had the still more fundamental effect of nearly demolishing pacifism and anti-interventionism in America. As Vandenberg put it, "that day [December 7] ended isolationism for any realist." Vandenberg meant that the dawn of air power ended America's historic safety from foreign attack. Like his contemporaries he also meant that America must never again be caught unprepared. There must be no more appeasement, no more "Munichs." The United States must stay armed and ready to meet potential threats all over the globe. Like a sleepy giant, America staggered to its feet in 1941, battered its enemies for four years, and kept on swinging.

Suggestions for reading

The major books covering foreign policy in the Hoover era are Robert Ferrell, *American Diplomacy in the Great Depression: Hoover-Stimson Foreign Policy, 1929–1933* (1957); Elting Morison, *Turmoil and Tradition: A Study of the Life and Times of Henry L. Stimson** (1960); and Richard Current, *Secretary Stimson: A Study in Statecraft* (1954). For the 1930s consult John E. Wiltz, *From Isolation to War, 1931–1941** (1968), an excellent brief interpretation; and Julius Pratt, *Cordell Hull,* 2 vols. (1964). Bryce Wood, *Making of the Good Neighbor Policy** (1954) expertly covers its subject. Lloyd Gardner, *Economic Aspects of New Deal Diplomacy* (1964) emphasizes economic considerations.

Four excellent books deal with isolationism and its manifestations in the 1930s. They are: John E. Wiltz, *In Search of Peace: The Senate Munitions Inquiry, 1934–1936** (1963); Robert Divine, *The Illusion of Neutrality** (1962), which focuses on congressional battles; Manfred Jonas, *Isolationism in America, 1935–1941** (1969), a study of ideas; and Wayne S. Cole, *America First* (1953). Coverage of America's response to the Spanish civil war is provided in Allen Guttmann, *The Wound in the Heart: America and the Spanish Civil War* (1962); and Richard P. Traina, *American Diplomacy and the Spanish Civil War* (1968). Beatrice Farnsworth, *William C. Bullitt and the Soviet Union* (1967), and Edward E. Bennett, *Recognition of Russia** (1970), deal with Soviet-American relations in the 1930s.

For American involvement in World War II, consult first Robert Dallek, *Franklin D. Roosevelt and American Foreign Policy* (1979); and the detailed volumes by William Langer and S. Everett Gleason, *Challenge to Isolation, 1937–1940** (1952), and *The Undeclared War, 1940–1941** (1953). See also Theodore A. Wilson, *The First Summit: Roosevelt and Churchill at Placentia Bay, 1941* (1969); and Arnold Offner, *America's Appeasement of Germany* (1968). An excellent brief interpretation is Robert A. Divine, *Franklin D. Roosevelt and World War II** (1969). Books that criticize the way in which Roosevelt maneuvered the country into war include Charles A. Beard's older revisionist accounts, *American For-*

eign Policy in the Making, 1932–1940 (1946) and *President Roosevelt and the Coming of War, 1941* (1948); and a provocative brief interpretation by Bruce Russett, *No Clear and Present Danger** (1972). See also Alan Bullock, *Hitler** (1952); and Alton Frye, *Nazi Germany and the Western Hemisphere, 1933–1941* (1967).

Diplomacy involving Asia is covered in Dorothy Borg, *The United States and Far Eastern Crises of 1933–1938* (1964); Herbert Feis, *Road to Pearl Harbor** (1950); Waldo H. Heinrichs, *American Ambassador: Joseph C. Grew and the Development of the United States Diplomatic Tradition* (1966); Charles E. Neu, *The Troubled Encounter: The U.S. and Japan** (1975); Robert Butow, *Tojo and the Coming of the War* (1961); and Paul Schroeder, *The Axis Alliance and Japanese-American Relations* (1958). For Pearl Harbor see Robert Wohlstetter, *Pearl Harbor** (1962), a brilliant study of intelligence problems; and Walter Lord, *Day of Infamy** (1957), a popular account.

10

World War II:
the great divide

Around 1939, the social historian John Brooks concluded, America began a "Great Leap" toward the future. The critic Irving Kristol added that the 1930s were governmentally the "last amateur decade." Both writers properly stressed the incalculable impact of World War II on American life. In every area—military and diplomatic affairs, politics, social and economic relations—the war greatly accelerated the processes of economic change, political centralization, and international involvement that were the grand themes of American twentieth-century life.

The military effort

America's primary task after the attack on Pearl Harbor was of course to settle on the quickest, most effective way of defeating the enemy. This problem, in turn, ultimately raised four major questions, all of which had profound long-range implications.

Which adversary, Germany or Japan, was to be dealt with first? Should the enemy be totally defeated or, as in 1918, be permitted to reach an armistice? What emphasis should Britain and the United States place on strategic bombing, thought by some to be a way of avoiding the bloodbath of World War I? Where, and when, should Allied ground forces actually attack Germany and Japan?

The answer to the first question aroused little controversy at the time. Roosevelt always considered Germany the number one enemy, and in March 1941 British and

Whether nations live in prosperity or starve to death interests me only so far as we need them for slaves for our Kultur; otherwise it is of no interest to me. Whether 10,000 Russian females fall down from exhaustion while digging an anti-tank ditch interests me only in so far as the anti-tank ditch for Germany is finished. We shall never be rough and heartless when it is not necessary, that is clear. We Germans, who are the only people in the world who have a decent attitude toward animals, will also assume a decent attitude toward these human animals. But it is a crime against our blood to worry about them and giving them ideals, thus causing our sons and grandsons to have a more difficult time with them. When someone comes to me and says: "I cannot dig the anti-tank ditch with women and children, it is inhuman, for it will kill them," then I have to say "You are the murderer of your own blood, because if the anti-tank ditch is not dug German soldiers will die, and they are the sons of German mothers. They are our own blood."

Heinrich Himmler, head of the Nazi SS, explains the nature of modern war.

American military leaders agreed. After the attack on Pearl Harbor, Prime Minister Winston Churchill came to the United States for the first of many summit conferences, and the agreement became official policy.

At times during the war Roosevelt appeared to depart from this position. In mid-1942, American naval forces scored unexpectedly quick victories at the battles of Midway and Coral Sea, and Admiral Chester Nimitz, commander in the central Pacific, was authorized to mount offensives against Japanese-held islands. By the spring of 1943 Nimitz's forces had captured the Solomon Islands; and by October 1944, after desperate island battles, American soldiers were invading the Philippines. This military progress in the Pacific caused a few critics to argue later that America should have concentrated its efforts against Japan, thereby leaving Hitler and Stalin to destroy each other in the West.

Roosevelt refused to do that. He recognized that any American invasion of Japan's home islands would encounter fanatical resistance. He also had to respond to the incessant pleas of Josef Stalin, his wartime ally, for aid against Germany. And like most of his contemporaries, the President was anxious to destroy the scourge of Hitler first and forever. For all these reasons he paid little attention to the ''Asia-firsters'' (whose counsel might have left Stalin free to overrun all of Europe).

The second question—should the enemy be allowed to sue for peace?—was answered formally at the Casablanca conference in January 1943, at which Roosevelt proclaimed the policy of unconditional surrender. Later, America deviated slightly from it: Italy was permitted to lay down its arms in 1943, and Japan was ultimately allowed to retain its emperor. But the total defeat of the enemy remained at the heart of Roosevelt's thinking. ''I do not want them to starve to death,'' he said of the Germans, ''but, as an example, if they need food to keep body and soul together, they should be fed three times a day with soup from army soup kitchens.'' In late 1944 he even initialed the unrealistically harsh Morgenthau Plan aimed at ''converting Germany into a country primarily agricultural and pastoral in character.'' Though he later dropped the plan, he adhered consistently to the central goal, that of beating the enemies so thoroughly that they could never again threaten the peace.

To many postwar critics the policy of unconditional surrender seemed a tragic mistake. Supposedly, it steeled the resolve of the enemies, discouraged leaders of the resistance in Germany and Japan, and left power vacuums in central Europe and Manchuria—vacuums filled by the Soviets. Roosevelt, it appeared, forgot the fundamental maxim that wars are fought for political as well as military objectives.

Some of these criticisms were convincing. American insistence on Japan's unconditional surrender proved the major stumbling block to peace in July 1945, before the dropping of the atomic bombs on Hiroshima and Nagasaki. Otherwise, however, the critics were unfair. No policy, no matter how generous, could have swayed the leaders of Germany and Japan from their destructive course. The threat of unconditional surrender did not prevent dissidents in Germany from attempting to overthrow Hitler—an officers' plot almost succeeded in 1944. And Russia charged into central Europe because its armies were powerful, not because of the policy of unconditional surrender. If Roosevelt had shown the slightest tendency to negotiate a truce with Hitler—which he did not—Stalin would probably have kept on fighting—and have ended up with more territory than he did.

The critics of unconditional surrender also forgot the ruthless nature of modern war. In 1917 it was possible for ''Yanks'' to believe that they were fighting a war to save democracy; there were ideals to be achieved. In World War II, American soldiers were ''GIs''—''government issued'' machines sent abroad by a much more organized society that remembered Pearl Harbor and loathed Hitler. Like Willie and Joe, cartoonist Bill Mauldin's dirty, unshaven infantrymen, they fought because they had to, and they had few aims save destroying the enemy quickly and coming home. General Lesley J. McNair, director of the training program for all American ground forces, put it this way to a radio audience in 1942: ''We must lust for battle; our object in life must be to kill; we must scheme and plan night and day to kill.'' What McNair meant, and what every American understood, was that Germany and Japan must be totally defeated. No Allied leader in World War II could have pursued a policy that promised otherwise.

The quest for total victory helps explain Roosevelt's support of scientific research into the development of atomic weaponry. This effort began in October 1939, when Leo Szilard, Enrico Fermi, and other emigré scientists, worried about Nazi progress in the field of atomic physics, persuaded Albert Einstein to write a letter to Roosevelt. The letter urged the President to engage the United States in the race to harness atomic energy. Though responsive to the scientists' pleas, the President moved slowly, and it was not until the summer of 1941 that the administration established a ''uranium section'' in the National Defense Research Committee.

The attack on Pearl Harbor gave renewed urgency to the program, and in 1942 Secretary of War Henry Stimson placed General Leslie Groves, a tough, secretive administrator, in charge of the Manhattan District Project, code name for bomb development. The project's purpose was to beat the Nazis in the race for atomic weaponry. Japan, concentrating on more conventional weapons, was never seriously engaged in the race.

From 1942 on, American and emigré scientists working on the program received more than $2 billion in federal funds. All of it was appropriated for unspecified military purposes by a Congress that heeded Stimson's requests not to probe closely into how it was going to be used. Top military leaders, including generals Douglas MacArthur and Dwight Eisenhower, America's army commanders in the Pacific and Atlantic, were kept almost as much in the dark. Meanwhile, some 540,000 people worked on the project during the war. This incredibly vast, secret operation enabled the United States to pass Germany, which diverted much of its expertise to jet planes and rocketry. The Manhattan project testified amply to America's desire to win the war by whatever means necessary, and to the willingness of the nation's elected representatives to turn over authority, no questions asked, to the executive branch.

The passion for total victory also helped to sustain the argument for strategic bombing—mass raids against enemy cities, factories, storage facilities, military bases, and transportation complexes. Theoretically, these raids could do such a thorough job of weakening enemy strength (and morale) that ground forces could complete the job with minimal loss of American life. "Strategic air power," General Henry ("Hap") Arnold claimed, "is a war-winning weapon in its own right, and is capable of striking decisive blows far behind the battle line, thereby destroying the enemy's capacity to wage war."

Though Arnold did not get all the planes he wanted until late in the war, he could hardly complain. As early as 1940 Roosevelt astounded Congress by asking for production of 50,000 planes per year. By 1942, B-17's and B-24's were already being flown over to Great Britain; by 1943 they were taking off on steady raids against the enemy; and by late 1944 they were smashing the Japanese home cities. Before the end of the war the strategic bombing attacks had leveled many industrial cities in both enemy nations.

Whether strategic bombing was as effective as Arnold claimed was another matter. Undoubtedly, it forced the enemy nations to divert manpower and equipment to reconstruction. In crowded, urban Japan it was so effective that neither the atomic bombs nor an invasion may have been necessary. But until late 1944 it was also terrifically costly to the United States. Only 28 of 120 bombers that took off for a raid on Berlin in July 1943 made it to the target. Between February 20 and 26, 1944, America lost 226 bombers, 28 fighter planes, and 2,600 crewmen. Only in the last year of the war, when American fighter planes finally gained air supremacy, did these raids become reasonably safe for planes and crew.

Strategic bombing enthusiasts were also far too optimistic about the possibility of "pinpoint" bombing. The British bombed mostly at night and could not be too precise about their targets. Americans were scarcely more accurate. Often it was too overcast to see much; often German fighters or antiaircraft artillery forced American pilots to hurry in and off. Either way, the bombs all too frequently blasted civilian areas. And the British and Americans sometimes resorted to indiscriminate firebombing. One raid against Tokyo killed an estimated 84,000 people and left a million homeless. The city, said one observer, was a "midden of smoking flesh." Another attack by the British and Americans, against nonindustrial Dresden in 1945, killed more than 100,000 people.

By the time the U.S. entered the war, the nation was mass producing planes for the air force.

Even when the bombs hit their targets, they caused much less disruption than many strategists supposed. Against Japan in 1945 they were devastating, for by then many key targets were defenseless. However, Germany always maintained surplus factory space and labor, and the bombers caused more inconvenience than crisis. Die-hard enthusiasts of bombing argued later that America's mistake was only in not staging enough raids against German oil reserves, necessary for most forms of production. Perhaps so. But because that was not done, it cannot be proved that bombing the oil reserves would have made a significant difference. What is known is that Germany's productive capacity increased until the last weeks of the war.

Dresden, Germany, after Allied bombing.

These limitations of bombing should have suggested that modern war requires great flexibility in response, that not only bombers but also fighters, tanks, and—as ever—infantry are essential to victory. Strategic bombing nonetheless continued to offer an almost fatal allure after the war. To many people anxious for quick solutions to complex international problems it seemed a ''surgical'' way to dispose of troublesome opponents.

The fourth military question—where and when to attack the enemy—was ultimately avoided in the Asian theater, where a land invasion of Japan's home islands proved unnecessary. Regarding Europe, however, it sparked heated debate.

At first it was assumed that Britain and the United States would attack Germany's western front as soon as possible. Stalin, whose people were suffering horribly, insisted on help right away. He was supported by American army leaders like Marshall and Dwight D. Eisenhower, commander of the war plans division. ''We've got to go to Europe and fight,'' Eisenhower said in January 1942, ''and quit wasting resources all over the world—and still worse, wasting time.''

With men like Marshall so optimistic, Roosevelt led Stalin to believe that America would stage a second front before the end of 1942. But he then had to confront Churchill, whose cooperation was essential to the success of a cross-Channel invasion. Churchill vividly remembered the frightful British losses in World War I. He was also persuaded, probably correctly, that the Allies lacked sufficient men and equipment, especially landing ships for vehicles. Accordingly, he insisted on smaller attacks against Germany's periphery in the Mediterranean. Churchill's stand infuriated American leaders. But FDR, needing British cooperation before undertaking a cross-Channel invasion, relented and accepted the British plan for an offensive in North Africa in late 1942.

When the North African campaign proved successful, Marshall and Eisenhower hoped for a cross-Channel invasion in 1943. However, Churchill still posed objections, and at Casablanca in January he persuaded Roosevelt to agree to assaults against Sicily and Italy. Marshall observed angrily that "we lost our shirts . . . we came, we listened, and we were conquered." Moreover, the Italian campaign proved costly: at war's end in 1945 Allied troops were still battling their way up the peninsula. So the months slipped by without the long-anticipated invasion. Not until the Teheran summit conference of November 1943 did the Russians receive a guarantee for an attack early in 1944.

Churchill was probably right in arguing that a second front in 1943, when the Allies lacked full control of the air, would have been costly. But the political ramifications of postponing "D-day" to June 1944 were unfortunate, for Stalin, having been assured of aid in 1942 and again in 1943, grew ever more suspicious of his English-speaking allies. During this time the Soviet Union suffered catastrophic damage and lost millions of its people (perhaps 20 million by the end of the war). Moreover, when the second front finally materialized, his armies were already poised on Germany's eastern borders. At war's end he had little reason to be trustful of the "friends" who were so slow to help in his time of trial.

Roosevelt's handling of these military questions subjected him later to complaints that he was a short-sighted opportunist during the war. If he had thought more often about the postwar world, critics argued, he would have insisted on a second front in 1943 and done all he could to build up ground forces capable of getting into eastern Europe before the Russians. Barring that, he should have agreed to a conditional surrender before the Russians moved into Germany. These arguments ask the impossible. Neither the American public nor Roosevelt's allies would have tolerated such a conditional surrender, and Churchill stood in the way of a harmoniously organized invasion prior to 1944. In acting to safeguard the anti-Axis alliance and to keep the voters behind him in a long and bloody struggle, FDR did what he had to do.

Wartime diplomacy

Complaints about Roosevelt's military leadership were but part of broader attacks on his diplomacy. Left-wing critics later charged him with refusing to stand up to imperialists like Churchill and with cooperating with decadent forces in China and France. Right-wingers countered by accusing him of naiveté concerning the Soviet Union. Whatever he did, it seemed he could not win.

The left-wing critics focused first on Roosevelt's dealings with Vichy France, the pro-Nazi collaborators who controlled much of France following Hitler's victory in 1940. First he recognized the puppet regime. Then, in planning the North African invasion he (and Eisenhower) worked carefully with Admiral Jean Darlan, head of the Vichy fleet. The "deal" secured Darlan's noninterference with the Allied invasion. But it also antagonized General Charles de Gaulle, the extremely sensitive leader of the French resistance forces, and it outraged many American progressives. The United States, they thought, was tainted by association with fascists.

The American Left also disliked his handling of China. During the war Chiang Kai-shek, the Nationalist leader, angered American officials by fighting harder against the communist Chinese than against the Japanese. Corruption and mismanagement within Chiang's regime were undermining what little hold he retained on the peasantry. By 1943, General Joseph ("Vinegar Joe") Stilwell, America's military commander in China, was so disgusted that he referred to Chiang as "Peanut." Roosevelt urged Chiang to mend his ways. However, Chiang ultimately responded by demanding Stilwell's recall. Roosevelt acceded. When he named General Patrick Hurley, a Republican anticommunist with little knowledge of China, as ambassador in 1944, he played further into Chiang's hands.

Other liberals grumbled that FDR failed to appreciate the anticolonial stirrings of the nonwhite world. Why didn't the President make it clear to Churchill, who had been so anxious for American aid in 1941, that the price was surrender of India, Malaya, and other colonial possessions? Roosevelt did not, his biographer James MacGregor Burns concluded, because he was too "soft and pasty" to risk unpleasantness in negotiations, and because he was content to let occasional rhetorical outbursts against colonialism substitute for the effective use of American power.

These critics agreed with spokesmen of the Right (and the center) that Roosevelt possessed many traits ill suited for the business of diplomacy. One of these was his legendary reliance on his own charm. This led him, critics charged, to jolly his way through conferences instead of standing up to Stalin or Churchill. Worst of all, FDR's detractors pointed out, it caused him to rely on summit meetings and on personal emissaries like Hopkins instead of on briefings by experts. "I know you will not mind my being brutally frank," he told Churchill in 1944, "when I tell you that I think I can personally handle Stalin better than either you or your Foreign Office or my State Department. Stalin hates the guts of all your top people. He thinks he likes me better, and I hope he will continue to do so."

These habits appeared to make Roosevelt into a Great Procrastinator who preferred to keep everyone happy by committing himself to nothing. Unlike Wilson, he gave little encouragement before 1945 to supporters of a United Nations organization. He refused to be specific about America's postwar commitments, except to imply that the United States would go home after the war. At the Teheran conference he told Stalin that the American people would chafe at stationing soldiers in Europe after 1947. And in early 1944 he wrote, "I do not want the United States to have the post-war burden of reconstituting France, Italy, and the Balkans. This is not our natural task at a distance of 3,500 miles." Attitudes such as these caused some observers to wonder if the President had any purposeful postwar goals at all.

Critics on the Right insisted that Roosevelt's desire to avoid unpleasantness led him to be "soft on the Soviets." If Roosevelt had not been such a procrastinator, they argued, he could have exacted promises from the Russians in 1942, when they were calling anxiously for American assistance. If he had understood the peculiar ruthlessness of Stalin's regime, he would have seen the futility of dealing with him. If he had not been so anxious to win friends at the conference table, he would have refused to make damaging and unnecessary concessions.

The culmination of this foolish approach, critics grumbled, was at the Yalta Conference of February 1945. There, Roosevelt allegedly betrayed American interests by permitting Russia three seats in the UN General Assembly, by settling for a vague agreement on reparations (which later permitted Russia to paralyze eastern Germany), by doing nothing to assist Polish boundary claims, and by failing to secure a noncommunist Polish government. Without consulting China, Roosevelt also reached a secret accord with Stalin that gave the Soviets Southern Sakhalin, the Kurile Islands, and joint operation of the Chinese-Eastern and Southern Manchurian railways, and which recognized Russia's "preeminent interests" in Manchuria. In return for these concessions Roosevelt secured only the vague Soviet promise to hold free elections in eastern Europe, and the assurance that Russia would enter the war against Japan within three months of Germany's surrender.

Many of these complaints, from both the Left and the Right, were partly justified. Roosevelt placed far too much faith in Chiang Kai-shek, and he overestimated the value of personal diplomacy. His hopes for the democratic governments in eastern Europe were misplaced: by 1948 all of them had fallen under the thumb of the Kremlin. His failure to secure precise guarantees of access routes to western zones in postwar Berlin caused no end of conflict later on. And successful development of atomic energy later made the Asian deal at Yalta unnecessary.

But FDR's options were restricted. As commander-in-chief his first concern, properly enough, was to win the war with as little suffering to America as possible. The deal with Darlan, therefore, seemed necessary; the alternative might have subjected Allied forces to substantial fighting against the French. Playing along with Chiang was less wise. But cutting off aid to Chiang, who threatened to quit the war unless America kept the dollars flowing, was politically hazardous. And in combating colonialism what was the President to do with Churchill, who proudly proclaimed, "I did not become the King's first minister in order to preside over the

Churchill, Roosevelt, and Stalin at Yalta in 1945, where the "Big Three" worked out international distribution of power.

liquidation of the British empire''? If preserving wartime unity was the primary goal, it made little sense for America to issue demands to such an important ally. In assuming that the United States could have forced its will, Roosevelt's detractors presumed an omnipotence that America has never possessed.

Complaints about the President's Russian diplomacy falsely assumed that Soviet designs were both evil and clear at the time. In fact, FDR's advisers included men like Hopkins, Hull, and Eisenhower, who reported that "nothing guides Russian policy so much as a desire for friendship with the United States." The critics also exaggerated America's potential to influence postwar eastern Europe. The Soviets overran the area by force of arms, just as the United States and Great Britain took France and the low countries. Recognizing the American sphere of influence, Stalin expected the United States, which had historically shown little concern for the fate of eastern Europe (witness the Munich accord, or the division of Poland in 1939) to leave him alone in his sphere of interest. This meant letting Russia protect itself against unfriendly governments on its borders. And it meant permitting Stalin to subjugate the East Germans, who had invaded Russian territory twice since 1914. In this sense Roosevelt did well to get any Soviet "assurances" whatever about eastern Europe. Americans at the time applauded his "success" at Yalta.

Roosevelt was right also in recognizing that America could secure free elections in eastern Europe only by force, which he had neither the will nor the power to apply. His attitude was best expressed in an exchange with Admiral William Leahy, his top military aide. Leahy complained that the Polish accord was so vague that Russia could "stretch it all the way from Yalta to Washington without ever technically breaking it." Roosevelt nodded, but replied, "I know it, Bill—I know it. But it's the best I can do for Poland at this time." This was not naiveté, but an accurate appreciation of military reality in Europe. It was therefore unfortunate that Roosevelt, seeking political credit for a "victory" at Yalta, did not explain to Americans the limitations of the accord. Stalin, he implied, had agreed to promote democracy in eastern Europe. When that did not happen, Americans were quick to cry that the Russians had broken a promise.

Roosevelt could even be forgiven his concessions to the Soviet Union in Asia. In February 1945 the Japanese were obviously headed for defeat, with or without Russian intervention. But no one could be sure at the time that the atomic bomb, untested until July 1945, would work. What Roosevelt did know was that Japan was fighting fanatically to hold all its possessions. He was further advised (probably wrongly) that America might suffer as many as a million casualties in an invasion of the home islands. To avoid such a catastrophe, he determined to secure Russian help, which Stalin would have given grudgingly, if at all, without securing concessions for himself.

In these ways Roosevelt's Russian diplomacy revealed not softness but perceived political and military necessity. Despite strains over the second front, his policies managed to sustain Allied cooperation. Roosevelt may also have been correct in assuming that Stalin was more concerned for his nation's security (and for traditional Russian territorial gains) than in fomenting worldwide communist revolution. Stalin gave little support to communist forces under Marshal Tito of Yugoslavia; he recognized Chiang in China (then, as always, Stalin was ambivalent about Mao Tse-tung); and he kept a bargain made with Churchill in the fall of 1944, by which Britain recognized Russia's paramount interests in much of southeastern Europe in return for a Soviet hands-off policy in Greece (which became scarcely more "democratic" than Poland). Stalin also cruelly disappointed the communist parties in Italy and France, which had hoped for Russian postwar aid.

All these Soviet actions suggested to some moderates in America that Stalin's territorial ambitions—at least to 1945—were limited, and that postwar cooperation with the Soviet Union was possible. In making these assumptions Roosevelt took risks, and he exaggerated, for political effect at home, his diplomatic "triumphs" at Yalta. But he also perceived that Soviet-American détente in the postwar world was indispensable for world peace. Compared to Wilson's millenial visions, Roosevelt's view struck anticommunist Americans as amoral. But given the realities of military power in 1945—the Soviets, after all, already occupied eastern Europe—Roosevelt's options were limited.

The expansion of government

FROM WELFARE PROGRAMS TO WARTIME POWERS

In December 1943 Roosevelt explained that he was no longer "Dr. New Deal," but "Dr. Win the War."

His remark confirmed that the exciting days of domestic reform were past. Though Roosevelt continued to work for his programs, he was necessarily preoccupied with military problems. And Congress grew even more obstructive than it had been in his second term, especially after the Republicans made further inroads in 1942. The conservative coalition of Republicans and rural Democrats killed the WPA, the CCC, and the National Resources Planning Board. It defeated bills for federal aid to education, national health insurance, and public power development, and it ignored groups crusading for civil rights. As responsive as ever to well-organized interest groups, it approved legislation granting farmers 110 percent of parity and exempting many agricultural laborers from the draft.

The conservatism of the wartime Congresses was most pronounced in the areas of labor legislation and taxation. In 1943 Congress approved, over Roosevelt's veto, the Smith-Connally Act, which authorized the president to seize strike-bound defense plants and to impose thirty-day "cooling off" periods before labor could go on strike. In the same year it enacted a plan that introduced the principle of withholding taxes, but at the cost of forgiving taxpayers an estimated 75 percent of 1942 taxes. The plan especially benefited high-income people. Then in 1944 Congress passed a tax bill that raised only $2 billion more than before. FDR, who had called for an increase of $10 billion, snapped publicly that it was "not a tax bill, but a tax relief bill providing relief not for the needy but for the greedy." His blunt remark angered even his congressional supporters, who helped to pass the bill over his veto. Long before FDR's death in 1945, relations between Capitol Hill and the White House were cold indeed.

The balance of power within the parties also shifted toward the Right during the war. In 1944 the GOP nominated New York governor Thomas E. Dewey as its presidential candidate. Though Dewey accepted much of the New Deal, he waged an abrasive campaign. Other Republican orators engaged in a demagogic effort to link the Roosevelt administration with communism. The Democrats, meanwhile, refused to renominate the liberal Henry Wallace for the vice-presidency. Instead, Harry Truman, a dependable middle-of-the-roader from Missouri, received the prize. Thanks to the power of the Democratic voting coalition, and especially to the efforts of organized labor (which provided $2 million to party funds), Roosevelt and Truman won handily. But their margin of 3.6 million votes fell well short of the Democratic lead of 5 million votes in 1940 and 11 million in 1936. Republicans understandably looked forward to 1948, when they expected to triumph at last.

Despite these blows against the New Deal, the war years did not witness any triumph for reaction. Many of the defeated programs, such as the WPA or the CCC, truly seemed unnecessary in the midst of a revived wartime economy. More important reforms—TVA, social security, the minimum wage, even the NLRB—emerged intact. Nondefense spending actually increased during the war from $7.2 billion to $17 billion, thus remaining at about 8 percent of the Gross National Product. Having helped to build a partial welfare stat?, Congress was not about to dismantle it.

The growth in domestic expenditures was but one manifestation of a virtual explosion in the size of government during the war. Thanks primarily to defense spending, the federal budget jumped from $9 billion in fiscal 1940 to $98 billion in 1945, or from 9 percent to 46 percent of the GNP. The number of civilian employees of the federal government increased during the same period from 1 to 3.8 million. Federal taxes leaped ahead from $5 billion to $44.5 billion, and millions of Americans felt the bite of the Internal Revenue Service for the first time. With so much money at its command, and with virtual armies of bureaucrats staffing such new agencies as the Office of Price Administration, the War Production Board, the War Labor Board and the Selective Service, the federal government enjoyed more power than the most avid New Dealers ever envisioned in the 1930s.

The impact of this expansive fiscal policy was little short of revolutionary. By increasing federal spending more than tenfold within six years, the government ran up deficits averaging more than $30 billion per year, or ten times the average deficits during the New Deal. Chiefly because of this spending, the economy finally surged back. Unemployment virtually disappeared (thanks in part to the draft), and the GNP (in 1929 prices) shot forward from $121 billion in 1940 to $181 billion in 1945. Few politicians dared to endorse this Keynesian approach as a matter of regular policy, and deficits were modest (except during war) from 1946 through 1963. Still, the power of public spending had been demonstrated beyond doubt. Thereafter all but the most hardened fiscal conservatives admitted that a little pump priming in times of recession was desirable.

The war witnessed an almost equally revolutionary growth in the power of the presidency. Only the White House seemed able to carry on the war and manage the nation's more complex international responsibilities. As Professor Edward Corwin noted ruefully, phrases describing the presidency as the "great engine of democracy" and "the American people's one authentic prophet" began appearing in textbooks. The diplomatic historian Thomas Bailey spoke for many scholars in 1948 by stressing the need for a strong presidency. "Just as the yielding of some of our national sovereignty is the price we must pay for effective international organization," he wrote, "so the yielding of some of our democratic control of foreign affairs is the price we may have to pay for greater physical security." If TR began the twentieth-century American infatuation with the presidency, World War II transformed it into a long-lived affair.

BIG GOVERNMENT: BLESSING OR CURSE?

Most reformers welcomed this explosion in the power of the presidency. Congress, after all, was in the hands of conservatives, and the Supreme Court had until 1937 stood in the way of social legislation. By 1945 belief in an activist central administration was a cardinal tenet of modern American liberalism.

Even during the war, however, some people worried about the concentration of enormous power in the hands of a few. One concern was the Office of War Information, which was formed to apprise the public of the course of the war. The *New York Times* observed that it was "feeding us bad news when it was thought we could stand it and good news when it was thought we needed it." Even Elmer Davis, the experienced newsman who headed the agency, fought regularly with military brass who refused to give him accurate, up-to-date information. Admiral King's idea of war information, Davis complained, "was that there should be just *one* communique. Some morning we would announce that the war was over and that we won it." These charges were accurate in recognizing the government's close-mouthed monopoly on sources of important news.

The administration's handling of civil liberties during the war was equally unsettling. The 12,000-odd conscientious objectors who refused to accept noncombatant military service were placed in so-called Civilian Public Service camps, where the courts refused to extend the protection of the first and fifth amendments. They did not receive pay. The administration imprisoned some 5,500 other conscientious objectors, including Jehovah's Witnesses, who claimed exemptions as ministers.

Roosevelt was especially harsh in handling allegedly profascist dissenters. In 1942 the Justice Department charged twenty-six "native fascists" with conspiring against the government. The accusations were based in part on the arbitrary Smith Act of 1940, which made it an offense even to advocate the overthrow of the government. After much legal wrangling, which revealed no evidence of conspiracy, the government finally had to drop the cases in 1944.

Defenders of the administration rightly pointed out that Roosevelt treated dissenters more even-handedly than Wilson had in World War I. But this improvement did not necessarily signify that America was growing more tolerant or more mature. Rather, it reflected the relative absence of dissent in a war precipitated by the "sneak attack" on Pearl Harbor. As one congressman phrased it a week after the attack, "This war had to come. It is a war of purification in which the forces of Christian peace and freedom and justice and decency and morality are arrayed against the evil pagan forces of strife, injustice, treachery, immorality, and slavery. . . ."

This kind of passion erupted quickly in open racism against Japanese-Americans. A California barber advertised "free shave for Japs," but "not responsible for accidents." A funeral parlor proclaimed, "I'd rather do business with a Jap than with an American." In a 1944 poll that asked Americans to say which enemy, Germany or Japan, the United States could "get along with better after the war" only 8 percent picked Japan.

Popular thinking such as this reinforced flagrantly unconstitutional policies. In 1942 the government began systematically to round up Japanese-Americans and to place them in detention centers. These were really concentration camps guarded by soldiers and situated in remote areas of the West. In all, they contained some 112,000 people for the duration of the war. Most of these (perhaps 70,000) were second-generation Nisei who were American citizens. When a few brought suit, the Supreme Court sanctioned the government's action (during wartime) in 1944. Only later, when passions had subsided, did Americans realize the truth of Justice Frank

---

The Japanese, because they are unassimilable, because the aliens have been denied the right to own real property in California, because of the marked differences in appearance between Japanese and Caucasians, because of the generations of training and philosophy that makes them Japanese and nothing else—all of these contributing factors set the Japanese apart as a race, regardless of how many generations have been born in America. Undoubtedly many of them intend to be loyal, but only each individual can know his own intentions, and when the final test comes, who can say but that "blood will tell"?

Los Angeles Mayor Fletcher Bowron arouses passions against Japanese-Americans, February 1942.

Murphy's dissent labeling the evacuations "one of the most sweeping and complete deprivations of constitutional rights in the history of this nation."

Those who feared the excesses of big government could content themselves with the hope that ominous wartime developments like the Office of War Information and detention centers were temporary phenomena. However, the administration's handling of defense contracting led first to bureaucratic confusion and then to the development of a military-industrial complex. Together these exposed the dangers of the governmental expansion produced by modern war.

Bureaucratic confusion began as early as 1939, when Roosevelt created the War Resources Board to oversee defense needs. It received only limited support from the administration before being replaced after the fall of France by the Advisory Commission of the Council of National Defense. This, in turn, gave way in 1941 to the Office of Production Management. All these agencies had to contend with other sources of power, such as Secretary of the Interior Harold Ickes, who was also oil administrator, and Jesse Jones, the imperious banker who headed the Reconstruction Finance Corporation. Critics demanded that Roosevelt create a more permanent agency and give it real authority.

When the President established the War Production Board in January 1942, it appeared that he recognized the need for centralization. But he still refused to make Donald Nelson, the WPB chief, a "czar" over production. His stand was deliberate. As he told Labor Secretary Frances Perkins, "there is something to be said . . . for having a little conflict between agencies. A little rivalry is stimulating . . . . the fact that there is somebody else in the field who knows what you are doing is a strong incentive to strict honesty." Moreover, the President did not want to turn over such power to a potential rival to himself. So he gave only sporadic support to Nelson's efforts at concentrating authority in the WPB. From the beginning Nelson, like almost all later civilian officials in charge of defense planning, was unable to prevent interagency fighting or to override the military, which Roosevelt permitted to control the crucially important matter of procurement.

Despite these problems, American production leaped ahead with astonishing speed. After procrastinating in 1940 and 1941 to assure themselves of markets,

---

The President is the poorest administrator I have ever worked under in respect to the orderly procedure and routine of his performance. He is not a good chooser of men and he does not know how to use them in coordination.

The inevitable result is that the Washington atmosphere is full of acrimonious disputes over matters of jurisdiction. In my own case a very large per cent of my time and strength, particularly of recent months, has been taken up in trying to smooth out and settle the differences which have thus been created.

Secretary of War Henry Stimson, March 1943, complains of FDR's administrative habits.

American manufacturers converted rapidly to war production. Many assumed direction of plants built almost overnight with public funds. The enormous airplane manufacturing facilities at Willow Run, Michigan, were larger than the combined prewar plants of Boeing, Douglas, and Consolidated Aircraft. More than a mile long, they included 1,600 machine tools and 7,500 jigs and fixtures. The story of rubber production was equally amazing. The government built fifty-one synthetic rubber-making plants, which by 1944 made close to a million tons per year. (The German peak, in 1943, was 109,000 tons.) These fantastic increases in output created a virtual overabundance of weaponry by late 1943. Thereafter many contractors began scrambling for the privilege of reconverting to civilian production.

The production miracle unfortunately led many businessmen to praise themselves for accomplishing so much. Conveniently overlooking the role of government spending, they extolled the virtues of capitalistic free enterprise, and they rejected arguments that more government supervision might have secured better results. This claim had some merit, for even a "czar" might have found it impossible to fine-tune an economy so huge and complex as America's. Businessmen may have been equally correct in asserting (Roosevelt agreed) that a degree of voluntarism was necessary for morale in such a long war. For social reformers, however, the self-assured hostility of many businessmen to government "interference" proved a formidable obstacle to change in the 1940s and 1950s.

Reformers worried also about the lasting connections developed in wartime between big business and the military. For it was the big operators to whom the army, the navy, and the newly created Office for Scientific Research and Development turned for help. These large organizations had the capital, the research potential, and the equipment to produce quickly. They could afford to free middle-management specialists and white-collar workers to handle government red tape. Above all, big institutions could be dealt with quickly. Government officials liked to work with a handful of experienced operators instead of with a host of smaller entrepreneurs.

Top government officials made sure that big business was at home in its developing relationship with Washington. Many of these officials had been recruited by the supposedly "radical" New Deal from corporations, and they agreed that producing for defense ought to bring a handsome profit. "If you are going to . . . go to war, . . . in a capitalist country," Stimson observed, "you have got to let business make money out of the process." Stimson and others offered contractors cost-plus contracts and generously renegotiated deals when businesses complained. The government also provided low-interest federal loans for plant expansion and easy tax writeoffs. Patents for processes developed with government aid generally reverted to the manufacturer. Such massive assistance assured big corporations of commanding positions in areas formerly handled by subcontractors.

There was no easy way for government to reverse the long-range movement toward concentration in business. Still, progressives not surprisingly complained about government's enthusiastic hand on the tiller. The observed that big business and the military, eclipsed by other contenders for federal favor in the 1930s, used the war to surpass other interest groups like big labor and big agriculture. They prophesied also that the military-industrial complex, as it came to be known, could lock the nation on a martial course. Among the baneful results of political centralization, the military-industrial nexus perhaps was for them the most frightening of all.

The war and American society

Stuart Chase, a liberal economist, surveyed American society at the end of the war and concluded that prosperity had worked wonders undreamed of during the New Deal. "The facts," he said, "show a better break for the common man than liberals in 1938 could have expected for a generation."

Almost every economic indicator supported Chase's conclusion. Despite rationing of gasoline, coffee, tin, and other goods, few Americans suffered much at home. National income jumped from $81 billion in 1940 to $182 billion five years later, or from $573 to $1,074 per capita. Improvements in diets and health care during the same period caused life expectancy to increase by three years to sixty-six. (However, poor teeth and eyes, symptoms of malnutrition, still caused more than 50 percent of young men in some regions to fail preinduction physicals.) Thanks in part to the GI Bill, 8 million young people learned a trade or attended college after the war, while bonuses for American veterans totaled more than $2 billion.

The war even slightly improved the distribution of income. This was not because the rich were getting poorer, but because workers were regularly employed and drawing extra pay for overtime. The average wages of workers employed full-time in manufacturing rose from $28 per week in 1940 to $48 in 1944; in construction, wages in those years rose from $26 to $50. These were unprecedented advances. Accordingly, the share of income owned by the richest 5 percent declined from 23.7 to 16.8 percent. As these figures suggest, the United States remained a country with sharp disparities in wealth. Still, World War II did much to accelerate one of the major trends of modern American society: the development of a large middle class. It was the only time in modern American history that income distribution improved.

Important social changes accompanied this return to prosperity. One was even greater movement of an already mobile people. Those who moved included 12 million men in uniform, dependents who pulled up roots to follow them to training bases, and millions more who left their homes to work in war plants. The migrations slightly increased urbanization, which had slowed during the depression years. The number of people living in towns with populations of 25,000 or more increased from 53 million in 1940 to 63 million ten years later, or 42 percent of the total 1950 population of 152 million.

The total classified as "rural farm" decreased during the decade, from 30 to 23 million. A few states, well-favored in the granting of war contracts, virtually exploded in population. California alone gained 2 million people during the four years of war.

This is the last time
This time we will all make certain
That this time is the last time!
    For this time we are out to finish
    The job we started then
    Clear it up for all time this time
    So we won't have to do it again

The words to a wartime song by Irving Berlin suggest the no-nonsense thoroughness with which Americans approached the war.

The status of women also changed considerably during the war. In 1940 only 14 million American women (26 percent of the total work force) were employed; by 1945, 19 million (or 36 percent) were. Moreover, 22 percent of these working women in 1945 were married, as opposed to 15 percent five years earlier. Most of these married workers were mothers. Contemporaries thought these trends were temporary, for the numbers of regularly employed women dipped in 1946. Polls also suggested that Americans still considered it unnatural for women to enter the labor force: a woman's place, the ladies' magazines added, was at home. But increasing numbers of women disagreed, and by 1951 the number of women in the work force was already higher than at any time in World War II.

The jobs that they took presaged a sharp departure from traditional patterns of women's work. Abandoning jobs as domestics, waitresses, and laundresses, they headed for aircraft plants and shipyards. Hundreds of laundries had to close for lack of female help. Some 400,000 women dropped domestic service to labor in the factories. The percentage of black women who did paid housework declined from 69 to 35 percent; for the first time, many found work in industrial occupations, which (despite pay scales lower than those for men) paid about 40 percent more than the traditional jobs for women workers. The public seemed to welcome this great change. A popular cartoon character, Rosie the Riveter, appeared on many magazine covers and newspapers.

These trends in female employment were significant. In the short run, the working women contributed much to the war effort. The wages they brought home fattened the budgets of working-class people, who began to put aside money for wartime (and postwar) purchases of consumer goods, including houses. Consumption of household furniture, equipment, and supplies jumped from $4.9 million in 1940 to $16.6 million in 1950. In the long run, the growth of female employment widened the public sphere of women and challenged older notions relegating women to the home. Henceforth, women ventured into the working world in ever-increasing numbers, thereby providing an economic and ideological underpinning to later movements for women's liberation.

Wartime developments led to yet other changes in the American family. Thousands of young people who had postponed marriage or family in the depression

Women left the home for the factory during World War II. Here women are using welding equipment to cut and shape armor plating. It was this sort of work that gave rise to the popular figure of Rosie the Riveter.

refused to wait in the 1940s. Thousands more, confronted with the draft and overseas service, did the same. The result was a trend toward younger marriages and a baby boom that began in 1940 and continued irregularly throughout the war. Demographers who assumed the increase in birth rates would end with the war were wrong, for the baby boom lasted until the early 1960s. Rising birth rates helped stimulate demand in a host of consumer-goods industries; they prompted great growth in postwar home building and in suburban development; and they all but swamped educational institutions until the 1970s. By 1965, when the early boom babies had reached their late teens or early 20s, the baby boom culminated in the growth of a "youth culture," which baffled and frightened older generations.

To many observers during the war (and since) these developments were unfortunate. Young people, it seemed, were hurrying irresponsibly into marriage and parenthood. They were pulling up roots to live in ill-constructed housing developments without proper socializing institutions for children. Some women were "abandoning" their children in order to enter the work force, while others—"allotment Annies"—deserted their soldier husbands as soon as their dependence allowances stopped coming. A rapidly increasing divorce rate appeared to be one unhappy result of these patterns of behavior. Juvenile delinquency involving "wolf packs" in housing developments and "zoot suit" gangs in large cities appeared to be another. Some people foresaw a new "Lost Generation."

Above all, the war prompted anxieties about the future. Having survived ten years of depression, Americans entered the 1940s already searching for security. With regular employment, they seemed at last to have found it. But could it endure? Many felt certain that depression would recur, that hard-earned gains would be wiped out, that the status of other groups would rise at the expense of their own. The writer Bernard de Voto observed that this anxiety rarely received "public expression, and little direct expression even in private." But "it exists and it may well be the most truly terrifying phenomenon of the war. It is a fear of the coming of the peace."

One group that clearly displayed this anxiety was organized labor—in part because it gained so much. In a strong bargaining position at the start of the war, unions received government support of "maintenance of membership" clauses in contracts. These required members to stay in the union for the duration of the war. Unions then drove ahead to recruit the 7 million new workers who found jobs between 1940 and 1945. Accordingly, union membership increased from 9 million in 1940 to almost 15 million in 1945, a growth more rapid than at any time in American history. Management generally acquiesced in this union activity: with

Jim Crow laws enforced strict separation of the races.

great profits to be made and a war to be won, it did not seem wise to goad militant workers into strikes.

Despite these gains, workers remained uneasy. John L. Lewis and other leaders led dramatic walkouts for better pay during the war. Work stoppages, though usually short-lived, increased from 2,968 in 1942 to 4,956 in 1944. In 1945, 4,750 stoppages affected 12 percent of the labor force and involved 3.4 million workers. And 1946, when wartime frustrations exploded, witnessed a record 4,985 stoppages involving 4.6 million laborers. Unionists, having begun to taste power and increased income, were insisting upon more in the future.

A similar revolution in expectations affected blacks, who made unprecedented gains during the war. Some of these advances were essentially symbolic—in 1943 the first black joined the American Bar Association; in 1944 the first black was admitted to a presidential press conference. Other changes were vitally important. The number of blacks who secured jobs in the federal government increased from 50,000 in 1939 to 200,000 six years later, and the appeal of jobs in northern and western cities pulled more than a million blacks out of the South.

This mass migration, one of the greatest in American history, persisted in the postwar period, dramatically changing the demographic, economic, and political world of black America. As late as 1940, 6.6 million of the nation's 12.8 million blacks lived in rural areas, the vast majority in the South (which was still the home for three-fourths of the black population). There, the color line remained rigid indeed. Jim Crow laws enforced strict separation of the races—in waiting rooms, movie theaters, restaurants, beaches, restrooms, even drinking fountains. Schools, of course, were segregated. Poll taxes, all-white primaries, and other discriminatory methods effectively disfranchised all but a handful of determined black southerners. And widely understood social conventions reinforced blacks' low standing. Whites did not shake hands with blacks, or tip their hats. They did not dream of letting a black person into their homes through the front door. They regularly called blacks—no matter their ages—by their first names, or they addressed them as "boy," or "girl," or "aunty." Blacks, of course, were expected to address all whites formally.

Southern life was harsh on blacks in countless other ways. Blacks went without decent medical care and rarely if ever entered a hospital. Their mortality rate was twice that of whites; their average life span was twelve years less. They were poorly educated. Of those over twenty-five years of age in 1940, only one in 100 was a college graduate; one in ten had no schooling at all. There was scarcely a black middle class in the South. Alabama, for instance, had four black lawyers (compared to 1,600 white lawyers); Mississippi had six (compared with 1,200). Blacks suffered all sorts of physical intimidation, abuse, and violence and were without legal recourse. "A white man," one scholar observed, "can steal from or maltreat a Negro in almost any way without fear of reprisal, because the Negro cannot claim the protection of the police or courts." Indeed, blacks played no role in southern law enforcement. In 1940 there were no black policemen in Mississippi, South Carolina, Alabama, Louisiana, Georgia, Arkansas, and Virginia. When arrested,

> While the March on Washington Movement may find it advisable to form a citizens committee of friendly white citizens to give moral support . . . it does not imply that these white citizens . . . should be taken into the March on Washington Movement as members. The essential value of an all-Negro movement such as the March on Washington is that it helps to create faith by Negroes in Negroes. It develops a sense of self-reliance with Negroes depending on Negroes in vital matters. It helps to break down the slave psychology and inferiority-complex in Negroes which comes and is nourished with Negroes relying on white people for direction and support. This inevitably happens in mixed organizations that are supposed to be in the interest of the Negro.
>
> A. Philip Randolph promotes black power, 1942.

blacks could expect physical beatings, harsh sentences, and barbaric prison conditions.

The wartime and postwar migrations to the North and to cities (where 14 million of America's 20 million blacks lived by 1960) meant great changes in their lives. While they faced discrimination in the North—notably in employment and housing—they usually managed to find better-paid work than on the farms of the South, and they were free of southern-style racism. Though confined to northern ghettos, they inched ahead economically and began to develop a substantial middle class. Their very concentration (in Washington, Detroit, Newark, and other cities they comprised a majority or near majority of the population by 1960) gave them the chance for political power. As early as 1944, their votes were important in securing Roosevelt's fourth term. This geographical concentration—along with developments in mass communications—also facilitated community organization. In all these ways the war, by unleashing the migrations, had a deep and lasting impact on the status of blacks and on race relations in the United States.

As in the years between 1914 and 1919, this combination of migration and relative prosperity created mounting militancy among black leaders. The Congress on Racial Equality, an interracial organization devoted to pacifism as well as to civil rights, was founded in 1942. The NAACP, the largest of the interracial organizations, increased its membership during the war from 50,000 to 500,000. Most alarming of all to whites was the potential political power demonstrated by A. Philip Randolph, the porters' union leader who threatened to call for a mass march on Washington in 1941 unless Roosevelt acted to prevent racial discrimination in employment. After much procrastination (for Roosevelt still hesitated to offend southern Democrats), the President relented far enough to issue an executive order setting up a Fair Employment Practices Commission. Easily his most significant contribution to racial justice, it stemmed entirely from black pressure. The lesson was not lost on later leaders of the black cause.

These advances merely reminded blacks how far America had to go. The poorly financed, understaffed FEPC was able to resolve only one-third of the 8,000 complaints it had time to hear. Of its forty-five compliance orders, thirty-five were ignored. Despite a Supreme Court ruling against white primaries, most blacks in the South continued to be disfranchised through poll taxes, literacy tests, and other ruses. The armed forces, which were under federal control, flagrantly discriminated against blacks. The marines and army air corps simply excluded them, the navy gave them menial tasks, and the army segregated them under white officers. "Leadership," Secretary of War Stimson explained, "is not imbedded in the negro race yet, and to try to make commissioned officers to lead men into battle—colored men—is only to work a disaster to both." It was not until 1944 that the navy integrated the crews of a few of its ships or that the army sent blacks into combat. By then the top brass was worrying about black unrest in the services. "My God! My God!" General Marshall exclaimed, "I don't know what to do about this race question in the army. Frankly, it is the worst thing we have to deal with. . . . We are getting a situation on our hands that may explode right in our faces."

As Marshall prophesied, the humiliations suffered by blacks (in and out of the army) created many conflicts during the war years. In 1943 blacks in Harlem rioted against discrimination. A race riot in Detroit the same year killed 34 and injured more than 700. The antiwhite Black Muslims began to make modest gains among the dispossessed. CORE leaders experimented with sit-ins (only in the North) and other forms of direct action. And countless blacks expressed themselves bitterly against a society that fought fascism abroad while ignoring injustice at home. One told Gunnar Myrdal, the Swedish social scientist investigating race relations, "just carve on my tombstone, here lies a black man killed fighting a yellow man for the protection of a white man." A "Draftee's Prayer" in a black newspaper added,

> Dead Lord, today
> I go to war:
> To fight, to die,
> Tell me what for?
> Dear Lord, I'll fight,
> I do not fear
> Germans or Japs;
> My fears are here.
> America!

Such attitudes among workers and blacks captured one essential aspect of life on the home front. So long as the enemy fought on the field, a common goal of victory secured domestic peace most of the time. But it was a restless, increasingly factious peace. Blacks and blue-collar workers, like farmers, businessmen, veterans, and others, had sensed the chance for a better life, and they pressed urgently to enjoy it as the war came to a close. Better organized, they sought to advance their own interests with the same grim single-mindedness that they showed in battle. This militancy amid plenty, this revolution of expectations, this scramble not only for security but for slices of an ever-larger pie—all these were among the major social developments of the "Great Leap" of World War II.

Suggestions for reading

The key books covering American politics and diplomacy in World War II are James M. Burns, *Roosevelt: Soldier of Freedom** (1970); and A. Russell Buchanan, *The United States and World War II*, 2 vol.* (1964). See also W. H. McNeill, *America, Britain, and Russia* (1953); Gaddis Smith, *American Diplomacy During the Second World War, 1941–1945** (1965); John Snell, *Illusion and Necessity: The Diplomacy of World War II** (1963); Herbert Feis, *Churchill, Roosevelt, Stalin** (1957); and the revisionist account by Stephen Ambrose, *Rise to Globalism: American Foreign Policy Since 1938** (1971). Gabriel Kolko, *The Politics of War: The World and U. S. Foreign Policy, 1943–1945* (1969) stresses economic motives.

Other relevant studies are Raymond O'Connor, *Diplomacy for Victory: FDR and Unconditional Surrender** (1971); Trumbull Higgins, *Winston Churchill and the Second Front, 1940–1943* (1957), and *Soft Underbelly: The Anglo-American Controversy over the Italian Campaign, 1939–1945* (1968); Diane Shaver Clemens, *Yalta* (1970); and Robert Divine, *Second Chance: The Triumph of Internationalism During World War II* (1967). Important books on military policy are Kent Roberts Greenfield, *American Strategy in World War II: A Reconsideration** (1967); and Louis Morton, *Strategy and Command* (1962). For science policy consult James P. Baxter, *Scientists Against Time** (1946); Richard G. Hewlett and Oscar E. Anderson, *The New World* (1962), and *The Atomic Shield* (1969), on atomic development; and the highly readable narrative by Robert Jungk, *Brighter Than a Thousand Suns: A Personal History of the Atomic Scientists** (1958). An essential source is Martin Sherwin, *A World Destroyed: The Atomic Bomb and the Grand Alliance* (1975).

Books dealing with Asia are John Toland, *The Rising Sun** (1970); Robert Butow, *Japan's Decision to Surrender* (1954); Tang Tsou, *America's Failure in China, 1941–1950** (1963); and Barbara Tuchman, *Stilwell and The American Experience in China, 1911–1945** (1971). Important books on wartime sources of the Cold War include John Gaddis, *The United States and the Origins of the Cold War, 1941–1946** (1972); and George C. Herring, Jr., *Aid to Russia, 1941–1946* (1973).

The starting points for life in the United States during the war are Richard Polenberg, *War and Society: The United States, 1941–1945** (1972); and John M. Blum, *V Was for Victory* (1976). Other surveys are Richard Lingeman, *Don't You Know There's a War On?* (1970); Geoffrey Perrett, *Days of Sadness, Days of Triumph* (1973); and William Ogburn, ed., *American Society in Wartime* (1943). For economic policy consult Eliot Janeway, *Struggle for Survival* (1951); John M. Blum, *From the Morgenthau Diaries: Years of War, 1941–1945* (1967); and Bruce Catton, *War Lords of Washington* (1948). See also Davis Ross, *Preparing for Ulysses* (1969), which deals with manpower and military policies; Walter Wilcox, *The Farmer in the Second World War* (1947); and Joel Seidman, *American Labor from Defense to Reconversion* (1953). Useful biographies of labor leaders include Saul Alinsky, *John L. Lewis* (1949); and Matthew Josephson, *Sidney Hillman* (1952). William Chafe's book on American women, cited in the bibliography for chapter 6 is indispensable. See also Allan Winkler, *The Politics of Propaganda: The Office of War Information 1942–45*

(1979); and George Flynn, *The Mess in Washington: Manpower Mobilization in World War II* (1979).

The experiences of blacks during the war are detailed in Richard Dalfiume, *Desegregation of the Armed Forces, 1939–1953* (1969); August Meier and Elliott Rudwick, *CORE . . . 1942–1968* (1973); Robert Shogan and Thomas Craig, *The Detroit Race Riot* (1964); and Gunnar Myrdal, *An American Dilemma** (1944, rev. ed. 1962), a classic sociological account. The fate of Japanese-Americans is well told in Jacobus ten Broek, et al., *Prejudice, War, and the Constitution* (1945); and in Roger Daniels, *Concentration Camps** (1971). Lawrence S. Wittner, *Rebels Against War: The American Peace Movement, 1941–1960* (1969) covers its subject sympathetically. For constitutional developments see Edward S. Corwin, *Total War and the Constitution** (1947); Francis Biddle, *In Brief Authority* (1962), by Roosevelt's wartime attorney general; and J. Woodford Howard, *Mr. Justice Murphy* (1968).

11

Acrimony at home and abroad

1945–1952

When Roosevelt died in April 1945, liberals were distraught. TVA director David Lilienthal shuddered to think of "that Throttlebottom Truman. The country and the world doesn't deserve to be left this way." Remembering Truman's rise in the corrupt politics of Kansas City, the journalist Max Lerner asked, "can a man who has been associated with the Pendergast machine be able to keep the panting politicians and bosses out of the gravy?"

Millions of Americans appeared to share this anxiety. After all, Roosevelt had been president for as long as many people could remember. Yet now, with the Germans still fighting, with Japan to be invaded, and with postwar problems yet to be tackled, the country seemed saddled with an uninspiring border state senator whom the party had plucked from relative obscurity. Truman himself seemed frightened about the responsibilities ahead. "Boys," he told reporters, "if you ever pray, pray for me now. I don't know whether you fellows ever had a load of hay fall on you, but when they told me yesterday what had happened, I felt like the moon, the stars, and all the planets had fallen on me."

Actually, people worried too much; the American political system was stable enough to withstand sudden shocks to the presidency. While Truman tried to master his office, delegates in San Francisco completed the task of devising a United Nations charter, which the Senate adopted by a vote of eighty-nine to two in July. In Europe, Allied forces overwhelmed the Germans, who surrendered on May 8. And in Asia, Americans pressed forward into Iwo Jima and Okinawa. The country's awesome military-industrial machine surged ahead, largely unaffected by personalities in the White House.

If you judge from the articles and editorials which have been written in the past twenty years, and all the prayers which have been prayed, and all the mourning and preaching that has been going on, you would judge that we crossed some kind of moral boundary with the use of these weapons. The assumption seems to be that it is much more wicked to kill people with a nuclear bomb, than to kill people by busting their heads with rocks.

General Curtis Le May, a staunch advocate of nuclear weaponry, ridicules the "moralists" who complained about Hiroshima and Nagasaki.

Truman also showed himself capable of acting decisively. His most far-reaching decision in these early months was to authorize the dropping of atomic bombs on Hiroshima (August 6) and Nagasaki (August 9). Later, critics argued persuasively that in reaching this decision he did not ask advice on *whether* the bomb should be used but on *how,* and that he listened only to scientists and government officials who could have been expected to favor its use in war. In the process he ignored the pleas of scientists who urged him to warn the Japanese or to demonstrate the bomb in an uninhabited area. Instead, Truman merely told the Japanese on July 26 to surrender unconditionally or face "prompt and utter destruction." Since this was what they had already been receiving from fire raids, it was not surprising that they kept on with the war.

The use of the atomic bombs may have been unnecessary. By July 1945 the Japanese knew they were doomed, and their moderates were exploring avenues to peace. If Truman had told them that they could retain their emperor, they might have agreed to surrender, particularly after Russia joined the war against them on August 8. At least, he could have awaited the impact of the Russian declaration, and of further fire bombings, which many later observers felt would have won the war without an American invasion. He definitely should have paused after incinerating close to 100,000 people in Hiroshima, instead of authorizing the air force to go ahead on its own and kill 40,000 to 75,000 more at Nagasaki. Truman's actions showed that he was more decisive—more impetuous, even—than reflective.

Truman never wavered in defending his decision. Warning the Japanese or demonstrating the bomb seemed risky. The Japanese, he reasoned, would ignore the warning and concentrate their remaining defenses against air attacks. Japan might even succeed in shooting down the plane carrying such a bomb. Moreover, there was the chance that a bomb dropped in a demonstration might not work. How foolish the United States (and Truman) would look if that happened, especially as there were only two bombs ready for use in early August! For Truman, therefore, the decision involved little soul-searching. The United States had spent six years and billions of dollars developing the weapon, and once it had been successfully tested, he thought, it was silly not to use it.

Later, some critics contended that Truman authorized use of the bombs to demonstrate America's power to the Soviet Union and to end the war before the Russians could join it. Such concerns did influence men like James Byrnes, who be-

Victims of the atomic blast at Hiroshima await aid a few hours after the explosion.

Seven weeks later I returned to Alamogordo after I had watched the same model of the A-bomb devastate the city of Nagasaki. On that return visit I saw for the first time what the bomb had done to the desert. Over a radius of four hundred yards the ground has been depressed to a depth ranging from ten feet at the periphery to twenty-five feet in the center. All life within a mile, vegetable as well as animal, had been destroyed. There was not a rattlesnake left in the region, nor a blade of desert grass. The sand in the depression had been fused into a glasslike substance the color of jade, all of it radioactive. Eight hundred yards away a steel rigging tower weighing thirty-two tons had been turned into a twisted mass of wreckage. The one-hundred-foot-high steel tower at the top of which the bomb was exploded was completely vaporized. A herd of antelope that had been grazing several miles away had vanished. It was believed they had started on a mad dash for the wilds of Mexico. A number of cows at a similar distance developed grey spots from deposits of radioactive dust. These radioactive cows and their progeny became the nearest equivalent to "sacred cows" in the United States, being carefully studied for the effects of radiation.

William Laurence, a leading American reporter, recalls the power of the first atomic bomb, detonated in Alamogordo, New Mexico, in July 1945.

came secretary of state in 1945. They also moved General Leslie Groves, head of bomb development, who recalled, "Russia was our enemy . . . and the project was conducted on that basis." But Truman was focusing mainly on Japan, not on the Soviet Union. Like Roosevelt, he was more preoccupied with short-run military concerns than with postwar diplomacy. At the time, the Japanese seemed prepared to fight to their last man, and in Okinawa they lost 110,000 men in eighty-three days, while killing 12,500 Americans, or 150 per day. (Later, in Vietnam, it was a bad *week* when 200 Americans died.) It was primarily to stop such losses as these, and to prevent the still more unthinkable bloodletting anticipated in an invasion of the home islands, that Truman did what he did.

At the time, Americans had no chance to debate the alternatives and no idea of Truman's options. But they did know that the bombs had worked and that Japan had finally surrendered. So they reacted not with horror at what had been done but with profound relief that the war was over. In this way Truman's popularity was further enhanced, his judgment seemingly vindicated. For the time being, there appeared little question of Truman's capacity to rule.

Domestic controversies

1945–46

With characteristic briskness, Truman wasted little time after Japan's surrender before turning to problems at home, and on September 6, four days after V-J Day, he asked Congress to enact a "second Bill of Rights" for the American people. Among these rights, Truman declared, were "useful and remunerative" jobs for all, government assistance to farmers, protection for small businessmen against monopoly, decent housing for every family, "adequate medical care," "protection from the economic fears of old age, sickness, accident, and unemployment," and the "right to a good education." These rights, he said, echoing Roosevelt, "spell security."

Truman's requests, to be known as the Fair Deal, aimed at consolidating the partial welfare state built during the Roosevelt years. Indeed, in calling for such measures as national health insurance he went beyond the New Deal. Inevitably his requests provoked controversy. To secure them from a conservative Congress, the new president was to need all the skill he could muster.

As the struggle developed, it was clear that Truman possessed some of the qualities necessary to win. One of these was his awareness that the president must lead. As he liked to say, "the buck stops here." Another was his initially friendly relations with congressmen of both parties. A senator for ten years, he had pleased New Dealers by supporting most of Roosevelt's policies, while his impartial chairmanship of a wartime committee investigating defense contracting ingratiated him with moderates and conservatives.

Truman made gestures to improve congressional-executive relations, which had deteriorated badly during the war. To placate the GOP, he named Senator Theodore Burton, an Ohio Republican, to the first vacancy in the Supreme Court. He resur-

President Truman with three leading politicians from Texas, Senator Lyndon B. Johnson, former Vice-President John Nance Garner, and Congressman Sam Rayburn.

rected Herbert Hoover by appointing him to head a commission studying governmental reorganization. His appointment of Byrnes, a former congressman and senator from South Carolina, as secretary of state and of Fred Vinson, a popular Democratic congressman from Kentucky, as secretary of the treasury (and in 1946 as chief justice) were especially well received on the Hill. More than FDR, Truman appeared to appreciate congressional advice and counsel.

But Truman also left himself open to criticism. In making lesser appointments he showed a tendency to favor old friends from his days in the national guard (he had been a captain in World War I) and in Missouri politics, where he had belonged to the malodorous Pendergast machine of Kansas City. To observers used to the intellectuals and brain trusters who had flourished under Roosevelt these appointees seemed an undistinguished lot. "The composite impression," the journalist I. F. Stone wrote, "was of big-bellied, good-natured guys who knew a lot of dirty jokes, spent as little time in their offices as possible, saw Washington as a chance to make 'useful' contacts, and were anxious to get what they could for themselves out of the experience. . . . The Truman era was the era of the moocher. The place was full of Wimpys who could be had for a hamburger."

The liberal admirers of FDR were especially offended by some of Truman's conservative appointees to important positions. These included Charles Snyder, a Missouri banker who held several major jobs before becoming secretary of the treasury in 1946, and Tom Clark, a conservative Texan who became attorney general and then a Supreme Court justice. By the end of 1946 almost all the important New Dealers whom Truman had inherited had resigned or been fired. Roosevelt's intimates, he told a friend, were "crackpots and the lunatic fringe." He added, "I don't want any experiments; the American people have been through a lot of experiments, and they want a rest." Harry Dexter White, assistant secretary of the treasury under FDR and Truman, explained that when Roosevelt was alive, "we'd go over to the White House for a conference on some particular policy, lose the argument, and yet walk out of the door somehow thrilled and inspired to go on and do the job the way the Big Boss had ordered." Now, he added, "you go in to see Mr. Truman. He's very nice to you. He lets you do what you want to, and yet you leave feeling somehow dispirited and flat."

Truman also failed to maintain order within his administration during his first two years in office. Perhaps no one could have done so very well, for the transition from war to peace inevitably caused confusion. But Truman, still feeling his way, too often allowed bureaucratic battles to take place. Harold Smith, Truman's budget director, expressed the dismay of many government officials. "I don't know what goes on around here," he confided to his diary in February 1946, "and that is a rather dangerous situation for all of us to be in. . . . The top people in government are solving problems in a vacuum, and the vacuum is chiefly in their heads."

Moreover, Truman's approach to Congress lacked finesse. Instead of working purposefully for one or two goals at a time, he outlined grandiose programs and left Congress to its devices. "What the country needed in every field," he said, "was up to me to say . . . and if Congress wouldn't respond, well, I'd done all I could in a straight-forward way." TRB, the progressive columnist for the *New Republic,* later saw a disturbing pattern: "Truman would ask Congress for about 120 percent more than he expected. Congress, with a great show of indignation, would slash it to 75 percent. Truman would smile his little-man smile and bounce back with something else. It's a funny way to run a country."

Piecing these criticisms of Truman together made a most unflattering portrait. The new president, it appeared, was a poor judge of people, an anti-intellectual, a sloppy administrator, a rhetorical liberal, a heavy-handed manager of Congress. Possibly, he felt unprepared and insecure in the White House and overcompensated by sounding tough and decisive. Perhaps so. In any event, he possessed little of the deftness and none of the charisma that had characterized Roosevelt at his best.

In retrospect it is equally clear that Truman (like most of his contemporaries among politicians) did not address himself carefully to some domestic problems. Though he carried liberalism slightly beyond the bread-and-butter issues of the Roosevelt era—as in his support of civil rights—he was insensitive to the prevalence of poverty and the continuing maldistribution of income. Instead, he concentrated on meeting the presumed threat from the Soviets. To a degree, of course, any president in the late 1940s would have had to do the same. With Truman, however, the focus on foreign affairs meant that many domestic problems received low priority.

But most of the progressives who blamed Truman for the nation's troubles had to concede that he faced formidable obstacles. By 1945 the Democratic party was almost as sharply divided between its northern-urban and southern-western-rural wings as it had been in the 1920s. Though outnumbered, the rural wing, which opposed the urban liberalism of the New Deal, coalesced successfully with Repub-

America's mood:
the public's view
of the most important problem
facing the country,
according to Gallup Poll results,
1949–52

1949	High cost of living
1950	War and the threat of war
1951	War and foreign policy
1952	Korean War

SOURCE: Adapted from *U.S. Foreign Policy: Context, Conduct, Content* by Marian Irish and Elke Frank. © 1975 by Harcourt Brace Jovanovich. Reproduced by permission of the publisher.

licans to dominate both houses of Congress. For example, GOP House leader Joseph Martin and Charles Halleck, his right-hand man from Indiana, worked closely with southern conservatives like Howard Smith of Virginia, a rural reactionary who was a power on the House Rules Committee. The Senate was dominated by southern conservative Democrats, among them Harry Byrd of Virginia and Richard Russell of Georgia, and by Republican leaders like Robert Taft of Ohio.

A still greater barrier to domestic reform was the national mood. Having sacrificed during four years of war (and ten years of depression), Americans looked forward to enjoying the good life. They chafed at shortages, and they yearned for material goods. In doing so they helped build up enormous demand for a host of products that had barely existed, if at all, in 1940: television, heat-and-serve dinners, automatic transmissions, tubeless tires, air conditioning, hi-fis, filter cigarettes, dishwashers, freezers, detergents, tape recorders, and fiberglass. Americans began to fly in four-engine planes, to drive on superhighways, to live in ranch-style homes, to shop in supermarkets. With such a comfortable world within grasp it was easy, as it had been in the 1920s, for Americans to turn to their own private concerns.

This mood, however, was different from the "normalcy" of the 1920s, when people praised the virtues of rugged individualism. By 1945 the modest welfare state of FDR had come to stay, and special-interest groups fought single-mindedly to broaden their share of it. Veterans demanded benefits, farmers higher prices, unions better wages and working conditions, consumers more goods and lower prices. Where Harding and Coolidge could win acclaim by leaving people alone, Truman (and his successors) had to act to sustain these groups in a standard of living that no society in world history had ever enjoyed before. He was confronted with one of the most powerful forces of the postwar era: the revolution in expectations.

Like Roosevelt, Truman had to rely on an essentially nonideological, indeed almost apathetic, electorate. As studies of voters were beginning to show, most Americans did not act as "liberals" or as "conservatives." Rather, they voted as their parents or their peers did. Millions (some 40 percent of the eligible electorate) failed to vote at all even in presidential elections. It was therefore difficult for Truman (and for reformers in the next fifteen years) to mobilize a mass following or a Democratic party that would consciously demand enactment of a "liberal" program. Instead, he had to work with constituency-oriented congressmen and senators, few of whom felt much pressure from home for progressive legislation.

THE ISSUES

These obstacles, with Truman's own limitations, combined to defeat all of the Fair Deal goals in 1945–46. Congress brought an end to the wartime Fair Employment Practices Commission and filibustered to death efforts to create a new one. It failed to pass measures against poll taxes. It ignored or defeated bills for public housing and federal aid to education. Though it approved the Employment Act of 1946 (which established a Council of Economic Advisers and proclaimed the government's responsibility to step in against economic declines), it rejected amendments to commit the government to using Keynesian fiscal policies.

The most pressing issues of Truman's first two years barely touched on his Fair Deal proposals. Rather, they concerned the economic consequences of the war. In trying to deal with them Truman received little but blows for his pains.

The pressures for a return to civilian life were overwhelming by mid-1945. Business interests demanded lower taxes, immediate demobilization, and the end of lend-lease and other measures assisting foreign competitors in international markets. Soldiers insisted on being allowed to come home, and office-holders were swamped with postcards from Asia labeled, "No boats, no votes." Under such pressure the politicians of both parties simply collapsed. In November 1945 Congress approved a $6 billion tax cut, even though it would obviously contribute to inflation. The administration quickly disposed of most of its war plants, usually by turning them over to private interests on very generous terms. It let business move ahead quickly into civilian production. Given no choice by Congress, it cut lend-lease shipments. And—feeling secure with an atomic monopoly—it brought the boys home. The armed forces, 12 million strong in 1945, had only 3 million by mid-1946 and but 1.6 million by mid-1947.

This rapid demobilization was popular enough at first. But by the end of 1945 its costs were already becoming apparent. The return of so many soldiers to the domestic scene created great competition for jobs and enormous demand for housing. One veteran complained, "six months ago I was piloting a B-29 against the Japs. Now I am trying to build a home in my home town. The first fight was easier. . . ." Though the economy opened up quickly enough to provide most veterans with jobs, the housing market, depressed since 1928, fell far short of demands.

Truman tried to alleviate the housing shortage. Through existing agencies such as the Federal Housing Agency he (and his successors) helped millions of Americans get government-insured mortgages at moderate rates of interest. He also called for more generous appropriations for public housing, but even the backing of Robert Taft failed to stop a predominantly rural coalition from blocking the proposal until 1949. Meanwhile, Truman made matters worse by authorizing John Snyder, his director of reconversion, to remove federal controls on building materials. This action, one of many that attempted to placate private interests, sabotaged central direction of housing policy. It also meant that materials flowed into the areas that would bring builders immediate profit. These areas, as often in the construction business, were commercial, not residential or industrial.

The housing crisis, though serious, seemed almost trivial compared to the problem of inflation. To a large degree this too was inevitable after the war, because demand for consumer goods had been pent up since 1941, during which time Americans had saved unprecedented sums. The baby boom and the sudden return of so many soldiers made this demand still more formidable. During the year and a half following the end of the war in September 1945, the consumer price index jumped almost 25 percent. This was a rate of increase greater than at any time since World War I. It seemed destined to wipe out all the hard-earned economic gains of war.

Truman, of course, could hardly bring prices down. That would happen on a broad front only when supply caught up with demand—in 1948. Moreover, he was again stymied by the conservative coalition in Congress, which did away with firm price controls. Prices therefore rose almost uncontrollably during the summer of 1946. By November 1946 Truman removed the few controls that remained.

Truman's handling of inflation made this difficult situation worse. Instead of demanding strong controls from the start, he belatedly stepped in to veto a bill establishing weak controls. His actions angered not only conservatives but also some of his own party leaders, who had advised him to accept the bill as the best to be had under the circumstances. "The government's stability policy," a top adviser complained, "is not what you have stated it to be, but is instead one of improvising on a day-to-day, case-by-case method, as one crisis leads to another—in short . . . there is really no policy at all."

In dealing with labor-management controversies Truman faced perhaps the profoundest domestic problems of the era. It was his political misfortune to confront an acrimonious situation in which unions tried to make up for wartime restraint by demanding sizable wage increases. Management refused, and millions of American workers went out on strike in late 1945 and early 1946. Both sides then turned to Truman, who had the power (stemming from the war) to authorize price increases. After a show of firmness, Truman gave way under business pressure by permitting price hikes of approximately 19 percent. Management then granted workers pay increases of 18 to 19 percent. Truman's actions settled some of the strikes, but only by encouraging the first of many postwar rounds of inflationary wage-price agreements between powerful interest groups. Consumers paid the bill in higher prices.

John L. Lewis then led the soft-coal miners out on strike on April 1, 1946. American industry, very dependent on coal, seemed threatened by what promised to be a long and divisive confrontation. At the same time railway engineers and trainmen also served notice of their intention to strike. Furious, Truman went before a joint session of Congress to demand emergency powers. As he was reading his message, he was handed a note advising him that the railwaymen had come to terms. But he went on with his address, which called on Congress to give him power to order federal troops into strike-bound industries, and even to draft strikers into the armed services.

John L. Lewis, the defiant, outspoken leader of the United Mine Workers, inspecting mine conditions.

It was a sign of the hysteria of the times that the House quickly approved this violation of labor's civil liberties. However, the Senate ultimately listened to calmer men like Taft, the supposed enemy of organized labor, and rejected Truman's appeal. The episode showed how hard it was for Truman (and later presidents) to impose their will on organized labor. It revealed that he could be hot-tempered to the extent of endangering the liberties of working people. Few of his actions were more ill-considered or counterproductive.

Truman's frustrations in dealing with labor-management relations also revealed the political power that the labor movement had developed as a pressure group during the war. In some states, such as Michigan, industrial workers in the CIO virtually controlled the Democratic party. Elsewhere, labor's power was nowhere nearly so powerful as anguished conservatives contended (only a third of nonagricultural workers belonged to unions), but it was potentially formidable. The CIO's Political Action Committee served as an important source of funds and votes for prolabor candidates. The postwar era, some contemporaries thought, offered the chance for a fundamental political and social realignment, with political leftists and laborers uniting with increasingly militant civil rights activists to forge a social-democratic movement in the United States. In any event, the unions seemed strong; the sociologist C. Wright Mills called them the "new men of power."

But Mills accurately noted another characteristic of the postwar labor movement: it had lost much of the old militancy of the 1930s. In the late 1940s a few union leaders (many of them communists) tried to sustain the drive for social justice that had marked the sit-down strikers. However, an increasing majority of union members wished to steer clear of radical associations. Earning three or four times as much in real dollars as in the 1930s, often with wives bringing in added income, they were anxious to enjoy the good life. In 1948 the pollster Samuel Lubell interviewed a class-conscious local of the United Automobile Workers that he had visited eleven years before, and he found that most of the members owned their own homes. These workers were consumers first—"haves," not "have-nots." They had cars, savings, many expensive household appliances. Like many similarly placed blue-collar workers, they lent their support to union leaders such as Philip Murray and Walter Reuther, who successfully purged the CIO of communist members by 1949. This bitter internal struggle, which raged within the union movement for much of the 1940s, sapped the unity of organized labor.

The new men of power, indeed, proved themselves willing to sacrifice many demands in order to secure what their members seemed to want: better pay and benefits. Few union leaders—Reuther was an exception—paid much attention to the claims of blacks, who were discriminated against by unions as well as by employers. Fewer still heeded the complaints of the millions of women who continued to work at lower wages than did men with comparable skills. In focusing on bread-and-butter issues, the unions soft-pedaled their once bitter demands for greater control over the processes of production. The "speedup" of assembly lines persisted. Other unions negotiated contracts that traded away the right to strike for big wage increases (which employers then passed on to consumers). By the late 1940s many of the once-militant unions had become large, sometimes sluggish bureaucracies without close contact with the rank and file. Though liberal on political issues, the unions were in many other important ways similar to other large pressure groups.

The fact remained, however, that as pressure groups the unions alarmed many contemporaries, who blamed Truman for labor-management problems. These problems, along with struggles over reconversion and price controls, badly damaged Truman's standing with the voters by late 1946. Gleeful opponents circulated cruel jokes about the President's blundering. One conjectured how Roosevelt would have handled matters by asking, "I wonder what Truman would do if he were alive." Republicans proclaimed that "to err is Truman" and repeated, "Had Enough?" In November, with meat shortages provoking fury among consumers, they succeeded in winning control over Congress for the first time since 1930. With liberals in disarray and with the conservative coalition riding high, Truman seemed doomed to electoral extinction in 1948.

THE EIGHTIETH CONGRESS

During the 1948 campaign Truman sounded one theme almost endlessly: the Eightieth Congress of 1947–48 had been "good-for-nothing." Like most politicians at election time, he distorted the past, for the Congress had actually compiled a significant list of foreign policy legislation, including military assistance to Greece and Turkey, the Marshall Plan of foreign aid to Europe, and the National Security Act, which attempted to reduce interservice rivalries by setting up the Joint Chiefs of Staff and the Defense Department. The law also established the National Security Council and the Central Intelligence Agency. These agencies vastly increased the role of the military and intelligence services in subsequent decision making.

In giving the impression that the Eightieth Congress was totally obstructive, Truman also distorted the truth. What he should have said was that the majority of congressmen opposed labor union power, deficit spending, high taxes, and wage and price controls—that is, progressive fiscal policy and state regulation of private enterprise. Otherwise, they were often conciliatory. In the 1940s and 1950s most of them supported, though often belatedly, increases in social security and the minimum wage. In battling for tax cuts many of them were in effect conservative Keynesians who agreed that federal policies could and should promote consumer spending. Taft, the conservative leader, spearheaded the battle for federal aid to education and public housing, both of which passed the Republican Senate in 1948, only to fail in the House. Not just a brave and lonely Harry S. Truman but also conservatives and moderates helped sustain the partial welfare state of the New Deal in the 1940s: it offered too much to too many groups to be abolished.

Truman also conveniently overlooked his own equivocations in 1947–48. After doing little for civil rights in the first two years of his presidency, he used the election campaign to outline (but not to work hard for) a broad program which he knew Congress would never pass. He demanded national health insurance, about which he had said little during Democratic control of Congress in 1946. To appear forceful concerning inflation, he called for presidential power to control prices—authority he did not really want and knew he could not get. Overreacting to fears about communist subversion, he established loyalty boards, which had the power to ignore civil liberties of governmental employees. It was not surprising that many people thought that Truman cared less about broadening human rights than about getting himself reelected in 1948.

Still, Truman was correct in claiming that the Eightieth Congress was both conservative and partisan. Among its new members—the "class of '46"—were such Red-hunters as Richard Nixon of California and William Jenner of Indiana, opportunists like Joseph McCarthy of Wisconsin (who replaced Robert La Follette, Jr.), and conservatives like John Bricker of Ohio and William Knowland of California. Led by Taft, one of the hardest-working, best-prepared Senate leaders of the postwar era, they were formidable foes to the administration.

In this frame of mind they joined with conservative Democrats to defeat the entire Fair Deal program. The Eightieth Congress rejected public housing, aid to education, and Truman's appeal for universal military training. It refused to relax immigration quotas or to aid displaced persons. Though it did not challenge well-established interest groups such as farmers and veterans or dismantle the social welfare programs of the New Deal, it complained loudly (and most unfairly) about Truman's "lavish" spending. To ensure that there would be no more four-term presidents, as Roosevelt had been, it set in motion a constitutional amendment limiting presidents to two terms that was later ratified in 1951.

Congress reserved its heaviest ammunition for tax and labor policies. Twice in 1947 it passed tax cuts, only to watch Truman veto them with the claim that they favored the wealthy and imperiled the budget. In the election year of 1948, however, enough of Truman's supporters deserted him to override a third presidential veto. In the area of labor law Congress approved, again over Truman's veto, the Taft-Hartley Act of 1947. The measure enumerated unfair labor practices, outlawed the closed shop, required union officers to sign noncommunist oaths to secure access to the NLRB, and authorized the president to impose eighty-day "cooling off" periods before workers could start strikes threatening national health or safety. Furious, the unions called the act a "slave-labor law."

Neither the tax cut nor the Taft-Hartley law was as retrogressive as Truman and his supporters claimed. The tax cut, which administration economists had thought would be inflationary, helped sustain purchasing power during a recession in 1949, while the labor law proved a workable, if clumsy, measure that Truman himself employed in attempts to head off strikes in key industries. For all their complaints, unions were able to live with Taft-Hartley for decades thereafter.

But the struggles of the Eightieth Congress, especially over Taft-Hartley, did make a difference in American politics. In 1945–46 Truman had often seemed aimless and complacent. In battling against Taft-Hartley and the tax bills, his combative, partisan spirit arose. Progressives, though remaining suspicious of his motives, cheered him on. "Let's come right out and say it," one exulted. "We thought Truman's labor veto message thrilling." If it did nothing else, the strife of the Eightieth Congress enabled Truman to strike a pose—for that in part is what it was—for the "people" against the "interests." This fighting image, which gained him the support of many New Dealers, was valuable in an election year.

Cold war, 1946–48

The closing months of 1945 brought no respite from the tension that had been gathering between the United States and the Soviet Union. For the next three years—indeed for the next two decades—this Cold War, as it became known by 1947, was the paramount issue not only of international relations but of domestic politics.

Of the many forces that helped to foment tensions, the most important was Stalin's determination to safeguard Russian interests. By the end of 1945 it was clear that he had no intention of relinquishing his hold on eastern Europe. At the same time he systematically stripped East German industrial potential and shipped thousands of German citizens—Nazis, Stalin claimed—to forced-labor camps. He pressured Turkey for control of the straits leading from the Black Sea to the Mediterranean, and Iran for oil rights in Azerbaijan. In February 1946 he alarmed American observers by proclaiming that communism and capitalism were incompatible. Eric Sevareid, a progressive journalist, concluded that the speech made it "clear as daylight that the comintern, formalized or not, [was] back in effective operation. If you can brush aside Stalin's speech . . . you are a braver man than I."

Churchill, Truman, and Stalin at Potsdam, Germany, July 1945.

These events led Western leaders to stiffen their response to Stalin. In a timely cable sent two weeks after Stalin's speech, George Kennan, a top American diplomat in Moscow, argued that Stalin was "only the last of that long succession of cruel and wasteful Russian rulers who have relentlessly forced their country on to ever new heights of military power. . . . " Churchill, out of power but widely admired in America, spoke two weeks later in Missouri of an "iron curtain" descending around eastern Europe. The Soviets, he declared, sought the "indefinite expansion of their power and doctrines." An approving Truman sat on the platform as Churchill delivered this speech. The President, convinced that he had to talk and act tough, also took decisive steps. By dispatching an American battleship to the eastern Mediterranean, he warned against further Russian pressure on Turkey, and by sending stiff notes protesting against Soviet behavior in Iran, he helped stave off Russian encroachment. The American people obviously supported this get-tough policy: 71 percent said they disapproved of Russia's international conduct, and 60 percent thought America "too soft" in dealing with Moscow.

American leaders reflected this hardening of opinion in 1946. In September, Secretary of State Byrnes proclaimed that the United States would henceforth forget about trying to secure Russian cooperation in the occupation of Germany. America would unilaterally strengthen its own zone. Russia, with good reason to fear a revitalized Germany, was understandably alarmed. Within a year and a half of the end of the European war, Germany, once the scourge of the Atlantic world, was

Legend:
- Areas annexed by USSR
- Areas once German, now controlled by Poland
- NATO Allies of U.S., 1955
- Allies of USSR, 1955
- Independent communist states, 1955
- Countries not allied with U.S. or USSR

REYKJAVIK • ICELAND

SWEDEN

FINLAND

NORWAY
OSLO •
HELSINKI •
STOCKHOLM •
LENINGRAD •

North Sea

Baltic

ESTONIA

RIGA •
LATVIA •

IRELAND

Sea

DENMARK

UNITED
KINGDOM
LONDON •

EAST
PRUSSIA
LITHUANIA

MOSCOW •

Atlantic
Ocean

NETHERLANDS

EAST

U.S.S.R.

BELGIUM
BONN •
BERLIN •
WARSAW •

PARIS •
GERMANY

POLAND

LUXEMBOURG

WEST
GERMANY

FRANCE
SWITZERLAND
CZECHOSLOVAKIA
VIENNA •
AUSTRIA

HUNGARY

PORTUGAL

ITALY
BELGRADE •
RUMANIA
ODESSA •

• MADRID

YUGOSLAVIA

SPAIN

ROME •

Adriatic Sea

BULGARIA

ALBANIA

ISTANBUL
ANKARA •

Mediterranean Sea

GREECE
ATHENS •

TURKEY

CRETE

CYPRUS

Division of Europe, 1945–1955

becoming the front line of Western defense, while Russia, one of the Big Three, became the enemy.

In the same month Truman blundered into an impasse that resulted in the firing of Secretary of Commerce Henry Wallace. While Byrnes was negotiating with the Soviets in Paris, Wallace gave a speech that said the Russians were trying to "socialize their sphere of interest just as we try to democratize our sphere of interest. . . . Only mutual trust would allow the United States and Russia to live together peacefully, and such trust could not be created by an unfriendly attitude and policy." Truman had looked at the speech beforehand, but too perfunctorily to realize how sharply it contradicted his own anti-Soviet position. Senator Arthur Vandenberg, with Byrnes in Paris, cabled "we Republicans can cooperate with only one secretary of state at a time." Having maneuvered himself clumsily into a corner, Truman thereupon fired Wallace. In so doing he cut an important tie with left-wing American opinion on foreign policy.

Truman proved especially unbudging on the crucial question of atomic energy. Moderates such as former Secretary of War Stimson had been arguing that Russia would soon be able to develop the bomb on its own and that America ought to earn Soviet good will by sharing scientific secrets. Having done so, the United States and the Soviet Union could develop plans for international supervision and inspection. "The chief lesson I have learned in a long life," Stimson said, "is the only way you can make a man trustworthy is to trust him; and the surest way you can make a man untrustworthy is to distrust him and to show your distrust."

Even during the war, however, America had withheld atomic secrets not only from Russia but from England—in part to secure industrial advantages in the postwar world. Truman, who reflected this attitude, ignored Stimson and listened instead to anticommunist advisers like financier Bernard Baruch and future Secretary of State Dean Acheson. They called for international inspection and for the gradual sharing of scientific information (which could not be kept secret anyway). But they opposed letting the Soviet Union in on American technical expertise. Russia, in short, was to be subjected to prying into her military installations while the United States retained a monopoly of bomb manufacture. Stalin, demanding that America begin by destroying its stockpile, rejected the American proposal, and by the end of 1946 chances for international control of atomic weapons had disappeared.

A series of crises in the next year and a half intensified the Cold War. Indigenous communist guerillas in Greece threatened British influence in the eastern Mediterranean, and communist parties capitalizing on severe economic discontent seemed about to gain office in France and Italy. Seizing the opportunity to toughen American policy, Truman called in March 1947 for $400 million in military aid to Greece and Turkey. This Truman Doctrine stated that "it must be the policy of the United States to support free peoples who are resisting subjugation by armed minorities or by outside pressures. . . . we must assist free peoples to work out their own destinies in their own way." He then defended the breathtaking scope of this doctrine by doing what Vandenberg recommended—"scaring hell out of the country." In May the same Republican Congress that was blocking Truman's domestic program granted his request.

A month later George Marshall, who had replaced Byrnes as secretary of state in January, called for massive aid to Europe. Seeking to deflect criticisms that America focused on providing military aid to shore up nations against communism, Marshall explained that his aid program was "directed not against any country or doctrine but against hunger, poverty, desperation, and chaos." But the President admitted that the Truman Doctrine and the Marshall Plan (both of which bypassed the United Nations) were "two halves of the same walnut." Marshall himself observed that American economic aid was aimed at permitting the "emergence of political and social conditions in which free institutions can exist." He also made European cooperation (and sharing of information about resources) a condition of getting aid—a requirement that inevitably discouraged Russian and eastern European participation in the plan. And Kennan, whose memorandums had influenced Marshall's thinking, published an article in July (written in January) that urged America to embark on "long-term, patient but firm and vigilant containment of Russia." The Marshall Plan, like the Truman Doctrine, embraced this doctrine of containment.

Congress moved slowly in considering Marshall's request, but the Soviets played into the administration's hands by controlling Czechoslovakia in early 1948. In June they reacted to Western plans to create a more autonomous Federal Republic of Germany by blockading West Berlin. Truman responded with an airlift to relieve West Berlin. Congress then acquiesced by approving a peacetime draft—which lasted until 1973—and by passing the first of many authorizations for foreign aid.

These grants, so sharp a contrast to America's stinginess after World War I, helped restore European economic health. They showed how far the Cold War had dragged the country from isolation. But they were not altruistic. On the contrary,

American enterprise abroad, 1925–55

	FOREIGN TRADE (In millions of current dollars)					INTERNATIONAL INVESTMENTS (In billions of current dollars)		
	EXPORT		IMPORT					NET INVESTMENT
	AMOUNT	% OF GNP	AMOUNT	% OF GNP	BALANCE (+ OR −)	U.S. INVESTMENTS ABROAD	FOREIGN INVESTMENTS IN U.S.	POSITION (+ OR −)
1925	5,272	5.4	4,419	4.6	+ 852	10.9[a]	3.9[a]	+ 7.0
1930	4,013	4.2	3,500	3.4	+ 514	17.2	8.4	+ 8.8
1935	2,304	3.1	4,143	5.7[b]	− 1,839	13.5	6.4	+ 7.1
1940	4,030	4.0	7,433	7.4[b]	− 3,403	12.3	13.5	− 1.2
1945	10,097	4.9	4,280	1.9	+ 5,816	16.8	17.6	− 0.8
1950	10,816	3.6	9,125	3.1	+ 1,691	32.8	19.5	+ 13.3
1955	15,563	3.9	11,562	2.9	+ 4,001	44.9	29.6	+ 15.3

SOURCE: Adapted from *Historical Statistics of the United States*, pp. 537, 542, 564
[a]Data for 1924   [b]Percentages recomputed from Census data

recipients of aid (which totaled some $100 billion in the next quarter century) were required to buy American goods in return. For Truman and his successors, preserving "free" institutions meant assisting American "free" enterprise. It also meant circling the Soviet Union with military force to ensure that such "freedoms" would thrive.

THE SOURCES OF AMERICAN ANTICOMMUNISM

To a degree, Russian-American rivalry was inevitable. As Alexis de Tocqueville had pointed out more than a century earlier, Russia and the United States were becoming the "two great nations in the world. . . . each seems marked out by the will of heaven to sway the destinies of half the globe." By 1945, with power vacuums in Europe and Asia, Tocqueville's prophecy came true, for the two superpowers found themselves head-to-head for the first time in history. Conflict between such different societies was to be expected.

As Wallace pointed out at the time, however, America's attitude toward the Soviet Union after 1945 was unusually truculent, especially in contrast to its patience with Hitler from 1933 to 1940. Though dictatorial, suspicious, often ruthless, Stalin was not bent on world conquest, or even (as French and Italian communists discovered to their dismay) on controlling western Europe. Despite Truman's assertions, the USSR did little to assist the Greek communists. Rather, Stalin seems—Soviet secrecy makes his ambitions unclear—to have sought traditional Russian goals: expanded influence in Iran to the south, in Manchuria to the east, in Turkey in the southwest. Above all, he hoped to preserve Russian power in eastern Europe as protection against a rearmed Germany. In this sense Wallace was probably correct in stating that Russia wished to protect and communize its sphere of influence in much the same way that the United States wished to expand its interest in Latin America and western Europe.

Why then did America act with such a show of energy and determination against the Soviet Union? The answer lay not only in Russian behavior, but also in domestic tensions and pressures within the United States.

Some of these stemmed from America's historical experience as the world's leading democratic nation. Until 1917, when Lenin led the Bolshevik revolution, Americans had confidently cherished their experience; it was their "manifest destiny" to serve as an example to the world. However, the rise of communism in Russia was a frightening specter—so much so that America refused even to recognize the new regime until 1933. Like fascism, communism threatened democratic government and individual freedom. It also struck at private property. It possessed a prophetic strain in its ideology—worldwide proletarian revolution—which lent credence to the American notion that communism and aggression were much the same. Americans, once so sure of their revolutionary appeal, now felt insecure and defensive, for they had to contend not only with Russian power but with a rival ideology of enormous appeal. Insecure nations, as both Russia and the United States revealed, often act impatiently and provocatively.

Americans especially feared communism's threat to capitalism. Already, it had cut off the markets (such as they were) of eastern Europe. What would happen if it crept into Asia, Latin America, or—as seemed possible in 1947—into Greece and western Europe? The answer, Truman's advisers thought, was that America's exports would suffer. A communistic world would therefore undermine America's dearly loved standard of living. This is not to say that economic motives dominated Truman's policies. They did not. But it was true that Truman, his advisers, corporate leaders, labor unions, and Americans generally sought the widest possible "Open Door" for American enterprise abroad. After all, capitalism and democratic government had expanded almost as one; the decline of one might mean the ultimate collapse of the other.

The presumed threat from Russia also aroused what Kennan later called the "American urge to the universalization or generalization of decision." By this he meant that the United States had frequently talked in sweeping, moralistic terms. Cherished principles—of constitutional government, individual liberty, and capitalistic free enterprise—were universally good. It followed that the United States must spread the blessings of capitalism and democracy around the world. This "globalism" was at the root of Truman's doctrine supporting all "free peoples." By late 1948 it virtually silenced people who sought a more limited response to international problems.

As in the past, the "lessons" of history affected policy. In the 1930s, Truman now thought, appeasement had encouraged aggressors to provoke a war. There must be no more "Munichs." Moreover, World War II had disposed people to think in all-or-nothing terms. Coexistence, to use a term the hard-liners hated, had been impossible with Hitler; Stalin, too, had to be battled at every turn. Some Americans even demanded a "preventive war" with the Soviet Union. Though responsible leaders never endorsed such a plan, their rhetoric grew almost as apocalyptic by the mid-1950s.

Domestic politics in America added to these pressures for firmness. Many of the most outraged anticommunists, including Polish-Americans, were Democrats whom Truman had to satisfy. So were many Catholics, who loathed the atheistic anticlericalism of Bolshevism. Moreover, isolationism virtually vanished, a casualty of war. Republicans like Vandenberg wondered if America could be isolated in the age of air power. Others feared to sound like appeasers. And conservative Republicans were quick to oppose left-wing ideologies whether at home or abroad. The defection of such groups from the isolationist cause meant that Truman, unlike Roosevelt in the 1930s, was safer politically when he struck back at the Soviet Union than he was when he turned the other cheek.

But Truman was no simple prisoner of public opinion. On the contrary, he had displayed his feelings toward Stalin as early as July 1941, when he said, "if we see that Germany is winning we ought to help Russia, and if Russia is winning we ought to help Germany." In office only a few weeks in 1945, he took such a firm line that Foreign Minister Molotov complained that he had never been spoken to so harshly in all his life. "Carry out your agreements," Truman snapped undiplomatically, "and you won't get talked to like that." Once America became the sole possessor of the A-bomb, he felt safer than ever in adopting an unbending line. Thereafter Truman made little effort to carry on Roosevelt's earlier policy of cooperating with the Russians.

These preconceived notions helped Truman to talk tough without qualms. They made him unreceptive to Soviet requests for economic aid. They enabled him to talk of "saving" eastern Europe, an area traditionally outside America's national interest. They induced him to overlook the fact that the bomb, which was of limited value except to blast Soviet cities, was not a credible deterrent in case of military clashes in western Europe. As the historian John Gaddis put it, the bomb represented the Impotence of Omnipotence. Truman's anticommunism also led him deliberately to exaggerate the Soviet threat. This was the approach that he used in 1947 in getting Congress to approve the Truman Doctrine. Far from trying to change the contours of public opinion, Truman exploited the prevailing anticommunist fears of most Americans. In so doing he helped escalate the Cold War.

Truman could have employed subtler ways of serving his ends. Indeed, the containment policy of the world's only nuclear power made Stalin even more suspicious than he already was. If Truman had really hoped to defuse the Cold War (and after 1946 there is no evidence that he did), he might have spent less time in futile talk about getting the Russians out of eastern Europe. He might have recognized the foolishness of trying to keep knowledge of atomic energy from Russian scientists. He might have conceded the truth of the argument that the Truman Doctrine shored up undemocratic regimes in Greece and Turkey.

Truman's failure to follow potential avenues to détente attracted relatively little notice at the time. Instead, he and his fellow warriors struck most Americans as patriots combating a worldwide communist conspiracy that was as "immoral" as that of fascism a few years before. Blunt, moralistic, and anticommunist, Truman probably reflected the sentiments of most of his countrymen. As the election campaign approached, his determined foreign policy was an asset, not a liability.

Truman's second term

TRUMAN IN 1948

In early 1948 many liberal Democrats rebelled at the thought of renominating Truman for the presidency. Franklin D. Roosevelt, Jr., Hubert H. Humphrey, the young, progressive mayor of Minneapolis, and others backed General Eisenhower. The *New Republic* editorialized, "As a candidate for President Harry Truman should quit." "If Truman is nominated," the columnists Joseph and Stewart Alsop wrote, "he will be forced to wage the loneliest campaign in history."

After the conventions Truman's chances seemed little better. Though he secured the Democratic nomination (Eisenhower refused to be considered), a few left-wing leaders gave their support to Henry Wallace, who broke away to form the Progressive party. Their defection appeared likely to hurt Truman in key urban areas. And Republicans, rejecting Taft, named what appeared to be a strong ticket composed of the popular vote-getting governors Thomas Dewey of New York and Earl Warren of California. The derisive slogan "We're Just Mild About Harry" appeared an accurate description of Truman's appeal to voters.

Truman also had to contend with a party split over the ever more contentious issue of civil rights for blacks. By 1948, blacks were demanding a host of changes, including the end of job discrimination and of the Jim Crow laws segregating public accommodations. Led by lawyers like Thurgood Marshall (later the first black Supreme Court justice), they were then mounting legal challenges in the lower courts to school segregation and other forms of discrimination. Enlisting the aid of white liberals, they insisted on a strong Democratic civil rights platform in 1948. Party leaders were aware of the voting potential of blacks in key northern states and grudgingly acceded. Their action prompted many southern Democrats to bolt the convention. These formed their own States Rights Democratic (Dixiecrat) party and named Governor J. Strom Thurmond of South Carolina as their presidential candidate. The split over civil rights revealed the sharp divisions that rent the national Democratic party and exposed the growing groundswell for racial justice.

Until election day the public opinion polls showed Dewey with a strong lead. But it turned out they were wrong. The Dixiecrats failed to gain much support outside the Deep South. Indeed, their very presence in the campaign forced blacks and other civil rights advocates to recognize Truman's efforts, however limited, in their behalf. In November Thurmond won only four states, while Truman ran up large margins in black wards in the North.

Wallace's campaign disintegrated just as rapidly. Some observers, including many who backed his policies, found him vague and mystical. Others worried that he had become a tool of the communists and that many top Progressives were party members or fellow travelers. Labor leader Walter Reuther, a committed reformer, spoke for many anticommunist liberals in concluding that "Henry is a lost soul. . . . Communists perform the most complete valet service in the world. They

Election, 1948

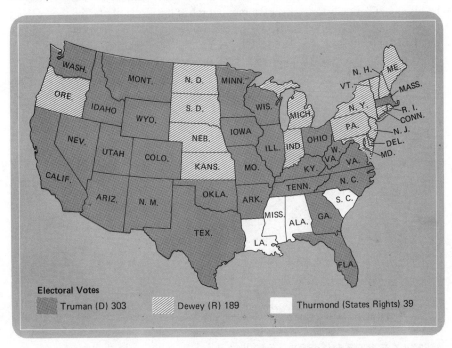

Electoral Votes

Truman (D) 303   Dewey (R) 189   Thurmond (States Rights) 39

write your speeches, they do your thinking for you, they provide you with applause, and they inflate your ego.'' Wallace's pro-Soviet line at the height of the Cold War ultimately left most liberals with no one to turn to save Truman.

Dewey, too, failed to excite the voters. A trim, dapper little man, he struck one critic as a ''certified public accountant in search of the Holy Grail.'' Others found him cold, curt, and aloof—it was said that ''you have to know him really well to dislike him.'' Certain of victory, Dewey ran a bland campaign aimed at offending the smallest possible number of people. In the process he was vague and unclear on the issues, and he ignited little grass-roots enthusiasm. Fewer Republicans came to the polls in 1948 than in either 1940 or 1944.

Finally, Truman himself proved a feisty, opportunistic campaigner. At the convention he electrified the faithful by calling the ''do-nothing'' Eightieth Congress back into special session to act on Fair Deal legislation. He kept up the offensive. Republicans, he charged, were ''just a bunch of old mossbacks . . . gluttons of privilege . . . all set to do a hatchet job on the New Deal.'' He then set off on a series of whistle-stop tours, always on the attack. This partisan strategy developed by his aide, Clark Clifford, was extreme, but it had the virtue of placing the GOP on the defensive. It exploited Democratic ties with labor and the ''have-not'' coalition that had four times elected Roosevelt.

For all these reasons Truman surprised almost everyone by winning in Novem-

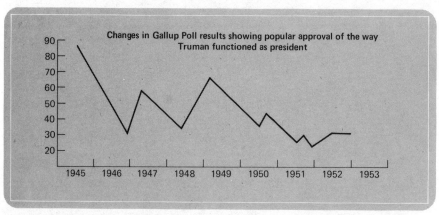

SOURCE: Adapted from p. 104 of *U.S. Foreign Policy: Context, Conduct, Content,* by Marian Irish and Elke Frank. © 1975 by Harcourt Brace Jovanovich, reproduced by permission of the publisher.

ber, with 24.1 million votes to Dewey's 22 million. Thurmond got less than 1.2 million, and Wallace only 1,157,000 and no electoral votes. The remarkably low turnout, more than a million less than in 1940, suggested that voters did not find either Truman or Dewey particularly attractive. Truman, in fact, failed to get 50 percent of the vote. But it also showed that the Democratic voting coalition forged during the depression remained intact and that the reforms of the New Deal were safe from attack. These were impressive reminders of the chronic weakness of the GOP and of the stability of American politics.

PROBLEMS, HOME AND ABROAD, 1949

President in his own right, Truman in January 1949 called on Congress to enact a broad-ranging program. It included health insurance, repeal of Taft-Hartley, extension of social security, increases in the minimum wage, civil rights legislation, federal aid to education, and larger appropriations for public housing. In foreign policy he broached the idea of supplying underdeveloped nations with technical assistance. Point Four, as it was called, suggested that the administration was beginning to worry about communism not only in western Europe but throughout the uncommitted world.

During the next two years Truman secured a few of these goals. Some of them, such as progress toward desegregation of the armed forces, came by executive order. Truman also strengthened the Civil Rights Division of the Department of Justice. Other reforms actually broke through the bottleneck on Capitol Hill. Congress passed a housing act including funds for public housing. It increased the minimum wage from forty cents to seventy-five cents, extended rent controls through 1950, and approved a displaced persons act admitting some 400,000 refugees to the United States. It raised social security benefits and broadened the program to cover 10 million new Americans. These were the most liberal measures passed by any Congress since 1935.

But the conservative coalition in Congress still held its own. This was a disparate group composed of most southern Democrats, representatives of many rural and small-town areas, and all but a handful of the Republicans. It was never monolithic, and it sometimes broke ranks. But it consistently fought Truman's requests for civil rights legislation, national health insurance, and federal aid to education. It proved slow in providing funds for Point Four. It showed itself willing to revise Taft-Hartley, but when Truman insisted on repeal, Congress balked, and the act remained as it was. After 1949 it proved very stingy in appropriating funds for the public housing program, which never even approached the expectations of reformers. It also rejected an administration proposal to reform the farm subsidy programs inaugurated by the New Deal.

In the area of foreign policy Truman secured a major goal when Congress approved American participation in the North Atlantic Treaty Organization, a mutual defense pact that bound twelve signatories to fight against aggression. It was the first time in American history that Congress had ratified a military alliance with European nations. Later in 1949 Congress added teeth to the pact by authorizing

Mao-Tse-tung with army commander General Chu-Teh on a tour of Peiping, the new Communist capital of China.

money for military aid to member nations. Because Stalin had no plans to attack western Europe, the NATO pact was of questionable military value. The military assistance plan, still more provocative, propelled America further into the business of supplying arms to other nations. At the time, however, both NATO and military aid were described as essential to sustain the morale of western Europe. They proved highly popular measures during the struggle to win the Cold War.

Events in Asia all but obscured Truman's policies in Europe. Since 1945, when American marines had helped Chiang Kai-shek strengthen his claims on North China, Truman had pursued Roosevelt's illusory hope for a peaceful, noncommunist China. But Chiang's corruption, and his failure to fight hard against the Japanese during the war, had already damaged his claim to rule, and Communist forces under Mao Tse-tung pressed forward. In 1946 Truman dispatched General George C. Marshall to China in an attempt to bring American influence to bear on the situation. Marshall, like other emissaries before him, sought to reconcile Chiang and Mao. When the two sides agreed to a truce, it seemed that his patient efforts had succeeded. But by late 1946 the truce had broken down. Mao's forces pushed on, and Marshall returned home to become secretary of state.

Truman then requested a report from General Albert Wedemeyer, America's chief military emissary in China. Wedemeyer's advice, to escalate aid to Chiang and to send 10,000 American military "advisers" to China, received a cool reception from Marshall and others in the State Department, and Truman not only rejected Wedemeyer's report but kept it from Congress. Within a year and a half, in 1949, Chiang's forces collapsed, and in December he fled to Formosa. China, land of more than 500 million people, was now a communist country.

Truman responded calmly to the "fall of China." His secretary of state after 1948, the tough, aristocratic Dean Acheson, spoke for the administration in defending America's policy since 1945. Sending in "advisers," he pointed out, would lead only to unnecessary loss of American life. Defeating Mao would require a major land war on the Asian continent, a war that the United States had neither the men nor the will to fight, especially at a time when Stalin seemed to pose a threat in Europe. Chiang's own maladministration, not American neglect, had led to the communist victory. "Nothing this country did or could have done within the reasonable limits of its capabilities," Acheson argued, "would have changed the result, nothing that was left undone by this country has contributed to it."

The Truman-Acheson argument was irrefutable. Few Americans before 1949 had demanded any sizable commitment to Chiang, and the administration, which was focusing its attention in Europe, would have had serious trouble trying to mobilize support for massive aid in China as well. Moreover, almost no one at the time expected economic or military aid to do much good. Even Wedemeyer had conceded that Chiang was losing because of corruption and "lack of spirit, primarily lack of spirit. It was not lack of equipment. In my judgment they could have defended the Yangtze if they had had the will to do it." In opting for limited aid to Chiang between 1945 and 1949 the Truman administration followed Roosevelt in backing the wrong horse. But it had sense enough not to waste more money than it did (perhaps $2 billion by 1949), and to keep American men out of what would have been an endless blood-bath.

The fall of so much territory to communism was not easy for Americans to accept. The United States, the history books said, had never lost a war. It had beaten both the Germans and the Japanese. It had sole possession of the bomb. Why then had it "lost" China? Why had it not acted to preserve the Open Door policy? Sensible observers replied that China was an ancient civilization that had never been America's to lose. They explained that the Open Door doctrine did not apply, for Mao had triumphed on his own, with little aid indeed from Stalin. But many people refused to listen to reason. Deluded by the illusion of American omnipotence, they continued to ask where and how Truman had gone wrong.

Some of Truman's critics concluded that he had merely made mistakes. Others were "Asia-firsters" or members of the so-called China lobby. Many of these people, especially partisan Republicans, grew nasty. Truman, they charged, had been duped by procommunist sympathizers in the State Department. Moreover, the Russians exploded their own atomic bomb in September 1949: perhaps procommunist scientists working for America had turned over secrets to Stalin? By 1950, Truman had to confront a resurgence of popular fears about the spread of communism.

McCARTHYISM

Senator Joseph McCarthy of Wisconsin, the demagogue who capitalized on these fears, began his Red-hunting campaign in February 1950 by claiming in a speech in Wheeling to hold in his hand the names of 207 (or 57—accounts differ) communists in government. Though few people paid him much notice at first, he repeated, expanded, and varied his charges in succeeding speeches, and by March he was front-page news across the country. At last, it seemed to Truman's critics, a responsible person had evidence not only of procommunist sympathy in high places but of disloyalty and treason.

Before McCarthy and fellow Red-haters overreached themselves in late 1954 they broadened their cause into a powerful witch hunt that swept into every corner of American life. McCarthyism destroyed morale in the State Department, cowed the Department of the Army, and exposed America's hysterical anticommunism to the scorn of civilized people throughout the world.

McCarthyism reached deeply into the fabric of American government. The Supreme Court in 1951 upheld the Smith Act of 1940, which had made it a crime even to advocate revolution. Its decision, in *Dennis* v. *U. S.*, resulted in the conviction and imprisonment of eleven top Communists and encouraged the Justice Department to proceed with further prosecutions. Ordinarily decent conservatives, such as Taft, also jumped on the anti-Red bandwagon as a means of courting votes and of avenging the bitterly disappointing defeat in the election of 1948. McCarthy, he said, was a "fighting Marine who risked his life to preserve the liberties of the United States." If accusations proved unfounded, Taft advised, McCarthy should keep trying. Liberal politicians joined conservatives to approve the Internal Security Act of 1950. It required Communists to register with the Attorney General, and it set up the Subversives Activities Board to review the loyalty of government employees. In vetoing it Truman correctly contended that the act was obscure, unfair, and unworkable. But 1950 was an election year, and practically no one dared to oppose the anticommunist onslaught. Congress quickly passed the act over Truman's veto.

Heartened by such responses, the Red-baiters became almost unbelievably extreme in 1951–52. McCarthy charged that the Democratic party was "the property of men and women . . . who have bent to the whispered pleas from the lips of traitors . . . who wear the political label stitched with the idiocy of a Truman, [and] rotted by the deceit of a Dean Acheson." Marshall, he added, was "a man steeped in falsehood . . . who has resorted to the lie whenever it suits his convenience . . . [and who was part of a] conspiracy so immense and an infamy so black as to dwarf any previous venture in the history of man." Not to be outdone, Senator William Jenner of Indiana concluded that America was "in the hands of a secret inner coterie which is directed by agents of the Soviet Union. . . . Our only choice is to impeach President Truman and find out who is the secret inner government."

These statements were wholly undocumented. The Red-baiters produced no evidence to support their accusations, and they never exposed a communist in

> *What the phenomenon of McCarthyism did . . . was to implant in my consciousness a lasting doubt as to the adequacy of our political system. . . . A political system and a public opinion, it seemed to me, that could be so easily disoriented by this sort of challenge in one epoch would be no less vulnerable to similar ones in another. I could never recapture, after these experiences of the late 1940s and early 1950s, quite the same faith in the American system of government and in traditional American outlooks that I had had, despite all the discouragements of official life, before that time.*

One veteran diplomat (George Kennan) recalls the devastating impact of McCarthyism on American life.

government. Indeed, McCarthy himself made little effort to follow up his scattershot accusations. On the contrary, he remained a profane, often unshaven, half-drunk individualist whose crusade against communism was aimed at securing the recognition he would need for his reelection campaign in 1952, and for higher political ambitions to follow. "That's it," he told friends who suggested anticommunism as an issue. "The government is full of communists. We can hammer away at them."

McCarthy's charges were as unnecessary as they were irresponsible, for Communists in America were weaker in 1950 than at any time since the 1920s. Anticommunist labor leaders had deprived them of positions of strength that they had enjoyed in the CIO. The government, especially after Truman created loyalty boards in 1947, had launched systematic (and often unconstitutional) security checks on federal employees. Russian moves such as the coup in Czechoslovakia and the blockade of West Berlin had driven all but the avid Stalinists out of the party. By the time McCarthy started his crusade, the Communist party had already fallen into the decline that cut its membership from a high of around 80,000 in 1945 to less than 3,000 in the late 1950s. Perhaps one-half of these were FBI agents.

Because McCarthy himself was so crude and reckless, and because communism at home was dwindling, it was hard for contemporary defenders of civil liberties to explain his appeal. In retrospect, however, it is clear that several forces combined to make him the dangerous demagogue that he was.

Among these was McCarthy himself. His very irresponsibility made him a frightening foe, for he thought nothing of charging his critics with communist sympathies. Politicians, therefore, were careful not to antagonize him. McCarthy was also a master at using the press, which treated his sensational charges as page-one news. Shrewdly, he called press conferences early in the morning to tell reporters that earth-shaking disclosures were soon to be announced. Alerted, the afternoon papers printed banner headlines, "McCarthy New Revelations Expected Soon." Newsmen for morning papers then besieged him for the latest developments, and McCarthy obliged by leading them to believe a key witness was about to be found. Hence the morning headlines, "Delay in McCarthy Revelations: Mystery Witness Sought." Tactics such as these brought McCarthy maximum publicity.

McCarthy was also fortunate in his timing. Before he seized on the communist issue to advance his political fortunes, other Red-baiters, notably the reckless House Un-American Activities Committee (HUAC), had set the stage for a crusade against alleged domestic subversion. In this way, McCarthy was an opportunistic Johnny-come-lately to the Red scare of the late 1940s. Just as he inaugurated his campaign, Alger Hiss, a former State Department official accused of espionage, was convicted of perjury—after two widely publicized trials. His conviction, which followed on a congressional investigation spearheaded by Representative Richard Nixon of California, appeared to prove that communists infested the government. McCarthy was further helped by the revelation that Klaus Fuchs, a British physicist, had passed American atomic secrets to the Soviets. Legal proceedings stemming from the Fuchs case culminated three years later in the conviction and execution for espionage of Julius and Ethel Rosenberg, American communists allegedly involved in the atomic plot. Actually, these cases did not prove much. If Hiss was a communist agent—which he steadfastly denied—he appears to have given the Russians nothing of value. Fuchs helped the Russians along on research that they were mastering on their own. The Rosenbergs, whose guilt was still being hotly debated many years later, were in no way associated with the government. Still, the Fuchs case was proof of the need for security. McCarthy, many Americans told themselves, might be a little rough in his methods, but his goals were noble. If permitted to continue, he would uncover the "traitors" in government.

Powerful interest groups further assisted McCarthy's campaigns. Among these were defense contractors and the military forces that had suffered from demobilization. Not all these groups thought well of McCarthy's methods—indeed, he later infuriated the army brass by accusing it of harboring communists. But until then his virulent campaign obviously assisted their demands for defense spending. With such potent forces supporting McCarthy's goals, or at least acquiescing in them, he had advantages lesser demagogues would have lacked.

McCarthyism also seemed to offer simple answers to the complex questions of the Cold War. China went communist, he explained, because State Department "traitors" willed it so. Russia developed the A-bomb because people like Fuchs told them how to do it. Because McCarthy's road to salvation seemed so quick and easy, it exercised an appeal that more complex, more accurate explanations failed to provide.

This conspiracy theory appealed in particular to superpatriotic Americans who responded warmly to McCarthy's attacks on intellectuals, left-wing sympathizers, New Dealers, and well-educated, upper-class easterners like Acheson. "I watch his smart-aleck manner and his British clothes and that New Dealism," Senator Hugh Butler of Nebraska exclaimed of Acheson, ". . .and I want to shout, Get out. Get out. You stand for everything that has been wrong with the United States for years." Butler, a Republican, had partisan reasons for welcoming assaults on the "striped-pants boys" in the State Department. But like many Americans he suspected the worst of the Eastern Establishment. In this way McCarthy had the best of two worlds: by hammering at communism he could appeal to conservatives, and by slashing at intellectuals and the Eastern Establishment he could win the approval of ordinary people.

Others who reacted positively to McCarthy included many ethnic Americans, especially blue-collar Catholics. By 1950 most of these people were second- or third-generation Americans. Many had fought in World War II. But as ethnics and Catholics they frequently suffered discrimination, and they were rarely accepted as "100 percent Americans." McCarthy, himself a Catholic, seemed one of them. By supporting his movement, ethnics could prove their patriotism, indeed their super-patriotism. Catholics could demonstrate their support of a movement directed against atheistic communism. For these reasons McCarthyism was strong in many heavily Catholic urban areas and in Catholic states like Massachusetts, where some politicians shared his concerns. "McCarthy," said John F. Kennedy, "may have something."

Not all political figures acted like Kennedy. Some, especially those who represented rural, Protestant states, felt freer to speak out in defense of civil liberties. But most office holders, including many liberals, were almost as anticommunist as McCarthy himself. They might deplore his methods, but they were committed to a hard-line Cold War policy. This is not to suggest, as some historians have, that Truman's exaggerations about Soviet designs made McCarthyism inevitable. But it is to say that the Cold War waged by the administration after 1945 helped develop the atmosphere of fear in which McCarthy thrived. To this extent McCarthyism was a broad-based (though unorganized) phenomenon, urban-ethnic as well as rural, and promoted by the rhetoric of liberal as well as conservative politicians.

In this sense McCarthyism was but the latest of many eruptions of intolerance in American history. Federalists had tried to silence their "radical" Jeffersonian foes by introducing the Alien and Sedition acts of 1798. Know-Nothings, nativist politicians of the 1850s, had developed considerable support in their campaign against Catholics and foreigners. Waves of prejudice against aliens had swept the country in tense periods since the 1870s. The Red scare of 1919, the sharpest explosion of all, had broken out against foreigners as well as leftists. By the early 1950s the "hyphenated-Americans" no longer seemed much of a threat. But the communists did. In such turbulent times, it was easy to make them a scapegoat for the nation's problems.

McCarthyism was above all the product of partisan politics at midcentury. For years American politicians had courted favor by preaching against the evils of communism. Some, such as Nixon, had built political careers by doing it. Like McCarthy, these people wanted desperately to run the Democrats out of the White House, and anticommunism, by 1950, seemed the most effective issue to employ to that end. Thus it was that when McCarthy ran again in 1952 he scored best in areas that had traditionally been Republican. This connection between McCarthyism and Republicanism was important in giving purpose and direction to the anticommunist crusade.

To counter such implacable opposition, Truman might have been well advised to take it seriously. This would have involved giving a bipartisan congressional committee access to classified executive documents concerning alleged security risks. Without publicizing information about individuals, the committee might have established the facts concerning McCarthy's charges. Deprived of the claim that Truman was hiding pertinent data, McCarthy would have had to quiet down, or to watch his accusations be torn to shreds.

Truman, however, hardly considered such a strategy. McCarthy, of course, would have insisted on being named to such a committee. If Democrats in Congress had refused to grant his demand, McCarthy would have shouted that he had been excluded. If they had agreed to it, they chanced having McCarthy give classified (and probably misleading) evidence to the press. Either way, the administration—to say nothing of the alleged security risks—might suffer.

Accordingly, Truman resorted to the doctrine of executive privilege: McCarthy would get no documents from him. He stepped up his campaign to rid the government of alleged security risks. Henceforth employees had to furnish proof, beyond a "reasonable doubt," of their loyalty. He encouraged Democrats in Congress to pursue their own counterinvestigation of McCarthy's charges. But these approaches merely suggested that Truman had something to hide. And in November 1950, Senator Millard Tydings of Maryland, the conservative Democrat who had chaired the investigation, went down in defeat before a Red-baiter who came close to outdoing McCarthy himself. Thereafter few Democrats wanted to sling stones at the Goliath of American politics. From February 1950 until the end of his tenure in the White House, President Truman had to endure his Wisconsin tormenter.

THE TRAVAIL OF KOREA

On June 25, 1950, communist forces from North Korea poured across the thirty-eighth parallel and attacked the pro-Western government of South Korea. Acting quickly, Truman authorized American forces under General Douglas MacArthur to go to South Korea's aid. At first it seemed as if MacArthur's troops might be destroyed. But the Americans and South Koreans held on until September, when MacArthur engineered a brilliant amphibious counterattack north of the enemy's lines. His forces then drove across the thirty-eighth parallel and smashed northward until they came within reach of the North Korean border with China.

If MacArthur's counteroffensive had stopped near the parallel, or if it had moved less precipitously toward China, the war might have ended there and then, a glorious triumph for Truman and for the anticommunist cause. As it was, the Chinese threw masses of men into battle, and American soldiers fell back into South Korea. General Matthew Ridgway, who replaced MacArthur in April 1951, restored order, but the conflict dragged on until a truce was arranged in July 1953. It divided the country along lines similar to those in force before the 1950 invasion

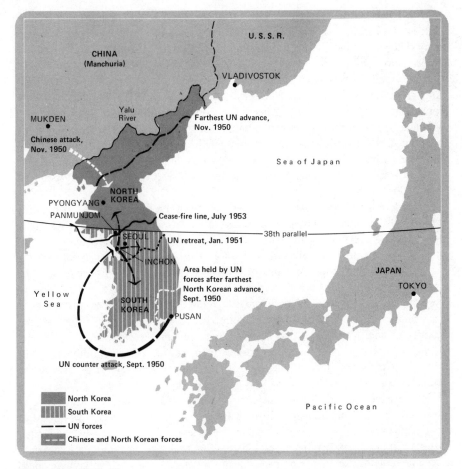

Korean War, 1950–53

and sustained in power Syngman Rhee, the anticommunist ruler of South Korea. For the West, therefore, the war had succeeded in preventing communist gains; Truman's intervention had not been wasted. It also resulted in a huge escalation of defense spending from approximately $14 billion in 1949 to $44 billion in 1953. This figure, some 60 percent of the federal budget, sparked a boom in the economy lasting until 1954. But the conflict left 54,000 Americans dead and 103,000 wounded. It wholly diverted attention—and funds—from domestic reforms. It greatly strengthened the role of the military and of defense contractors in American society. And because Truman refused to escalate the war still faster, he played readily into the hands of McCarthyites, who demanded total victory. The war applied the *coup de grace* to the administration's standing with the electorate.

Such a protracted war naturally prompted sharp debate over the wisdom of Truman's actions. Some critics complained that American policies had helped provoke the war in the first place. Others questioned his decisions to involve the United States in the fighting and then to press on over the thirty-eighth parallel. Many others denounced him for refusing to broaden the war once the Chinese had jumped into it.

The complaint that America helped to provoke the war was favored by right-wing critics at the time. Truman, they argued, had practically invited a North Korean invasion by removing American occupation troops from South Korea in 1949 and by leaving Rhee's government almost defenseless against the well-drilled forces of the North. Dean Acheson, they emphasized, had outlined an American "defense perimeter" in Asia that appeared to exclude Korea. With such a "soft spot" exposed, the communists, supplied by the Soviet Union, naturally pounced on it in June 1950.

Later left-wing critics, revisionists who renewed the debate over Korean policy in the 1960s, challenged Truman's policies from a different perspective. Rhee, they argued, was a dictatorial nationalist who had regularly vowed his intention to reunite Korea, by force of arms if necessary. His very presence antagonized the North. When he lost support in the May 1950 elections, revisionists suggested, he determined to provoke border incidents to reestablish his image and perhaps to force the United States to defend his regime. Other revisionists went still further in chastising the Truman administration. Pointing to a position paper of the National Security Council (NSC-68), they showed that Truman's leading defense planners had agreed early in 1950 to seek enormous increases in American military might. How better to get the money out of Congress than by tempting or provoking the North Koreans to attack?

Because the relevant documents are unavailable to historians, it is impossible to know why North Korea attacked in June 1950. It is therefore hazardous at best to evaluate the critiques of Truman. But some facts seem clear. Obviously, the United States was unwise in leaving Rhee's forces so weak and in implying that South Korea lay outside America's primary lines of defense. Conceivably, Truman could have assisted moderate factions to take over in South Korea. Such a policy—military preparedness allied to political and diplomatic moderation—might have preserved peace on the peninsula.

Still, Truman and Acheson had sound reasons for their prewar policies. The President's military advisers, including General MacArthur, had regularly called for the removal of American troops from South Korea, a place they considered costly to defend and of little strategic value. The military also needed all the strength it could find to bolster NATO. Moreover, arming Rhee properly seemed impossible—Congress would not have supplied the funds—and unwise, for Rhee might then have staged his own attack on the North. And though Truman might have worked to dispose of Rhee, whose power was slipping in early 1950, North Korea acted first. For better or worse, America and Syngman Rhee were thrust together against a common foe.

The revisionist case distorts two other essential points. First, for whatever reasons, it was not South Korea but North Korea that mounted the attack, which was too well planned and coordinated to pass as a mere border incident. Second, though many American military leaders wanted to increase defense spending, there is no evidence to suggest that they yearned for a war in Korea, which they continued to dismiss as of little importance. Indeed, such a war would drain Western defenses in Europe, which was Washington's major concern. The Korean War was a conflict that few people in America had expected and that fewer still were very happy to be involved in.

Truman's decision to resist the North Korean invasion prompted other criticisms. If Korea was hard to protect and of little military value, why bother to defend it? Key senators like Taft demanded to know why Truman did not consult Congress or ask for a formal declaration of war. Instead, Truman merely secured United Nations sanction (possible because the Soviets were boycotting the Security Council at the time) for common "police action" against the aggressor. Later, when the war deteriorated into an apparently endless stalemate, Truman's failure to consult Congress cost him dearly. Still later it offered an excuse for Presidents Kennedy and Johnson to send American troops to Vietnam without congressional sanction.

Truman easily brushed aside such complaints. The North Korean invasion, he declared, was part of a communist design to test America's will in the Cold War. The United States must fight to show that it would hold the line, that it would not repeat the disastrous appeasement policy of the 1930s. There must be no more Munichs. He added that he had to act quickly. If America waited for Congress to debate the issue, the North Koreans would overrun the peninsula.

Truman's arguments were a little self-serving, for no one could prove that either China or the Soviet Union had masterminded the invasion. And while it was true that Truman had to act quickly, he could still have requested congressional approval at any time in the early weeks of the war. But the speed of the invasion made his arguments so hard to refute that even critics like Taft grudgingly supported American intervention. In responding as he did Truman acted decisively, even courageously. Years later it is possible to fault his disregard of Congress, but harder to question the wisdom of the basic decision itself.

Truman's most controversial decision was authorizing MacArthur to push on toward the Yalu River, North Korea's northern border with China. His action seemed sensible at the time, for MacArthur had the enemy on the run. It also reflected the almost unanimous counsel of his top military and diplomatic advisers and of Allied leaders. The Chinese, Truman was reassured, were too tired to get involved in Korea. Moreover, Asian peoples were no match for America's technological superiority. "We are no longer fearful of their [Chinese] intervention," MacArthur told Truman at a special meeting on Wake Island in October. "The Chinese have 300,000 men in Manchuria. . . . Only 50,000 to 60,000 could be gotten across the Yalu River. They have no air force. Now that we have bases for our air force in Korea, if the Chinese tried to get down to Pyongyang [the North Korean capital near the thirty-eighth parallel] there would be the greatest slaughter."

The astonishingly successful intervention of the Chinese in November 1950, of course, quickly proved the tragic foolishness of such advice. Truman's advisers, including not only MacArthur but also the Central Intelligence Agency, deserved criticism for predicting that the Chinese would stay out. But Truman himself might have paused before accepting such counsel, for the Chinese had implied through diplomatic channels that they would attack UN forces that pushed north of the thirty-eighth parallel. In ignoring such a possibility Truman and his advisers displayed exaggerated faith in Western technology and contempt for Oriental military potential. As George Kennan pointed out at the time, Truman and his aides were also bemused by the insidious belief, another product of the modern age, that total victory is the purpose of war. In urging MacArthur to drive toward the Yalu, Truman went rashly beyond containment to seek what later became known as a policy of liberation.

The conflict with China accelerated the war's most dramatic clash of wills—between Truman and MacArthur. As the Chinese advanced, the general became progressively more restive and querulous. Truman, he complained, should escalate the war. The administration must blockade mainland China, "unleash" Chiang Kai-shek for raids in Korea or South China, and authorize air-sea attacks on Chinese "sanctuaries" in Manchuria. Without such steps, MacArthur insisted, America could never win the war.

Truman, however, shrank from embarking on such a course. He recognized that any attempt to blockade China's long coastline would tie up a substantial part of America's navy, which was needed elsewhere. A blockade might also lead to confrontation with other nations, including Russia. In any event, a blockade could do nothing to stop the flow of supplies that came overland from the Soviet Union.

With similar prudence, Truman rejected the idea of helping Chiang raid China. Contrary to MacArthur's assumption, such attacks would not have prompted native uprisings against the communist regime—Chiang remained too unpopular. Rather, Nationalist incursions, to be at all effective, would have required an enormous American commitment. The United States might have become involved in a renewal of the Chinese civil war, an eventuality that MacArthur himself shied away from.

Truman was equally wise to refrain from bombing Chinese "sanctuaries." Strategic bombing during World War II had suggested that such attacks rarely worked wonders. In Korea they would have done nothing to stop China's major asset, masses of foot soldiers who needed only the most meager rations to keep pressing toward the south. Employing bombers would also have frightened America's Western allies, who needed no reminding that Russian territory touched the Yalu. As General Omar Bradley, the army chief of staff, put it, they would have involved the nation in "the wrong war, at the wrong place, at the wrong time, and with the wrong enemy."

MacArthur, however, was an imperious egotist who could barely conceal his contempt for the likes of people such as Truman. Having served in the Pacific for much of his life, he failed to comprehend the administration's primary concern for Europe. He had equally little understanding of the sensitivities of the Western allies, whom he considered unreliable. He was a passionate globalist who believed that the United States, all by itself, should protect the world against the tide of Marxism. "I believe we should defend every place from communism," he declared. "I believe we are able to. . . . I don't admit that we can't hold communism wherever it shows its head." For all these reasons he was among the most sincere of the Asia-firsters. "It seems strangely difficult for some to realize," he wrote House Minority Leader Martin in April 1951, "that here in Asia is where the Communist conspirators have elected to make their play for global conquest. . .that here we fight Europe's war with arms while the diplomats there still fight it with words; that if we lose the war to communism in Asia the fall of Europe is inevitable; win it and Europe would probably avoid war and yet preserve freedom." With characteristic flourish, MacArthur closed his letter by proclaiming, "there is no substitute for victory."

As MacArthur had intended, Martin made the letter public. A classic confrontation then ensued between civilian and military authority. Truman had already tired of MacArthur's insubordination. He had also doubted MacArthur's handling of the war. Now MacArthur had gone the limit, ignoring presidential orders to keep quiet and challenging the very essence of administration policy. Certain of the course he had to follow, Truman nonetheless requested the advice of his chiefs of staff, who agreed that MacArthur had to go. The President then relieved him from command. If he hoped to preserve civilian rule, he could hardly have done otherwise.

The news of MacArthur's dismissal prompted critics to heap abuse on Truman's head. The GOP National Committee proclaimed that the President had perpetuated a "super Munich." McCarthy grumbled, "the son of a bitch ought to be impeached." MacArthur then began a triumphal return to the United States, where throngs of people crowded to sing his praises. To an emotional session of Congress he pulled out all the stops: "I still remember the refrain of one of the most popular barracks ballads of that day which proclaimed most proudly that 'Old soldiers never die; they just fade away.' And like the old soldier of that ballad, I now close my military career and just fade away—an old soldier who tried to do his duty as God gave him the light to see that duty. Good-bye."

General Douglas MacArthur in Korea, 1950.

Truman wisely did not attempt to counter such theatrics. But he did work to strengthen America's military posture in Asia and elsewhere. In 1951 America signed separate bilateral defense pacts with Japan and with the Philippines. It agreed to the so-called ANZUS treaty, a mutual defense pact involving Australia and New Zealand. In part to secure French agreement to the inclusion of West Germany in NATO, it stepped up aid to French forces in Indochina. By 1954 the aid had totaled $1.2 billion in a losing cause.

Truman also called upon loyalists in Congress to expose MacArthur's bombast. Led by Senator Richard Russell, they brought out the fact that all three chiefs of staff had rejected MacArthur's argument. By the summer of 1951 Truman's patience began to bring modest results, and MacArthur disappeared to the back pages. But MacArthur's dismissal had served as a public acknowledgment that total victory was impossible, that "limited war" would continue to be the policy of the administration. And limited war, as one writer put it, was like a slight case of pregnancy. In their heads Americans might understand the necessity for restraint; in their hearts they wanted to win, as their country always had. Or they wanted to get out. Unless the administration could find an honorable way to end the fighting, it would suffer dearly at the polls in 1952.

Early in 1952 Truman announced he would retire at the end of his term. He could hardly have done otherwise, for almost no one in his party wanted him to run again. Since 1950 he had suffered not only at the hands of McCarthyites and MacArthurites but also from corruption among some of his own friends and aides. Only 23 percent of the American people, a record low, signified their approval of his administration in late 1951.

With their albatross out of the way, the Democrats turned to Governor Adlai Stevenson of Illinois. Though a relative newcomer to electoral politics, Stevenson had already captured the affection of many reporters and intellectuals, who deeply admired his intelligence, his liberalism, and his patrician cultivation. Urban bosses liked his stand on labor and welfare issues and noted his apparent strength at the polls in Illinois. Upright, witty, articulate, Stevenson could be expected to carry on the New Deal–Fair Deal tradition and to defend Truman's internationalist policies. Though Stevenson was perhaps too intellectual for mass taste, he seemed a fresh contrast to the tired old regulars who had surrounded Truman. To the columnist Marcus Childs, the governor was "Lincolnian"; to David Lilienthal he was a tower of "wisdom and wit and strength"; to Max Lerner, a liberal writer, he was the "first figure of major stature to have emerged since Roosevelt."

Republicans, meanwhile, took no chances. Rejecting Taft, the controversial favorite of the Right, they selected General Eisenhower as their nominee. "Ike" was genial, nonpartisan, and widely admired as a war hero; he was expected to offend no one. As Truman's appointee to develop a NATO army, he was clearly a "Europe-firster," whom no one could accuse of being an isolationist or a McCarthyite. Only the nomination of Richard Nixon as Eisenhower's running mate—creating a ticket that one critic likened to an alliance between Ulysses S. Grant and Dick Tracy—suggested that the GOP had pursued an abrasively partisan line for the past four years.

As the campaign developed, Eisenhower edged closer to his party's right wing. At the so-called Surrender on Morningside Heights in New York City, he met Taft,

It would be very very fine if one could command new and amusing language—witticisms to bring you a chuckle. Frankly, I have no intention of trying to do so. The subjects of which we are speaking these days, my friends, are not those that seem to me to be amusing. . . . Is it amusing that we have stumbled into a war in Korea; that we have already lost in casualties 117,000 of our Americans killed and wounded; is it amusing that the war seems to be no nearer to a real solution than ever; that we have no real plan for stopping it? Is it funny when evidence was discovered that there are Communists in government . . . ?

Eisenhower, stepping up his crusade against communism and the war in Korea, slashes at Stevenson's attempts at humor.

who had been nursing his grievances in silence, and agreed to support a conservative domestic policy if elected. He endorsed (with some qualifications) the party's platform calling for the "liberation" of countries under communist control. With other partisan orators he stressed the anti-Truman slogan of K_1C_2—Korea, Communism, and Corruption. Nixon denounced Stevenson as "Adlai the appeaser," who "carries a Ph.D. from Dean Acheson's cowardly college of communist containment." Leaving nothing to chance, Eisenhower tried to secure McCarthyite support by deleting a paragraph from a Wisconsin speech praising his old boss, General Marshall. He closed the campaign by promising to go to Korea if elected. Ike, it appeared, would get the country out of the "mess" that Truman had caused in Asia.

Stevenson countered Eisenhower's attacks with wit and energy. But as a Democrat he was inevitably associated with Truman's policies. No one, therefore, was surprised when he was overwhelmed in November. Though he got 27.3 million votes, 3.2 million more than Truman received in 1948, he still trailed Eisenhower, who attracted a record 33.9 million voters, 12 million more than Dewey's total four

The Eisenhowers and the Nixons receiving the GOP nomination, July 1952.

ACRIMONY AT HOME AND ABROAD 1945–1952

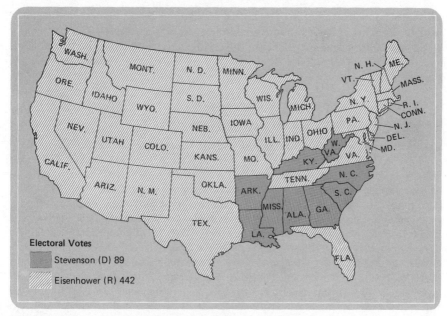

Election, 1952

Electoral Votes

Stevenson (D) 89

Eisenhower (R) 442

years earlier. Breaking deeply into the Democratic coalition, Eisenhower swept all the big urban states and carried four states in the ordinarily Democratic South. Republicans even won majorities in both houses of Congress, for the second time since 1930. The result not only ended twenty years of Democratic dominance; it appeared to be a virtual revolution overthrowing the electoral universe that Al Smith and Franklin D. Roosevelt had forged in the previous generation.

Democratic gains in congressional elections throughout the 1950s revealed that no such revolution had taken place. Republicans, weakened in the depression years, remained the minority party. But the election of 1952 suggested the enormously important effect that an attractive candidate could have, and the degree to which formerly partisan voters were prepared to split their tickets. It also showed that the South, which had begun to rebel against Truman in 1948, was heading toward the Republican column. These trends toward electoral independence and discontinuity were to expand in the 1960s. Above all, the election of 1952 left little doubt that voters wanted a change in the White House. Like Hoover in 1933, Johnson in 1969, and Nixon in 1974, Truman joined the group of modern American presidents who left office under clouds of disapproval.

Such a verdict, if that is what it was, was unfair, for Roosevelt's "Throttlebottom" had proved a competent if uninspiring leader. Though partisan in dealing with Congress, he had managed to broaden the partial welfare state of the New Deal. Though inflexible and unsophisticated in diplomacy, he had occasionally proved enlightened, as in his support of foreign aid for Europe, and sometimes decisive as in his intervention in Korea. As he left office in early 1953, it remained to be seen whether the GOP could do much better.

Suggestions for reading

Among the many accounts of foreign policy in the Truman years are Daniel Yergin, *Shattered Peace: The Origins of the Cold War and the National Security State* (1977); Herbert Feis, *From Trust to Terror: The Onset of the Cold War, 1945–1950* (1970); and the revisionist interpretation by Walter LaFeber, *America, Russia, and the Cold War, 1945–1971** (1972). See also the books by Gaddis and Ambrose mentioned at the end of chapter 10. Revisionist accounts include Thomas Paterson, *Soviet-American Confrontation* (1974); and Lloyd Gardner, *Architects of Illusion . . . 1941–1948* (1970). Important memoirs are George Kennan, *Memoirs, 1925–1950** (1967); and Dean Acheson, *Present at the Creation* (1969). Gaddis Smith, *Dean Acheson** (1972), is a useful biography. A revisionist account of the decision to drop the atomic bomb is Gar Alperovitz, *Atomic Diplomacy: Hiroshima and Potsdam** (1965). But see also Herbert Feis, *The Atomic Bomb and the End of World War II** (rev. ed., 1966), which refutes Alperovitz. A general study of Soviet-American relations is Adam Ulam, *The Rivals: America and Russia Since World War II** (1971).

Books on more specialized aspects of foreign policy include Tang Tsou, *America's Failure in China, 1941–1949** (1963); Herbert Feis, *The China Tangle* (1953); James Jones, *Fifteen Weeks** (1955), on the Truman Doctrine and the Marshall Plan; and Harry B. Price, *The Marshall Plan and Its Meaning** (1955). For the Korean War, consult David Rees, *Korea** (1964); Ronald Caridi, *The Korean War and American Politics* (1968); William Manchester, *American Caesar* (1978), on MacArthur.

The most balanced book on the Truman administration is Alonzo Hamby, *Beyond the New Deal: Harry S. Truman and American Liberalism* (1973). Bert Cochran, *Harry S. Truman and the Crisis Presidency* (1973) is critical. Barton Bernstein and Allen Matusow, eds., *Politics and Policies of the Truman Administration** (1970), is revisionist. Also, Richard Kirkendall, ed., *The Truman Period as a Research Field: A Reappraisal* (1974), offers conflicting interpretations. Richard Neustadt, *Presidential Power** (1960), includes case studies from the Truman administration. For political trends see V. O. Key, Jr., *Southern Politics* (1949); and the book by Samuel Lubell cited at the end of chapter 6. For the 1948 campaign consult Norman Markovitz, *Rise and Fall of the People's Century* (1973); and Irwin Ross, *The Loneliest Campaign** (1968). James T. Patterson, *Mr. Republican: A Biography of Robert A. Taft** (1972) is a biography. Susan Hartmann, *Truman and the 80th Congress* (1971), competently covers its subject.

Books dealing with aspects of domestic policy are Edmund Flash, Jr., *Economic Advice and Presidential Leadership* (1965), on the Council of Economic Advisers; R. Alton Lee, *Truman and Taft-Hartley* (1967); Allen Matusow, *Farm Policies and Politics of the Truman Administration* (1967); Richard O. Davies, *Housing Reform During the Truman Administration** (1966); and A. E. Holmans, *United States Fiscal Policy, 1945–1959* (1961). For labor, see Bert Cochran, *Labor and Communism: The Conflict that Shaped American Unions* (1977); Maeva Marcus, *Truman and the Steel Seizure* (1976); and David Brody, *Workers in Industrial America* (1980). For civil rights see William Berman, *The Politics of Civil Rights* *in the Truman Administration* (1970); and Donald McCoy and Richard Ruetten, *Quest and Response* (1973).

The subject of anticommunism has attracted many writers. Among the important books are David Shannon, *The Decline of American Communism* (1959); Earl Latham, *The Communist Conspiracy in Washington** (1966); Alan D. Harper, *The Politics of Loyalty, 1946–1952* (1969); Richard Rovere, *Senator Joe McCarthy** (1959), a brilliant study; and Robert Griffith, *The Politics of Fear** (1970), which focuses on the role of the Senate. Books highly critical of the Truman administration's anticommunism are Athan Theoharis, *Seeds of Repression: Harry S. Truman and the Origins of McCarthyism* (1971); Richard Freeland, *The Truman Doctrine and the Origins of McCarthyism* (1971); and David Caute, *The Great Fear: Anti-Communist Purge Under Truman and Eisenhower* (1978). Daniel Bell, ed., *Radical Right** (1963), includes essays stressing the role of social tensions in causing anticommunist hysteria.

12

The middle-class world
of the 1950s

"We've grown unbelievably prosperous and we maunder along in a stupor of fat," the historian Eric Goldman wrote in 1960. "We live in a heavy, humorless, sanctimonious, stultifying atmosphere, singularly lacking in the self-mockery that is criticism. Probably the climate of the late 1950s was the dullest and dreariest in all our history." The journalist William Shannon agreed. The decade, he wrote, was one of "flabbiness and self-satisfaction and gross materialism. . . . The loudest sound in the land has been the oink and grunt of private hoggishness. . . . It has been the age of the slob."

Many liberals echoed Goldman and Shannon. The decade of the 1950s, these critics recognized, was a period of unprecedented prosperity. It was like the 1920s, they said: materialistic, self-satisfied, conformist, politically conservative, and apathetic.

The case against the 50s

Primary targets of such criticism were the suburban middle classes, which expanded dramatically in the postwar years. In 1940, 74.4 million of America's 132 million people (57 percent) had lived in cities, then defined by the census as places with 2,500 or more people. By 1950, the Census Bureau recognized that this arbitrary definition excluded millions who lived in suburbs; so it broadened its definition of cities to include "densely settled urban fringes . . . around cities of 50,000 inhabitants or more." The number of urbanites then rose to 96.5 million in 1950, 124.7 million in 1960, and 149.3 million in 1970—73.5 percent of America's rapidly expanding population of 203 million. Meanwhile the number classified as "rural farm" dropped precipitously, from 30 million in 1940 to 23 million in 1950 to only 13.4 million in 1960.

These figures did not mean that central cities were growing. Quite the contrary, many of America's largest cities lost people between 1950 and 1960. These one-time city people, plus millions more from the countryside, were flocking to the "settled urban fringes," which—thanks to the ubiquitous automobile—grew three times as rapidly as the overall population. By 1960 a "megalopolis" stretched much of the way between Boston and Washington. Suburban areas around newer cities of the "Sun Belt"—Los Angeles, Dallas, Houston, Phoenix, San Diego— expanded fantastically. By 1970 some 80 million Americans lived in "suburbs." This was approximately 15 million more than lived in central cities, and more than the nation's entire population in 1900.

Naturally, the motives that inspired so many migrants varied widely. Millions fled the urban cores to escape countermigrations of blacks: in the 1950s alone America's twelve largest cities lost 2 million whites while gaining 1.8 million nonwhites. Millions more sought to better their social and economic status, to improve educational opportunities for their children, and to secure space and privacy. Some of these migrants were wealthy business and professional people who lived in style many miles from downtown sections. Others were blue-collar workers of limited means—people who borrowed heavily to buy tiny houses or to rent flats in hastily constructed apartment houses. Such suburban areas, sometimes heavily industrial, offered few of the amenities ordinarily associated with life outside the central city. The variety of suburbs, and of the motivations of the people who caused them to grow, almost defy description.

Generally, however, it is fair to identify most of the suburbanites as belonging occupationally to the middle classes, which grew rapidly during the postwar era of bureaucratization, specialization, and technological change. As the number of farmers declined, and that of manual workers increased only slightly, the number of Americans classified as white-collar workers rose rapidly throughout the decades since 1940. By the mid-1950s such people outnumbered blue-collar laborers for the first time in American history. By 1970 they were close to 40 million strong, compared to 28.5 million blue-collar workers, 11 million service workers, and 3 million farm workers. Having escaped blue-collar status, many of these white-collar families sought the space, the privacy, and the life styles of the older middle classes. In this way suburbanization and the process of becoming middle-class tended to develop together, and to establish themselves as significant demographic movements of the 1950s.

These middle-class suburbs distressed some contemporary critics. Places like Levittown, Pennsylvania, one of the many monotonous, mass-produced communities catering to lower- and middle-income groups, received special criticism. So did more costly but aesthetically dull developments plastered on the once rural landscape. John Keats, author of the antisuburban book *The Crack in the Picture*

Window (1961), dismissed them as "developments conceived in error, nurtured by greed, corroding everything they touch." To him as to other observers it seemed almost criminal that once picturesque countrysides should be bulldozed for houses and apartments, each with a TV antenna scarring a treeless sky. It seemed that a conspiracy of mercenary builders and ignorant architects was fastening a noose of vulgarity around the nation's cities.

Critics worried also about the human values nurtured by such humdrum surroundings. The "heroes" of Keats's book were John and Mary Drone—bored, purposeless materialists. Richard and Katherine Gordon, authors of *The Split-Level Trap* (1961), thought that the monotony of suburban existence promoted mental anguish and "Disturbia." And William H. Whyte, Jr.'s, widely discussed *Organization Man* (1956) bemoaned the fate that met the middle-class suburbanites of Park Forest, Illinois. Though Whyte considered Park Forest a pleasant, friendly place where newcomers were made to feel at home, he concluded that it was hell for people who valued privacy and nonconformity. The middle classes, Whyte implied, were losing themselves in a vast suburban sprawl (what others called "slurbs") of mediocrity and conformity.

The sociologist David Riesman made many of the same points in his book *The Lonely Crowd* (1950), which described the growth of conformist pressures not only in suburbia but in all areas of middle-class life. To Riesman, America had moved from an "inner-directed" culture in which people (through parental guidance) de-

Whereas the inner-directed middle-class boy often had to learn after twenty to adjust, to surrender his adolescent dreams and accept a burgher's modest lot, the other-directed boy never had such dreams. In a profound sense he never experiences adolescence, moving as he does uninterruptedly with the peer-group, from the nursery years on. He learns to conform to the group almost as soon as he learns anything. He does not face, at adolescence, the need to choose between his family's world and that of his own generation or between his dreams and a world he never made.

David Riesman laments the passing of "inner direction."

DRAWING BY CLAUDE. COPR. © 1956 THE NEW YORKER MAGAZINE, INC.

The alleged conformity of suburbia.

veloped individualized goals, to an "other-directed" society molded by peer-group pressures. Such a society, Riesman realized, could be more stable and even more tolerant than one composed of self-made men. But it helped create unventuresome little people like the boy who was asked, "Would you like to be able to fly?" and who answered, "I would like to be able to fly if everybody else did."

To writers like Dwight Macdonald the alleged deadness of contemporary life was especially clear in the arts. Unlike Great Britain or other Western societies, Macdonald thought, America could not sustain a High Culture. Instead, it had purely commercial television and radio, comic books and cartoon strips that sold by the millions, and "masscult," a parody of High Culture that featured sentimental painters like Norman Rockwell and pseudotheologians like Norman Vincent Peale. Worst of all, America was becoming swamped by "midcult," which Macdonald thought "watered down and vulgarized" the standards of High Culture. Examples of midcult were Hemingway's *Old Man and the Sea* (1952) and selections by such purveyors of "culture" as the Book-of-the-Month Club. Macdonald, an intellectual snob, thought that America was a nation of cultural philistines.

Many of these critics focused on what they saw as the self-indulgence, purposelessness, and lack of discipline in American society during the 1950s. The United States, wrote the novelist John Updike, "is like an unloved child smothered in candy. God doesn't love us any more. He loves Russia. He loves Uganda. We're fat and full of pimples and always yearning for more candy. We've fallen from grace." The economist John Kenneth Galbraith, in his book *The Affluent Society* (1958), showed that Americans spent billions on consumer goods—TV sets, home freezers, household gadgets, and above all, automobiles—while scrimping on necessary public services. Conservatives worried that the consumer society of the 1950s was inducing national flabbiness. "If you ask me," George Kennan wrote,

I drive my car to supermarket,
The way I take is superhigh,
A superlot is where I park it,
And Super Suds are what I buy.

Supersalesmen sell me tonic—
Super-Tone-O, for relief.
The planes I ride are supersonic.
In trains I like the Super Chief.

Supercilious men and women
Call me superficial—me.
Who so superbly learned to swim in
Supercolossality.

Superphosphate-fed foods feed me;
Superservice keeps me new.
Who would dare to supersede me,
Super-super-superwho?

The writer John Updike echoes complaints about American materialism, 1954.

. . . whether a country that is in the state this country is in today: with no highly developed sense of national purpose, with the overwhelming accent of life on personal comfort and amusement, with a dearth of public services and a surfeit of privately sold gadgetry . . . if you ask me whether such a country has, over the long run, a good chance of competing with a purposeful, serious, and disciplined society such as that of the Soviet Union, I must say that the answer is "No."

Other critics, including the distinguished sociologist Pitirim Sorokin, worried that Americans, lacking a sense of purpose, were wallowing in sex. He concluded: "Unless we develop an inner immunity against these libidinal forces, we are bound to be conquered by the continuous army of omnipresent sex stimuli." Sorokin's worries were exaggerated. Though Alfred Kinsey, an Indiana University researcher, published tomes (*Sexual Behavior in the Human Male* [1948] and *Sexual Behavior in the Human Female* [1953]) showing that large numbers of young people were indulging in premarital sex, he scarcely supported the notion that sexual immorality was sweeping the nation. His researches suggested that American sexual behavior had been changing since the 1910s and 1920s, not only in the supposedly degenerate postwar years. The very alarm displayed at the publication of Kinsey's "statistical filth" underlined the continued power of conventional ideas concerning sex, indeed of prudery, in the American consciousness.

The broadsides against philistinism were equally exaggerated. Scores of previous observers had lambasted America's material greed and cultural crudity. Like Macdonald, they tended to be elitists who refused to accept the simple fact that people in most societies prefer personal comfort to High Culture. As one sensible writer pointed out, "the critic waves the prophet's long and accusing finger and

. . . youngsters, instead of being sheltered and disciplined as they once were, are now exposed to the seamy side of sex in its rawest forms before they have the faintest concept of its total meaning in life. We have only to look about us to realize that, as a nation, we are preoccupied—almost obsessed—with the superficial aspects of sex, with sex as a form of amusement. This is not true sex, with the corollaries of love, marriage and child-bearing. It is an almost hysterical bandying about of sex symbols, coming close to fetish worship. (Consider the present over-emphasis of the breast, the stressing of erotic qualities in perfume.)

Dr. Goodrich C. Schauffler, a gynecologist, joins others in the 1950s in bewailing the triumph of sex.

warns: 'You may *think* you're happy, you smug and prosperous striver, but I tell you that the anxieties of status mobility are too much; they impoverish you psychologically, they alienate you from your family'; and so on. And the suburbanite looks at his new house, his new car, his new freezer, his lawn and patio, and to be sure, his good credit, and scratches his head, bewildered.'' Postwar Americans were not more materialistic than earlier generations—just incomparably richer. They were able to buy and to enjoy things that their parents could only dream about.

As careful critics recognized, it was also simplistic to paste labels—such as conformist or materialistic—on a society as diverse as the United States. What might apply to the corporate middle class (or some part of it) did not necessarily describe farmers, blacks, ethnics, blue-collar people, or many others in the enormously varied middle classes. What may have been true of some suburbanites was not in the least true of others—who resembled each other (if at all) primarily in their dependence on the automobile and their geographical mobility. It was equally hazardous to contend that "other-directedness" was new or on the upswing. Indeed, peer group pressures in nineteenth-century American towns may have been more formidable than in the ever-changing suburbs of the 1950s. Those who perceived only conformity also overlooked the continuing stress on personal achievement and—especially in the prosperous postwar years—the yearning for self-growth. The very attention accorded such books as *Organization Man* suggested that many Americans, including the middle classes who were supposedly so mindless, were as anxious as their ancestors had been to surmount the homogenizing pressures of life.

A similar yearning for self-expression prompted some of the major trends in art forms during the decade. Poets and dramatists reacted against the social realism of the 1930s and insisted on writing for themselves, not for causes. "A successful poem," the writer Leslie Fiedler explained, "is a complete and final act; if it leads outward to other action, it is just so far a failure." The director Alan Schneider later added, "we all have got to stop looking at all our plays as though they were socialist realism. . . . We can no longer go back to the well-made play because we haven't got a well-made world."

In the same way young painters like Jackson Pollock developed a wholly nonrepresentational style variously called Abstract Expressionism and Action Painting. Reflecting existentialist beliefs, they argued that a work of art must embody the spontaneous, individual emotions of the creator. Art was a process of expression, not a static final product. Pollock, indeed, came to stand on his canvasses, flinging paint on them with apparently reckless abandon. "What was to go on the canvas," the critic Harold Rosenberg explained approvingly, "was not a picture but an event. . . . It is the artist's existence . . . he is living on the canvas. . . . What gives the canvas meaning is . . . the way the artist organized his emotional and intellectual energy as if he were in a living situation."

This desire to be one's self, to overcome organizational constraints, helped to explain the critical acclaim bestowed in the 1950s on novelists otherwise as diverse as J. D. Salinger, Saul Bellow, and John Updike. In *Catcher in the Rye* (1951) Salinger's "hero" is Holden Caulfield, a supersensitive adolescent bent on preserving innocence against "perverts" and "phonies" who wanted him to conform. Most of Bellow's protagonists, in books such as *Dangling Man* (1946), *Adventures of Augie March* (1949), and *Herzog* (1961), are bemused men who revolt against what Augie called the "shame of purposelessness." Like Huckleberry Finn (who also had "adventures"), they tried to be true to themselves. Updike's Rabbit Angstrom in *Rabbit Run* (1961) is a similarly confused young man who looks desperately—and unsuccessfully—for ways to bring back the excitement and meaning of his high school days. Characters like these were fearful, confused, buffeted about—passive victims of larger forces. But they did not surrender. Some were existentialist antiheroes who at least survived.

These thrusts against conformity led in the late 1950s to a vogue among more radical students for books like C. Wright Mills's *Power Elite* (1956), Jack Kerouac's *On the Road* (1956), and Paul Goodman's *Growing up Absurd* (1957). The three men held differing social philosophies: Mills was a Marxist sociologist, Kerouac a "beat" novelist who celebrated free-wheeling nonconformity, Goodman a philosophical anarchist who combined Veblen's passion for productive labor, Freud's stress on the need for physical love, and the urban planner Ebenezer Howard's vision of decentralized communities and garden cities. Yet all three men agreed that America—in Goodman's words a "rat race," in Mills's a "great

---

The quest, I am beginning to think, whether it be for money, for notoriety, reputation, increase of pride, whether it leads us to thievery, slaughter, sacrifice, the quest is one and the same. All the striving is for one end. I do not entirely understand this impulse. But it seems to me that its final end is the desire for pure freedom. We are all drawn toward the same craters of the spirit—to know what we are and what we are for, to know our purpose, to seek grace. And, if the quest is the same, the differences in our personal histories, which hitherto meant so much to us, become of minor importance.

Saul Bellow's character Joseph in *Dangling Man* (1946) expresses a feeling later echoed by many of the most memorable characters in postwar American fiction.

> *. . . we get a clear but exaggerated picture of our American society. It has: slums of engineering—boondoggling production—chaotic congestion—tribes of middlemen—basic city functions squeezed out—garden cities for children—indifferent workmen—underprivileged on a dole—empty "belonging" without nature or culture—front politicians—no patriotism—an empty nationalism bound for a cataclysmically disastrous finish—wise opinion swamped— enterprise sabotaged by monopoly—prejudice rising—religion otiose—the popular culture debased—science specialized—science secret—the average man inept—youth idle and truant—youth sexually suffering and sexually obsessed—youth without goals—poor schools.*

Paul Goodman, in *Growing Up Absurd* (1957), expresses a radically unhappy view of American society.

salesroom, an enormous file, an incorporated brain, a new universe of management and manipulation''—stifled creative talent. For them, as for many less radical thinkers, large-scale organization was the enemy. Their appeal to young nonconformists suggested that the 1950s were less serene and complacent than they sometimes appeared.

CAUSES FOR ALARM

Still, there was no denying that many aspects of American life in the 1950s supported the critics of conformity and materialism. One of these was the growth of the huge, bureaucratic corporation. As Adolf Berle and Gardiner Means had pointed out in the early 1930s—and as James Burnham had stressed in his *Managerial Revolution* (1939)—''faceless'' bureaucrats were dominating the ever-growing corporations. These early writers had worried more about the power of such organizations than about the psyches of their employees. But by the 1950s it was clear that many corporations (to say nothing of government, the biggest bureaucracy of all) stressed ''teamwork'' and frowned on mavericks. Some, such as IBM, even outlined acceptable standards of dress and decorum. Alarmed, Mills perceived the coming of a ''white collar'' society in which people would be ''estranged from community . . . in a context of distrust and manipulation, alienated from work and, in the personality market, from self, expropriated of individual rationality, and politically apathetic.'' Mills exaggerated the capacity of organizations to transform people's minds. But he was perceptive in pointing to the growth of propagandists for ''togetherness'' and the ''need to belong.''

The call for togetherness also helped sustain a cult of domesticity in the 1950s. More than ever before—or so it seemed—Americans yearned to enmesh themselves in the ''tender trap'' of marriage, parenthood, and the nuclear family. During the late 1940s and early 1950s people continued to marry young and to have children quickly. As a result the baby boom, which demographers had expected would decrease shortly after World War II, continued until 1964. The nation's population increased from 151 million to 180 million people between 1950 and 1960. This was

the largest growth in any decade of American history (before or since). The rate of
increase (19 percent) was the greatest since 1910, when heavy immigration had
helped to swell the pace of growth.

Few people during the 1950s expressed much alarm about the ecological results
of such expansion. The baby boom, they said, helped to sustain prosperity, especially in the construction industry, which was kept busy building approximately 1
million new homes per year throughout the 1950s. By 1960 more Americans owned
their homes (with mortgages) than rented, for the first time in the twentieth century.
The majority of such homes had the creature comforts that the media promoted as
the joys of domesticity and parenthood.

The presumed blessings of domesticity helped to weaken feminism in the
1950s. Feminists, the Women's Bureau of the federal government had announced a
few years earlier, were a "small but militant group of leisure class women [giving
vent] to their resentment at not having been born men." Adlai Stevenson added,
"the assignment for you, as women and mothers, you can do in the living room
with a baby in your lap or in the kitchen with a can opener in your hand. . . . there
is much you can do about our crisis in the humble role of housewife. I could wish
you no better vocation than that." Dr. Benjamin Spock, whose *Baby and Child
Care* (1946) was a huge seller in the 1950s and 1960s, urged the government to pay
mothers so they would not leave the home for employment.

Such defenders of domesticity overlooked continuing growth in female employment, a profound demographic development that helped sustain the movement for
women's liberation a decade later. But movies and magazines undercut feminism.
Hollywood glorified sweet types like Doris Day and Debby Reynolds or sex objects
like Marilyn Monroe. Fashion designers popularized spike-heeled shoes, crinolines,
and the "baby doll" look. The "ladies" magazines extolled the satisfactions of
motherhood and home management. Women, like men in the apparently
unventuresome postwar era, seemed to know and accept their status.

There was cause also to worry about the impact of the mass media, particularly
television, which one critic labeled the "cheekiest, vulgarest, most disgraceful
form of entertainment since bear-baiting, dog-fighting, and the seasonal Czarist
Russian pogrom." Like others, he lamented the omnipresence of violence, the
virtual absence of serious drama, above all the pandering to the commercial nature
of the medium. Like the mass-circulation magazines and newspapers, TV con-

stantly flashed expensive luxury goods before the consumer. No one, of course, could prove that TV or the other media actually caused people to buy certain goods, much less to become conformists. Indeed, it was possible that the bombardment of varied images undercut provincialism and broadened the vision of millions. But by 1960 it was also clear that TV, by invading practically every American home for several hours a day, was projecting a peculiarly consumerist and middle-class world. It was also ignoring (or stereotyping) the millions who belonged to minority groups.

Another sign of blandness in the 1950s was what some contemporaries labeled the "new piety." By 1960 this was reflected in a rise in the percentage of Americans (63 percent) who identified with a religious denomination. (Only 48 percent had so identified in 1940.) Lesser manifestations of this trend abounded: a new stamp issue proclaimed "In God We Trust"; "under God" was added to the pledge of allegiance; the Eisenhower administration regularly opened meetings with a prayer. Subway posters proclaimed, "Go to church. You'll feel better. Bring your troubles to church and leave them there." Capitalizing on this search for faith, the evangelist Billy Graham efficiently utilized modern techniques of merchandizing and salesmanship in speaking to millions during the postwar era, while Bishop Fulton J. Sheen and the Reverend Norman Vincent Peale reached out to the middle classes over the radio and in magazine columns. "Flush out all depressing, negative, and tired thoughts," Peale told his readers in *Look* magazine. "Start thinking faith, enthusiasm, and joy."

This kind of exhortation was nothing new in the American experience, where faith in faith had long enjoyed support. Peale's "power of positive thinking" was a religious version of the quest for individualism. Nor was the search for faith strictly confined to the middle classes: the rapid growth of evangelical and fundamentalist churches during the postwar era suggested that millions of Americans, including many migratory blacks and poor whites, earnestly sought comfort against the forces of urbanization and technological change. But the theologian Will Herberg was correct in stressing, in *Protestant Catholic Jew* (1956), that for many Americans religion had lost its theological meaning. Instead, the churches supported a "civic religion," which sustained the status quo and the "American Way of Life." Far from promoting a deeply religious Great Awakening, the search for piety often revealed a quest for social status and identity.

Like the churches, schools reflected this concern for helping people find their place in mass society. This focus on "life adjustment" challenged many earlier pedagogical theories, including the stress on the Three R's, Dewey's idea that schools could promote social reform, or the progressive hope that teachers might stimulate the latent creativity of children. Instead, some schools offered subjects like "How can I look my best?" "How can I get along better with others?" and "How can hobbies contribute to my social growth?" The historian Richard Hofstadter complained that one New York community required a course in "Home and Family Living" for all children in grades seven through ten. The course featured such topics as "developing school spirit," "clicking with the crowd," and "what can be done about acne?" Other reformers worried that college youth in the 1950s had become the "Silent Generation," interested in football, fraternities, and, upon graduation, in well-paid security with General Motors, Wall Street, and Madison Avenue. Campus radicalism was so hard to detect that Kenneth Keniston, an acute observer of American youth, complained as late as 1962, "I see little likelihood of American students ever playing a radical role, much less a revolutionary one, in our society."

Hofstadter and others exaggerated the staying power of "life adjustment" in the curriculum. Indeed, traditionalists (who complained that students weren't "learning" anything) successfully counterattacked in the late 1950s, especially after the Soviet Union beat the United States in the race to outer space. Diatribes against campus complacency were short-sighted, for American university students, sons and daughters of the more affluent classes, had historically shown little sustained interest in social reform. It is also clear that some critics of American education placed too much faith in the potential of schools to transcend environmental forces. Schools, after all, are rarely much different from society at large. But that was partly Hofstadter's point: schools, like churches, like corporations, seemed bent on preserving the existing order.

This focus on sustaining social stability found approving interpreters among America's leading intellectuals of the 1950s. These included the historian Daniel Boorstin and the sociologist Daniel Bell. Both welcomed what they considered the consensus of American society. In *The Genius of American Politics* (1953) Boorstin described the national experience as one in which compromise and practicality overcame ideologies and class conflicts. Bell, a prolific writer, gathered many of his essays into a volume entitled *The End of Ideology* (1960). America, he said, was a flexible, pluralistic nation in which many groups vied for position. It was a much more humane society than the Soviet Union, which vividly exposed the dangers of absolutist ideology. These defenders of "consensus" underrated the degree of ethnic, racial, and class conflict in the American past, and they falsely assumed that ideology—or at least activism—was dead. "It's like an old man proclaiming the end of sex," one youthful rebel later sneered. "Because he doesn't feel it anymore, he thinks it has disappeared."

Bell was right, however, in arguing that leftist thinkers made little headway in the 1950s. Thanks to the Cold War, and especially to Korea, the Communist and Socialist parties virtually disappeared. The Progressive party lost what little hope it had had for survival as a political force when Henry Wallace deserted it to back the Korean War. Liberal groups such as the Americans for Democratic Action continued to press for progressive domestic reforms, but they remained on the defensive against McCarthyites who branded intellectuals as "parlor pinks" or communists. As if to prove otherwise, the ADA insisted loudly that it, too, hated the Reds. The weakness of the Left in the 1950s revealed the pervasive impact of the Cold War, the intimidating force of McCarthyism, and the dominance of "middle American" values.

AFFLUENCE

The primary support for such attitudes was the unparalleled affluence of the decade. In constant prices the GNP had already jumped from $205 billion in 1940 to $318 billion in 1950. During the 1950s it leaped again, to $440 billion in 1960. In per capita terms this meant an increase from $1,550 in 1940 to $2,100 in 1950 to

Economic growth, 1950–60, compared to selected years before and after this period

NATIONAL PRODUCT AND INCOME
(in billions of current dollars)

	GNP	PERCENT CHANGE FROM GNP OF PRECEDING YEAR (+ OR −)	NATIONAL INCOME	DISPOSABLE PERSONAL INCOME	PER CAPITA DISPOSABLE INCOME (in current dollars)
1929	103.1	n.d.	86.8	83.3	683
1933	55.6	− 4.2	40.3	45.5	362
1940	99.7	+10.2	81.1	75.7	573
1944	210.1	+ 9.7	182.6	146.3	1,057
1946	208.5	− 1.6	181.9	160.0	1,132
1950	284.8	+11.0	241.1	206.9	1,364
1951	328.4	+15.3	278.0	226.6	1,469
1952	345.5	+ 5.2	291.4	238.3	1,518
1953	364.6	+ 5.5	304.7	252.6	1,583
1954	364.8	+ 0.1	303.1	257.4	1,585
1955	398.0	+ 9.1	331.0	275.3	1,666
1956	419.2	+ 5.3	350.8	293.2	1,743
1957	441.1	+ 5.2	366.1	308.5	1,801
1958	447.3	+ 1.4	367.8	318.8	1,831
1959	483.7	+ 8.2	400.0	337.3	1,905
1960	503.7	+ 4.1	414.5	350.0	1,937
1970	977.1	+ 5.0	800.5	691.7	3,376
1973	1,294.9	+11.8	1,065.6	903.7	4,295
1978	2,107.6	+11.7	1,703.8	1,452	7,810

SOURCE: Adapted from Council of Economic Advisers, "Annual Report, January 1975" in *Economic Report of the President* (Washington, D.C., 1975), pp. 249, 267, 269

$2,435 in 1960. It was reflected in striking advances in life expectancy, education levels, and disposable income. In the 1950s, consumer credit rose from $8.4 billion to $45 billion. Workers, who had labored an average of forty-five hours a week in the 1920s, were on the job less than forty hours by 1960. Most received annual vacations of at least two weeks. The simplest way to describe the affluence of the 1950s is to note that the average American had twice as much real income to spend (and more time to spend it in) in the mid-1950s than in the boom times of the late 1920s.

Many forces produced this growth. Among them was the willingness of the private sector to risk funds for investment. Between 1946 and 1958, when a slump hit the economy, Americans pumped an average of $10 billion per year into new plant and equipment. Another was technological change including computers, which became important by the early 1960s. Labor-saving devices wiped out many jobs, especially in agriculture and in such industries as textiles, where the labor force declined by more than 30 percent between 1945 and 1960. Indeed, technological unemployment disproportionally hit poor farmers, miners, and blue-collar industrial workers in the urban Northeast and Midwest. There, large regions comprising millions of people became "depressed areas." But technological advances also created jobs, especially for white-collar "service" workers. Such areas as electronics and plastics expanded phenomenally during the years between 1945 and 1960.

The public sector played an indispensable role in promoting this prosperity. Much of the economic growth of the period stemmed from governmental expenditures for World War II and Korea. Military spending, which approached $40 billion per year in the peacetime years of the 1950s, accounted for approximately 60 percent of federal budgets and 10 percent of the GNP. Overall public expenditures—federal, state, and local—had amounted to only 10 percent of the GNP in 1929; by the mid-1950s they accounted for more than 25 percent. Governments directly employed more than 8 million people by 1957, double the number in 1940. Government work, overwhelmingly white-collar, was the fastest-growing area of the economy.

Books like Galbraith's *Affluent Society* accurately exposed many limits to this affluence: technological unemployment, depressed areas, slums, inadequate health care, decaying urban schools, racial injustice. The distribution of income remained inequitable; in 1955 the poorest fifth of American families earned 4.8 percent of the national income, while the top fifth earned 20.3 percent. Also, the rate of economic growth slowed down considerably late in the decade. In 1960, nearly 40 million Americans lived below a "poverty line" of $3,000 for a family of four. This was 22 percent of the population. Galbraith's *Affluent Society* also stressed the power of consumerism. Americans, he observed, were caught in an often frantic effort to accumulate as many consumer goods—especially automobiles—as they could. This quest imposed great pressures on working families. Millions of such families ran up large debts and had to work extremely hard to maintain the ever more expensive life styles enjoyed by the upper middle classes and promoted by the mass media. To a considerable extent, consumerism also tended to blind middle-class people to the needs of less fortunate Americans for tax-supported public services, most of which increased only slightly during the 1950s. Busy trying to amass personal possessions, these middle-class people tended to ignore the poor.

In history, however, what people think is often more important than reality. Sure that ever-greater prosperity lay ahead, Americans remained blind to the signs of poverty and stagnation. Moreover, there was no denying the fact of economic growth or of the boundless supplies of gadgetry available (on credit) to the majority of people. The United States, the richest nation in world history, was wealthier than it had ever been and incomparably more prosperous than in the 1930s. In such a world it was not at all surprising that self-satisfaction and materialism seemed stronger than in many periods of the American past.

THE ASCENDANCY OF THE RIGHT

Those who hoped for social reform found this complacency ominous indeed. As progressives were forced to recognize, people were tired of the Korean War and of partisan controversy. They wanted to be left alone to enjoy their material rewards.

Though Americans voted Democratic in congressional elections (even in 1956), they did not coalesce to demand progressive legislation. Like the 1920s, the decade was the despair of reformers.

In such an atmosphere McCarthyism continued to thrive. Because the GOP controlled the Congress in 1953, McCarthy became chairman of his own investigating committee, which he used to step up his accusations of communist subversion in government. His top aide, Roy Cohn, and Cohn's friend, G. David Schine, undertook a reckless and widely publicized tour of American embassies in Europe, where they searched for leftist books in government libraries and made a laughingstock of the State Department. A few books were actually burned. McCarthy even cowed the new administration into permitting endless security checks on high-ranking employees, some of whom were forced to resign not because they were disloyal but because they were what the government now vaguely termed "security risks." Among these was J. Robert Oppenheimer, "father of the atomic bomb," whose security clearance was taken away in December 1953, on the grounds that he opposed development of the H-bomb and had associated with left-wingers in the 1930s. A newsman who returned to Washington after an extended absence in 1954 was appalled. "I let myself into the State Department," he wrote, "and there encountered a few 'Acheson holdovers' cowering in their corners. They were aged and their voices were low. But oddly enough, some of the new Republican appointees whom I met seemed to have muffled voices too. . . . it was like Vienna all over again, where we had learned to beware of eavesdroppers."

McCarthy then turned his guns on the army, which had refused to give preferential treatment to Schine, a draftee. When the army proved slow to cooperate,

The McCarthy-Army hearings. Senator Joe McCarthy presenting dubious "facts" to the obvious disbelief of special counsel for the Army, Joseph Welch, on the left.

McCarthy exploded. "You are a disgrace to the uniform," he told Brigadier General Ralph Zwicker. "You're shielding communist conspirators. You're not fit to be an officer. You're ignorant." Attacks such as these made the hearings, which were televised in the spring of 1954, the most compelling entertainment of the year.

In making such accusations, McCarthy overreached himself. Seeing McCarthy on TV, many Americans began to realize how crude he was. Conservative supporters of the military establishment stiffened. As his appeal ebbed, the Senate roused itself against his insults. (He had described Senator Robert Hendrickson of New Jersey as a "living miracle in that he is without question the only man who has lived so long with neither brains nor guts.") In December 1954 the Senate at last voted, sixty-seven to twenty-two, to "condemn" McCarthy for bringing the Congress into disrepute. McCarthy remained in the Senate, but he was burned out, a casualty of his exaggerations, his alcoholic tendency, and his tiresome repetitions. Three years later, at the age of forty-eight, he died.

McCarthy's downfall, however, did not deter the extreme right wing, which became ever more shrill by the early 1960s. It included members of such superpatriotic groups as the John Birch Society and the Christian Anti-Communist Crusade. Robert Welch, founder of the John Birch Society, insisted that the Soviets were proceeding against America "on the soundest of strategy. It calls for paralyzing their enemy and their enemy's will to resist by internal subversion before ever striking a blow." Eisenhower, Welch concluded, was a "dedicated, conscious agent of the communist conspiracy."

This "Radical Right," as it was called, was much too extreme to be taken seriously by the voters. Unlike McCarthyism, which had some grass-roots support, it appealed primarily to superpatriots and reactionaries who had been ranting against "big government" since 1933. Still, by 1961, a Gallup poll reported that the goals of the John Birch Society were approved by 7 million Americans. The far Right's hostility to big government also had the backing of aggressive conservatives in Congress.

By mid-decade many of these men were focusing their attacks on the Supreme Court, which they said was "coddling" communists and other undesirables, including blacks. Led by Chief Justice Earl Warren, whom Eisenhower appointed to the court in 1953, the judges revealed their liberal orientation in 1954 by ruling unanimously (in *Brown* v. *Board of Education*) against school segregation. The decision capped years of litigation by lawyers for black families in several states—families that suffered abuse and economic hardship during their ordeals in the courts. "Separate educational facilities," the Court said in reversing precedents dating from *Plessy* v. *Ferguson* (1896), "are inherently unequal . . . segregation is a denial of the equal protection of the laws." The Court in 1955 then called for school desegregation with "all deliberate speed." Outraged, Senator Eastland denounced the Court's "monstrous crime. . . . These antagonistic decisions are . . . bent upon the destruction of the American form of government and the mongrelization of the white race." Led by Eastland, nineteen southern senators and seventy-seven representatives signed a manifesto in 1956 that bound them to "use all lawful means to bring about a reversal of this decision which is contrary to the Court and to prevent the use of force in its implementation." Among southern senators only Lyndon Johnson of Texas and Estes Kefauver and Albert Gore of Tennessee refused to sign.

Having infuriated the South, the Court then asked for trouble from zealous anticommunists and advocates of what President Richard Nixon was later to celebrate as "law and order." In *Service* v. *Dulles* (1957) it reinstated John Service, a State Department expert on China who had been dismissed in 1951 after six loyalty clearances. The decision forced the administration to clarify its procedures concerning so-called security risks in government. In *Mallory* v. *U.S.* (1957), it ruled that an accused rapist had been illegally charged because he had been held too long before being brought before a magistrate. Alleged criminals, the Court ruled, must be arraigned "without unnecessary delay." And in *Yates* v. *U.S.* (1956) the Court reversed the conviction of fourteen Communists jailed under the Smith Act of 1940. Mere advocacy of revolution, the Court stated, did not constitute grounds for convictions. The government must prove that defendants had "organized" revolution and that they had succeeded. The ruling caused the government to drop plans for further prosecutions of Communists.

These decisions began a judicial trend, much accelerated in the 1960s, toward greater federal guarantees for accused criminals and subversives. They showed that the Court had moved beyond the paralyzing anticommunism of the McCarthy era. The Bill of Rights, it seemed, meant what it said. But the decisions also prompted right-wingers to finance "Impeach Earl Warren" billboards along the nation's highways. Edward Corwin, professor of constitutional law at Princeton, wrote The *New York Times* to complain that the Court had gone on a "virtual binge" and "should have its aforesaid nose tweaked." Most alarming to liberal friends of the Court, a bipartisan congressional coalition almost put through legislation in 1958 that would have stripped the Court of its appellate jurisdiction in cases dealing with loyalty programs, contempt of Congress, state sedition statutes, regulations of employment and oaths of allegiance in schools, and admission to state law practice. Only careful maneuvering by Majority Leader Lyndon Johnson managed the forty-nine to forty-one vote that prevented the law from passing the Senate.

A handful of liberal Democratic senators struggled against these right-wing pressures of the 1950s. They included Hubert Humphrey of Minnesota, a crusader for civil rights; Estes Kefauver of Tennessee, who battled for curbs on monopoly and false advertising; and Paul Douglas, an innovative reformer who developed in the 1950s much of the economic legislation of Kennedy's New Frontier and Johnson's Great Society. Still influential in the national party, these liberals nominated a progressive ticket composed of Stevenson and Kefauver in 1956. (Senator John F. Kennedy, less experienced and less liberal than Kefauver, sought the vice-presidency and failed.) The prominence of such men suggested that liberalism was not dead in the 1950s.

But it remained on the defensive. In 1956 Democrats feared to mention national health insurance in their platform. Stevenson, attempting to placate the South, exclaimed during his campaign that the federal government must not send in money or troops to enforce desegregation. "I think that would be a great mistake," he said. "That is exactly what brought on the Civil War. It can't be done by troops, or bayonets. We must proceed gradually, not upsetting habits or traditions that are older than the Republic."

Stevenson lost more heavily to Eisenhower in 1956 than he had in 1952, even though his foe had suffered a heart attack in 1955. But if he had won, he would have had no chance of putting a liberal program through Congress. There the power lay, as it had since the Democrats won majorities in 1954, with moderates led by Johnson in the Senate and by his Texan friend, Sam Rayburn, Speaker of the House. Shrewd and tireless, both men were cool to liberals like Humphrey or Douglas. Even in 1959, when a band of young liberals entered Congress, and in 1961, when President Kennedy launched his New Frontier, these moderates remained in control. This "Four-Party Government," as political scientist James Macgregor Burns described the coexistence of the more conservative congressional wings of both parties with their more liberal national wings, remained a basic reality of American politics in the 1950s.

President Eisenhower

Dwight D. Eisenhower, who presided during the years of these developments, was the nation's most admired war hero in 1945. Decent, democratic, decisive, he had seemed a nonauthoritarian officer as well as a just and likeable man. Truman had told him at Potsdam, "General, there is nothing that you may want that I won't try to help you get. That definitely and specifically includes the presidency in 1948."

By that time, of course, Truman had changed his mind. But politicians of both parties yearned to nominate their hero, both then and in 1952. Like the American people, they were taken by his presence, his air of command, by what the reporter Robert Donovan called his "leaping and effortless smile." People responded also to his moderation, his balanced judgment, and his apparent aloofness from the intrigue of politics. The new president, it appeared, was heaven-sent to deliver the nation from the acrimony of the early 1950s. Like a benign father bringing peace to a quarrelsome tribe, Eisenhower seemed untouchable at the polls.

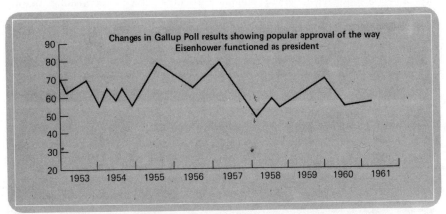

Changes in Gallup Poll results showing popular approval of the way Eisenhower functioned as president

SOURCE: Adapted from p. 104 of *U.S. Foreign Policy: Context, Conduct, Content,* by Marian Irish and Elke Frank. © 1975 by Harcourt Brace Jovanovich, reproduced by permission of the publisher.

Even liberals were prepared to accept him at first. Though to the right of Stevenson, he seemed to provide a sharp contrast to the conservatives in his party who had supported Taft. This image was more appearance than reality, for the new president considered Taft socialistic on such issues as public housing and aid to education. Nevertheless, Eisenhower was apparently willing to maintain the government's active role in the economy. "Never again," he said during the campaign, "shall we allow a depression in the United States." As soon as we "foresee the signs of any recession and depression . . . the full power of private industry, of municipal government, of state government, of the Federal Government will be mobilized to see that that does not happen." This "Modern Republicanism," as his liberal supporters in the eastern wing of the party liked to call it, suggested that the GOP had left Hooverism far behind.

In the late 1960s and 1970s historians of his administration began to appreciate still another of Eisenhower's virtues. This was his shrewdness. Far from having been a placid father figure (a "counterrevolutionist entirely surrounded by men who know how to profit from it," the journalist Elmer Davis had complained in the 1950s), he seemed in retrospect to have been in purposeful control of his administration at all times. Even his convoluted syntax, which had been laughable at the time, seemed part of a deliberate plan. "Don't worry, Jim," he allegedly told his press secretary James Hagerty, who was nervous about an imminent session with reporters. "If that question comes up, I'll just confuse them." As the liberal writer Murray Kempton put it (with some exaggeration) in 1967, Ike "was the great tortoise upon whose back the world sat for eight years. We laughed at him; we talked wistfully about moving; and all the while we never even knew the cunning beneath the shell."

Writers like Kempton, however, could not ignore qualities that prevented Eisenhower from making maximum legislative use of his personal popularity. Among these was a passivity and lack of sophistication that astonished veteran observers in Washington. The best way to prevent selfishness in labor unions or management, he told the cabinet at one point, was to appeal to their sense of fair play. The way to deal with McCarthy was to ignore him. "I will not get into the gutter with that guy," he remarked, as if keeping himself pure would cleanse the country. Eisenhower also told political aides that he would not descend into making "idiotic promises or hints about elect-me-and-I-will-cut-your-taxes-by-such-and-such-a-date! If it takes that kind of foolishness to get elected, then let them find someone else for the job." In fact, Eisenhower was neither so unsophisticated nor so non-

---

I haven't checked these figures, but eighty-seven years ago, I think it was, a number of individuals organized a governmental setup here in this country, I believe it covered eastern areas, with this idea that they were following up based on a sort of national independence arrangement and the program that every individual is just as good as every other individual.

Liberals frequently parodied Eisenhower's inelegant syntax. This parody imagines him delivering Lincoln's Gettysburg Address.

---

partisan as he sounded. Even his handling McCarthy—as he may have suspected—had the virtue of letting his adversary find the rope to hang himself. However, his passive approach to important questions was hardly purposeful leadership.

This approach rested on his view that the presidency must not become too expansive. "I am not one of those desk-pounding types," he explained, "that likes to stick out his jaw and look like he is bossing the show. I don't think it is the function of a President of the United States to punish anybody for voting as he likes." He told his cabinet appointees, "you have full authority. I expect you to stand on your own two feet. Whatever you decide goes. The White House will stay out of your hair." Because big government, like large corporations, had to rely on bureaucrats and managers, his approach had the virtue of freeing him from details. But the deliberate dispersal of power led also to inertia and procrastination. Eisenhower, in I. F. Stone's words, would be a "president in absentia, with a sort of political vacuum in the White House which other men will struggle among themselves to fill." .

Eisenhower's administration reflected his instinctive distaste for involving himself in the legislative process. He rarely applied pressure, and he often sounded ignorant even of important matters. After a Senate committee unanimously reported out to the floor a significant education bill in 1954, he blurted to newsmen, "I do not know the details of that particular legislation. . . . I'd suggest you go to [HEW] Secretary [Oveta Culp] Hobby to find out where we stand." At a press conference following introduction of his Justice Department's civil rights bill in 1957 he told reporters, "I was reading part of that bill this morning, and I—there were certain phrases I didn't completely understand. . . . I would want to talk to the Attorney General." No president since Coolidge had been more poorly informed about what was happening on the Hill.

His practice of paying little attention to details let aides like Sherman Adams, his chief assistant, and top cabinet officials handle many important decisions. Adams, a former governor of New Hampshire, was abrupt, flinty, as cold to self-important officials as New Hampshire granite in winter. Until 1959, when ruffled politicians drove him from power by showing that he had used his influence for personal gain, he made more enemies for Eisenhower than friends. On presidential orders, he kept many important questions from receiving top-level discussion and debate. If the "buck" stopped in the Oval Office under Truman, it floundered in the anterooms from 1953 to 1959.

Other important decisions were left in the hands of conservative businessmen more notable for their wealth than for their political experience. Democrats, indeed, wisecracked that Eisenhower's cabinet consisted of eight millionaires and a plumber (union leader Martin Durkin, who lasted less than a year as secretary of labor). Newsman James Reston added that "there is scarcely a member of the cabinet who can make a moving extemporaneous speech. It is humorless, obvious, unintellectual (almost anti-intellectual), and lacking in the one thing it has talked so much about—a crusading spirit."

Chief among these men, especially during the first term, were Secretary of Agriculture Ezra Taft Benson, Treasury boss George Humphrey, and Charles E. Wilson, who assumed command of the Defense Department. Benson, who served for the entire eight years of Eisenhower's presidency, was a devout Mormon who opened cabinet meetings with a prayer. He was an equally devout economic reactionary who vowed to get the government out of the business of supporting farm prices. In so doing, he hoped that marginal farmers would quit the land, overproduction would cease to be a problem, and federal aid would be unnecessary. This approach infuriated all farmers, marginal or otherwise, who demanded government assistance to 90 percent parity or more. The aroused farm bloc in Congress coalesced to defeat most of his efforts. For all Benson's persistence, overproduction escalated during the decade, and prices sagged. To keep pace, federal spending for agriculture rose from $1 billion in 1952 to $5.1 billion in 1961. Benson, like his predecessors, failed to change the course of American farm policy.

George Humphrey was an old-fashioned fiscal conservative who considered it his job to reduce spending. "We have to cut one-third out of the budget," he said in 1953, "and you can't do that just by eliminating waste. This means, wherever necessary, using a meat axe." In 1957, when Eisenhower announced a mildly expansionary budget for the coming year, Humphrey bluntly called for restraint, saying that without it "we're gonna have a depression which will curl your hair." This contradiction created total confusion over the administration's economic program until 1958.

Wilson was equally anxious to cut back governmental expenditures. During the congressional elections of 1954 he went to Detroit, where thousands of unemployed were clamoring for aid, to celebrate individual initiative. "I've got a lot of sympathy for people where a sudden change catches them," he said, "but I've always liked bird dogs better than kennel-fed dogs myself. You know, one who'll get out and hunt for food rather than sit on his fanny and yell." As this remark suggests, Wilson had an affinity for impolitic statements. One, in 1953, expressed his economic philosophy: "What was good for our country was good for General Motors, and vice versa." In short, the nation had no interests other than those of GM. Another avowed his belief in nuclear weaponry, chiefly because it cost less than large standing armies. "We cannot afford to fight limited wars," he said. "We can only afford to fight a big war, and if there is a war, that is the kind it will be." Appalled by such remarks, James Reston suggested that Wilson had invented the automatic transmission so he would have one foot free to put in his mouth.

Men like Wilson and Humphrey were not out of place in Eisenhower's administration. On the contrary, they reflected the President's fiscal conservatism. Ike once told the cabinet, Sherman Adams reported later, that "if he was able to do nothing as President except balance the budget he would feel that his time in the White House had been well spent." During his eight years as president, federal spending rose by only $8 billion, or 11 percent, while the population as a whole increased by approximately 18 percent. This reluctance to pursue an expansionary fiscal policy cost him dearly by the late 1950s, when his attempts to limit spending helped to promote the deepest recession since the 1930s. Unemployment, which had remained at approximately 4 percent in the peacetime years of 1955 to 1957, suddenly jumped to 6.8 percent in 1958, a figure that involved close to 5 million people. The economy continued to flounder until 1961, so badly that it caused large drops in tax revenue—which in turn created huge budget deficits. Not surprisingly,

Democrats insisted that only they could "get the country moving again." Economic recession did more than anything else to harm the GOP in the election of 1960.

Random quotations from Eisenhower during the decade suggest his conservative views on other issues. On welfare: "If all Americans want is security, they can go to prison." On national health insurance: "I have been against compulsory insurance as a very definite step toward socialized medicine. I don't believe in it, and I want none of it myself." On the appointment of Warren as chief justice: "biggest damn fool mistake I ever made." On the TVA (privately): "I'd like to sell the whole thing, but I suppose we can't go that far." On the *Brown* v. *Board of Education* ruling (publicly): "I think it makes no difference whether or not I endorse it. What I say is—the Constitution is as the Supreme Court interprets it; and I must conform to that and do my very best to see that it is carried out in this country;" and (privately): "I personally think the decision was wrong."

Occasionally, of course, Eisenhower proved flexible enough to accommodate pressure groups. Reactionaries like Barry Goldwater, in fact, grumbled that he was promoting a "Dime Store New Deal." Eisenhower assented to modest increases in social security and in the minimum wage, and to small appropriations for public housing. In 1958 he approved the National Defense Education Act, which Congress hurried through in response to Russia's successful satellite, the Sputnik. The NDEA program provided federal aid for science and language training. In 1960 Eisenhower signed the Kerr-Mills Bill, which offered federal matching money to states that enacted their own health insurance plans for the elderly poor. And in perhaps the most important measure of his administration he readily signed a multi-billion-dollar federal highway construction act in 1956. The measure passed because it satisfied all the important interest groups: state highway officials, who sought federal money; trade unions, who needed jobs for their members; farmers, who wanted better roads to market their goods; and city officials, who yearned for faster links with other urban centers. Unlike social welfare legislation, it commanded bipartisan majorities, for everyone thought well of the automobile. It passed Congress with ease.

The civil rights movement

The quest for civil rights, much accelerated in the 1950s, was the most revealing test not only of Eisenhower's philosophy but also of white America in general. After the Court's rulings in 1954–55 reformers thought optimistically that a new era of race relations was at hand. But Jim Crow statutes continued to enforce racial discrimination in southern housing, transport, and public accommodations. Overtly racist organizations—Citizens Councils, White Americans, Incorporated, the Society for the Preservation of White Integrity—sprang up throughout the South. Moreover, the Court's school decisions did nothing to change the pattern of race relations in the North. There, blacks continued to face systematic job discrimination. There, too, discrimination in housing, along with racially determined school districting, had long resulted in de facto school segregation. Blacks especially

I am convinced that the Supreme Court decision set back progress in the South at least 15 years. . . . It's all very well to talk about school integration—if you remember that you may also be talking about social disintegration. Feelings are deep on this, especially where children are involved. . . . You take the attitude of a fellow like Jimmy Byrnes. We used to be pretty good friends, and now I've not heard from him in the last eighteen months—all because of bitterness on this thing. . . . We can't demand perfection in these moral things. All we can do is keep working toward a goal and keep it high. And the fellow who tries to tell me that you can do these things by force is just plain NUTS.

Eisenhower expresses himself on the issues of school desegregation and civil rights.

resented their exclusion from white residential areas, many of which were developing modern educational facilities to cope with the population explosion. Levittown, Pennsylvania, one of developer William Levitt's mass-produced lower-middle-class housing projects, had 60,000 residents in 1957, not one of whom was black. That was because Levitt, fearful of "white flight" if blacks were permitted to move in, had steadfastly refused to open the development to Negroes. When a black family bought a house that year from a white owner there, sullen mobs of local residents milled about the house. A rock shattered the home's picture window. Cars, bedecked with Confederate flags, tore by noisily in the night. After two months of this kind of intimidation, the governor made it clear that he would tolerate no more such harassment, and the trouble stopped. But it was not until three years later, after blacks brought suit charging that discrimination in the sale of homes purchased with federally assisted mortgages was unconstitutional, that Levitt himself finally began selling homes directly to blacks.

Meanwhile, "massive resistance" in the South proved especially effective in stalling all efforts to end Jim Crow laws and school segregation. To subvert the Court, southern leaders employed countersuits, economic pressures, physical intimidation, and violence to stop black children from entering their white schools. Whites also resorted to a variety of legal ruses to evade the Court's rulings. One was to establish state-supported "private" schools—of course, for whites only. Another was "pupil placement" laws. These authorized local school boards to assign students to schools on the basis of their ability to adjust to new surroundings, their "mental energy," or their "morals, conduct, health, and personal standards." Some of these measures even secured later legal sanction. In 1958, in *Shuttlesworth* v. *Birmingham Board of Education,* the Court upheld Alabama's pupil placement law. This ruling, permitting the white South to subvert the meaning of "all deliberate speed," enraged civil rights militants.

The modern civil rights movement, which reflected the anger and impatience of blacks at these evasions, surfaced on a broad scale in Montgomery, Alabama, in December 1955. There a black woman named Rosa Parks, tired of Jim Crow laws on the city's buses, refused to surrender her seat to a white man, and was fined for breaking the law. Local black leaders responded by developing a boycott of the buses. Led by a charismatic young minister, the Reverend Martin Luther King, Jr., the city's 50,000 blacks carried out the boycott for almost a year. In doing so, they practiced nonviolent protest. The city's whites, by contrast, responded by denouncing King as a dangerous radical (he was not; he did not demand that blacks sit where they pleased, only that seating be done on a first-come, first-serve basis, with blacks filling in seats from back to front and whites from front to back). Extremists went further, bombing black homes and churches.

Beset, King's followers seemed destined for defeat, especially after the courts upheld a suit brought by whites against black car pools. But King and his followers held firm, and the Supreme Court ruled in November 1956 that Alabama's laws requiring segregation on buses were unconstitutional. Shortly thereafter, following more violence by whites, the buses were finally integrated. The bus boycott marked the first large-scale, well-publicized, and successful use of direct-action tactics on behalf of civil rights in the South.

The boycott also marked the rise to national prominence of King, who thereafter spread the gospel of nonviolent protest. In the next thirteen years, King's eloquence, faith, and commitment to nonviolence provided inspirational leadership for blacks and for ever-increasing numbers of whites. Many of these people maintained ties with older, established organizations such as the NAACP and the National Urban League. But they also grew increasingly impatient with strictly legal assaults on discrimination, and they came to distrust governmental figures—judges, congressmen, politicians generally. For them, direct-action tactics such as King's were much more attractive means of protest. Their courageous activities, indeed, were necessary to prod an often reluctant and slow-moving government into trying to better race relations in America.

The President was not wholly blind to these developments. In a series of executive actions he moved to improve conditions in the District of Columbia and in military camps. In 1957, when Governor Orval Faubus of Arkansas directly defied federal authority, thereby encouraging hostile mobs to bar nine blacks from entering a previously all-white school in Little Rock, Eisenhower sent in troops to sustain token desegregation. He signed civil rights acts in 1957 and 1960, the first passed since Reconstruction. These laws established a federal commission on civil rights. They also gave the government added powers to promote equal voting rights in the South. Most important, Eisenhower's attorney general, Herbert Brownell, was careful to appoint competent, indeed courageous, men to federal judgeships in the South. In the next few years these men did much to strike down legal precedents promoting racial segregation in the South.

But Eisenhower honestly believed that only changing attitudes, not government, could alleviate racial tensions. When it came to changing personal values, he said, ''we cannot do it by cold lawmaking, but must make these changes by appealing to reason, by prayer, and by constantly working at it through our own efforts.'' Accordingly, he did nothing to counter racial injustice in the North and said nothing against southern violence, including the lynching of Emmet Till, a young black boy found brutally murdered. Eisenhower's refusal to applaud the Court's decisions also encouraged the southern resistance. Indeed, Faubus acted defiantly because he assumed that the White House would do nothing to stop him. In 1958 and 1959 the governor closed Little Rock's high school altogether rather than submit again to the law of the land. As reformers had warned, the Deep South easily circumvented the civil rights acts of 1957 and 1960, which Eisenhower did nothing to promote. In his attitude toward civil rights the President revealed that he, like many contemporaries, failed to perceive the revolution in expectations that had been growing among blacks since World War II.

Popular complacency, to say nothing of the barriers posed by the Right and by Congress, would have prevented even the most charismatic of leaders from accomplishing very much during the 1950s. Therefore, Eisenhower was not to blame for the decade's rather barren legislative record. Moreover, he proved responsible in his use of presidential power. No postwar president was as respectful of the constitutional prerogatives of Congress. Particularly in his second term, however, he failed to respond to economic stagnation, to urban blight, and especially to the movement for racial justice. Within a few years that movement escalated into militant protest that forced the hands of Eisenhower's successors.

The Cold War continues, 1953–61

Containment, the Republican platform announced in 1952, was "negative, futile, and immoral." It abandoned "countless human beings to a despotism and Godless terrorism." The United States, the party implied, must take steps to "liberate" these downtrodden masses from their oppressors.

The atmosphere in Moscow was hardly more promising for détente. When George Kennan arrived in May 1952 to take up his duties as ambassador, he found Soviet personnel at the embassy too terrified even to help him with his bags, much

---

America's mood:
the public's view
of the most important problem
facing the country,
according to Gallup Poll results,
1953–60

1953	Korean War
1954	Threat of war
1955	Working out a peace
1956	Threat of war
1957	Keeping out of war
1958	Economic conditions
1959	Keeping peace
1960	Relations with Russia

SOURCE: Adapted from *U.S. Foreign Policy: Context, Conduct, Content* by Marian Irish and Elke Frank. © 1975 by Harcourt Brace Jovanovich. Reproduced by permission of the publisher.

---

less talk with him. He discovered that five guards had been assigned to follow him, that he was prevented from talking privately with people, and that his residence was electronically bugged. When he complained of such treatment, he was declared *persona non grata* by the Soviet government. Not until the spring of 1953, when Charles ("Chip") Bohlen was finally confirmed as the new ambassador, did America get around to replacing him.

During Eisenhower's years in the White House several developments promised to soften this frigid state of affairs. Most important of these was the death of Stalin in March 1953 and his replacement by new figures, including Nikita Khrushchev, who became the major power in Russia by 1956. Another was the Korean armistice in July 1953. Most important, though little realized at the time, China, Japan, and western Europe were developing into powers in their own right. By the 1960s the bipolar confrontation between Russia and America was giving way to a multiplication of power blocs.

Both nations acted sporadically to take advantage of these forces for coexistence. In 1953 Eisenhower startled hard-liners by calling for disarmament, and in 1955 he appealed for a condition of "open skies" over Russia and the United States, a proposal aimed at promoting meaningful arms control. In 1955 Russia attended a summit conference at Geneva—the first between Soviet and American heads of state since the meeting at Potsdam ten years earlier. Though the conference settled nothing, it showed that the Russians were willing to mingle with American diplomats. In 1956, when Khrushchev denounced Stalin as a "distrustful man, sickly and suspicious," and recounted his "crimes" and "tortures" while head of state, it seemed certain that the Soviet Union was taking a more conciliatory course.

Despite this potential for mutual understanding, relations between Russia and the United States remained cold throughout the 1950s. The Soviet suppression of the Hungarian revolution in 1956, its threats to isolate West Berlin, and finally its apparent support of revolutionary activity in Cuba and other parts of Latin America, all antagonized the Western powers. America's containment policy, which encircled Russia with naval power and military bases and which included the use of high-level reconnaisance planes to spy on Soviet territory, kept the Russians uneasy and resentful. Persistent American talk about liberating eastern Europe was more provocative still. As both sides developed hydrogen bombs and intercontinental missiles, the tension mounted.

Assigning blame for these tensions to individuals is neither easy nor especially helpful. Eisenhower and Khrushchev led societies whose fundamental differences prompted widespread feelings of insecurity and mutual distrust. Neither man had the freedom of action to end the Cold War. Indeed, as McCarthy's influence suggested, domestic obstacles to changing American attitudes were stronger than ever. The military, defense contractors, and the leading labor unions continued to promote a tough line. Influential politicians, including Republican Senate Leader William Knowland, constantly demanded that the administration act more firmly than it did. By contrast, advocates of détente were weak and scattered, and disarmament groups such as the Committee for a Sane Nuclear Policy (SANE) seemed almost subversive. In foreign affairs, as in domestic policy, Eisenhower had to operate under popular, institutional, and political constraints.

I'll be glad to restore peace in the Middle East too

In contending with these forces, however, Eisenhower named as his secretary of state John Foster Dulles, one of America's most outspoken anticommunists. The nephew of Robert Lansing, Wilson's secretary of state, and the grandson of John Foster, secretary of state under Benjamin Harrison, Dulles has been intimately involved in the making of foreign policy since 1907, when as a Princeton undergraduate he served as secretary to the Hague Peace Conference.

But if Eisenhower seriously hoped for détente, he would have done well to choose someone else. For it was Dulles who drafted the "liberation" plank for the party in 1952. A stern Presbyterian, Dulles loathed "atheistic communism," and he took a moralistic approach to foreign policy. A skilled lawyer, he handled negotiations like a prosecutor in a criminal trial, not like a diplomat hoping for compromise. His rigid, humorless approach made him the butt of wits, who dubbed him "Dull, Duller, Dulles." It earned him the cordial dislike not only of the Soviets but also of many French and British statesmen of the period. He was hardly the man to promote international good will.

Dulles was ambitious for himself and his party. He was acutely aware of the fate that had befallen Acheson, his predecessor, at the hands of men like McCarthy. He resolved therefore to give the Right no cause for suspicion. This meant actively supporting self-styled security experts, who terminated the appointments of some 5,000 State Department employees by August 1953, and ignoring advisers—no matter how expert—who might appear to be at all "soft" on communism. Among those who were not reassigned, and who therefore retired early, was Kennan, America's foremost expert on the Soviet Union. Sherman Adams, who tried to be objective, later conceded that Dulles' "point of view was often negative" and that he had induced a "strong aversion among foreign service career men to anything imaginative and original."

While purging the State Department, Dulles also acted to commit the new administration to hard-line policies. In January he succeeded in getting Eisenhower to insert a section in his state of the union message calling in effect for the "unleashing" of Chiang Kai-shek. Such a policy appeared to be aimed at promoting the "liberation" of mainland China from communism. In March Dulles made no effort to work for détente following the death of Stalin. At the same time he let the Chinese Communists know, again with Eisenhower's blessing, that the United States might use nuclear weapons in Korea if they did not soon agree to an armistice. When China backed off in July, it appeared that his nuclear blackmail (perhaps assisted by a more moderate Soviet line following the death of Stalin) had helped to end the war.

By 1954, when he enjoyed Eisenhower's full confidence, it was clear that Dulles planned to rely on two related policies to sustain his anticommunist world view. One, which he spelled out in April, was already implicit in Secretary of Defense Wilson's policy of the "new look"—heavy dependence on nuclear weapons and strategic bombing. A potential aggressor, Dulles explained, "should know in advance that he can and will be made to suffer for his aggression more than he can possibly gain by it. This calls for a system in which local defensive strength is reinforced by more mobile deterrent power. . . . the main reliance must be on the power of the free community to retaliate with great force by mobile means at places of its own choice." In simpler language this policy of "massive retaliation" meant "more bang for the buck," an approach that Russia emulated in policies dubbed "more rubble for the ruble."

The related policy, which critics labeled "brinkmanship," was part of the Eisenhower-Dulles approach from the time it was first used against the Chinese concerning Korea. Its central assumption was that potentially unfriendly nations understood nothing but force, especially nuclear force. Therefore, the United States must be prepared to threaten war. "The ability to get to the verge without getting into the war," Dulles wrote, "is the necessary art. If you cannot master it, you inevitably get into war."

In applying these doctrines Dulles and Eisenhower paid particular attention to Asia. It was there that Republican stalwarts like Senator Knowland demanded firmness. It was there, too, that threats seemed worth making, for Asian communists lacked the nuclear might of the Soviet Union. The first test was in Indochina, where rebels were gaining in their long war against French colonialism. Responding to French pleas, the Truman administration had already pumped millions of dollars into the area. But the forces of Ho Chi Minh, a Communist who led a broad-based nationalist coalition, trapped the French at Dien Bien Phu in May 1954 and threatened to drive them out of the country.

Many high-ranking members of the Eisenhower administration joined Dulles in recommending the use of American naval and air power—perhaps including atomic weapons—to assist the French. These included Admiral Arthur Radford, chairman of the joint chiefs of staff, and Vice-President Nixon. Eisenhower, too, believed that the loss of Indochina to communism would be contagious. "You have a row of dominos set up," he observed, "and you knock over the first one, and what will happen to the last one is the certainty that it will go over very quickly. So you have a beginning of a disintegration that would have the most profound influences." Before pursuing this "domino theory," however, Eisenhower insisted that Dulles consult congressional leaders and the Allies. As Eisenhower perhaps anticipated, they rejected the idea of using American force against a popular revolutionary movement on the other side of the globe. Bowing to the inevitable after the ensuing fall of Dien Bien Phu, the United States accepted (but refused to sign) an accord worked out at Geneva. It created the countries of Laos, Cambodia, and Vietnam, the last to be divided temporarily at the seventeenth parallel pending elections in 1956 that were to determine the government of a unified nation.

To counter this loss to the West, Dulles embarked on what later critics termed "pactomania": formation of the South East Asia Treaty Organization later in 1954. Its signatories, the United States, Great Britain, France, Australia, New Zealand, the Philippines, Pakistan, and Thailand, contracted to consult in the event of a communist attack on one of them. A separate protocol covered Laos, Cambodia, and Vietnam. However, SEATO did not include such important Asian nations as India, Indonesia, and Burma; it set up no military force like that which was being developed under NATO; and it required the members only to consult, not to fight. It became little more than a convenient excuse for American participation in Asian affairs.

The next test of administration policy in Asia involved China, where the Nationalists, who had fled to the island of Formosa, and the mainland Communists had been threatening each other since 1950. The administration continued the futile policy of nonrecognition of Communist China. In 1954 Dulles also negotiated a treaty that committed the United States to defend Formosa and the neighboring Pescadore Islands against attack from the mainland. The Communists responded by lobbing shells at Quemoy and Matsu, two Nationalist-held islands close to the mainland. Eisenhower then asked Congress for blanket authority to use force in the area as he, the commander-in-chief, saw fit. This was a shrewd maneuver, for it left him armed in advance—as Truman never had been in Korea—with congressional sanction. Nine years later President Johnson was to employ a similar tactic following alleged attacks on American ships in the Tonkin Gulf. As the more avid Asia-firsters complained, however, Eisenhower's action stopped short of "unleashing" Chiang Kai-shek or of adopting massive retaliation against the communists. Mao Tse-tung's forces bombed the islands sporadically throughout the 1950s and took the Tachens, a small group of islands north of Quemoy and Matsu, without any countermove from the United States. As in Indochina, Eisenhower stopped short of getting America's military involved.

The failure to dislodge Mao Tse-tung in China revealed the inappropriateness of the "liberation" policy. Liberation proved equally futile in eastern Europe, where the Soviets tightened their control throughout the 1950s. When Poland and East Germany rebelled against Russian rule, America did nothing. In 1956, when Russian tanks quashed a revolution in Hungary, the Eisenhower administration again stood by helplessly. Liberation, like massive retaliation, was useful for domestic political consumption. But it was too extreme to receive widespread endorsement either at home or among America's allies. And in the absence of large ground forces, which Eisenhower was cutting back, it was too incredible to be believed by the communists.

Moving into Hungary would have been particularly difficult, for two days before Soviet tanks rolled into Budapest, the Western allies broke openly over policy in Egypt. Here, too, Dulles' moralistic style contributed to America's difficulties. In 1954, General Gamal Abdal Nasser, the nationalistic strong man who had taken over in Egypt, induced Great Britain, which controlled the Suez Canal, to remove its troops from the area by 1956. Nasser then turned to the United States, Britain, and the World Bank for a loan to build the High Aswan Dam to harness the Nile River. At first Dulles encouraged the project, which appeared settled at the end of 1955.

Nasser, however, made threatening statements to Israel, which had relied on America for its sustenance ever since Truman proffered it instant recognition in 1948. In May 1956 Nasser recognized Communist China. He also negotiated an arms deal with Czechoslovakia, one result of which was to permit the arrival in Egypt of hundreds of Soviet technicians. To Dulles, the prospect of communist infiltration was disturbing enough, but Nasser also mortgaged Egypt's cotton crop—the nation's primary source of revenue—to pay for the arms. How, Americans asked, was Egypt to repay the loan for Aswan? Southern senators in particular grumbled that the United States was promoting foreign competition against American cotton. Their complaints revealed the thrust of economic considerations in postwar foreign policy. All these developments caused the United States to procrastinate in authorizing the loan. Egypt, impatient, then let it be known it would turn to the Soviet Union. This form of blackmail infuriated Dulles. Without consulting experts in the State Department, the Western allies, or World Bank officials, he simply announced that the loan was off. He hoped his action would call Russia's bluff and show have-not nations they could not push the United States around.

His decision merely infuriated Nasser, who immediately nationalized the Suez Canal and closed it to Israeli shipping. Tolls, Egypt said, would help pay for the dam. The Soviet Union then came through with the aid that Dulles had refused. And two months later, after communications between Dulles and the Western allies had all but broken down, Israeli troops stormed into the Sinai Peninsula. Britain and France, in what was obviously a well-planned move, assisted Israel.

When Russia stood behind Egypt, it looked as if World War III was on the horizon. Eisenhower, however, determined not to aid the Western allies, and America sponsored a United Nations resolution condemning Israel, Britain, and France, and proposing that UN forces be dispatched to stabilize the situation. Without American backing, the invaders had no choice but to pull out.

Eisenhower's action revealed his essential good judgment concerning military affairs. Fighting a war, even a limited one, to promote Western colonialism in Egypt would have been unwise. But the confrontation exposed the rifts in the

Western alliance that Dulles' cavalier diplomacy had helped to develop. In the Arab world it enormously expanded the popularity of Nasser, who resented his treatment at the hands of the West. And it enabled Russia to claim that it had come to the aid of anticolonialism in the Middle East.

The Suez crisis also exposed the Eisenhower administration's lack of understanding of the forces animating the Third World. To Dulles, as to most Americans at the time, nations like Egypt were important only in terms of the Cold War. "Neutralism," he said, "was immoral." America's task was to prop up pro-Western regimes, whether dictatorial or not—not to work for social reforms. Governments that turned to the Left, as Egypt's did under Nasser, must be restrained or, like Iran's in 1953 or Guatemala's in 1954, overthrown with the connivance of the CIA. Reflecting this attitude, the administration attempted to preserve its influence in the Middle East by proclaiming the so-called Eisenhower Doctrine, approved by Congress in 1957. This promised military aid to friendly governments, thus helping to promote arms sales in that already explosive region. It also authorized Eisenhower to dispatch troops to counter communist advances. Using this authority, the President helped preserve anticommunist factions in Jordan in April 1957. In the summer of 1958 he went still further, by sending marines into Lebanon to preserve a right-wing government that was unconstitutionally clinging to power. These actions temporarily sustained Western influence in the area. But they did nothing to come to terms with the forces of nationalism and reform in the Middle East.

Eisenhower's administration also encountered sharp anti-American feelings in Latin America. Vice-President Nixon, visiting Venezuela in 1958, was stoned as his car drove through the streets of Caracas. Cuba's Fidel Castro, relying heavily on anti-American diatribes, overthrew the dictatorial regime of Fulgencio Batista in 1959. "Revolution," the president's brother Milton Eisenhower concluded in 1960, "is inevitable in Latin America. The people are angry. They are shackled to the past with bonds of ignorance, injustice, and poverty. And they no longer accept as universal or inevitable the oppressive prevailing order. . . ."

These events in Latin America symbolized the Eisenhower administration's troubled life in foreign affairs during the second term. In 1957 the Soviets electrified the world by being the first to fire a satellite into space. Americans, once secure and arrogant in their presumed scientific superiority, reacted with surprise and shock. In 1958 Dulles grew ill (he died of cancer in 1959), and Eisenhower assumed more direct control of policy, working harder than before for détente; in 1959 Khrushchev even paid a celebrated visit to the United States, and another summit conference was scheduled for Paris in May 1960. On the eve of the conference, however, the Soviets shot down an American U-2 reconnaisance plane that had been photographing Russian installations. In this atmosphere the summit conference broke up on the very first day, and the Soviets withdrew an invitation for Eisenhower to visit Moscow later in the year. For the remainder of Eisenhower's presidency Soviet-American relations were more frigid than ever.

A summary judgment of the Eisenhower administration's foreign policy must begin by reiterating the constraints under which he had to operate: unreasoning anticommunism among the public, economic pressures against détente, the power of the military-industrial complex, and, not the least important, Russian provoca-

Eisenhower and Khrushchev enjoying a light moment during the latter's visit in 1959. Those sharing in the joke are from left to right: Vice President Richard M. Nixon, U.N. Ambassador Henry Cabot Lodge, Jr., President Eisenhower, Secretary of State Christian Herter, and Soviet Premier Khrushchev.

tions such as the suppression of the Hungarian revolt. Moreover, Eisenhower himself ordinarily showed balanced judgment—in Vietnam, over Quemoy and Matsu, over Suez. To his credit, he secured peace in Korea, and he kept the country from war for the next seven and a half years. Rhetoric aside, he continued, rather than reversed, the major policies of the Truman administration. As revisionists have rightly observed, he seems among the least bellicose of America's postwar presidents.

But questions remain. What if he had consistently pursued détente in the aftermath of Stalin's death? Suppose he had never named Dulles secretary of state, or, having named him, had taken command himself, as he began to do in 1958? And suppose further that he had appreciated the strivings of the Third World? If he had done these things, he might have succeeded in educating the citizenry about the dangers of rocket-rattling in the nuclear age.

The end of the Eisenhower order

John F. Kennedy's victory over Richard Nixon in the presidential election of 1960 appeared a striking repudiation of the past. After all, Kennedy was only forty-three when he took office—the first president to be born in the twentieth century, and the second youngest (next to TR) in American history. He was the first Roman Catholic to be elected president: Americans, it seemed, had progressed far since repudiating Smith in 1928. Most important, he imparted an air of vigor and purpose to the country. By struggling for a progressive program of domestic policies, he pledged to get the country moving again. He was to help the nation cross a "New Frontier."

People who expected wonders from the new president, however, would have done well to observe several aspects of the campaign. Kennedy was not the liberals' favorite—that had been either Humphrey or Stevenson, who still commanded widespread support in a third bid for the nomination. In selecting Lyndon Johnson as his running mate, Kennedy merely underlined the political caution he had displayed in four years as a representative and eight years as an uninfluential senator from Massachusetts. "I'm not a liberal at all," he told an interviewer. "I never joined the ADA [Americans for Democratic Action] or the American Veterans Committee. I'm not comfortable with those people." Reassuring conservatives, he added, "I believe in the balanced budget," except in a *"grave* national emergency or *serious* recession." Eleanor Roosevelt, speaking for many liberals who distrusted Kennedy, explained, "I would hesitate to place the difficult decisions that the next President will have to make with someone who understands what courage is and admires it, but has not quite the independence to have it."

People like Eleanor Roosevelt were especially critical of some of Kennedy's statements. In 1949 he had said that Truman had "lost" China. "Those responsible for the tragedy of China must be searched out and spotlighted," he proclaimed. ". . . What our young men had saved, our diplomats and presidents had frittered away." Pursuing this anticommunist line during the campaign in 1960, he berated the Eisenhower administration for its "softness" regarding Quemoy and Matsu and appealed to Cold War passions. "The enemy," he told an audience in Salt Lake City, "is the communist system itself—implacable, insatiable, unceasing in its drive for world domination. For this is not a struggle for the supremacy of arms alone—it is also a struggle for supremacy between two conflicting ideologies: Freedom under God versus ruthless, godless tyranny."

During his unprecedented television debates with Nixon—debates that probably enhanced his appeal with millions of voters who did not know him as well as Nixon—Kennedy also adopted a bellicose stance regarding Cuba's Fidel Castro, who was pursuing an anti-American line. When Eisenhower clamped an embargo on Cuba, Kennedy complained that it was "too little too late" and that it followed an "incredible history of blunder, inaction, retreat, and failure." The United States, he proclaimed, must "strengthen the non-Batista exiles in the United States and in Cuba itself." This was a demagogic statement, for he knew that anti-Castro exiles were even then being trained by the Eisenhower administration. In making it he exposed the passion for winning that critics perceived in the Kennedys. He showed that Cold War rhetoric was not the preserve of Nixon alone.

The results of the election failed also to produce much of a mandate for anyone. Kennedy did poorly in Protestant sections, where the political scientist V. D. Key detected "massive shifts" away from the Democratic ticket. Overall, his Catholicism hurt him more than it helped. Kennedy's total vote of 34.2 million exceeded Nixon's by only 118,000. Without very narrow victories in crucial states such as Pennsylvania, Missouri, and Illinois (where vote frauds in Democratic Cook County may have made the difference), Kennedy would have lost the election. And his new Congress, while nominally Democratic, had twenty additional Republicans in the House to bolster the conservative coalition.

It is hazardous to speculate on the major reasons for Kennedy's victory. Among them, however, was probably Nixon himself, who proved an energetic but unattractive candidate. Kennedy benefited also from Eisenhower's foreign policy setbacks, especially the U-2 affair. His constant focus on the nation's economic stagnation probably helped him most of all. He scored well—like many northern Democrats since the 1930s—in the populous black, ethnic, and industrial wards of

Election, 1960

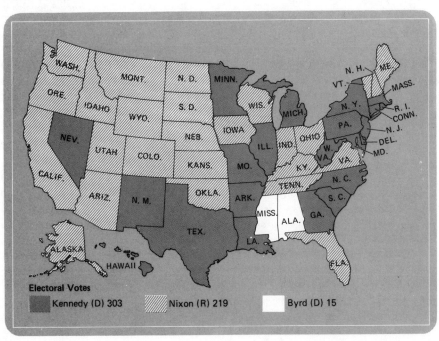

Electoral Votes
Kennedy (D) 303   Nixon (R) 219   Byrd (D) 15

urban America. He carried twenty-seven of the nation's forty-one largest cities, including all the biggest ones, where he rolled up a plurality of 2.7 million votes. This continuity in voting patterns reveals that Eisenhower's triumphs in 1952 and 1956 had been aberrations attributable to his unique personal appeal, and that Kennedy won because normally Democratic America reverted to form.

For these reasons the election suggests that voters in 1960 harkened as much to the past as to the future. The nation remained essentially Democratic, as it had since Franklin D. Roosevelt perfected the art of blaming Hoover for the world's problems. It remained divided, though less so than in the past, along religious lines. It responded, or so it seemed, as strongly as ever to appeals for fiscal conservatism, and to candidates of the political center. And it listened as attentively as before to inflammatory Cold War rhetoric. For all the talk about a New Frontier, it was fair to say in 1960, as it had been in 1952, that America, affluent and middle-class, still yearned as much for stability and consensus as for dramatic change.

Suggestions for reading

An important aid in understanding American life since 1945 is William Leuchtenburg, *A Troubled Feast** (1973). Books covering economic change in the 1940s and 1950s include John Brooks, *The Great Leap** (1966); H. P. Miller, *Rich Man Poor Man** (1964), a study of income distribution; Michael Harrington, *The Other America** (1962), a vivid account of poverty; David Potter, *People of Plenty** (1954), a far-ranging book concerning the effect of abundance on the American character; and E. L. Dole, *Conservatives in Power* (1960), which deals with government budgetary policy. Two books by John Kenneth Galbraith offer challenging interpretations of economic life: *American Capitalism** (1952) and *The Affluent Society** (1958). Richard Polenberg's *One Nation Divisible: Class, Race, and Ethnicity in the United States Since 1938* (1980) is especially valuable. Finally, see Godfrey Hodgson, *America in Our Time: From World War II to Nixon* (1976), an interpretive survey of the era.

Social trends are the subject of S. M. Lipset and Reinhart Bendix, *Social Mobility in Industrial Society* (1959); Peter M. Blau and Otis D. Duncan, *The American Occupational Structure* (1967); Robert C. Wood, *Suburbia** (1959); Scott Donaldson, *The Suburban Myth** (1969); William Dobriner, *Class in Suburbia** (1963); and William H. Whyte, *Organization Man** (1956). Like Whyte and Potter, David Riesman discusses the American national character in his widely read *Lonely Crowd** (1950). Books covering aspects of thought in the 1950s also include Lawrence Lipton, *The Holy Barbarians* (1959), on the "beats"; Sam Hunter and John Jacobus, *American Art of the Twentieth Century* (1974); and Richard Kostelanetz, ed., *The New American Arts* (1967).

For religious trends see Will Herberg, *Protestant Catholic Jew** (2nd ed., 1960), a challenging sociological analysis; and Digby Baltzell, *The Protestant Establishment: Aristocracy and Caste in America** (1964). C. Wright Mills offers sharp critiques of American society in *White Collar** (1951), and *The Power Elite** (1956). Edward Banfield, *The Unheavenly City Revisited** (1974), gives a provocative critique of policies to aid the cities. So do Martin Anderson, *The Federal Bulldozer* (1967), and Herbert Gans, *The Urban Villagers** (1962), both of which show the unhappy results of urban renewal. For the role of the military see Edward B. Glick, *Soldiers, Scholars, and Society* (1971); and Samuel Huntington, *The Soldier and the State* (1957). A critique of the military-industrial complex is Seymour Melman, *Pentagon Capitalism* (1970).

Books on politics in the 1950s are Peter Lyon, *Eisenhower** (1974); Herbert Parmet, *Eisenhower and the Great Crusades* (1972); James T. Patterson, *Mr. Republican: A Biography of Robert A. Taft* (1972); and especially James Sundquist, *Politics and Policy: The Eisenhower, Kennedy, and Johnson Years** (1968). Useful accounts by members of the Eisenhower administrations are Arthur Larson, *Eisenhower: The President Nobody Knew** (1968); and Emmet John Hughes, *The Ordeal of Power* (1963), which is unflattering. I. F. Stone, *The Haunted Fifties** (1964), contains articles highly critical of the Eisenhower administration. Political trends are surveyed in Samuel Lubell, *The Revolt of the Moderates* (1956); and in Norman Nie et al., *The Changing American Voter* (1979), an authoritative study of voting in the postwar era. Biographies are Kenneth Davis, *Adlai Stevenson** (1957); and Joseph Gorman, *Kefauver: A Political Biography* (1971).

For the civil rights revolution see Steven S. Lawson, *Black Ballots: Voting Rights in the South, 1944–1969* (1976); J. Harvie Wilkinson, *From Brown to Bakke: The Supreme Court and School Integration, 1954–1978* (1980); David Lewis, *King: A Critical Biography** (1970); and Robert Brisbane, *Racial Revolution in the United States, 1954–1970* (1974). Excellent on the status of blacks is Talcott Parsons and Kenneth Clark, eds., *The Negro American** (1966). J. W. Anderson, *Eisenhower, Brownell and the Congress* (1964), and Walter Murphy, *Congress and the Court* (1962), describe congressional opposition to decisions such as *Brown* v. *Board of Education*. Southern resistance is described in Numan Bartley, *The Rise of Massive Resistance* (1966); and Neil R. McMillen, *Citizens' Council . . . 1954–1964* (1971). Other books dealing with the Supreme Court are G. Theodore Mitau, *Decade of Decision . . . 1954–1964** (1968); John D. Weaver, *Warren* (1967); and Paul Murphy, *The Constitution in Crisis Times, 1918–1969** (1972).

Useful books on foreign policy include Robert A. Divine, *Eisenhower and the Cold War* (1981); Justus Doenecke, *Not to the Swift: The Old Isolationists in the Cold War Era* (1979); Seyon Brown, *Faces of Power; Constancy and Change in U. S. Foreign Policy from Truman to Johnson** (1968); Townsend Hoopes, *The Devil and John Foster Dulles* (1973); and the books on the Cold War cited at the end of the previous chapters. See also Norman Graebner, *The New Isolationism* (1956); David Wise and T. B. Ross, *The U-2 Affair* (1962); J. C. Campbell, *In Defense of the Middle East* (1960); and Henry Kissinger, *The Necessity for Choice** (1961), on military policies. Two books dealing with the CIA are L. B. Kirkpatrick, *The Real CIA* (1968); and the less flattering account by David Wise and T. B. Ross, *The Invisible Government** (1964).

13

The 1960s:
from altruism
to disenchantment

Many idealists found the early 1960s the most exciting time in modern American history. Young civil rights activists were staging interracial sit-ins and freedom rides. The Reverend Martin Luther King, Jr., was dramatizing the crusade for racial justice. The folksinger Bob Dylan was composing memorable ballads for peace and justice. Chief Justice Earl Warren was leading the Supreme Court toward breakthrough decisions broadening the Bill of Rights. And John F. Kennedy, youthful, energetic, articulate, was in the White House. Despite his assassination in November 1963, many progressives kept the faith, and under Lyndon Johnson's leadership they enacted a remarkably wide-ranging body of reforms in 1964 and 1965. The 1960s, it seemed, were to witness the triumph of social justice in America.

The New Frontier

Kennedy's upbringing offered clues to anyone who wished to predict his behavior as president. His maternal grandfather had been a colorful mayor of Boston, his paternal grandfather a politically active saloonkeeper. Both had been upwardly mobile Irish Catholics anxious to gain acceptance in America. Kennedy's father, Joseph, made millions in a variety of speculative endeavors, contributed generously to the Democratic party, and was rewarded with the coveted ambassadorship to Great Britain. Fiercely competitive, Joseph instilled his own energy and ambition in his children. As president, Kennedy was to exalt activity and vigor almost as ends in themselves and to insist that the United States compete strenuously against its enemies. Though fatalistic in many ways—he thought of himself as an "idealist without illusions"—he clothed his doubts in an altruistic rhetoric that captured the mood of the time. "Ask not what your country can do for you," he proclaimed. "Ask what you can do for your country."

In seeking to implement his goals Kennedy deliberately rejected Eisenhower's low-key approach. He revealed—at least in his rhetoric—that he planned to use all the tools at his command and that opponents could expect retaliation from the White House. Kennedy replaced Eisenhower's businessmen with a corps of academicians, intellectuals, and dynamic younger executives, and he rejected the staff system. "Whereas Eisenhower wanted decisions brought to him for approval," one political scientist has written admiringly, "Kennedy wanted problems brought to him for decision."

Such an administrative style had obvious pitfalls. The reporter Joseph Kraft thought that Kennedy, like Truman, was rather too fond of action for action's sake. The President's "bang-bang" style, he complained, "favors people who know exactly what they want to do. It is tough on people who have dim misgivings— even if those misgivings happen to be very important." But most observers praised the new president's methods. Under Eisenhower, I. F. Stone wrote, "teamwork was conducted much in the manner of a football game—frequent huddles, great attention to coordinating everybody, and interminable periods spent catching breath between plays." Kennedy's approach, by contrast, resembled basketball. "Everybody is on the move all the time . . . . The President may throw the ball in any direction, and he expects it to be kept bouncing."

Reporters responded especially favorably to Kennedy's sense of humor. Told of Vatican unhappiness with his politics, the President quipped, "now I understand why Henry the Eighth set up his own church." When people grumbled that his brother Robert was too young to be Attorney General, he joked that Bobby might as well get some experience before practicing law. Reporters also welcomed his mental quickness and his accessibility, and people who saw him on television were immediately struck by his poise and good looks. In the TV age of the 1960s, when style and image frequently counted for as much as substance, Kennedy enjoyed great advantages.

These assets appeared to help in his dealings with a still-conservative Congress. In early 1961 his followers in the House succeeded, by the narrow margin of 217 to 212, in liberalizing the obstructive Rules Committee. Later, Congress increased the federal minimum wage, set aside funds for manpower training and area redevelopment, and passed a trade expansion act that promised to lower tariffs throughout the industrialized noncommunist world. Before his death the House approved a multi-billion-dollar tax cut, which the Senate passed early in 1964. This was a Keynesian measure that deliberately risked short-term budgetary deficits in the hope of promoting purchasing power. Kennedy's willingness to embrace this "New Economics" was the most striking manifestation of his gradual receptiveness to unorthodox ideas.

Kennedy also kept his promise to pull the country out of its economic slump. Increases in defense spending pumped new billions into the economy. So did his

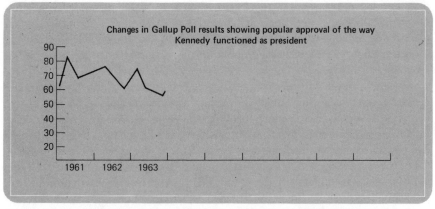

Changes in Gallup Poll results showing popular approval of the way Kennedy functioned as president

SOURCE: Adapted from p. 104 of *U.S. Foreign Policy: Context, Conduct, Content* by Marian Irish and Elke Frank. © 1975 by Harcourt Brace Jovanovich. Reprinted by permission of the publisher.

Kennedy's popularity in office reached a peak in mid-1961 when 83 percent of respondents approved of his presidency. He reached a low of 57 percent shortly before his assassination in 1963.

program to place a man on the moon: by 1969, when Neil Armstrong got there, the government had spent some $25 billion on space exploration. In part because of these expenditures, an upswing in the economy developed in 1961 and lasted until the early 1970s—the longest uninterrupted period of growth in modern American history. During this time some 15 million of 40 million American poor rose above the "poverty line" established statistically by the government, and median family income increased from $4,000 to $8,000, a jump in real dollars of more than 80 percent. Though these unprecedented advances did not change the maldistribution of income, they were widely hailed. By developing faith in the government's ability to promote socioeconomic change, these impressive, indeed fantastic, gains smoothed the way for Johnson's Great Society programs in 1964–65.

Though most liberals favored the tax cut, they observed that it was part of a generally cautious economic policy. During his tenure Kennedy made no serious effort to improve the distribution of income or to plug notoriously large loopholes in the tax laws. He worked harder for increases in defense spending than for social welfare. He encouraged Congress to enact tax breaks for big business. Even the tax cut, John Kenneth Galbraith grumbled, was "reactionary Keynesianism" that helped people spend more on unnecessary gadgetry. "I am not sure what the advantage is," he said, "in having a few more dollars to spend if the air is too dirty to breathe, the water too polluted to drink, the commuters are losing out on the struggle to get in and out of the cities, the streets are filthy, and the schools so bad that the young, perhaps wisely, stay away, and hoodlums roll citizens for some of the dollars that they save in taxes."

By late 1963 reformers were recognizing the limitations of other New Frontier laws. Efforts for tariff reduction, for instance, foundered amid disagreements among the Western allies. The manpower training program could barely keep pace with technological change, and it made no attempt at all to attack hard-core poverty—a problem neglected until the end of Kennedy's presidency. Area redevelopment encountered opposition from business interests, which protested the granting of aid to potential competitors, and from labor leaders, who complained when money went to nonunion employers. In 1963, only two years after passage of the act, these pressure groups succeeded in killing a proposed increase in funds for the program.

Congress prevented many other measures from passing at all. These included medicare, aid to education, funds for mass transit, and creation of the Department of Urban Affairs. Some people thought that the lawmakers would have to be more responsive in 1964, an election year. But at the time of Kennedy's death the legislative logjam seemed as imposing as in the 1950s. The *New York Times* commented: "Rarely has there been such a pervasive attitude of discouragement around Capitol Hill and such a feeling of helplessness to deal with it. This has been one of the least productive sessions of Congress within the memory of most of its members."

Those who blamed Kennedy for this unproductive record were a little unfair. Like Truman before him, he lacked three advantages necessary for success on Capitol Hill: reliable progressive majorities, the support of pressure groups, and a popular mandate as expressed at the polls. Congressmen, accordingly, paid more attention to well-organized constituents than to presidential persuasion. "You can twist a fellow's arm once or even twice," a Kennedy aide explained. "But the next time he sees you coming he starts to run."

Kennedy's efforts on behalf of a bill for aid to education revealed the power of these forces to sustain the status quo. As Kennedy well knew, opponents included many Republicans and southern Democrats. Some of them objected to spending large sums of money for social programs; others feared that government aid would lead to federal dictation of curricula. In packing the House Rules Committee in early 1961, the President weakened these conservatives at their main bastion of defense. He also succeeded in dissuading Representative Adam Clayton Powell, a Harlem congressman, from attaching his antisegregation amendment to the bill. A similar provision, which denied aid to segregated schools, had forced almost all southerners, liberal or conservative, into opposing aid to education in the 1950s.

With these obstacles surmounted, Kennedy ran into yet another pressure group: the Catholic Church. As a Catholic, he felt he had to deny aid to parochial and private schools. Otherwise, angry Protestants would have accused him of religious favoritism. However, this decision led prominent Catholic churchmen to oppose the bill. After much maneuvering, the measure sank under such pressure. Only later, in the more ecumenical spirit of the mid-1960s—and under a Protestant president who favored aid to parochial schools—did the bill command sufficient support to pass.

Kennedy's relations with influential spokesmen for big business provided another example of the way in which pressure groups could stymie presidential power. The President took office hoping to conciliate corporate leaders. "I'm not against business," he said, "I want to help them if I can." To prove his point, he named Douglas Dillon, a prominent banker who had been undersecretary of state in the Eisenhower administration, as secretary of the treasury, and Robert McNamara, head of the Ford Motor Company, as secretary of defense. But many business leaders remained uneasy, and when prices dipped on the stock market, they were quick to blame the White House. Annoyed, Kennedy commented, "I understand every day why Roosevelt, who started out such a mild fellow, ended up so ferociously antibusiness. It's hard as hell to be friendly with people who keep trying to cut your legs off."

His struggle with steel executives in 1962 merely intensified this hostility. This controversy began when Roger Blough, head of U. S. Steel, raised prices in defiance of an understanding previously reached with the White House. Other large steel companies followed Blough's example. Angry, Kennedy bared the weapons of the modern presidency. Antimonopolists in Congress, led by Kefauver, threatened an investigation. The Federal Trade Commission announced it would look into price agreements among large producers. McNamara implied that the Defense Department might deny contracts to corporations that refused to cooperate with Washington. The FBI appeared to be using its formidable powers to gather information against Blough's allies. Kennedy himself made it clear that he would have to review his policies favoring generous tax allowances to business. He observed, "my father always told me that all businessmen were sons of bitches, but I never believed it 'til now." Shortly after this display of strength Blough backed down slightly.

Kennedy's actions were not so potent as they appeared. Blough's retreat stemmed less from fear of the administration (though that mattered) than from the decision of Inland Steel, a dangerous competitor, to keep its prices at existing levels and therefore to bid for a larger share of the market. Inland's action showed that some competitive pressures existed even in an industry as oligopolistic as steel. Simplistic talk about a monolithic "power elite" overlooked these fissures within the business community. But Inland's decision also revealed that leading business executives often possessed more power than Big Government or the presidency. Few confrontations offered a clearer example of the institutional obstacles facing elected officials.

As if these obstacles were not burden enough, Kennedy had personal liabilities that hurt his chances on the Hill. Some congressmen remembered him as a former colleague who had spent as much time socializing and promoting his personal ambition as he had fulfilling the duties of committee work. For these reasons he had never been an "insider" in Congress. Others sensed correctly that he was much more interested in foreign affairs than in domestic policy and that he found many congressmen long-winded and boring. As James Reston pointed out, Kennedy disliked "blarneying with pompous congressmen and simply would not take the time to do it." Still others were put off by the elitist tone of his administration. "All that Mozart string music and ballet dancing down there," one congressman remarked, "and all that fox hunting and London clothes. He's too elegant for me." This populistic reaction to Kennedy's style showed that hostility to the Eastern Establishment—an ill-defined entity—remained a force in American politics. It suggested further that the very traits assisting the president in his dealings with the media and with eastern urban elites could become liabilities in managing Congress.

Kennedy also showed rather less forcefulness than he had led some progressives to expect. Always a pragmatic politician, he shied away from promoting controversial programs. "There is no sense in raising hell and then not being successful," he said. This caution led him to rely on congressional magnates like Speaker of the House Sam Rayburn or senators Richard Russell of Georgia and Everett Dirksen of Illinois, the GOP leader. By avoiding confrontations, he hoped to win the massive victory in 1964 that might give him the mandate he needed.

The revolution in civil rights

Progressives found Kennedy particularly cautious in the area of civil rights, where dramatic and far-reaching events were rapidly outdistancing the politicians. In February 1960 black students in Greensboro, North Carolina, kicked off a new, more militant phase of the civil rights movement by sitting down at a segregated lunch counter and refusing to move until served. After an hour the management closed the counter, and the students left. Their forthright action, reminiscent of the sit-ins conducted by blue-collar workers in the 1930s, quickly attracted the attention of other southern blacks and of liberal whites. Within weeks, members of the three large militant civil rights groups—King's Southern Christian Leadership Conference, the rapidly growing Congress on Racial Equality (CORE), and the newly formed Student Nonviolent Coordinating Committee (SNCC)—were conducting similar sit-ins throughout the South. More militant than the older, established organizations such as the NAACP and the Urban League, these impatient groups rejuvenated the movement for civil rights.

This militancy intensified and spread during the next three years of Kennedy's presidency. As early as May 1961 CORE activists began staging integrated "freedom rides" into the South in order to desegregate transportation facilities. Angry mobs stoned their buses, set them afire, and beat the demonstrators. Southern authorities arrested the freedom riders, while federal authorities, fearful of further mob action, acquiesced. Though the freedom rides, like the sit-ins, largely failed to achieve the immediate goal of striking down Jim Crow, they exposed again the extremism of southern whites and steeled the resolve of the civil rights crusaders.

America's mood:
the public's view of the most important
problem facing the country,
according to Gallup Poll results,
1961–63

1961	Prices and inflation
1962	War, peace, and international tensions
1963	Racial problems

SOURCE: Adapted from *U.S. Foreign Policy: Context, Conduct, Content* by Marian Irish and Elke Frank. © 1975 by Harcourt Brace Jovanovich. Reproduced by permission of the publisher.

The Birmingham, Alabama police use dogs against civil rights demonstrators, 1963.

Of the many protests and demonstrations that broke out in the South during the next two years, two were especially dramatic. The first involved the effort in 1962 of James Meredith, a black man, to enroll as a student at the University of Mississippi. Meredith was challenged by Governor George Barnett and by angry crowds of whites, who went on a rampage of protest in September. In a night of violence on the campus, two people were killed and 375 injured, including 166 federal marshals belatedly sent in to prevent trouble. Barnett's demagogic stand, like that of Alabama governor George Wallace, revealed the presumed political advantages to be reaped by overtly racist white politicians in the South.

The other demonstration, in Birmingham in April 1963, was a major milestone in the history of the American civil rights movement. The protest was carefully planned by King and other leaders. Civil rights workers trained volunteers in the techniques of nonviolence and schooled them (through staged "socio-dramas") to endure verbal abuse and beatings. The protestors then engaged in weeks of peaceable marches, sit-ins, and pray-ins. When arrests thinned their ranks, school children filled their places. If southern whites had employed restraint, they might have outlasted the demonstrators. But local authorities led by Eugene "Bull" Connor lost their patience, repelling the nonviolent activists with cattle prods, high-pressure water hoses, and dogs. The ferocity of Connor's countermeasures, shown to nationwide television audiences, unleashed a wave of revulsion throughout the country and immeasurably aided King's cause. Shortly afterward, white authorities in Birmingham agreed to desegregate stores and to upgrade some black workers.

Many forces combined to unleash this activist phase of the movement. Basic to the activism was the impatience of southern blacks, whose expectations had escalated following the Brown decisions in the 1950s, and whose rage was intense. Angry and idealistic, they were impatient with what they considered the calculations of the politicians and the legalism of groups such as the NAACP. Led skillfully by King and others, they received much support from the churches, from the federal courts, and from increasing numbers of whites, many of whom were moved by religious commitments. The protestors benefited—especially at Birmingham—from TV. "Before television," an NBC official exclaimed, "the American public had no idea of the abuses blacks suffered in the South. We showed them what was happening: the brutality, the police dogs, the miserable conditions. . . . We made it impossible for Congress not to act." This statement, while exaggerated, was accurate in pointing to the need of King and his allies in the South to secure the backing of white liberals in the North.

Overtaken by these events, Kennedy seemed vaguely sympathetic with the movement. During the 1960 campaign he had insisted that a presidential "stroke of the pen" could wipe out racial discrimination in federally supported housing. He had helped get Martin Luther King, Jr., out of jail in Georgia—an act that solidified his vote among blacks in the North. Once in office, he appointed blacks to important offices—such as Robert Weaver as head of the Housing and Home Finance Agency, and Thurgood Marshall, a top NAACP lawyer, to a judgeship on the United States Circuit Court. When confronted by recalcitrant governors like Ross Barnett and George Wallace of Alabama, he reluctantly used federal authority. The Justice Department, under his brother Robert, successfully attacked segregation in southern airports, and it brought more suits in support of voting rights than the Eisenhower regime had done since passage of the Civil Rights Act of 1957.

But the Kennedys remained too cautious to suit the activists. Forgetting the rhetoric of the 1960 campaign, the President waited until after the midterm elections of 1962—by which time hundreds of pens had been sent to him through the mail—to issue his order against discrimination in housing. The order, carefully limited and gently applied, had little impact. Bowing to men like James Eastland of Mississippi, chairman of the Senate Judiciary Committee, he appointed several segregationists to southern judgeships. And he disappointed activists by refusing to introduce a civil rights bill. "When I feel that there is a necessity for a congressional action, with a chance of getting that congressional action," he said in early 1961, "then I will recommend it to the Congress." For the next two years he adhered to this opportunistic course.

By mid-1963 the actions of men like Bull Connor forced Kennedy to take a stronger stand. He did so for several reasons. One was revulsion: during the trouble at Birmingham he remarked that a photograph of a German shepherd leaping at a black woman made him "sick." He also had practical reasons for acting. The trouble, he recognized, harmed America's image abroad. It threatened to move beyond his control, perhaps into wholesale racial violence throughout the country. When Alabama authorities in June 1963 refused to register two black students who sought to enter the university, he decided he had to act. In a nationwide TV address,

Martin Luther King, Jr., tells the throngs attending the march on Washington (1963), "I have a dream. . ."

he called for a federal civil rights law to attack racial injustice. Congress, he implored, must see to it that "race has no place in American life or law."

As Kennedy had foreseen, however, Congress was in no hurry to respond. Indeed, southern senators clearly planned an all-out filibuster against the bill. Restless blacks then determined to "march on Washington." Worried about violence, Kennedy tried to discourage the demonstrators from marching; failing in that effort, he labored hard behind the scenes to minimize the role of the most militant members of the march. In these efforts he was largely successful, and the 200,000 who assembled remained true to the cause of nonviolence. The highlight of the event was the impassioned, memorable speech by King pressing the goal of racial integration, and focusing on his "dream" of the future. "I still have a dream" he exclaimed. "It is a dream chiefly rooted in the American dream." He anticipated that "one day on the red hills of Georgia, the sons of former slaves and the sons of former slave owners will be able to sit together at the table of brotherhood."

Even in these last months of his life, however, Kennedy failed to grasp the intensity behind the drive for racial justice. His proposed civil rights bill was moderate. It limited the Justice Department's injunctive powers against racial discrimination to the area of schools. Its public accommodations section affected only those enterprises having a "substantial" impact on interstate commerce. Recognizing these loopholes, progressives in the House toughened the bill by authorizing the Attorney General to intervene in any civil rights suit initiated by private parties. It was this tougher bill, not Kennedy's milder version, that the House passed in January 1964, two months after the assassination in Dallas.

Both then and later, many observers criticized Kennedy for his caution concerning civil rights (and other domestic reforms). To a degree, these critics underestimated the formidable political obstacles facing him, especially in Congress before mid-1963. As late as March of that year—before the demonstrations at Birmingham—almost all people agreed that Congress would have hotly resisted any civil rights proposal. In moving cautiously Kennedy probably was in tune with majority opinion. Moreover, he proved flexible enough to change in 1963. At that time he not only pushed for civil rights legislation but also set his staff to work on proposals that ultimately—in the hands of President Johnson—emerged as a "war against poverty." He could justifiably argue that his rhetoric for a New Frontier helped develop popular support for domestic reforms that were passed later.

Of course, he never got the chance to prove what he might have done later. Moreover, it was not surprising that activists grew impatient. Kennedy, they said, was not so much altruistic as manipulative. He displayed more style than substance, more profile than courage. His rhetoric, other critics added, aroused exaggerated hopes and ultimately weakened the credibility of government. Though these criticisms were harsh, they revealed the disenchantment of many people late in 1963. Kennedy, James Reston concluded, had "touched the intellect of the country but not the heart."

New Frontiers abroad

Perhaps no twentieth-century president was readier than Kennedy to engage the nation in world affairs. "Let every nation know," he proclaimed, ". . . that we shall pay any price, bear any burden, . . . support any friend, oppose any foe to assure the survival . . . of liberty." Confident about his expertise in the realm of foreign policy, he accelerated the centralization of policy making in the White House, where McGeorge Bundy, a former Harvard dean, played an important role as national security adviser. Kennedy's secretary of state, Dean Rusk, was expected to have a lesser part. Bundy and Rusk, like Kennedy himself, tended to approach the world in the dualistic terms of the Cold War. "Our first great obstacle," Kennedy said, "is still our relations with the Soviet Union and China. We must never be lulled into believing that either power has yielded its ambitions for world domination."

Kennedy's globalism, his anticommunism, and his self-assured activism led him into one of the greatest blunders in the history of American foreign relations: the attempt in April 1961 to overthrow Fidel Castro in Cuba. The reasons for this decision seemed compelling enough beforehand. By 1961 Castro was welcoming Soviet aid and influence. Eisenhower's administration had been training anti-Castro exiles in Guatemala—clearly, Kennedy felt, the military training should be made use of. The Central Intelligence Agency under Allen Dulles (John Foster's brother) warned that it was "now or never" in the struggle against Castro's growing power in Latin America. Dulles outlined a plan calling for American logistical support of an invasion by the exiles. Anti-Castro guerillas in Cuba, they implied, would rise in support of the invasion and topple the regime. When the Joint Chiefs of Staff supported the CIA's argument, the administration had every reason to anticipate success.

A few people expressed doubts about the wisdom of the plan. Among them were Senator J. William Fulbright, head of the Senate Foreign Relations Committee, and Marine Commandant David Shoup. Castro, Fulbright said, was a thorn in the flesh but not a dagger in the heart. Shoup was more dramatic. He prepared an overlay map of Cuba and laid it on one of the United States. It showed that Cuba stretched some 800 miles, from New York to Chicago; clearly, it could not be conquered quickly. Shoup then placed a second overlay on the others. It was of a tiny island. What is that? he was asked. "That, gentlemen," he replied, "represents the island of Tarawa [where Shoup had won a Medal of Honor in World War II] and it took us . . . 18,000 marines to take it." The military lesson could not have been more obvious.

Kennedy's top people, however, were activists by temperament. Placing great faith in America's superior technological capacity, they assumed that a preinvasion air strike would wipe out Castro's defenses and assure the success of the landing. They also thought that an invasion would unleash popular discontent with the government. These characteristically American attitudes—exaggerated faith in technology, blindness to nationalism in the Third World—left Fulbright and Shoup without significant support. With little hesitation, the National Security Council approved the plan on April 4.

The invasion—at the Bay of Pigs on April 17—was an unrelieved disaster. The open movement beforehand of exiles both in Guatemala and in Florida made it easy for Castro to anticipate the attack. Moreover, the air strike failed to destroy Castro's air force. With only six operational fighters he was able to knock out five of twelve planeloads of paratroopers, to strafe ground troops, and to disable a munitions ship loaded with exile soldiers. Richard Bissell and others then tried to persuade Kennedy to authorize the use of American planes as air cover. Kennedy refused, for he knew it was too late to salvage success. Castro then mopped up the remaining invaders.

The New Frontiersmen showed a less bellicose side on other foreign questions in 1961 and 1962. Greatly expanding initiatives begun under Eisenhower, the Kennedy administration promoted the Alliance for Progress in the Western Hemisphere. The Alliance promised to outlay some $20 billion by 1970 in American aid for social and economic programs. Other priorities, among them the war in Vietnam, later prevented the program from amounting to much. But Kennedy's apparent hostility to right-wing elites in Latin America suggested that he sympathized with progressive forces. His support of the Peace Corps, which promoted educational, technological, and social change in the area (and in underdeveloped regions throughout the world), further enhanced his reputation abroad. By 1964 America's relations south of the border were temporarily warmer than they had been in 1960.

Elsewhere in the Third World, Kennedy showed more restraint than he had in Cuba. In Laos, where communists, moderates, and right-wing forces struggled for control, he resisted the temptation to involve American manpower and supported instead a neutral coalition. After extended talks in Geneva, Averell Harriman, America's chief negotiator, worked out such an arrangement in 1962. The Pathet Lao, the native communist forces supported by Russia and North Vietnam, soon resumed the fighting, and Laos remained a war-torn land. But Kennedy had at least avoided direct American participation. His toleration of neutralism in the Third World, while limited, contrasted sharply with Dulles' hostility in the 1950s.

Kennedy also exhibited toughness with Khrushchev, who treated his young American adversary contemptuously at a brief meeting in Vienna in June 1961. America, the Soviet leader warned at the time, must agree to a German peace treaty by December. Otherwise, Russia would sign a separate agreement permitting East Germany to control access routes into West Berlin. Kennedy responded by reaffirming America's commitment to Berlin, by mobilizing reserve units, and by using the confrontation to get higher defense appropriations from Congress. He even endorsed, though only temporarily, erection of fallout shelters. Russia reacted by raising barriers (later to become the Berlin Wall) preventing the flow of East German refugees to the West. Suddenly, American and Russian tanks faced each other at the line between the zones. Fighting, perhaps leading to nuclear war, appeared at hand. But the military forces avoided incidents, Khrushchev let his deadline pass without further action, and tensions gradually subsided. Kennedy's management of the confrontation showed that he was ready to employ brinkmanship to secure his ends.

The young president's handling of the Cuban missile crisis in 1962 revealed even more clearly his tendency to toughness and brinkmanship. The crisis began in

One cartoonist's view of the Berlin Wall, 1961.

See how many are staying on our side.

Wright, *The Miami News.*

BERLIN WALL
ERECTED
AUG. 13, 1961

October when U-2 planes discovered that the Soviets were emplacing offensive missiles on Cuban soil. Many angry American officials counseled for an air strike to prevent completion of the missile sites, and for a time it appeared that the President would authorize it. After tense discussions, however, this option was postponed. Such a strike, Robert Kennedy recalled, would have made his brother the Tojo of the 1960s. Instead, the administration proclaimed a "quarantine," or blockade, of the island. For two days Russian ships headed for the blockade, and the United States stood "eyeball to eyeball" with the Soviet Union. It was the most frightening confrontation of the Cold War. However, Khrushchev proved wise enough to avoid naval engagements thousands of miles from Russian territory. He ordered the ships to turn about and promised to remove the missiles if the United States ended the blockade and renounced any intention of invading Cuba. The next day he changed his mind and sent a much more hostile message. Kennedy, however, shrewdly pretended that the second cable had never arrived. America acceded to Khrushchev's initial deal, and the crisis was over.

The President's defenders have emphasized his restraint during this confrontation. Kennedy, they point out, resisted pleas for an immediate air strike, then had the cunning to ignore the second Soviet note. Moreover, the President's admirers add, he showed wisdom as well as restraint. Permitting the installation of offensive missiles in Cuba, they insist, would have altered the balance of power by giving the enemy greater "first strike" potential. They argue also that JFK had to prove his toughness to Khrushchev, who had (presumably) found him indecisive at Vienna and during the Bay of Pigs fiasco. Kennedy, they conclude, had to act firmly or risk more provocative Soviet behavior concerning Berlin and western Europe.

These arguments are difficult to disprove—for Khrushchev's behavior seemed both antagonistic and erratic. But it is questionable whether his brinkmanship was necessary. Though Khrushchev acted provocatively, his policy in Cuba would have made little difference in the existing military situation: offensive missiles were already well emplaced on Soviet soil. Indeed, in one sense Khrushchev was merely emulating the United States, which had missiles pointing at the Soviet Union from nearby Turkey.

Recognizing this parallel, Adlai Stevenson, who was Kennedy's ambassador at the UN, had recommended tentatively during the crisis that America avoid confrontation by suggesting an exchange. Russia would pull its missiles out of Cuba, and the United States would dismantle its bases in Turkey. Because the Turkish installations were not needed—Kennedy had previously ordered them removed, only to be disobeyed by the Pentagon—Stevenson's idea seemed a more measured response than a blockade. In any event, as Stevenson and others pointed out at the time, there was little to lose by trying to negotiate first. If Russia proved obdurate, there was still time for sterner stuff. But though the Russians were led to believe that the Turkish bases would be dismantled once the crisis was over, the administration's main—and public—response was the blockade. People like Stevenson, White House aides implied, lacked backbone.

Ironically the missile crisis had the unanticipated effect of sobering both sides in the Cold War. Shaken, both Kennedy and Khrushchev paid more attention to nuclear disarmament, and in the summer of 1963 Averell Harriman succeeded in negotiating a Russian-American ban on nuclear testing on land, on the seas, and in the atmosphere. The measure did not permit on-site inspection, nor did it prohibit underground testing, which continued virtually unchecked. Would-be nuclear powers like France and China refused to ratify it. But Kennedy properly called it "an important first step toward peace, a step toward reason, a step away from war." At the time of his assassination in Dallas a few months later, Russian-American relations were more relaxed than they had been since the end of World War II. For this improvement Kennedy's administration could take some of the credit. George Kennan was one of many who praised him accordingly. "I am full of admiration, both as an historian and as a person with diplomatic experience," he wrote before Kennedy's death, "for the manner in which you have addressed yourself to the problems of foreign policy. . . . I don't think we have seen a better standard of statesmanship in the present century."

Kennan did not foresee the legacy of Kennedy's administration in two key areas of foreign policy: defense planning and Vietnam. In the former Kennedy was both opportunistic and demagogic. He came to office having argued on insufficient evidence that America was on the short end of a "missile gap." By February 1961 he knew otherwise. The United States, in fact, had an edge over the Soviets. Yet he acted immediately to improve America's airlift capacity, to speed up Polaris submarine development, and to "accelerate our entire missile program." Using the Berlin stalemate as an excuse, he asked for and received $6 billion in additional defense appropriations in the next six months alone. Russia's response, naturally enough, was to accelerate the production of its own weaponry.

Throughout his administration Kennedy stressed the necessity of balanced defenses—which meant readying America for guerilla warfare as well as nuclear conflict. It was with such wars in mind that he created, over Pentagon protests, the Green Berets, and that he flew himself to Fort Bragg to pick their special equipment. Given these actions, it was ironic that his admirers praised Secretary of Defense McNamara for restoring civilian control over military policy. McNamara's feat, a triumph of managerial expertise, could make a difference only if the "civilians" approached the Cold War differently from the "military." Under Kennedy they ordinarily did not. Far from curbing the potential of the military-industrial complex, the Kennedy administration left it better equipped to fight on land, at sea, or in the air—anywhere, it seemed, in the world.

That "anywhere" was Vietnam. Since the Geneva accord of 1954, which had promised elections in 1956 to determine the political nature of a unified country, conditions there had steadily deteriorated. The Eisenhower administration, recognizing that Ho Chi Minh would win such elections, conspired with South Vietnam to see to it that they were never held. Instead, America spent some $2 billion by 1960 to support South Vietnam's Ngo Dinh Diem, a vehemently anticommunist Catholic nationalist. But Diem lacked Ho Chi Minh's popular acceptance, and by 1957 his opponents in the south, derisively labeled the Vietcong (Vietnamese Communists), were starting to rebel. When Kennedy took office, civil war was raging, and the Diem regime, though dictatorial and repressive, could not control roads more than 100 yards from urban centers—and these only at night.

Kennedy was perceptive enough to recognize the excesses of Diem's regime, especially its repressive treatment of Buddhists. In September 1963 he stated, "I

Vietnam represents the cornerstone of the Free World in Southeast Asia, the keystone to the arch, the finger in the dike. Burma, Thailand, India, Japan, the Philippines and, obviously, Laos and Cambodia are among those whose security would be threatened if the red tide of Communism overflowed into Vietnam. . . . Moreover, the independence of Free Vietnam is crucial to the free world in fields other than the military. Her economy is essential to the economy of all of Southeast Asia; and her political liberty is an inspiration to those seeking to obtain or maintain their liberty in all parts of Asia—and indeed the world. The fundamental tenets of this nation's foreign policy, in short, depend in considerable measure upon a strong and free Vietnamese nation.

Kennedy on Vietnam, 1956.

don't think that unless a greater effort is made to win popular support that the war can be won out there. In the final analysis it is their war. They are the ones who have to win it or lose it." When Diem balked at instituting reforms, Kennedy cut back economic aid. A month later, in November, a military coup overthrew and killed Diem. Though Kennedy had not foreseen Diem's assassination, he knew in advance of the plot and made no attempt to prevent it. By letting the coup take place, the President showed that he did not want to associate America with ineffectively repressive regimes.

But Kennedy's growing disillusion with Diem never meant support for Ho Chi Minh. On the contrary, JFK strongly opposed the rebels in the south. "The Free World," he said, "must increasingly protect against and oppose communist subversive aggression as practiced today most acutely in Southeast Asia." His vice-president, Lyndon Johnson, underscored America's commitment by going to Vietnam and publicly hailing Diem as the Winston Churchill of Southeast Asia. General Maxwell Taylor, a forceful advocate of larger American ground forces, and Walt W. Rostow, a top presidential adviser, insisted that Kennedy must step up aid to the Diem regime. By early 1963 McNamara and others were reporting confidently about favorable "kill ratios" and "actual body counts." By November America had some 17,000 military "advisers" in Vietnam, some of whom were engaging in combat and getting killed. This was more than eight times the number that had been stationed there at the end of Eisenhower's administration.

This escalation was not a prelude to an inevitable American involvement under President Johnson. Kennedy did not want to engage in a ground war in Southeast Asia. Had he lived, he might have acted with restraint. But the fact remains that Kennedy's stand on Vietnam, like his defense policy, was disingenuous. Far from crossing "new frontiers" in foreign policy, he traveled over much old terrain.

The Johnson years, 1963–68

Few presidents have received as much abuse as Lyndon Johnson, Kennedy's successor. By the late 1960s stories circulated about his towering ego, his crudity, his cruelty to members of his staff. The historian Eric Goldman, who served briefly as

> *I dreamed about 1960 myself the other night, and I told Stuart Symington [Democratic Senator from Missouri] and Lyndon Johnson about it in the cloakroom yesterday. I told them about how the Lord came into my bedroom, anointed my head and said, "John Kennedy, I hereby appoint you President of the U.S." Stuart Symington said, "That's strange, Jack, because I too had a similar dream last night in which the Lord anointed me and declared me, Stuart Symington, President of the United States and of Outer Space." Lyndon Johnson then said, "That's very interesting, gentlemen, because I too had a similar dream last night and I don't remember anointing either one of you."*

Kennedy jokes about Johnson's egotism prior to the 1960 campaign.

a consultant to the White House, repeated an alleged exchange between Johnson and a friend. Upset by criticism, the President supposedly asked, ''why don't people like me?'' The friend replied: ''because, Mr. President, you are not a very likeable man.''

Liberals especially distrusted Johnson. From 1948, when he squeaked into the Senate by eighty-seven votes, through the 1950s, when he worked with conservatives of the Eisenhower administration, they had found him uncooperative. They also observed his assiduous protection of southwestern oil and gas interests, his coolness to civil rights, and his close relations with hustlers like Bobby Baker, a top aide during his Senate years. In his fondness for wheeling and dealing, for long pointed collars and shiny suits, and for backroom stories, Johnson seemed like a riverboat gambler, albeit with the drawl and the swagger of a Texas tycoon.

These unflattering portrayals overlooked other sides of Johnson. Though he alienated liberals, it was not because he was instinctively conservative but because he had to satisfy his Texas constituency. Indeed, he had begun his political career in the 1930s as an ardent New Deal congressman. Roosevelt himself had regarded him as future presidential material. Thereafter Johnson became an extraordinarily effective Senate majority leader from 1954 to 1960. As he grew more secure in his political base, he tentatively accepted many liberal programs, including the civil rights bill of 1957—which could not have become law without his patient negotiations on Capitol Hill.

Johnson's detractors also tended to ignore traits that made him one of the most dynamic chief executives in American history. One of these was his unflagging energy in working with Congress. Unlike Kennedy and Eisenhower, who disliked the hard negotiating involved in securing legislation, he undertook it himself. By 1968 this passion to be at the center of the action had worn him out. It deprived him of the assistance of men of ideas, who found him increasingly domineering. But it enabled him to know exactly how congressmen stood on issues and to move quickly in rewarding his friends and punishing his foes. No president since Roosevelt, his idol, had shown such careful attention to the details of legislation.

LBJ often resorted to what was known as the ''Johnson Treatment,'' described by one senator as a ''great overpowering thunderstorm that consumed you as it closed in on you.'' Johnson, the columnists Rowland Evans and Robert Novak

President Johnson gives Harold Wilson, Prime Minister of Great Britain, the "Treatment."

explained, bore in on people he wished to convince, "his face a scant millimeter from his target, his eyes widening and narrowing, his eyebrows rising and falling. From his pockets poured clippings, memos, statistics, mimicry, humor, and the genius of analogy [which] made the Treatment an almost hypnotic experience and rendered the target stunned and helpless."

In applying such methods Johnson had advantages denied Kennedy. Among these were friendships with many powerful figures on the Hill. Senators like Richard Russell of Georgia and Harry Byrd of Virginia had had little reason to help Kennedy; with Johnson, a crony of many years' standing, it was harder to be obstructive. Another advantage was his southern background, which made his support of civil rights all the more impressive. His Protestantism gave him an edge that Kennedy had lacked in handling the explosive question of aid to parochial schools. Above all, Johnson came to office at a time when Americans were shocked by Kennedy's assassination. As in 1933, they were yearning for purposeful leadership.

Johnson used these advantages brilliantly in late 1963 and 1964. On November 27, five days after the assassination, he made Kennedy's program his own by appearing before Congress and reminding it of the unfinished New Frontier, especially in the realm of civil rights. "No memorial oration or eulogy," he said, "could more eloquently honor President Kennedy's memory than the earliest possible passage of the civil rights bill for which he fought so long. . . . I urge you again, as I did in 1957 and again in 1960, to enact a civil rights law so that we can move forward to eliminate from this nation every trace of discrimination and oppression that is based upon race or color.''

In 1964, Johnson persisted in similar appeals to carry out Kennedy's program—with breathtaking results. Congress approved the $13.5 billion tax cut Kennedy had called for in June 1963. It passed a controversial bill authorizing federal funds for mass transit. It quickly enacted an $800 million ''war against poverty'' program. And it passed the first effective civil rights bill since Reconstruction. The Civil Rights Act of 1964 created a Fair Employment Practices Committee, banned discrimination in public accommodations, gave the Attorney General injunctive powers in cases involving school segregation as well as voting rights, and authorized the government to withhold funds from public authorities practicing racial discrimination.

Given the national mood, these measures might have passed in any event. Still, Johnson made a difference. The poverty program, though originally conceived in the closing weeks of the Kennedy administration, owed its shape and scope to LBJ's efforts. The tax cut escaped the Senate Finance Committee only after he shrewdly promised Senator Byrd, the committee chairman, that he would cut federal spending. The bill then passed the Senate, seventy-seven to twenty-one, with the consensus that he demanded. Johnson was most effective of all in shepherding the civil rights bill. Instead of settling for half a loaf, he encouraged House liberals to tack on tougher amendments to Kennedy's original bill. As moderates had warned, his action provoked a Senate filibuster. But Johnson held firm, and fence-sitting senators soon began to feel the pressure from home. After fifty-seven days the Senate invoked cloture for the first time in the history of civil rights legislation.

As if to ensure Johnson's continued success, the Republicans then nominated Senator Barry Goldwater of Arizona to oppose him in November. Right-wingers hailed the choice, for Goldwater was an avowed reactionary who opposed civil rights legislation and progressive federal taxation, and who called for bombing in Vietnam. At the GOP convention he antagonized moderates in his own party by courting support from the right-wing John Birch Society. ''Extremism in defense of liberty is no vice,'' he proclaimed. His partisans proclaimed, ''In Your Heart You Know He's Right,'' but opponents countered with ''In Your Guts You Know He's Nuts.''

In fact, Goldwater's nomination suggested a major trend of the future: the rise of ideology (especially of conservatism) in American politics. The successes of other right-wing politicians of the late 1960s and 1970s—Governor George Wallace of Alabama, Governor Ronald Reagan of California—revealed that many Americans were dissatisfied not only with liberalism but with the center as well. In 1964, however, Goldwater's ideology seemed particularly extreme. No major-party candidate for the presidency had ever seemed farther from the mainstream of American political thought.

Johnson took full advantage of Goldwater's exposed position on the issues. The GOP stance on Vietnam, LBJ implied, was irresponsible. ''We are not going South and we are not going North,'' he said on September 28. ''We are going to continue to try to save their own freedom with their own men, with our leadership and our officer direction.'' On October 21 he added (in the same vein as FDR in 1940), ''we are not going to send American boys nine or ten thousand miles away from home to do what Asian boys ought to be doing for themselves.'' On domestic questions he emphasized his liberal sympathies by naming Hubert Humphrey as his running mate, and he appealed to the center by reminding people of Goldwater's extremism. ''Right here is the reason I'm going to win this thing so big,'' he told a friend. ''You ask a voter who classifies himself as a liberal what he thinks I am and he says 'a liberal.' You ask a voter who calls himself a conservative what I am and he says 'a conservative.' You ask a voter who calls himself a middle-roader, and that is what he calls me. They all think I'm on their side.''

To no one's surprise Johnson won overwhelmingly, by 43.1 million to 27.1 million. Goldwater carried only Arizona and five southern states. The GOP, once moribund in Dixie, now seemed wrecked everywhere else. Democrats also secured huge majorities of 68 to 32 in the Senate and 295 to 140 in the House. The enormous shifts in voting since 1960 showed that the electorate was becoming unpredictable and unstable in presidential elections.

Exhilarated, LBJ interpreted the election as a mandate for further domestic reform. ''Hurry, boys, hurry,'' he told his aides. ''Get that legislation up to the Hill and out. Eighteen months from now ol' Landslide Lyndon will be Lame-Duck Lyndon.'' Driven at a furious pace, the Democratic Congress responded with the most far-reaching legislation since 1935. Chief among its accomplishments were medicare and aid to elementary and secondary education. Medicare, funded by an increase in social security taxes, provided for health care to the aged. A corollary program, medicaid, offered free care to poor people who qualified for public assistance. The education act set aside an initial appropriation of $1 billion. Much supplemented in succeeding years, it gave the federal government an unprecedented role in educational policy.

Hardly pausing for breath, Congress approved many other reforms in 1965. It appropriated generously for manpower training, authorized $900 million to improve conditions in Appalachia, passed a housing act that included provisions for rent supplements, set aside $1.6 billion more for the war against poverty, and

---

A supreme congressional politician, President Johnson was an incompetent and ineffective national politician. This should not have been too surprising. After all, he had had experience in only two national campaigns: one when he was the vice-presidential candidate, the other when he was running for President against a man Noam Chomsky [a radical antiwar intellectual] could have beaten. In his political instincts he was more a South American caudillo than a North American leader. . . . The President as a man impressed increasing numbers of Americans as high-handed, devious and disingenuous, the embodiment of a political system that wilfully deceived the people and denied them a voice in vital decisions.

Arthur Schlesinger, Jr., a liberal historian and Kennedy partisan, offers a widely held view of Johnson, 1969.

Selma, Alabama, 1965. The Civil Rights Act of that year prompted an intense and often imaginative effort to get blacks to register to vote.

established the Economic Development Act for depressed areas with the potential for growth. It created the Department of Housing and Urban Development and the National Endowment for the Arts and the Humanities, authorized an additional $2.4 billion for education, including colleges and universities, and approved a new immigration law ending quotas based on pseudoscientific theories.

When police in Selma, Alabama, roughed up blacks seeking to register to vote, new outrage exploded among civil rights advocates. Prodded by Johnson, Congress then approved the Civil Rights Act of 1965. This far-reaching piece of legislation authorized federal examiners to register voters, and it banned literacy tests. Along with passage of the twenty-fourth amendment (1964), which outlawed the poll tax in federal elections, it enabled thousands of formerly disfranchised people to register, to vote, and later to elect black officials in record numbers throughout the South. It was a fitting capstone to a congressional session of unparalleled productivity, and it made Johnson—once the whipping boy of liberals—the greatest champion of progressivism since FDR.

DISILLUSIONMENT WITH LIBERALISM

That very year, however, the euphoria began to disappear. Altruism turned to frustration, then to disenchantment. By 1966 Americans were tiring of listening to the "best and brightest"—the journalist David Halberstam's apt phrase describing the liberals, intellectuals, and "experts" who had ruled since 1961. Explaining this rapid change in mood tells much about the strengths and limitations of modern liberalism, about the stubbornness of the nation's problems, about the relative weakness of governmental institutions, and—in the last analysis—about the role of traditional attitudes.

This change of mood gradually affected Capitol Hill. Between 1966 and 1968 the lawmakers increased the minimum wage, created a Department of Transportation, and established a Model Cities program. In 1968 they approved another civil rights act—against discrimination in housing. But by then Congress was already cautious in authorizing funds for rent supplements, housing, and the war against poverty. For the next decade congressional advocates of reform remained as stymied as they had been from 1937 to 1963.

Johnson's programs, by falling far short of expectations, were partly to blame for these developments. Funds for Appalachia, many people observed, went primarily for short-run projects and to road-building, which gave out-of-state profiteers access to valuable raw materials. Aid to education failed to provide money for teachers' salaries or for renovation of urban schools, which continued to deteriorate. Medicare, too, left reformers dissatisfied, for it assisted only the elderly, was financed by regressive social security taxes, and failed to bring about reforms in the medical establishment.

The urban poor complained about federal welfare policies. Many government programs, such as aid to the blind, to the disabled, and to dependent children, continued to require state contributions—stipulations that resulted in wide variations and (especially in the poorer southern states) in wholly inadequate standards. Welfare recipients had to meet strict residency requirements (declared unconstitutional in 1969) and unnecessarily demeaning tests. These provisions required an ever-increasing bureaucracy of social workers. Though dedicated and humane, these workers offended militants who demanded an end to "snooping" and to governmental "paternalism" in general. Social workers, one young slum dweller protested, "are rat fink types. They act like they think we're not human. They think they've got all there is, and all they do is convert us to think and do what they think and do."

Easily the most controversial of the Great Society programs was the much ballyhooed "war on poverty," which Johnson hailed as a "milestone in our 180-year search for a better life for our people." This broad-ranging program operated under a newly created Office of Economic Opportunity (OEO), which received close to $10 billion in federal money between 1965 and 1970. Among its programs were loans for farmers and rural coops, aid to migrant workers, and adult education. More significant were VISTA (Volunteers in Service to America), which was a "domestic peace corps" of young people who lived with and provided services to the poor; the Job Corps, residential centers offering counseling and job training for unskilled young people; and the Neighborhood Youth Corps, a program providing work and on-the-job training for students and dropouts. Most important of all were the community action agencies under the Community Action Program (CAP). These agencies, of which there were 1,000 by the end of the decade, sought to develop neighborhood solutions to the problems of poverty. Some focused on educational programs such as Head Start for preschool children and Follow-Through for elementary school students. Others concentrated on developing legal services for the poor. Still others worked hard to develop family planning services or to provide day care centers for children. All the community action agencies were supposed to avoid "paternalism" by giving poor people "maximum feasible participation" in planning.

An antipoverty worker tutors a child in Alabama.

By the late 1960s, it appeared that the war on poverty was facing severe problems. Of all its efforts, only the Neighborhood Youth Corps and work experience programs were actually providing jobs to help the employable poor. Indeed, the war in Vietnam, by heating up the economy, did much more than did the OEO to create jobs. The unemployable poor—the aged, crippled, and, above all, nonsupported mothers and their dependent children—had to turn to the nation's creaking welfare "system." By 1969 the plight of such people (the number of mothers and dependent children on relief had risen from 3.5 million to 8 million since 1961) was so desperate that the Nixon administration proposed (unsuccessfully) a program of assistance payments setting a floor below which family incomes would not be permitted to fall.

Many of the limitations of the war on poverty (and other programs) stemmed from lack of funds. Average expenditures per year by the OEO were approximately $1.7 billion. Even when added to the $5 billion per year for medicare and the $1 billion per year for poor school districts under the education act of 1965, this was a piddling sum (approximately $250 per poor person), which could not begin to take care of the 25 to 35 million Americans who were classified as poor in the middle and late 1960s.

Even with proper funding, the war on poverty would have had political problems. The community action programs were a case in point. Though most of them were well run, a few fell into the hands of the wrong kinds of entrepreneurial leaders: in Syracuse, an extreme example, $7 million of the $8 million expended by mid-1967 went for salaries and administration—and only $1 million to the poor. Leaders in some communities soon adopted the fashionable revolutionary rhetoric and the racial separatism of the late 1960s (see chapter 14). Such leaders alarmed local politicians, who moved quickly to prevent federal money from flowing toward those rivals for power. In 1967 these politicians succeeded in getting Congress to require state approval of community action initiatives. Thus expired—in two years—the much-acclaimed stress on local administration and on "maximum feasible participation."

The CAPs suffered also from misconceptions. One of these was the assumption that poverty could be fought on a neighborhood basis. This view, useful in promoting participation by the poor, underestimated the mobility in and out of slums. The warriors against poverty also assumed—again with little evidence to guide them—that poor people could organize themselves. This was not always the case; in many areas, racial and ethnic groups confronted one another. In retrospect, it is reasonably clear that the poor would have benefited more from WPA-like public employment programs or from legislation guaranteeing a minimum annual income for all. Such programs would have done more to give poor people pride, economic security, and the ability to think of the future.

Some of these misconceptions stemmed from Johnson's passion for rapid accomplishment. He simply did not give Congress time to contemplate its actions. As the sociologist Nathan Glazer observed later, the war on poverty was enacted with "nothing like the powerful political pressure and long-sustained intellectual support that produced the great welfare measures of the New Deal." Other critics complained that Johnson, like most New Deal liberals, relied too heavily on the presumed benefits of federal spending. Throw money at problems, he seemed to say, and they will go away. The journalist David Broder observed, "His primary purpose was to provide all the tangible benefits that Federal initiative could devise and Federal money could buy. There was no pause to consider how each of the new Federal programs meshed with all the others, or whether the function was one the national government could most appropriately undertake." To Broder and others Johnson's programs merely encouraged pressure groups (including welfare mothers) to demand ever-greater sums from Uncle Sam.

To the extent that these critics perceived Johnson as a lavish spender they were unfair. As the war on poverty revealed, the money expended on domestic programs between 1965 and 1968 was modest. Much more was needed to attack social problems. Critics were closer to the mark, however, in suggesting that spending on welfare services—as opposed to providing public employment or a guaranteed minimum income—was no panacea. In this sense Johnson was indeed something of a paternalist—a politician trying to develop middle-class behavior and values in poor people whose primary needs were jobs and money.

Johnson's greatest error—and Kennedy's before him—may have been to promise so much. Kennedy had talked about getting the country moving again, about crossing new frontiers. Johnson went still further: there was to be a "war" on poverty, an end to racial injustice, a "Great Society." Such high-sounding rhetoric was inspiring, at least for a while. But it helped to arouse unrealistic expectations, radical protest, middle-class backlash, and political conservatism. It led others, including many young radicals, to blame Johnson for "running out of ideas" and to attack liberals in general. "Liberalism," one militant said, "drifts in smug self-

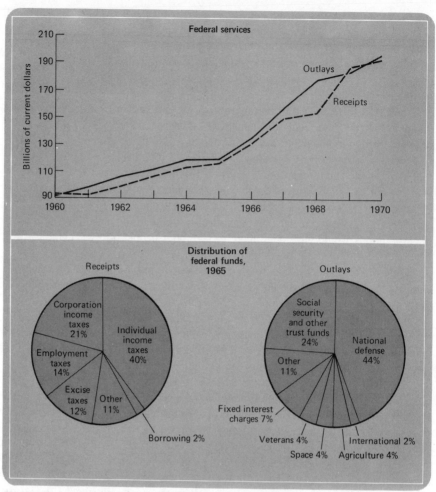

Federal services

Billions of current dollars

Outlays

Receipts

1960 · 1962 · 1964 · 1966 · 1968 · 1970

Distribution of federal funds, 1965

Receipts

Corporation income taxes 21%
Individual income taxes 40%
Employment taxes 14%
Excise taxes 12%
Other 11%
Borrowing 2%

Outlays

Social security and other trust funds 24%
National defense 44%
Other 11%
Fixed interest charges 7%
Veterans 4%
Space 4%
Agriculture 4%
International 2%

SOURCE: U.S. Bureau of Census, *Statistical Abstract of the United States: 1974,* 95th ed. (Washington, D.C., 1974), p. 220; distribution of funds projected by *Statistical Abstract of the United States: 1964,* p. 387.

Growth of federal services, 1960–70, and percent distribution of federal funds by function, 1965.

satisfaction, preening itself with its pragmatic and value-free cleverness in social problem solving. . . . The time for radicalism has struck.''

Most of these criticisms were unperceptive. LBJ was much more than a simple opportunist, and his policies, especially in the realms of health and education, offered much to ordinary people. The civil rights acts of 1964 and 1965 were among the most far-reaching pieces of legislation passed in American history. In criticizing such reforms many radicals could do little more than demand more of the same; other radicals called for changes that were simply unrealizable within the framework of American values and institutions.

Still, by the late 1960s the disillusion with Johnsonism was not wholly ground-less. LBJ's Vietnam policy (see chapter 14) was an unmitigated disaster that drained support—and funds—from domestic programs and divided the country.

Moreover, like his idol FDR, Johnson stopped short of fundamental social change. He made no effort to reform the tax laws, to redistribute income, or to attack monopoly. He was slow to perceive the flaws in welfare and urban programs.

Accordingly, many thoughtful observers began to question the state's ability to solve social problems. "There is mounting evidence," the writer Peter Drucker said, "that government is big rather than strong; that it is fat and flabby rather than powerful; that it costs a great deal and does not achieve much. . . . The citizen less and less believes in government and is increasingly disenchanted with it." James Sundquist, a liberal political scientist, added in 1968: "There are many signs that the capacity of the United States to make policies and establish programs in the domestic field has outrun its capacity, or its determination, to finance and administer them." Amid doubts such as these about welfare statism, it is not surprising that reformers were forced onto the defensive after 1965.

PRACTICALLY INSUPERABLE PROBLEMS

Poverty in the cities Johnson's critics also underestimated the size of the problems to be confronted. These, by the mid-1960s, revealed a socially divided nation. Poverty, as books like Michael Harrington's *The Other America* (1962) revealed, affected as much as one-fifth of America's population, or nearly 40 million people, in 1960. Moreover, racial tensions pervaded American life. The rapid migrations to the North of southern blacks posed especially large problems in the cities. Between 1950 and 1970 the black population in metropolitan areas increased by 7 million. Yet these cities offered fewer blue-collar jobs than had been available in earlier years. Thus the densely crowded cores of cities teemed with unemployed rural migrants. In New York City, where the migrations were especially large, the welfare load increased from 530,000 in 1965 to 1.2 million in 1972, or one-sixth of the city's population. New York's ghettos, like those in other cities, also suffered from high rates of drug abuse, infant mortality, and family breakup. To outsiders, the ghettos also seemed to be hotbeds of crime.

White alarmists probably exaggerated the extent of crime in the ghettos. Often hostile to cities generally, they also failed to recognize the positive side of the cities, which offered wider economic opportunities than did farming regions or small towns, which languished in the postwar era. Compared to the black rural areas in the South, poverty-stricken Puerto Rico, or rural Mexico, America's cities seemed heaven-sent. But these Americans were correct in recoiling in fear from the spread of hard drugs on the streets and in recognizing that many ghetto areas were dangerous to outsiders, especially after dark. These fearful whites anxiously fled such areas—in a "white flight" that accelerated the growth of nearby suburbs. Confronted with such widespread hostility to cities—and to the blacks with which they were intimately identified—Johnson and urban reformers had difficulty finding support.

Those who continued to press for urban programs in the late 1960s were divided about what to do. Some, like Lewis Mumford, complained of the density of cities; others, such as Jane Jacobs, author of *The Death and Life of Great American Cities* (1963), thought that heterogeneous, closely settled neighborhoods such as Greenwich Village in New York were the ultimate in civilized living. Some reformers continued to press for public housing, but others complained that slums were a reflection, not a cause, of racial prejudice and lack of economic opportunities. Others despaired. "Once upon a time," one reformer mused sadly, "we thought that if we could only get our problem families out of those dreadful slums, then papa would stop taking dope, mama would stop chasing around, and junior would stop carrying a knife. Well, we've got them in a nice new apartment with modern kitchens and a recreation center. And they're the same bunch of bastards they always were."

Advocates of racial justice were equally divided by the end of the decade. Most reformers continued to favor federal initiatives to promote desegregation in housing, schools, and employment. Destroy the legal basis for discrimination, they said, and tensions would abate. However, some liberals developed doubts about cherished beliefs. In 1965, Daniel Moynihan authored a study for the government, *The Negro Family*. It stressed the social disorganization of black families. Despite increases in black income, he argued, illegitimacy afflicted a larger percentage of nonwhite families than in the 1950s. Many activists challenged these findings, which they said resurrected old stereotypes about fun-lovin', indolent "darkies" who drifted from woman to woman. Find economic opportunities for black men, they argued, and families would stabilize. To others, however, reports such as Moynihan's were unhappy reminders that class and cultural forces as well as "white racism" would continue to plague attempts to promote racial harmony.

The Great Society reformers also had the formidable task of trying to maintain harmony within the West's most polyglot society. According to the 1960 census, America had more than 19 million nonwhites (a term that included Orientals and American Indians as well as blacks), 9.3 million foreign-born whites, and 23.8 million people of mixed or foreign-born parents. The white ethnics, including millions of Mexicans who crossed the border as illegal aliens, comprised nearly 20 percent of the nation's population of 183 million in 1960. Most of them lived unobtrusively, hoping to become accepted. But many faced sharp hostility from older-stock Americans. Shut off from the mainstream, these ethnic Americans responded by jealously guarding their cultural identities or by demanding redress. Obviously, the melting pot had failed to boil away America's religious, cultural, and ethnic divisions. So long as these existed, it remained difficult to mobilize a reform coalition based on class or occupational lines.

Economic interest groups further divided the potential progressive coalition. Unions, businessmen, farmers, and professional groups joined self-conscious blacks and ethnics in competing for governmental favor. Almost all had pipelines to Congress or to the bewilderingly large federal bureaucracy that had "modernized" the American political system since the 1930s. Neither Johnson nor other postwar American presidents really had the power to control these groups or the bureaucrats who assisted them. Indeed, it was to fight back against these forces that Kennedy and Johnson dramatically increased the White House staff and that Nixon, even more anxious for control, resorted to a range of illegal intelligence-gathering activities.

Large corporations were by far the most powerful of these groups. By mid-decade one-half of the productive assets of American manufacturing was controlled by 150 corporations; two-thirds was held by 500. General Motors, America's largest corporation, made $2 billion in profits after taxes in 1965, a sum greater than the revenue for forty-eight of the fifty states. Its sales exceeded the Gross National Product of all but nine nations in the world. Other big companies spread into far corners of the world during the 1960s. By 1970 American firms sold some $200 billion worth of goods abroad, three-fourths of which was made in American-owned overseas plants. United States private investment abroad (including portfolio investment in overseas securities) grew from $19 billion in 1950 to $49 billion in 1960, and to $101 billion in 1968. International Telephone and Telegraph, among the largest of these "multinational" corporations, had operations in ninety countries, 400,000 employees, and a president who earned $812,000 a year in salary. Like other such corporations, it possessed enormous potential influence over American foreign policies.

Corporate influence at home was still more obvious. The large firms not only employed millions of Americans but also served as important social and welfare institutions. Their investments in pension funds, which increased from $4 billion in 1940 to $100 billion in 1965, deeply affected the stock market and the level of general economic activity. The large corporations also continued to depend on, and to influence, government defense spending. Frequently unrestrained by competition, they remained free to increase prices, thus promoting inflation even in times of recession. As John Kenneth Galbraith argued in 1968, large corporations formed a potent "technostructure" that undermined the free market and made many of the nation's most fundamental decisions concerning production, wages, and technological change. J. P. Morgan would have been gratified.

By all but the pathologically romantic, it is now recognized that this is not the age of the small man. But there is still a lingering presumption among economists that his retreat is not before the efficiency of the great corporation, or even its technological proficiency, but before its monopoly power. . . . This, by the uncouth, would be called drivel. Size is the general servant of technology, not the special servant of profits. The small firm cannot be restored by breaking the power of the larger ones. It would require, rather, the rejection of the technology which since earliest consciousness we are taught to applaud. It would require that we have simple products made from readily available materials by unspecialized labor. . . . If the market thus reigned, there would be, and could be, no planning. No elaborate organization would be required. The small firm would then, at last, do very well. All that is necessary is to undo nearly everything that, at whatever violence to meaning, has been called progress in the last half century. There must be no thought of supersonic travel, or exploring the moon, and there will not be many automobiles. . . .

J. K. Galbraith analyzes the "technostructure," 1968.

If Johnson had been disposed to challenge the corporations—which he was not—he would have been unable to rely on their historic adversaries, the labor unions. Though union membership increased slightly in absolute numbers during the postwar years, the labor movement was hurt by the migration of many industries to the South, which was traditionally antiunion, and by the rapid expansion of the middle class, which limited the growth in blue-collar employment. Between 1955 and 1968 the percentage of unionized people in nonagricultural employment declined from 33 to 28 percent. Some of the stronger unions, such as the Teamsters (which had almost 2 million members by 1970), were plagued by corruption. The writer Norman Mailer concluded that such unions "sat closer to the Mafia than to Marx." Though Mailer exaggerated (as usual), he—and other critics—were right in noting the continuing decline of labor militancy, which had been a cutting edge for reform in the 1930s.

The relative complacency of unions did not mean that industrial workers enjoyed lives of comfort, or even that they felt secure. On the contrary, they were among the first to be laid off during hard times. Their work on the assembly line seemed ever more tedious and alienating as definitions of the "good life" focused on the desirability of creative labor. Still, regularly employed industrial workers, like skilled craftsmen at the turn of the century, comprised the privileged elite of blue-collar labor. Those in strong unions enjoyed economic "clout" undreamed of in the 1930s. Like many other interest groups, they used it to advance their own goals, not to promote the social welfare of the less fortunate. The proliferation of such well-organized groups in America tended to fragment the political parties, to embattle the Congress, and to stymie efforts after 1965 to alleviate the nation's racial, ethnic, and urban divisions.

THE WARREN COURT: A CENTER OF CONTROVERSY

Reformers took some comfort from the most activist Supreme Court in American history. Liberal justices like Earl Warren, Hugo Black, William O. Douglas, and William J. Brennan, Jr., validated the sit-ins of the early 1960s and the civil rights

---

Legislators represent people, not trees or acres. Legislators are elected by voters, not farms or cities or economic interests. As long as ours is a representative form of government, and our legislatures are those instruments of government elected directly by and directly representative of the people, the right to elect legislators in a free and unimpaired fashion is a bedrock of our political system.

Reynolds v. Sims (1964), the Court's decision requiring reapportionment of state legislatures.

---

acts of 1964 and 1965. In *Engel* v. *Vitale* (1962) and subsequent decisions they ruled against required prayers and Bible reading in public schools. In a series of cases starting with *Baker* v. *Carr* (1962) the Court struck at legislative malapportionment on both the state and national levels. Only population, it declared, could be the basis for representation. The Court then acted to broaden the rights of accused criminals. In *Gideon* v. *Wainwright* (1963) it declared that indigents charged with felonies in state courts had the right to free counsel; in *Escobedo* v. *Illinois* (1964) it stated that police must permit alleged offenders to consult with lawyers during interrogation; and in *Miranda* v. *Arizona* (1966) it required police to warn suspects that any statements they made could be used against them, and that they had the right to remain silent and to get free legal counsel. The Court ruled against state laws banning the use of contraceptive devices, and it delivered a number of decisions against laws censoring allegedly pornographic material. All these cases marked significant departures from past judicial decisions.

But these decisions infuriated conservatives. Southerners reacted as angrily as they had to *Brown* v. *Board of Education* in the 1950s. Traditionalists predicted (with some truth) that the apportionment decisions would involve the Court in what Justice Felix Frankfurter, a dissenter, called the "political thicket" of legislative districting. Catholics, fundamentalists, and others heatedly denounced the decisions concerning Bible reading in the schools, censorship, and contraception. Advocates of "law and order" complained that the Court was "coddling" criminals and hampering effective police work. In 1968 they passed the Crime Control and Safe Streets Act, which sanctioned so-called voluntary confessions in federal courts even if suspects were not informed of their rights. The act also authorized police to hold suspects for up to six hours before arraigning them, and to utilize wiretapping for a variety of purposes.

Most of these complaints were considerably exaggerated. Far from opposing religion, the Court permitted states to supply textbooks to parochial schools. It continued to hold that church property was exempt from taxation. Its decisions concerning criminals merely gave indigents in state courts the rights that they already possessed in federal courts and that wealthier law-breakers such as the Mafiosi had long enjoyed. The apportionment rulings were unprecedented—Warren himself regarded them as the most significant judgments of his tenure. But by the 1960s they seemed long overdue. By then only the Court could have broken the political logjams that had permitted gross overrepresentation for rural areas. Warren also exaggerated the impact of these decisions, for while they gave more political power to the growing suburban areas, they did relatively little to strengthen minority groups. The nation's most deliberately malapportioned institution, the United States Senate, remained constitutionally sacrosanct.

What mattered, however, was what people thought the Court was doing. With crime disturbing America's cities it was convenient to blame the Court's decisions concerning police behavior. As blacks became more "uppity," segregationists were quick to chastise the judges, especially for decisions striking down laws against intermarriage and against sexual relations between blacks and whites. By

1966 a Harris poll discovered that 65 percent of Americans opposed the tribunal's actions concerning criminals. What they probably feared most was not only crime but the different life styles of some blacks and long-haired whites. But the liberal decisions of Warren provided a convenient scapegoat for these cultural concerns.

These criticisms were the more forceful because the Court was an appointive institution whose jurisdiction in sociopolitical issues was unclear. Indeed, it was hard to ignore Justice Frankfurter's complaint that the Court was concerning itself with nonjudicial matters. Problems such as malapportionment, he insisted, were for popularly elected presidents and legislators to cure. To such critics, democratic institutions—Congress, the presidency, the states—ought to deal with these social problems. The courts, they insisted, ought to mind their own business.

Affluence—bane of social change?

Affluence also accounted for some of the disenchantment of the late 1960s. For a time the unprecedented economic growth of the period assisted the activists. The New Economic Policy, reformers were able to maintain, proved that purposeful government did make a difference. Moreover, prosperity freed thousands of Americans, especially college students, from preoccupation with earning their daily bread. The altruism of the early 1960s, like that of the progressive era (but unlike that of the New Deal) coincided with a decided upswing in the business cycle and with the movement of thousands of people into the middle classes.

But affluence was a mixed blessing, for it prompted great expectations. Poor people, blacks, ethnics, though better off than ever before, knew from TV and other modern communications how much they were missing. Indeed, the gap between black income (rising) and white income (rising faster) was widening, not narrowing. Lower-income groups therefore grew restless and demanding.

Rising affluence also had an ambivalent impact on the spirit of reform among the politically influential middle and upper middle classes. On the one hand, they

Economic growth, 1961–70, compared to selected years before and after this period

NATIONAL PRODUCT AND INCOME
(In billions of current dollars)

	GNP	PERCENT CHANGE FROM GNP OF PRECEDING YEAR (+ OR −)	NATIONAL INCOME	DISPOSABLE PERSONAL INCOME	PER CAPITA DISPOSABLE INCOME (In current) dollars
1940	99.7	+10.2	18.1	75.7	573
1945	211.9	+ 0.9	181.5	150.2	1,074
1949	256.5	− 0.4	217.5	188.6	1,264
1961	520.1	+ 3.2	427.3	364.4	1,984
1962	560.3	+ 7.7	457.7	385.3	2,065
1963	590.5	+ 5.4	481.9	404.6	2,138
1964	632.4	+ 7.1	518.1	438.1	2,283
1965	684.9	+ 8.3	564.3	473.2	2,436
1966	749.9	+ 9.5	620.6	511.9	2,604
1967	793.9	+ 5.9	653.6	546.3	2,749
1968	864.2	+ 8.9	711.1	591.0	2,945
1969	930.3	+ 7.6	766.0	634.4	3,130
1970	977.1	+ 5.0	800.5	691.7	3,376
1971	1,054.9	+ 8.0	857.7	746.4	3,605
1972	1,158.0	+ 9.8	946.5	802.5	3,843

SOURCE: Adapted from *Economic Report of the President*, 1975, p. 249, 267, 269

sensed that the country could afford more generous social welfare policies. Poverty, indeed, was "un-American." On the other hand, the pervasive appeal of consumer goods was seductive. Gains in real income meant the chance to buy big cars and stereo sets, to travel, or simply to buy a home and settle down. This privatism helps to explain why support for social change did not run deep.

This is another way of saying that American attitudes toward the needy had really changed rather little since the 1930s. Although people continued to believe that the state ought to help those who could not help themselves, they also retained much of their historic distrust of Big Government. Thus, when the have-nots attempted to secure social as well as legal equality, this "silent majority" balked. This instinctive retreat from social reform complicated the problems Johnson faced in trying to reduce racism, poverty, and injustice.

For all these reasons Johnson had to strike quickly. If he had waited for lengthy studies or debate, he would have missed the first chance in thirty years to get significant domestic legislation on the statute books. His dilemma suggests the plausibility of the cyclical theory of American reform, which holds that bursts of social legislation, long blocked by Congress, by unstable parties, by state and local governments, by the affluence of the politically influential middle classes, by historic fears of Big Government, suddenly cascade over the barriers, only to be followed by troughs of complacency. This theory is not helpful in predicting when or why such bursts occur, but it helps explain why they dissipate so quickly. It suggests that Johnson, for all his limitations, deserves credit for appealing to the mood of altruism while it lasted.

Suggestions for reading

William Leuchtenburg's *A Troubled Feast** (1973) is a readable account of domestic developments in the United States during the 1960s and early 1970s. Other helpful books are William O'Neill's idiosyncratic *Coming Apart* (1971); and Godfrey Hodgson, *America in Our Time* (1976). James Sundquist's *Politics and Policy** (1968) is the most thorough account of policy making; Richard Polenberg's *One Nation Divisible* (1980) is a fine study of social trends.

Other books on politics include Arthur Schlesinger, Jr., *A Thousand Days** (1965), and Theodore Sorenson, *Kennedy* (1965). Both are pro-Kennedy accounts written by insiders. James M. Burns, *John Kennedy** (1960), is a remarkably objective campaign biography. The same author's *Deadlock of Democracy** (1963) is an engaging interpretation of executive-congressional relations and presidential leadership from the late eighteenth century on. Herbert Parmet, *Jack: The Struggle of John F. Kennedy* (1980), covers Kennedy until 1960. Books on electoral trends include Theodore White, *Making of a President, 1960** (1961), and *Making of a President, 1964* (1965); and Norman Nie et al., *Changing American Voter* (1979). Other books dealing with aspects of the Kennedy administration are Lawrence Fuchs, *John Kennedy and American Catholicism* (1967); Grant McConnell, *Steel and the Presidency—1962** (1963); Seymour Harris, *Economics of the Kennedy Years** (1964); and Carl M. Brauer, *John F. Kennedy and the Second Reconstruction* (1977).

Lyndon Johnson's memoirs, *Vantage Point**(1971), are a self-serving account of his presidency. More critical is Robert Novak and Rowland Evans, *Lyndon B. Johnson: The Exercise of Power** (1966). A psychologically oriented study is Doris Kearns, *Lyndon Johnson and the American Dream* (1976). For welfare policy see James T. Patterson, *America's Struggle Against Poverty, 1900–1980* (1981); and Gilbert Steiner, *State of Welfare* (1971). See also Frances F. Piven and Richard A. Cloward, *Regulating the Poor: The Functions of Public Relief** (1972); and Ben Seligman, *Permanent Poverty** (1968). Jane Jacobs, *Death and Life of Great American Cities** (1961), is a provocative discussion of cities and urban policy, while Daniel Moynihan and Nathan Glazer, *Beyond the Melting Pot** (1963), reveals the ethnic dimensions of life in New York City. Mark Gelfand's *A Nation of Cities: The Federal Government and Urban America, 1933–1965* (1975), is authoritative. For civil rights in the early 1960s see Benjamin Muse, *The American Negro Revolution: From Nonviolence to Black Power, 1963–1967** (1968); Charles Silberman, *Crisis in Black and White** (1964), a very well-written and provocative analysis; Howard Zinn, *SNCC: New Abolitionists, 1964–65* (1964); William Chafe, *Civilities and Civil Rights: Greensboro, North Carolina, and the Black Struggle for Freedom* (1980) and Harvard Sitkoff, *The Struggle for Black Equality, 1954–1980* (1982).

Books on foreign policy in the 1960s include Warren I. Cohen, *Dean Rusk* (1980); Peter Wyden, *The Bay of Pigs* (1979); and Richard Walton, *Cold War and Counterrevolution**

(1972), which is critical of Kennedy. Roger Hilsman, *To Move a Nation* (1967), is an interpretive account by a former member of the Kennedy administration. David Halberstam, *The Best and the Brightest* (1972), is a sustained critique of liberal foreign policy under Kennedy and Johnson. H. B. Johnson, *The Bay of Pigs* (1964), is helpful. For the missile crisis see Robert Kennedy, *13 Days* (1969); Elie Abel, *Missile Crisis** (1966); and especially Graham Allison, *Essence of Decision** (1971).

For Vietnam in the 1950s and early 1960s consult George M. Kahin and J. W. Lewis, *The United States and Vietnam** (1967); and Bernard Fall, *The Two Vietnams** (2nd rev. ed. 1967). Also helpful are Marvin Gettleman, ed., *Vietnam: History, Documents, and Opinions** (1970); and Neil Sheehan et al., *The Pentagon Papers** (1971). See also Richard Barnet and Ronald Müller, *Global Reach: The Power of the Multinational Corporations* (1974).

14

Turmoil

1965–1968

On March 31, 1968, a deeply lined, worn-looking Lyndon Johnson appeared on television to announce his retirement from the presidency at the close of his tenure in January 1969. He said, "I shall not seek, and I will not accept, the nomination of my party for another term as president."

Though his announcement came as a surprise, it was greeted with relief by millions of Americans. By that time Gallup polls were reporting that only 36 percent of the people approved of his conduct of the presidency. Militants were so angry and threatening that Johnson hardly dared appear in public. Like Hoover before him, he had fallen victim to his own stubbornness and to unusually chaotic and turbulent times.

Among the many manifestations of this discord, which rent the country after 1965, three were outstanding. The first, the breakdown of the interracial civil rights movement, culminated in explosive social unrest, including race riots in the cities. The second, escalation of the fighting in Vietnam, led to massive antiwar activity. The third, the rise of radical protest movements and of the "counterculture," was in part the consequence of the other two and in part the cause of further divisions in society. Together these three forces produced domestic turmoil unprecedented in twentieth-century American history.

From interracialism to black power

Since 1960, when the sit-ins first attracted national attention, the civil rights movement had been the vanguard of domestic reform. In providing a cause worthy of sacrifice it sustained the idealism that assists broader movements for change. The

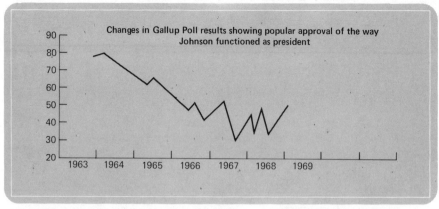

Changes in Gallup Poll results showing popular approval of the way Johnson functioned as president

SOURCE: Adapted from *U.S. Foreign Policy: Context, Conduct, Content* by Marian Irish and Elke Frank. © 1975 by Harcourt Brace Jovanovich. Reproduced by permission of the publisher.

Johnson reached the peak of his popularity shortly after he assumed the presidency in 1964, when 80 percent of respondents approved of the way he conducted his office, and reached a low in mid-1967 when only 32 percent approved of his presidency.

activists who gave up their work or their studies and who risked their lives to participate in the sit-ins, freedom rides, and demonstrations between 1960 and 1963 forged, in interracial organizations such as SNCC, an inspiring "beloved community."

As early as 1963, however, internal divisions were beginning to split the interracial coalition. By 1966 this disintegration produced widespread disruption and disillusion.

One source of discord was the militants' ever-intensifying awareness of the limits of legal action in combating racial discrimination in the South. More black children attended segregated schools in the Deep South in 1964 than in 1954, the year of the supposedly epochal *Brown* decision. Jim Crow laws flourished throughout the region. Despite legal guarantees, blacks (and many poor whites) still were denied the vote. Though the civil rights acts of 1964 and 1965 eventually rectified some of these abuses, they came too late to pacify activists.

Militants in the North grew equally angry by 1965. Whites, they complained, discriminated against all blacks in the crucially important areas of education and housing, where de facto segregation was the rule. Urban renewal, activists added, usually meant "Negro removal." James Baldwin commented bitterly that housing projects "are hated almost as much as policemen, and that is saying a great deal. And they are hated for the same reason: both reveal, unbearably, the real attitude of the white world, no matter how many liberal speeches are made." Like many others, Baldwin recognized that the civil rights acts did nothing to assist social welfare or racial justice in the North, where more than half of America's blacks lived by 1970.

Even before 1965 growing discontent among Negro slum dwellers led to an increase in the strength of the Black Muslims. Led by their Messenger, Elijah Muhammed, the Muslims combined faith in Islam with vehement separatism, anti-Semitism, and black racism. Like Marcus Garvey (and Booker T. Washington), they called for black self-help. Whites, they said, were agents of the devil; blacks must consider them enemies and refuse to mingle with or intermarry with them. Integrationists such as Martin Luther King, Jr., Elijah Muhammed argued, were tools of white society.

This black racism did not become a mass movement: perhaps no more than 20,000 people belonged to the Muslims during the mid-1960s. But it appealed to some people whom the interracial organizations failed to attract. It enlisted Cassius Clay (later Muhammed Ali), the heavyweight boxing champion of the world. It promoted the rise of Malcolm X, a charismatic leader who broke with Elijah Muhammed in 1963 to form the Organization for Afro-American Unity before he was assassinated by black gunmen in February 1965. At that point he had renounced his black racism and begun to encourage interracial cooperation such as he thought existed under Islam. Though he had not been able to put his ideas into practice when he died, he had attracted a considerable following. His death made him a martyr. His appeal, like that of the Muslims, exposed the bitterness affecting many blacks even at the peak of interracial cooperation in the early 1960s.

By 1964 racial and sexual tensions began to divide civil rights workers in the South. The idealistic white activists endured great discomfort and real danger in trying to register blacks to vote. Two of them, Andrew Goodman and Michael Schwerner, were killed along with James Chaney, a black, in Mississippi in 1964. But some northern white girls were shocked by what they perceived as the sexual aggressiveness of their black co-workers. Others—relatively affluent, upwardly mobile college students—were staggered by what they thought to be the ignorance and laziness of blacks in the rural South. "I really don't understand how they [blacks] can sit on the porch from six in the morning until nine in the evening without crossing their legs," one white wrote. Another added, "[Negroes] speak our same language but they look at things differently. Religion, Sex. It's sort of a different culture." Still other whites, accustomed to assuming positions of leadership in biracial movements, grew resentful as blacks sought to direct their own revolution.

Blacks easily detected these white attitudes. The white activists, they countered, returned to exclusive northern suburbs when the registration drives were over, leaving blacks to face the angry segregationists in the South. Blacks complained also about the mass media, which exalted the idealism—and exaggerated the contributions—of the whites while taking the blacks for granted. Some black militants developed misconceptions of their own about sex. "I think all those white girls down here sat up North dreaming about being raped by some big black Negro." a southern black said, "and came down here to see what it was like." The problem of leadership was especially divisive. Only black people, the militants argued, could understand the black experience. Whites, in any event, had no business trying to tell blacks what to do.

Militant young blacks came vehemently to distrust "paternalistic" white liberals as much as segregationists. President Kennedy, they believed, coopted the movement by preventing militants from taking a prominent role in the march on Washington in 1963. SNCC leaders from Mississippi complained—with much justice—that liberals had blocked their Freedom Democratic party delegation to the

1964 Democratic Convention. Integration and nonviolence, these blacks believed, were goals for "Uncle Toms." "Do I really want to be integrated into a burning house?" Baldwin asked. Whites, he added, would give in only under the threat of force—"the fire next time."

Baldwin was prophetic. One consequence of this bitterness was racial violence in northern cities. This began on a relatively small scale in Harlem and in Rochester in 1964. In August 1965, five days after Johnson signed the civil rights law, black rioting broke out anew in the Watts district of Los Angeles. It caused the death of thirty-five people and property damage estimated at more than $30 million. In 1966 minor disturbances occurred in Chicago and other places, and in 1967 the greatest explosions of all took place in Newark, where 26 died and more than 1,000 were injured, and in Detroit, the worst conflagration since the Chicago race riot of 1919. At Detroit 43 died and 2,000 were hurt. Much of the city's black belt was burned or destroyed. In 1967 alone 83 people were killed in 164 disorders (8 of them major), causing more than $100 million in property damage.

To many observers, envy of white prosperity and consumer culture seemed to motivate the rioters. "The rebellion," one rioter conceded, ". . . was all caused by the commercials. I mean you saw all those things you'd never be able to get. . . . Men's clothing, furniture, appliances, color TV. All that crummy TV glamor just hanging out there." These observers pointed out accurately that black rioters in the 1960s, unlike those of 1919, did not physically assault white people; they retaliated instead against businesses in ghetto areas. The rioters, indeed, were generally careful not to harm people and usually confined their destructive behavior to their own communities.

Other people blamed the disturbances on destitute migrants—"riffraff" cast adrift in strange cities. Or they said that the rioters were engaged in fun and games, like students tearing up Fort Lauderdale during spring vacation. Firm police action, it was believed, would restore order. Still others suggested that class conflict lay at the root of the trouble. Most of the troublemakers, they argued, were poor blacks, sometimes joined by poor whites.

Many of these explanations contained some truth, for motives varied. But one major cause of the rioting was what the blacks called "police brutality." Many of the riots were sparked by reports of harsh police behavior toward blacks in the ghettos. The study commissions also noted that the rioters included few "riffraff"—these were too disorganized and marginal to play much of a part. Rather,

Detroit riots, 1967. National Guardsman patrols in front of a store devastated by burning and looting.

the majority of rioters were upwardly mobile blacks who felt most deeply what President Johnson's commission called "white racism." Though these blacks had gained economically, they sensed that they had far to go to close the widening gap that separated them from the white middle classes, and that whites would never let them move out of the ghetto. Thus it was that some of the worst riots, as in Watts and Detroit, occurred where blacks were relatively well off and relatively well treated—where expectations had been whetted the most.

Another cause—and consequence—of the riots was the developing cry for "black power." This phrase, which frightened whites throughout the late 1960s, first gained currency in June 1966, when James Meredith was shot and wounded while making a demonstration walk from Memphis, Tennessee, to Jackson, Mississippi. King and others then moved in to complete the march. But Stokely Carmichael, the head of SNCC, rejected King's faith in white liberals and in nonviolence. "We have got to get us some black power," he said. "We have to organize ourselves to speak for each other. That's black power. We have to move to control the economics and politics of our community."

White and nonwhite family income, 1950–70
(Percent distribution of families, by race of head of family)

WHITE FAMILIES	(In current dollars)			
	UNDER $2,000	$2,000–$5,999	$6,000–$9,999	OVER $10,000
1950	22.2	62.6	11.6	3.5
1955	15.3	54.1	23.8	6.8
1960	11.0	41.3	32.5	15.3
1965	7.7	30.1	35.3	27.1
1970	3.8	18.7	25.9	51.6
NONWHITE FAMILIES				
1950	53.4	43.2	3.2	0.3
1955	39.7	51.7	7.9	0.6
1960	31.7	47.9	15.4	4.9
1965	20.7	49.7	20.5	9.0
1970	11.1	35.0	25.6	28.2

SOURCE: Adapted from *Statistical Abstract of the United States*, 1974, p. 382

To some extent, the development of black power organizations after 1965 merely exposed openly what had existed for some time: divisions among black leaders in the movement. Many blacks, while recognizing the indispensable contributions of Martin Luther King, Jr., resented the way in which he seemed to receive the credit (from white-dominated media) for the movement's successes. Local leaders of black communities in southern towns were especially bitter when King and other spokesmen for the interracial organizations "took over" the organizing drives, only to leave town when the publicity subsided. Still other advocates of black power, including some young activists from the North, did not share the religious style or the evangelical manner of leaders like King—"de Lawd," they sneered. In these ways, the quest for black power reflected formerly obscured divisions—by age, by region, by social class—within the heterogeneous American black community itself.

The major force behind the drive for black power, however, was the rage that men like Carmichael felt against white attempts to dominate a movement which after all was supposed to affect black people. Some black power spokesmen, in-

The media claims that I teach hate. Hate, like love, is a feeling. How can you teach a feeling? If Black people hate white people it's not because of me, it's because of what white people do to Black people. If hate can be taught, ain't no better teacher than white people themselves. I hate oppression. I am anti anybody who is anti-Black. Now if that includes most white people in America, it ain't my fault. That's just the way the bones break. I don't care whether or not white people hate me. It's not essential that a man love you to live. But "the man" has to respect you.

H. Rap Brown of SNCC offers his view of race relations.

deed, made Carmichael sound like a moderate. H. Rap Brown, who took over as head of SNCC in 1967, explained that "John Brown was the only white man I could respect and he is dead. The Black Movement has no use for white liberals. We need revolutionaries. Revolutions need revolutionaries." Julius Lester, a SNCC field secretary, published a book entitled *Look Out Whitey! Black Power's Gon' Get Your Mama!* "Now it is over," he said, "the days of singing freedom songs and the days of combatting bullets and billy clubs with love. We Shall Overcome (and we have overcome our blindness) sounds old, outdated, and can enter the pantheon of the greats along with the IWW songs and the union songs. As one SNCC veteran put it after the Mississippi march, 'Man, the people are too busy getting ready to fight to bother with singing any more.'" Huey Newton, a leader of the Black Panthers, founded in 1966, added that blacks must arm themselves in defense against the police and the military. "We make the statement," he said, "quoting from Chairman Mao, that Political Power comes through the Barrel of a Gun."

In the cultural realm "black power" did much to develop pride among black people. Carmichael said, "The only thing we own in this country is the color of our skins. . . . We have to stop being ashamed of being black. A broad nose, a thick lip, and nappy hair is us, and we are going to call that beautiful whether they like it or not." This "Black Is Beautiful" theme (which Langston Hughes and others had promoted forty years earlier) cut down the sale of bleaches, hair straighteners, and other cosmetics that blacks had bought for decades in attempts to hide their racial characteristics. It affected advertising, films, art, and poetry. It led to courses in black history, to renewed appreciation for African culture, and to growing confidence among black people generally. As James Brown's popular song proclaimed, "Say It Loud—I'm Black and I'm Proud."

By using the rhetoric of violence, however, spokesmen like H. Rap Brown cut deep divisions into the civil rights movement. Roy Wilkins of the NAACP, whose legal defense fund had been indispensable to civil rights activists—and who was far from being an "Uncle Tom"—said that such rhetoric was the "father of hatred and the mother of violence." A. Philip Randolph, who had threatened an all-black march on Washington in 1941, considered the new version of black power a "menace to peace and prosperity." King complained that "returning violence for violence multiplies violence, adding deeper darkness to a night already devoid of stars. Darkness cannot drive out darkness; only light can do that."

These nonviolent leaders stressed that blacks, working with white allies, could attain power through economic organization and voter solidarity. They insisted also that Carmichael, Brown, and other extremists represented only a very small minority of blacks. The moderates in the movement made other telling points against the separatist argument. First, they said, a few of the separatists were ideologically empty-headed and romantic. Others, they said, spouted violent rhetoric that intensified white "backlash." Above all, the moderates said, separatism was unrealistic. Blacks, comprising some 11 percent of the population, needed white help if they were to succeed. And blacks could be destroyed if they forsook nonviolence. Hatred and violence, King said, "intensify the fears of the white majority, and leave them less ashamed of their prejudices against Negroes."

King, however, could not wish away either the urban riots or the extremist rhetoric of the militant minority, both of which antagonized whites. As early as June 1966, 85 percent of whites thought blacks were too demanding, compared to only 34 percent in 1964. House Republican leader Gerald Ford asked, "how long are we going to abdicate law and order—the backbone of our civilization—in favor of a soft social theory that the man who heaves a brick through your window or tosses a fire bomb into your car is simply the misunderstood and underprivileged product of a broken home?" Johnson himself grew peevish, especially when Rap Brown branded him a "white honky cracker." After appointing a commission to study the riots, he rejected its call in 1968 for far-reaching federal reforms. "They always print that we don't do enough," he snapped. "They don't print what we do."

Reactions like these did not mean that a white backlash was overrunning the country or that the civil rights movement had failed. Polls in the more peaceful years after the riots revealed that most Americans approved of the gains that had been made. The civil rights laws remained on the books, blacks registered and voted in unprecedented numbers, school and universities were desegregated, especially in the Deep South. By 1970 southern blacks enjoyed as much legal protection as blacks in the North, where de facto segregation had long prevailed. But black spokesmen began pressing for more social and economic equality, including the end of discrimination in housing, and busing to achieve racial balance in the schools. At this point many whites balked, and the struggle for racial justice entered a period of stalemate. The drive that had characterized the civil rights movement in the early 1960s seemed eons past by 1968.

Vietnam, 1964–68

Three days after Kennedy's assassination President Johnson conferred with Henry Cabot Lodge, Jr., America's ambassador to South Vietnam. Lodge confirmed what people already sensed: the assassination of Diem earlier in the month had increased political instability in South Vietnam, while doing nothing to facilitate the military struggle. Another president, recognizing that South Vietnam was engaged in a civil war, might have refrained from increasing America's commitment of 17,000 men. But not Johnson, who persisted in blaming North Vietnam and China for the fighting in the south. Johnson told Lodge, "I am not going to be the president who saw Vietnam go the way China went."

In 1964 Johnson did his best to conceal this determined attitude from the electorate. Troop levels were increased, but only to 21,000. During the election campaign he ridiculed the notion that he might escalate the number of American soldiers in Vietnam. After the Vietcong attacked American facilities at Bien Hoa in October, he declared, "We are not going to drop bombs."

Even before the 1964 election, however, signs appeared of the Johnson deceptions that lay ahead. Early in August he announced that North Vietnamese torpedo boats had attacked American destroyers in the Tonkin Gulf thirty miles off North

Vietnam war and fall of Indochina, 1954–75

Vietnam. He suppressed the truth: that the American warships had been assisting
South Vietnamese commando raids; that the destroyers had been in combat zones
close to shore; and that the alleged assaults, on dark nights in rough seas, may have
been imagined by nervous American officers. The supposed attacks, in any event,
caused no damage. Feigning outrage, Johnson ordered American planes to smash
North Vietnamese torpedo bases and oil installations—targets picked carefully two
months earlier. He also asked Congress to authorize him to take ''all necessary

measures to repel any armed attack against the forces of the United States and to prevent further aggression." An alarmed (and uninformed) Congress acceded, unanimously in the House and eighty-eight to two in the Senate. Like Truman after the North Korean invasion, Johnson never troubled to ask for a declaration of war. The Tonkin Gulf resolution gave him latitude to increase the American presence there over the next four years.

The escalation itself occurred early in 1965 after the Vietcong rebels killed 7 Americans and wounded 109 at Pleiku. Within twelve hours of getting the news, American planes retaliated by dropping bombs in the north. Three days later Johnson authorized regular bombing, again on targets chosen in 1964. In April, after Vietcong attacks had almost succeeded in blowing up the American embassy in Saigon, he stepped up the dispatch of ground troops. By early 1966 the United States had nearly 200,000 soldiers in South Vietnam.

When critics complained of American escalation, Johnson reminded them of his efforts for peace. In April 1965 he promised both sides long-term economic aid. On December 24, 1965, he called a bombing halt, which lasted until January 31, 1966. He made Averell Harriman an ambassador-at-large and sent him on well-publicized missions in search of peace. In October 1966 Johnson went to Manila to pledge that the United States would pull out of Vietnam within six months of the end of the shooting. Later in the year secret negotiations to end the war started in Poland.

It is unlikely that Johnson really expected these overtures to succeed. Instead, he remained fixed in his central goal: to keep South Vietnam within the noncommunist orbit. Because its pro-American puppet governments had little popular support, this policy required further escalation, which destroyed chances for accommodation. By mid-1966 America had 265,000 troops in South Vietnam; by the end of 1967 it had more than 500,000. The war cost an estimated $100 billion per year by 1968—the amount spent yearly on *all* federal expenditures as recently as 1964. Bernard Fall, the best-informed writer on Vietnam at the time, estimated that it cost the United States between $300,000 and $500,000 per enemy death as of early 1966.

Johnson relied heavily on massive bombing of North Vietnam. The attacks sought to destroy military installations, oil reserves, and railway lines and to slow down the flow of supplies from the north to the Vietcong. However, the raids were counterproductive. North Vietnam, which had given little aid to the Vietcong before 1965, responded to the attacks by stepping up its delivery of goods. The raids also smashed urban areas and killed countless North Vietnamese civilians. Frequently American bombers used napalm, an incendiary substance that set human flesh aflame.

In the south, American military action was equally devastating. "Pacification" programs to secure the countryside entailed burning of villages, forcible uprooting of civilians, and desecration of ancestral burial grounds. "Search and destroy" missions killed thousands of villagers. Overwhelming American firepower defoliated forests, destroyed rice crops, and shattered the economy. Some American troops perpetrated atrocities, such as the one in the village of My Lai in 1968, which resulted in the killing of 347 civilian men, women, and children. During Johnson's presidency the war caused the deaths of some 28,000 Americans, per-

A scene from Vietnam

haps 100,000 South Vietnamese, and untold numbers of Vietcong rebels. Civilian deaths approached a million.

Long before Johnson left office, opponents of the war inveighed against these policies. Like the more progressive isolationists in 1917 and 1940, they complained that the war was undermining support for reform at home. They protested the immorality of bombing civilians, the abuse of presidential power, and the impact of the war on America's relations with the rest of the world. Other critics, such as Walter Lippmann and the political scientist Hans Morganthau, pointed out that the United States had no economic or strategic interests in Vietnam worth such a commitment.

Johnson remained deaf to such arguments. He brusquely dismissed dissidents within his administration. "Kennedy," one observer explained, "didn't mind disagreement. It didn't bother him. But disagreement really bothers this president. He is going to do what you dislike anyway; so let's not upset him by having an argument in front of him." In such an atmosphere it was not surprising that few top-ranking officials dared dispute him, or that those who did, like McNamara in 1967–68, left office. As late as March 16, 1968, six weeks after the devastating "Tet" offensive by the Vietcong, which brought pleas for de-escalation from the new secretary of defense, Clark Clifford, Johnson held to his position. "Let's get one thing clear," he said. "I am not going to stop the bombing. I have heard every argument on the subject, and I am not interested in further discussion." Though he finally softened his stance two weeks later—announcing the end of bombing in the north (save near the demarcation line) and reporting that America was beginning peace talks in Paris—these were not concessions to his advisers but changes in tactics. The rebels demanded that America withdraw, and the talks in Paris went nowhere.

Johnson's stubbornness derived from many misconceptions. Among them was his characteristically American view of communism as a united, worldwide conspiracy. This attitude led him to ignore opportunities for Soviet-American détente. In Latin America it caused him to neglect the Alliance for Progress and, in 1965, to send marines to challenge left-wing forces in the Dominican Republic. In Southeast Asia it prompted him to ignore the simple fact that the conflict in South Vietnam was a civil war. Communist China, he said, was responsible for the "aggression" of Ho Chi Minh from the north. By focusing on China, Johnson vastly underestimated the tenacity of the South Vietnamese rebels. Theirs was a war of revolution, not only against puppets like Diem but against decades of Western imperialism. This revolutionary nationalism helped to explain why superior American firepower, to say nothing of 500,000 men, failed utterly to control the countryside.

Johnson also placed exaggerated faith in money and technology. When the North Vietnamese ignored his offer of economic aid in 1965, he was uncomprehending. "I don't understand it," he said. "George Meany [head of the AFL] would've grabbed at a deal like that." Encouraged by the statistics of Secretary of Defense McNamara, he persisted in believing that American air superiority would eventually destroy the enemy. But the bombing failed to stem the flow of supplies from the north. Vietnam, an agricultural country where supply routes wound through dense cover, was singularly ill-suited for strategic bombing.

Ironically, the appalling cost of these misconceptions prompted doubts in America about long-held liberal dogmas. Among these was the view that a strong presidency was a positive good. In domestic policy, this remained an article of liberal faith. In foreign affairs, however, it seemed that isolationists like Charles Beard and Robert Taft had been wise in demanding an important role for Congress. This distrust of the presidency added immeasurably to the discord that tore the nation apart after 1965.

Another partial casualty of the war was globalism—the view that the United States must preserve "freedom" everywhere. To many Americans, the war in Vietnam ultimately proved that this was not possible. America was not omnipotent; it had to think about priorities. Most of those who turned against globalism were not isolationists—they supported the United Nations, NATO, and aid to Israel. But they demanded a reduced presence in Asia, and they looked for ways to defuse the Cold War. They pointed especially to the split between the Soviet Union and China. This break, already deep in the 1960s, led both communist nations to look for détente with the United States. Thanks in part to the rethinking of foreign policy engendered by Vietnam, even hard-liners like Richard Nixon were later induced to respond.

THE ANTIWAR MOVEMENT

Second thoughts such as these were but small consolation to Americans who by 1968 were suffering under the travails of the longest war in the nation's history. Besides devastating Vietnam, it shattered the reform coalition in the United States

America's mood:
the public's view of the most important
problem facing the country,
according to Gallup Poll results,
1964–68

1964	Integration
1965	Vietnam
1966	Vietnam
1967	Vietnam
1968	Vietnam

SOURCE: Adapted from *U.S. Foreign Policy: Context, Conduct, Content* by Marian Irish and Elke Frank. © 1975 by Harcourt Brace Jovanovich. Reproduced by permission of the publisher.

and ultimately promoted the most alarming inflation since 1946. As much as any other development of the decade, the war eclipsed the idealism and hopefulness of the Kennedy era and precipitated the unrest that gripped the country between 1965 and 1968.

Prompting this unrest was the most militant antiwar movement in American history. By late 1965 students were already starting to stage mass demonstrations, to conduct "bleed-ins" seeking blood for the Vietcong, to burn their draft cards, and to chant, "hey, hey, LBJ, how many kids did you kill today?" A stop-the-bombing march in Washington in November 1965 attracted 20,000 protestors, including Norman Thomas, the veteran socialist leader, James Farmer, the head of CORE, and Dr. Benjamin Spock.

Many developments helped to swell the antiwar movement after 1965. One, of course, was the enormous American escalation, which became too obvious to hide by 1966. Another was the coverage—in news photographs and on television—of American patrols burning Vietnamese villages, of refugees fleeing the smoke of battle, of horribly burned and wounded women and children, of mutilated American soldiers. These scenes of bloodletting, plus the mounting casualty figures, made it increasingly difficult for Americans to believe the White House and the Pentagon. The "credibility gap" added desperation and fury to the protests.

Young people, especially college students, provided much of the energy behind the antiwar movement. Many of these activists were veterans of the civil rights struggle, where they had learned the tactics of nonviolent mass protest. Most agreed with Martin Luther King, Jr., who proclaimed that the United States was "the greatest purveyor of violence in the world."

Other young people had more personal reasons for joining the struggle against war: they did not want to fight in Vietnam. As draft calls mounted (from 5,000 per month in 1965 to 50,000 per month in 1967), graduate students—who had previously secured exemptions—began to be inducted. Alarmed, they moved from quiet disagreement with the war to participation in "teach-ins" on campus to mass protests. Their parents often supported them. By 1967 the antiwar crusade had become a broad-based movement including pacifists, leftists, civil rights activists, draft-age students, and substantial numbers of previously apolitical middle-class parents. By

BROOKS, BIRMINGHAM NEWS

I have to speak to some college students about Vietnam—could you rig up a tank with a loudspeaker?

By 1968 Johnson hardly dared appear in public.

1968, after the Tet offensive, these people were angry enough to demonstrate against the Pentagon, to challenge LBJ himself in the political arena, and to turn college campuses into cockpits of turmoil.

The youth rebellion

The growth of education in the postwar period was staggering. In 1940 the average level achieved by Americans was grade eight. At that time one out of six people of college age attended colleges or universities; one in twelve graduated. By the late 1960s the average grade level was twelve; 50 percent of college-age youth went on to college; and more than 20 percent graduated. The nation's colleges and universities reflected the major themes of twentieth-century American history: affluence, professionalization, and the rise of the middle class.

Until the early 1960s the campuses were peaceful, and students appeared to worry more about fraternities and football than about social issues. In the Kennedy years, however, many students became more politicized. Some joined New Leftist groups like the Students for a Democratic Society. Others led civil rights demonstrations, served in the Peace Corps, or volunteered in the war against poverty. These altruists were not a majority of students, let alone of young people generally: only 12 percent of students identified themselves as part of the "New Left" even at the peak of campus unrest in 1970. But the protestors attended some of the nation's largest and most prestigious universities. They were articulate. Their role in civil rights demonstrations at Birmingham and Selma suggested that they could make a difference in the world.

By the end of the decade, many of these campuses displayed the same turmoil that affected society at large. Beginning with a demonstration for free speech at Berkeley in 1964, youthful protest became steadily more radical. In 1968, agitators at Columbia seized the president's office and forced the university to shut down. Elsewhere, militants littered campus offices, stormed buildings, shouted down visiting speakers, staged strikes, and battled police ("pigs") called in to restore order. In all, 221 major demonstrations took place on the campuses between January and June 1968. Until 1971, America's universities seemed to be centers of revolution.

Among the forces prompting such unrest were the social divisions outside the university. Like the radicals in the 1930s, activists protested against racism, concentration of wealth, and the "power elite." Like many conservatives, they complained about bureaucratic government, "snooping" by federal agencies, the draft, and "globalism." Like radical students elsewhere—for unrest gripped universities throughout the world at the time—they tended to question all authority. Their enemies were not the universities but racism, social inequality, and the military-industrial complex promoting war in Vietnam.

Other students concentrated their assaults on the universities. In this way they differed from the youthful radicals of the 1930s, who had tried to protect the campus from external pressures. Places like Berkeley, the new rebels complained, had become enormous bureaucratic institutions—"multiuniversities" that treated students like IBM cards. Urban universities like Harvard and Columbia, students protested, gobbled up surrounding areas once occupied by poor people. As the Vietnam war escalated, militants also protested against campus institutions such as ROTC. Others busied themselves exposing the connections between multiuniversities and the CIA. For all these students, universities were the most visible and vulnerable manifestations of a repressive Establishment.

Idealistic students complained especially that universities were degree mills where young people had to do what they were told so that they could enter the Establishment at the age of twenty-two. Other critics, like Paul Goodman, went further and opposed compulsory education. "We have been swept on a flood-tide of public policy and popular sentiment," he argued, "into an expansion of schooling and an aggrandizement of school-people that is grossly wasteful of youth and effort and does positive damage to the young."

The restlessness that Goodman perceived helped explain why so many otherwise nonradical students lent their support to (or at least acquiesced in) the demands of antiestablishment minorities. It also helped to account for the lack of consistent ideology among the youthful militants. Unlike the radicals of the 1930s, many of whom were moved by Marx, the New Left of the 1960s (except for a handful who admired China's Mao or Cuba's Ché Guevara) eschewed programmatic approaches to revolution. Rather, they focused on tactics. Inspired by the civil rights demonstrations, and then by the attention given to advocates of black power, they moved quickly into confrontation strategies against the Vietnam war and the "power elite."

It later became almost fashionable to deride these militants. The campus unrest of the late 1960s, people began to argue, was orchestrated by a small minority, most of whom were sons and daughters of radicals in the 1930s. The militants, critics added, were affluent, self-indulgent hypocrites who were quick to join the Establishment after graduation; antiwar protestors wanted to escape the draft. Conservatives also argued that transitory demographic imperatives prompted the campus unrest. High birth rates in the 1940s and early 1950s, they contended, created a uniquely large percentage of college-age people by the late 1960s. No such revolt of youth, these analysts concluded, was likely to recur.

Though there was some truth in these observations, conservatives had to admit that the young people scored a few victories. Students forced administrative and curricular changes in some universities. Off campus they were the backbone of the civil rights and antiwar movements. Many of the protestors made permanent commitments to social change by fighting against environmental pollution, by enlisting in Common Cause, or by backing Ralph Nader and other foes of commercial and governmental exploitation. Many worked for antiwar political candidates in 1968 and 1972. The student movement, like the struggle for black power, was neither wholly negative nor wasted.

It was a fact, however, that many student victories were pyrrhic by 1968. Indeed, youthful excesses appalled many reformers as well as conservatives. These reformers agreed that many American institutions needed changing. But they lamented what they considered the anti-intellectualism and fundamental disrespect for rational discourse that characterized some of the youthful extremists. The reformers also resented the rhetoric of the young radicals. Slogans such as "Don't Trust Anyone Over Thirty," to say nothing of well-publicized campaigns like the "Filthy Speech" movement at Berkeley, were hardly calculated to appeal to the majority of Americans. Neither were insults to "pigs" and other symbols of authority. Excesses such as these created backlash, divided the movement, and sapped its effectiveness.

The counterculture

Some young people did not content themselves with unsettling the universities. They embraced what became known in the late 1960s as the counterculture. The overlapping of the two movements, radical protest and rebellion against the life styles and values of the 1950s, gave unprecedented visibility to the youth movement of the 1960s.

A "hippy" commune. Much communal living took place in the kitchen.

The surface manifestations of the counterculture in themselves alienated traditionalists. Increasing numbers of young men (and some adults) let their hair grow long, donned love beads, and dressed in faded jeans, work shirts, and sandals. Young women, slouching about without bras or shoes, talked of sexual freedom. Many of these people took marijuana or other more dangerous drugs, and they lived as "hippies" in rural communes or in seedy urban areas like San Francisco's Haight-Ashbury district. The very sight of such apparently unkempt people was offensive to many more staid Americans.

Traditionalists also grew alarmed at the taste in popular music shared by many young people in the late 1960s. Earlier in the decade idealistic youth had flocked to hear folk musicians like Bob Dylan, Malvina Reynolds, and Joan Baez sing gentle lyrics of social protest. Reynolds asked (in complaining about radioactivity), "What Have They Done to the Rain?" Pete Seeger chimed in, "Where Have All the Flowers Gone?" Though lyrics such as these were socially conscious, they did not much worry most Americans. One radical complained that Baez talked only about "clouds, flowers, butterflies . . . and the like." Arlo Guthrie, a leading folksinger, conceded that "you don't accomplish very much singing protest songs to people who agree with you. Everybody just has a good time thinking they're right."

Within the next three years social protest songs gave way to "acid rock." John Lennon, one of the Beatles, scored a hit with "Lucy in the Sky with Diamonds," and Dylan himself wrote "Mr. Tambourine Man." Both frankly embraced the use of drugs. Another singer explained, "You take the drugs, you turn up the music real loud, you dance around, you build up a fantasy." By the late 1960s the most popular entertainers included groups like the Doors and the Rolling Stones. Jim

Morrison of the Doors relied primarily on sexuality for his effect and was twice arrested for indecent exposure. Mick Jagger, leader of the Rolling Stones, unleashed not only sexual instincts but also violence. In 1969 at Altamont in California he called on the Hell's Angels, a gang of motorcyclists, to keep order at one of the Stones' concerts. When the crowd grew unruly, the Angels stomped a black man to death on the stage.

Advocates of the counterculture neither sought nor welcomed such violence. By the end of the decade, however, they flocked happily to extravaganzas such as the "Woodstock" concert at Bethel, New York, in 1969. This attracted some 400,000 people. For three days the majority seemed content to lie about in the mud, to share marijuana, and even to fornicate in the open. "Everyone swam nude in the lake," a journalist wrote. "Balling was easier than getting breakfast, and the 'pigs' just smiled and passed out the oats."

There was much more to the counterculture than lovebeads and rock concerts. True believers posed sharp challenges to existing values. For them there was a "generation gap." Like Dustin Hoffman, "hero" of the hit movie *The Graduate* (1969), they rejected what they considered the hypocrisy of people over thirty. Paul Simon's song *Sound of Silence* symbolized the gigantic gap that prevented understanding between young people and their parents. The "revolution," these youths believed, was cultural and generational. Young people must advance to new thresholds of freedom. To Charles Reich, whose *Greening of America* (1969) celebrated the new culture, this meant rejecting the materialism and competitiveness of previous epochs and creating a world of love, beauty, and peace. The counterculture, another writer suggested, meant a "vision of a new American identity—a collective identity that will be blacker, more feminine, more oriental, more emotional, more intuitive, more exuberant—and, just possibly, better than the old one."

Central to the ideas of these true believers was the conviction that older people were repressed. Adults, caught in what Paul Goodman called the "rat-race," were supposedly afraid to let themselves go. Herbert Marcuse, whose books appeared to support the counterculture, argued that affluence was abolishing poverty in society. Eros, the symbol of affluence and the end of scarcity, would ultimately conquer aggression. The avant garde must transcend repression to live by an "aesthetic ethos." As the historian John P. Diggins pointed out, beliefs such as these aligned the counterculturists more closely with the "lyrical left" that had challenged middle-class values prior to World War I than with the "old" Marxist left of the 1930s. Like Randolph Bourne, the New Leftists believed that "imagination is revolution." Some added that drugs helped to explode repressions. The key was "not politics but psychedelics."

Surmounting repression meant rejecting taboos about sex. If Eros was to conquer, people must feel free to indulge in premarital sex, to challenge nuclear families, even to practice homosexuality or lesbianism. It followed—to some—that censorship was wrong. By 1970 traditionalists were appalled at the spread of "X-rated" movies, of "gay liberation," and even of "swingers" magazines featuring photos of naked people advertising their wares. One such magazine had a circulation of 50,000 by 1972. As never before, sexuality was becoming a virtue, and pornography a consumer durable.

If sex was one avenue to transcendence, rejection of science was another. Theodore Roszak, a leading proponent of the counterculture, argued that American society resembled a "world's fair in its final days, when things start to sag and disintegrate behind the futuristic façade." To overcome this technological debauch, people needed to reject scientism, computerism, reason generally. Roszak and others sought a more decentralized, less industrialized, less competitive cosmos. It was to discover such an Eden that the true believers moved to rural communes and scratched at the soil with hand-made tools.

In this way the foes of contemporary culture joined others in the 1960s who swelled the age-old chorus against materialism. "American civilization," Norman Mailer cried, "had moved from the existential sanction of the frontier to the abstract ubiquitous sanction of the dollar bill." Another writer added, "people no longer have opinions: they have refrigerators. . . . The only way to catch a spirit of the times is to write a handbook on home appliances." Like Andy Warhol, a "pop" artist who occupied himself painting such commercial symbols as Campbell's soup cans and Marilyn Monroe, these critics thought that consumerism was the essence of American culture.

To replace material values, Roszak and others called for a return to spiritualism. By this they did not mean orthodox religious faiths. Rather, like Henry Thoreau and the transcendentalists, they wanted human beings to achieve enlightenment through communion with nature. People, Roszak said, must develop a "new culture in which the nonintellective capacities of personality" will predominate. This faith in intuition underlay the growing popularity in the 1960s of mysticism, astrology, and Oriental philosophy. Human beings, these people believed, must seek harmony with, not victory over, the natural world.

Such faith in nature assisted a broader movement for ecological balance, which gripped thousands of Americans who otherwise had little use for the counterculture. Among these were scientists who raised frightening visions. Barry Commoner, a Washington University biologist, argued that nuclear explosions, automobiles, detergents, and pesticides polluted the environment and increased the percentage of carbon dioxide in the atmosphere. Soon, he warned, temperatures would increase, the polar ice caps would melt, and water would inundate the world's great seaports. Paul Ehrlich, author of *Population Bomb,* crusaded for birth control, the ultimate guarantee of environmental protection. Mothers' milk contained so much DDT, he said, that it would be banned if sold on the market. He added, "we must realize that unless we are extremely lucky everybody will disappear in a cloud of blue steam in twenty years."

Many scientists challenged such forecasts of doom. While conceding the misery caused by population growth in underdeveloped nations, they observed that the American birth rate was declining in the 1960s to the lowest level, except for the 1930s, in American history. Others insisted that pesticides such as DDT were necessary to grow food for the world's hungry masses. Alarmists like Commoner, they thought, failed to grasp Theodore Roosevelt's central point—that resources must be used wisely for orderly growth.

Still, there was no denying one important theme of many of the ecologists: that modern American society was incredibly wasteful and destructive. Awareness of such demands on resources led many people to recycle glass and paper, to join consumer movements, and to push the Pill. Others challenged the desirability of growth itself. The counterculturists could hardly take full credit for awakening these activists to the nation's wastefulness—conservation, after all, was not new to the 1960s. But their passion for the harmonious life helped the movement for ecology to spread. It was their most lasting legacy.

By the end of the decade it became increasingly clear that sharp differences divided the youth movement. While many members of the counterculture held vaguely New Left views on social issues, they were essentially nonpolitical. Their primary grievance was with bourgeois life styles, not with capitalism. New Leftists and black power advocates, accordingly, accused the "flower children" of trying to cop out of society, instead of fighting it. The crusade for sexual liberation, C. Wright Mills grumbled, was a "gonad theory of revolution." These differences, resembling nineteenth-century divisions between transcendentalists and abolitionists, split the young radicals in manifold ways and left them considerably less potent than alarmists perceived.

Extremists further undercut the appeal of the youthful counterculturists—just as they hurt the New Left. Among these were Jerry Rubin and Abbie Hoffman, self-styled leaders of the Yippies. They were long-haired, unkempt, savagely expressive. "When in doubt, BURN," Rubin counseled in 1967. "Fire is the revolutionary's god. . . . Burn the flag. Burn churches. Burn. Burn. Burn." People should "farm in the morning, make music in the afternoon, and fuck wherever and whenever they want to." Rubin and Hoffman were essentially antipolitical; they were indulging themselves, not organizing a revolution. Yet their rhetoric— overcovered by the media—disgusted many men and women of peace. It was easy for the public to lump together the hippies and the New Leftists and to perceive a united movement against the established ways of life.

People like Rubin especially appalled some of America's older leftists, who complained that the counterculture was anti-intellectual, self-indulgent, and elitist. One critic observed that Rubin and others mistook "vividness, intensity, and urgency for cultural sensitivity and responsible morality." Paul Goodman, commenting on his experiences with members of the counterculture, said, "they did not believe there was such a thing as the simple truth. To be required to learn something was a trap by which the young were put down and coopted. Then I knew that I could not get through to them. I had imagined that the worldwide student protest had to do with changing political and moral institutions, to which I was sympathetic, but I now saw that we had to do with a religious crisis of the magnitude of the Reformation in the fifteen hundreds, when not only all institutions but all learning had been corrupted by the whore of Babylon."

Calm observers of the counterculture later perceived these excesses. They recognized that the huge majority of Americans still cherished the work ethic, nuclear families, and censorship of pornography. They also noted that the media, playing up the bizarre and colorful aspects of the hippie world, vastly exaggerated the numbers involved. Indeed, it became steadily more obvious that there was a larger gap between blue-collar young people and the college elitists than there was between the generations.

In 1968, however, few people could be sure that the youth movements would lose momentum by the early 1970s. With the media playing up extremists like Rubin and Hoffman, with long-haired demonstrators battling police outside the Pentagon, with campuses in turmoil, with hippies advocating free and open sex, with blacks tearing up the ghettos, it seemed that traditional values and institutions were endangered. By 1968 "backlash" among "middle Americans," a vague term embracing blue-collar workers, conservatives, and others who were angry and frightened by domestic turmoil, was growing throughout the country.

Black power, red power, women's power

The rise of protest movements and of the counterculture alerted other aggrieved Americans to the potential of group solidarity. By the end of the decade these too had become highly vocal and increasingly demanding. Their outbursts added to the turmoil of the times.

Among these were many ethnic leaders. Though the more acculturated groups—Irish-Americans, Italian-Americans—tended to work within the existing "system," others shared the rage that animated blacks. Leaders of the Puerto Ricans, who were treated as badly as blacks, staged strikes and demonstrations. American Indians, hidden away on arid reservations, conducted sit-ins to demand revision of old "treaties" with the government. Cesar Chavez, the charismatic leader of the National Farm Workers, championed the cause of "Chicanos" in California. With the aid of eastern sympathizers, who helped boycott nonunion produce, he secured modest concessions from the landowners.

Chavez, an organizer in the old CIO tradition, did not endorse separatism. Other disgruntled leaders did. Some Indians raised the flag of "red power." Radical Chicanos called for "brown power," or *La Raza,* a culture divorced from white American society. Like the advocates of black power, they represented minorities within their movements. But their militance forced the moderates to take tougher stands, and their tactics of direct action created confrontations with civil authorities. Their rage exposed the continuing power of ethnocultural divisions in American society and of the obstacles that had prevented proscribed groups from developing more than the rudiments of a middle class.

"Power" ideologies also helped to promote a revival of feminism, which had been quiescent since the 1920s. As Betty Friedan pointed out in *The Feminine Mystique* (1963), an influential demand for equal rights, the intervening decades had actually witnessed setbacks for the feminist cause. Smaller percentages of women were in colleges in 1960 than in the 1920s. Women formed steadily lower percentages of the professionally employed (which included teachers) and of holders of M.A. and Ph.D. degrees. As late as the mid-1960s, 90 percent of school board members were men, although the school board was considered a woman's "place." Studies revealed that poverty and unemployment among women, especially among black women, were widespread in the 1960s and that the gap separating men's and women's wages was widening. Friedan and others protested particu-

This healthy, normal baby has a handicap. She was born female.

When she grows up, her job opportunities will be limited, and her pay low. As a sales clerk, for instance, she'll earn half of what a man does. If she goes to college, she'll still earn less than many men with a 9th grade education. Maybe you don't care—but it's a fact—job discrimination based on sex is against the law. And it's a waste. Think about your own daughter—she's handicapped too.

Womanpower. It's much too good to waste.

The National Organization for Women makes a case.

larly against the plethora of state laws discriminating against women. These prohibited women from serving on juries, from making contracts, and even from holding property. And women who wanted to enter politics were regularly rebuffed. Shirley Chisholm, a black congresswoman from New York, recalled that her sex was a larger obstacle than her color. "I was constantly bombarded by both men and women," she said, "that I should return to teaching, a woman's vocation, and leave politics up to men."

Long-developing demographic and economic trends helped feminists like Friedan to be heard. Thanks in part to birth control pills, which permitted women to plan their lives with some assurance, and in part to the huge expansion of clerical opportunities, the growth in female employment accelerated. By 1965 more than 25 million women were regularly employed. Of married women with young children almost 40 percent held jobs by 1968—a startling increase of nearly 15 percent since the mid-1950s. The majority of these women worked because they needed the money, not because they wished to liberate themselves from the home. But the existence of such an army of female wage-earners virtually assured a decent reception to arguments for equal justice in work.

At this point the civil rights and peace movements offered models for "women's power." They helped train women in direct action tactics. They revealed also that many male activists were chauvinists who expected women to wash dishes and cook the meals while others "manned" the barricades. The position of women in the struggle for racial justice, Carmichael had sneered, should be prone. Friedan explained, "the absolute necessity for a civil rights movement for women had reached such a point of subterranean explosive urgency by 1966, that it took only a few of us to get together to ignite the spark—and it spread like a chain reaction." With others she helped form the National Organization for Women in 1966. Soon NOW and other more militant groups were employing the same aggressive tactics—sit-ins, demonstrations, protest meetings—that had inspired activists for other causes.

A variety of causes engaged the feminists. Some focused on changing what they considered the corrosive effect of sexism on the psychological health and morale of women. "Consciousness-raising" sessions proliferated to explore and attack the sources of male domination. Other feminists concentrated on promoting sexual

Median annual earnings, by sex and occupation: 1962 to 1972
(In current dollars. Covers persons 14 years old and over as of March of following year.
Earnings are for year-round full-time workers)

OCCUPATION GROUP	1962		1966		1970[a]		1972[a]	
	MALE	FEMALE	MALE	FEMALE	MALE	FEMALE	MALE	FEMALE
Total earnings	5,754	3,412	6,856	3,946	8,966	5,323	10,202	5,903
Professional, technical, kindred workers	7,621	4,840	9,203	5,779	12,255	7,850	13,542	8,744
Teachers, primary and secondary	6,584	5,183	7,629	5,910	9,883	7,856	11,310	8,706
Managers, officials, proprietors	6,907	3,744	8,826	4,472	11,665	6,369	13,486	7,024
Clerical and kindred workers	5,613	3,826	6,542	4,315	8,652	5,539	9,716	6,054
Salesworkers	6,225	2,607	7,553	3,066	9,765	4,174	11,610	4,445
In retail trade	4,956	2,573	6,150	3,002	7,633	3,874	8,254	4,137
Other Salesworkers	7,137	(B)	8,294	4,153	10,853	5,967	12,838	5,775
Craftsmen, foremen, and kindred workers	6,249	(B)	7,161	4,213	9,253	4,955	10,413	5,545
Foremen	7,350	(B)	8,104	4,250	10,531	5,223	11,497	5,972
Craftsmen	6,056	(B)	6,981	4,161	9,051	4,772	10,196	5,317
Operatives and kindred workers	5,335	3,156	6,135	3,387	7,644	4,465	8,747	5,004
Manufacturing	5,422	3,260	6,219	3,467	7,580	4,559	8,754	5,114

[a]Data may not be strictly comparable with those of previous years. (B) Not computed; base less than minimum required for reliability.
SOURCE: Adapted from *Statistical Abstract of the United States*, 1974, p. 361

freedom, including lesbianism. Many demanded an end to antiabortion statutes. They also criticized male gynecologists for recommending "unnatural" childbirth and surgeons for performing excessive operations for cancer of the breast and of the uterus. Women, they insisted, must be free to control their own bodies. Still others demanded changes in traditional family patterns that, they said, relegated women to subordinate domestic roles. Most of these causes were neither new nor necessarily "radical." But in challenging family patterns they worried and offended many American women as well as men.

Less alarming to traditionalists were the feminists who focused on the need for equal treatment—in hiring, in universities, on the job. These women, strong in NOW, worked hard for an equal rights amendment to the Constitution, a dream of militant feminists since 1920. Like blacks and ethnics, the activists crusaded for recognition of their past accomplishments, for courses in women's history, and for coeducation in sex-defined courses, such as woodworking for boys and home economics for girls. They made especially effective use of the prohibition of discrimination on grounds of sex in Title VII of the 1964 Civil Rights Act. This title had been added by segregationists who had hoped to weaken support for the entire bill. It later enabled women to employ the full force of the government in the struggle against discrimination in federally assisted employment and education.

For a variety of reasons, "women's liberation" did not prove so frightening in the 1960s as the related movement for black power. Women, after all, were already working in large numbers: to cede them equal rights was only reasonable. The growth in female white-collar employment may also have altered traditional concepts of masculinity and blurred sex roles. If men feared job competition, they were prepared at least to admit that not all women must languish at home. Most important, the movement for women's liberation was nonviolent, and it was led by middle-class people. For all its vehemence, it was not likely to overturn society.

By 1968 traditionalists could take further comfort in the fissures that divided the movement. From the beginning many black women devoted their energies to the cause of civil rights for black men. Women's liberation, they insisted, was a diversion. Some working-class women objected that the Equal Rights Amendment, which proposed to wipe out sex-oriented laws, would deprive them of protective labor legislation. Such splits were hardly surprising, for women comprised 51 percent of the population. Nor were the splits entirely new—similar divisions had weakened the feminist cause since the nineteenth century. Still, they permitted opponents of "women's lib" to anticipate further disagreements in the 1970s.

But these cracks in the movement could not hide the fact that the new feminism was more widespread than campaigns earlier in the century. Even women who called themselves moderates were free in criticizing the glorification of marriage and domesticity. For militant women, as for blacks and other minorities, agitation and turmoil were to be welcomed if they accelerated social change. For some traditionalists, therefore, the "new" women seemed threatening. To such conservatives, the future of the nation seemed to hinge on the forthcoming electoral campaign of 1968.

The incredible campaign of 1968

On January 3, 1968, Senator Eugene McCarthy of Minnesota surprised the pundits by announcing he would challenge President Johnson on an antiwar platform. In many ways he seemed ill-suited to such a formidable task. A devout Catholic who had seriously considered becoming a monk and an intellectual who numbered the poet Robert Lowell among his advisers, he was hardly a typical representative of American politics. But for many people his stand on the war and his courage in challenging an incumbent president were qualifications enough. And when the Vietcong blasted American installations (including the embassy at Saigon) during the daring Tet offensive beginning January 31, the bankruptcy of Johnson's foreign policies became painfully obvious. With thousands of student volunteers making campaign arrangements, McCarthy came close to beating Johnson in the New Hampshire primary on March 12. He seemed likely to win the next important confrontation, in Wisconsin on April 2. Johnson's awareness of McCarthy's popularity helped to precipitate his startling announcement on March 31 that he would not run for renomination.

Though McCarthy won with ease in Wisconsin, he immediately faced challenges within the Democratic party. Centrists in the Democratic coalition, including many labor leaders, leaned toward Vice-President Hubert H. Humphrey. Right-wingers flocked to Governor George Wallace of Alabama, who was anti-intellectual, openly racist, and hawkish on the war. No one doubted that Wallace commanded widespread support among segregationists in the South and among advocates of escalation. But he displayed much more than a sectional appeal. By denouncing the counterculture, the New Left, and the Eastern Establishment, he appealed to many "middle Americans," ethnics, and blue-collar workers. His impressive showings in northern primaries—34 percent in Wisconsin, 30 percent in Indiana, 43 percent in Maryland—suggested that backlash was widespread indeed.

As the campaign progressed, McCarthy demonstrated his lack of appeal to blacks. In the best of times the weakness would have been a liability for a prospective Democratic candidate. But after April 4 it became doubly serious. On that day James Earl Ray, a white exconvict, shot and killed Martin Luther King on the balcony of a Memphis motel. Outraged blacks responded immediately by rampaging through ghettos in Chicago, Washington, and other American cities. McCarthy was naturally appalled by the assassination. But most blacks continued to regard him as the candidate of the white student elite—which in large part he was. Someone else would have to be found who could unite the black masses and antiwar activists and appeal to the center as well.

That someone was Robert Kennedy, who announced his candidacy after the New Hampshire primary. His belated entry earned him few plaudits for courage, and McCarthy supporters abused him for his opportunism. But Kennedy possessed useful assets. He was rich, intelligent, highly organized, and charismatic. More than all other candidates in 1968, he aroused passionate support among blacks, Chicanos, and many Catholics and blue-collar workers. By calling for de-escalation of the war he gradually cut into McCarthy's support among the white student Left. Though he lost to McCarthy in a primary in Oregon, he won impressively everywhere else. He peaked on June 4 when he won the biggest test of all in California.

Whether he could have gone on to win the nomination is hard to judge. Perhaps not, for the Johnson loyalists hated him. In any case, he never got the chance. On the night of the California primary, as he walked down a kitchen corridor in a Los Angeles hotel, he was shot and killed by Sirhan Sirhan, a crazed Jordanian immigrant. To millions of blacks and poor people his assassination, following so closely on the murder of King, was "proof" of the violence and divisions that rent American society.

Kennedy's death eliminated the last chance for the triumph of the antiwar forces at the Democratic convention in Chicago. McCarthy stayed in to the end, but his defeat in California exposed his limitations as a vote getter. Kennedy partisans tried to make a candidate of Senator George McGovern, an antiwar liberal from South Dakota. At that late date, however, McGovern excited little enthusiasm. After bitter struggles over the seating of delegates, the party regulars excluded most of the insurgents. They then chose Humphrey by a margin of more than two to one over McCarthy and McGovern and balanced the ticket by naming liberal-leaning

Left-wing students protest during 1968 Democratic National Convention in Chicago.

Edmund Muskie, a senator from Maine, as the vice-presidential nominee. As in most Democratic conventions since the 1920s, the slightly left-of-center coalition within the party had triumphed.

These nominations seemed almost worthless as a result of the tumult that convulsed Chicago. As the convention opened, left-wing protesters moved into the city. Most of them were nonviolent whites working for McCarthy. Others, however, were determined to provoke confrontations with Mayor Richard Daley, who had earned notoriety after King's assassination by ordering his police to "shoot to kill" arsonists and to "shoot to maim" looters. Daley erected chain-link fences and barbed wire to protect the convention site and surrounded it with police. Some of the activists responded by taunting and insulting the "pigs," who then charged wildly into crowds, clubbing and gassing passersby as well as demonstrators. The "police riot," as the Walker Report later described it, shattered what hope had remained for rapprochement between the Democratic center and the youthful Left. For Humphrey, "beneficiary" of this police activity, the convention was a disaster.

Richard Nixon, the Republican nominee, seemed certain to profit from this Democratic disarray. His victory at the GOP convention was a triumph of ambition, persistence, and party loyalty. After losing to Kennedy in 1960, he had failed in a race for the governorship of California in 1962. Tired and petulant in defeat, he had told reporters, "You won't have Nixon to kick around any more, because, gentlemen, this is my last press conference." Thereafter, he had been a conscientious party worker, supporting Goldwater in 1964 and traveling widely for GOP congressional candidates in 1966. His smooth performance during the preconvention campaign bested right-wingers who had supported California governor Ronald Reagan and liberals who had favored governors Nelson Rockefeller of New York and George Romney of Michigan. It also misled many who had disliked him in the past. "The Nixon of 1968," said Theodore White, chronicler of presidential elections, "was so different from the Nixon of 1960 that the whole personality required reexplanation. . . . There was . . . a total absence of bitterness, of the rancor and venom that had once colored his remarks."

As the campaign developed, Nixon failed to generate enthusiasm. Despite his appeals for "law and order," a rightist slogan, it was clear that George Wallace, running as the presidential candidate of the American Independence party, would capture much of the right-wing vote. Nixon also waffled on Vietnam. In 1966 he had proclaimed, "we believe this is a war that has to be fought to prevent World War III." By early 1968 he was saying that America must "end the war," but refusing to say how or when he would do it. And many people, remembering his partisan, Red-baiting past, refused to believe there was a "new Nixon." As if these were not handicaps enough, he yoked himself to Governor Spiro Agnew of Maryland, his choice for vice-president. Inexperienced and maladroit, Agnew repeatedly insulted ethnic groups. He was one of the most ill-qualified vice-presidential candidates in modern times.

Humphrey, meanwhile, labored earnestly to salvage what he could from the discord of the convention. Many union leaders, distrusting the GOP, gave him their support. So did some black spokesmen, who recalled his enthusiasm for civil rights as far back as the 1948 convention. Humphrey built bridges with the antiwar supporters by edging away, though much too slowly for McCarthy, from Johnson's policies. And he benefited from the energetic campaigning of Muskie, a Catholic who appealed to many ethnic voters. On October 31, when Johnson announced that he was stopping all bombing in North Vietnam, it seemed that Humphrey might have a chance.

Johnson's move came too late. On election day Nixon and Agnew triumphed over the Democrats. Considering the woeful state of the GOP in 1964, their victory was impressive. It suggested that voters were becoming much less partisan, indeed, more independent, than they had been in the heyday of the Democratic coalition under Roosevelt.

However, the results hardly gave Nixon much cause for rejoicing. In winning he got 31,770,222 votes, less than 1 percent more than Humphrey's 31,267,744. He took only 43 percent of the total vote, the smallest share for a victor since Wilson's in 1912. Like Eisenhower before him, he failed to dent the large Democratic majorities in Congress. Analysts concluded that a higher turnout among blacks would have given Humphrey the margin for victory, and that the Democratic coalition, though slipping, had not disappeared. Voters, they added, had not been attracted to Nixon. As in so many presidential elections since World War II, they had rejected the loser.

This negativism showed most clearly in the votes for Wallace and his warlike running mate, General Curtis LeMay. Although Wallace carried only five states (all in the Deep South), he won 9.9 million votes. This was 13.5 percent of the turnout, the highest for any third-party candidate since Robert La Follette in 1924, and the highest ever for a candidate on the Right. Wallace's supporters included large numbers of northerners as well as southerners, young people as well as old, blue-collar workers (who defied union spokesmen) as well as wealthy conservatives. His appeal proved that a significant cross section was disgusted with the major parties, with radical youth, with liberalism generally. It showed also that millions still wanted to win the war, even if it meant adopting LeMay's suggestion of bombing North Vietnam into the Stone Age. For people such as these Nixon's victory over Humphrey was small consolation.

The Left was especially discouraged by the campaign of 1968. Nixon had proclaimed the slogan of "Bring Us Together Again." But he had shown little discernible longing to include in his happy circle the antiwar activists, the blacks, or young people generally. He had denounced the liberal Supreme Court, talked threateningly (though vaguely) about restoring "law and order," and hinted (again vaguely) about cutting back Great Society programs. Given the frustration, indeed the fury, felt by many activists, his victory did not augur well for social peace in the years ahead.

The result of the election should presumably have comforted the center. To a degree it did. Moderates considered it cause for congratulation that the American people had gone peaceably to the polls and had authorized without protest a transfer

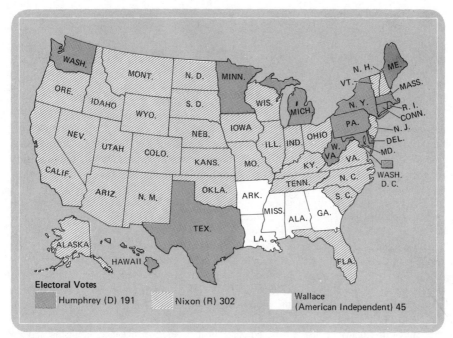

Electoral Votes

Humphrey (D) 191	Nixon (R) 302	Wallace (American Independent) 45

Election, 1968

of great political power from one party to the other. As so often in the American past, the two-party system had helped to undermine extremes and to sanction the legitimacy of elected officials. This stability was impressive amid such turbulent events.

But thoughtful analysts also asked: stability for what? In being forced to choose between two middle-of-the-road candidates (Wallace was never a plausible winner) the voters had been given no real opportunity to express themselves. And in remaining so vague, Nixon had done little to enlighten them. Millions probably voted for him because of the violence they associated with the radicals in the Democratic party. But did they want Nixon to dismantle the Great Society? Polls suggested not. Millions also supported him because they were tired of "Johnson's war." But did that mean they expected Nixon to stop the fighting or to escalate it? Here the polls were disturbing, for they showed that Americans were confused by the war. McCarthy's supporters, for instance, included many who wanted to end the conflict by moving in with the full force of American military power.

This confusion and ambiguity was the most unsettling feature of the campaign of 1968. Far from toning down the discord of the previous three years, it frustrated reactionaries as well as radicals and reduced even the center to apprehensiveness and uncertainty. As Americans were shortly to discover, the stability they had bought by letting Nixon "Bring Us Together Again" was to be short-lived indeed.

Suggestions for reading

Useful starting points for understanding Johnson's foreign policy are Philip L. Geyelin, *Lyndon B. Johnson and the World* (1966); and Richard J. Barnet, *Intervention and Revolution: U.S. and the Third World** (1969), a far-ranging analysis. For the intervention in the Dominican Republic see Theodore Draper, *Dominican Revolt** (1968); and Jerome Slater, *Intervention and Negotiation* (1970). Vietnam policy is covered in Townsend Hoopes, *Limits of Intervention** (1973); Chester Cooper, *Lost Crusade* (1971); Guenter Lewy, *America in Vietnam* (1978); and Lawrence Baskir and William A. Strauss, *Chance and Circumstance: The Draft, the War, and the Vietnam Generation* (1978). See especially Frances Fitzgerald, *Fire in the Lake** (1972), which exposes the impact of war on Vietnamese culture.

Books on domestic unrest include the Report of the National Advisory Commission on Civil Disorders* (1968); and the report of the Scranton Commission on Campus Violence* (1970). Hugh Davis Graham and Ted Gurr, *Violence in America** (1969), provides some historical background. See also Robert Fogelson, *Violence as Protest* (1971); and Robert Conot, *Rivers of Blood, Years of Darkness** (1968), which deals with the riot in Watts. Two eye-witness books by Norman Mailer are *Armies of the Night** (1968) on the demonstration at the Pentagon in 1968; and *Miami and the Siege of Chicago** (1968) on protest at the national conventions. Morris Dickstein, *Gates of Eden: American Culture in the 1960s* (1977), is a readable survey of its subject.

Among the many books on young people in the 1960s are Kenneth Keniston, *Young Radicals** (1968); Lewis Yablonsky, *Hippie Trip* (1968); Lewis Feuer, *The Conflict of Generations* (1969); and Seymour Lipset, *Rebellion in the University* (1972). Books read widely at the time are Theodore Roszak, *Making of a Counter Culture** (1969); and Charles Reich, *Greening of America** (1970). Paul Goodman, *Growing Up Absurd** (1960), is a lucid account of what alienated young people. Charles Silberman, *Crisis in the Classroom** (1970); and David Riesman and Christopher Jencks, *The Academic Revolution* (1969), cover their subjects thoroughly. Paul Jacobs and Saul Landau, eds., *New Radicals** (1966), is a useful anthology. Books dealing with left-wing ideology include Kirkpatrick Sale, *SDS* (1973); Peter Clecak, *Radical Paradoxes: Dilemmas of the American Left, 1945–1970* (1973); Edward Baccioco, *The New Left: Reform to Revolution* (1974); and Irwin Unger, *The Movement: A History of the American New Left, 1959–1972** (1974). See also John Diggins, *The American Left in the Twentieth Century** (1973).

For the attitudes of militant blacks in the 1960s see James Baldwin, *The Fire Next Time** (1963); Malcolm X, *Autobiography** (1965); Stokely Carmichael and Charles Hamilton, *Black Power** (1967); and Julius Lester, *Look Out Whitey* (1968). Peter Coleman, *The Death and Life of Malcom X* (1973), is excellent. E. U. Essien-Udom, *Black Nationalism** (1962), describes the Black Muslims. See also David J. Garrow, *Protest at Selma: Martin Luther King, Jr. and The Voting Rights Act of 1965* (1978). Surveys of other minorities include Matt Meier and Feliciano Rivera, *The Chicanos** (1972); Stan Steiner, *La Raza** (1970); and Oscar Lewis, *La Vida** (1966), on Puerto Ricans. Michael Novak, *Rise of the Unmeltable Ethnics* (1970), describes the failure of the melting pot.

Books that help in understanding the rise of feminism are Robert Lifton, ed., *The Woman in America** (1965); Lois Banner, *Women in Modern America** (1974); and the book by William Chafe cited in chapter 6. Important feminist statements are Betty Friedan, *The Feminine Mystique** (1963); and Germaine Greer, *The Female Eunuch** (1972). See also Sara Evans, *Personal Politics: The Roots of Women's Liberation in the Civil Rights Movement and the New Left* (1979).

For politics, especially in 1968, consult the thorough account by Lewis Chester, et al., *An American Melodrama** (1970). Theodore White, *Making of a President, 1968** (1969), is useful. Marshall Frady, *Wallace** (1970), is entertaining and provocative. David Halberstam, *The Unfinished Odyssey of Robert Kennedy* (1968); and Jeremy Larner, *Nobody Knows: Reflections on the McCarthy Campaign of 1968* (1970), add insights. Richard Scammon and Ben Wattenberg, *The Real Majority* (1970), is a well-written, balanced account of recent electoral trends. Arthur M. Schlesinger, Jr., *Robert F. Kennedy and His Times* (1977), is a highly readable biography.

15

Unsettling times:
from Nixon to Reagan

In his first inaugural President Nixon repeated the "bring us together" note he had sounded during his campaign. "We are torn by division," he said. "To a crisis of the spirit, we need an answer of the spirit. And to find that answer, we need only look within ourselves. . . . We cannot learn from one another until we stop shouting at one another—until we speak quietly enough so that our words can be heard as well as our voices. For its part, government will listen."

Limited advances, 1969–73

During the first few years of Nixon's tumultuous presidency, there were some signs that he was succeeding in promoting domestic harmony. Racial unrest seemed to subside. Contrary to expectations, the ghettos had quieted in the summer of 1968, and they stayed relatively peaceful throughout the 1970s. Some people attributed the calm to prosecutions that had driven militants like Carmichael and Rap Brown into jail or exile. Others concluded that blacks had come to doubt the wisdom of destroying their own property. As one Watts leader put it, "the rioting phase, where we burn down businesses in our own areas, is over. The whole movement is in another direction—toward implementing black power and finding our own dignity as a people."

Blacks did not obtain much "power," but they did score some successes. Thanks to the Supreme Court, which ruled in 1969 *(Alexander v. Holmes)* that

Feminists on the march, New York City

school desegregation must proceed "at once," the percentage of blacks in formerly all-black schools fell from 68 percent to 18 percent between 1968 and 1970. Statistics revealed that blacks, though still failing to capture a larger share of the national income, were developing a sizable middle class. The number who attended college rose between 1966 and 1970 by 85 percent—to 434,000. And blacks began to make use of the vote. By 1971 there were 13 black congressmen, 81 mayors, 198 state legislators, and 1,567 black local office holders. These advances were significant. Few people in 1960 could have predicted them. Nevertheless, discrimination still plagued the nation. The controversy over busing in the schools, perhaps the most acrimonious domestic issue of the early 1970s, showed that many white Americans still refused to accept residential integration or to go much beyond tokenism in the schools.

Feminists, too, made modest gains in the 1970s. Writers like Robin Morgan, author of *Sisterhood Is Powerful* (1970), and Germaine Greer, author of the *Female Eunuch* (1971), offered forceful briefs for women's liberation. In 1972 activists founded *Ms.*, the first feminist magazine to attract a sizable circulation. In the same year Congress approved legislation banning sex discrimination in colleges and universities receiving federal aid. In 1973 the Supreme Court *(Doe* v. *Bolton, Roe* v. *Wade)* ruled against state laws prohibiting abortions, and both houses of Congress approved the Equal Rights Amendment, which feminists had been seeking for fifty years. A total of twenty-two states—of thirty-eight needed—ratified the amendment the same year.

Thereafter, feminism suffered reverses. Many black women continued to be cool to the movement. So did large numbers of married working women—who were too intent on keeping their jobs (or on earning enough money to return to the home) to spend time on campaigns for women's rights. NOW moderates complained that lesbians and sexual radicals exposed the movement to distortion and ridicule. Other articulate women led a countermovement. One of their most forceful leaders, Phyllis Schlafly, was a conservative whose idols were Thomas Edison, Elias Howe (inventor of the sewing machine), and Clarence Birdseye, all of whom had promoted comforts of domesticity. "A man's first significant purchase," she said, "is a diamond for his bride, and the largest financial investment of his life is a home for her to live in." Reflecting this attitude, Nixon vetoed a bill in 1973 that would have provided funds for day-care centers. Meanwhile, antifeminists campaigned against ratification of the ERA, which they said would destroy the "special place" of women in the home.

Yet feminists, like blacks, could take some comfort in the progress they had made since the early 1960s. A majority of women told pollsters that they approved the general goals of the movement. Of all the protest movements that started in the 1960s—for peace, for black power, for brown power—women's liberation seemed most durable.

Other reformers took limited pleasure in accomplishments of the Democratic Congresses between 1969 and 1972. The legislators voted huge increases in social security benefits and extended the life of the 1965 Voting Rights Law. They approved an act regulating campaign spending and authorized eighteen-year-olds to vote in federal elections. The Twenty-sixth Amendment to the Constitution, ratified in 1971, extended the voting rights of eighteen-year-olds to state and local elections. Though Congress fell far short of attacking the nation's festering urban and racial problems, it did increase funding for some domestic purposes. In part because of a recession that descended on the economy in 1969, spending for food stamps—to go to 11 million poor people—rose from $250 million in 1969 to $2.2 billion in 1971. Nonmilitary federal expenditures as a percentage of the GNP almost doubled between 1969 and 1972. This dramatic rise in social welfare spending suggested to many that the nation could afford butter as well as guns.

The lawmakers occasionally proved responsive to the pressures for environmental conservation applied constantly by Ralph Nader and others in the early 1970s. Among the important measures approved were the Water Quality Improvement Act, which attempted to control pollution caused by industry and power companies; the Clean Air Act, which called for changes in the manufacture of automobiles; and the Resource Recovery Act, which promoted recycling of solid wastes. Congress also refused funds for the Super Sonic Transport (SST), a huge, noisy airplane that the administration had strongly favored. In 1971 Congress created the Environmental Protection Agency and empowered it to bring suits against corporate or municipal leaders who violated federal standards. Despite these laws, many corporations (especially in the automobile industry) found ways to evade or to postpone stringent regulation. Careless oil drilling and pumping continued to cause damage. Most alarming, Americans continued to squander resources at an alarming rate. But as the birth rate approached the point of zero population growth, advocates of ecological balance continued to hope that the nation could learn to exist without destroying its environment.

Nixon could claim little credit for these developments. Indeed, he was cool to legislation for social welfare or environmental protection. But many observers welcomed his apparent expertise in the realm of foreign affairs. Here he, like Kennedy, paid little attention to the State Department. Its secretary until late 1973, William Rogers, played an insignificant role in policy making. Nixon relied instead on Dr. Henry Kissinger, his national security adviser. Kissinger, a German immigrant who had become a professor of government at Harvard, was a highly skilled negotiator and a persuasive exponent of power politics. The way to avoid nuclear catastrophe, he believed, was to seek détente with the Soviet Union and China. These powers, with Japan and western Europe, could cooperate with the United States to prevent brush fires from escalating into World War III.

Kissinger's policies did not work wonders in 1969–71. In the Middle East they failed to end tensions heightened by Israel's stunning victory over Arab countries in the Six-Day War of 1967. Nixon and Kissinger also did not deserve much credit for the limited détente that did develop with Russia and China by 1972. Rather, these communist powers, at odds with each other, assumed considerable initiative for developing better relations with the West. Still, the administration helped to defuse the Cold War and to reverse the tide of postwar American foreign policy. Nixon, once the cold warrior extraordinaire, had revealed his capacity for change.

The President even seemed to make progress toward de-escalating the war in Vietnam. In 1969 he announced the Nixon Doctrine, which proclaimed that allies could expect American aid, but not troops, when confronted with internal revolt. He added that he would end the draft within two years. Encouraged by Secretary of Defense Melvin Laird, he propounded Vietnamization, as it became called. The United States, Nixon said, would build up the Vietnamese military so that it could stand on its own. To institute this policy, the President began withdrawing American troops. In 1968 there had been 543,000; by September 1972 there were 39,000. Though later developments revealed the serious limitations of Vietnamization, the troop withdrawals were a popular step toward disengagement.

From the beginning of Nixon's presidency, however, the discord of the Johnson years persisted. For the universities, in fact, the spring of 1969 was the most disruptive to date. Police moved in to restore order at Howard, Massachusetts, Pennsylvania State, and San Fernando State. Conflicts between black and white students erupted in violence at the University of Wisconsin and City College of New York. Harvard students invaded University Hall, rifled files, and were thrown out by state police. And at Cornell armed blacks seized the student union, leading the university president to capitulate to their demands. The backlash that followed such demonstrations—perpetrated by a small minority of students—was one of many forces that culminated in scanty funding for colleges and universities in the early 1970s.

Meanwhile, unrest among workers mounted. The 1970s were for public service employees what the 1930s had been for industrial workers. Teachers, nurses, policemen, garbage collectors, firemen, and transit employees formed militant unions, picketed city hall, and staged walkouts that would have seemed revolutionary in Calvin Coolidge's day. A strike of postal workers tied up the nation's mails for a week and forced the National Guard to take charge in New York City. Despairingly, Congress established an independent postal service that was expected to soften discontent. Inflation stemming from a war-heated economy accounted for much of this conflict. So did new visions of the "good life" and meaningful work. White-collar and service workers in the 1970s, like so many Americans in the prosperous postwar years, were joining the revolution of rising expectations.

Continuing violence was particularly frightening. In early 1970 bombs tore up the Manhattan offices of IBM, General Telephone and Electronics Corporation, and Mobil Oil. Antiwar revolutionaries claimed credit for the explosions. Shortly thereafter two black militants, followers of Rap Brown, were killed when one of their homemade bombs went off prematurely. And in March 1970 three young radicals, one of them a socially prominent young woman who had recently graduated from Swarthmore, were blown to pieces in their "bomb factory" in Greenwich Village. Two other revolutionaries, cut and bleeding, fled from the scene.

These were but the most striking manifestations of apparent social upheaval in the years after 1968. In New York City bomb threats averaged 1,000 a month in 1969–70. Within fifteen months 368 bombs actually exploded. In 1970 the FBI reported 35,202 asssults on policemen, four times the number in 1960. People were not even safe in the air: skyjacking diverted seventy-one planes in 1969 alone. The drug traffic seemed particularly frightening. When rock stars Jimi Hendrix and Janis Joplin died from overdoses, some of the worst fears seemed confirmed.

The most shocking violence of the early 1970s took place in prisons, many of which were breeding grounds for racial confrontations between convicts and authorities. One such outbreak occurred in August 1971 at San Quentin prison, where George Jackson, one of the three black "Soledad brothers" (actually not related), was caged for allegedly killing a white guard at Soledad prison a year earlier. Using a smuggled pistol, Jackson broke out of his cell and demanded the release of twenty-seven prisoners. He then murdered three white guards and two trusties before falling in a rain of shots himself. Militants, outraged by his death, dressed him in a Black Panther uniform and gave him a martyr's funeral.

Jackson's death helped to trigger the most bloody prison riot in American history. This occurred at Attica, New York State, home of 2,254 convicts, 75 percent of whom were black or Puerto Rican. All the 383 guards were white, and racial incidents were common. In September 1971 angry blacks staged a rebellion that was quickly joined by more than 1,200 inmates. They grabbed 39 hostages, seriously hurt a guard, barricaded themselves in a cell block, and issued demands on the warden. When the prisoners threatened to cut the throats of their hostages, the authorities waited no longer. In the assault which followed, police gunfire killed 30 prisoners and 10 guards. To some observers, like *New York Times's* Tom Wicker, the Attica riot displayed the callousness of officials like Governor Rockefeller, the violence of police, and the urgent need for prison reform. To many others it was "proof" of the savagery of the criminal population—especially of blacks—and of the need for "law and order."

NIXON AT BAY, 1969–71

Nixon, of course, was not to blame for such violence. But to many Americans— progressives, college activists, blacks—he was an unsympathetic figure. Between 1969 and mid-1971 they grew increasingly hostile to the President. They focused on four themes: his personal style, his domestic policies, his "southern strategy," and Vietnam.

Objections to Nixon's style ranged from the frivolous to the profound. Americans who had looked to the White House for cultural leadership disliked his patronage of pro football, middlebrow music, and Norman Vincent Peale. Others considered him banal, hypocritical, and sanctimonious. People wondered about his close friendships with C. G. ("Bebe") Rebozo, a wealthy real estate operator, and with Robert H. Abplanalp, a businessman, who helped Nixon finance the purchase of property worth $600,000 at Key Biscayne, Florida, and San Clemente, California. Nixon's taste for regal living, it was revealed later, cost the government $10 million in improvements and security measures. To his critics, "Tricky Dick" was becoming "King Richard."

Nixon's style was above all secretive and suspicious. Extremely sensitive to criticism, he avoided contacts with the press. Faced with important decisions, he frequently slipped off to the presidential retreat at Camp David, Maryland, or to one of his tightly guarded compounds in Florida and California. Even his cabinet found him remote and unsupportive. Two of the more popular among his appointees, Secretary of the Interior Walter Hickel and HEW Secretary Robert Finch, left or were fired by the end of 1970. Like reporters, they complained that Nixon surrounded himself with a much-expanded White House staff of ambitious, unscrupulous young lawyers, public relations men, and advertising executives. Nixon's closest domestic advisers, H. R. Haldeman and John D. Erlichman, had no experience in government. Tough, cold, and devoted to their boss, they excluded visitors, insulted important politicians, and narrowed the circle of decision making. Not even Lyndon Johnson at his most highhanded had seemed so inaccessible as Nixon.

The President's economic policies aroused special concern. Some of his angriest critics, susprisingly enough, were conservatives. When Nixon proclaimed, in January 1971, "I am now a Keynesian," they were appalled. They were equally shocked to discover that the budget deficit for the 1970–71 fiscal year amounted to more than $23 billion, only $2 billion less than the record set during Johnson's last year in office. Nixon's endorsement of unbalanced budgets provided added evidence of his flexibility (critics said of his lack of principle), and of the political clout enjoyed by pressure groups.

Conservatives had other complaints about Nixon's domestic policies. They resented Hickel's rigorous enforcement of the laws protecting the environment. They grumbled especially about the influence of Daniel Patrick Moynihan, a Harvard professor whom Nixon named to head the newly created Urban Affairs Council. Under Moynihan's persistent coaching Nixon endorsed the controversial Family Assistance Plan, which would have guaranteed an income of $1,600 a year (plus food stamps valued at $800 or more) to a family of four. The plan promised cash payments to the hitherto neglected working poor. Michael Harrington, a socialist, termed FAP "the most radical idea since the New Deal." But Democrats in Congress ultimately sidetracked the measure—in part because they demanded more generous benefits, in part because they disliked Nixon, in part because the President (to gain conservative support) appeared to threaten able-bodied heads of households with loss of benefits if they failed to register for job training or to accept work. Congress's rejection of the measure meant that America's creaking welfare "system" staggered on.

Most criticism of the President's domestic policies came from liberals. They recognized that Nixon, like Kennedy, was primarily interested in foreign affairs. Indeed, Nixon once commented, "I've always thought this country could run itself domestically without a President." He added, "all you need is a competent cabinet to run the country at home." This attitude antagonized reformers, most of whom could not get past the "Berlin Wall" erected by Haldeman and Erlichman. Long before Congress counterattacked in 1973–74, many of its most influential members were barely on speaking terms with the White House.

The liberals were particularly critical of Nixon's handling of the economy, which grew ragged and unstable between 1969 and 1972. The administration's tight money policy, they claimed, harmed investment and impeded construction. The failure to set forth price and wage guidelines encouraged round after round of inflationary settlements between management and labor. A $2.5 billion tax cut, which Nixon signed in December 1969, further fed inflation. By 1971 the country was experiencing the worst of all possible worlds: "stagflation." Inflation (5.3 percent in 1970) coexisted with recession (6 percent unemployment). At fault, said Democratic party chieftain Lawrence O'Brien, were, "Nixonomics." O'Brien explained, "All the things that should go up—the stock market, corporate profits, real spendable income, productivity—go down, and all the things that should go down—unemployment, prices, interest rates—go up."

NIXON'S SOUTHERN STRATEGY

Most objectionable of all to progressives was the administration's "southern strategy." In its broad outlines this reflected the argument of Kevin Phillips, a Justice Department aide who wrote *The Emerging Republican Majority* in 1969. To Phillips the preeminent need of the GOP was to outflank men like Governor Wallace by 1972. This meant securing the votes of "middle Americans"—southern whites, blue-collar workers, Catholic ethnics, suburbanites, conservatives. It meant stressing the theme of "law and order," discrediting activist students, and paying relatively little attention to the wishes of blacks, Hispanic-Americans, and others who were predominantly Democratic anyway.

This southern strategy helps to explain Nixon's civil rights policies. These were a predominantly conservative mixture of forward and backward movements. To assist blacks, Nixon instituted the so-called Philadelphia Plan, which required unions working on federal projects to accept quotas of blacks as apprentices and to admit them when training was completed. To secure black support, he named James Farmer, a leading activist, as an assistant secretary of HEW. He told Farmer that he wanted to do "what's right" for blacks. "I care," he added. "I just hope people will believe that I DO care."

During the two years that Farmer stayed with HEW, however, he was unable to do much. Like other advocates of civil rights, he confronted the influence of Attorney General John Mitchell, a Nixon law partner who emerged as the strongest figure in the new cabinet. Under Mitchell the Department of Justice attempted (unsuccessfully) to prevent extension of the Voting Rights Act of 1965. He also brought suit to delay school desegregation guidelines in Mississippi. Outraged attorneys in the civil rights divisions of the Justice Department and HEW protested vigorously. Though the Supreme Court's ruling for desegregation "at once" foiled Mitchell's effort, he had shown the white South that the administration cared.

Mitchell's passion for "law and order" led him into several other blunders between 1969 and 1971. One was his attempt to prosecute antiwar demonstrators. Among the many activists he had arrested were the "Harrisburg Seven," the "Gainesville Eight," and others who were tried in groups. Capping efforts to stifle dissent, Mitchell brought suit in 1971 to stop publication of the so-called Pentagon papers, a forty-seven-volume, 2.5-million-word summary that documented the escalation of the war in Vietnam prior to 1969. However, the Supreme Court ruled against prior restraint of publication in the press, and lower courts sustained the antiwar demonstrators. The court decisions revealed the continuing independence of the judiciary from executive activity. They suggested also Mitchell's disregard for civil liberties. For a guardian of "law and order" it was an unedifying performance.

The southern strategy came gradually to dictate the administration's choice of justices to fill vacancies in the Supreme Court between 1969 and 1972. The first nominee, Warren Earl Burger of Minnesota, was a moderate named to replace Chief Justice Warren, who retired after sixteen years on the bench. The Senate confirmed him quickly. Mitchell's next choice was Judge Clement F. Haynsworth, Jr., a South Carolinian. Union leaders, civil rights advocates, and progressives opposed him. Early supporters wavered when they learned of conflict-of-interest charges marring Haynsworth's judicial record. In November 1969 the Senate, including seventeen Republicans, rejected him.

The Senate's action infuriated Nixon, who called the attacks on Haynsworth "brutal, vicious . . . and unfair." His temper high, he carelessly nominated Mitchell's next choice, G. Harrold Carswell, a Floridian who served on the court of appeals. Suspecting Nixon's political motives, opponents produced evidence to show Carswell's racial bias. Law professors throughout the country exposed his mediocrity as a judge. Accordingly, the Senate, including thirteen Republicans, rejected him in April 1970. Adhering to the southern strategy, Nixon burst out, "I understand the bitter feelings of millions of Americans who live in the South. They have my assurance that the day will come when judges like Carswell and Haynsworth can and will sit on the High Court."

After circulating the names of other mediocre candidates, Nixon finally searched for qualified nominees who could command congressional support. By 1972 he had named three. The first, Judge Harry Blackmun of Minnesota, held views that resembled Burger's. The second, Lewis F. Powell, Jr., had been a president of the American Bar Association. The third, Assistant Attorney General William H. Rehnquist, was a young Goldwater Republican who was developing a reputation as a thoughtful exponent of conservative jurisprudence. The Senate confirmed all three.

Nixon's actions enhanced his standing in the South. But they antagonized Congress. And they failed to produce a tractable Court. Though the four new appointees often voted together, they showed little disposition to reverse the decisions of the Warren Court, and they did not constitute a majority. In addition to the abortion and Pentagon papers cases—both of which annoyed the administration—the Burger Court voted unanimously in 1971 that busing was necessary and proper if other means failed to achieve school desegregation. Though later decisions concerning busing left the issue in doubt, it was clear that Burger and his associates would not block the movement for racial justice.

In the next few years the Court continued to antagonize conservatives. In 1972 it held, five to four, that state laws authorizing the death sentence were unconstitutional because they gave too much discretion to judges and juries. The decision did not outlaw the death sentence per se—thirty-two states passed new laws authorizing it by 1975—but it stopped executions for the time being, and it prompted renewed litigation that branded the death penalty unconstitutional "cruel and unusual punishment." The Court also ruled that the government had to get a court order before employing wiretapping against suspected subversives. And in 1974 it ruled, eight to nothing, that Nixon must turn over damning tape recordings to a district court. The President, like many of his predecessors in the White House, experienced the rugged independence of the judicial branch.

Vietnam, Cambodia, and Laos

Nixon's most divisive policies before 1973 were in the realm where he had seemed so assured: foreign policy. His problem was simple: Vietnamization was not working. As American troops were withdrawn, the North Vietnamese and the Vietcong proved more than a match for the forces of South Vietnam's dictator, Nguyen Van Thieu. To compensate, Nixon authorized unpublicized bombing raids on neighboring Cambodia, which the enemy was using as a sanctuary. These raids, some 3,600 beginning early in 1969, failed to stop the communists. Encouraged by the Joint Chiefs, Nixon then sent American troops into Cambodia in April 1970. The fact that the soldiers were invading a neutral nation did not seem to trouble him. On the contrary, he spoke fiercely. "We will not be humiliated," he explained. "We will not be defeated. If when the chips are down the United States acts like a pitiful helpless giant, the forces of totalitarianism and anarchy will threaten free nations and free institutions throughout the world. It is not our power but our will that is being tested. . . ."

Nixon miscalculated badly. In Cambodia the attack was of dubious military merit. By reducing some of the military pressure on Thieu's forces, it may have given Vietnamization a little more time. But allied casualties were 1,138 dead and 4,911 wounded. The invasion failed to drive the enemy out of Cambodia. Worst of all, the assault dragged Cambodia itself into full-scale civil war, one that tore its society to pieces by the early 1980s.

INTENSIFICATION OF ANTIWAR SENTIMENT

At home Nixon's action prompted stirrings of independence in Congress, which repealed the 1964 Gulf of Tonkin resolution. The invasion also led to tragedy in Ohio. Two nights after Nixon announced his move, students at Kent State University firebombed the ROTC building, causing Ohio Governor James Rhodes to call in the National Guard. For a time it seemed that calm would return. But on May 4

Kent State University, 1970

students threw rocks and bottles at the guardsmen, who responded with tear gas. When the soldiers ran out of gas, they retreated nervously up a hillside. They were out of range of rocks, and in no danger. Some of the guardsmen then stopped, turned, and began to shoot. A girl screamed, "my God, they're killing us." When the firing stopped, four students lay dead and eleven were wounded. The Justice Department, acting under Mitchell's orders, failed to call a federal grand jury to review the tragedy, and it was not until 1974 that eight guardsmen were indicted (and acquitted) on criminal charges of violating the students' civil rights.

The deaths at Kent State unleashed a torrent of protest, especially on the campuses, which erupted for the third consecutive spring. Within the month demonstrations disrupted more than 400 universities; more than 250 had to be closed down before the end of the semester. By May 9 weekend, some 100,000 students descended on Washington in protest. A week later at Jackson State College in Mississippi two black students were killed and eleven wounded when police fired indiscriminately into a dormitory. President William J. McGill of Columbia University commented accurately that it was the "most disastrous month of May in the history of American higher education."

Nixon's first reaction was to discredit the students. "These bums . . . blowing up the campuses," he said, " . . . burning up the books, storming about." After the bloodshed at Kent State he commented that the shootings should "remind us once again that when dissent turns to violence it invites tragedy." But the protests worried him, and before dawn on May 9 he got out of bed and stole off to talk to demonstrators camped near the Lincoln Memorial. He intended to be responsive, conciliatory, understanding. But the ensuing dialogue exposed the gulf that separated him from the demonstrators. To California students he talked about surfing; to those from Syracuse he posed questions about the college football team. When he left to eat breakfast in a Washington hotel, he had done nothing to placate his opposition.

The campus disorders also heightened the President's desire to curb dissent. Already he had arranged to tap the phones of thirteen top government officials whom he suspected of leaking stories about the bombings in Cambodia, and of four journalists who had published them. Now, in June 1970, he tried to form a special national security committee composed of top people from the CIA, FBI, and Defense Intelligence Agency, and headed by FBI chief J. Edgar Hoover. The committee was to have the power to engage in electronic surveillance, stage break-ins, open mail, and infiltrate college campuses. However, Hoover spiked the plan by refusing to serve. Disappointed, Nixon had to put the plan aside for a while.

Instead, he relied on the vitriolic rhetoric of his vice-president, Spiro Agnew, who outdid himself during the congressional campaigning of 1970. Dissidents, Agnew said, were "parasites of passion," "ideological eunuchs," an "effete corps of impudent snobs who characterize themselves as intellectuals." The press was an "unelected elite," a "tiny and closed fraternity of privileged men . . . enjoying a monopoly sanctioned and licensed by the government." Agnew's assaults dovetailed neatly with the southern strategy and appealed to "middle Americans" who disliked the radical students and the "metromedia" of the eastern seaboard. But Agnew was practically threatening the media with censorship. Not since the days of the sedition and espionage acts during World War I had an administration acted so menacingly toward its opponents.

Agnew, however, did little to help the administration. The GOP lost ground in the 1970 elections, and Nixon struggled unsuccessfully against worsening stagflation early in 1971. The press carried alarming stories of drug addiction, desertion, and mutiny among the troops in Vietnam. Courting further confrontations with antiwar spokesmen, Nixon had charges of stealing government property brought against Daniel Ellsberg, a McNamara protégé and Rand Corporation employee who had released the Pentagon papers to the press. Some of Nixon's aides even drew up an "enemies list." It included such threats to the state as James Reston, Jane Fonda, Barbra Streisand, Paul Newman, and many others.

Nixon compounded his difficulties with yet another adventure in Southeast Asia. This was an invasion of Laos by South Vietnamese troops in February. Its aim, like the assault on Cambodia in 1970, was to cut off sanctuaries and supply routes winding into Vietnam. The incursion was also to display the fighting capacity of the South Vietnamese, who were to go it alone this time. When the attack was over in April, Nixon announced proudly, "tonight I can report that Vietnamization has succeeded." Press accounts showed otherwise. The enemy inflicted 50 percent casualties—3,800 South Vietnamese killed and 4,500 wounded—in six weeks. Only heavy bombing by the United States—again in a neutral country—prevented still more shocking losses.

Predictably, the invasion of Laos provoked demonstrations. This time the universities were relatively quiet—perhaps because students remembered Kent State, perhaps because protest on the campuses had seemed ineffective in the past. Instead, students and antiwar veterans—by then a growing lobby—headed for Washington. Their protests were nonviolent but disruptive, and Mitchell sent in police, national guardsmen, and army troops. Using truncheons and tear gas, they arrested 12,614 people in four days and penned them in open spaces like Robert F. Kennedy Memorial Stadium. Mitchell said that the government had "stopped a repressive mob from robbing the rights of others." The courts, appalled, threw out the arrests as violations of civil rights. Once again the Nixon administration, which had promised to bring the nation together, had helped to drive it apart.

The great turnabout, 1971–72

In mid-1971 the administration began a turnabout that dramatically improved its fortunes. Nixon began it in July by announcing that he was to visit the People's Republic of China early in 1972. Critics grumbled that the proposed trip was a public relations stunt. Others complained that Chiang Kai-shek was being abandoned—indeed, the General Assembly of the United Nations voted three months later to seat Mao Tse-tung's regime. Still others pointed out that the visit would poison American relations with Japan, the most highly industrialized nation in Asia. But most Americans were as pleased as they were surprised by Nixon's announcement. Kissinger's efforts for détente with the great powers were apparently paying off. The Cold War was thawing at last.

A month later Nixon made an equally dramatic announcement: the New Economic Policy. To improve the nation's balance of payments, he said, the United States would permit the dollar to find its own level—to "float" in the international exchange markets. He also called for a 10 percent tax on many imports, the repeal of important excise taxes, and tax breaks for industries that undertook new investment. To bring inflation to a halt, wages, prices, and dividends were to be frozen for ninety days, and controlled thereafter.

These changes were startling. Permitting the dollar to float in its weakened condition was largely the same as devaluing it. To many Americans this was a rude shock. Establishing controls seemed even more incredible, for Nixon, who had served unhappily as a young lawyer with the Office of Price Administration in World War II, had adamantly rejected such a policy earlier in the year. But if Americans were surprised, they were pleased by the administration's show of resolve—and by the gains that appeared to follow. As the dollar declined in value (eventually by about 9 percent), American exports became cheaper, and the balance of trade seemed to improve. Controls temporarily slowed down the rate of inflation. Stock prices jumped encouragingly, until the Dow Jones industrial average broke 1,000 for the first time in history, in November. The President's amazing turnabout was literally paying off.

In the next few months Nixon's economic policy seemed less assured. The government's wage and price commissions began to give way before the pressure of unions and of business interests. Inflation, which controls had checked, began to accelerate again. Disgruntled, the AFL-CIO refused to cooperate any longer in March 1972. For the rest of the year—indeed for the next decade—the rising cost of living became an increasingly vital concern.

But Nixon's pyrotechnic diplomacy in early 1972 helped conceal the faults of his economic policies. His visit to China in February 1972, though accomplishing little that was concrete, was elaborately staged for the American television audience. It greatly enhanced his stature. Kissinger's handling of Moscow was even more dazzling. When North Vietnam mounted an offensive on March 30, Nixon responded by bombing the north for the first time in three years, and by dropping mines in the harbor of Haiphong, a provocative step that not even Johnson had dared to take. Yet the Soviet Union, anxious not to drive the United States and China closer together, posed no objections. On the contrary, it welcomed Nixon with open arms when he visited Moscow in May. The trips to Moscow and Peking marked the high points of the Nixon-Kissinger foreign policy.

By this time the President's campaign for reelection was well underway. Here he took no chances. In 1971 he had already formed the Special Investigations Unit. It hired "plumbers," outfitted illegally by the CIA, to burglarize the office of Daniel Ellsberg's psychiatrist in an unsuccessful attempt to find compromising evidence. In 1971 Nixon had also formed the Committee to Re-elect the President. CREEP disbursed funds for "dirty tricks" aimed at embarrassing potential opponents like Wallace and Muskie. It arranged to tap the phone of the secretary of Lawrence O'Brien, chairman of the Democratic National Committee. And it collected a record $60 million, much of it in violation of existing laws against corporate contributions to political campaigns.

In mapping out his campaign the President had more than the usual amount of luck. Senator Edward Kennedy of Massachusetts, once the most popular Democratic challenger, had seriously harmed his chances in 1969 when he had driven his car off a bridge on the island of Chappaquiddick near Martha's Vineyard. The crash caused the death by drowning of a passenger, Mary Jo Kopechne. Senator Edmund Muskie, the frontrunner early in 1972, was damaged politically by his tearful response to a letter contrived by a "dirty trickster" in the employ of CREEP and published during the New Hampshire primary. George Wallace, who scored well in Democratic primaries in the North as well as in the South and seriously threatened Nixon's chances in November, was shot on May 15 by a deranged white youth, Arthur H. Bremer. Though Wallace survived, the shots paralyzed him for life and removed him from the presidential race. As it turned out, Wallace's withdrawal practically guaranteed Nixon the election.

The Democratic convention further played into Nixon's hands. It adopted a quota system that favored blacks, women, and young people while lessening the power of labor unions, urban political machines, congressional leaders, and ethnic groups. It thereby alienated the backbone of the Democratic party and exposed the ultimate nominee, George McGovern, to the charge that he (like Goldwater in 1964) was the candidate of a lunatic fringe. As if to ensure McGovern's defeat, the delegates nominated as his running mate Senator Thomas Eagleton of Missouri. Eagleton then disclosed that he had twice been hospitalized for psychiatric care. Under enormous pressure to reject Eagleton, McGovern at first proclaimed his support of the vice-presidential candidate, only to reverse himself and secure Eagleton's withdrawal. R. Sargent Shriver, a Kennedy brother-in-law who had headed the Peace Corps and the war on poverty, took Eagleton's place. McGovern, whose integrity had been a major asset, now struck many people as indecisive and self-righteous.

In an effort to redeem himself, McGovern moved to the attack. He criticized Nixon's handling of the war, which had caused 15,000 American deaths since January 1969. He rapped the administration's economic policies. He charged the President with dropping an antitrust suit against ITT in return for a campaign contribution of $400,000. And he tried to implicate Nixon in a burglary on June 17 of the Democratic National Committee headquarters in Washington's Watergate Hotel.

The Watergate affair, as it became known, deeply worried Nixon, who knew of CREEP's involvement in it. Citing national security reasons, he got Haldeman to stop the FBI from investigating the incident. Later in the campaign he authorized payments of more than $460,000 in hush money to keep the plumbers from implicating higher-ups in the administration. Publicly, he and other ranking Republicans disclaimed any involvement in the affair. Nixon said inaccurately in late August that his counsel, John Dean, had conducted a "complete investigation" that showed that "no one in the White House staff, no one in this administration, presently employed, was involved in this very bizarre incident." Nixon concluded: "what really hurts in matters of this sort is not the fact that they occur, because over-zealous people in campaigns do things that are wrong. What hurts is if you try to cover them up."

Americans apparently believed such protestations of innocence. Indeed, they had little choice, for the Democrats lacked evidence at the time to implicate the White

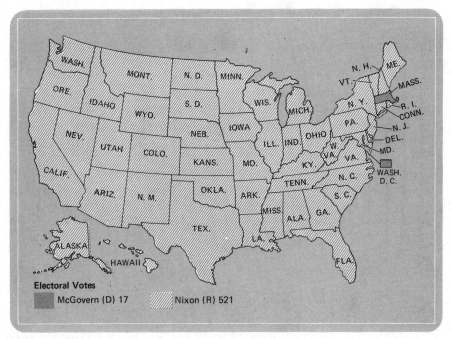

Electoral Votes
McGovern (D) 17   Nixon (R) 521

Election, 1972

House. The voters also seemed impressed with Nixon's conduct of foreign policy. Despite the failures of Vietnamization, troop withdrawals were continuing, and casualty lists, which had shown around 300 American deaths per week in late 1968, totaled near zero by September 1972. A month later, on October 26, Kissinger held a televised press conference to announce a breakthrough in the negotiations he had been conducting with the enemy in Paris. "Peace," he declared grandiloquently, "is at hand."

Kissinger's misleading announcement perhaps clinched victory for the team of Nixon and Agnew, which took 47 million votes to 29 million for McGovern and Shriver. This was 60.7 percent of the vote, the highest percentage in modern American history except for that won by Johnson in 1964. Nixon carried every state except Massachusetts and the District of Columbia, for a margin in the electoral college of 521 to 17. Nixon's critics bravely explained that turnout had been low and pointed out that Democrats still held wide margins in Congress. But it was impossible to deny that the voters had endorsed the President. At least for the time being Nixon was a resounding political success.

Acrimony again, 1973–75

INTERNATIONAL PROBLEMS

Those who hoped for harmony after the election were immediately disillusioned. Kissinger's forecast of peace, it developed, was inaccurate, primarily because General Thieu refused to agree to the deals the United States and North Vietnam were making without his participation. By mid-December the prospects for peace seemed as remote as ever.

Nixon, safely reelected, reacted sharply by authorizing the most savage bombing of North Vietnam in the twelve-year history of American involvement in the war. General Alexander Haig, Kissinger's deputy, described it aptly as the ''brutalizing'' of the north. Some of the bombs hit a hospital in Hanoi; others damaged a camp holding American prisoners of war. The enemy, better defended than in the past, shot down fifteen B-52 planes (each costing $8 million) and captured ninety-eight American airmen in two weeks.

The resumption of bombing may have achieved its aim: two weeks after starting it Nixon announced that peace negotiations were soon to resume. At the same time, he stopped the raids. More important in North Vietnam's attitude may have been pressure to settle from Russia and China, both of whom were tired of the war. In any event, the negotiations succeeded in establishing a cease-fire beginning January 28. An agreement signed by the United States, North Vietnam, South Vietnam, and the Vietcong's Provisional Revolutionary Government (PRG) decreed that in the next sixty days America would remove its 23,700 remaining troops, and the enemy would return 509 prisoners of war. The future of Vietnam—left vague—was to be determined by negotiations, not by force.

The agreement brought to an end, after twelve years, the presence of American combat troops in Vietnam. In that time the dead included 56,000 Americans, 5,200

Desperate Vietnamese refugees try to board an American evacuation plane at Da Nang, April 1975.

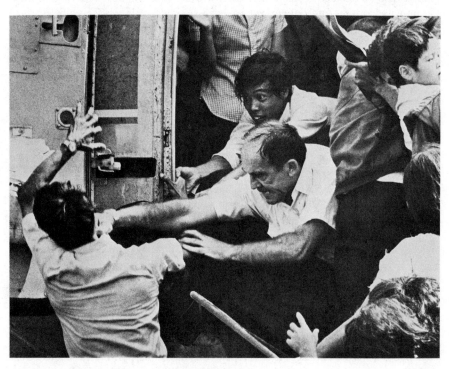

allied soldiers, 184,000 South Vietnamese, and an estimated 925,000 North Vietnamese. Approximately five times these numbers were wounded. The total of refugees, and of civilian deaths, in Vietnam, Laos, and Cambodia could only be guessed at—probably many millions. In the face of such statistics it is not surprising that many Americans, relieved at the prospect of withdrawal, accepted Nixon's statement that he had bought "peace with honor."

Thoughtful observers knew better. In part because Nixon had secretly assured Thieu of military support in the event of communist gains, South Vietnam refused from the start to recognize the PRG, to consider communist participation in a coalition government, or to work earnestly to restrain its combat forces. Faced with this all-or-nothing attitude, the PRG and North Vietnam pressed on for a military solution, and fighting ravaged the country again. In response America dispatched bombing raids over Laos and sent billions more in military equipment to sustain Vietnamization. For a time in early 1973 Nixon even considered resuming saturation bombing of North Vietnam, refraining only for fear of domestic turmoil. Russia and China, meanwhile, aided Hanoi and the Vietcong.

Whether America learned the correct "lessons" from the war also remains to be seen. World War I, after all, had taught the "virtues" of noninvolvement; World War II had encouraged globalism. By 1973 Americans seemed fairly sure about two things: first, that they could not protect the whole world; and second, that Southeast Asia should fight its own civil wars. Holding to such views, Congress forbade the President to undertake any military action whatever in Indochina after August 15, 1973. It also approved, over Nixon's veto, the War Powers Act of 1973. Henceforth the White House was to give Congress a full explanation within forty-eight hours for the dispatch of American troops abroad. Presidents must withdraw such troops within sixty days unless Congress specifically authorized them to stay. In 1975, when the administration wanted to intervene again in Cambodia and Vietnam, the War Powers Act stood in its way. As in 1919, the presidential excesses prompted a resurgence of congressional will.

It was too much to expect, however, that the withdrawal of American troops could end the nation's problems. On the contrary, continuing deficits in the balance of payments resulted in further devaluation of the dollar—this time of 10 percent—by February 1973. Rising inflation forced Nixon to reintroduce price controls, first on petroleum products and meat, and then (in June) on all retail prices. The controls lasted sixty days. At the same time, militant Indians on the Oglala Sioux reservation in South Dakota reminded Americans of injustice at home. Rising in anger at Wounded Knee, site of a massacre of Indians eighty-three years before, they seized eleven hostages and demanded redress of their grievances. Federal authorities responded by surrounding the Indians and blocking the flow of food. Before the siege ended eleven weeks later, outbreaks of shooting had killed one Indian and wounded one FBI man. The protracted confrontation settled nothing of consequence.

Withdrawal from Vietnam also failed to deliver the nation from complicated overseas involvements. These became obvious in October 1973, when Israel and the Arab states went to war again. As in 1948, 1956, and 1967, the Israelis showed their military superiority. But this time the Arabs inflicted costly losses on their

America's mood:
the public's view of the most important
problem facing the country,
according to Gallup Poll results,
1969–74

1969	Vietnam
1970	Reducing crime
1971	Inflation
1972	Vietnam
1973	High cost of living
1974	Energy crisis

SOURCE: Adapted from *U.S. Foreign Policy: Context, Conduct, Content* by Marian Irish and Elke Frank. © 1975 by Harcourt Brace Jovanovich. Reproduced by permission of the publisher.

enemies, and it became clearer than ever that the future of Israel depended on continuing American support. In the next two years Kissinger, who became secretary of state in October 1973, shuttled back and forth to the Middle East in an effort to promote some understanding between the antagonists. Though he made progress with Egypt, he found Israel reluctant at first to return territory gained in the 1967

Middle East, 1947–78

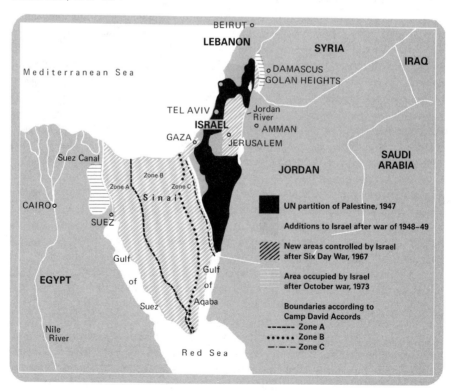

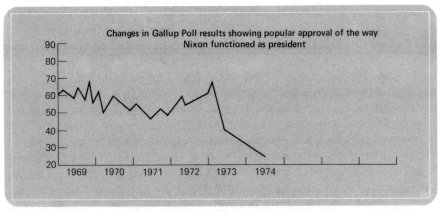

Changes in Gallup Poll results showing popular approval of the way Nixon functioned as president

SOURCE: Adapted from p. 104 of *U.S. Foreign Policy: Context, Conduct, Content* by Marian Irish and Elke Frank. © 1975 by Harcourt Brace Jovanovich. Reproduced by permission of the publisher. And from *Gallup Opinion Index*, no. 111, Sept. 1974, p. 11.

Nixon's popularity peaked in late 1969 and early 1973 when 68 percent of respondents approved of his handling of the presidency, and reached a low of 24 percent shortly before he resigned in 1974.

war. He also could not placate the Palestine Liberation Organization, which represented the million-plus Arabs uprooted from their lands in Israel. Meanwhile the Soviet Union continued to provide arms to the Arabs and to persecute Jews at home. Soviet-American détente was obviously limited.

The Middle East war had the further effect of drawing the often quarrelsome Arab states closer together. Using oil as a weapon, they cut back on shipments of oil to their enemies, including the United States. Thereafter, they hiked their prices. These actions dramatically exposed the dependence of the industrialized nations on oil—the great powers, one observer cracked, were now the United States, Russia, Saudi Arabia, Kuwait, and Abu Dhabi. The increase in oil prices was also followed by the most frightening wave of inflation to date throughout much of the industrialized noncommunist world. Nixon called for voluntary restraint in the use of gasoline and heating oil. But he refused to impose rationing, to investigate high oil company profits, or to develop a long-range policy for the conservation of energy resources. Inflation continued to mount, the stock market to plummet, and the economy to stagnate.

A popular president might have been able to act resourcefully against these problems. But a host of revelations in 1973–74 combined to undermine Nixon's standing. One showed that the CIA had been involved in a military coup in September 1973 that overthrew Chile's Salvador Allende, the Western Hemisphere's first popularly elected Marxist leader. Though the CIA denied the charges, other rumors about the agency's excesses placed it also on the defensive. (One such rumor, that the CIA had hired Mafiosi to kill Fidel Castro in 1961, was later confirmed.)

WATERGATE

Charges of corruption further harmed the administration in 1973–74. In October 1973 Vice-President Agnew, champion of law and order, had to resign when it was revealed that he had cheated on his income taxes and had taken more than $100,000 in payoffs from contractors between 1966 and 1972. The IRS then disclosed that Nixon himself owed more than $400,000 in back taxes and penalties. Other critics showed that CREEP had solicited huge corporate campaign contributions, illegal under the 1972 campaign financing law, that the government had spent millions on improvements to the presidential properties in Florida and California, and that the administration had raised subsidies to milk producers, who thereupon gave $527,500 to the Republican party. The trail of corruption surrounding the election was winding dangerously close to the Oval Office.

The President's major problem was the Watergate burglary. Though he did his best to cover up his involvement in the affair, hard-working reporters from the *Washington Post* and other papers gave him no rest. Neither did the Senate Select Committee on Campaign Practices headed by folksy Sam Ervin of North Carolina. Judge John Sirica of the United States district court of the District of Columbia, which heard the cases of the burglars in early 1973, was perhaps the most persistent of all. Imposing stiff sentences in March, he disclosed a letter from one of the plumbers that involved higher-ups in the administration.

A series of revelations between April and July of 1973 sustained this allegation. Patrick Gray, who had been acting chief of the FBI since Hoover's death a year earlier, resigned after admitting that he had burned incriminating documents concerning Watergate and related matters. Evidence linking the White House to the cover-up forced the resignations of Haldeman and Erlichman. In June, White House counsel John Dean testified that the President himself had been involved in the cover-up. And a month later a White House aide revealed that Nixon had taped many of the conversations concerning the affair. This disclosure set off a year-long war in which the Senate, Judge Sirica, and federal prosecutors fought the President for access to the tapes.

In an attempt to promote public confidence in his conduct the President brightened the image of his administration. To head the FBI he picked William Ruckelshaus, an Indianan who then headed the Environmental Protection Agency. To run the Justice Department, the prosecuting arm of the government, he named Elliot Richardson, his secretary of defense. Both men had reputations for courage and integrity. The President even accepted Richardson's choice for a special Watergate prosecutor. This was Archibald Cox, a Harvard law professor. Cox, Nixon said, would have full cooperation from the White House.

When Cox insisted on going to court for the tapes, however, Nixon demanded that Richardson fire him. Claiming executive privilege, the President added that he would personally edit a summary of the transcripts. Richardson refused to do Nixon's bidding and resigned in late October. Ruckelshaus, who had become Richardson's deputy, agreed with Richardson, and was fired. The solicitor general, next in command at the Justice Department, then discharged Cox. In the ensuing uproar, Nixon felt compelled to yield some of the tapes, to name a new special prosecutor, Leon Jaworski of Texas, and to tell the public over TV, "I am not a crook." But he refused to give up all the tapes, and Jaworski, as tenacious as Cox, kept up the legal struggle in late 1973 and early 1974.

During this time the President continued to profess his innocence. On April 29, 1974, he appeared on TV again to announce that he was releasing transcripts of the tapes. These, he said, "will at last, once and for all, show that what I knew and what I did with regard to the Watergate cover-up were just as I described them to you from the very beginning." On other occasions he angrily blamed the press for his dilemma and insisted that impeachment, which the House Judiciary Committee began considering seriously in May 1974, would "jeopardize" world peace and endanger the American political system. As if to prove his indispensability, he toured the Middle East and Moscow in June and July. Though he attracted sizable crowds, he accomplished little, in part because the Watergate affair was undermining his effectiveness abroad as well as at home. "Every negotiation," Kissinger said later, "was getting more and more difficult because it involved the question of whether we could, in fact, carry out what we were negotiating."

By this time the pressure on Nixon to release all the tapes was overwhelming. But he had good reason to refuse such requests, because he knew that they proved his obstruction of justice. Accordingly, he cited "executive privilege" and national security as his reasons for keeping the recordings. His lawyers, none of whom were told the facts, were instructed to resist Jaworski's requests for the tapes and to appeal the matter to the Supreme Court.

On July 24 a unanimous Court gave its answer. It agreed that a president could withhold "military, diplomatic, or sensitive national security material." To this extent executive privilege gained explicit judicial sanction for the first time. But the judges went on to insist that the Court, not the president, had the right to "say what the law is," and that the Watergate affair, a criminal proceeding, did not involve "national security." The claim for executive privilege, therefore, had to "yield to the demonstrated, specific need for evidence in a pending criminal trial," and the President must turn over "forthwith" the sixty-four recordings demanded by his foes. Judge Sirica could listen to the tapes and release relevant portions to Jaworski, who could give them to Congress.

A few days later the House Judiciary Committee acted against the President by voting to impeach him on three counts. The first, passed twenty-seven to eleven, charged him with obstruction of justice. Nixon, the committee said, had made or caused to be made false statements, withheld relevant and material evidence, interfered with investigations by the FBI, the Justice Department, special prosecutors, and Congress, approved the payment of hush money to witnesses, and lied to the American people. The second charge, approved twenty-eight to ten, accused Nixon of abusing his presidential authority by resorting to illegal wiretapping and by using the FBI, CIA, and Internal Revenue Service against American citizens. A third charge hit him for refusing to turn over the tapes, after receiving a congressional subpoena, to the committee. The committee had deliberated long and responsibly, and its concluding debates, carried on radio and TV, did much to restore faith in Congress as an institution. There was little doubt that the House would endorse the committee's conclusions by wide margins. If the Senate could corral a two-thirds majority for conviction—and that seemed entirely possible—Nixon would have to leave office.

Nixon, trapped, procrastinated until August 5, when he finally released the tapes that proved his involvement in the cover-up. He admitted that he had concealed them, even from his own lawyers, but insisted that he had done nothing to

I have discovered that according to a secret tape of June 23, 1972, I AM a crook.

warrant conviction by the Senate. The Senate clearly disagreed. So did the American people, who felt betrayed by the President's lies over the previous twenty-six months. In the next few days Republicans as well as Democrats indicated they would vote for conviction. Deprived of support, the President resigned on August 9, 1974. Vice-president Gerald Ford of Michigan, whom Nixon had appointed to succeed Agnew earlier in the year, was immediately sworn in as the next president.

Nixon's resignation, while welcomed by many people at home and abroad, enabled him to avoid the Senate trial that might have established clearly the extent of his involvement in the Watergate affair. It also left many questions unanswered. What self-incriminating documents had the administration hoped to steal at Watergate? Also, suppose Nixon had never taped the conversations? Having done so, suppose he had destroyed the tapes, along with logs that showed what they contained? What if some future president, having committed some egregious act, concealed such misconduct by claiming executive privilege based on the existence of "military, diplomatic, or sensitive national security material?" Such questions suggested that future presidents might still find ways of acting above the law. The imperial presidency, which the founding fathers had feared—and which twentieth-century chief executives from TR on had done so much to create—might again endanger constitutional processes and lead to paralysis of the state.

Subsequent disclosures did little to dispel such fears. These disclosures revealed a new kind of corruption. The men around Grant, Harding, and other scandal-stained presidents had acted primarily for financial gain. Many of Nixon's criminal subordinates, however, truly believed that their ends—defined as everything from reelection of the President to the maintenance of world peace—justified the means. They had no qualms about subverting democratic institutions and civil liberties. Charles Colson, Nixon's counsel, had exclaimed, "for the President I would walk over my grandmother if necessary." A plumber, Gordon Liddy, added that Watergate was "an intelligence-gathering operation of one group of persons who were seeking to retain power against another group of persons who were seeking to acquire power. That's all it was. It's like brushing your teeth. It's basic." Defending the cover-up, CREEP director Jeb Magruder added that "after the Democrats nominated Senator McGovern, we felt that we were protecting the honorable peace that the President was bringing to Vietnam. . . . We were not covering up a burglary, we were safeguarding world peace." He concluded, "we wanted to win the election and we wanted to win it big. Just as a corporation wants to dominate its market, our reelection committee wanted to dominate that year's election. . . . We were past the point of halfway measures or gentlemanly tactics."

In the aftermath of Watergate

The resignation of Nixon brought to the fore problems that excitement over Watergate had helped to obscure. The afflictions that had troubled the nation in the twentieth century—racial injustice, urban blight, economic inequality, sex discrimination, oppression of Indians and Hispanic-Americans—persisted. So did stagflation, which proved chronic and serious into the 1980s. In April 1975, the North Vietnamese won their civil war against the South, forcing General Thieu and his supporters to flee. But the ending of Western influence there did not bring peace to Southeast Asia. In the ensuing years, Cambodia fell victim to cruel authoritarianism and famine, and sporadic fighting broke out between China, Cambodia, and Vietnam.

Americans worried about the capacity of their new leaders to deal with these problems. In his lengthy political career Ford had shown little interest in fighting urban or racial problems. He was largely uninformed concerning fiscal policy. He was handicapped also by his lack of a popular mandate. Both he and his new vice-president, former Governor Nelson Rockefeller of New York, were Republicans facing the most aroused and self-assertive Democratic Congresses in recent memory. Thanks to the Twenty-fifth Amendment (1967), which authorized presidents to nominate (and Congress to confirm) vice-presidents, both men were nonelective officials. The United States, which had done so much to advance the cause of political democracy 200 years earlier, had to wait more than 2 years before being governed by a popularly elected president.

President Ford then compounded doubts about his ability by pardoning his predecessor. He did so, he said, because he wanted people to forget the recent past and because Nixon had suffered enough. A few weeks later, when Nixon almost died after an operation on his leg for phlebitis, Ford's compassion seemed appropriate. Whether the pardon was proper was another matter. Men like Erlichman, Haldeman, Mitchell, Dean, and Magruder—and many lesser officials—were either in jail or appealing convictions for crimes ranging from perjury to obstruction of justice. These people, like many Americans, wondered about the fairness of a system that punished the little fish while the shark escaped scot-free. Americans found it equally difficult to forget the deceit and hypocrisy that had contaminated governmental institutions since the mid-1960s. As one magazine phrased it earlier, the United States seemed to have swung half circle in the 200 years of its existence: "from George Washington, who could not tell a lie, to Richard Nixon, who could not tell the truth."

As if to register their alienation, the voters showed little interest in the off-year elections of 1974. Democrats gained throughout the nation. But only 45 percent of eligible voters cast their ballots. In a nation supposedly governed by popular majorities, this was hardly encouraging. The turnout of youth was especially poor: only 21 percent of people aged eighteen to twenty bothered to vote. This apparent political apathy (or alienation?) persisted into the 1980s. Indeed, students seemed remarkably quiescent in contrast to a few years earlier. Confronting a sluggish economy, they worried about finding jobs or getting into graduate schools and seldom engaged in sustained protest. The historian C. Vann Woodward commented, "Rarely in history has publicized activism been replaced so rapidly by apparent apathy, student dissent by silence."

Many Americans in the late 1970s and early 1980s shared the students' worries about the future. Though the nation was calmer than it had been in the turbulent years of the late 1960s, no one could be confident that domestic tranquility would last. Some observers feared that the approach of zero population growth, for the first time in American history, signaled not only the end of economic expansion but also a more general loss of confidence. The last frontiers, it appeared, had been conquered; it was time to consolidate and pull back. Others, lamenting the continuing coexistence of inflation and recession, foresaw increasing government control over a stagnant economy. Robert Lekachman, a respected economist, wrote, "I think we are entering a long period of slower growth. I take seriously the resource scarcities. We've reached the end of cheap energy. . . . The prospects for improvement in the American standard of life thus are much less than they've been."

Reflecting these doubts, many observers concluded that the nation was becoming a "business civilization" like that of the 1920s: materialistic, hollow, lacking in securely held values or sense of purpose beyond individual self-aggrandizement. The rise of such a society, critics said, exposed the mixed blessings of modernization, which had unleashed a revolution in expectations along with economic growth and technological progress. Restless, cranky, divided, Americans seemed psychologically unfulfilled and impossible to satisfy.

American foreign policy gave special cause for concern. In 1975 the United States operated a defense budget of $104 billion—an increase of $15 billion over the amount needed during the years of involvement in Vietnam in 1972–74. America also sold arms to more than 130 countries and maintained military commitments with forty nations. Most of these forty were NATO or Latin American countries. Other commitments included South Korea, a repressive dictatorship, Japan, Taiwan, the Philippines, Australia, and New Zealand. Two danger zones, West Berlin and Israel, were not covered by treaty but appeared to be integral parts of America's worldwide defense perimeter. With naval vessels circling the globe, planes ever in the air, 8,500 strategic nuclear weapons in full deployment, and more than 400,000 troops stationed overseas in the cause of Pax Americana, the once uncommitted United States ran the risk of constant military involvement.

The Ford administration quickly showed its readiness to use part of this formidable arsenal. In May 1975 Cambodia captured the *Mayaguez,* an American merchant vessel sailing near its shores. When the anti-American government of Cambodia was slow to answer United States protests, Ford authorized an attack by 350 marines on Koh Tang, a nearby island where the crew was wrongly believed to be held. The assault, accompanied by bombing in Cambodia, marked a heavy overreaction to a minor incident. It cost the United States fifteen dead, three missing, and fifty wounded. It was probably unnecessary, for Cambodia was in the process of returning both ship and crew at the time. But many Americans exulted in Ford's show of steel. The incident suggested that they cared little for consultation, that they had learned almost nothing from ten years of trauma over Vietnam, and that deep down they were uncertain and insecure.

It was nonetheless possible in the mid-1970s to contemplate the future with guarded optimism. Whatever the President's faults, he appeared honest and open. Some people hailed him as a Republican Harry Truman. Ford also proved willing to compromise. When Congress rebuffed his conservative economic policies in late 1974, he reversed himself to favor a multibillion-dollar tax cut, an increase in unemployment benefits, and a Keynesian budget that envisaged a deficit of $52 billion. His turnabout did little to arrest inflation—it may in fact have made it a little worse—and it failed to end the worst recession since the 1930s. Unemployment, hovering at around 9 percent in 1975 (affecting more than eight million people) had not been so high since 1940. Still, Ford's flexibility relieved observers who had feared a return to Hooverism. Congress acted quickly to expand on his proposals.

Americans with a sense of history also recognized that the strife of the immediate past had brought progress as well as pain. The forces of technology, industrialization, and economic growth had made the nation incomparably richer than it had been in 1776, or—more to the point—than in 1940 or 1960. The civil rights revolution had brought the most impressive gains for blacks since emancipation. Supreme Court decisions had broadened the civil rights and civil liberties of the people. The Cold War, with its attendant threat of nuclear catastrophe, had softened. The country's political institutions, apparently so flawed, had remained stable under pressure of war, assassinations, and incomparable presidential abuse. The virtues of a free press, an independent judiciary, and an alert Congress had rarely been so clearly revealed. For all the nation's problems, it had withstood a public airing of its deficiencies that would have disrupted many other countries in the world. For these and some other blessings the United States could take cautious pride.

Bicentennial and after: social problems

In contrast to some of the bleaker periods of American history, the years from the bicentennial in 1976 into the early 1980s offered many grounds for optimism. Public opinion polls revealed that 70 to 75 percent of Americans were happy in their own lives and optimistic about the future as it was likely to affect them personally. These feelings of individual well-being were understandable in a country that had seen real personal income double since the 1940s. The phenomenal prosperity of spectator sports, the vogue for blockbuster films, and the growth of the travel business suggested the continuing existence of affluence for the favored middle classes.

Technological and scientific developments promised the conquest of further frontiers in the near future. Scientists attempting to unravel genetic strands of deoxyribonucleic acid (DNA) and to recombine the strands with others were changing the instructions governing living cells; by 1980 they had succeeded in transferring genes into living animals. Other scientists were moving ahead rapidly in the field of fiber optics, which some thought could revolutionize the field of communications. Scientists working for the space program succeeded in 1981 in reusing a space vehicle, thus indicating the possibility of space shuttles in the long-range future. Progress in computer technology was especially startling. In 1970, 16 "bits" (or pieces of information) could be packed on one silicon chip in a computer. By 1985, the capacity of a chip was expected to be at least 250,000 bits. The age of the minicomputer (at no increased cost)—for the home, libraries, stock market, medical services—was at hand.

Optimists could argue even that progressive developments were improving the lives of groups that had long been deprived. Huge increases in appropriations for social security greatly reduced poverty among old people and the disabled. Higher spending for food stamps and for Medicaid (until cuts in 1981) helped alleviate destitution among millions of other Americans. While some 30 million Americans continued to live in households earning less than the official poverty line in the early 1980s, this statistic represented progress of a sort in a country that had had 40 million designated as poor in 1960.

Black Americans, too, had some reason to be encouraged by trends of the period. Various developments stemming from the civil rights movement, including affirmative action programs administered by the federal government, led to real changes in the occupational and economic status of blacks. "We have a truly visible black middle class," the National Opinion Research Center concluded in 1980. "Twenty percent of blacks earn more than the median white income, and proportionally, the rates of going to college are higher for blacks than for whites."

To sustain this progress, the Supreme Court seemed willing to sharpen the teeth of affirmative action guidelines. In 1978 it upheld the suit of Alan Bakke, a white who had been refused admission to the medical school at the University of California at Davis, where there existed an explicit quota system for admitting blacks and other minority students. The Court ruled in favor of Bakke, who had shown that his examination grades and other intellectual qualifications were superior to those of many blacks who had been admitted. But it did so on the relatively narrow ground that such explicit quotas violated the equal protection clause of the Constitution when used by state-funded institutions. It said that admissions schemes which take race into account as one factor among many, and use informal targets rather than strict quotas, were legal. In the Weber case of 1979 the Court added that private industries were free to apply voluntary racial preference programs in hiring. These decisions seemed to safeguard affirmative action in practice. Many Americans, indeed, worried that the Court left the door too far open for reverse discrimination.

The promising developments of the period, however, were neither large nor solid enough to satisfy most Americans. Polls showed that while people were optimistic about their own personal futures, they were very dissatisfied with the way the nation as a whole was going. Contemporary commentators perceived a general malaise in the late 1970s and early 1980s. Some blamed the hangover of Vietnam. "That goddam war really soured the country," one survey researcher concluded. Another social scientist added, "the trauma and scars [of the war] had the same psychological impact on America that the loss of empire had on Britain." Many others blamed the sluggish economy. "I have a growing feeling," one man said, "that we are close to the edge. I don't see how we can continue the way we did in the last ten years—it really scares me."

Others seemed profoundly alienated by what they perceived as the persistent injustice of American society. More than three-fourths of Americans polled in 1977 agreed that "the rich get richer and the poor get poorer." More than 60 percent agreed that "what you think doesn't count any more" and that "most people with power try to take advantage of people like yourself." These figures represented sizable increases over the percentages responding to the same questions in 1972. The responses appeared to reveal a growing gulf between expectations and realities. The American dream, it seemed, was fading as the country entered its third century.

Many worried Americans perceived a crisis of social instability—centered, perhaps, in the decay of the traditional nuclear family. Thanks in large part to a rapidly rising divorce rate (33 percent of first marriages failed during the period, and 40 percent of second marriages), the number of households headed by women rose to more than 25 percent by 1980. At that time some 12 million children under the age of 18 lived in divorced families. Traditionalists worried also about the continuing liberation of sexual behavior. By the late 1970s, more than 1 million couples lived together without the blessing of marriage. Of people aged 18 to 24, 95 percent of men and 80 percent of women acknowledged having indulged in premarital sexual intercourse. The number of legal abortions increased from 18,000 in 1968 (before the Supreme Court legalized them) to 1.3 million in 1977. These statistics—along with the rapid expansion of the pornography business—convinced some people that traditional standards of morality were collapsing.

Still more alarming was the violence of American society in the late 1970s and early 1980s. During this time, the political activist Allard Lowenstein and the

Beatle John Lennon were killed. Would-be assassins tried to kill President Ford and wounded President Ronald Reagan. The rate of violent crime in cities with populations over 250,000 had been 300 per 100,000 people in 1960; by 1978 it was 1,100. Rates of homicide, assault, rape, and robbery were higher in the United States than in other Western democratic nations; the American rate of gun murders was about 50 times as high. Citizens complained that they could not walk about freely on the streets, or sit securely in their homes. "They don't just rob you any more," one complained. "Now they gotta beat you up." Calling for tougher measures against criminals, President Reagan in 1981 declared that crime was "an American epidemic—it takes the lives of 23,000 Americans, it touches nearly one-third of American households, and it results in at least $8.8 billion in financial losses."

Those who advanced suggestions for coping with such violence included advocates of a strict federal gun control law. Such legislation, they argued, might at least impose controls on the sale of handguns, or "Saturday night specials." Opponents of such legislation, however, managed to defeat such efforts. Many other Americans demanded tougher treatment of criminals. Reflecting this mood, the Supreme Court seemed to edge slightly away from its landmark decisions of the 1960s dealing with criminal justice. In 1976 it held that the death penalty did not violate the Eighth Amendment's ban against cruel and unusual punishment. Executions, Justice Stewart said, were "an extreme sanction, suitable to the most extreme of crimes." A total of 37 states thereupon restored the death penalty in the late 1970s; three death row inmates were executed. Cities also attempted to strengthen their police forces, including SWAT teams specially trained to deal with violent crimes. Such measures, however, remained controversial. Some critics claimed that they facilitated police brutality. Others argued that they did nothing to attack the causes of criminal activity, including poverty and drug addiction. Amid continuing debate over such measures, violence persisted as a serious blight on American society in the early 1980s.

The status of blacks also gave many contemporaries great cause for concern. Numbering around 25 million in the total 1980 population of 220 million, blacks seemed to be dividing sharply along class lines. Many of those in the middle classes, and in intact two-parent families, were achieving impressive gains. But 40 percent of black families were female-headed, most of them very poor. Partly for this reason, the gap between overall black income and white income increased in the late 1970s. Poverty afflicted some 30 percent of blacks. Unemployment among blacks was much higher than among whites; for black teenagers it approached 40 percent in many areas. In one such area, the Liberty City ghetto of Miami, rioting broke out in 1980, following the acquittal of four white policemen on charges of killing a black businessman. The riot lasted four days and caused great destruction to property in the area.

Moreover, blacks were not the only group facing severe social and economic problems by the early 1980s. The status of American Indians—or native Americans as many preferred to be called—remained as economically deprived as ever. So did the status of many Puerto Ricans, whose living conditions in New York City were as bad as or worse than those of poor blacks. Contemporaries worried also about the rising influx of immigration—much of it illegal—from Latin America (mainly

Mexico). Careful observers estimated that the number of Hispanics in the United States increased from around 3 million in 1960 to 19 million in 1980, perhaps 7 million of whom were illegal aliens. These migrants succeeded in building cohesive neighborhoods in many parts of America, notably in the Southwest. Still, their numbers threatened to disrupt established institutions and to deprive some native white workers of employment. Moreover, many Chicanos suffered from exploitation and poverty. How to deal with the influx of illegal aliens promised to become one of the most divisive political issues of the 1980s.

Overall, the status of women as a group was better than that of these minority groups. The movement for women's rights, indeed, proved broader and more durable than those for black or Indian power. But it was clear that much sexual discrimination persisted. In part because many working women held beginning-level jobs, their income on the average was only about 60 percent of that of men. The percentage of managerial and professional positions held by women seemed to decline slightly. Advocates of women's rights demanded a host of improvements in the conditions of work, including better provision for maternity leave, more public funding for day care, and legislation making child care costs tax deductible. They complained bitterly about the Supreme Court decision of 1977 that said the government need not pay for abortions for the poor under the provisions of Medicaid. And they lamented the refusal of the requisite number of states to approve the Equal Rights Amendment by 1982. The failure of the amendment (which said that "equality of rights under the law shall not be denied or abridged by the United States or by any State on account of sex") revealed the political power of anti-feminist lobbyists, many of them women. The fate of the ERA suggested also that the women's movement in the 1980s, like the civil rights movement in the 1970s, might be stalling—at least until the gains of the recent past could be assimilated and institutionalized.

The condition of blue-collar and white-collar workers seemed equally unpromising by the early 1980s. Factory workers showed some signs of rebelling against "blue-collar blues"—the monotony and hectic pace of assembly line work. They demanded greater control of the work process itself. Similarly, white-collar workers began turning increasingly to labor unions. The United Federation of Teachers became a potent union in some places, notably New York. The American Federation of State, County, and Municipal Employees emerged as one of the largest in the AFL-CIO. Despite such efforts, unions did not flourish. Indeed, the percentage of nonfarm workers in unions declined from 31 percent in 1960 to 25 percent in 1980. Other indicators—notably the unchanging distribution of income in America (the wealthiest 20 percent of Americans had 40 percent of personal income, the poorest 20 percent had 5 percent—suggested that the structure of American capitalism and the power of American corporations faced no great challenges from below in the 1980s.

THE INSECURE ECONOMY

The status of all these groups—blacks, immigrants, women, workers—and of other, more fortunate groups depended ultimately on the functioning of the American economy. This, however, remained as shaky as it had been since the early

1970s. Public opinion polls regularly revealed that Americans worried above all in the postbicentennial years about the future of the economy.

These worries reflected profound general questions about America's future development. Could economic prosperity—readily assumed by most Americans since the 1940s—be sustained, or had the country at last staggered to its final frontier? Was the nation, indeed the whole Western industrialized world, now engaged in a zero-sum game in which as many were to suffer as to prosper? And if the economy was to stagnate, could the United States maintain its dynamic, expansive role in the world?

One especially alarming problem concerned the high costs and threatened shortages of energy sources. Several forces produced this situation, including the policies of the OPEC nations, which joined together to increase prices of their oil exports. Oil prices quintupled between 1972 and 1979. Attempting to cope with these pressing problems, experts called for various solutions. Some insisted that the answer was to develop solar energy. As of the early 1980s, however, cheap and effective methods of producing solar energy on a large scale were yet to be found. Others hailed the potential of atomic-based power. But a frightening accident at the atomic power plant at Three Mile Island, Pennsylvania, in 1979 dramatized the potential dangers involved in the widespread development of such installations. Other experts called for greater production of coal, of which abundant resources remained. Coal, however, had its disadvantages. Much of the cheapest and most available coal had to be strip-mined, thereby savaging the landscape and polluting surrounding streams. Much of this coal burned "dirty," polluting the atmosphere. Attempting to encourage further exploration for energy sources, Congress instituted a policy of gradual deregulation of natural gas and funded efforts aimed at developing oil from shale in the western mountains. Whether these efforts promised a real answer, however, was debatable. Surely, they were leading to even higher energy costs in the short-run. Meanwhile, until oil prices dipped sharply in 1982, the oil companies were reaping record profits. By the early 1980s the United States had failed to develop anything like a coherent energy policy.

To many observers it seemed that the only long-range answer to the "energy crisis," as it was coming to be called, was conservation. Americans, they pointed out, drove long distances in gas-guzzling automobiles and heated their homes to high temperatures. They consumed much more energy per capita than did people of other nations. As gasoline and oil prices rose in the late 1970s, many Americans had no choice but to begin conserving on a small scale. They turned to smaller automobiles, and they heeded advice about ways of improving home insulation. But old habits did not die quickly, for the exploitation of apparently abundant natural resources, and the attendant comforts that this exploitation made possible, were widely regarded as fundamental to the American way of life. Cutting back on energy, in fact, necessitated sacrifices and sharpened the struggle between groups for slices of a smaller pie. As Arthur Schlesinger, Jr., put it, "our national development has been premised on the assumption of limitless supplies of low cost energy. But the age of cheap energy is over. The realization of this fact, as it slowly sinks in, will bring painful readjustments not only in energy policy and in economic management but in our very habits of thought and ways of life."

The most hotly discussed economic problem, caused in part by the higher price of energy, was inflation. The cost of living doubled between 1968 and 1978 and continued thereafter to rise at an alarming rate. Interest rates reached record heights, dampening investment. Worse, rising unemployment accompanied this inflation, and some of the nation's leading industrial enterprises teetered on the brink. The situation in automobile production was especially serious. In 1980 the federal government chose to bail out Chrysler Corporation, which lost a record $1.7 billion. General Motors also lost money in 1980—for the first time since 1921. Ford ended the year with a $1.2 billion deficit, as Japan outproduced and outsold the "Big Three" American auto manufacturers for the first time. A total of 200,000 American auto workers were unemployed in 1980. Perhaps the most frightening aspect of this crisis in American manufacturing was that it stemmed in part from an apparently inexorable decline in productivity. Production had grown at around 3 percent per year in the prosperous 1960s. After 1973 the rate of increase dropped to virtually zero in real dollars and lagged badly in comparison to continuing growth in economies such as Japan's and West Germany's.

Frustrated by "stagflation," Americans searched for simple solutions to it. Some, blaming the problem on escalating government budgets at all levels, responded by calling for tax reductions. In 1978 Californians voted for Proposition 13, which called for dramatic cuts in state taxes. Massachusetts residents demanded reductions in taxes, and therefore in state services, two years later. In 1981 Congress approved record tax cuts, even though these promised to add to an already record-high federal deficit. Partly because of such efforts, government employment—federal, state, and local—actually declined in 1981, for the third time in modern American history. (The others had been in the recession of 1920–21, in the depression year of 1932–33, and during demobilization in 1945–47.) But these efforts provided no answer to the insidious fall in productivity, which appeared to be caused by deeper forces, including reliance on aging plant and equipment and slow rates of spending on capital investment. Moreover, cutting taxes meant cutting often important services and adding to poverty and unemployment.

Many Americans, fearful of the economic future, acted to maximize their pleasure in the present. "It's important to maintain the quality of life," one mother with four children commented. "I'll continue to dip into savings so we can go on trips and out to dinner." A young worker added, "I may not earn much, but I'm making it count. I'm planning a trip to Central America next month. There's no point in letting money sit in the bank." An executive concluded, "we'll spend money on household furnishings that will increase in value—antiques, lamps, and rugs." Reactions such as these were not possible, of course, for the millions of Americans who lived close to the line of poverty. But they were apparently widespread among the more affluent middle classes. They reflected a sense that the economy would continue to be unsteady and that inflation would remain a permanent part of life. In such a world, they believed, old-fashioned virtues such as frugality no longer applied.

How deep was this pursuit of individual pleasure? One contemporary critic, the historian Christopher Lasch, thought it was pervasive; he said America had developed a "culture of narcissism." Other observers labeled the 1970s the "Me Decade.'' Americans, they argued, showed little interest in social reform; even the campuses remained relatively quiet. Instead, they turned to more solitary pleasures, such as jogging, which enjoyed a phenomenal rise in popularity. (James Fixx's *The Complete Book of Running* sold almost 800,000 copies in hardback between 1977 and 1979.) According to some contemporary critics, Americans became even more obsessed with sexual pleasure than ever. Alex Comfort's illustrated ''how-to'' book, *The Joy of Sex,* was a best seller, with 1 million hardback copies and 2.4 million paperback copies sold from 1972 to 1979. So were ''M's'' *The Sensuous Man* (4.5 million paperback copies sold from 1971 to 1979) and Marabel Morgan's *The Total Woman* (2.7 million copies from 1973 to 1979). In fiction, best sellers included Erich Segal's escapist *Love Story* (9.8 million paperback copies), Peter Benchley's *Jaws* (9.2 million copies), and Richard Bach's *Jonathan Livingston Seagull* (7.3 million). *Seagull* celebrated the wonders of individual freedom.

Whether such cultural signs betokened a more hedonistic or narcissistic nation was impossible to prove. (Best sellers, for instance, tend to be escapist in all periods.) Still, it seemed fair to say that middle-class Americans did not want to make major alterations in their unprecedentedly comfortable life styles. When Paul Volcker, chairman of the Federal Reserve Board, said in 1979 that the ''standard of living of the average American has to decline,'' his advice fell on hostile ears. Instead, Americans characteristically persisted in believing that some way could be found—must be found—to improve the economy. As one commentator noted, ''most Americans would say there is something that can be done about inflation. They don't know what it is, but the notion that nothing can be done— that's un-American. They think the problems can be solved, and they are mad at institutions because they're not solving them.'' In this somewhat cranky yet not despairing mood, Americans entered their third century of independence. Whether new economic frontiers yet beckoned remained an unanswered question.

POLITICS: FROM 1976 TO 1982

Political developments in any democratic nation ordinarily reflect underlying attitudes. So it seemed to be in the United States in the years from 1976 into the 1980s. Beset by economic instability, Americans alternately expected great answers from public officials, then blamed governmental institutions for ineffectiveness. This gulf between expectations and official performance led to increasing dissatisfaction with political leaders, a dissatisfaction that expressed itself by 1980 in an apparent disillusion with liberalism generally.

This dissatisfaction was apparent during the 1976 election campaign. President Ford, after barely overcoming a challenge from Governor Ronald Reagan of California for the GOP nomination, seemed doomed to defeat. Though Americans thought him an honest man (many compared him to the forthright Harry Truman), they also perceived him as Nixon's appointee and as the man who had pardoned the chief Watergate conspirator. Moreover, Ford seemed prone to politically hurtful statements, such as his remark that ''there is no Soviet domination of eastern Europe.'' As the incumbent, Ford inevitably drew criticism for the then very shaky nature of the economy. In mid-summer 1976, few observers gave him a chance in November.

Ford's challenger, however, was a virtual outsider to national politics, Jimmy Carter of Georgia. Carter was a former naval officer, a successful businessman and peanut farmer, and a former one-term governor of Georgia. He won his party's presidential nomination easily, in part because he managed to convince party members that only an outsider such as he could clean up the mess in Washington. "I will never lie to you," he told people who remembered Watergate. Avoiding substantive issues, Carter promised people a "new era of honest, compassionate, responsive government." His appeal rested also on his moderate—indeed bland—approach to issues. Democratic leaders recalled the disastrous McGovern campaign of 1972 and yearned for a candidate who was both conservative and safe. Carter, perhaps the most conservative Democratic presidential nominee since Alton Parker in 1904, appeared to fit the bill. His nomination signaled the disarray and uncertainty of liberalism by the mid-1970s.

The results of the election revealed that voters did not have much enthusiasm for either candidate. There was much talk at the time, in fact, of a "clothespin vote—hold your nose and vote for one or the other." Carter won, but in so doing lost almost all of the huge margin that he had enjoyed in mid-summer. He received only 50.1 percent of the popular vote, compared to 48 percent for Ford and 1 percent for Eugene McCarthy of Minnesota, who ran as an independent. Polls revealed that as many as 20 percent of voters made up their minds in the last week of the campaign and that only 40 percent trusted either candidate to "do the right thing most of the time." The turnout, 53 percent of eligible voters, was the lowest since 1948. It appeared that Carter won mainly because he was able to hold onto many traditional areas of Democratic strength in the North and because he regained the South. His appeal to blacks, among whom he was especially popular, was perhaps crucial to his cause.

President Carter offered a somewhat contradictory image. As a "born again" Christian who taught Sunday school classes, he appeared to represent a growing wave of evangelical Protestantism in America. At the same time, however, he was an efficient, somewhat colorless technocrat—in some ways a characteristic representative of the new South, not the old. Rejecting the aid of old Washington hands, he surrounded himself with advisers from his campaign team, mostly fellow Georgians. He presented a folksy image, appearing dressed in sweaters for TV "fireside chats" to the American people. He also ran a phone-in "talk show" of sorts from the Oval Office of the White House.

Cultivation of the art of public relations, however, could not work wonders in the long run. Indeed, the commentator Eric Sevareid noted as early as 1977 that Carter and his somewhat inbred team might lose their appeal before long. "He has the mind of an engineer," Sevareid said. "He's very bright, has an enormous capacity and is a quick study. He's got a lot of little filing cabinets in his mind that he seems able to use as needed. But he doesn't seem to have much stylistic change of pace, and I fear he will become less and less stimulating."

Sevareid's judgment proved accurate. Lacking special charisma and facing deep problems, Carter compounded his difficulties by refusing to try to cultivate amicable relations with Congress. He tended increasingly to disappoint Democratic liberals, notably Senator Ted Kennedy of Massachusetts, who demanded more resolute federal action to counter the nation's economic and social problems. For these reasons Carter did not succeed in securing passage of those few measures that he requested, such as comprehensive welfare reform that aimed to set a minimum floor under the income of most American families. During the Carter years, the Democratic Congresses also failed to reach agreement on other domestic issues, such as national health insurance (for which Carter and Kennedy offered rival plans) or energy policy. Most damaging, Carter never developed a consistent "game plan" to deal with rising unemployment and inflation. The zero-sum economy, it seemed, was at hand. By 1980 Carter faced sharp criticisms from all sides. The columnist George Will cracked, "Carter has on his desk Truman's sign, 'THE BUCK STOPS HERE.' The resemblance stops there."

Criticisms such as these, while witty, reflect a widespread tendency of Americans to blame their presidents for the assorted ills of the body politic. The reality was that the major issues defied simple solutions. Indeed, they existed in most Western democratic nations in the late 1970s and early 1980s. For all of Carter's limitations—and he was both a poor manager of Congress and an uninspiring, inconsistent leader—he came to office at a time when the presidency as an institution had been badly damaged by Vietnam and Watergate. Unlike Nixon, he could not get far by trying to wave the flag. Carter also presided over a badly divided Democratic party and over a political arena dominated by single-interest pressure groups. As the political scientist Richard Neustadt explained in 1980, "the next man's problems will be much like Carter's. Those who put their hopes on 'charismatic' leadership from the United States government, on a par with Roosevelt or Eisenhower, are just heading for disappointment."

In foreign policy Carter scored a few successes, notably the Senate's narrow ratification of a treaty with Panama in 1978. The treaty promised to turn over the Canal Zone to Panama by the year 2000. Carter also sought to regularize relations with the People's Republic of China, which was finally recognized formally in December 1978. His most notable success, or so it seemed at the time, was the Camp David accord worked out between Egypt, Israel, and the United States. This accord, for which the patient diplomacy of Carter and his top advisers was partly responsible, resulted in Egypt's recognition of Israel and in Israel's promise to turn over much of the Sinai to Egypt by 1982. Though subsequent developments (including the assassination of Egyptian leader Anwar Sadat in 1981) renewed tension in the area, thereby destroying the "spirit of Camp David," Carter's efforts were impressive at the time.

Carter, however, did not succeed in defusing the Cold War. To a limited degree his own policies prevented such a result, for he brought to his public utterances a moralistic element that broke with the *Realpolitik* of Henry Kissinger and that harmed chances for détente with the Soviet Union. In his inaugural address in 1977, the President proclaimed his "absolute commitment to human rights." "Because we are free," he added, "we can never be indifferent to the fate of freedom elsewhere." When Carter then denounced the Soviet Union for its treatment of dissidents like the nuclear physicist Andrei Sakharov, while simultaneously maintaining relatively cordial relations with repressive regimes elsewhere, he irritated Soviet leader Leonid Brezhnev. Carter nonetheless attempted to develop détente in defense policies, working for Senate ratification of SALT II, an agreement that promised to bring about some limitations on the development of nuclear weapons. The Senate,

Prime Minister Begin and Presidents Carter and Sadat enjoy a joke together after signing the Camp David Accords.

however, was suspicious of the Soviets, and delayed. The Soviets then destroyed all chances for détente by invading neighboring Afghanistan in December 1979. Outraged, Carter called the invasion the "most serious threat to world peace since World War II." He then cut off various agreements with the Soviet Union and staged an American boycott of the 1980 Olympics in Moscow. For the remainder of his administration, Soviet-American relations were cold indeed. Détente, such as it had been before 1976, perished.

Events in Iran, however, overshadowed all other aspects of America's foreign relations during the last year of Carter's presidency. Early in 1979, revolutionaries overthrew the long-standing, pro-American regime of the Shah of Iran. Amid great instability, Moslem fundamentalists loyal to the Ayatollah Ruhollah Khomeini gained control of the country. When the Shah came to the United States for treatment of cancer (which killed him in 1980), fiercely nationalistic, anti-American Iranians seized the U.S. embassy in Iran and held 52 Americans hostage. At least one of these Americans represented the CIA. The Khomeini government supported the takeover and refused to free the hostages until America pledged to keep out of Iranian affairs, to return the Shah's wealth (given an astronomical value by the Khomeini government), and to unfreeze Iranian assets. Carter refused, and later he approved a dramatic airborne expedition to free the hostages. The raid was badly conceived and proved a dismal failure. Appalled, Secretary of State Cyrus Vance resigned in protest, and the war of nerves dragged on through 1980. Finally, on the

Americans from the U.S. embassy in Tehran are held hostage by Iranian students. This photograph was taken on the day the U.S. embassy was captured by Islamic revolutionary students and clergy.

day that Carter left office in January 1981, the hostages were freed, after 444 days in captivity.

The lengthy imprisonment of the hostages deeply angered Americans at home. Frustrated by failure in Vietnam, seemingly unable to control events anywhere abroad, Americans erupted in sharp displays of xenophobia. Texans paraded with pictures of John Wayne and placards reading, "Don't buy Iranian oil." One poster read, "They can take their students and shove them up their pipeline." The *Wall Street Journal* said that Washington should "put obstreperous Iranian students on the next plane for Iran." Other Americans chafed openly at American impotence. "America today needs a tough-talking and tough-acting leader," one exclaimed. "America's strength was built on national pride and morale, and both of these have dropped under the weight of the defeat in Vietnam, the scandal of Watergate, and the catastrophic policies of Jimmy Carter." When the hostages finally came home, the nation turned out in an orgy of welcome that contrasted sharply with the neglect shown returning Vietnam veterans a few years earlier. By 1981, the stage was set for a more militaristic, anticommunist, and nationalistic foreign policy. That was the short-run legacy of the trauma of the hostages in Iran.

Reagan and the 1980s

After losing the 1980 presidential election to Ronald Reagan, Carter announced that he would "avoid any significant action for the rest of my term." A columnist responded, "this is ironic . . . he has been doing just that since 1977."

President and Mrs. Reagan leaving White House for inaugural balls. The Reagans' enthusiasm for the symbols of wealth contributed to the President's reputation as someone who was sympathetic to the rich, and heartless toward the poor.

Though unfair, this response helps explain the decisive victory of Reagan in that election. On the surface a stunning triumph for the Republican party (which even regained control of the Senate for the first time since 1954), and for conservatism generally, the election can more simply be explained as a repudiation of Carter and the Democrats. Americans, personalizing their foreign and domestic problems, took out their frustrations on the man, and the party, that had occupied the White House for four years of economic stagnation and overseas frustrations. That interpretation was the view of many political scientists, who stressed the ability of Reagan, a consummate media politician, to exploit Democratic failures and who rejected the GOP claim that the election represented a "sea change" in public sentiment. They showed that there was no increase in the number of voters identifying themselves as Republicans and no party realignment. Though Reagan won a large margin in the electoral college, he captured only 51 percent of the voters, 3 percent more than Ford had in 1976. Carter got 41 percent, John Anderson, an independent, got 6.6 percent, and eighteen other candidates divided the remainder among themselves. The election of 1980, like many since the early 1960s, seemed to reflect widespread distrust of both parties. It exposed anew the unreal expectations of people who at once suspected that politicians could do little and yet blamed them when they didn't do much.

As if to confound these pessimists, Reagan took office with a flurry of activity, especially in domestic policy. Affable, politically astute, the President showed remarkable command over Congress, including the nominally Democratic House of Representatives. During the 1981 session Congress cut more than $35 billion from domestic programs, including medicaid, medicare, welfare, and food stamps. Most of these cuts threatened to harm those most in need and thereby occasioned loud but futile protests from liberals. Congress, going further than Reagan had requested, also enacted an enormous tax cut totaling at least $750 billion over the next five years. Though it refused to consider Reagan's request for major cuts in social security, it did his bidding by increasing spending for defense. More than any president since Lyndon Johnson before 1966, Reagan succeeded in outlining and securing passage of significant changes in domestic spending priorities. Commentators began likening Reagan's impact on government to FDR's, his popularity to Eisenhower's. There was talk of a "Reagan Revolution." His performance, said the writer Jeff Fishel, was "virtually unparalleled in the modern presidency."

These actions marked Reagan as decidedly conservative in temper. That was no surprise, for Reagan had campaigned as a political conservative who believed that domestic programs cost too much, and as a friend of the military, whose needs he ardently supported. Reagan, however, proved shrewd enough not to ally himself too closely with the "New Right," a loose confederation of increasingly assertive pressure groups that opposed the ERA, abortion, welfare, busing of blacks to schools, and modernist religion. They demanded tough measures against criminals, curbs on the "liberal" Supreme Court, and confrontation policies against the Soviet Union. Many of the New Right wished to impose their own brands of Protestant fundamentalism on the country. During the campaign Reagan had benefited from the support of such groups, but in 1981 he deflected sensitive issues such as abortion and school prayers from the political arena. He even went so far as to appoint Sandra Day O'Connor, an Arizona judge who had earlier supported a law legalizing abortion, as the nation's first female Supreme Court justice. Frustrated, advocates of the New Right regrouped for future battles.

By 1982, however, it seemed clear that Reagan's economic policies were not working. The combination of tax cuts and increased military expenditures merely increased already staggeringly high budgetary deficits, projected at $100 billion a year for 1982–83 and more thereafter. These deficits, along with conservative monetary policies, kept interest rates high and discouraged investment. Conservative businessmen, souring on Reaganomics, grumbled that deficits were ruining the country. The economy continued to stagnate, and inflation, while a little less severe than during the 1970s, remained a divisive and intractable problem.

Confessing failure, David Stockman, Reagan's influential director of management and budget, blurted in late 1981 that "none of us really understands what's going on with all these numbers. You've got so many budgets out and so many different baselines and such complexity." He complained especially of the power of special-interest groups able to get their way in Congress. The tax cuts grew huge, he said, because "they got so goddamned greedy that they got themselves strung way out there on a limb." He concluded, "I have a new theory—there are no *real* conservatives in Congress."

Reagan's foreign policies took a back seat in 1981 compared to domestic concerns. Congress authorized large military expenditures with little debate and narrowly approved the sale of sophisticated radar planes to Saudi Arabia, thereby irritating the Israelis. But Reagan, like his predecessors, found that he could not impose America's will on the world. Though he talked tough with the Soviet Union, thereby scrapping SALT II for all practical purposes, it was beyond American capacity to prevent a harsher military regime from taking over in Poland in late 1981. Nor could he shout the Soviets out of Afghanistan, where Russian troops still remained in 1982. Reagan also could not prevent the renewed escalation of tensions in the Middle East, especially after Israeli Prime Minister Menachem Begin engineered the annexation of the Golan Heights in 1981, and invaded Lebanon, sanctuary for enemy forces of the PLO, in 1982.

Many observers worried about the apparent bellicosity of the Reagan administration, whose policies deeply alarmed western European nations. Critics complained also about the inarticulateness of his foreign policies. This stemmed in part from Reagan's inexperience in this area, and in part from open fighting between his Secretary of State, Alexander Haig, and Reagan's White House staff, and other top officials. Haig, increasingly out of step with such rivals, resigned in 1982.

The hawkish stance of the Reagan administration in Latin America especially worried some of his critics by 1982. Among the many tense regions there was El Salvador, which was racked by guerilla war. The president in early 1982, José Napolean Duarte, claimed to be less repressive than the military men who had preceded him in power, and the Reagan government attempted to provide him with substantial military aid in his struggle against leftist guerillas. If El Salvador fell to Marxists, Reagan believed, a "domino" effect might threaten Central America. But the Duarte government proved unwilling or unable to stop its own forces from killing thousands of civilians. As the battle wore on, some Americans feared that the United States might be stumbling into another Vietnam. Others were simply torn. "If we turn down additional aid [to Duarte], one Senator remarked, "we could be helping the Communist guerilla takeover of the country. But on the other hand, we'd be aiding a government we're not happy with. The bottom line is, which is the lesser of two evils?" This dilemma, painfully familiar in the era of Pax Americana, was certain to persist as long as American governments considered it in the national interest to stop left-wing activities, real or perceived, in many nations throughout the world.

Unshaken by such worries, the Reagan administration in 1982 hewed to its earlier course of attempting to cut back on social programs benefitting the poor while increasing the military budget. His budget message for fiscal 1983 therefore outraged liberals. It also alarmed many economic conservatives, for Reagan, once the apostle of balanced budgets, estimated a federal deficit of $91.5 billion, only slightly less than the one for fiscal 1982. Some observers, notably the nonpartisan Congressional Budget Office, said that the actual deficit for fiscal 1983 would be much higher—around $157 billion. Other observers noted that while the rate of inflation might subside a little, unemployment, which was nearly 10 percent and involved perhaps 10 million people, was expected to remain at high levels for at least the next few years. Whether Reaganomics could succeed remained very questionable.

Though these events eroded some of Reagan's great personal popularity, liberals did not seem ready to wage an effective counterattack. The domestic programs and economic policies of the Democratic administrations since 1960 had not, after all, worked wonders. Many people thought they had hastened inflation and created built-in federal deficits of unprecedented magnitude. Moreover, the record of earlier Democratic presidents was stained by revelations in 1982 that FDR had secretly taped press conferences in 1940, probably from a microphone concealed in his Oval Office desk lamp. Not to be outdone, President Kennedy had secretly taped some 600 White House meetings between June 1962 and November 1963. Whatever these tapes might reveal (Kennedy's remained unavailable to researchers), it was clear that wiretapping and secretive behavior were not the exclusive preserve of Richard Nixon. The American presidency, one of the most powerful offices in the world, was obviously a deeply troubled, and troublesome, institution. Whether it could be harnessed in ways that could help revive the uncertain economy and act as a reliable agent for peace were matters of deep concern not only to Americans but to billions of people throughout the world.

Suggestions for reading

Useful starting places for the politics of the Nixon era include Jonathan Schell, *Time of Illusion* (1976); Godfrey Hodgson, *America in Our Time* (1976); and Otis Graham, Jr., *Toward a Planned Society: From Roosevelt to Nixon* (1976). Studies of policy include Henry Aaron, *Politics and the Professors* (1978); and James T. Patterson, *America's Struggle Against Poverty, 1900–1980* (1981). For political trends in the late 1970s, see James Duffy, *Domestic Affairs: American Programs and Problems* (1979); Haynes Johnson, *In the Absence of Power* (1980), on the Carter administration; and Peter Steinfels, *The Neoconservatives* (1979). Books on Richard Nixon include Earl Mazo and Stephen Hess, *Nixon: A Political Portrait** (1968); Jules Witcover, *The Resurrection of Richard Nixon* (1970), which covers the years 1960–68; and Gary Wills, *Nixon Agonistes** (1970). Other books that deal with politics and policies of the 1970s are Leonard Silk, *Nixonomics** (1972); Jules Witcover, *White Knight: The Rise of Spiro Agnew* (1972); Robert S. Ansom, *McGovern* (1972); and Daniel Moynihan, *Politics of a Guaranteed National Income** (1973).

Important books on political trends include Walter Dean Burnham, *Critical Elections and the Mainsprings of American Politics** (1972), a stimulating analysis of twentieth-century developments; Walter De Vries and V. L. Torrance, *The Ticket Splitters* (1972); Samuel Lubell, *The Hidden Crisis in American Politics** (1970); Frederick G. Dutton, *The Changing Sources of Power* (1971); and David S. Broder, *The Party's Over** (1972). See also Theodore White, *Making of a President, 1972** (1973); Kevin Phillips, *The Emerging Republican Majority** (1969); and Richard Scammon and Ben Wattenberg, *The Real Majority** (1970). Among the books on Watergate are Carl Bernstein and Bob Woodward, *All the President's Men** (1974), a devastating account by two *Washington Post* reporters; and Raoul Berger, *Impeachment: The Constitutional Problems* (1974).

Sources for foreign policy include Henry Brandon, *The Retreat of American Power*

(1973); David Landau, *Kissinger* (1972); R. W. Tucker, *The Radical Left and American Foreign Policy** (1971); and Arthur Schlesinger, Jr., *The Imperial Presidency* (1973), which narrates the impact of foreign policy on the executive branch. See also V. Brodine and Mark Seldon, eds., *Open Secret: The Nixon-Kissinger Doctrine in Asia* (1972); Lloyd Gardner, ed., *The Great Nixon Turnaround* (1973); Morton Halperin, *Defense Strategies for the Seventies* (1971); Leonard Mosley, *Power Play* (1973), on oil companies in the Middle East; and Adam Yarmolinsky, *The Military Establishment: Its Impact on American Society* (1971).

Domestic unrest in the 1970s is the subject of many books, including J. A. Michener, *Kent State: What Happened and Why* (1973); I. F. Stone, *Killings at Kent State* (1971); George Jackson, *Soledad Brother: The Prison Letters of George Jackson* (1970); Tom Wicker, *A Time to Die* (1975), on the Attica riot; Ramsey Clark, *Crime in America* (1970); and Robert C. Wood, *The Necessary Majority: Middle America and the Urban Crisis* (1972). An important book dealing with the growth of corporate power is J. K. Galbraith, *The New Industrial State** (1971). Books dealing with social and economic trends include Andrew Levison, *Working Class Majority* (1974); Charles Silberman, *Criminal Violence, Criminal Justice* (1978); Orlando Patterson, *Ethnic Chauvinism* (1977); and Albert Camarillo, *Chicanos in a Changing Society* (1979). Differing accounts of American culture in the 1970s include Daniel Bell, *The Cultural Contradictions of Capitalism* (1976); and Christopher Lasch, *The Culture of Narcissism* (1979).

Among the books that focus on environmental issues are Paul Erlich, *Population Bomb** (1968); Barry Commoner, *The Closing Circle** (1971); Garrett De Bell, ed., *The Environmental Handbook* (1970); and R. F. Buckhorn, *Nader: The People's Lawyer* (1972). See also Emma Rothschild. *Paradise Lost: The Decline of the Auto-Industrial Age* (1973).

Unrest among American Indians is the subject of: A. M. Josephy, ed., *Red Power** (1971); Stan Steiner, *The New Indians** (1968); and Sar Levitan and Barbara Hetrick, *Big Brother's Indian Programs** (1971).

The Constitution
of the
United States
of America

We the people of the United States, in Order to form a more perfect Union, establish Justice, insure domestic Tranquility, provide for the common defence, promote the general Welfare, and secure the Blessings of Liberty to ourselves and our Posterity, do ordain and establish this Constitution for the United States of America.

ARTICLE I

Section 1. All legislative Powers herein granted shall be vested in a Congress of the United States, which shall consist of a Senate and House of Representatives.

Section 2. The House of Representatives shall be composed of Members chosen every second Year by the People of the several States, and the Electors in each State shall have the Qualifications requisite for Electors of the most numerous Branch of the State Legislature.

No Person shall be a Representative who shall not have attained to the Age of twenty-five Years, and been seven Years a Citizen of the United States, and who shall not, when elected, be an Inhabitant of that state in which he shall be chosen.

The Constitution and all amendments are shown in their original form. Parts that have been amended or superseded are bracketed and explained in the footnotes.

[Representatives and direct Taxes shall be apportioned among the several States which may be included within this Union, according to their respective Numbers, which shall be determined by adding to the whole Number of free Persons, including those bound to Service for a Term of Years, and excluding Indians not taxed, three fifths of all other Persons.][1] The actual Enumeration shall be made within three Years after the first Meeting of the Congress of the United States, and within every subsequent Term of ten Years, in such Manner as they shall by Law direct. The Number of Representatives shall not exceed one for every thirty Thousand, but each State shall have at Least one Representative; and until such enumeration shall be made, the State of New Hampshire shall be entitled to chuse three,

[1] Modified by the Fourteenth and Sixteenth amendments.

Massachusetts eight, Rhode Island and Providence Plantations one, Connecticut five, New-York six, New Jersey four, Pennsylvania eight, Delaware one, Maryland six, Virginia ten, North Carolina five, South Carolina five, and Georgia three.

When vacancies happen in the Representation from any State, the Executive Authority thereof shall issue Writs of Election to fill such Vacancies.

The House of Representatives shall chuse their Speaker and other Officers; and shall have the sole Power of Impeachment.

Section 3. The Senate of the United States shall be composed of two Senators from each State, [chosen by the Legislature thereof,][2] for six Years; and each Senator shall have one Vote.

Immediately after they shall be assembled in Consequence of the first Election, they shall be divided as equally as may be into three Classes. The Seats of the Senators of the first Class shall be vacated at the Expiration of the second Year, of the Second Class at the Expiration of the fourth Year, and of the third Class at the Expiration of the sixth Year, so that one-third may be chosen every second Year; [and if Vacancies happen by Resignation, or otherwise, during the Recess of the Legislature of any State, the Executive thereof may make temporary Appointments until the next Meeting of the Legislature, which shall then fill such Vacancies].[3]

No Person shall be a Senator who shall not have attained to the Age of thirty Years, and been nine Years a Citizen of the United States, and who shall not, when elected, be an Inhabitant of that State in which he shall be chosen.

The Vice-President of the United States shall be President of the Senate, but shall have no vote, unless they be equally divided.

The Senate shall chuse their other Officers, and also a President pro tempore, in the absence of the Vice-President, or when he shall exercise the Office of the President of the United States.

The Senate shall have the sole Power to try all Impeachments. When sitting for that purpose, they shall be on Oath or Affirmation. When the President of the United States is tried, the Chief Justice shall preside. And no person shall be convicted without the Concurrence of two thirds of the Members present.

Judgment in Cases of Impeachment shall not extend further than to removal from Office, and disqualification to hold and enjoy any Office of honor, Trust, or Profit under the United States: but the Party convicted shall nevertheless be liable and subject to Indictment, Trial, Judgment, and Punishment, according to Law.

Section 4. The Times, Places and Manner of holding Elections for Senators and Representatives, shall be prescribed in each state by the Legislature thereof; but the Congress may at any time by Law make or alter such Regulations, except as to the Places of Chusing Senators.

The Congress shall assemble at least once in every Year, and such Meeting shall [be on the first Monday in December,][4] unless they shall by Law appoint a different Day.

Section 5. Each House shall be the Judge of the Elections, Returns and Qualifications of its own Members, and a Majority of each shall constitute a Quorum to do Business; but a smaller number may adjourn from day to day, and may be authorized to compel the Attendance of absent Members, in such Manner, and under such Penalties, as each House may provide.

Each House may determine the Rules of its Proceedings, punish its Members for disorderly Behavior, and, with the Concurrence of two thirds, expel a Member.

Each House shall keep a Journal of its Proceedings, and from time to time publish the same, excepting such Parts as may in their Judgment require Secrecy; and the Yeas and Nays of the Members of either House on any question shall, at the Desire of one fifth of those Present, be entered on the Journal.

Neither House, during the Session of Congress, shall, without the Consent of the other, adjourn for more than three days, nor to any other Place than that in which the two Houses shall be sitting.

Section 6. The Senators and Representatives shall receive a Compensation for their Services, to be ascertained by Law, and paid out of the Treasury of the United States. They shall in all

[2] Superseded by the Seventeenth Amendment.
[3] Modified by the Seventeenth Amendment.

[4] Superseded by the Twentieth Amendment.

Cases, except Treason, Felony, and Breach of the Peace, be privileged from Arrest during their Attendance at the Session of their respective Houses, and in going to and returning from the same; and for any Speech or Debate in either House, they shall not be questioned in any other Place.

No Senator or Representative shall, during the Time for which he was elected, be appointed to any civil Office under the Authority of the United States, which shall have been created, or the Emoluments whereof shall have been increased, during such time; and no Person holding any Office under the United States shall be a Member of either House during his continuance in Office.

Section 7. All Bills for raising Revenue shall originate in the House of Representatives; but the Senate may propose or concur with Amendments as on other bills.

Every Bill which shall have passed the House of Representatives and the Senate, shall, before it becomes a Law, be presented to the President of the United States; If he approve he shall sign it, but if not he shall return it, with his Objections, to that House in which it shall have originated, who shall enter the Objections at large on their Journal, and proceed to reconsider it. If after such Reconsideration two thirds of that House shall agree to pass the bill, it shall be sent, together with the objections, to the other House, by which it shall likewise be reconsidered, and if approved by two thirds of that House, it shall become a Law. But in all such Cases the Votes of both Houses shall be determined by Yeas and Nays, and the names of the Persons voting for and against the Bill shall be entered on the Journal of each House respectively. If any Bill shall not be returned by the President within ten Days (Sundays excepted) after it shall have been presented to him, the Same shall be a Law, in like Manner as if he had signed it, unless the Congress by their Adjournment prevent its Return, in which Case it shall not be a Law.

Every Order, Resolution, or Vote to which the Concurrence of the Senate and House of Representatives may be necessary (except on a question of Adjournment) shall be presented to the President of the United States; and before the Same shall take Effect, shall be approved by him, or being disapproved by him, shall be repassed by two thirds of the Senate and House of Representatives, according to the Rules and Limitations prescribed in the Case of a Bill.

Section 8. The Congress shall have Power To Lay and collect Taxes, Duties, Imposts and Excises, to pay the Debts and provide for the common Defence and general Welfare of the United States; but all Duties, Imposts and Excises shall be uniform throughout the United States;

To borrow money on the credit of the United States;

To regulate Commerce with foreign Nations, and among the several States, and with the Indian Tribes;

To establish an uniform Rule of Naturalization, and uniform Laws on the subject of Bankruptcies throughout the United States;

To coin Money, regulate the Value thereof, and of foreign Coin, and fix the Standard of Weights and Measures;

To Provide for the Punishment of counterfeiting the Securities and current Coin of the United States;

To establish Post Offices and post Roads;

To promote the Progress of Science and useful Arts, by securing for limited Times to Authors and Inventors the exclusive Right to their respective Writings and Discoveries;

To constitute Tribunals inferior to the Supreme Court;

To define and punish Piracies and Felonies committed on the high Seas, and Offenses against the Law of Nations;

To declare War, grant Letters of Marque and Reprisal, and make Rules concerning Captures on Land and Water;

To raise and support Armies, but no Appropriation of Money to that Use shall be for a longer Term than two Years;

To provide and maintain a Navy;

To make Rules for the Government and Regulation of the land and naval forces;

To provide for calling forth the Militia to execute the Laws of the Union, suppress Insurrections and repel Invasions;

To provide for organizing, arming, and disciplining the Militia, and for governing such Part of them as may be employed in the Service of the United States, reserving to the States respectively, the Appointment of the Officers, and the

Authority of training the Militia according to the discipline prescribed by Congress;

To exercise exclusive Legislation in all Cases whatsoever, over such District (not exceeding ten Miles square) as may, by Cession of particular States, and the acceptance of Congress, become the Seat of the Government of the United States, and to exercise like Authority over all Places purchased by the Consent of the Legislature of the State in which the Same shall be, for the Erection of Forts, Magazines, Arsenals, dock-Yards, and other needful Buildings;—And

To make all Laws which shall be necessary and proper for carrying into Execution the foregoing Powers, and all other Powers vested by this Constitution in the Government of the United States, or in any Department or Officer thereof.

Section 9. The Migration or Importation of such Persons as any of the States now existing shall think proper to admit shall not be prohibited by the Congress prior to the Year one thousand eight hundred and eight, but a tax or duty may be imposed on such Importation, not exceeding ten dollars for each Person.

The privilege of the Writ of Habeas Corpus shall not be suspended, unless when in Cases of Rebellion or Invasion the public Safety may require it.

No Bill of Attainder or ex post facto Law shall be passed.

[No capitation, or other direct, Tax shall be laid unless in Proportion to the Census or Enumeration herein before directed to be taken.][5]

No Tax or Duty shall be laid on Articles exported from any State.

No Preference shall be given by any Regulation of Revenue to the Ports of one State over those of another: nor shall Vessels bound to, or from, one State, be obliged to enter, clear, or pay Duties in another.

No Money shall be drawn from the Treasury, but in Consequence of Appropriations made by Law; and a regular Statement and Account of the Receipts and Expenditures of all public Money shall be published from time to time.

No Title of Nobility shall be granted by the United States: And no Person holding any Office of Profit or Trust under them, shall, without the

[5] Modified by the Sixteenth Amendment.

Consent of the Congress, accept of any present, Emolument, Office, or Title, of any kind whatever, from any King, Prince, or foreign State.

Section 10. No State shall enter into any Treaty, Alliance, or Confederation; grant Letters of Marque and Reprisal; coin Money; emit Bills of Credit; make any Thing but gold and silver Coin a Tender in Payment of Debts; pass any Bill of Attainder, ex post facto Law, or Law impairing the Obligation of Contracts, or grant any title of Nobility.

No State shall, without the Consent of the Congress, lay any Imposts or Duties on Imports or Exports, except what may be absolutely necessary for executing its inspection Laws: and the net Produce of all Duties and Imposts, laid by any State on Imports or Exports, shall be for the Use of the Treasury of the United States; and all such Laws shall be subject to the Revision and Control of the Congress.

No State shall, without the Consent of Congress, lay any duty of Tonnage, keep Troops, or Ships of War in time of Peace, enter into any Agreement or Compact with another State, or with a foreign Power, or engage in War, unless actually invaded, or in such imminent Danger as will not admit of delay.

ARTICLE II

Section 1. The executive Power shall be vested in a President of the United States of America. He shall hold his Office during the Term of four years, and, together with the Vice-President, chosen for the same Term, be elected, as follows:

Each State shall appoint, in such Manner as the Legislature thereof may direct, a Number of Electors, equal to the whole Number of Senators and Representatives to which the State may be entitled in the Congress: but no Senator or Representative, or Person holding an Office of Trust or Profit under the United States, shall be appointed an Elector.

[The Electors shall meet in their respective States, and vote by Ballot for two persons, of whom one at least shall not be an Inhabitant of the same State with themselves. And they shall make a List of all the Persons voted for, and of the Number of Votes for each; which List they shall sign and certify, and transmit sealed to the Seat of the Government of the United States, directed to the President of the Senate. The President of the Senate shall, in the Presence of the Senate and House of Representatives, open all the Certificates, and the Votes shall then be counted. The Person having the greatest Number of Votes shall be the President, if such Number be a Majority of the whole Number of Electors appointed; and if there be more than one who have such Majority, and have an equal Number of Votes, then the House of Representatives shall immediately chuse by Ballot one of them for President; and if no Person have a Majority, then from the five highest on the List the said House shall in like Manner chuse the President. But in chusing the President, the Votes shall be taken by States, the Representation from each State having one Vote; a quorum for this Purpose shall consist of a Member or Members from two-thirds of the States, and a Majority of all the States shall be necessary to a Choice. In every Case, after the Choice of the President, the Person having the greatest Number of Votes of the Electors shall be the Vice-President. But if there should remain two or more who have equal votes, the Senate shall chuse from them by Ballot the Vice-President.][6]

The Congress may determine the Time of chusing the Electors, and the Day on which they shall give their Votes; which Day shall be the same throughout the United States.

No person except a natural-born Citizen, or a Citizen of the United States, at the time of the Adoption of this Constitution, shall be eligible to the Office of President; neither shall any Person be eligible to that Office who shall not have attained to the Age of thirty-five years, and been fourteen Years a Resident within the United States.

[In Case of the Removal of the President from Office, or of his Death, Resignation, or Inability to discharge the Powers and Duties of the said Office, the same shall devolve on the Vice-President, and the Congress may by Law provide for the Case of Removal, Death, Resignation, or Inability, both of the President and Vice-President, declaring what Officer shall then act as President, and such Officer shall act accordingly, until the disability be removed, or a President shall be elected.][7]

The President shall, at stated Times, receive for his Services a Compensation, which shall neither be increased nor diminished during the Period for which he shall have been elected, and he shall not receive within that Period any other Emolument from the United States, or any of them.

Before he enter on the execution of his Office, he shall take the following Oath or Affirmation:—''I do solemnly swear (or affirm) that I will faithfully execute the Office of President of the United States, and will, to the best of my Ability, preserve, protect, and defend the Constitution of the United States.''

Section 2. The President shall be Commander in Chief of the Army and Navy of the United States, and of the Militia of the several States, when called into the actual Service of the United States; he may require the Opinion, in writing, of the principal Officer in each of the executive Departments, upon any subject relating to the Duties of their respective Offices, and he shall have Power to Grant Reprieves and Pardons for Offenses against the United States, except in Cases of Impeachment.

He shall have Power, by and with the Advice and Consent of the Senate, to make Treaties, provided two thirds of the Senators present concur; and he shall nominate, and by and with the Advice and Consent of the Senate, shall appoint Ambassadors, other public Ministers and Consuls, Judges of the supreme Court, and all other Officers of the United States, whose Appointments are not herein otherwise provided for, and which shall be established by Law: but the Congress may by Law vest the Appointment of such inferior Officers, as they think proper, in the President alone, in the Courts of Law, or in the Heads of Departments.

The President shall have Power to fill up all Vacancies that may happen during the Recess of the Senate, by granting Commissions which shall expire at the End of their next Session.

Section 3. He shall from time to time give to the Congress Information of the State of the

---

[6] Superseded by the Twelfth Amendment.

[7] Modified by the Twenty-fifth Amendment.

Union, and recommend to their Consideration such Measures as he shall judge necessary and expedient; he may, on extraordinary occasions, convene both Houses, or either of them, and in Case of Disagreement between them, with respect to the Time of Adjournment, he may adjourn them to such Time as he shall think proper; he shall receive Ambassadors and other public Ministers; he shall take Care that the Laws be faithfully executed, and shall Commission all the Officers of the United States.

Section 4. The President, Vice-President and all civil Officers of the United States, shall be removed from Office on Impeachment for, and Conviction of, Treason, Bribery, or other high Crimes and Misdemeanors.

ARTICLE III

Section 1. The judicial Power of the United States, shall be vested in one supreme Court, and in such inferior Courts as the Congress may from time to time ordain and establish. The Judges, both of the supreme and inferior Courts, shall hold their Offices during good Behaviour, and shall, at stated Times, receive for their Services, a Compensation, which shall not be diminished during their Continuance in Office.

Section 2. The judicial Power shall extend to all Cases, in Law and Equity, arising under this Constitution, the Laws of the United States, and treaties made, or which shall be made, under their Authority;—to all Cases affecting ambassadors, other public ministers and consuls;—to all cases of admiralty and maritime Jurisdiction;—to Controversies to which the United States shall be a Party;—to Controversies between two or more States;—[between a State and Citizens of another State;]—between Citizens of different States,— between Citizens of the same State claiming Lands under Grants of different States, and between a State, or the Citizens thereof, and foreign States, Citizens or Subjects.

In all Cases affecting Ambassadors, other public Ministers and Consuls, and those in which a State shall be Party, the supreme Court shall have original Jurisdiction. In all the other Cases before mentioned, the supreme Court shall have appellate Jurisdiction, both as to Law and Fact, with such Exceptions, and under such Regulations as the Congress shall make.

The trial of all Crimes, except in Cases of Impeachment, shall be by Jury; and such Trial shall be held in the State where the said Crimes shall have been committed; but when not committed within any State, the Trial shall be at such Place or Places as the Congress may by Law have directed.

Section 3. Treason against the United States, shall consist only in levying War against them, or in adhering to their Enemies, giving them Aid and Comfort. No Person shall be convicted of Treason unless on the Testimony of two Witnesses to the same overt Act, or on Confession in open Court.

The Congress shall have power to declare the Punishment of Treason but no Attainder of Treason shall work Corruption of Blood, or Forfeiture except during the Life of the Person attainted.

ARTICLE IV

Section 1. Full Faith and Credit shall be given in each State to the public Acts, Records, and judicial Proceedings of every other State. And the Congress may by general Laws prescribe the Manner in which such Acts, Records and Proceedings shall be proved, and the Effect thereof.

Section 2. The Citizens of each State shall be entitled to all Privileges and Immunities of Citizens in the several States.

A Person charged in any State with Treason, Felony, or other Crime, who shall flee from Justice, and be found in another State, shall on demand of the executive Authority of the State from which he fled, be delivered up, to be removed to the State having Jurisdiction of the crime.

[No Person held to service or Labour in one State, under the Laws thereof, escaping into another, shall, in Consequence of any Law or Regulation therein, be discharged from such Service or Labour, but shall be delivered up on Claim of the Party to whom such Service or Labour may be due.][9]

Section 3. New States may be admitted by the Congress into this Union; but no new State shall be formed or erected within the Jurisdiction of any other State; nor any State be formed by the Junction of two or more States, or parts of States,

[8] Modified by the Eleventh Amendment.
[9] Superseded by the Thirteenth Amendment.

without the Consent of the Legislatures of the States concerned as well as of the Congress.

The Congress shall have Power to dispose of and make all needful Rules and Regulations respecting the Territory or other Property belonging to the United States; and nothing in this Constitution shall be so construed as to Prejudice any Claims of the United States, or of any particular State.

Section 4. The United States shall guarantee to every State in this Union a Republican Form of Government and shall protect each of them against Invasion; and on Application of the Legislature, or of the Executive (when the Legislature cannot be convened) against domestic Violence.

ARTICLE V

The Congress, whenever two-thirds of both Houses shall deem it necessary, shall propose Amendments to this Constitution, or, on the Application of the Legislatures of two-thirds of the several States, shall call a Convention for proposing Amendments, which, in either Case, shall be valid to all Intents and Purposes, as part of this Constitution, when ratified by the Legislatures of three-fourths of the several States, or by Conventions in three-fourths thereof, as the one or the other Mode of Ratification may be proposed by the Congress; Provided that no Amendment which may be made prior to the Year One thousand eight hundred and eight shall in any Manner affect the first and fourth Clauses in the Ninth Section of the first Article; and that no State, without its Consent, shall be deprived of its equal Suffrage in the Senate.

ARTICLE VI

All Debts contracted and Engagements entered into, before the Adoption of this Constitution, shall be as valid against the United States under this Constitution as under the Confederation.

This Constitution, and the Laws of the United States which shall be made in Pursuance thereof; and all Treaties made, or which shall be made, under the Authority of the United States, shall be the supreme Law of the Land; and the Judges in every State shall be bound thereby, any Thing in the Constitution or Laws of any State to the Contrary notwithstanding.

The Senators and Representatives before mentioned, and the Members of the several State Legislatures, and all executive and judicial Officers, both of the United States and of the several States, shall be bound by Oath or Affirmation to support this Constitution; but no religious Test shall ever be required as a qualification to any Office or public Trust under the United States.

ARTICLE VII

The Ratification of the Conventions of nine States shall be sufficient for the Establishment of this Constitution between the States so ratifying the same.

Done in Convention by the Unanimous Consent of the States present the Seventeenth Day of September in the Year of our Lord one thousand seven hundred and Eighty seven, and of the Independence of the United States of America the Twelfth. In Witness whereof We have hereunto subscribed our Names.

Articles in Addition to, and Amendment of, the Constitution of the United States of America, Proposed by Congress, and Ratified by the Legislatures of the Several States, Pursuant to the Fifth Article of the Original Constitution.

AMENDMENT I[10]

Congress shall make no law respecting an establishment of religion, or prohibiting the free exercise thereof; or abridging the freedom of speech, or of the press; or the right of the people peaceably to assemble, and to petition the Government for a redress of grievances.

AMENDMENT II

A well regulated Militia, being necessary to the security of a free State, the right of the people to keep and bear Arms shall not be infringed.

AMENDMENT III

No Soldier shall, in time of peace, be quartered in any house, without the consent of the Owner, nor in time of war, but in a manner to be prescribed by law.

[10] The first ten amendments were passed by Congress September 25, 1789. They were ratified by three-fourths of the states December 15, 1791.

AMENDMENT IV

The right of the people to be secure in their persons, houses, papers, and effects, against unreasonable searches and seizures, shall not be violated, and no Warrants shall issue, but upon probable cause, supported by Oath or affirmation, and particularly describing the place to be searched, and the persons or things to be seized.

AMENDMENT V

No person shall be held to answer for a capital or otherwise infamous crime, unless on a presentment or indictment of a Grand Jury, except in cases arising in the land or naval forces, or in the Militia, when in actual service in time of War or public danger; nor shall any person be subject for the same offence to be twice put in jeopardy of life or limb; nor shall be compelled in any criminal case to be a witness against himself, nor be deprived of life, liberty, or property, without due process of law; nor shall private property be taken for public use, without just compensation.

AMENDMENT VI

In all criminal prosecutions, the accused shall enjoy the right to a speedy and public trial, by an impartial jury of the State and district wherein the crime shall have been committed, which district shall have been previously ascertained by law, and to be informed of the nature and cause of the accusation; to be confronted with the witnesses against him; to have compulsory process for obtaining witnesses in his favor, and to have the Assistance of Counsel for his defence.

AMENDMENT VII

In suits at common law, where the value in controversy shall exceed twenty dollars, the right of trial by jury shall be preserved, and no fact tried by a jury, shall be otherwise reexamined in any Court of the United States, than according to the rules of the common law.

AMENDMENT VIII

Excessive bail shall not be required, nor excessive fines imposed, nor cruel and unusual punishments inflicted.

AMENDMENT IX

The enumeration in the Constitution, of certain rights, shall not be construed to deny or disparage others retained by the people.

AMENDMENT X

The powers not delegated to the United States by the Constitution, nor prohibited by it to the States, are reserved to the States respectively, or to the people.

AMENDMENT XI (1798)[11]

The Judicial power of the United States shall not be construed to extend to any suit in law or equity, commenced or prosecuted against one of the United States by Citizens of another State, or by Citizens or Subjects of any Foreign State.

AMENDMENT XII (1804)

The Electors shall meet in their respective States and vote by ballot for President and Vice-President, one of whom, at least, shall not be an inhabitant of the same State with themselves; they shall name in their ballots the person voted for as President, and in distinct ballots the person voted for as Vice-President, and they shall make distinct lists of all persons voted for as President, and of all persons voted for as Vice-President, and of the number of votes for each, which lists they shall sign and certify, and transmit sealed to the seat of the government of the United States, directed to the President of Senate;—The President of the Senate shall, in the presence of the Senate and House of Representatives, open all the certificates and the votes shall then be counted;—The person having the greatest number of votes for President, shall be the President, if such number be a majority of the whole number of Electors appointed; and if no person have such majority, then from the persons having the highest numbers not exceeding three on the list of those voted for as President, the House of Representatives shall choose immediately, by ballot, the President. But in choosing the President, the votes shall be taken by states, the representation from each state having one vote; a quorum for this purpose shall consist of a member or members from two-thirds of the states, and a majority of all the states shall be

[11] Date of ratification.

necessary to a choice. [And if the House of Representatives shall not choose a President whenever the right of choice shall devolve upon them, before the fourth day of March next following, then the Vice-President shall act as President, as in the case of the death or other constitutional disability of the President.][12]—The person having the greatest number of votes as Vice-President, shall be the Vice-President, if such number be a majority of the whole number of Electors appointed, and if no person have a majority, then from the two highest numbers on the list, the Senate shall choose the Vice-President; a quorum for the purpose shall consist of two-thirds of the whole number of Senators, and a majority of the whole number shall be necessary to a choice. But no person constitutionally ineligible to the office of President shall be eligible to that of Vice-President of the United States.

AMENDMENT XIII (1865)

Section 1. Neither slavery nor involuntary servitude, except as a punishment for crime whereof the party shall have been duly convicted, shall exist within the United States, or any place subject to their jurisdiction.

Section 2. Congress shall have power to enforce this article by appropriate legislation.

AMENDMENT XIV (1868)

Section 1. All persons born or naturalized in the United States, and subject to the jurisdiction thereof, are citizens of the United States and of the State wherein they reside. No State shall make or enforce any law which shall abridge the privileges or immunities of citizens of the United States; nor shall any State deprive any person of life, liberty, or property, without due process of law; nor deny to any person within its jurisdiction the equal protection of the laws.

Section 2. Representatives shall be apportioned among the several States according to their respective numbers, counting the whole number of persons in each State, excluding Indians not taxed. But when the right to vote at any election for the choice of electors for President and Vice-President of the United States, Representatives in Congress, the Executive and Judicial officers of a State, or the members of the Legislature thereof, is denied to any of the male inhabitants of such State, being twenty-one years of age, and citizens of the United States, or in any way abridged, except for participation in rebellion, or other crime, the basis of representation therein shall be reduced in the proportion which the number of such male citizens shall bear to the whole number of male citizens twenty-one years of age in such State.

Section 3. No person shall be a Senator or Representative in Congress, or elector of President and Vice-President, or hold any office, civil or military, under the United States, or under any State, who, having previously taken an oath, as a member of Congress, or as an officer of the United States, or as a member of any State legislature, or as an executive or judicial officer of any State, to support the Constitution of the United States, shall have engaged in insurrection or rebellion against the same, or given aid or comfort to the enemies thereof. But Congress may by a vote of two-thirds of each House, remove such disability.

Section 4. The validity of the public debt of the United States, authorized by law, including debts incurred for payment of pensions and bounties for services in suppressing insurrection or rebellion, shall not be questioned. But neither the United States nor any State shall assume or pay any debt or obligation incurred in aid of insurrection or rebellion against the United States, or any claim for the loss or emancipation of any slave; but all such debts, obligations, and claims shall be held illegal and void.

Section 5. The Congress shall have the power to enforce, by appropriate legislation, the provisions of this article.

AMENDMENT XV (1870)

Section 1. The right of citizens of the United States to vote shall not be denied or abridged by the United States or by any State on account of race, color, or previous condition of servitude—

Section 2. The Congress shall have power to enforce this article by appropriate legislation.

AMENDMENT XVI (1913)

The Congress shall have power to lay and collect taxes on incomes, from whatever source

---

[12] Superseded by the Twentieth Amendment.

derived, without apportionment among the several States, and without regard to any census or enumeration.

AMENDMENT XVII (1913)

The Senate of the United States shall be composed of two Senators from each State, elected by the people thereof, for six years; and each Senator shall have one vote. The electors in each State shall have the qualifications requisite for electors of the most numerous branch of the State legislatures.

When vacancies happen in the representation of any State in the Senate, the executive authority of such State shall issue writs of election to fill such vacancies: *Provided,* That the legislature of any State may empower the executive thereof to make temporary appointments until the people fill the vacancies by election as the legislature may direct.

This amendment shall not be so construed as to affect the election or term of any Senator chosen before it becomes valid as part of the Constitution.

AMENDMENT XVIII (1919)[13]

Section 1. After one year from the ratification of this article the manufacture, sale, or transportation of intoxicating liquors within, the importation thereof into, or the exportation thereof from the United States and all territory subject to the jurisdiction thereof for beverage purposes is hereby prohibited.

Section 2. The Congress and the several States shall have concurrent power to enforce this article by appropriate legislation.

Section 3. This article shall be inoperative unless it shall have been ratified as an amendment to the Constitution by the legislatures of the several States, as provided in the Constitution, within seven years from the date of the submission hereof to the States by the Congress.

AMENDMENT XIX (1920)

The right of citizens of the United States to vote shall not be denied or abridged by the United States or by any State on account of sex.

Congress shall have power to enforce this article by appropriate legislation.

[13] Repealed by the Twenty-first Amendment.

AMENDMENT XX (1933)

Section 1. The terms of the President and Vice-President shall end at noon on the 20th day of January, and the terms of Senators and Representatives at noon on the 3d day of January, of the years in which such terms would have ended if this article had not been ratified; and the terms of their successors shall then begin.

Section 2. The Congress shall assemble at least once in every year, and such meeting shall begin at noon on the 3d day of January, unless they shall by law appoint a different day.

Section 3. If, at the time fixed for the beginning of the term of the President, the President elect shall have died, the Vice-President elect shall become President. If a President shall not have been chosen before the time fixed for the beginning of his term, or if the President elect shall have failed to qualify, then the Vice-President elect shall act as President until a President shall have qualified; and the Congress may by law provide for the case wherein neither a President elect nor a Vice-President elect shall have qualified, declaring who shall then act as President, or the manner in which one who is to act shall be selected, and such person shall act accordingly until a President or Vice-President shall have qualified.

Section 4. The Congress may by law provide for the case of the death of any of the persons from whom the House of Representatives may choose a President whenever the right of choice shall have devolved upon them, and for the case of the death of any of the persons from whom the Senate may choose a Vice-President whenever the right of choice shall have devolved upon them.

Section 5. Sections 1 and 2 shall take effect on the 15th day of October following the ratification of this article.

Section 6. This article shall be inoperative unless it shall have been ratified as an amendment to the Constitution by the legislatures of three-fourths of the several States within seven years from the date of its submission.

AMENDMENT XXI (1933)

Section 1. The eighteenth article of amendment to the Constitution of the United States is hereby repealed.

Section 2. The transportation or importation into any State, Territory, or possession of the

United States for delivery or use therein of intoxicating liquors, in violation of the laws thereof, is, hereby prohibited.

Section 3. This article shall be inoperative unless it shall have been ratified as an amendment to the Constitution by conventions in the several States, as provided in the Constitution, within seven years from the date of the submission hereof to the States by the Congress.

AMENDMENT XXII (1951)

Section 1. No person shall be elected to the office of the President more than twice, and no person who has held the office of President, or acted as President, for more than two years of a term to which some other person was elected President shall be elected to the office of the President more than once.

But this Article shall not apply to any person holding the office of President when this Article was proposed by the Congress, and shall not prevent any person who may be holding the office of President, or acting as President, during the term within which this Article becomes operative from holding the office of President or acting as President during the remainder of such term.

Section 2. This article shall be inoperative unless it shall have been ratified as an amendment to the Constitution by the legislatures of three-fourths of the several States within seven years from the date of its submission to the States by the Congress.

AMENDMENT XXIII (1961)

Section 1. The District constituting the seat of Government of the United States shall appoint in such manner as the Congress may direct:

A number of electors of President and Vice-President equal to the whole number of Senators and Representatives in Congress to which the District would be entitled if it were a State, but in no event more than the least populous State; they shall be in addition to those appointed by the States, but they shall be considered for the purposes of the election of President and Vice-President, to be electors appointed by the State; and they shall meet in the District and perform such duties as provided by the twelfth article of amendment.

Section 2. The Congress shall have power to enforce this article by appropriate legislation.

AMENDMENT XXIV (1964)

Section 1. The right of citizens of the United States to vote in any primary or other election for President or Vice-President, for electors for President or Vice-President, or for Senator or Representative in Congress, shall not be denied or abridged by the United States or any State by reason of failure to pay any poll tax or other tax.

Section 2. The Congress shall have power to enforce this article by appropriate legislation.

AMENDMENT XXV (1967)

Section 1. In case of the removal of the President from office or of his death or resignation, the Vice-President shall become President.

Section 2. Whenever there is a vacancy in the office of the Vice-President, the President shall nominate a Vice-President who shall take office upon confirmation by a majority vote of both Houses of Congress.

Section 3. Whenever the President transmits to the President pro tempore of the Senate and the Speaker of the House of Representatives his written declaration that he is unable to discharge the powers and duties of his office, and until he transmits to them a written declaration to the contrary, such powers and duties shall be discharged by the Vice-President as Acting President.

Section 4. Whenever the Vice-President and a majority of either the principal officers of the executive department or of such other body as Congress may by law provide, transmit to the President pro tempore of the Senate and the Speaker of the House of Representatives their written declaration that the President is unable to discharge the powers and duties of his office, the Vice-President shall immediately assume the powers and duties of the office as Acting President.

Thereafter, when the President transmits to the President pro tempore of the Senate and the Speaker of the House of Representatives his written declaration that no inability exists, he shall resume the powers and duties of his office unless the Vice-President and a majority of either the principal officers of the executive department or of such other body as Congress may by law provide, transmit within four days to the President pro tempore of the Senate and the Speaker of the House of Representatives their written declaration that the President is unable to discharge the powers and duties of his office. Thereupon Congress shall decide the issue, assembling within forty-eight hours for that purpose if not in session. If the Congress, within twenty-one days after receipt of the latter written declaration, or, if Congress is not in session, within twenty-one days after Congress is required to assemble, determines by two-thirds vote of both Houses that the President is unable to discharge the powers and duties of his office, the Vice-President shall continue to Discharge the same as Acting President; otherwise, the President shall resume the powers and duties of his office.

AMENDMENT XXVI (1971)

Section 1. The right of citizens of the United States, who are eighteen years of age or older, to vote shall not be denied or abridged by the United States or by any State on account of age.

Section 2. The Congress shall have power to enforce this article by appropriate legislation.

Presidential elections, 1900–1980

YEAR	NUMBER OF STATES	CANDIDATES	PARTIES	POPULAR VOTE (In thousands)	ELECTORAL VOTE	PERCENTAGE OF POPULAR VOTE[a]
1900	45	WILLIAM McKINLEY	Republican	7,218	292	51.7
		William J. Bryan	Democratic; Populist	6,356	155	45.5
		John C. Wooley	Prohibition	208		1.5
1904	45	THEODORE ROOSEVELT	Republican	7,628	336	57.4
		Alton B. Parker	Democratic	5,084	140	37.6
		Eugene V. Debs	Socialist	402		3.0
		Silas C. Swallow	Prohibition	258		1.9
1908	46	WILLIAM H. TAFT	Republican	7,675	321	51.6
		William J. Bryan	Democratic	6,412	162	43.1
		Eugene V. Debs	Socialist	420		2.8
		Eugene W. Chafin	Prohibition	253		1.7
1912	48	WOODROW WILSON	Democratic	6,296	435	41.9
		Theodore Roosevelt	Progressive	4,118	88	27.4
		William H. Taft	Republican	3,486	8	23.2
		Eugene V. Debs	Socialist	900		6.0
		Eugene W. Chafin	Prohibition	206		1.4
1916	48	WOODROW WILSON	Democratic	9,127	277	49.4
		Charles E. Hughes	Republican	8,533	254	46.2
		A. L. Benson	Socialist	585		3.2
		J. Frank Hanly	Prohibition	220		1.2
1920	48	WARREN G. HARDING	Republican	16,143	404	60.4
		James N. Cox	Democratic	9,130	127	34.2
		Eugene V. Debs	Socialist	919		3.4
		P. P. Christensen	Farmer-Labor	265		1.0
1924	48	CALVIN COOLIDGE	Republican	15,718	382	54.0
		John W. Davis	Democratic	8,385	136	28.8
		Robert M. La Follette	Progressive	4,831	13	16.6
1928	48	HERBERT C. HOOVER	Republican	21,391	444	58.2
		Alfred E. Smith	Democratic	15,016	87	40.9
1932	48	FRANKLIN D. ROOSEVELT	Democratic	22,809	472	57.4
		Herbert C. Hoover	Republican	15,758	59	39.7
		Norman Thomas	Socialist	881		2.2

SOURCE: Adapted from *Historical Statistics of the United States*, p. 682; *Statistical Abstract of the United States: 1974*, p. 422
[a]Candidates receiving less than 1 percent of the popular vote have been omitted. For that reason the percentage of popular vote given for any election year may not total 100 percent.

YEAR	NUMBER OF STATES	CANDIDATES	PARTIES	POPULAR VOTE (In thousands)	ELECTORAL VOTE	PERCENTAGE OF POPULAR VOTE[a]
1936	48	FRANKLIN D. ROOSEVELT	Democratic	27,752	523	60.8
		Alfred M. Landon	Republican	16,674	8	36.5
		William Lemke	Union	882		1.9
1940	48	FRANKLIN D. ROOSEVELT	Democratic	27,307	449	54.8
		Wendell L. Willkie	Republican	22,321	82	44.8
1944	48	FRANKLIN D. ROOSEVELT	Democratic	25,606	432	53.5
		Thomas E. Dewey	Republican	22,014	99	46.0
1948	48	HARRY S. TRUMAN	Democratic	24,105	303	49.5
		Thomas E. Dewey	Republican	21,970	189	45.1
		J. Strom Thurmond	States' Rights	1,169	39	2.4
		Henry A. Wallace	Progressive	1,157		2.4
1952	48	DWIGHT D. EISENHOWER	Republican	33,936	442	55.1
		Adlai E. Stevenson	Democratic	27,314	89	44.4
1956	48	DWIGHT D. EISENHOWER	Republican	35,590	457	57.6
		Adlai E. Stevenson	Democratic	26,022	73	42.1
1960	50	JOHN F. KENNEDY	Democratic	34,227	303	49.9
		Richard M. Nixon	Republican	34,108	219	49.6
1964	50	LYNDON B. JOHNSON	Democratic	43,126	486	61.1
		Barry M. Goldwater	Republican	27,176	52	38.5
1968	50	RICHARD M. NIXON	Republican	31,785	301	43.4
		Hubert H. Humphrey	Democratic	31,275	191	42.7
		George C. Wallace	American Independent	9,906	46	13.5
1972	50	RICHARD M. NIXON	Republican	47,170	520	60.7
		George S. McGovern	Democratic	29,170	17	37.7
1976	50	JIMMY CARTER	Democratic	40,830	297	50.0
		Gerald R. Ford	Republican	39,147	240	47.9
1980	50	RONALD W. REAGAN	Republican	43,899	489	50.8
		Jimmy Carter	Democratic	36,481	49	41.0
		John B. Anderson	Independent	5,719	0	6.6

INDEX

A&P, 145
Abbott, Grace, 54
Abortion: in late 1970s, 465;
  Supreme Court ruling on, 440,
  467
Abplanalp, Robert H., 444
Abrams v. *U.S.*, 126
Abstract Expressionism, 343
Accommodationism, 58
Acheson, Dean, 310, 319, 322,
  362; and Korean War, 326
Acid rock, 423
Action Painting, 343
Adams, Henry, 5, 20, 21
Adams, Sherman, 355, 356, 363
Addams, Jane, 10, 46–47, 84, 126,
  134–135
Adding Machine (Rice), 144
*Adolescence: Its Psychology and
  Its Relation to Physiology,
  Anthropology, Sociology, Sex,
  Crime, Religion, and Education*
  (Hall), 41
Adventures of Augie March
  (Bellow), 343
Advertising, in 1920s, 145–146
Affirmative action, 464–465
Affluence: in 1950s, 347–349; vs.
  social change, 402–403
The Affluent Society (Galbraith),
  340, 349
Afghanistan, Soviets in, 473, 477
Aged: health insurance for, 357;
  and Townsend plan, 1930s, 228.
  See also Social security
Agee, James, 201
Agnew, Spiro, 449, 450, 453; and
  election of 1968, 433; resigns,
  1973, 457–458
Agribusiness, 156
Agricultural Adjustment
  Administration (AAA), 215,
  217–220; Supreme Court ruling
  on, 233
Agricultural Marketing
  Administration, 206

Agriculture: boycott by Chicago
  farm workers, California, 427;
  and Coolidge, 158; government
  spending for, 1950, 356; grain
  production, 22; migrant
  workers, 1930s, 184. *See also*
  Farming
Agriculture Department, 156, 219
Airplanes, 21; crosscountry and
  transatlantic flights, 185;
  production, WWII, 282
Alabama, bus boycott in
  Montgomery, 1950s, 358–359
Aldrich, Nelson, 72–73, 80, 82
Alexander v. *Holmes*, 439
Alger, Horatio, 29
Ali, Mohammed, 409
Alien and Sedition Acts (1798),
  323
Alienation, late 1970s, 465
"The Aliens" (Tarkington), 10
Allende, Salvador, 457
Alliance for Progress, 383, 418
Allies, WWI, 106; Soviet
  occupation, postwar, 130–31
Allies, WWII, 248; and
  lend-lease, 252–253
Allotment Annies, 287
Alsop, Joseph and Stewart, 314
Amalgamated Clothing Workers
  Union of America, 49
Amendments. *See* Constitutional
  Amendments
America First, 250–251
American Association of School
  Administrators, 190
American Association of
  University Professors, 44
American Bankers Association,
  95
American Bar Association, 288,
  447
American Civil Liberties Union,
  125
American Commonwealth
  (Bryce), 9

American Defense Society, 126
American Economic Association,
  19
American Federation of Labor
  (AFL), 28, 29, 49; and CIO,
  225; Debs on, 52
AFL-CIO, 451
American Federation of State,
  County, and Municipal
  Employees, 467
American Independence Party,
  and election of 1968, 433
American Medical Association,
  44
American Protective Association,
  18
Americans for Democratic Action
  (ADA), 347, 368
American Sociological Society,
  40, 44
American Telephone and
  Telegraph Co. (AT&T), 145
American Tobacco Co., 77
American Tragedy (Dreiser), 162
American Union Against
  Militarism, 126
American Veterans Committee,
  368
American Vigilante Patrol, 126
"Amos 'n Andy" (radio
  program), 200
Anacostia Flats, Bonus Army at,
  210
Anderson, John, 51, 475
Anderson, Sherwood, 7, 40
Angell, Norman, 105
Angelus Temple, Los Angeles,
  167
Anna Karenina, 36
Anthony, Susan B., 54
Anthropology, cultural, in 1920s,
  153
Anti-Comintern Pact, 246
Anticommunism, sources of,
  312–314
Antin, Mary, 13

Anti-Saloon League, 44, 61
Anti-Semitism, 174–176; and
America First, 251; of Black
Muslims, 408
Antitrust, and Theodore
Roosevelt, 77, 78
Antiwar movement: in 1960s,
418–420; intensifies, 1970s,
448–450
Anti-War Week, 1934, 195
ANZUS treaty, 329
Appalachia, aid for, 391, 393
Appeal to Reason (newspaper), 50
Appeasement, 1930s, 245–247
Apportionment, Supreme Court
ruling on, 400–401
Arabic, liner, sunk, 109
Arbitration, coal strike, 1902, 28
Area redevelopment, in 1960s,
375–376
Armed services, 72, 94; blacks
discharged from, 1905, 79;
demobilization, post-WWII,
302; desegregration, 317;
discrimination in, WWII, 290;
GIs in, WWII, 269; Joint Chiefs
of Staff, 306, 448; and
McCarthyism, 320, 322; in
Soviet Union, post-WWI,
130–131; and trial of Billy
Mitchell, 154; and WWI, 111,
119
Arms embargo, 1930s, 244, 245,
248
Armstrong, Neil, 375
Arnold, Henry (Hap), 270
Arnold, Matthew, on American
cities, 9
Arnold, Thurman, 195–196
Art: in 1930s, 196–197; and High
Culture, 340; and
self-expression, 1950s, 342–343
Arthur, Chester, 93
Aryan Order of St. George, 19
Asia: FDR's diplomacy in,
261–263; TR's policy on, 94–98.
See also China; Japan; Korea;
Open Door policy; Philippines;
Vietnam War; World War II
Asia-firsters, 268
Assassination: of Robert
Kennedy, 431; of Martin Luther
King, Jr., 431; of Malcolm X
409; of McKinley, 75; of Sadat,
472
Aswan High Dam, 365
Atomic bomb, 248; dropped on
Hiroshima and Nagasaki, 296;
Laurence on, 297; Manhattan
District Project on, 269–270.

See also Nuclear weapons
Atrocities, in Vietnam, 416
Attica prison, riot, 1971, 444
Australia, and ANZUS treaty, 329
Austria: annexed, 1938, 246;
central bank collapses, 1931,
188
Automobile, 21, 22, 468; baneful
effects of, 147
Automobile industry: losses,
1980, 469; post-WWI, 143–144;
sales, 1920s, 188
Awake and Sing (Odets), 198
Axis powers. *See* World War II

Babbitry, and politics, 1920s,
161–165
Babbitt (Lewis), 61
Baby and Child Care (Spock), 345
Baby boom, 287, 344–345; and
prices, post-WWII, 303
Bach, Richard, 470
Back Door to War (Tansill), 259
Back-to-Africa movement, 172,
173
Baez, Joan, 423
Bailey, Josiah, on Democratic
party, 235
Bailey, Thomas, 280
Bakelite, 142
Baker, Bobby, 388
Baker, Newton, 35, 125, 126
Baker, Ray Stannard, 57, 119; on
TR, 78
Baker v. *Carr*, 400
Bakke, Alan, 464–465
Balance of payments, 451
Balance of trade, 451
Baldwin, James, 408, 410
Baldwin, Roger, 125, 126
Ballinger, Richard, controversy
with Pinchot, 82–84
Banks: closings, 1930s, 180–181,
188; and FDIC, 213–214;
holiday, 1933, 213; and stock
market crash, 186–188; turn of
century, 24; and Wilson, 87–88
Barnes, Harry Elmer, 259
Barnett, Ross, 379, 380
Baronial Order of Runnymede, 19
Barton, Bruce, 164
Baruch, Bernard, 120–121, 212,
310
Batista, Fulgencio, 366
Baum, L. Frank, 56; on Plains
life, 9
Bayer aspirin, 145
Bay of Pigs invasion, 382, 383, 385
Beard, Charles, 242, 244, 250, 251,
418; on new era, 153

Beatles, 423
Beecher, Henry Ward, 28
Beer, legalization, 1933, 214
Begin, Menachem, 473, 477
Bell, Daniel, 347
Bell, Thomas, on steel mill, 1930s,
185
Bellamy, Edward, 35, 44
Bellow, Saul, 343
Benchley, Peter, 470
Benedict, Ruth, 153
Bennett, Constance, 185
Benson, Ezra Taft, 355–356
Benton, Thomas Hart, 199
Berger, Victor, 125–126
Berle, Adolf, Jr., 145, 355
Berlin, Irving, 285
Berlin: blockade and airlift, 1948,
311; Wall, 384
Bernays, Edward, 146
Beveridge, Albert, 73, 96
Bicentennial, 464
Bicycle races, six-day, in 1930s,
190
Bien Hoa, Vietcong assault on,
414
Big Money (Dos Passos), 198
Birdseye, Clarence, 441
Birmingham, Alabama, civil
rights demonstration, 1963, 379
Birth control movement, and
women's rights, 52
Birth of a Nation (film), 60, 143,
168
Birth rate: baby boom, 287,
344–345; and environment, 425
Bissell, Richard, 383
The Bitter Cry of the Children
(Spargo), 26
Black, Hugo, 3, 4–5, 234, 400
Blacklist, of U.S. firms by Britain,
WWI, 107
Blackmun, Harry, 447
Black Muslims, 173, 290, 408–409
Black Panthers, 413
Black power, from interracialism
to, 407–414
Black racism, 408–409
Blacks: and civil rights
movement, 1950s, 357–360;
discharge from armed services,
1905, 79; and discrimination
under Wilson, 89; and election
of 1936, 232; and election of
1948, 315; gains, early 1970s,
439–440; in late 1970s, 464–465;
life in South, pre-WWII,
288–289; life style of women in
South, 1912, 54; in Macon
County, 1930s, 192; militancy,

in 1920s, 171–173; militancy, WWII, 289–291; and NRA, 231; and prison violence, 443–444; and racial justice, early 1900s, 56–60; and revolution in civil rights, 1960s, 378–382; and rise of ethnic consciousness, 1920s, 170–174; social problems, late 1970s, 466; tensions, turn of the century, 5; Wilson and discrimination against, 89; in WWII, 288. *See also* Riots

Black Star shipping line, 172, 173
Blind, categorical aid for, 222
Blockade, of Cuba, 1962, 385
Blough, Roger, 377
Blue-collar workers: in early 1980s, 467; and McCarthyism, 322; in 1920s, 165; in 1950s, 338; and rise of unions, 1930s, 227–228; turn of century, 26–29
Boaz, Franz, 40
Boeing Aircraft Corp., 282
Bohlen, Charles (Chip), 361
Bomb threats, early 1970s, 443
Bonus Army, 1932, 193–194; assault on, 209–210
Book-of-the-Month Club, 244, 340
Bootlegging, 166
Boorstin, Daniel, 347
Borah, William, 134, 155
Boston police strike, 1919, 127, 157
Boulder Dam, 156, 206
Bourne, Randolph, 38–39, 162, 424; on superpatriotism, 125
Bow, Clara, 148
Bowron, Fletcher, on Japanese-Americans, 282
Boycott: of buses in Montgomery, Alabama, 1950, 358–359; of produce by Chicano farm workers, California, 1960s, 427
Boy Spies of America, 126
Brace, Charles Loring, on crowding and sexual morality, 12
Bradley, Omar, 328
Brain trusters, 212
Brandeis, Louis D., 41, 88, 176, 233; and *Muller* v. *Oregon*, 42
Breezy Stories magazine, 148
Bremer, Arthur H., 452
Brennan, William J., Jr., 400
Brewer, David, 74
Brezhnev, Leonid, 472
Bricker, John, 306
Brinkmanship, 363
Bristol-Myers, 145
Broadcasting, concentration in, 145
Broder, David, 395

Brooks, John, 267
Brooks, Van Wyck, 39, 161, 200
Brotherhood of Sleeping Car Porters, 172
Brown, H. Rap, 413, 414, 439, 443; on race relations, 412
Brown, James, 413
Brown, John, 413
Brownell, Herbert, 359
Brown power, 427
Brown v. *Board of Education*, 351, 357, 380, 401, 408
Bryan, William Jennings, 8, 61, 101; and Scopes trial, 167; as Wilson's secretary of state, 106, 108
Bryce, James, on American cities, 9, 10
Buck, Pearl, 255
Bunau-Varilla, Philippe, 99–100
Bundy, McGeorge, 382
Bureaucracy: black employment in, WWII, 288; decline of, 1982, 469; and McCarthyism, 321; in 1910, 72; in 1920s, 155; in 1950s, 349; and political system, 1960s, 398; in WWII, 279. *See also* Government
Bureaucratic corporations, 344
Bureau of Corporations, 77
Burger, Warren Earl, 446, 447
Burleson, Albert, S., 124, 127
Burnham, James, 344
Burnham, Walter Dean, 67
Burns, James MacGregor, 274, 353
Burton, Theodore, 298
Bus boycott, Montgomery, Alabama, 1950s, 358–359
Business: black-run, 59; and Coolidge administration, 158; U.S. enterprise abroad, 1900–1920, 96; and Wilson, 121. *See also* Corporations; Economy; Industry
Businessmen, Keynes on, 235
Business Week, 182
Busing, Supreme Court ruling on, 447
Butler, Hugh, 322
Byrd, Harry, 301, 389, 390
Byrnes, James, 296, 298, 299, 398, 310, 358

Caesarism, 205
Cagney, James, 198
Caldwell, Erskine, 196, 198; on tenant farmers, 1930s, 184
California: boycott by Chicano farm workers, 1960s, 427;

Japanese immigrants and anti-Oriental riots, 1907, 98; Japanese restriction laws, 20; migrant agricultural workers, 1930s, 184; population, WWII, 285; progressivism in, 45; Proposition 13, 469; reform government, early 1900s, 63; suffrage for women, 53
Cambodia, authoritarianism in, 461; bombed and invaded, 448; and Geneva accord, 364; and SEATO, 364
Camp David, Maryland, 444
Camp David accord, 472
Caniff, Milton, 200
Cannon, Joseph (Uncle Joe), 72, 73, 82
Capitalism, Fay on, 164
Capone, Al, 166, 167
Capra, Frank, 199
Cardozo, Benjamin, 233
Caribbean. *See* Cuba; Latin America
Carmichael, Stokely, 171, 411, 412, 413, 429, 439
Carnegie, Andrew, 25, 28, 105
Carnegie, Dale, 202
Carnegie Steel Co., 24; Homestead Works, 23
Carranza, Venustiano, 103
Carrizal incident, 103, 104
Carswell, G. Harrold, 447
Carter, Jimmy, 475; as president, 471–474
Carter, John F., on youth culture, 1920s, 162
Carver, George Washington, 142
Casablanca conference, 1943, 268, 273
Castro, Fidel, 366, 368, 382, 383, 457
Casualties: in Cambodia, 448; at Hiroshima and Nagasaki, 296; in Laos, 450; in Okinawa, 298; Soviet Union, in WWII, 273; strategic bombing, WWII, 270; Vietnam War, 416–417, 454–455; in WWI, 119
Catcher in the Rye (Salinger), 343
Categorical assistance program, 222–223
Catholics: and election of 1960, 368, 369; immigrants, 15; and McCarthyism, 322–323; as 1960s pressure group, 376
Catt, Carrie Chapman, 53
Catton, Bruce, 4–5
Cellophane, 142
Censorship: of mail, WWI,

124–125; of movies, 1930s, 191
Central Intelligence Agency (CIA), 306, 327; and coup in Chile, 457; and Bay of Pigs, 382–383
Central Powers, WWI, 106
Chamberlain, Neville, 246, 247
Chandler, William E., 93
Chaney, James, 409
Chapin, Roy, 21
Chaplin, Charlie, 23
Charity Organization Society, 33
Chase, Stuart, 284; on advertising, 146
Chavez, Cesar, 427
Chevalier, Maurice, 185
Chiang Kai-shek, 242, 257, 258, 274, 275, 318, 319, 328, 363, 364, 450
Chicago: black population, 1920s, 59, 170; clothing workers' strike, 1910, 49; discrimination against blacks, early 1900s, 60; population, 1900, 6; and prohibition, 166; riot, 1919, 123; riot, 1966, 410; riot, 1968, 431
Chicago, Milwaukee and St. Paul Railway Co. v. *Minnesota*, 74
Chicago *Tribune*, 157, 158, 166, 231, 263
Chicanos, and brown power, 427
Child labor: abolished, 236; in 1900, 26
Children, dependent, categorical aid for, 222
Children's Aid Society, 12
Children's Bureau, 81
Childs, Marcus, 330
China: Communist takeover in, 318–319; and Eisenhower foreign policy, 363, 364; Japan invades, 1937, 246, 256; and Korean War, 324, 327, 328; and Manchurian crisis, 1931, 242; Nixon visit to, 450–451; Open Door policy in, 94–95, 97, 102, 255, 257, 319; and Suez crisis, 365; and Wilson's diplomacy, 102
China lobby, 319
Chinese: exclusion, 13; immigrants, 16
Chisholm, Shirley, 171, 428
Chomsky, Noam, 391
Christian Anti-Communist Crusade, 351
Christian Century, 241
Christianity and the Social Crisis (Rauschenbusch), 34
Chrysler, Walter, 148

Chrysler Corp., 145, 469
Churchill, Winston, 268; on appeasement, 247; iron curtain speech, 308; and second front in Europe, 272–273
Circuit Court, U.S., 380
Cities: Arnold on, 9; black population, 1910–1920, 59; and election of 1928, 160; growth, 1860–1970, 6; immigrants in, 15; and industrial development, 23; metropolitan sprawl, and automobile, 144; population, 1950s, 337–338; population, WWII, 285; poverty in, 1960s, 397–398; quality of life, 1900, 9–13; at turn of century, 5–9
Citizens Council, 357
City College of New York, campus unrest, 1969, 443
City government: reform, early 1900s, 61–63; spending, 1920s, 155
Civilian Conservation Corps (CCC), 214, 232, 278
Civilian Public Service camps, WWII, 280
Civil liberties, and WWI, 124–127
Civil rights: and election of 1948, 315; Johnson's policy on, 389–390; movement, 1950s, 357–360; Nixon policy on, 446; revolution in 1960s, 378–382; shift from interracialism to black power, 407–414; Truman's program, 306
Civil Rights Act: of 1957, 359, 380; of 1960, 359; of 1964, 390, 396, 400, 408, 430; of 1965, 392, 396, 400, 408, 410
Civil Works Administration (CWA), 214
The Clansman (Dixon), 56, 60
Clark, Champ, 93
Clark, Tom, 299
Clay, Cassius, 409
Clayton, Bill, 88
Clean Air Act, 442
Clemenceau, Georges, 130, 131, 132
Cleveland, Grover, 13, 71, 72, 85
Cleveland, Ohio: black population, 1910–1920, 59; reform government, 61–62
Clifford, Clark, 316, 417
Clothing industry, unions and strikes, early 1900s, 49
Coal mining, 20; strikes, turn of century, 26; strike, 1946, 303–304

Cohen, Benjamin, 229
Cohn, Roy, 350
Cold War, 463; and American anticommunism, 312–314; and Carter policy, 472–473; and Eisenhower policy, 1950s, 360–367; and McCarthyism, 322, 323; and Truman policy, 1946–1948, 307–312
Collective bargaining, and NRA, 215
Colleges and universities: blacks in, 440; campus unrest, 1960s, 421, 443; enrollments, 1920s, 152–153. *See also* Education
Colombia, and Panama Canal, 98–100
Colonial Dames, 19
Colored Advisory Committee, 170
Colored Farmers Alliance, 58
Colosimo, "Big Jim," 166
Colson, Charles, 461
Columbia Broadcasting Co. (CBS), 145
Columbia University, campus unrest, 1960s, 421
Columbus, New Mexico, burned by Villa, 1916, 103
Comfort, Alex, 470
Comic strips, in 1930s, 200
Commerce Department, 156, 206
Committee for a Sane Nuclear Policy (SANE), 361
Committee on Public Information, 124
Committee on Social Trends, 153
Committee to Aid the Allies, 250
Committee to Re-elect the President (CREEP), 451, 452, 458, 461
Commodity Credit Corp., 218
Common Cause, 422
Commoner, Barry, 425
The Common Law (Holmes), 41
Commons, John R., 20, 40
Communications industry, post-WWI, 142, 143
Communist Labor party, 127
Communist party, 127, 347; and *Dennis* v. *U.S.*, 320; and election of 1932, 213; and isolationists, 1940, 251; and McCarthyism, 1950s, 320, 321; in 1930s, 196; and *Yates* v. *U.S.*, 352
Communists: in Laos, 383; takeover in China, 318–319. *See also* Cold War; Soviet Union; Vietnam War
Community Action Program (CAP), 393, 394,395

The Complete Book of Running (Fixx), 470
Comptroller General, 156
Computers, 464
Concentration, corporate, post-WWI, 145
The Condition of the Working Class in England (Engels), 46
Conformity, of 1920s, 161–165
Congress, 72–73; censures McCarthy, 351; and civil rights legislation, 1960s, 380, 381; Eightieth, 305–308; and election of 1932, 212; and election of 1936, 232; and entry into WWII, 259; and Harding, 156; and hope for appeasement, 1936–1938, 246; and Johnson, 390, 391–392; and Kennedy policy, 374; and New Deal stalemate, 235–236; in 1969–1972, 441; and noninterventionism, 244–245; post-WWII, 300–301; and Reagan, 476; and strikes, post-WWII, 304; and TR, 79; and WWII legislation, 278–279
Congressional Budget Office, 478
Congress of Industrial Organizations (CIO): Political Action Committee, 304; and rise of unions, 1930s, 225–227
Congress of Racial Equality (CORE), 289, 290, 378, 419
Connor, Eugene (Bull), 379, 380
Conscientious objectors (C.O.'s): in WWI, 125–126; in WWII, 280
Conservation, 468; Ballinger-Pinchot controversy, 82–84; in early 1970s, 442; Newlands Act, 77; TR on, 83
Consolidated Aircraft Corp., 282
Constitution, text of, 481–492
Constitutional Amendments: Sixteenth, 81, 86; Seventeenth, 66; Eighteenth, 61; Nineteenth, 53, 54; Twenty-second, 306; Twenty-fourth, 392; Twenty-fifth, 461; Twenty-sixth, 441
Construction industry, 23, 188; 1920s, 142
Consumer goods industries, 23, 143
Consumer price index, post-WWII, 303
Consumption, conspicuous, 25
Containment, of communism, 311; and Eisenhower foreign policy, 361–366
Contraband, WWI, 107

Contraception, Supreme Court ruling on, 401
Contract labor, as peonage, 56–57
Cooley, Thomas M., 74
Coolidge, Calvin, 180, 206, 355; on advertising, 145; elected in 1924, 159; as president, 156, 157–158
Coral Sea, battle of, 268
Corcoran, Thomas, 229
Cornell University, campus unrest, 1969, 443
Corporations: bureaucratic, 344; interlocking directorates, 24; and Kennedy policy, 376–377; and modernization, 145; in 1960s, 399–400; and unions, 1930s, 226–227. *See also* Business; Economy; Industry
Corwin, Edward S., 251, 280, 352
Cost of living: and inflation, 469; turn of century, 45
Coughlin, Charles, 228; and election of 1936, 231
Council of Economic Advisers, 302
Council of National Defense Advisory Commission, 282
Counterculture, of 1960s, 407, 422–427
Counts, George S., 195
Courts: and labor unrest, 27. *See also* Supreme Court
Cowley, Malcolm, 196
Cox, Archibald, 458
Cox, James M., 159
The Crack in the Picture Window (Keats), 338–339
Crane, Stephen, 39
Credibility gap, 419
Credit, and stock market crash, 179–180
Creel, George, 124
Creel Committee, 146
Crime: in cities, late 1970s, 466; in ghettos, 1960s, 397; and prohibition, 166–167
Crime Control and Safe Streets Act (1968), 401
Criminals, Supreme Court rulings on rights, 401
Crisis magazine, 231
Cromwell, William, 100
Crosby, Ernest Howard, 95
Crowding, in cities, 1900, 10–12
Cuba: Bay of Pigs invasion, 382–383, 385; Castro takeover in, 366; Kennedy on Eisenhower policy in, 368–369; missile crisis, 384; protectorate ends, 1934, 243; and

Spanish-American War, 94. *See also* Latin America
Current Opinion magazine, 38
Czechoslovakia: arms deal with Egypt, 365; seized, 1939, 247; Soviet control of, 311; Sudetenland annexed, 1938, 246, 247

Daladier, Eduard, 247
Daley, Richard, 432
Dallas, in 1900, 5
Dance marathons, in 1930s, 190
The Dangerous Classes of New York (Brace), 12
Dangling Man (Bellow), 343
Dare the School Build a New Social Order? (Counts), 195
Darlan, Jean, 274
Darrow, Clarence, 35; and Scopes trial, 167
Daugherty, Harry, 157
Daughters of the American Revolution (DAR), 14, 19
Davis, Elmer, 280, 354
Davis, James J., 157
Davis, Jeff, 60
Davis, John W., 159, 230
Davis, Richard Harding, 106
Day, Clarence, 192
Day, Doris, 345
Dayton, Tennessee, Scopes trial, 167
D-day, WWII, 273
Dean, John, 452, 458, 462
The Death and Life of Great American Cities (Jacobs), 397
Death penalty: restored, late 1970s, 466; Supreme Court ruling on, 447
Debs, Eugene, 30, 86, 126, 156; on AFL, 52; and election of 1920, 159; on sedition, 125; and Socialist party, 50–51
Defense Department, 306, 377
Defense spending: Kennedy policy, 386; in 1940, 250; Reagan policy, 476, 477. *See also* Government spending
Deficits, government, 1946–1963, 279–280
Deflation, and wages, turn of century, 29
Defoliation, in Vietnam, 416
de Gaulle, Charles, 274
Dell, Floyd, 38, 162, 196
De Mille, Cecil B., 148
Democratic National Committee, 451, 452
Democratic party: Bailey on, 235; convention, 1964, 410;

convention, 1968, 432–433; and election of 1916, 88; and election of 1932, 210–213; and election of 1948, 315; and election of 1960, 369–370; and League of Nations, 135–136; and McCarthyism, 323–324; in 1920s, 159

Denmark, conquered, 1940, 248

Dennis v. *U.S.*, 320

Deoxyribonucleic acid (DNA), 464

Deportation, of aliens, post-WWI, 129

Depression: in mid-1890s, 19, 23, 96; in 1930s, 188–202; and stock market crash, 180–186

Destroyer deal, 1940, 250

Détente, 360, 362, 366, 442, 450, 472–473

Detroit: black population, 1910–1920, 59; reform government, 62; riot, 1943, 290; riot, 1967, 410

Devaluation of dollar: in 1933, 214; in 1971, 451; in 1973, 455

de Voto, Bernard, 287

Dewey, George, 71, 94

Dewey, John, 42–43, 195

Dewey, Thomas E., 279; and election of 1948, 314–317

Dick Tracy (comic strip), 200

Diem, Ngo Dinh, 386, 387, 414

Dien Bien Phu, 363

Diggins, John P., 424

Dillingham Commission, 19

Dillon, Douglas, 376

Diplomacy: dollar, of Taft, 101–102; of FDR, 261–263, 273–279; of Wilson, 102–105. *See also* Cold War; Foreign policy

Direct democracy, 65–67

Dirksen, Everett, 378

Dirty tricks, of Nixon, 451

Disabled, categorical aid for, 222

Disarmament: Eisenhower supports, 361; in 1960s, 385–386; Washington Conference, post-WWI, 154–155

Discount rate, rise in, 1931, 297

Disfranchisement of blacks, pre-WWI, 56

Disillusionment, post-WWI, 137–138

Dissenters, profascist, WWII, 280

Divide and conquer, management strategy of, 27

Divorce: in late 1970s, 465; in 1930s, 191; in WWII, 287

Dix, Dorothy, 150

Dixiecrat party, and election of 1948, 315

Dixon, Thomas, 56, 60

DNA (deoxyribonucleic acid), 464

Dodd, William, 245

Doe v. *Bolton*, 440

Dollar diplomacy, of Taft, 101–102

Domesticity, and feminism, 1950s, 344–345

Domino theory, 364

Donne, John, 198

Donovan, Robert, 353

"Don't Take My Darling Boy Away" (song), 106

Doors (singing group), 423

Dos Passos, John, 163, 196, 198, 200; and Sacco and Vanzetti, 164; on Unknown Soldier, 137

Douglas, Lewis, 214, 220

Douglas, Paul, 3, 4, 5, 352, 353

Douglas, William O., 153, 193, 234, 400

Douglas Aircraft Corp., 282

Draft, in 1940, 250

Dreiser, Theodore, 4, 8, 39, 40, 106, 162, 196, 199

Dresden, Germany, bombed, 1945, 270

Drucker, Peter, on government, 397

Drug, Inc., 145

Drugs, and counterculture, 423

Drug traffic, early 1970s, 443

Duarte, José Napoleon, 477

Du Bois, W. E. B., 43, 58–59, 170, 173

Duke, James B., 23

Dulles, Allen, 382

Dulles, John Foster, 367, 382, 384; and Cold War, 1950s, 362–366

Duluth, Missabe, and Iron Range Railroad, 23

Duncan, Isadora, 148

Durant, William C. (Billy), 145

Durkin, Martin, 355

Dutch East Indies, Japan dominates, 256

Dylan, Bob, 373, 423

Dynamo (O'Neill), 144

Eagleton, Thomas, 452

Eakins, Thomas, 36

Earnings, men vs. women, 1962–1972, 429

East Germany, rebellion, 1950s, 364

Eastland, James, 351, 380

Eastman, Max, 38

East St. Louis, race riot, 1917, 122

Economic Development Act (1965), 392

Economic growth: in 1919–1929, 142; in 1950s, 347–348; in 1961–1970, 403

Economic nationalism, and isolationism, 1930s, 243–244

Economic progress, in 1920s, 141–148

Economic warfare, with Japan, 257

Economy: and automobile, 143–144; collapses, 1929–1939, 180–181; in early 1970s, 451; in late 1970s, 467–470; in 1950s, 356–357; in 1960s, 375; in 1980s, 476–477; Nixon policy on, 445; and oil prices, 1973, 457

Economy Act (1933), 214

Eden, Anthony, on FDR, 275

Edison, Thomas A., 165, 441

Education: aid for, 1960s, 376; of blacks in South, 289; high school graduates, 1930s, 184; in 1920s, 152–153; in 1930s, 195–196; in 1950s, 346–347; progressive, 41–43; segregated schools, 56, 408; turn of century, 25. *See also* Colleges and universities

Education Act (1965), 394

Egypt, Suez crisis, 365

Ehrlich, Paul, 425

Ehrlichman, John D., 444, 445, 458, 462

Einstein, Albert, 269

Eisenhower, Dwight D., 270, 272, 314, 388, 434, 476; and civil rights movement, 357–360; and Cold War, 1950s, 360–367; and election of 1952, 330–332; on military-industrial complex, 368; as president, 353–357; and Radical Right, 351; reelected in 1956, 353

Eisenhower, Milton, 366

Eisenhower Doctrine, 366

Elderly. *See* Aged

Election: of 1896, 8; of 1904, 77; of 1912, 80, 84–86, 93; of 1916, 88, 111–112; of 1920, 156–157, 159; of 1924, 159; of 1928, 159, 160, 206; of 1932, 210–213, 231–232; of 1934, 220; of 1936, 226; of 1940, 252, 253; of 1944, 279, 289; of 1948, 314–317; of 1952, 321, 323, 330–333; of 1956, 352–353; of 1960, 367–370; of 1964, 390–391; of 1968, 430–435; of 1970, 449–450; of 1972, 451–453; of 1974, 462; of 1976, 470–471; of 1980, 474–476; summary, 1900–1972, 494–495

Electoral reform, and progressivism, 65–67
Eliot, Charles, 106
Elkins Act, 79
Ellsberg, Daniel, 450, 451
El Salvador, Reagan policy on, 477
Ely, Richard T., 30, 63
Embargo, and gasoline and scrap iron shipments to Japan, 1940, 257
Emergency Fleet Administration, 120
The Emerging Republican Majority (Phillips), 446
Employers, power over labor, 27–28
Employment Act (1946), 302
Encyclopaedia Brittanica, 174
The End of Ideology (Bell), 347
Enemies list, of Nixon, 450
Energy crisis, 468
Engels, Friedrich, 46
Engel v. *Vitale*, 400
Englebrecht, Helmuth, 244
Environmental protection, 425
Environmental Protection Agency, 442, 458
Episcopal Committee on Motion Pictures, 191
Equal Rights Amendment, 430, 440, 467, 476
Ervin, Sam, 458
Escobedo v. *Illinois*, 401
Espionage Act (1917), 50, 124, 125–126
Ethiopia, Mussolini invades, 1935, 243, 245
Ethnic consciousness, and black experience, 1920s, 170–174
Ethnic groups: conflict in melting pot, 174–176; in 1960s, 398; in politics, 17–18; tensions, turn of century, 5; and Versailles Treaty, 135; voting, 1920s, 160; in work force, turn of century, 29
Ethnocentrism, scientific, 19–20
Europe, division, 1945–1955, 309
Evans, Hiram Wesley, 169
Evans, Rowland, 388–389
Evans, Walker, 199, 201
Executive branch, government, in 1900, 71
Executive Office of the President, 236
Export-Import Bank, 243

Fair Deal, of Truman, 298, 302
Fair Employment Practices Commission, 289, 302, 390

Fall, Albert, 157
Fall, Bernard, 416
Family: in 1930s, 190–194; at turn of century, 3–5; in WWII, 287
Family Assistance Plan (FAP), 445
Farley, James A., 212
Farm bloc, and Eisenhower administration, 356
Farm Credit Administration, 218
Farmer, James, 419, 446
Farmers' Union, 44
Farming: mechanization, and growth of cities, turn of century, 6–7; migrant workers, poverty, 182–184; milk dumping, 1930s, 194. *See also* Agriculture
Farm Security Administration, 182, 219
Farrell, James T., 198, 200
Fascism, 196
Faubus, Orval, 359
Fay, Charles N., on capitalism, 164
Federal Bureau of Investigation, 458
Federal Deposit Insurance Corp., 213–214
Federal Emergency Relief Administration (FERA), 214
Federal funds, distribution, 1965, 396
Federal Highway Act (1916), 88
Federal Housing Agency, 302
Federal Radio Commission, 143
Federal Reserve Banks, 86
Federal Reserve System: and FDR, 214; and recession of 1937, 234; and stock market crash, 186–188
Federal Theatre Project, 222
Federal Trade Commission (FTC), 87, 88, 156, 377
Female Eunuch (Greer), 440
The Feminine Mystique (Friedan), 427
Feminism: and domesticity, 1950s, 344–345; gains, early 1970s, 440–441; and nativism, 55; in 1920s, 150–152; in 1960s, 427–430; and suffrage, 53–56
Fermi, Enrico, 269
Fiedler, Leslie, on successful poem, 342
Field, Stephen, 74
Filibuster, on civil rights, 1960s, 381, 390
Film industry: in 1930s, 197–198; post-WWI, 143
Finch, Robert, 444

Firebombing, WWII, 220
Fireside chats, of FDR, 238
Fishel, Jeff, 476
Fisher, Dorothy Canfield, 150
Fitzgerald, F. Scott, 161
Five-power treaty, 154–155; Japan abrogates, 243
Fixx, James, 470
Flappers, 148, 151
Flexner, Abraham, 86
Florida, land boom collapses, 1926, 180
Flower children, 426
Folklore of Capitalism (Arnold), 195
Folksingers, and 1960s social protest, 423
Follow-Through, educational program, 393
Fonda, Jane, 450
Food Administration, 120, 121, 206
Food Stamps, 441, 445, 464, 476
Foodstuffs, canned and processed, 22
Ford, Gerald, 414, 466, 475; and election of 1976, 470–471; pardons Nixon, 462; as president, 460, 461, 462, 463
Ford, Henry, 23, 162, 165, 174; and NRA, 217; stand on unions, 226
Ford Motor Co., 145, 376
Fordney-McCumber Act (1922), 154
Foreign affairs, and Hoover, 241–242
Foreign policy: in 1920s, 154–155; of Carter, 472–473; of Eisenhower, 362–367; of Ford, 463; of Kennedy, 382–387; of Reagan, 477. *See also* Cold War; Diplomacy
Forest Service, 77
Formosa, and Eisenhower foreign policy, 363, 364
Fortune, T. Thomas, 58
Fortune magazine, 202
For Whom the Bell Tolls (Hemingway), 198
Foster, John, 362
Foster, William Z., and election of 1932, 213
Four-power treaty, 155
Four-Square Gospel, 167
Fourteen Points, of Wilson, 130, 131, 132
France: casualties, WWI, 119; conquered, 1940, 248, 250; and Indochina, 363–364; and Suez crisis, 365; Vichy, 273–274; and

Washington Conference, 155
Franco, Francisco, 246
Frank, Jerome, 153, 195, 219
Frankfurter, Felix, 234, 401, 402
Frazier, E. Franklin, 170
Freedom Democratic Party, 409
Freedom rides, 378
French Indochina, Japan dominates, 256, 257
French Stories magazine, 148
Freud, Sigmund, 145, 146, 148–149
Friedan, Betty, 427, 429
Fuchs, Klaus, 322
Fuel Administration, 120
Fulbright, J. William, 383
Fundamentalists, in 1920s, 165, 167–168

Gaddis, John, 314
Gainesville Eight, 446
Galbraith, John Kenneth, 340, 349, 375; on technostructure, 399
Galveston Plan, 62
Garland, Hamlin, 7
Garner, John Nance, 210, 212
Garvey, Marcus, 171–172, 173, 408
Gary, Elbert, 128
Gasoline Alley (comic strip), 192
Gay liberation, 424
General Federation of Women's Clubs, 44
General Motors Corp., 145, 399, 469; and CIO, 225; stock prices, 1929–1932, 180
General Telephone and Electronics Corp., 443
Generation gap, 424
Geneva accord, on Indochina, 364
Geneva summit conference, 1955, 361
The Genius of American Politics (Boorstin), 347
Genteel Tradition, 35–37
Genteel values, assault on, 37–40
Gentleman from Indiana (Tarkington), 8
Gentlemen Prefer Blondes, 151
Gentlemen's Agreement (1907), 98
George, Henry, 35, 62
Germany: and freedom of seas, WWI, 107–109; signs Anti-Comintern Pact, 246; surrender, WWII, 295; Tripartite Pact with Italy and Japan, 1940, 255; and U.S. military effort, WWII, 267–273; and Versailles Treaty, 131–132. *See also* Hitler, Adolf

Getty, J. Paul, 184–185
Ghettos, northern cities, 56, 59, 170; crime in, 1960s, 397
GI Bill, 284
Gideon v. *Wainwright*, 401
Gilbreth, Frank, on nature of labor, 164
Gilman, Charlotte Perkins, 52–53, 56
Girdler, Tom, 227
Gladden, Washington, 34
Glass industry, 22
Glazer, Nathan, 395
Globalism, and Vietnam War, 418
GNP. *See* Gross National Product
Gold, Michael, 196, 197
Gold, Mike, on sexual emphasis, 150
Golden Bed (film), 148
Goldman, Emma, 52, 129
Goldman, Eric, 337, 387
Gold standard: and devaluation of dollar, 1933, 214; Hoover's policy on, 207, 208
Goldwater, Barry, 357, 390, 391, 452
Gompers, Samuel, 28, 29–30
Gone with the Wind (Mitchell), 200
Goode, Kenneth, 146
The Good Earth (Buck), 255
Good Housekeeping's Marriage Book: Twelve Ways to a Happy Marriage, 192
Goodman, Andrew, 409
Goodman, Paul, 343, 344, 421, 424, 426
Good neighbor policy, in Latin America, 243
Gordon, Richard and Katherine, 339
Gore, Albert, 352
Gore-McLemore resolutions, 109
"Gospel of Wealth" (Carnegie), 28
Government: black office holders, 440; executive branch, 1900, 71; expansion, WWII, 278–284. *See also* Bureaucracy; City government; Congress; Government spending; Supreme Court
Government spending: for agriculture, 1950s, 356; corporations, 399; and deficits, 1930s, 237–238; in 1920s, 155; in 1950s, 349; in 1969–1972, 441; and recession of 1937, 234; and unemployment, 1950s, 356; in WWII, 279. *See also* Defense spending; Government

The Graduate (film), 424
Graham, Billy, 346
Grand Coulee Dam, 206
Grant, Madison, 19–20, 174
Grant, Ulysses S., 461
Grapes of Wrath (Steinbeck), 190, 198
Gray, Patrick, 458
Great Britain; casualties, WWI, 119; and command of seas, WWI, 107–109; destroyer deal, 250; and Suez crisis, 365; and Washington Conference, 155; in WWII, 248
Great Depression, 188–190; repercussions, 190–202
Greater East Asia Co-Prosperity Sphere, 255, 261
The Great Illusion (Angell), 105
Great Society, of Johnson, 352, 375, 393–396
The Great Train Robbery (film), 21
Great War. *See* World War I
Greece, military aid to, post-WWII, 306, 310
Green Berets, 386
"The Green Hornet" (radio program), 200
The Greening of America (Reich), 424
Greensboro, N.C., lunch counter sit-ins, 378
Greer, Germaine, 440
Greer, destroyer, 254
Gregory, Thomas, 125, 126
Grew, Joseph, 257, 260
Grey, Sir Edward, 107, 109
Griffith, D.W., 60
Gross National Product (GNP); early 1900s, 95; and military spending, 1950s, 349; in 1920s, 141; in 1950s, 347–348; in WWI, 120; in WWII, 279
Groton School, 18
Group Theatre, 196, 200
Groves, Leslie, 269, 298
Growing Up Absurd (Goodman), 343
Guam, U.S. occupation, early 1900s, 94
Guevara, Ché, 422
Gun control, 466
Guthrie, Arlo, 423
Guthrie, Woody, 7, 198, 202

Hadley, Yale president, 25
Hagerty, James, 354
Haig, Alexander, 454, 477
Haiphong harbor, mined, 1972, 451

Haiti, U.S. occupation of, 102
Halberstam, David, 392
Haldeman, H. R., 444, 445, 452, 458, 462
Hall, G. Stanley, 36, 41
Halleck, Charles, 301
Hanighen, Frank, 244
Hanna, Mark, 75
Hanson, Ole, 127; on revolution, 128
Harding, Warren G., 121, 129, 138, 206, 461; and election of 1920, 159; as president, 156–157
Harlem: Hughes on, 170; riot, 1943, 290; riot, 1964, 410
Harlem Renaissance, 170, 173
Harper's magazine, 106
Harriman, Averell, 383, 385, 416
Harrington, Michael, 397, 445
Harrisburg Seven, 446
Harrison, Benjamin, 80, 362
Harvard *Crimson*, 127
Harvard University, campus unrest, 1960s, 421, 443
Hat industry, strike, turn of century, 26
Havemeyer, Henry, 28
Hawaii, Pearl Harbor attacked, 155, 258
Hawley-Smoot tariff (1930), 207
Hay, John, 94, 95, 96, 98
Haymarket affair, 26
Haynsworth, Clement F., Jr., 446, 447
Hays, Will, 191
Haywood, William (Big Bill), 49–50
Head Start, 393
Health, turn of century, 25
Health, Education, and Welfare Department, 446
Hearst, William Randolph, 230
Heflin, Thomas, on immigration, 175
Hell's Angels, 424
Hemingway, Ernest, 162, 198, 340
Hendrickson, Robert, 351
Hendrix, Jimi, 443
Hepburn Act, 77, 78, 79
Herberg, Will, 346
Herskovitz, Melville, 153
Herter, Christian, 367
Herzog (Bellow), 343
Hewitt, Abram, 61
Hickel, Walter, 444, 445
Hickok, Lorenz, on NRA, 217
Hicks, Granville, 196
Highway construction act (1956), 357
Hill, Napolean, 201

Hillis, Marjorie, 190
Himmler, Heinrich, on modern war, 268
Hippies, 426
Hirohito, Emperor of Japan, 258
Hiroshima, atomic bomb dropped on, 296
Hispanics, social problems, 1980s, 446–467
Hiss, Alger, 321, 322
Hitler, Adolf, 196; annexes Austria and Switzerland, aids Franco, 246, 247; assumes power, 1933, 243; declares war on U.S., 255; and nonaggression pact with Stalin, 247; and U.S., 1939–1941, 247–255. *See also* Germany; World War II
Ho Chi Minh, 363, 386, 387, 418
Hobby, Oveta Culp, 355
Hoffman, Abbie, 426, 427
Hoffman, Dustin, 424
Hofstadter, Richard, 346, 347
Holding companies, and stock market crash, 186
Holli, Melvin, 62
Holmes, Oliver Wendell, Jr., 41, 43, 126
Home building, post-WWII, 287
The Home Maker (Fisher), 150
Home ownership, in 1950s, 345
Home Owners Loan Corp., 214
Homestead strike, 26
Homosexuality, 424
Hoover, Herbert, 121, 153, 156, 157, 165, 250, 332, 370, 407; on economic progress, 148; and election of 1928, 159; and foreign affairs, 241–242; as president, 205–210
Hoover, J. Edgar, 128, 449
Hoovervilles, 181
Hopkins, Harry, 194, 214, 274; on Pearl Harbor, 262; on postwar cooperation, 277; and WPA, 220, 221
Hostages, in Iran, 473–474
Hours of work: maximum, 215, 236; in 1900, 26; in 1920s, 142–143; ten-hour day, 41
House, Edward, 107, 109, 135
House-Grey memorandum, 109
House Judiciary Committee, 459
House of Representatives, leadership, 72–73. *See also* Congress
House Rules Committee, 326
House Un-American Activities Committee (HUAC), 236, 321

Housing: discrimination, 1950s, 357–358; post-WWII, 302–303; segregation in, 408; tenements, New York, 1900, 11–13
Housing act, 317
Housing and Home Finance Agency, 380
Housing and Urban Development Department, 392
Houston: in 1900, 5; race riot, 1917, 122
Howard, Ebenezer, 343
Howard University, campus unrest, 1969, 443
Howe, Elias, 441
Howe, Frederic, 129
Howe, Louis, 212
Howells, William Dean, 36
How the Other Half Lives (Riis), 34
How to Win Friends and Influence People (Carnegie), 202
Huddleston, George, on starvation, 1932, 182
Huerta, Victoriano, 102, 103
Hughes, Charles Evans, 88, 111, 154, 156, 157, 234
Hughes, Langston, 173, 413; on Harlem, 170
Hull, Cordell, 243, 257, 258, 261
Hull House, Chicago, 46, 47
Humphrey, George, 355, 356
Humphrey, Hubert H., 314, 352, 353, 368, 391, 434; and election of 1968, 431, 432, 433
Hungary, revolution, 1956, 364–365
Hunter, Robert, on poverty, 25
Hunt Foods, 185
Hurley, Patrick, 274
Hutchins, Robert, 196

I Am a Fugitive from a Chain Gang (film), 197–198
IBM Corp., 344, 443
Iceland, U.S. occupies, 1941, 252
Ickes, Harold, 216, 232, 247
Idiot's Delight (Sherwood), 244
Illegitimacy, in 1950s, 398
Illiteracy, blacks, 1910, 56
I'll Take My Stand, 199
Immigrants: and employers' power, 27; illegal, 466–467; Japanese, Gentlemen's Agreement on, 98; and population, 1870–1930, 14–15; turn of century, 13–20; and unions, 29; women, in 1920s, 151
Immigration Restriction Act (1924), 175

Immigration Restriction League, 20, 44
Impeachment, of Nixon, 459–460
Imperialism: in Asia and Latin America under Taft and Wilson, 101–105; pressures, early 1900s, 95–105; and TR's *Realpolitik*, 97–101
Income, white vs. nonwhite, 1950–1970, 412
Income distribution: in 1920s, 189; in 1950s, 349; in 1960s, 375; in WWII, 284
Income tax, 74, 77, 81, 86
Indians: Oglala Sioux uprising at Wounded Knee, 455; and red power, 427
Indochina: aid to French in, 329; and Eisenhower foreign policy, 363–364; Geneva accord on, 364; Japan dominates, 257. *See also* Vietnam War
In Dubious Battle (Steinbeck), 198
Industrialization, turn of century, 20–23
Industry: growth, 1860–1920, 20–21; horizontal mergers and vertical combinations, 23; and military-industrial complex, 283–284; and NRA, 215–217; production, WWII, 282–283. *See also* Business; Corporations; Economy
Inflation: in early 1970s, 445; in late 1970s, 469; and oil prices, 457; post-WWII, 303; and wage and price controls, 1971, 451; WWI, 121–122
The Influence of Sea Power upon History (Mahan), 96
Inheritance tax, 77
Initiative, 65
Inland Steel Co., 377
Inland Waterways Commission, 77
Inner-directed culture, 339–340
Insull, Samuel, 186
Interest groups. *See* Pressure groups
Interest rates, and stock market crash, 187
Internal Revenue Service, 279, 458
Internal Security Act (1950), 320
International Ladies Garment Workers Union, 49
International Telephone and Telegraph Corp. (ITT), 399, 452
International Workers of the World (IWW, or Wobblies),

49–50, 413; leaders imprisoned, WWI, 126
Interracialism, to black power from, 407–414
Interstate commerce, and *Schechter* v. *U.S.*, 229
Interstate Commerce Commission (ICC), 79, 81
Intolerance, and McCarthyism, 323
Inventions, turn of century, 21
Investment trusts, and stock market crash, 186, 187
Iran, hostages held, 473–474
Irish, in urban politics, 17
Iron mining, 22–23
Isolationism, and America First, 250–251; and economic nationalism, 1930s, 243–244
Israel: Six-Day War, 442; and Suez crisis, 365; war with Arab states, 1973, 455–456
Italians: immigrants, 16; in urban politics, 17
Italy: Tripartite Pact with Germany and Japan, 1940, 255; and Washington Conference, 155
Iwo Jima, U.S. forces take, 295

Jackson State College, students killed by police at, 449
Jacobs, Jane, 397
Jagger, Mick, 424
James, Henry, on American cities, 9
James, William, 9, 33, 42–43
Janis, Elsie, 108
Japan: aggression in Asia and Pacific, 1931–1942, 256; atom bomb dropped on Hiroshima and Nagasaki, 296; bilateral defense treaty with, 1951, 329; hegemony in Korea, 98; invades China, 1937, 246; and Manchurian crisis, 1931, 242; signs Anti-Comintern Pact, 246; sinks *Panay*, 247; surrenders, WWII, 298; Tripartite Pact with Germany and Italy, 1940, 255; and U.S. military effort, WWII, 267–273; U.S. move toward war with, 255–259; and Versailles Conference, 130, 131; war with Russia, 1904, 97–98; and Washington Conference, 154–155; and Wilson's diplomacy, 102
Japanese: Gentleman's Agreement on immigration, 98;

restriction laws, 20
Japanese-Americans, internment, WWII, 281
Japan: Feet of Clay (Utley), 256
Jawboning, 206
Jaworski, Leon, 458, 459
Jaws (Benchley), 470
Jazz, 173
Jehovah's Witnesses, 280
Jenner, William, 306, 320–321
Jews, as immigrants, 15, 16
Jews Without Money (Gold), 196
Jim Crow Laws, 288, 408
Jim Jam Jems magazine, 148
Job Corps, 393
Jogging, 470
John Birch Society, 351, 390
John Reed clubs, 196
Johnson, Charles, 192
Johnson, Hiram, 63, 64, 133, 155, 232; on Wilson's wartime domestic policy, 122
Johnson, Hugh, 216, 217
Johnson, James Weldon, 60, 170
Johnson, Lyndon, 326, 333, 352, 353, 364, 368, 373, 382, 407, 453, 476; and affluence vs. social change, 402–403; and civil rights movement, 414; and disillusionment with liberalism, 392–397; and election of 1964, 390–391; popularity polls on, 408; as president, 387–392; problems, 397–400; and Vietnam War, 414–418; and Warren Court, 400–402
Johnson, Tom, 35, 61–62
Joint Chiefs of Staff, 306, 448
Jonathan Livingston Seagull (Bach), 470
Jones, Bobby, 165
Jones, Samuel (Golden Rule), 35, 62
Joplin, Janis, 443
Jordan, David Starr, 20
The Joy of Sex (Comfort), 470
The Jungle (Sinclair), 40
Jurisprudence, sociological, 41, 153
Justice Department, 128, 234, 280, 381, 446, 449, 458; Civil Rights Division, 317; and NRA, 215
"Just Plain Bill" (radio program), 200
Juvenile delinquency, in WWII, 287

Kansas City, population, 1900, 6
KDKA, radio station, 143
Kearney, destroyer, 254

Keats, John, 338–339
Kefauver, Estes, 352, 377
Kelley, Florence, 20, 46
Kellogg-Briand Pact (1928), 242
Kempton, Murray, 354
Keniston, Kenneth, 347
Kennan, George, 243, 311, 327, 360, 363, 386; on consumer society, 340–341; on McCarthyism, 320; on Stalin, 277, 308
Kennedy, Edward, 471, 472; and election of 1972, 452
Kennedy, John F., 323, 326, 353, 367, 478; elected in 1960, 367–370; and New Frontiers abroad, 382–387; and revolution in civil rights, 1960s, 378–382; on Vietnam, 387
Kennedy, Joseph, 212, 250, 251, 373
Kennedy, Robert, 374, 380, 385; and election of 1968, 431–432
Kennedy Memorial Stadium, Washington, 450
Kennedy-Nixon debates, 368–369
Kent State University, students killed by National Guardsmen, 448–449
Kerouac, Jack, 343
Kerr-Mills Bill (1960), 357
Key, V. D., 369
Key Biscayne, Florida, Nixon property at, 444
Keynes, John Maynard: on businessmen, 235; on Wilson, 86
Khomeini, Ayatollah Ruhollah, 473
Khrushchev, Nikita, 361, 367, 384, 385
King, Admiral, 280
King, Martin Luther, Jr., 373, 409, 419, 431; and Black Power movement, 411–414; and bus boycott, 358–359; and revolution in civil rights, 1960s, 378–381
Kinsey, Alfred C., 150, 341
Kipling, Rudyard, on Chicago, 9
Kissinger, Henry, 442, 450, 451, 453, 456, 459, 472
Kitchin, Claude, 111, 113
E. C. Knight case, 74
Knowland, William, 306, 361, 363
Know-Nothings, 323
Knox, Frank, 258
Knudsen, William, on NLRB, 225
Komisar, Lucy, on women's movement, 441
Konoye, Fumimoro, 257, 258, 261

Kopechne, Mary Jo, 452
Korea: Japanese hegomony in, 98; war, 324–330, 367; war ends, 1953, 361
Kraft, Joseph, 374
Kreditanstalt, collapses, 188
Kristol, Irving, 267
Krutch, Joseph Wood, 162
Kuhn-Loeb bank, 24
Ku Klux Klan, 60, 160; in 1920s 168–169

Labor: contract, as peonage, 56–57; Gilbreth on nature of, 164; legislation, post-WWII, 307; and Smith-Connally Act, 278. See also Hours of work; Labor force; Strikes; Unemployment; Union(s); Wages
Labor force: in 1900, 26; post-WWI, 143; women in, turn of century, 18. See also Labor
Labor-management relations: and NLRB, 224–225; post-WWII, 303–305
Labor movement. See Union(s)
Ladies Home Journal, 37
La Follette, Robert, 51, 63–64, 65, 73, 137, 434; on economic motives for war, 112–113; and election of 1924, 159; on Taft, 80; on TR, 78
La Follette, Robert, Jr., 228, 250, 306
La Guardia, Fiorello, 228
Laird, Melvin, 442
Land, single tax on, 35
Landon, Alfred M., 232
Lange, Dorothy, 199
Lansing, Robert, 107, 109, 362
Lansing-Ishii agreement (1917), 102
Laos: and Geneva accord, 364; invaded, 450; and SEATO, 364. See also Vietnam War
Lasch, Christopher, 469
Laski, Harold, 127; on New Deal, 237
Latin America: and Alliance for Progress, 383; and Eisenhower foreign policy, 366; good neighbor policy, 243; Reagan policy on, 477; TR's policy in, 100–101; U.S. investments, 1920s, 154; U.S. involvement, early 1900s, 101. See also Cuba
Laurence, William, on atomic bomb, 297
Law and order, 446

"Leaden-Eyed" (Lindsay), 25
League of Nations, 242; fight for, 129–137; and Versailles Treaty, 132–133, 134
League of Women Voters, 151
Leahy, William, 277
Lease, Mary Ellen, 7
Left: and election of 1932, 213; and election of 1968, 434–435; evaluation of FDR, 236; and FDR's wartime diplomacy, 273–274; in 1930s, 194–198; in 1950s, 347
Legion of Decency, 191
Lekachman, Robert, 462
LeMay, Curtis, 434; on nuclear weaponry, 296
Lemke, William (Liberty Bell), 231
Lend-lease, 252, 253, 254, 302
Lenin, V. I., 162, 312
Lennon, John, 423, 466
Lerner, Max, 330; on Truman, 295
Lesbianism, 424, 429
Lester, Julius, 413
Let Freedom Ring (Odets), 198
Let Us Now Praise Famous Men (Agee and Evans), 201
Leuchtenburg, William, 4
Levitt, William, 358
Levittown, Pennsylvania, housing discrimination in, 1950s, 358; mass-produced suburb, 338
Lewis, John L., 225, 250, 287, 303; and New Deal, 226
Lewis, Sinclair, 7, 61, 161; on Howells, 36
Liberalism: disillusion with, 1960s, 392–397; in 1950s, 352
Liberty League, 220
Liddy, Gordon, 461
Life Begins at Forty (Pitkin), 200
"Life Can Be Beautiful" (radio program), 200
Life expectancy: in 1930s, 184; turn of century, 25; in WWII, 284
Life style: of Negro women in South, 1912, 54; on Plains, 9; at turn of century, 3–4
Life with Father (Day), 192
Life with Mother (Day), 192
Liggetts stores, 145
Lilienthal, David, 215, 330; on Truman, 295
Lincoln, Abraham, 200
Lincoln Highway, 185
Lindbergh, Anne Morrow, 251
Lindbergh, Charles (Lone Eagle), 165, 250

Lindsay, Vachel, 25
Lippmann, Walter, 77, 162, 196, 230, 417; on new capitalist, 146
Literacy tests: banned for voters, 392; for immigrants, 13
Literature, naturalism, 39–40
Little Rock, Arkansas, schools integrated, 1957, 359–360
Live Alone and Like It (Hillis), 190
A Living Wage (Ryan), 26
Lloyd George, David, 130, 131, 132
Lochner v. *New York*, 41
Locke, Alain, 170
Lodge, Henry Cabot, 75, 97, 113; and Versailles Treaty, 134–137
Lodge, Henry Cabot, Jr., 367, 414
Lomasney, Martin, on political machines, 10
London, Jack, 51, 57
London Economic Conference, 1933, 243–244
The Lonely Crowd (Riesman), 339–340
"The Lone Ranger" (radio program), 200
Long, Huey (Kingfish), 194, 228, 229; and election of 1936, 231
Longworth, Alice Roosevelt, 158
Look magazine, 346
Looking Backward (Bellamy), 35
Look Out Whitey! Black Power's Gon' Get Your Mama! (Lester), 413
Lorentz, Pare, 197
Los Angeles: population, 1900, 6; Watts riot, 1965, 410
Louisville *Courier-Journal*, 84; on Dewey, 316
Love Story (Segal), 470
Low Countries, conquered, 1940, 248
Lowell, Robert, 430
Lowenstein, Allard, 465–466
Loyalty boards, post-WWII, 306
Loyalty programs, and Supreme Court, 352
Lubell, Samuel, 305
"Lucy in the Sky with Diamonds" (Lennon), song, 423
Lusitania, liner, sunk, 108
Lynching: of Emmet Till, 359; pre-WWI, 57
Lynd, Robert and Helen, 148, 153, 179, 191, 201; on automobile, 147

MacArthur, Douglas, 270; and Bonus Army, 210; and Korean

War, 324, 326, 327–330
Macdonald, Dwight, 340
MacMurray, John, 262
Macon County, Georgia, poverty in, 192
Madero, Francisco, 102
Mafia, 16
Magazines, pulps, in 1920s, 148
Maggie–A Girl of the Streets (Crane), 39
Magruder, Jeb, 461, 462
Mahan, Alfred Thayer, 96–97
Mail: parcel post, 23; Rural Free Delivery, 23
Mailer, Norman, 400, 425
Maintenance of membership clauses, union contracts, WWII, 287
Malapportionment, legislative, 400–401
Malcolm X, 409
Mallory v. *U.S.*, 352
Management: revolution, 145; scientific, 23, 164
The Managerial Revolution (Burnham), 344
Manhattan District Project, 269
Mann-Elkins Act (1910), 81
Manpower training program, 375, 391
"The Man with the Hoe" (Markham), 26
Mao Tse-tung, 278, 318, 319, 364, 422, 450
"Ma Perkins" (radio program), 200
Marcuse, Herbert, 424
Markham, Edwin, 26
Marriages, in WWII, 287
Marshall, George, 272, 290, 332; and Chiang vs. Mao in China, 318; and Marshall Plan, 306, 311; and Pearl Harbor, 260, 261
Marshall, Thurgood, 315, 380
Marshall Plan, 306, 311
Martin, Joseph, 301, 328
Marx, Karl, 422
Massachusetts: progressivism in, 45; tax cut demand, 1980, 469
Massachusetts, University of, campus unrest, 1969, 443
Masscult, 340
Masses magazine, 38, 125
Masters, Edgar Lee, 40
Mauldin, Bill, 269
May, Henry, 36
Mayaguez incident, 463
McAdoo, William G., 159
McCarthy, Eugene, 435, 471; and election of 1968, 430–433

McCarthy, Joseph, 194, 306, 354, 355, 361, 362; and McCarthyism, 319–324
McCarthyism, 319–324, 350–351
McCormick, Medill, 133
McGill, William J., 449
McGovern, George, 461, 471; and election of 1968, 432; and election of 1972, 452–453
McKay, Claude, 170, 171
McKinley, William, 8, 71, 75, 95–96; and Spanish-American War, 94
McNair, Lesley J., 269
McNamara, Robert, 376, 377, 386, 387, 417, 418, 450
McPherson, Aimee Semple, 167
McTeague (Norris), 39
Mead, Margaret, 4, 153, 201
Means, Gardiner, 145, 344
Meany, George, 418
Meat Inspection Act, 77, 79
Media, in 1950s, 345–346
Medicaid, 391, 464, 467, 476
Medicare, 391, 393, 394, 476
Megalopolis, 338
Mellon, Andrew, 157, 158, 189
The Melting Pot (Zangwill), 13
Mencken, H. L., 38, 40, 61, 161, 175; on Coolidge, 158, 159; on educated Negro, 57; on Harding's writing, 157; on TR, 79; on Wilson, 86
Merchants of Death (Englebrecht and Hanighen), 244
Meredith, James, 379, 411
Mergers, turn of century, 24
Mesabi Range, Minnesota, 22, 24
Messenger, 172
Messersmith, George, 245–246
Metropolitan Magazine, 106
Mexican-Americans, in California, 1930s, 184
Mexico, Wilson's intervention in, 102–105
Miami, riot, 1980, 466
Midcult, 340
Middle class: black, 59, 440, 464; in 1920s, 143; in 1950s, 337–344; in WWII, 284
Middle East: in 1947–1978, 456; Six-Day War, 442; war, Israel and Arab States, 1973, 455–456
Middletown (Lynd), 153
Midway, battle of, 268
Migrant, agricultural laborers, poverty of, 182–184
Migration, of blacks in WWII, 288
Military effort, WWII, 267–273
Military-industrial complex,

283–284, 386; Eisenhower on, 368

Military spending, Reagan policy, 476, 477

Millis, Walter, 244

Mills, C. Wright, 304–305, 343, 344, 426

Minicomputer, 464

Minimum wage, 357; established, 236; and NRA, 215; post-WWII, 306; Supreme Court ruling on, 233, 234; for women, 48. *See also* Wages

Mining: strike, mid-1930s, 194; and WWI, 49. *See also* Coal mining

Minneapolis, population, 1900, 6

Minor, Robert, 105

Minorities, militance of, 1960s, 427

Miranda v. *Arizona*, 401

Missile gap, 386

Mississippi, Jackson State University students killed by police, 449

Mississippi, University of, integrated, 1962, 379

Missouri Pacific Railroad, 182

Mitchell, Billy, 154

Mitchell, John, 446, 449, 450, 462

Mitchell, Margaret, 200

Mitchell, Wesley, 153

Mobil Oil Corp., 443

Model Cities program, 393

Modern Corporation and Private Property (Berle and Means), 145

Modern Times (film), 23

Mohawk Valley Formula, 226–227

Moley, Raymond, 212, 215, 231

Molotov, Vyacheslav, 313

Money market, turn of century, 24

Monopoly (game), 201

Monroe, Marilyn, 345, 425

Monroe Doctrine, 132; Roosevelt Corollary, 100, 241

Montgomery, Alabama, bus boycott, 1950s, 358–359

Montgomery Ward stock prices, 1929–1932, 180

Morgan, J. P., 24, 28, 77, 399

Morgan, House of, 24, 25

Morgan, Marabel, 470

Morgan, Robin, 440

Morgenthau, Hans, 417

Morgenthau, Henry, 247

Morgenthau Plan, 268–269

Morrison, Jim, 423–424

Moscow, Nixon visit, 451

Moses, "Grandma," 200

Movies: attendance in 1930s, 190; censorship, 1930s, 191

Moynihan, Daniel Patrick, 398, 445

Mr. Deeds Goes to Town (film), 199

Mr. Smith Goes to Washington (film), 199

"Mr. Tambourine Man" (Dylan), song, 423

Ms. magazine, 440

Muckrakers, 40

Muhammed, Elijah, 408, 409

Muir, John, 83

Muller v. *Oregon*, 42, 74

Multinational corporation, 399

Multiversities, 421

Mumford, Lewis, 130, 196, 397

Muncie, Indiana, in mid-1930s, 201

Munich Conference, 1938, 247

Munitions making, 244–245

Murphy, Charles, 10

Murphy, Frank, 281

Murray, Philip, 305

Muskie, Edmund, 451; and election of 1968, 432, 433; and election of 1972, 452

Mussolini, Benito, 162; invades Ethiopia, 1935, 243, 245

My Lai massacre, 416

Myrdal, Gunnar, 290

Nader, Ralph, 422, 442

Nagasaki, atomic bomb dropped on, 296

Nanking, slaughter by Japanese in, 256

Napalm, 416

Nasser, Gamal Abdel, 365, 366

Nathan, George Jean, 38

National Afro-American League, 58

National American Women's Suffrage Association, 53

National Association for the Advancement of Colored People (NAACP), 44, 46, 57, 58, 59, 231, 289, 359, 378, 380

National Association of Credit Men, 179

National Association of Manufacturers, 28

National Broadcasting Co. (NBC), 143, 145

National Business League, 44

National Civic Federation, 28, 44

National Civil Liberties Bureau, 125

National Consumers' League, 46, 151

National Defense Education Act (1958), 357

National Defense Research Committee, 269

National Endowment for the Arts, 392

National Endowment for the Humanities, 392

National Farm Workers, 427

National income: in 1920s, 141–142; in 1929–1932, 180; in WWII, 284

National Institute of Public Administration, 153

Nationalist clubs, 35

National Labor Relations Act. *See* Wagner Act

National Labor Relations Board, 224–225

National Organization for Women (NOW), 52, 428, 429, 430, 441

National Recovery Administration (NRA), 215–217; Supreme Court strikes down, 229

National Resources Planning Board, 278

National Rivers and Harbors Congress, 44

National Security Act, 306

National Security Council, 306, 325–326

National Student League, 195

National Urban League, 59, 359

National Youth Administration, 222

Nation magazine, 37–38

Native Son (Wright), 198, 200

Nativism, 13–14, 18–19, 175, 323; and feminism, 55

The Negro Family (Moynihan), 398

Negro World (newspaper), 171

Neighborhood Youth Corps, 393, 394

Nelson, Donald, 282

Neustadt, Richard, 472

Neutrality Act, of 1935, 245; of 1937, 246

Newark, riot, 1967, 410

New Deal: and CIO, 226; evaluation of, 236–238; and opposition, 228–231; stalemate, 232–236

New Economic Policy, of Nixon, 402, 451

New era, of 1920s, 148–154

New Freedom, of Wilson, 88

New Frontier, of Kennedy, 352, 368, 370, 373–378, 389; and

foreign affairs, 1960s, 382–387
Newlands Act, 77
New Left, 421, 422, 424, 426
Newman, Paul, 450
New Masses, 196, 197
New Nationalism, of Theodore
   Roosevelt, 78, 82
New Republic, 20, 135, 314
New Right, 476
Newton, Huey, 413
New York City: black population,
   1920s, 59, 170; clothing
   workers' strike, 1909, 49;
   crowding and tenements, 1900,
   10–13; Harlem riots, 290, 410;
   population, 1900, 6; Triangle
   Shirt Waist Company fire, 26
New York *Herald Tribune*, 233
New York State, progressivism
   in, 45
New York *Sun*, 93
The New York Times, 19, 84, 280,
   352, 376, 444
New York Women's Trade Union
   League, 49
New York World, 22
New Zealand, and ANZUS
   treaty, 329
Niebuhr, Reinhold, 35
Nimitz, Chester, 268
Nine-power treaty, 154
Nixon, Richard, 306, 321, 323,
   364, 367, 398, 418, 470, 472, 478;
   back taxes, 458; debates with
   Kennedy, 368–369; and election
   of 1952, 330–333; and election
   of 1968, 433–435; impeachment,
   459–460; and intensification of
   antiwar sentiment, 448–450;
   and international problems,
   453–457; and persistence of
   discord, early 1970s, 443–445;
   as president, 439–442;
   presidential pardon for, 462;
   reelected in 1972, 451–453;
   resigns, 460; southern strategy,
   446–447; turnabout, 1971–1972,
   450–453; and Vietnam War,
   447–450; and Watergate, 452,
   457–461
Nixon Doctrine, 442
Nixonomics, 445
Nonaggression pact:
   Russo-German, 247;
   Russo-Japanese, 257
Noninterventionism, rise of,
   1933–1936, 243–245
Nonwhites, life expectancy, turn
   of century, 25
Norris, Frank, 39

Norris, George, 73, 82, 112, 113;
   and TVA, 214, 215
Norris, J. Frank, 167
Norris-La Guardia Act (1932), 206
North Atlantic Treaty
   Organization (NATO), 317, 364,
   477
Northern Securities Co., 41, 74, 77
Norway, conquered, 1940, 248
Novak, Robert, 388–389
Nuclear accident, at Three Mile
   Island, 468
Nuclear fission, 185
Nuclear weapons: disarmament,
   1960s, 385–386; and
   Eisenhower foreign policy, 363;
   limitations on, 472. *See also*
   Atomic bomb
Nye, Gerald P., 244–245

O'Brien, Lawrence, 445, 451
Obsolescence, planned, 145
O'Connor, Sandra Day, 476
Odets, Clifford, 198
Office for Scientific Research and
   Development, 283
Office of Economic Opportunity
   (OEO), 393, 394
Office of Price Administration,
   279, 451
Office of Production
   Management, 282
Office of War Information, 280,
   281
Ohio, Kent State University
   students killed by National
   Guardsmen, 448–450
Oil industry, 20
Oil prices, in late 1970s, 468
Okinawa, U.S. forces take, 295
Old Age Revolving Pensions,
   Ltd., 228
The Old Man and the Sea
   (Hemingway), 340
Old Wives for New (film), 148
Oligopoly, 145
Olney, Richard, 93, 104
Olson, Floyd, 228
Olympic games, boycott, 1980,
   473
Omaha, race riot, 1917, 122
O'Neill, Eugene, 144
On the Road (Kerouac), 343
Open Door at Home (Beard), 244
Open Door policy, in China,
   94–95, 97, 102, 255, 257, 319
Oppenheimer, J. Robert, 350
Organization for Afro-American
   Unity, 409
Organization Man, 161

Organization Man (Whyte), 339,
   342
Orlando, Vittorio, 130
Ostrogorski, M. I., 72
The Other America (Harrington),
   397
Other-directed society, 340

Pacification, in South Vietnam,
   416
Page, Walter Hines, 107, 108
Pahlavi, Mohammed Reza, Shah
   of Iran, 473
Palestine Liberation
   Organization, 457
Palmer, A. Mitchell, 127, 128–129
Pan-Africanism, 170–171
Panama Canal, 98–100
Panama treaty, 472
Panay, gunboat, sunk, 247
Panic: of 1901, 24; of 1907, 24, 79
Paris: Eisenhower-Khrushchev
   summit conference, 1960, 366;
   Vietnam War peace talks, 418
Park, Robert, 153, 173
Parker, Alton B., 77, 471
Parker, Dorothy, 150; on
   Coolidge, 158
Parks, Rosa, 358
Parral incident, 103
Passing of the Great Race
   (Grant), 19–20, 174
Pathet Lao, 383
Payne-Aldrich Tariff (1909), 82
Payroll tax, and social security,
   223, 224
Peace Corps, 383, 421
Peace Fund, 1910, 105
Peale, Norman Vincent, 340, 346,
   444
Pearl Harbor: attack on, 155, 258;
   Hopkins on, 262; and
   revisionists, 259–261
Peek, George, 219
Pendergast machine, 299
Pennsylvania, University of, 46
Pennsylvania Railroad, 145
Pennsylvania State University,
   campus unrest, 1969, 443
Pension, old-age, 222–223
Pension funds, 399
Pentagon papers, 446, 450
Perkins, Frances, 217, 225, 282
Pershing, John J., 103
Pescadore Islands, 364
Petroleum, and automobile, 144
Philadelphia: black population,
   1920, 59; population, 1900, 6;
   unemployment, 1932, 181
Philadelphia Academy, 36

Philadelphia Plan, 446
Philippines: bilateral defense treaty with, 1951, 329; captured, 1944, 268; U.S. occupation, early, 1900s, 94
Phillips, David Graham, 10, 40, 73
Phillips, Kevin, 446
Pietism, in 1920s, 165–168
Pinchot, Gifford, 77; controversy with Ballinger, 82–84
Pingree, Hazen, 61–62
Pitkin, Walter, 200
Pittsburgh, population in, 1900, 6
Pleiku, battle at, 416
Plessy v. *Ferguson*, 74, 351
The Plow That Broke the Plains (film), 197
"Plumbers," White House, 451, 452
The Plum Tree (Phillips), 10
Plunkitt, George Washington, on political machines, 10
Point four, 317
Poland: invaded, 1939, 248; military regime, 477; rebellion, 1950s, 364
Political machines, turn of century, 10
Political science, in 1920s, 153
Politics: and Babbittry, 1920s, 161–165; ethnics in, 17–18; in 1920s, 155–161; of 1976–1982, 470–474; of Taft, 80–84; turn of century, 71–72
Pollack v. *Farmers' Loan and Trust Co.*, 74
Pollock, Jackson, 343
Poll tax, outlawed in federal elections, 392
Pollution, 425
Popular culture: and domesticity, 1930s, 192; in 1920s, 148–149; in 1930s, 200–201
Population: and baby boom, 344–345; cities, turn of century, 5–6; density, Manhattan, 1894, 10; and immigration, 1870–1930, 14–15; in 1900, 4; in WWII, 285
Population Bomb (Ehrlich), 425
Pornography, 424; Supreme Court ruling on, 401
"Portia Faces Life" (radio program), 200
Pound, devaluation of, 1931, 188
Pound, Roscoe, 41
Poverty: in cities, 1960s, 397–398; and Kennedy programs, 375; in late 1970s, 464; migrant agricultural workers, 182–184; in 1930s, 192–194; in 1950s, 349;

and social reform, 33; turn of century, 25
Poverty (Hunter), 25
Powel, Harford, Jr., 146
Powell, Adam Clayton, 376
Powell, Lewis F., Jr., 447
The Power Elite (Mills), 343
Pragmatism, 42–43
Prayers in schools, Supreme Court ruling on, 400, 401
Presidency, power, WWII, 280
Press conferences, of FDR, 238
Pressure groups, 30, 44; Anti-Saloon League, 61; and legislation, Eisenhower years, 357; and New Deal, 238; in 1960s, 376, 398–400; and progressivism, 44–46; women's suffrage, 53; WWI, 121
Prices: controls, 1970s, 451, 455; controls, WWI, 121–122; decline, 1930s, 180; post-WWII, 303; and steel industry, 1960s, 377; stocks, 1929, 180
Primary, direct, 65–67
Princeton University, 85
Prisons, violence, early 1970s, 443–444
Production, in WWII, 282–283
Productivity, decline in, 469
Profits, corporate, 1915–1929, 145
Progress and Poverty (George), 35
Progressive party, 53, 347; and election of 1912, 84, 86; and election of 1948, 314, 315; and Taft, 80–84; and TR, 77–78
Progressivism, 43–46; broad visions, 46–60; and electoral reform, 65–67; narrow visions, 60–65; and social justice, 46–52; successes and failures, 67–68; and women's rights, 52–56
Prohibition, 60–61
Prohibitionists, in 1920s, 165–167
The Promised Land (Antin), 13
Propaganda, WWI, 124
Proposition 13, 469
Prostitution, in 1930s, 191
Protestant Catholic Jew (Herberg), 346
"Protocols of the Elders of Zion," 174–175
Provisional Revolutionary Government (PRG), of Vietcong, 454, 455
Psychology, and advertising, 145–146
Public assistance, in 1934, 184
Public relations, in 1920s, 146–147

Public Utilities Holding Company Act (1935), 229
Public Welfare Department, 156
Public Works Administration, 214, 216, 232
Pulitzer Prize, 244
Pullman strike, 26, 28
Pupil placement laws, and school segregation, 358
Pure Food and Drug Act, 77, 79
Purity movement, 37

Quality of life, cities, turn of century, 9–13
Quarantine speech, of FDR, 246, 247
Quemoy and Matsu, 364, 367, 368

Rabbit Run (Updike), 343
Race relations, H. Rap Brown on, 412
Races of Man (Ripley), 19
Racism, black, 408–409
Radford, Arthur, 364
Radical protest, in 1960s, 407
Radical Right, in 1950s, 351
Radio, 21; in 1930s, 190, 200; post-WWI, 143
Radio Corp. of America, stock prices, 1929–1932, 180
Railroads, 20; interurban, 23; Pullman car, 21; Wisconsin commission on, 64–65
Rand, James H., 226
Rand Corp., 450
Randolph, A. Philip, 172–173, 289, 290, 413
Rankin, Jeannette, 259
Rationing, in WWII, 284
Rauschenbusch, Walter, 34
Ray, James Earl, 431
Rayburn, Sam, 353, 378
Rayon, 142
La Raza, 427
Reagan, Ronald, 390, 433, 466, 470; as president, 474–478
Reaganomics, 476
Realpolitik, of TR, 97–101
Rebellion, of youth in 1960s, 420–422
Rebozo, C. G. (Bebe), 444
Recall, 65
Recession: of early 1970s, 445; of 1937, 234; of 1949, 307; of 1969, 441
Reciprocal Trade Agreements Act (1934), 243
Reconstruction Finance Corp., 206, 282
Red power, 427

Red scare, post-WWI, 127–129, 323

Reed, James, 133–134

Reed, John, 38, 196

Referendum, 65

Reform: barriers, post-WWII, 300–302; city government, early 1900s, 61–63; electoral, 65–67; and Genteel Tradition, 35–40; in 1920s, 156; prohibition, 60–61; racial, 56–60; social, 46–52; and social Darwinism, 40–43; state government, early 1900s, 63–65; women's rights, 52–56

Reformers, turn of century, 33–35

Regionalist movement, 199

Rehnquist, William H., 447

Reich, Charles, 424

Religion: new piety, 1950s, 346; social gospel, 34–35

Remington Corp., 226

Rent strikes, in 1930s, 194

Republican party: and election of 1912, 80, 84–86; and election of 1936, 232; and election of 1964, 390–391; and League of Nations, 135–136; and McCarthyism, 323; in 1920s, 158

Republic of the Golden Rule, 35

Republic Steel Corp., 227

Resettlement Administration, 219

Resource Recovery Act, 442

Reston, James, 355, 356, 377, 382, 450

Restrictionism, 19–20

Retailing, 23; chain stores, 1920s, 145

Reuben James, destroyer, 254

Reuther, Walter, 226, 305, 315

Revenue Act (1916), 88

Revisionists, and Pearl Harbor, 259–261

Rexall Stores, 145

Reynolds, Debby, 345

Reynolds, Malvina, 339, 423

Reynolds v. *Sims*, 400

Rhee, Syngman, 324, 325

Rhodes, James, 448

Rice, Elmer, 144

Richardson, Elliot, 458

Ridgway, Matthew, 324

Riesman, David, 339–340

Right: ascendancy, 1950s, 349–353; and election of 1932, 213; and election of 1936, 231; and election of 1964, 390–391; and FDR's wartime diplomacy, 274–275; and Korean War,

325–326; opposition to New Deal, 229–231; and Reagan presidency, 476–478

Riis, Jacob, 5–6, 10, 34

Riots: anti-Oriental, California, 1907, 98; Chicago, 1968, 431; Miami, 1980, 466; in 1943, 290; in 1960, 410–411; pre-WWI, 57; prison, 444; WWI, 122–123

Ripley, William Z., 19

The River (film), 197

Rivers, Mendell, 401

Road to War (Millis), 244

Robber Barons, 28

Roberts, Kenneth, 174

Roberts, Owen, 234

Robinson, Edwin Arlington, 39

Rochester, New York, riot, 1964, 410

Rockefeller, John D., 127

Rockefeller, John D., Jr., 73

Rockefeller, Nelson, 444, 461; and election of 1968, 433

Rockwell, Norman, 340

Roe v. *Wade*, 440

Roethke, Theodore, 201

Rogers, Will, 186; on FDR, 213; on trickle down theory, 207

Rogers, William, 442

Rolling Stones, 423

Romney, George, and election of 1968, 433

Roosevelt, Eleanor, 198, 210, 232; on Kennedy, 368; on turn of century genteel values, 38

Roosevelt, Franklin D., 159, 185–186, 206, 289, 370, 377, 388, 391, 392, 397, 476, 478; and AAA, 217–220; Asian diplomacy, 261–262; closes banks, 1933, 180–181; elected in 1932, 210–213; and forgotten man, 220–225; and Hitler, 1939–1941, 247–255; and hope of appeasement, 1936–1938, 245–247; and military effort, WWII, 267–273; and move toward war with Japan, 255–259; and New Deal stalemate, 232–236; and noninterventionism, 243–245; and NRA, 215–217; and opposition to New Deal, 228–231; reelected in 1936, 231–232; and wartime diplomacy, 273–278

Roosevelt, Franklin D., Jr., 314

Roosevelt, Theodore, 22, 36, 37, 41, 47, 51, 75–77, 110, 425, 461;

on conservatism, 83; and election of 1912, 84–86; on labor agitation, 28; legacy of, 78–80; on muckrakers, 40; as progressive, 77–78; *Realpolitik* of, 97–101; rift with Taft, 81–82

Roosevelt Corollary, 100, 241

Root, Elihu, 76

Root-Takahiro Agreement (1908), 98

Rosenberg, Harold, 343

Rosenberg, Julius and Ethel, 322

Rosenfeld, Morris, 22

Rosie the Riveter, 286

Ross, Edward A., 20

Rostow, Walt W., 387

Roszak, Theodore, 425

Rubin, Jerry, 426, 427

Ruckelshaus, William, 458

Rural Electrification Administration, 218

Rural Free Delivery, 23

Rural life, and growth of cities, turn of century, 7–8

Rusk, Dean, 382

Russell, Richard, 301, 330, 378, 389

Russia: casualties, WWI, 119; war with Japan, 1904, 97–98. *See also* Soviet Union

Rustin, Bayard, 171

Rough Riders, 75

Round Robin, 132

Ruth, Babe, 165

Ryan, John A., 26

Saarland, and League of Nations, 131

Sacco, Nicola, 129, 163, 164

Sadat, Anwar, 472, 473

Saigon, attack on American embassy in, 416

Sakharov, Andrei, 472

Sales tax, and social security, 223

Salinger, J. D., 343

San Clemente, California, Nixon property at, 444

Sandburg, Carl, 200

San Fernando State, campus unrest, 1969, 443

San Francisco: general strike, 1900, 26; Haight-Ashbury district, 423

Sanger, Margaret, 12–13, 52

San Quentin prison, violence at, 443–444

Santayana, George, 35, 43

Santo Domingo: and Roosevelt Corollary, 100; U.S. occupation of, 102

Saturday Evening Post, 124
Savings, 23
"Say It Loud—I'm Black and I'm Proud" (Brown), song, 413
Schechter v. *U.S.*, 229
Schenck v. *U.S.*, 126
Schine, G. David, 350
Schlafly, Phyllis, 441
Schlesinger, Arthur, Jr., 468; on Lyndon Johnson, 391
School and Society (Dewey), 42
Schools: busing, 440; closings, 1930s, 180. *See also* Colleges and universities; Education; School segregation
School segregation: ends in Little Rock, Arkansas, 1957, 359–360; in 1950s, 357–358; in 1960s, 408; Supreme Court ruling on, 439–440
Schwab, Charles, 24
Schwerner, Michael, 409
Science, rejection of, 1960s, 425
Science magazine, 20
Scopes, John, 167
Search and destroy missions, in South Vietnam, 416
Sears, Roebuck & Co., 23
Seattle, general strike, 1932, 194
Securities Act (1933), 214
Securities and Exchange Commission (SEC), 220
Security risks, 350, 352
Sedition Act (WWI), 50, 125, 126
Sedition Slammers, 126
Seeger, Pete, 423
Segal, Erich, 470
Selective Service, 279
Self-respect, quest for, 1930s, 201– 202
Senate: leadership, 72–73; and Versailles Treaty, 132–137. *See also* Congress
Senate Finance Committee, 390
Senate Foreign Relations Committee, 134, 383
Senate Judiciary Committee, 380
Senate Select Committee on Campaign Practices, 458
Senators, direct election of, 65
The Sensuous Man, 470
Separate but equal doctrine, 74
Service, John, 352
Service v. *Dulles*, 352
Settlement houses, early 1900s, 47–48
Sevareid, Eric, 307, 471
Sex, taboos rejected, 1960s, 424
Sex discrimination, banned, 440
Sexes, relations between, turn of century, 36–37

Sexual behavior, in late 1970s, 465
Sexual Behavior in the Human Female (Kinsey), 341
Sexual Behavior in the Human Male (Kinsey), 341
Sexual liberation, and women's rights, 52
Sexual mores, in 1920s, 148–152; in 1930s, 190–194; in 1950s, 341–342
Sexual tensions, and civil rights movement, 409
Shahn, Ben, 163, 197
Shame of the Cities (Steffens), 40
Shannon, William, 337
"Share Our Wealth" crusade, 194, 229
Shaw, Anna Howard, 55
Sheen, Fulton J., 346
Sherman Antitrust Act, 74, 78, 82, 88
Sherwood, Robert, 244
Shipping Board, 120
Ships: armed, WWI, 112; armed, WWII, 254; and command of sea, WWI, 107–109; naval vessels as escorts, WWII, 252–254; sunk by submarines, WWI, 119
Shipyards, strike, post-WWI, 127
Shoup, David, 383
Shriver, R. Sargent, 452, 453
Shuttlesworth v. *Birmingham Board of Education*, 358
Siegfried, Andre, 143
Sierra Club, 83
Simmons, William J., 168–169
Simon, Paul, 424
Sinclair, Upton, 40, 51, 61
Sirhan, Sirhan, 431
Sirica, John, 458, 459
Sister Carrie (Dreiser), 39
Sisterhood Is Powerful (Morgan), 440
Sit-down strikes, 226, 227
Sit-ins, at lunch counters, 378
Six-Day War, 442
Skyjacking, early 1970s, 443
Skyscrapers, New York, 1900, 6
Slavs: immigrants, 16; in urban politics, 17
Sloan, Alfred P., 145
Slums, urban, 1900, 10–13
Smart Set magazine, 38
Smith, Alfred E., 159, 175, 206, 368; and election of 1932, 210, 212
Smith, Gerald L. K., 231
Smith, Harold, 300
Smith, Howard, 301
Smith Act (1940), 280, 320, 352

Smith-Connally Act (1943), 278
Smith-Lever Act (1914), 89
Snyder, Charles, 299
Snyder, John, 302
Soap operas, on radio, 1930s, 200
Social change, vs. affluence, 402–403
Social Darwinism, 28; under siege, 40–43
Social Frontier magazine, 195
Social gospel, 34–35
Social hygiene movement, 37
Socialist party, 347; and election of 1928, 159; and election of 1932, 213; and election of 1936, 232; and isolationists, 1940, 251; and social justice, 50–52
Social justice: and progressivism, 46–52; and women's rights, 52–56
Social lag, 44
Social problems, in 1976–1980, 464–470
Social programs, Reagan policy on, 476, 477–478
Social Register, 19
Social science, in 1920s, 152–153
Social Science Research Council, 153
Social security, 222–224, 306, 317, 441, 464, 476
Social services, growth, 1960s, 396
Social welfare, spending, 1969–1972, 441
Social workers, and welfare policies, 1960s, 393
Society: and WWII, 284–291; polyglot, in 1960s, 398
Society for the Preservation of White Integrity, 357
Society of Mayflower Descendants, 19
Sociology, in 1920s, 153
Soil Conservation Service, 218
Solar energy, 468
Soledad Brothers, 443
Solomon Islands, captured, 1942, 268
Sons of the Revolution, 18
Sorokin, Pitirim, 341
Soule, George, 198
Souls of Black Folk (Du Bois), 58
Sound of Silence (Simon), song, 424
South Dakota, Oglala Sioux uprising at Wounded Knee, 455
South East Asia Treaty Organization (SEATO), 364
Southern Christian Leadership Conference, 378
Soviet Union: Allied occupation,

post-WWI, 130–131; and Carter policy, 472–473; casualties, WWII, 273; and Eisenhower policy, 360–367; and FDR's wartime diplomacy, 275–278; joins Allies in Pacific, WWII, 296; and lend-lease, 253; Nixon visit, 1972, 451; and Suez crisis, 365; and U.S. anticommunism, 312–314; and U.S. containment policy, 1950s, 361; U.S. recognizes, 1933, 243. *See also* Cold War

Space exploration, in 1960s, 375

Space shuttle, 464

Spain, civil war, 246

Spanish-American War, 75, 94

Spargo, John, 26

Spear, Allan, 174

Special Investigation Unit, 451

Speculation, and stock market crash, 186, 188

The Spirit of '76 (film), 126

Spiritualism, in 1960s, 425

The Split-Level Trap (Gordon), 339

Spock, Benjamin, 345, 419

Spoon River Anthology (Masters), 40

Springfield, Illinois, race riot, 1908, 57

Springfield *Republican*, 100

Sputnik, 357

Square Deal, of Theodore Roosevelt, 77

Stagflation, 445, 450, 469

Stalin, Josef, 196, 268, 361, 363; and Cold War, 307–310; and nonaggression pact with Hitler, 247; and second front in Europe, 272–273

Standard Oil Co. case, 77

Stanton, Elizabeth Cady, 54

Starvation, and depression, 1932, 182

State Department, 350, 442; and McCarthyism, 320; purge, 1953, 362–363

State government: FERA grants, 1933, 214; reform, early 1900s, 63–65; and social security, 222–224; spending, 1920s, 155

States' Rights Democratic party, and election of 1948, 315

Staunton, Virginia, city manager, 62

Steel industry, 20; and labor unrest, 27; "little steel" companies, 227; in 1930s, 185; and prices, 1960s, 377; strike, post-WWI, 127, 128

Steffens, Lincoln, 35, 40, 147–148, 162, 163, 196

Steinbeck, John, 190, 192, 198; on poverty of migrants, 182–184

Stephenson, David, 169

Stevenson, Adlai, 345, 352, 353, 354, 368; and election of 1952, 330–332; and Cuban missile crisis, 385

Stewart, Potter, 466

Stilwell, Joseph (Vinegar Joe), 274

Stimson, Henry, 209, 241, 242, 247, 250, 258, 284, 310; on black leadership, 290; on FDR as administrator, 282; and Manhattan District Project, 269–270

Stockman, David, 476

Stock market crash, 1929, 179–186; reasons for, 186–188

Stock prices: in 1920s, 145; in 1929–1932, 180; in WWII, 120

Stokes, Rose Pastor, 126

Stone, Harlan, 233

Stone, I. F., 355; on Eisenhower vs. Kennedy, 374; on Truman era, 299

Stone, William J., 109

Strategic Arms Limitation Talks II, 472, 477

Strategic bombing, WWII, 270–272; and Eisenhower foreign policy, 363

Streisand, Barbra, 450

Strikes: cooling-off period, 278; in mid-1930s, 194; in 1970s, 443; post-WWI, 127; post-WWII, 303–305; sit-down, 225, 226, 227, 234; and social justice movement, 49–50; turn of century, 26–27; in WWII, 287–288. *See also* Union(s); Wages

Strong, Josiah, on slum life, 1900, 12

Student League for Industrial Democracy, 195

Student Nonviolent Coordinating Committee (SNCC), 378, 408, 409, 411, 413

Students for a Democratic Society, 421

Studs Lonigan (Farrell), 198, 200

Submarines: in WWI, 107–109, 119; in WWII, 254

Suburbs: and automobile, 144; in 1950s, 337–339; and WWII, 287

Subversive Activities Board, 320

Subway, in Boston, 1900, 6

Suez crisis, 1950s, 365

Suffrage, for women, 53–56

Sullivan, Louis, on Chicago, 9

Sullivan, Mark, 231

Summit conference: Eisenhower-Khrushchev, in Paris, 1960, 366; Geneva, 1955, 361; Kennedy-Khrushchev, in Vienna, 384; Roosevelt-Churchill, 268; Teheran, 223

Sumner, William Graham, 28

Sunday, Billy, 127, 167

Sundquist, James, on government, 397

Superpatriotism, WWI, 124–125

Super-Sonic Transport (SST), 442

Supreme Court, 41, 74–75; abortion ruling, 440, 467; affirmative action rulings, 464–465; Brandeis named to, 88; Clark named to, 299; and internment of Japanese-Americans, WWII, 281; and McCarthyism, 320; Nixon appointments to, 446–447; and Radical Right, 351–352; Roosevelt's effort to reform, 232–234; ruling on death penalty, 466; ruling on school desegregation, 439–440; ruling on segregation of buses, 359; ruling on white primaries, 289; and sit-down strikes, 225; and social security, 224; sustains wartime espionage and sedition statutes, 126; Truman names Burton to, 298; Vinson named chief justice, 299; under Warren, 400–402; woman appointed to, 476

Sussex, channel steamer, sunk, 109

Sweatshops, 49

Swift, Gustavus, 23

Swift and Co., 79

Symbols of Government (Arnold), 195

Symington, Stuart, 388

Synthetics, 142

Szilard, Leo, 269

Taft, Robert, 250, 301, 302, 304, 306, 314, 326, 327, 330, 354, 418; and McCarthyism, 320

Taft, William Howard, 80–82; and Ballinger–Pinchot controversy, 82–84; as chief justice of Supreme Court, 157; and dollar diplomacy, 101–102; and election of 1912, 84–86; on Pullman strike, 28

Taft-Hartley Act (1947), 307, 317
Tammany Hall, 10
Tansill, Charles, 259, 260
Tape recordings: Supreme Court ruling on, 447; Watergate, 458–459
Tariff: Fordney-McCumber (1922), 154; Hawley-Smoot (1930), 207; Payne-Aldrich (1909), 82; and Roosevelt-Taft rift, 82; Underwood-Simmons (1913), 86, 89
Tarkington, Booth, 8, 10
Tarzan (comic strip), 200
Taxes: cut, 1930, 206; cut, 1945, 302; cut, 1964, 374, 375, 390; cut, 1970, 445; cut 1981, 469, 476; in 1930s, 237; post-WWII, 306, 307; single, 35; social security, 393; in WWII, 278–279
Taylor, Frederick Winslow, 23, 164
Taylor, Maxwell, 387
Taylor, Myron, 189, 226
Teach-ins, 419
Teamsters, 400
Teapot Dome scandal, 157
Technology: in 1920s, 142; in 1930s, 185; in 1970s, 464; and unemployment, 1950s, 348–349; and urban growth, 1900, 6–7
Technostructure, 399
Teheran, summit conference, 273
Telephone, 22; post-WWI, 143
Television, in 1950s, 345–346
Tenant farmers, and AAA, 219
Tenement Housing Commission of New York, 12
Tennessee, Scopes trial, 167
Tennessee Coal and Iron Co., 82
Tennessee Valley Authority (TVA), 214–215
Terrible Threateners, 126
Terry and the Pirates (comic strip), 200
Tet offensive, 417
Textile industry: strikes, mid-1930s, 194; and WWI, 49
Theatre Union, 196
Thieu, Nguyen Van, 448, 453, 455
Think and Grow Rich (Hill), 201
Third International, 127
Thomas, Norman, 126, 250, 419; and election of 1928, 159; and election of 1932, 213; and election of 1936, 232
Thoreau, Henry, 425
Three Mile Island, Pennsylvania, nuclear accident, 468

Thurmond, J. Strom, and election of 1948, 315, 317
Till, Emmet, 359
Tillman, Benjamin, 56
Time magazine, 148
Tito, Marshal, 278
Tobacco Road (Caldwell), 198
Tocqueville, Alexis de, 312
To Have and Have Not (Hemingway), 198
Tojo, Hideki, 258, 261
Tokyo, bombed, WWII, 270
Toledo, Ohio, reform government, 62
Tonkin Gulf, 364
Tonkin Gulf resolution, 414–416; repealed, 448
The Total Woman (Morgan), 470
Townsend, Francis, 228; and election of 1936, 231
Townsend Plan, 228
Trade, with Allies vs. Central Powers, WWI, 106–107
Transportation, funds for mass transit, 1964, 390
Transportation Department, 393
Treason of the Senate (Phillips), 40
Triangle Shirt Waist Company fire, 1911, 26
Trickle down theory, 206–207
Tripartite Pact, 1940, 255, 257
Truman, Harry, 353, 355, 364, 368, 374, 376, 416, 472; and bombing of Hiroshima and Nagasaki, 296; and domestic controversies, post-WWII, 298–305; and Eightieth Congress, 305–308; elected vice-president, 279; and election of 1948, 314–317; and election of 1952, 330–333; and Korean War, 324–330; and McCarthyism, 319–324; and problems at home and abroad, 1949, 317–319; and U.S. anticommunism, 312–314
Truman Doctrine, 310–311, 314
Tugwell, Rexford, 153, 207, 212, 217; and AAA, 219; on TVA, 215
Tunney, Gene, 165
Turkey: military aid to, 306, 310; Soviet pressure on, 307, 308
Turner, Frederick Jackson, 3, 4, 30, 199
Tuskegee Institute, 192
Twain, Mark, 161
Twenty-one demands, 102
Twenty-Thousand Years in Sing Sing (film), 198
Tydings, Millard, 324

Unconditional surrender, Roosevelt's policy of, 268–269
Underdeveloped nations, and Point Four, 317
Underwood-Simmons Tariff (1913), 86, 89
Unemployment: and government spending, 1950s, 356; Hoover's policy on, 206, 208; in 1980s, 478; Philadelphia, 1932, 181; and poverty in cities, 1960s, 397; and recession of 1937, 234; and technology, 1950s, 348–349; and WPA, 220–222; in WWII, 279
Unemployment compensation, 222, 223
Union(s): black, 172–173; CIO formed, 225; collective bargaining, and NRA, 215; company-run, 28; in early 1980s, 467; and immigrants, 29; membership, WWI, 120; membership, 1920s, 164–165; in 1960s, 400; post-WWII, 305; rise of, 1930s, 225–228; and social justice, 46–47; turn of century, 26–28; in WWII, 287–288. *See also* Labor; Strikes; Unemployment; Wages
Union for Social Justice, 228
Union Party, and election of 1936, 231
United Auto Workers, 226, 305
United Federation of Teachers, 467
United Mine Workers, 157, 225
United Nations: charter, 295; and Korean War, 326; and Yalta Conference, 275
U.S. Employment Service, 207
U.S. Steel Corp., 24–25, 82, 128, 145, 377; and CIO, 225; stock prices, 1929–1932, 180
Universal Negro Improvement Association, 171
University of California–Berkeley, campus unrest, 1960s, 421
University of California–Davis, 465
Updike, John 343; on materialism, 340, 341
Uprising of the Twenty Thousand, 49
Urban Affairs Council, 445
Urban Affairs Department, 376
Urban League, 378
U.S.A. (Dos Passos), 198
Utley, Freda, 256
U-2 affair, 366, 369

Vance, Cyrus, 473
Vandenberg, Arthur, 213, 250,
    251, 263, 310
Vanderbilt family, 25
Vanzetti, Bartolomeo, 129, 163, 164
Vardaman, James K., 60; on war
    with Germany, 113
Veblen, Thorstein, 41, 42, 43
Venezuela, and Roosevelt
    Corollary, 100
Vera Cruz, Mexico, U.S.
    takeover, 103
Versailles Peace Conference,
    130–132
Versailles Treaty, and Senate,
    132–137
Veterans of Future Wars, 244
Vick Chemical Co., 145
Vienna, Kennedy–Khrushchev
    summit conference, 384
Vietnam: and Geneva accord,
    364; Kennedy policy on,
    386–387; and SEATO, 364
Vietnamization, 442, 447, 448
Vietnam War: and antiwar
    movement, 418–420; bombing
    resumes, 1972, 451, 454; and
    election of 1964, 391; ends,
    454–455; escalation, 1960s, 407,
    414–418; Johnson's policy on,
    396; Nixon's policy on, 442;
    troop withdrawals, 453
Villa, Francisco (Pancho), 103
Vinson, Fred, 299
Violence: at rock concerts, 424; in
    early 1970s, 443–444; in late
    1970s, 465–466; and TV,
    345–346
Virginia, progressivism in, 45
Volcker, Paul, 470
Volstead Act (1919), 61
Volunteers in Service to America,
    393
Vote: and black office holders,
    440; for eighteen-year-olds, 441;
    for women, 53–56
Voters League of Pittsburgh,
    62–63
Voting: decline in, 66–67;
    post-WWII, 301; turnabout in
    1920s, 159–160
Voting Rights Act (1965), 441, 446

Wages: blacks, pre-WWI, 56;
    controlled, 1971, 451; in 1900,
    26; in 1920s, 142; and strikes,
    post-WWII, 303; of women in
    WWII, 286; in WWI, 120, 121;
    in WWII, 284. See also
    Minimum wage

Wagner, Robert, 159, 225
Wagner Act (1935), 220, 224–225
Waiting for Lefty (Odets), 198
Walker, Francis, 19
Walker Report, 432–433
Wallace, George, 51, 379, 380,
    390, 446, 451; and election of
    1968, 431, 433, 434; and election
    of 1972, 452
Wallace, Henry, 279, 310, 312,
    347; and AAA, 217, 218, 219;
    and election of 1948, 314–317
Wall Street Journal, 474
Ward, Lester, 40
War debts, moratorium on, 206,
    242
Warhol, Andy, 425
War Industries Board (WIB),
    120–121
War Labor Board, 279
Warner Brothers, 197
War on poverty, 382, 391, 393–395
War Powers Act (1973), 455
War Production Board, 279, 282
Warren, Earl, 351, 352, 357, 373,
    446; and election of 1948, 314;
    Supreme Court under, 400–402
War Resources Board, 282
Washington, Booker T., 58, 171,
    192, 408
Washington, D.C.: antiwar
    protest, 1970, 449; antiwar
    protest, 1971, 450; Bonus Army
    in, 209–210; civil rights march
    on, 1963, 381, 409; disarmament
    conference, post-WWI,
    154–155; riot, 1968, 431;
    stop-the-bombing march on,
    1965, 419. See also Congress;
    Government
Washington (state), suffrage for
    women, 53
Washington Conference, 154–155
Washington Post, 458
Watergate affair, 452, 457–461
Water Quality Improvement Act,
    442
Watson, John B., 145–146
Wayne, John, 474
Wealth, turn of century, 25
Wealth tax (1936), 229–230
Weaver, Robert, 380
Weber case, 465
Wechsler, James, 195
Wedemeyer, Albert, 318, 319
Weinberger, Caspar, 477
Welch, Robert, 351
Welfare: in 1960s, 393, 394; and
    poverty in cities, 1960s, 397;
    and unemployment, 394

Welfare capitalism, 28, 164; and
    Mellon, 157
West, Mae, 191
Western Federation of Miners, 49,
    79
West Indian immigrants, 173
The Wet Parade (Sinclair), 61
What About Advertising? (Goode
    and Powel), 146
"What Have They Done to the
    Rain?" (Reynolds), song, 423
Wheeler, Burton, 3, 5, 228, 233,
    252, 263
"Where Have All the Flowers
    Gone?" (Seeger), song, 423
White, Harry Dexter, on
    Roosevelt vs. Truman, 300
White, Theodore, 433
White, William Allen, 57, 65, 76,
    250; on Hoover, 208
White Americans, Inc., 357
White-collar society, 344
White-collar workers, 29; in early
    1980s, 467; in 1950s, 338, 349;
    post-WWI, 143
White flight, from cities, 397
Whitlock, Brand, 35, 62
Whyte, William F., 202
Whyte, William H., Jr., 339
Wicker, Tom, 444
Wilder, Thornton, 196–197
Wilkins, Roy, 413
Will, George, 472
Willard, Frances, 61
Willkie, Wendell, 230, 252
Willow Run, Michigan, airplane
    production, WWII, 282
Wilson, Charles E., 355, 356, 363
Wilson, Edmund, 196, 199, 201
Wilson, Milburn, 217
Wilson, Woodrow, 13, 15, 51, 73,
    80, 206, 244, 245; Asian
    diplomacy, 102; domestic
    program, 86–88; and election of
    1912, 84–86; evaluation of,
    88–90; and fight for League of
    Nations, 129–137; intervention
    in Latin America, 102;
    intervention in Mexico,
    102–105; and Versailles Peace
    Conference, 130–132; and
    Versailles Treaty, 132–137; and
    WWI, 105–113
Winrod, Gerald B., 167
Wiretapping: of government
    officials, 1970, 449; and 1972
    election, 451; Supreme Court
    ruling on, 447
Wisconsin, reform government,
    early 1900s, 63–64

Wisconsin, University of, 63; campus unrest, 1969, 443
Wobblies (WWI), 49–50, 126, 413
Women: in cities, 1900, 12–13; gains, early 1970s, 440; immigrants, 18; liberation movement, 1960s, 427–430; minimum wage for, 48; in 1930s, 191; and sexual mores, 1920s, 150–152; social problems, late 1970s, 467; in work force, early 1900s, 26, 53; work week, 42; in WWII, 285–286
Women and Economics (Gilman), 52, 53
Women and Lovers (film), 148
Women's Bureau, 345
Women's Christian Temperance Union, 61
Women's International League for Peace and Freedom, 46
Women's Party, 151
Women's rights: early 1980s, 467; and progressivism, 52–56

Women's Trade Union League, 151
The Wonderful Wizard of Oz (Baum), 9
Wood, Grant, 199
Wood, Leonard, 127
Woods, Robert A., 20
Woodstock, 424
Woodward, C. Vann, 462
Work force. *See* Labor force
Workmen's compensation, 77
Works Progress Administration (WPA), 220–222, 232, 278
World Bank, and Suez crisis, 365
World War I, 105–114; burdens of, 121–123; and civil liberties, 124–127; U.S. policy reconsidered, 114–116; and women's suffrage, 53
World War II: begins, 1939, 248; ends, 1945, 296, 298; Germany surrenders, 295; government expansion, 278–284; military effort, 267–273; and society, 284–291; U.S. enters, 259

Wounded Knee, South Dakota, Indian uprising, 1973, 455
Wright, Frank Lloyd, 250
Wright, Richard, 196, 198, 200
Wright brothers, 21
Writers, in 1930s, 196–197

Yalta Conference, 275, 276
Yates v. *U.S.*, 352
Yellow dog labor contracts, 206
Yellow Peril, 20, 255
Yippies, 426
Young, Art, 110
Young Communist League, 195
Youth: counterculture, 1960s, 422–427; in 1920s, 162; post-WWII, 287; rebellion, 1960s, 420–422; voting rights for eighteen-year-olds, 441

Zangwill, Israel, 13
Zimmerman, Arthur, 112
Zoot suit gangs, in WWII, 287
Zwicker, Ralph, 351

B
C 4
D 5
E 6
F 7
G 8
H 9
I 0
J 1